Through the Eyes of Another

Through the Eyes of Another
Intercultural Reading of the Bible

Edited by
Hans de Wit, Louis Jonker, Marleen Kool, Daniel Schipani

Institute of Mennonite Studies
Vrije Universiteit, Amsterdam

Copyright ©2004 by Institute of Mennonite Studies
3003 Benham Avenue, Elkhart, Indiana 46517-1999
http://www.ambs.edu/IMS/
Published in collaboration with the Free University, Amsterdam.

Printed in the United States of America by Evangel Press, Nappanee, Indiana

Institute of Mennonite Studies ISBN 0-936273-36-4

Library of Congress Cataloging-in-Publication Data

Through the eyes of another : intercultural reading of the Bible / edited by Hans de
Wit ... [et al.].
    p. cm.
  ISBN 0-936273-36-4 (alk. paper)
  1. Bible. N.T. John IV—Reader-response criticism—Case studies. 2.
Multiculturalism—Religious aspects—Christianity—Case studies. 3.   Samaritan
woman (Biblical figure) I. Wit, Hans de (J. Hans de)
  BS2615.52.T47 2004
  226.7'06—dc22

                                        2004013087

Book design by Mary E. Klassen. Cover art: "At the Well" by Sadao Watanabe. Used by
permission of the Asian Christian Art Association (Jatimulya Yogyakarta, Indonesia).

Unless otherwise indicated, the Scripture quotations in this book are from the *New Revised
Standard Version Bible,* copyright ©1989 by the Division of Christian Education of the
National Council of Churches of Christ in the USA, and are used by permission.

Contents

Preface

This book documents an unprecedented three-year research study focused on the story of the encounter of Jesus with a Samaritan woman presented in the Gospel according to John.[1] Readers can appreciate the extraordinary nature of the study by noting three characteristics that researchers deliberately affirmed from the very beginning. First, the project needed to stem from and reflect a close collaboration among institutions and programs representing the academy, the church, and development and other organizations. Second, the study was to be carried out in sustained partnership involving diverse kinds of participants: committed and creative ordinary readers, expert teachers and other pastoral leaders, and Bible and theology scholars; those participants would also represent different cultures and languages and many countries on five continents. Third, the project was uniquely designed to consist of three phases: Bible study groups from around the world first read the John 4 story in their own terms. Then each group exchanged their carefully prepared hermeneutical report with another group from a completely different cultural background, thus making it possible for everybody to reread the text "through the eyes of another." Finally, each group responded locally to the readings and again addressed the partner group, including the possibility of further interaction and collaboration.

The book starts with a thorough description and explanation of the research project. It is followed by a number of *tableaux vivants*, colorful windows on the actual experience of groups who read the John 4 story and interacted with other readers from very diverse social and cultural settings.

The second part includes nine case studies centering on intercultural reading and communication. They discuss numerous specific dimensions of the experience. These studies supply extended illustrations meant to shed light and to deepen observations and understandings. Special attention is given to contextual and intercontextual dynamics at play in different social situations.

In the third part of the book, eleven critical analyses consider various aspects of the hermeneutical and communication processes involved in the experience. The authors employ a variety of perspectives and study tools resulting in a multidimensional interpretive view.

The fourth part includes five essays that point to a number of ramifications of the project. Implications are drawn for practical theology and theological education, hermeneutical practices and studies, and ecumenical and missiological endeavors.

The voices of the writers presented in this book nicely symbolize the polyphonic readings and conversations that took place around the text of John 4. English is a second or third language for the vast majority of these authors, and the editorial team of the Institute of Mennonite Studies made an effort to preserve the original characteristics of each individual contribution. That feature, together with the fact that the publication project consisted by design of different kinds of essays, has made of this book a heterogeneous collection of articles. Nevertheless, we trust that it will be possible to appreciate the comprehensive nature of the project and the integrity of the contributions.

It is our conviction that readers will find in this volume a special testimony to the fascinating nature of intercultural Bible reading and its potential contribution to the life of faith communities and to the work of church agencies and scholars. Far from considering this effort a finished product, the editors present it as an invitation to further reflection, dialogue, and collaboration.

The research project leading to the publication of this book was initially supported by the Uniting Protestant Churches in the Netherlands and the Faculty of Theology of the Free University in Amsterdam. Such support continued even after the formation of the Intercultural Bible Collective (IBC), the network responsible for providing overall coordination and supervision to the research project. The steering committee named on behalf of the IBC was chaired by Louis Jonker (South Africa). Other members included Eric Anum, Ghana (Africa representative); Sientje Merentek, Indonesia (Asia representative); Pedro Triana, Cuba (Latin America representative); John Riches, Scotland (Europe and USA representative). Hans de Wit and Piet Schelling, the Netherlands, served as ex-officio members representing the international and the Netherlands secretariats respectively. An editorial committee was appointed to be in charge of the publication project, and its four members—Hans de Wit, Louis Jonker, Marleen Kool, and Daniel Schipani—eventually became the editors of the present volume.[2]

Financial and other contributions were granted by two Dutch groups which became *project partners*: Solidaridad, a development organization, and ICCO (Interchurch organization for development cooperation). Further financial assistance was provided by the Dutch Bible Society, which became a valuable *project sponsor*.

Many nongovernmental organizations, church-associated bodies, and faculties and seminaries made it possible for their members to participate in the project in different capacities. They are scattered throughout Africa, Asia, Europe, and the Americas.

Heartfelt gratitude goes to the hundreds of women and men in more than twenty countries who participated in the Bible study groups focusing on the John 4 narrative.[3] They represent several kinds of church affiliations and denominations. Their commitment to reading scripture together and "through the eyes of another" for the sake of life and faith has made this study truly worthwhile. The work of group leaders, reporters, researchers, and regional coordinators has been particularly appreciated as well.[4] Special thanks go also to the writers of the different kinds of essays included in this volume; they were also active participants in the process of communal reading and intercultural communication and hermeneutics.

Preparing the book for publication was the task of the Institute of Mennonite Studies in the United States, which also provided funds to facilitate the editorial work. Its director, Mary Schertz, gave unqualified support to the project, which was managed by Barbara Nelson Gingerich with much competence and dedication. The expertise and collaborative spirit of Lois Siemens (overall clerical support), Sue Conrad and Christine Guth (copy editors), Rachel Epp (proofreader and indexing assistant), and James Nelson Gingerich (page layout, indexing, and technical support) are also gratefully acknowledged.

It is our hope and our prayer that the fruits of all these labors may encourage further Bible study and research. We also pray that they may nurture community building across sociocultural, ethnic, racial, and religious boundaries in the midst of our increasingly globalized world. May the Spirit who graciously illumines the story of the transforming encounter at the well continue to provide living water that we may enjoy and share.

Daniel Schipani, for the Editorial Committee

Pentecost 2004

Notes

[1] For especially prepared Greek and English versions of the text, see chapter 23 by Daniel Schipani and Mary Schertz, "Through the Eyes of Practical Theology and Theological Education," in part four of this volume.

[2] Hans de Wit, Bible scholar at the Faculty of Theology of the Free University in Amsterdam, was the lead researcher and main contributor to the overall project. He worked in close collaboration with Marleen Kool, also of the Free University. Louis Jonker, also a Bible scholar, is a member of the Department of Old and New Testament, in the Faculty of Theology of Stellenbosch, South Africa. Daniel Schipani is a practical theology scholar and professor at Associated Mennonite Biblical Seminary in Elkhart, Indiana, USA.

[3] See the appendix for a listing of participant groups.

[4] Readers are encouraged to visit the website of the Intercultural Bible Collective: www.bible4all.org

PART 1

Introduction to the project

CHAPTER 1

Through the eyes of another
Objectives and backgrounds
Hans de Wit

You can't send a kiss by messenger.

A tired man is sitting by himself at the foot of the hills. It is hot. He is thirsty. He needs help. There is water—he is sitting next to a well—but he has no urn and the well is deep. A woman is coming from the village to draw water. She is alone. We are not told what her name is. She is also thirsty. The man and the woman never met before. The things they share are their thirst and a common history. Beyond that there are vast differences. He is a man; she is a woman. They do not belong to the same people. The man crossed a border to get to the well; his people do not usually come to the place where he is now sitting. His people despise her people. The man addresses her and asks for water. She has brought an urn with her; she could help him quench his thirst. But she does not do it. She asks him a question: "Why are you talking to me? Your people do not talk with us!" Then everything changes. A conversation begins, about thirst and water, about who they really are and about the tradition that produced them, about salvation and healing. Something fundamental happens to both of them. He interrupts his journey to stay with her and her people. She changes her life. She no longer has to flee from her past. She begins to sow. They will never forget each other.

Over the past three years, hundreds of ordinary readers from more than twenty-five countries and the most varied communities of faith have been studying this scene, told in John 4. The title of this book, *Through the Eyes of Another*, is also the title of the project in the framework of which they did this reading. To the best of our knowledge, this is the first time that a project with this presentation and scope has been implemented. The text was first read in the intimacy of the small group.

Hans de Wit, Faculty of Theology, Free University (Amsterdam, the Netherlands)

Subsequently, contact was established with a partner group on the other side of the world, and the story was read again, this time through the eyes of the partner group. Profound contact was created between some groups; people wrote letters to each other, sent gifts or photos. Other groups terminated the process prematurely. Reports were made of the group meetings. Nearly 3,000 pages of text present how groups read the text; they are vernacular commentaries on John 4. The material is overwhelmingly rich. It provides a fascinating picture of what readers do with Bible texts and what Bible texts do to readers.

An international group of authors has been processing the reading reports. Many of them participated in the reading groups. This book presents the results of their studies. The core question of the project was: What happens when Christians from radically different cultures and situations read the same Bible story and start talking about it with each other? Can intercultural reading of Bible stories result in a new method of reading the Bible and communicating faith that is a catalyst for new, trans-border dialogue and identity formation?

The authors who contributed to this book tie in developments and challenges that have come to light in the past decades in the broad field of theology. They share a great concern about the negative effects of globalization and the increasing asymmetry in the world. They are convinced of the wealth of Bible reading practices of ordinary readers and of the fact that this is, in many aspects, a neglected terrain that offers tremendous opportunities. They are keenly aware of the diversity in the world and of the necessity of establishing new interactions that contribute to consciousness-raising and change. It is not the search for the ultimate meaning of Bible texts that takes center stage in this process, but rather the development of a new perspective.

The intention of this collection is to reflect the wealth of the project. Experiences of groups of ordinary readers are shown, but there is also scholarly reflection. The authors involved have looked at the project from different perspectives. Case studies are provided. Group-dynamic aspects of the project are analyzed, as is the interaction between the scholarly and vernacular readings of John 4. What lessons can be learned for theological education? What is the significance of the project for ecumenism and mission? What can the project actually contribute to consciousness-raising and empowerment, change of perspective and social transformation?

The scope of the project is broad. Certain objectives appeared feasible in the implementation and some hypotheses relevant and fertile; others faded into the background, turned out to be too diffuse, and will have to be defined more precisely. Testing a number of assumptions from an empirical point of view was one of the project's objectives.

In this introductory contribution, I will discuss the background and objectives of the project. First, I will describe the process that lay ahead for the participating groups. Then I will reflect on the intuition that formed the basis of the project. The central question I have just formulated contains four core components that require more detailed explanation. If (1) ordinary Bible readers from radically different situations and contexts (2) read the same Bible story and (3) enter into a conversation with each other about this reading, (4) what will happen? Such an extensive project has a long history of development and also of fallacies, which I then describe. Finally, I offer some conclusions.

The process

What was in store for participating groups? Each group had a discussion leader and a reporter at their disposal. The process consisted of three phases, described in a protocol that was available to all groups. In the first phase, which could consist of a number of meetings, the mostly small groups read the story of John 4. Groups did not know which partner groups they would be linked with. Reading was communitarian and done the way participants were accustomed to read a Bible story. The group had the power. A report was made of every meeting. In addition to a presentation of the interpretation of the text, the reports also contain information about the group: the context of participants, personal information, their church background. Sometimes the reports contain attachments: photos of the group, videos of the meetings, pictures of the Samaritan woman or songs composed especially for the occasion. The reports were then sent to the central coordinators in Amsterdam and translated. On the basis of reports received and a number of previously established criteria, groups were linked to a partner group. Reports were sent to partner groups. The interval between the first and second phases was sometimes filled with a number of meetings at which attention was focused on the context of the partner group, who had been identified by then.

Next, the second phase began. The group read the story once again, now through the eyes of the partner group. What were the similarities? What were the differences? What role did culture play in the reading? Could anything be learned from the partner group? Did people discover things in the text that they had not noticed at first? Did a change of perspective take place? A report was also made of the second phase. The group concluded the second phase with a response to the partner group, usually a letter.

In the third phase, the group responded to the responses of the partner group, looked back over the entire process, and decided whether they wished to have further contact.

Ordinary readers

The great majority of people who read Bible stories belong to the category of ordinary Bible readers. Ordinary Bible readers are the owners of the project that is described and evaluated here. Their reading reports were treated with great care. Their joy in reading, their knowledge, creativity, and vulnerability form the raw materials of the analyses given here. The participants come from all layers of society. So many occupations and professions are represented that we could build a new world with them. Ordinary readers have carried the project and brought the story of the Samaritan woman to life in a thousand ways from their own imaginations and situations. The concept *ordinary readers* touches the heart of this project and also presents the developments with which this project links up.

Why were ordinary Bible readers put into contact with each other in this manner? To answer that, I first must focus the magnifying glass on a development that has been taking place in all kinds of disciplines since the 1970s. We can call it the beckon of the ordinary reader. Since then, what has happened in the past few decades in the Southern hemisphere has been especially important for biblical hermeneutics. Attention to ordinary readers in particular is much more in demand there than in the circles of Western biblical scholars.

What should we understand by *ordinary readers*? After all, the differences in social status, income, culture, education level, occupation, church background, and religious conviction are enormous. On reflection, the term, which seemed so transparent, needs an explanation. *Ordinary reader* is a dynamic, complex concept. At least four melodies converge in the concept. In the first place, it has a spiritual dimension. In the second place, and in the same line as the previous one, it is an important technical term in hermeneutics and literary scholarship that indicates a certain manner of reading, an attitude toward the text. Third, when the term is used in the world of scholarly explanation of the Bible, it often sounds harsh; it is a critical term. In the fourth place, where used in a normative sense—as something that should be decisive in Bible reading—the term has an almost metaphorical meaning. In that sense, the ordinary reader is a source of wisdom and knowledge.

The spiritual dimension

Quite a collection of terms has been created around ordinary readers in recent years: ordinary reader, grassroots readings, *lectura popular*, spontaneous readings, *pueblo, povo, volkse lezing, pre-kritische Leser, naïve Leser, Bibellektüre durch das Volk*.

When authors from the Southern hemisphere talk about ordinary readers, they mean the many millions of people who live in situations of poverty, exclusion, persecution, illness, and apartheid—and read the Bible. Their reading is with a wounded heart, from the experience and perspective of life itself. These writers speak of people who are desperate and still read the Bible. In religious traditions, many references are found to this manner of dealing with fundamental texts. Terms used are *lectio contemplativa*, *lectio divina*, and *sensus spiritualis* in the Patristics; *dhvani* (the approach of the heart) in the Indian tradition; *Semoya* (of the spirit) in the African tradition; and *lectura orante* in the Latin American tradition. Ignatius wrote of *sentire et gustare res interne*, the feeling and tasting of the heart. This reading is the hermeneutic counterpart of what is called, in liberation theologies, theologizing from the experience of the poor, the *no-persona*. This spiritual dimension of theologizing and Bible reading was what Gustavo Gutiérrez referred to with the expression, "Spirituality is our method."

We encounter plenty of the spiritual dimensions of Bible reading by ordinary readers, so extensively documented in Latin American, African, and Asiatic literature, in non-Western reading reports but also in Western ones. The encounter with this dimension of Bible reading is perhaps one of the most valuable aspects of our project. Readers approach the text full of expectation. An interaction is created between the text and the readers that focuses on life, innovation, healing. "African Bible readers," says Musa Dube, "who live in life-sapping and paralyzing situations of oppression, necessarily view the Bible as a life-giving and empowering resource. Ordinary African readers go to the Bible . . . to tap this potency, this life-giving power."[1] When we leaf through the hundreds of pages of reading reports, we are overwhelmed by the confrontation with this dimension: clearly the Bible is not primarily a gift to academics but to the people. This understanding from the wounded heart stands out as fragile and delicate in contrast to the activity of professional readers. The effect on ordinary readers of dealing with the Bible in a scholarly way is often devastating, not because scholars intend it to be, but because the instruments used to approach the text are so different: power and knowledge rather than expectation and hope. Ordinary readers often clam up like an oyster if an "expert" comes forth in the group. The slow, careful approach of the scholar is often difficult to understand in places where the quest for life is urgent.

The spiritual dimension is also expressed in the fact that for the groups, reading is more than a cerebral process. I will give a few examples of how, during the meetings, people celebrate, eat, sing, dance, pray, commemorate, and are concerned about what oppresses people and what hurts them. "They met four times in order to study the passage. All meetings started with a liturgical time: chants, hymns, dynamics, prayers," says a Cuban group. "Meetings always begin with a hymn, after members have had the opportunity to greet and inform [one another] about their health. One of the members led in prayer and asked the blessing of the Lord on the procedures," says the reporter of the meeting of the group in KwaZulu Natal, South Africa. A second Cuban group comments, "For us, the Bible reading meetings are true celebrations. We sing accompanied by the guitar, we develop group dynamics, we pray, we bring along symbolic objects. All this creates an atmosphere that enables us to share and imagine. In this way, a plastic water bottle can take on the value of a large, antique earthenware pot." People in El Salvador composed a new song for the occasion of the project: "La Samaritana." Group members brought symbolic objects along to the meetings. In a report from Nigeria we read: "The group members bring along with them such symbolic objects as bottled water, cross, candle, and pieces of white cloth. The group considers these objects symbolic of life, purity, and light, which Christ radiates in the life of Christians, etc. In addition, members of the group brought symbolic objects such as the Ikenga or Ofo, cowries, clay pots, fowl feathers, and other objects of worship believed to be accepted by the ancestors in the African cultural setting." A group from the Netherlands reports: "Some members of the group brought along symbolic objects: A cut crystal. A crystal has many facets.

Likewise, the scripture also has many facets and its own message in each context. The Rembrandt Bible. This contains a print of an etching by Rembrandt representing Jesus in conversation with the Samaritan woman. It is clearly visible that Rembrandt had his own outlook on the scene of the story. Likewise, individuals also have their own views and outlook on the texts." A report from Brazil gives another nice example:

> There is water, and then there is water! Two transparent water bottles are standing on the table. Two bottles of water, in common transparent glass. One bottle has water from the public water supply. This water is collected from the Sinos River, which is very polluted with heavy metals from the tanneries and with the sewerage of the city. A complex process officially guarantees that this water is technically drinkable. Because of this treatment the water becomes very transparent. The other bottle had water from an artesian well. The water from this well [is subjected] to regular chemical tests to guarantee its purity. The bottles were passed from hand to hand. Every participant had the task of discovering the origin of the water. Only a few made the right decision. The pure water from the artesian well was less transparent than the water that was submitted to chemical treatment. There was a dialogue about it. The more transparent water is not always the water of life.

The examples underline the spiritual dimension of reading processes in which ordinary readers have the power. What people bring to the text and what people expect from the text are often radically different from what motivates scholars. Therefore, it is the interaction between the two approaches that is so important.

The ordinary reader as a hermeneutic concept

The concept of *ordinary reader* is also a technical concept that plays an important role in hermeneutics. The terms used are precritical, prefigurative, naïve, spontaneous. These terms do not constitute a value judgment, but indicate a certain manner of dealing with the biblical text. This approach involves an attitude. What ordinary readers do with texts is not a contamination or an unimportant addition; no, theirs is a reading attitude that is completely legitimate, from the point of view of the text. It is something the text demands.

In a classic essay, Paul Ricoeur explained that literary texts enable (at least) two reading attitudes.[2] Texts are configurations of linguistic components that can be examined critically and scientifically. Literary texts have a structure, a phonetic aspect, syntax, a literary composition. They have a rhetorical dimension; they are intended to stir something in the reader. Texts have a historical background outside the text that is sometimes explicitly referred to. All this can be examined methodically and scientifically. Such a study, usually called exegesis when Bible texts are concerned, especially serves the interests of the text. People want to unfold the meanings that the text could have had in its historical setting. This activity requires knowledge, expertise, and an objectifying attitude on the part of the researcher. Ricoeur calls this the analytical attitude.

In addition, texts demand a different attitude, an existential one, an attitude focused on appropriation. Readers bring their situation, demands, and experiences to the text and seek to elicit a word from the text for their own situation. The historical reference of the text is replaced by a new one, the actual moment of the new reader. Again, texts not only make this existential attitude possible, but actually require it. Texts are meant to be read again and again and are capable of illustrating new situations that were not foreseen by the author. This fresh reading is possible when the text is liberated from being tied to the past and "the author's intention." Reading, Ricoeur writes, is a response to written texts. The primary effect of reading is that autonomy, an independent existence, is bestowed on a text. The author is not available and can no longer be interviewed; his or her intention cannot be found anywhere else but in the text. In this manner, the text can open itself up for further development and enrichment by new readers. This process is important to the meaning of the text itself. Later rereading may enrich the meaning of the text, may even have an effect on it: As Gregory the Great said, scripture grows with its readers. What becomes clear in this process is that the interpretation process is not limited to "restoring the source text all along this sequence or sequences of repeated actualization, rather this process re-invents, re-figures, and re-orients the model."[3]

Precisely because the text, in this process of recontextualization, becomes fertile for new readers' lives, understanding takes on the nature of a fundamental event in this process. This event deepens the hermeneutic circulation and changes the text for its readers from a historical object into a friend and an ally. The event-nature of reading also implies that appropriating or actualizing must not be regarded, as in classical hermeneutics, as a third—separate or added, and because of that metaphoric—phase of the understanding process, but as an essential dimension of understanding. Therefore, ordinary readers are not a category to be disregarded; they should be fully involved in the interpretation of biblical texts.

By turning to ordinary readers, the project takes up the challenges of modern hermeneutics that had been, in practice, responded to only sporadically. The term used is a paradigm change in modern hermeneutics that has taken place since the 1960s and 1970s. The paradigm shift has everything to do with contextualization and the role of the reader. It can be summarized in the insight that understanding is always contextual, but that contextualization is not an obstacle and can instead lead to enrichment and new meanings of a text. Recognition of the legitimacy of contextualization in the understanding process guards against the continuous temptation of objectifying tradition. Recognition of the importance of the (new) situation guards readers from fundamentalism.

Context, culture, and situation have a large effect on understanding biblical texts. They determine the space within which the ordinary readers appropriate the text. If we want to discover how context and culture affect reading processes, we have to enter this space. This effect is also one of the reasons why the project ties in with reading experiences of ordinary readers.

The concept of ordinary reader has a second meaning in hermeneutics. Spontaneous reading is intent on appropriation. The text is brought forward to the present, the historical context is replaced by the current one; the oppressor of those days is given the facial features of the current oppressor. This process is often rich and creative, but may also have egocentric, narcissistic tendencies. Reading then becomes annexation, a closed process. Readers only hear the echo of their own voices, and always take the side of the good and just. To interrupt this circularity, confrontation with other reading and readers is of fundamental importance. One of the core objectives of the project is effecting interaction and confrontation. This process already takes place in the group itself—the text is read communally!—but takes on a new dimension because of the intercultural encounter.

Ordinary readers and exegesis

A great deal of research has been done on the writers of the most-sold book in the world, but we know very little of most readers. How do Bible readers on the African plains or in the Andean highlands deal with the Bible? How do people on the European continent read Bible stories? Here we are confronted with one of the biggest embarrassments and gaps in modern biblical scholarship. Research on the question of how readers deal with their texts is done in literature sociology and sociolinguistics. Remarkably, this territory is still undeveloped in biblical scholarship and hermeneutics. Of course, a great deal of research was done on the foreground or *Wirkungsgeschichte* of biblical texts. However, the question is almost always how classic readers, the Church Fathers or Reformers, deal with classic texts. How present-day readers do this in their different contexts is a new question. Empirical research, carried out primarily in Latin America and Africa, allows this large, hidden, and severely neglected group of ordinary Bible readers to slowly come out of the shadows. The field of research on their reading habits—empirical hermeneutics—is just as complex as it is challenging. The project Through the Eyes of Another is intended to contribute to that research.

The relationship between ordinary readers and exegesis has been under scrutiny by biblical scholars in the Southern hemisphere, where most of the hermeneutics of the new subject have been designed, since the 1970s. Ordinary readers have a central role in this hermeneutics and constitute a concept that is critically related to the established exegetical methods that originated in Europe. The list of these hermeneutics is long and the quantity of literature overwhelming: hermeneutics of liberation, black hermeneutics, feminist hermeneutics, Dalit hermeneutics,[4] Caribbean or Calypso hermeneutics,[5] hermeneutics of indigenous peoples of North and South America,[6] postcolonial hermeneutics.[7] The authors share the conviction that a gap exists between exegesis and the reading habits of ordinary readers. That gap has come into being since the Enlightenment, but it is becoming more problematic as scientific biblical studies appear to go ever less frequently into topical questions. In particular, people in situations where the Bible is of great social importance, and who expect scientific biblical research to contribute to the alleviation of affliction, see the gap as a drama. The blame for the fact that the gap is not being bridged—Carlos Mesters dedicated his well-known "parable of the house of the people" to this problem exactly thirty years ago[8]—is laid, by and large, at the doorstep of Western exegesis. This drama has everything to do with the ethics of the interpretation of the scripture. The opinion is that Western exegesis is stuck in a ghetto position. These hermeneutics, whether black, liberation, Dalit, Minjung, Calypso, or Rastafari, emphasize the urgency of biblical research that focuses on questions that are relevant in their own context of exclusion, poverty, and premature death, and that, in the general opinion, are seldom the point of orientation of Western exegetes. Biblical scholarship must be decentralized[9] or decolonized;[10] the relation between the text being interpreted and the community in behalf of which this is done must be analyzed critically. Interpretation *of* is, after all, also always the interpretation *for*.[11] A new awareness of their own situation leads exegetes to long to make a break with the universal presumptions of Western theology and the dominance of Western methods. For their exegesis to be capable of being contextual, Eurocentrism must be superseded:

> Such Eurocentrism is said to match the patriarchal nature of the discipline and to reflect not only the broader Eurocentric character of theological education in general but also the strong Eurocentric control over culture. Its characteristics are variously identified as follows: (a) confinement of the task of interpretation to the past; (b) focus on the discovery of the original meaning of the text, the meaning back then; (c) emphasis on the impartation and absorption of information; (d) insistence on a particular method or cultural understanding; (e) predilection for christological and soteriological questions, such as the issue of religious salvation; (f) a view of instruction as universal and undifferentiated. In the end, such a view of the discipline is regarded as profoundly ironic: a worldview that is highly cultural in nature—Western or Eurocentric—presents itself as without cultural bias and hence as normative, as the centre, resulting in the exaltation of a particular worldview above all others.[12]

The questions that are up for discussion here touch the heart of the Through the Eyes of Another project. The basic structure of the project takes the issue formulated here exceptionally seriously. The project is intended to stimulate interaction, not only among ordinary readers, but also between ordinary and professional readers of the scripture. The intercultural nature should make it clear that the project is meant to escape Eurocentrism. At the same time, one does not want the project to become stranded in the sometimes fierce and infertile polemics described, but to take it one step further. There are also components in the structure of the project that will criticize the criticism of European ways of dealing with the Bible. Let's consider a few of these now.

First, criticism of Western methods of exegesis must be qualified. Elsewhere, I have demonstrated for the Latin American context that, as vehement as the resistance is against European methods, there is not an exegete who does not use them.[13] If my perceptions are accurate, the same is true for the Asiatic and African regions. An even more important point is that at the level of dealing with the Bible in a scientific manner, there is no such thing as the Latin Americans' own method. They have a high hermeneutic sensitivity for ordinary readers; they intend to do relevant research, to have new questions, but the methods are very European. A method such as the sociological reading of the Bible, so beloved in Latin America, is thoroughly Western and historicized. We touch here on one of the most important challenges for those who would like to break through the hegemony of Western methods. How is it possible to develop methods that are truly African or Asiatic, are scientific and that depart entirely from criteria prevailing in the West or imposed by the West, for dealing scientifically with the scripture? Or should one say that it is precisely those Western methods that enable interpreters working in non-Western contexts—which are, for that matter, also abundant in the West!—to reach quite adequately the result they wish to attain? Furthermore: what methods are we talking about? Over the past few decades, the number of methods generated from literature science, ideology criticism, postmodernism, feminism, narratology, semiotics, and cultural studies has increased to the extent that every general judgment on Western methods easily will suffer from what in sociology is called strategic essentialism.[14] This increase in methods and new readers, all with their own sociopolitical perspectives, must be considered as a process of liberation and decolonization, as justly observed by Fernando Segovia.[15] The West contributed a great deal to this. The debate on the ethics of reading and the responsibility of the exegete is also slowly warming up in the West.[16]

Second, we must be very careful with the boundary of Western–non-Western, first world–third world, where practice of exegesis is involved. We should actually leave this path. Over the past few decades, the situation has changed to such an extent that anything being said about the West and Western reading of the Bible is almost always a caricature.[17] Non-Western situations abound in the West. If the concept of a poor or excluded person were to be defined somewhat more broadly than in solely economic terms, it would be clear that there are also many millions of poor people in the West. The project makes it clear that there are indeed differences between Western and non-Western methods of reading the Bible, but that those differences run much less along the familiar lines of poor-rich, oppressed-free, than we had thought. Church affiliation appears to be just as important as social status.

Third, for those who live and work in the West, doing exegesis out of the experience of the unimaginable suffering in the third world requires great sensitivity. It requires what Buber once called "reading with your soul." I do not mean to suggest that exegetes in the West, however oriented, never reflected on suffering, inequity, and persecution. Moreover, it is true that wherever Western exegetes are not sensitive or are less sensitive to the new readers and methods and do not want to know about that worldly, multicolored community of interpreters, they end up ever more frequently on the sidelines of their profession. The discipline of biblical scholarship is becoming less popular all the time at an increasing number of European universities.

Fourth, we must be on guard against a mistake that is often made, which we could call the "fallacy of comparison": the reading habits of ordinary readers in the Southern hemisphere should not be compared with the reading habits of exegetes in the Northern hemisphere.

Fifth, exegesis is a different way of dealing with Bible texts than that encountered in ordinary reading. Exegesis implies a different but not less meticulous attitude, as the project clearly demonstrates. If respect for the texts and defending their importance is involved, exegesis often treats the texts with more respect than the spontaneous reading focused on actualization. Every actualization, no matter how creative and fertile, is an adventure from the point of view of the text. Sometimes it is necessary to ask oneself what the text was actually intended to convey.

Furthermore, every hermeneutic design, every definition of how processes of understanding have to develop and what their effect must be, is culture-specific. Not a single hermeneutic design escapes cultural definition.[18] Indeed, Western European exegesis and Bible hermeneutics often show strong colonial, imperialistic, rationalistic, and individualistic traits.[19] The interpretation model is often oriented hierarchically (with strong emphasis on validation by the expert) and historically. Latin American liberation hermeneutics, Rastafari hermeneutics from the Caribbean area, and certain variants of black hermeneutics show strong masculine, nationalistic, and collectivist traits. They are unilaterally focused on the current context. They have preference for sociological and economical questions, while more culturally determined problems such as gender and race are only now being focused on. Masculine values such as violence, resistance, rebellion, heroic action, revolution, and martyrdom play a large role. The cultural definition of hermeneutic designs also implies that the vision of the "usefulness" of a Bible text depends, for personal faith or social praxis, to a great extent on the cultural values adhered to. Which values will lead to the choice of the power of violence or armed resistance, and which lead to the option for the drip that hollows out the stone or to banging on pots and pans?

Back to the ethics of the interpretation that this project primarily concerns. The gap between exegesis and prefigurative understanding touches a deep-seated ethical issue. I will make this ethical dimension clear by examining the two concepts of plurivocity and plenitude. Hermeneutics that focus on the reception history of texts, on what readers do with the texts, will carefully take their inconvertible plurivocity into account. If there is one thing that our project demonstrates, it is that the same single text can be read in many ways. This multicoloredness is hard data. There is a difference beginning from the moment readers read a text and interpret their own existence by means of the text. It happens only rarely that a text does not produce different reading communities. Texts are multidimensional and are simultaneously read at different levels by communities with different interests.

This difference brings up the problem of validation, about which so much has been written in the past few decades. Who is to judge the differences? Exegesis is often presented as the referee, and the relationship between exegesis and spontaneous understanding is understood to be hierarchic. The recent developments have led to a severe problem of the concept of validation. Our project also shows that the limits of what texts may mean are often more relaxed than the professional exegete thought possible. However that may be, a validation strategy, especially necessary where the use of religious texts does not produce life but death, would rather obey the dynamics of probability than logic of empirical verification.[20] Authentic interpretation will reflect the conflict of interpretations, test it, listen carefully to alternative interpretations, striving for consensus, although direct consensus is out of reach.

The interpretation that includes the maximum number of facts offered by the text, including possible connotations, is the most probable. Quality interpretation will honor the principle of plenitude. As Ricoeur has said, "The poem means all it can mean." In spontaneous understanding, a different reading strategy and often a result other than what we encounter in scientific approach are involved. All possible and impossible connotations of texts have a vote in spontaneous understanding. Exactly for that reason, it is not easy to realize why spontaneous understanding of the texts should not be systematically involved in the discussion on the meaning of biblical texts. If an overwhelming majority of readers are excluded from the process of giving meaning, as meant in a scientific sense, and there is no systematic interaction, the principle of plenitude is not met, and the issue of the ethics of the interpretation is up for discussion.

Exclusion also means impoverishment here. That is exactly the reason the new hermeneutics that we have just discussed have emphasized so strongly the importance of "working with the people" and the interaction between exegesis and "the people." There is no single scientific reason why exegetes should not listen to the people, should not work to serve the people or read the scripture with ordinary readers. Gerald West gives a simple answer to the question of why exegetes should do these things: because you are asked to, and because it enriches you. It changes you. Reading with ordinary readers is anything but a *sacrificium intellectus*. On the contrary, it implies an exciting process of reorientation of the exegete. West summarizes the experience of many exegetes who read the Bible "with the people": What is particularly exciting and challenging about reading the Bible with ordinary readers is that it is quite legitimate for ordinary readers and trained readers to emerge from the reading process with different elements of interest. The readings produced in this interface affect ordinary and trained readers differently, and this is not surprising because we come to the text from different places and after the reading encounter return to our different places. Our subjectivities as trained and ordinary readers are differently constituted, so the effect that the corporate reading has on our subjectivities will be different. However, and this is extremely important, we will have been partially constituted by each other's subjectivities. And this should always be a constituent element of the contextual Bible study process: a desire to be partially constituted by those from other communities. And not only does such a reading process enable us to be partially constituted by the other, "the other" who is usually absent from biblical studies, but our readings now bring to the academic stage glimpses of readings that are to be found offstage among the poor and marginalized and which call us to share their struggle with the God of life against the forces of death.[21]

A great deal has already been written about the benefits to exegesis of the interaction between the professional and ordinary reader. This relationship is complicated. It means functioning in two realities, as it were. Bible readers not included in the academic guild are examined, and the results of their interpretation are intended to be made fruitful to the guild. Moreover, the guild participates in the reading group it analyzes, and thus works in two realities in which the meaning of texts is constructed in sometimes radically different ways. What is required from Bible scholars here looks like what is called *methodological ludism* in cultural anthropology. This is the capacity to look at two different ways in which reality is constructed at the same time. This involves:

> the capacity to deal simultaneously and subjunctively with two or more ways of classifying reality. Though primarily playful, this capacity can be used in a very serious manner too: play is not "just a game." The reference to simultaneity reflects connectionist ideas about the parallel processing of schemas. . . . Methodological ludism is a way of exploring the ambiguity of participant observation as a research attitude in which the field worker goes beyond subjectivity and objectivity, is both here and there—or perhaps neither here nor there! The ethnographer plays with two realities—is existentially involved but at the same time is constructing an image of what is actually being experienced.[22]

What applies to ethnologists applies in our case to Bible scholars. They are existentially involved, but at the same time are describing what is actually happening and are trying to make this fertile. This capacity is the essence of "reading with" and is what West means by the expression "being partially constituted by work with others." One tries to connect insights from different realities to each other and to relate them to each other critically.

It is not only new questions that exegetes ask about the texts nowadays that benefit exegesis through the interaction with ordinary readers. The process also involves a critical attitude toward their own guild and the narrow definitions of exegesis that prevail there. More important yet, it concerns the willingness to contribute to what Severino Croatto calls "the unforgettable task of softening and opening Bible texts to ordinary readers, opening the text towards the front, towards life."[23] It also involves reorientation of the manner in which the discipline of exegesis is taught. While meticulous education in methods is often sacrificed at academies in the Southern hemisphere because they wish to be relevant, we often see in faculties in the North that the question of how one wishes to actualize texts, use them in church or open them up to life, is completely ignored. For example, we see that some German and Dutch groups participating in the project are wrestling with the question of how one can appropriate the text, how it can be actualized. "You know a lot about the historical background of the text, but where can one find the Samaritan woman in your village?" writes a group from El Salvador to a Dutch group. The tradition within which biblical education is taught in Dutch and German academies is strongly reflected in this struggle.

I will make one last comment about the interaction between ordinary and professional readers. When surveying the field, one encounters a paradox. While ordinary readers in the West are rarely involved by exegetes in the process of giving meaning to biblical texts, a voluminous quantity of popular readings of the Bible has been collected, especially in the Southern hemisphere, without any systematic research ever having been done on it. Systematic analysis of the reading reports is new to many of us, and we lack a theoretical framework and coding system, as well as the time to do the analysis meticulously. This lack is remarkable, especially if one is aware that the presumption of many liberation hermeneuts is that reading the Bible can contribute to the transformation of society. In that case, one would also like to know how those social changes come about, what role reading the Bible plays in this process, what factors are decisive, and which ones impede it.

The ordinary reader as a metaphor

Since the advent of what people in Latin America have started to call the Bible movement (*movimiento bíblico*), exegetes have been impressed by the force of this movement. José Luis Caravias writes, at the end of the 1980s: "Something entirely new is happening here, something that never happened before in the history of our continent: the Bible and the People have met each other and the two of them, united, have started on their path. It seems like the embrace of two old friends that had been separated from each other by a great distance for a long time. The one is there for the other."[24]

When looking back over twenty years of Bible movement in Latin America, Carlos Mesters writes: "Nobody can explain exactly how it happened. The Catholic Church in Brazil was suddenly involved in an interest of the people for the Bible, as never had been the case in its entire history. This interest exceeds all that was foreseen and seems improbable for those who do not live here. If somebody had predicted this twenty years ago . . . no one would have believed him. The Bible seems like an herb, suitable for every meal. The people use the Bible for everything."[25]

In the early days of the movement, as is the case with many genitive hermeneutics, people are optimistic and approach the text, along with the poor, full of confidence. The hermeneutic model is a combination of trust and suspicion. The suspicion is focused on how others—for example, the church or the West—read the text; the trust is focused on the poor, the ordinary readers. Only later will the suspicion be focused on the text itself; the text becomes part of the problem for some people; the text appears to be an anti-text, and the Bible must first be liberated by the poor and oppressed before they can be liberated.[26]

Especially among Latin American authors there is the conviction that when you read the scripture with the poor, you touch the essence of the text and arrive at what was originally intended. What had been stolen, embezzled, or hidden reappears. The result is that a type of cult is created around the ordinary reader. The poor, the Dalit, Indian, woman, rasta-man become metaphor. These terms are no longer descriptive; they become standardizing concepts. They preeminently become the hermeneutic subject; they are privileged readers, the best interpreters of the Bible message.[27] Authors such as Pablo Richard base this conviction on the following analogy. The Bible was written by the poor and contains the subversive memoirs of the poor;[28] the situation of today's poor people in Latin America seems very similar to that of the poor in Palestine during biblical times.

The metaphoric use of the ordinary reader is a consequence of the richness of the movement, and is therefore completely understandable, but it is also a fallacy and shows the traits of strategic essentialism. At second glance, the concept *poor*, as a standardizing concept, a hermeneutic category, appears to actually also have a strongly excluding nature. Too often *the poor* refers to a certain category. To Latin American authors, *the poor* means Catholic, politically aware Christians who participate in base communities and are willing to participate actively in social change. Other poor people are left off the boat.

In the Through the Eyes of Another project, we tried to avoid this fallacy by letting the ordinary readers do the talking themselves. No schemes or methods were imposed. The group had the power. The empirical material, the many hundreds of pages with ordinary or spontaneous reading of the story of the Samaritan woman, makes it clear how multicolored and conflicting—sometimes shallowly, at other times profoundly—is biblical interpretation among the poor.

The ordinary reader as assignment

The project considers the ordinary reader as assignment. The ordinary reader is a category, a space, that must be cherished. Entering the world of ordinary Bible readers is fruitful and necessary. It forces Bible scholars into an encounter with the unknown, into an encounter with a counterstrategy that takes place, bypassing the rules of the guild, and often as if exegesis does not exist. In his beautiful hermeneutics of the New Testament, Klaus Berger, imitating Gadamer, penetratingly points out the importance of the unknown in the interpretation process. By this he mainly refers to experiences that are unknown to part of modern Western humanity: experiences of acute emergency, experiences of permanent suffering, the voice of the ones sacrificed. The truth, in Berger's opinion, is among those being sacrificed, because only they can expose which way does not lead to life. Innocent suffering is often more right than power is. The discovery of the unknown, Berger states, is the condition for arriving at a new and productive understanding of the biblical text.[29]

I agree with Berger. In the encounter with ordinary Bible readers, the unknown and the unconventional, the often bizarre experience, and the completely concrete ordinary reading of the Bible become fruitful. This encounter asks of exegesis the question, To what extent does the theoretical correctness of exegesis contribute to clarifying the truth?[30]

If one gives the *ordinary reader* the definition it often has in the Southern hemisphere—the poor and sacrificed ones—the concept also takes on soteriological and theological meaning. If our basic assumption is that God's liberating action is also especially directed toward them, and this is one of the supporting themes of Bible testimony, we can expect a great deal from their understanding of scripture.

And another thing: the reading processes of the small groups are characterized by great intimacy. A Dutch group writes, "The conversation sometimes became very personal, and that was possible because we felt very safe." A space is created in which faithful people feel safe because they have escaped from what they experience as imposed: dominance of church lectures, dogmas, the things one is supposed to believe. In quite a few reading reports, we find references to those safe spaces, the importance of which is so emphasized by West et al., appealing to Scott.[31]

While the first response in many Bible study groups is often the "missionary response" or the dogmatically correct response—the public transcript—critical modes of reading enable ordinary people from poor and marginalized communities to begin to articulate their working readings and theologies, what is incipient and usually deliberately hidden from public view. The latter is clearly dangerous. What is hidden from the dominant is hidden for good reason, and can and should only be openly owned in a context of trust and accountability. But within such a context, the intersection of community and critical resources enables the recognizing, recovering, and arousing of dangerous memories (Metz), subjugated knowledge (Foucault), and hidden transcripts.[32]

The reading reports demonstrate that communitarian Bible reading in a small group, in mutual trust and intimacy, creates a new culture. This process is delicate and fragile. People get to know each other in a different way. *Counterstrategy* is given a more profound meaning here, and not only positions itself critically and complementarily with respect to the scholarly reading, but also with respect to congealed, bleached lectures from church traditions. Things come up that were not supposed to be said; people express things they were not allowed to think or feel; they doubt where they weren't allowed to doubt. Participating in this process requires great sensitivity and knowledge by the "expert." Carlos Mesters has noted:

> Another obstacle that crops up at times is the lack of tact on the part of pastoral workers among the people. They are in a hurry and have no patience. They ride roughshod over some of the natural resistance that people have to our interpretations of the Bible. One time a nun went to give a course on the Old Testament. Halfway through she had to close down the course because no one was showing up. The people said: "Sister is destroying the Bible!" . . . A certain priest offered an explanation of the Exodus. Many people never came back. "He is putting an end to miracles," they complained. . . . Meddling with the faith of the people is very serious business. You must have deep respect and a delicate touch. You must try to feel as they would and intuit their possible reaction to what you are going to say. The people should be allowed to grow from the soil of their own faith and their own character.[33]

To summarize: Many nice things can be said about the complex relation between ordinary readers and exegetes. In the end, it all boils down to how this pact can be made fruitful for the local community of faith.[34]

The power of the story

One of the core objectives of the project is getting people from different situations into a conversation with each other about what moves them profoundly, what motivates them, the way they give form to their lives, where they find God. Participants are invited to read a Bible story together. This goal provides the project with an exceptionally powerful component, the story, the religious story in particular. Religious stories stimulate the imagination, cause people to decide the question of how they stand in life, and may determine the behavior of the reading community of faith.

In the past few decades, a rediscovery of the power of stories took place, also in theology. Stories are important carriers of world contemplation, yes, even making an essential contribution to its shape. In the literature, we find expressions such as "our universe itself is storied," "storied knowledge," "story-like knowledge."

> Our lives are ceaselessly intertwined with narrative, with the stories that we tell and hear told, those we dream or imagine or would like to tell, all of which are reworked in that story of our own lives that we narrate to ourselves in an episodic, sometimes semiconscious, but virtually uninterrupted monologue. We live immersed in narrative, recounting and reassessing the meaning of our past actions, anticipating the outcome of our future projects, situating ourselves at the intersection of several stories not yet completed.[35]

Knowledge and experience are passed on in the form of stories: they have a narrative structure. Stories are important to people because awareness, knowledge, culture, experience, community, and personal identity flow together in them. Between memory and anticipation, stories set the conversation in motion about tradition and the future, about where we came from and where we are going. Ricoeur sees the story, the narrative, as the basic structure of our experience of time and reality.

Stories are of eminent importance in all cultures, as is passing them on. Stories create identity in the same way that a sculptor forms shapes by cutting away material. A few of the many possibilities of being are offered here as worthwhile. Stories interpret life and found communities. From the perspective of African culture, Musa Dube writes:

> Stories are told and retold repeatedly to depict life, to transmit values, and to give wisdom for survival in life. The art of telling and retelling stories remains central to African societies. For example, a grandmother can tell the same story differently depending on her audience and the issues she wants to address. Thus characters in a story may change to suit the listeners and their circumstances, as the teller sees fit. A story may also be told to a group of listeners who add their comments and questions. This makes storytelling itself (and the story itself) a moment of *community writing* or *interpretation of life*, rather than an activity of the teller or author. The teller or writer thus does not own the story or have the last word, but rather the story is never finished: it is a page of the community's fresh and continuous reflection.[36]

What is true for stories in general applies to an even greater degree to religious stories. The story is also essential for the Christian tradition. "The center of the Christian message is not a proposition, but a narrative: the story of the passion, death and resurrection of Jesus."[37] The Bible, Christianity's basic document, contains all kinds of texts, but the story dominates. The stories make the Bible a Bible. "With respect to the Bible as such, the important texts, the texts that are the most relevant to religion, are stories," writes Ricoeur. The community of Christians at its deepest is primarily also a community of storytellers.[38]

Religious stories are experienced by people as ground-laying, as fundamental to their existence. Religious stories have authority; they belong to a canon. This quality means that the communities of faith, whether they want this or not, are led back to these stories time and again. And it also means that the meaning-reserve of these stories is explored time and again; these stories become "tested stories." Religious stories are the central component of traditions. The fact that they were told in this manner in the past is a reason to tell them once again, forming a dialectic between the new and the one from tradition, between servile repetition and creative innovation. Bible stories are liturgical in the sense that reenactment in the liturgic situation gives them an unprecedentedly profound meaning. Thus we see in our project that celebration is an important part of reading. Reading is laid in the cradle of celebration. One begins with it and ends with it. A Cuban group says: "These Bible meetings are true celebrations for us. We sing together accompanied by the guitar, we pray. Personal experiences and those of the group as a whole are made fruitful. Via the celebrations, the texts are connected to our own lives."

Communal reading of Bible stories stimulates crystallization on fundamental questions of life. "Reading the Bible together, reading together and asking questions, listening to each other, what strikes one person, what strikes another, is found meaningful; this is already valuable enough to the group, although we are not receiving any response from the partner group," says a group from Halle (the Netherlands). In mutual exchange, vague convictions and ideas are shown in the light of Bible stories that help people deal with the ambiguity of existence. "I wish to link concrete Bible stories with my own situation. I hope to be inspired. It is of essential importance to read Bible stories in the midst of problems you have to deal with on a daily basis," comments a participant in Zutphen (the Netherlands). Contrary to what people often experience in their lives, these stories paint pictures of the good life, life the way it should be.[39] "I feel in a moment of pain. When reading the Bible I find hope, some options that generate life," says an Indian woman in a Bolivian group. A group in Stellenbosch (South Africa) says: "We come to the Bible study to gain more knowledge of the Bible and God's purpose for our lives, to share our ideas and to understand that people have different points of view, but most of all we share a lot of that which is good and honest within us. By sharing experiences and ideas, the distance between people that city life brings is bridged. This is not only a learning process, but also a healing process—spiritually and physically."

Reading religious stories stirs up a great deal in people. The researchers who contribute to this collection are overwhelmed by this awareness. The story of the Samaritan woman stirred up so much! Communitarian reading of John 4 is experienced as enriching: "At the end of the reading of the passage, after two meetings, we concluded that it is very valuable to read a passage together with other people" (Wichmond, the Netherlands). People get to know each other in a new, profound manner. There is not one group that is not struck by the possibilities offered by communitarian reading of a Bible story. "Every participant experienced the conversation as exceptional," says a group in the Netherlands. "Each time anew a Bible story appears to come to life if you prepare for it together. You discover new, unsuspected sides of the story, and you discover the essence together." When reading a Bible story together, people share experiences, search for identity. "During the discussion on John 4, the group grew together and there were a lot of times when we laughed and reflected together. Afterwards, people said spontaneously that this text had taken on a different meaning for everyone" (Zutphen, the Netherlands). "On the whole, the group said they enjoyed the process, learned much from the passage because during the 'sharing' time, their own understanding was enriched by others' insights. Members said they gained fresh insights from a familiar biblical incident," reports a group from the Philippines.

We notice that the effect that stories as such can cause is intensified in reading the story of the Samaritan woman; in fact the identity of the reading community is being discussed. How do people relate to each other, with all mutual differences; what is their position in the world? The community of faith finds its reason for existence and identity in the story it tells and cherishes. As the story goes, so goes the community telling about it. The relationship between the reading community and the story it selects is tight. It seems as if the texts and the reading community choose one another; in a teaching-learning process the identity of the one is transferred to the other. "Nourishing and nutritious. A story like this one . . . it will sustain you for quite some time. It is like food that satisfies hunger," someone in a Dutch group comments.

In this process of searching for meaning, especially when it happens in the safe space of the small group, the longing for liberation, healing, delivery, and radical change appear stronger than all types of professed "Christian" schemes. "There is too little discussion about faith in church communities. It seems like it is no longer possible to have a heart-to-heart talk with one another," says one Dutch participant. "The participants found both the Bible study sessions so interesting, so enriching and educative, that they decided to do this kind of spontaneous, participatory Bible study in their regular biweekly Bible study sessions. All the members spontaneously participated in the discussion *freely*," says a group in Chennai (India). "In sum, the group had an interesting time during the number of times we met. At every session, members *freely* expressed their opinions," comments a group in Ghana. "They also felt comfortable with this method because it gives them the opportunity of expressing themselves in *confidence* and *brotherhood*, in their humble or cultured way of saying things, without false theories; with the blessing of human sharing," says a group in Cuba. "The cohesion in the group created a reading environment where everybody felt *free* to participate," says a group in Stellenbosch (South Africa).

Freely, confidence, and *brotherhood* touch on what is described by Ricoeur as one of the central tasks of a narrative theology. The assignment of narrative theology is to save the playfulness, stubbornness, incoherence, and ambiguity of the story from the hands of dogmatic argument, absolute certainty, closed formulas. Story and dogma are critically related to each other. Stories demonstrate more affinity for wisdom and sensible action than for the theoretical reason of dogma. When "the story" is liberated from the shackles of all types of Christian salvation-historical patterns, or from answers acceptable from a social and religious point of view, "then memory and hope would be delivered from the visible narrative that hides that which we may call, with Johann-Baptist Metz, the dangerous memories and the challenging expectations that together constitute the unresolved dialectic of memory and of hope."[40] In a time when tradition loses its authority and there no longer seems to be time for the stories that recall to mind the suffering and premature death of so many, keeping alive the dangerous memory is an urgent task for the community of faith. Cherishing the memory of those sacrificed, those forgotten, "the poor of YHWH," is a central theme of theological ethics. One could say that the Bible stories need a storytelling community capable of remembering and for which reinterpretation of this memory is a key to a different way of life. Scripture creates more than a world; it shapes a community that is the bearer of that world. Claims about the authority of scripture make sense only in that the world and the community it creates are in fact true to the character of God.

The reading reports show us that in the safe space and intimacy of the small group, the conversation about the dangerous memory of John 4 flows into the hope for a new future. "What we do here feeds our hopes. Making the decision to want to be an instrument of God and be on our way," says an Argentinean group.

This happens in almost all groups that participate in the project: keeping the memory alive that things became different with Jesus in those days and that therefore things can be done differently now. There is no group that does not discover how cultural codes get broken down in the story of John 4 and how boundaries are moved. Among all differences, this discovery is something all groups shared. I will give an example. In John 4:20, the question is asked whether people can worship God only in the temple. This question addresses an enormous problem for untouchables in India, who are not permitted to enter the temple. "Why does the woman start talking about worshiping?" asks someone in a group of Dalit women. "The Samaritan woman probably did not fit in with the existing forms of worship," answers another. "Maybe she was not allowed to enter as an outcast." "But wherever people suffering pain are excluded, God cannot be found either, right?! God would never be in a place where there is no place for us!"

Another feature of stories is important for the project, and that is the cohesion between story, imagination, and behavior. We see this coherence in expressions such as the following: "We meet because of God's Word, but also to share our personal needs and problems, to help each other and encourage each other," says a women's group in Bolivia. "Dear Lord, as we start to study the Gospel of John, let us see what this Gospel is for our lives, how it is transforming and orienting us," prays a Brazilian group. "We think this story is very real in our world full of conflicts. Will we be capable of finding common ethics? How will they look then?" says a Hungarian group. "In two lively sessions, participants saw different facets of a model for life-changing evangelism, and Jesus's inclusive approach to the lowly and the outcasts," comments a group in Chennai (India). In all these statements, the link between reading a story and associated behavior is an immediate one: there is an old story, the plot or the message of which is felt to be current, which calls for action. In Latin American hermeneutics, this association is often expressed in the scheme: seeing, judging, acting (*ver, juzgar, actuar*). Whether this relationship is as fluid as often presented is another question. The point to be made here is that stories are carriers of potential behavior. This is emphatically underscored in philosophy and sociolinguistics. A text is then referred to as "behavior potential": "A text . . . does not have a single, closed meaning, but a 'meaning potential,' or more appropriately in a functional framework, 'behavior potential.' The text, from this point of view, is a range of possibilities, an open-ended set of options in behavior that are available to the individual interpreter."[41]

This behavior takes on form where the plot of the old story and the imagination of the current reader meet. The components of a story—characters, actions, background—are anchored in space and time. This anchoring makes identification possible. Moreover, stories always have a plot, "the very organizing line, the thread of design, that makes narrative possible because it is finite and comprehensible. . . . Plot is a constant of all written and oral narrative. . . . Plot is the principle of interconnectedness and intention," "the design and intention of narrative, what shapes a story and gives it a certain direction or intent of meaning."[42]

The plot is what differentiates one story from another. It gives shape to a conviction, an outlook on life: it offers a way to be. Stories are not only the visible text; they can also become a perspective, a way of looking at things. When readers read a text, the capacity of the plot to change experiences is actualized. A story is actualized through analogy and imagination. Stories also have an elliptical nature. The story cannot capture the entire reality. There are gaps, things that were not said, details the reader must fill in. How old was the Samaritan woman? What was she wearing? How deep was the well? How many people lived in Sychar? Why did the village people believe her? A reporter in El Salvador writes: "The group developed a great deal of imagination to fill in the gaps in the story where it was short on information. People invented conversations and situations, gestures and attitudes, a beginning and an end."

Stories are always open. They stimulate the imagination of the readers and challenge them to finish the story. In this process, a new context and culture begin to operate, the original referent of the text is replaced by a new one, the situation of the current reader. The text is recontextualized, to use an ugly term. Before a new praxis is established in reading an old text, recognition and imagination are at issue. Imagination precedes praxis.

The relationship between story and praxis must especially be sought in the fact that stories offer schemes and possibilities for action. Praxis always assumes a minimum of decision, analysis, and imagination. Recognition via analogy and imagination that precede praxis forms the space in which possibilities and impossibilities of current praxis are pre-practiced. The old story may lead to a new project. The project, directed toward the future, and the story, directed towards the past, exchange their schemes and patterns in the area of recognition and imagination. The project derives its structuring force from the story; the story derives the possibility of projecting itself forward from the project. Thus, imagination is the area in which the "we could" of the story can become a "we can" of the project.

The link between the interpretation of the story of John 4 and the subsequent praxis—wished for or real—is tight; it appears from the project. "All of the participants, without exception, hold the normative conviction that the biblical text read in the community of believers is essential for growth in the life of the Christian faith and therefore fully reliable and trustworthy. They expect to be affected in different ways (inspired, nurtured, challenged, comforted, invited, empowered for action, etc.). It is for that reason that they are committed to studying the Bible together," says a group in Elkhart, Indiana (USA). "What do we ourselves thirst for?" an Argentinean group asks. "This text helps us see our own reality. We must leave the urn behind, go out to preach the gospel, leave safety behind. We must change our hearts." Someone in a Dutch group comments: "Jesus often does surprising things. He tackles things differently than we would, in unexpected ways. We should also try this, whether it involves faith or other groups of people whom you don't often see or visit. Learning to look at things differently." A woman participating in a Philippine group confesses: "Me, I identify myself with the Samaritan woman. She had many men in her life, and I was like her in the past. I was angry with the world, too, until I heard lessons from God from my reading of the Bible. Now I am not that angry anymore, just a little bit. Something changed in the life of the Samaritan woman; I also have changed."

Exactly how the line runs from reading the story to a new social or faith praxis is a complicated question. The reading reports offer the possibility of getting a more precise picture of that line.

Intercultural

With the concept *intercultural* we happen upon the third central component of the project. Like *ordinary reader*, *intercultural* is an umbrella concept. It can be divided into two concepts. *Cultural* means the question of influence of the local situation on reading biblical texts—culture is an important component here. *Inter* means comparison, exchange, confrontation, meeting, conversation. The two concepts together also represent the question of what possibilities are offered by the project in the world of ecumenics and mission.

Culture

In the protocol that accompanies the project, and elsewhere, we have already dwelt extensively with the manner in which the component culture and the term *intercultural* are defined in the project.[43] Culture is not the only and all-determining factor when people read the Bible. Social status, gender, ethnicity, power, level of education, and church background also play important roles. Therefore, the project not only focuses on culture but assumes that culture is also an essential and often neglected factor in hermeneutic processes. The term *intercultural* was chosen because culture, often more than the concept of context, offers the opportunity for finding a grid, a number of calibration points, which are necessary for discovering and converting differences between interpretations. The concept of culture, as used here, can be made operational—better than context.

What water is for fish

Cultures are powerful. They do change, but rather as an octopus than as fast-flowing water, as Clifford Geertz has noted. Over the past few decades, the weight of culture has also been discovered in theology, and intercultural theologies are popping out of the ground like mushrooms. Hans-Georg Gadamer says about tradition that "what water is for fish, tradition is for people." This observation also applies to culture. Precisely because one is in the middle of taking hold of one's own cultural values, problematizing them is difficult and can only really be done successfully via confrontation. Charles Larson tells how he wrestled with that question when he started teaching English literature in 1962 in Nigeria. The analysis of one of Thomas Hardy's passionate novels, in which kissing is an important characteristic of the behavior of some of the actors, led one of the students to an important question. Larson reports:

> "Excuse me, sir, what does it mean, 'to kiss'?" That was a much more difficult question to answer than the usual ones relating to the plot or the characters of the novel—a real shock when it was brought to my attention that I had a rather naïve boy in my class. So I brushed the question off until it was repeated a number of times and I slowly began to realize that all of my students had no real idea of what it meant to kiss. This seemed an extremely odd thing to me because most of my students were upper-form boys in their late teens—some in their early twenties—and I had, of course, heard them talking on occasion about their girl friends. It was also rumored that several of the boys were married, although by school regulations they were not supposed to be. Nevertheless, that question and others of a like nature kept recurring—in part, no doubt, because we were reading Thomas Hardy's *Far from the Madding Crowd*. Why did Hardy's characters get so flustered when they were kissed (or more likely, when they weren't kissed)? When I asked one of the European-educated African teachers why my students always seemed ready to return to that same question, I was more than surprised to learn that Africans, traditionally at least, do not kiss; to learn that what I thought was "natural" in one society is not natural at all, but learned, that is, cultural. Not all peoples kiss. Or, stated more appropriately, not all peoples have learned to kiss. . . . How was one to read a Thomas Hardy novel with all those frustrated kisses without ever having been kissed?[44]

The insight that culture to a large extent determines the behavior of people, their values and standards, and their view of life, has meanwhile also been adopted in theology. The discovery of "culture," cultural differences, and cultural identity has its positive side. It removes the existence of different ways of thinking and acting from the realm of hierarchic patterns. It emphasizes the legitimacy of differences. Differences can exist equivalently. In previous generations the appeal to a common humanity and neglect of cultural differences have often been severely repressive.

What was presented as universal was actually no more than an aggregate of European standards that were considered to be standardizing.[45]

If we wish to verify the role that culture plays in interpretation processes and insights into faith, a warning is in order, important for a project in which people with so many different backgrounds and so many different situations participate. Cultures do not function in a vacuum but develop in a social context in which other factors also are decisive. Not everything can be explained from a cultural point of view. Every culture has subcultures: certain patterns in what Oscar Lewis called poverty culture are part and parcel of the behavior of the poor, in any culture.

In our project, the idea is not to find the best definition of the more than 150 existing ones. The idea here is to be able to recognize culture where it crops up in reading the Bible, the Mediterranean culture in which the Bible was created, and the culture of the reader himself or herself. In keeping with Clifford Geertz,[46] culture is interpreted not as a static unit, a closed house, but as "a permanent activity of sense construction, where new connections between the old and the new are made all the time."[47] For the project, the question of how the influence of culture can be made visible in the interpretation of biblical texts is important. For this we need a cultural theory that gives us a set of instruments for empirical research. The well-known cultural theory by Hofstede can help us.[48] According to Hofstede, culture is chiefly mental programming, software of the mind. Hofstede agrees with the cultural-anthropological insights of the first half of the twentieth century, to wit: that all societies, modern or traditional, have to do with identical fundamental problems; the answers, however, are different. A number of these problems can be considered of a fundamentally cultural nature. Hofstede calls these fundamental problems *dimensions*. One may call them cultural depth dimensions. Hofstede argues that there are a fixed number of such dimensions. There are systematic differences in the manner in which people deal with (1) power and inequality, (2) the relationship between the individual and the greater collective one belongs to, (3) expected social roles of men and women, (4) the fear and uncertainty of existence, and (5) time and tradition.

Hofstede has been reproached for having too static an opinion of culture. The importance of Hofstede's research for the project is that a number of calibration points are found that can be used to analyze the reading reports for cultural specificity. Hofstede's set of instruments only covers some of the codes that can be used to analyze the reports—once again, not everything is culture!—but it appears to be fertile. John 4 is full of cultural depth dimensions. The story involves a question of power, a man-woman meeting, tradition versus radically new religious insights (the place of worship, for example), social groups that Jesus and the Samaritan woman are involved with (disciples and village people), social exclusion, ethnic differences and discrimination, a difference in social status. Culture has an immediate impact on the interpretation of Bible stories. While some groups are struck by the unusual nature of the meeting between Jesus and the Samaritan woman—they are alone, at a strange time of the day, a man addresses an unknown woman—others read without noticing these features at all. Some groups dwell on the comment that the meeting takes place at the sixth hour. Others are barely aware of the fact that this verse is unusual. The perception of the Samaritan woman's attitude is also determined culturally, as is that of Jesus and his disciples. It is fascinating to see not only how differently groups focus on ("focalize") the story (i.e., the relationship between the way the story presents its elements and the way the reader responds), but also how culturally determined their manners of meeting and reading are.

While some groups go into the mountains for a weekend to read John 4 and turn the meeting into a celebration, taking along symbolic objects, a Dutch group says: "During this first meeting we noticed that we actually don't use symbolic objects. No one thought about this in advance. We concluded from this that we aren't very symbol-oriented people. . . . We noticed that what we bring along to such a meeting in the Netherlands does say something about our culture. Everyone has brought along a pen, a notepad, and an agenda book. The minutes are taken on a laptop. Apparently, pragmatism and efficiency make us feel good."

A clear distinction can be made between collective and more individualistic reading. Certain groups, e.g., from Central America and Africa, read collectively. This means that in the group discussion, one does not go into the text so much, but rather goes into what the other people in the group mentioned, and endorses it, takes the line further. Western reading reports are often found to be very individualistic by non-Western partners. Groups compare these reports with a chicken coop where people peck around themselves and one never arrives at a communal opinion or project. A number of reading reports breathe the presence of what can be called, along the lines of Walter Ong, *listening readers*: illiterates whose interpretations have the characteristics of oral tradition.[49]

Intercultural

The use of the concept *intercultural* underlines that we intend to go toward exchange, confrontation, interaction. Intercultural implies that the project is intended to go a step beyond detecting differences. Intercultural is more than multicultural. Regarding the differences between the terms *intercultural, intracultural,* and *cross-cultural,* I agree with the definitions that apply in anthropological research.

> If intercultural communication refers to communication between people from different cultures, then intracultural communication refers to communication between people from the same culture. . . . If we observe communication between a Japanese and a German . . . we are looking at intercultural communication. . . . Another term that needs to be clarified is cross-cultural. While this term often is used as a synonym for intercultural, the term cross-cultural traditionally implies a comparison of some phenomena across cultures. If we examine the use of self-disclosure in Japan and

Germany, for example, we are making a cross-cultural comparison. If we look at how Japanese use self-disclosure when communicating with Germans and how Germans use self-disclosure when communicating with Japanese, in contrast, we are looking at intercultural communication.[50]

The new aspect of the project is, on the one hand, the comparative aspect, the opportunity to compare interpretations of the same biblical text originating from different cultural and social contexts, and on the other hand, the aspect of interaction. Participants are asked to examine radically different interpretations of the same text. Are they willing to exchange perspectives? Why? Thus, the *inter* represents the insight that confrontation with the difference may lead to a new, productive understanding of texts. The *inter* implies a discussion on the question of whether a structure and hierarchy can be detected in the differences in such a way that the weight of the differences is cancelled, can be explained and put into perspective in the light of a common engagement, a common assignment. Thus, interaction is a goal, and at the same time it is a quality for which an analytical instrument is necessary to test in what way that interaction manifests itself, whether it is experienced as successful or whether it fails.

Multicultural reading of the Bible as a fact

Over the past few years, an overwhelming quantity of material has been published about Bible reading in non-Western situations. It seems more is known about ordinary readers in Latin America and Africa than in Europe or the U.S. Christians, also in the West, "know" that the Bible is read "multiculturally." But this vague awareness is not the same thing as being present at the moment when that reading happens. Everybody who sees or hears this phenomenon occurring is struck by the possibility of so many interpretations, even of rather classical and central passages from the Old and New Testament. And they are struck by the weight culture carries in the interpretation process.

An example can help me describe the complexity of the problem. At the Free University in Amsterdam, we receive a considerable number of students from all over the world every year. As part of the class "Text and Context" on modern, postmodern, and third world hermeneutics, students participate in a short experiment on intercultural reading of the Bible. These exercises are, we think, eloquent. The astonishing fact is not only that of the diversity of interpretations and emphasis but also that of the complexity of factors that orient and mediate the interpretation process. Of course, every participant is very aware of the differences in the perception of what is central to the text. Nevertheless, there always is a degree of acceptance of that diversity; an almost natural space for polysemy or plurivocity and differences is allowed.

However, tension mounts when different cultural codes and values are linked to the text. Acceptance of diversity makes way for a struggle for truth when cultural practices are legitimized by means of specific interpretations of the text. Sometimes the very existence of the group as a small interpretive community is threatened. Thus, in our multicultural interpretation exercise two major problems always arise. First is the fact of plurality itself. However, the real conflict of interpretation arises only there where conflicting social and cultural practices are legitimized by the interpretation of the (same) text. The second problem is the lack of criteria with which to determine the weight to be given to each of the mediating factors. How can we establish a hierarchy of values for a proper intercultural reading strategy? And that is, of course, precisely what we always need as a group. While every individual is entitled to have his or her own application of the text, as a group—as an interpretive community—we need to come to grips with the differences; we have to resolve the tensions that arise. It is not so difficult for the participants to apply the text to their own local contexts. They do so all the time. What happens is that our very existence as a group, as a recently established multicultural interpretive community, is in terrible need of a more profound, more enriching interpretation process. In order to survive as a community, we need to take another step, beyond diversity. A new interaction is necessary, not so much between each individual member of the group and the text, but rather between the text and the group as a group. We have to practice a communitarian reading of the text, and triggered by the text, a critical interpretation of the cultural practices we are used to. In order to survive, a new sort of catholicity is needed. We have to broaden the scope of our interpretation. In order to reach a consensus, we cannot avoid a conversation about culture and life itself.

Transforming reading

This analysis takes us to another aspect of the intercultural: the question of under what conditions a change of perspective takes place. What is the motive for people to listen to others' religious outlooks in order for an exchange of perspective to take place? The presumption of the project is not that changes automatically occur if Bible readers from different cultural situations are put in contact with each other. On the contrary, intercultural communication is an unruly process and often proceeds with difficulty. Instead, we explore under what conditions change takes place. What happens in reading groups that actually come to new insights in the interaction with other groups? What factors are responsible for this change? Can biblical texts change people? A great deal has been written about that question in the recent past. The term used is *transforming reading*. Anthony C. Thiselton's book on new horizons in hermeneutics is subtitled *The Theory and Practice of Transforming Biblical Reading*.[51] This question is of essential importance within all hermeneutic designs, especially in liberation hermeneutics. There, especially, one finds the presumption that Bible reading contributes to social transformation.

Thus, a lot has been written about transforming reading but very little about the conditions that reading (the Bible) must meet if change is intended. I have in mind here the reader response movement that originated in the science of literature, in which again great emphasis is placed on the reader. Some people go so far as to consider the reader the co-author of the text. Reading communities (interpretive communities), with their own conventions and interests, are decisive to interpretation, according to Stanley Fish. Interpretation is the source of texts, facts, authors, and intentions. All is the result of interpretation.[52] However, no matter how much one talks about the reader, and how many endless debates are held on the profile of the reader—the implicit reader or the model reader—reader response criticism will continue to move, as does sociopragmatic hermeneutics, on the abstract level of reading strategies in general, reading communities in general, and general relationships between texts and readers. This drives Hans Robert Jauss, a student of Gadamer, to lament: "In biblical studies [one] has not yet begun to attend seriously to the reception history of biblical texts. As long as biblical reader-response critics concentrate on the implied reader and narratee in the biblical texts, they will continue to neglect the reception of biblical texts by flesh-and-blood readers."[53]

With his aesthetic reception, Jauss focuses attention on the horizon of expectation of the reader. Each reader introduces a certain point of view, a perspective, to the text. This point of view is charged from a reference framework, from experiences and expectation. Jauss carefully moves to the new area of empirical hermeneutics. He develops a model for the analysis of identification patterns between readers and characters from a story (association, admiration, and sympathy), but he also does not progress beyond the analysis of the motivation for the identification.

In *The Double Perspective*, David Bleich makes a plea for more interaction between professional and ordinary readers.[54] However, the perspective remains theoretical and North American. Bleich's double perspective does not include the interaction between the rich and the poor, or between Western and non-Western readers. Ideology critics such as Louis Althusser and Terry Eagleton have also been preoccupied with the reader. Every reader confronts a text with expectations and interests. The engagement with the text is almost always conflicting: the expectations are not met, and tension and splits are created. Ideology criticism intends to follow this interaction. How are things explained or adapted; how are eliminations made? What criteria guide the process? Why does this component of the text have preference, and why is another one suppressed? Also true of ideology criticism, however, is that it was developed in the area of theory and rarely listens to ordinary readers.

Transforming reading is possible, but as Gadamer emphasized, a process of change, adjusting expectations, and change of perspective does not always take place. If it does happen, the process is not automatic.[55] Traditions are capable of absorbing new insights; traditions can also lead to reading the fundamental texts in a petrified or gastronomic manner (Umberto Eco). The space that tradition allows readers regarding its fundamental texts can sometimes be so minute that interpretations and reading processes are institutionalized. This constriction reduces the original vision that the texts were intended to serve to nothing.

Diversity, confrontation, and distance are conditions for productive and creative reading. Readers are separated from Bible texts by historical distance. One factor responsible for the change in paradigm in modern hermeneutics is the insight that distance is a positive factor. Distance is not an obstacle that leads to hermeneutic powerlessness. Because of distance, prejudices may disappear, or instead may manifest themselves. However, when reading biblical texts, Distance (*Distanz*) is always accompanied by its sister, Partner (*Zugehörigkeit*). Readers are also always part of a reading and interpretive tradition, often without being aware of it. The situation in which we find ourselves relative to the text we wish to understand is already hermeneutic and partially determined by tradition. Historical awareness itself is affected by the *Wirkungsgeschichte* of the text. The relationship between *Distanz* and *Zugehörigkeit* is dialectic. Sometimes the opportunities of distance are nullified by tradition. Wherever reading traditions allow only reproduction of meaning, and not a creative and renewing association with texts, wherever *Distanz* has lost its power, only pale, flat interpretation will take place. In that case, opportunities for broadening horizons or changing perspective must be felt out by involving new factors in the game. One of those factors is cultural diversity. Diversity can be given shape, and confrontation can be organized by designating the hermeneutic function of distance, chronological but also cultural, and making it operative. This is exactly what is attempted in the Through the Eyes of Another project. Cultural diversity is introduced as a hermeneutic factor; confrontation is organized. The basic assumption of the project is that it can have added value when diversity is taken seriously in this manner.

Implications for ecumenism and mission

I come to the last aspect. What are the implications and possibilities of the project for the world of mission and ecumenism? The conviction is that the project provides opportunities for enriching relationships of mission and service between Christians, especially at the grassroots level of the churches. We could call this the ecumenical aspect. Next, these Christians will not wish to avoid also involving non-Christians in the discussion on the good world and the merciful God. This conversation is the missionary aspect.

The situation Christians have among themselves can be compared with the image Geert Hofstede uses in opening his study on cultural differences. Twelve members of a jury are sitting together. The cultural differences are great; they have never met each other before, but they must arrive together at resolving the matter imposed on them before they will be allowed to leave. "Like the twelve members of the jury," Hofstede writes, "people, groups and nations are confronted with communal problems that can only be solved by co-operation."[56]

Groups that participated in the project are intensely engaged with their faith, but in a situation of great differences. The differences involve insight into faith, church traditions, and socioeconomic conditions. Seventy percent of the participants in the project consider themselves poor. There are groups that meet in stately houses or churches, in safe neighborhoods, and in villages where society is described as homogeneous and calm. There are also groups that meet in slums, have to reckon with youth gangs, cannot come because of the rain that paralyzes transportation; some must make long and dangerous journeys. One of the Bolivian groups reports that all participants come from the slum districts of La Paz. "All members have to deal with social problems that get worse every day," states the report. A Dutch group says: "If we look at our social and economic position, globally, and compare it to those of the poor, we are members of the powerful." A Colombian group reports: "Nobody has a permanent job; most of us work as salespeople in small neighborhood stores, others babysit the neighbor's kids, others are housewives and depend on the support of their children."

The discussion about those differences touches the heart of the project. The project targets interaction and not just reporting differences. We do not want to end up in what has been described sometimes as the multicultural fallacy: Everything is allowed as long as it is different; deviations are all right as long as they are not really profound. Detection of the fact of cultural plurality and fundamental equality of cultures is not sufficient. After all, this plurality occurs within the framework of a dramatic inequality that directly determines the lives of people. Therefore, intercultural Bible reading is important, because those differences not only clearly surface in the encounter between groups but are also directly involved in the discussion. Often more concrete and more existential than abstract theological debate, intercultural Bible reading turns out to be a space where consensus, balance, and identity are sought in a broad ecumenical perspective.

The special position of the scripture hereby comes fully to the fore. We see things happen that are expressed so well by de Groot: Returning to the scripture is always turning to the communal future of the separated churches as well. There is a conviction that unity is not a lost cause as long as the scripture continues to be opened, read, and preached in all Christian churches.[57] Groups discover they need each other when formulating and experiencing the essentials of Christian faith. One realizes that multicoloredness and complementarity are profound evangelical values. Thus, intercultural Bible reading may effect a form of meeting that is profound and eminently reciprocal. A glance into the second phase of the project, where interaction takes place, presents this effect clearly. Without further analysis, I will provide examples that touch the core moments of ecumenical learning. More extensive analyses are provided elsewhere in this volume.

People (1) get to know each other's context, (2) similarities are discovered, (3) prejudices are adjusted, (4) from longing to unity, and (5) the situation of asymmetry is critically involved in the discussion. (6) One tries to discover a structure and origin in the differences, (7) puts them into perspective and searches for what can bind them. (8) One looks critically at one's own context. (9) Mechanisms of exclusion from the partner group are criticized.

(1) Before sharing your reflection, we read the context of the village you live in and found it very interesting. This context helps situate your group in Dutch reality. Then, after several meetings, we invited a person who has traveled to your country to open a panorama of your culture for us. We admire your solidarity with the world and your respect for people, ecology, and human rights. (El Salvador to the Dutch partner group)

(1) We started by pointing to the island of Cuba on the map of the world. The discussion leader asked what we knew about Cuba. That was not much. We know that it is one of the few communist countries left and that Fidel Castro is its ruler. Also that the relationship with the U.S. is not that good, although America is very nearby. (Macassar, Indonesia, to Cuba)

(2) The experiences of the women of our partner group have been similar to ours. This is very interesting, because like us, they are located in countries with huge social problems, displaced by violence and heavy economic problems. (Colombia to a North American group of Mexican immigrants)

(3) The people of the partner group are more involved with God than we ever thought. (Colombian group to the Dutch partner group)

(3) At the start, the group thought that the Dutch partners were boasting about what they have in their houses. Slowly, the group realized that they were simply explaining their contexts and natural environment to help the Samaritana group have a better understanding of their background. (Philippines to a Dutch group)

(3) The group was surprised by the demographics of the partner group from Colombia: They are young, well educated, and from diverse cultural backgrounds—a stark contrast to our group of elderly people, with at the most secondary education (except for two teachers) and mostly from the same cultural group. The fact that most of the participants from the partner group are single was referred to in passing; most of the women in the South African group are widows. (Durban, South Africa, to Colombia)

(4) The issue of prejudice is discussed in detail and evaluated with a clear focus on unity. (Durban, South Africa, to the Colombian partner group)

(5) We believed that we have helped our Dutch partners to have some understanding of what it means to be poor. They, in fact, commented and reminded us that the poor tend to be closer to the Lord. We feel we have been able to encourage them to trust God, because people whose needs are sufficiently met tend to forget God. We are glad that they acknowledged their need for God even as they enjoy what they have materially. (Philippine group to a Dutch partner group)

(5) What are you thirsty for? The insecurity you show about "losing the car" sounds strange to us. Our insecurities are related to survival: What to eat? How to support our children? We don't even think about having a car here. (Cuba to a North American group)

(5) They dedicate time to the nuclear problem. We have other things to worry about, which are related to reflection: the massacres, the displaced people, the social insecurity, the armed groups, and our economic instability. (Colombia to a Dutch group)

(6) Our group realized the difference of their socioeconomic standing from the Dutch partners and that this difference may have had an impact on the way we read and understood John 4. Our group centered on the woman at the well because we can identify with the woman's background. Her life is similar to what most of us in the group have also gone through. The Dutch partners did not look at the woman's reputation as something bad, which our group did. (Philippine group to a Dutch partner group)

(6) Their interpretation also deals with outcasts from their society, such as prostitutes, homosexuals, colored or dark people, those who are afflicted with AIDS, the poor, and the like. I remember we also drew a parallel between the woman of Samaria and outcasts in our culture. But we tended to focus on the woman as one who committed adultery and was marginalized, while they drew a wider parallel between the woman and the poor, as well as other outcasts in their society. (Indonesia to Cuba)

(7) Our counterpart in the Netherlands analyzed the passage more intellectually. We used our hearts and feelings more. But we understand that the difference lies in our background and situation. (Philippines to the Netherlands)

(7) The most important is to seek our similarities in Jesus and from them work for the kingdom, without looking for that which divides us, separates us, because the world needs us united. "May they be one so that the world may believe," Jesus said. We embrace you in loving kinship. (an Argentinean group to a Nicaraguan Pentecostal group)

(8) As you grew up, who were the people you were told to avoid? When we were young (in the 1980s), we were told to avoid religious people, homosexuals, people against the Cuban revolution, and alcoholics. We were also prevented from going to slums. (Cuba)

(9) Though we read that the group consists of the same number of men and women, we could not hear the voice of women. Young Hee: Is there no

discrimination against women in Colombia? Hee Soon: Was there no right for Colombian women to speak out in public? (Korean group to their Colombian partner group)

From a theological and hermeneutic point of view, interaction sometimes leads (1) to reorientation of the group's own initial interpretation; (2) to a broadening of horizons; (3) to critical questions about the church that the partner group belongs to; (4) to critical questions about the reading method: one wants to copy the method of the partner group, one blames the partner group for not involving their lives in the reading to a great enough extent, the partner group does not allow women to speak, one finds the partner report too superficial or too open; (5) to adjustment of the group's attitude toward other local churches; (6) to beginning small intercultural relations of friendship.

(1) and (2) The Colombian group did not focus on the water and bread as extensively as we did. But their interpretation gave deeper meaning to the text, making it personal and helping us develop the theme more fully. We are like dams that will break if we don't have a release. The living water needs to be shared but also received from others. Pride makes people think there is nothing they can receive from others. We cut ourselves off, but maybe we need to be more creative in bridging the boundaries we set for ourselves by thinking there is nothing we can learn from the Samaritan woman, as the disciples thought. We were acting on instinct and learned patterns of thought. Even the comment about how sorry we feel for rural women who have to carry water is a sign of this. We can learn from these women, because we are all women of Africa. We need each other and need to be less self-absorbed. We need to return to the truth of our situation and let go of false truths. False truths are created by pride. But we rationalize it and say it is fear or whatever lie we want to believe to remain comfortable without truly living in the world and appreciating our situation and other people. But we still think we are something special and know everything. (Durban to Colombia)

(1) and (2) I was surprised when I read the document, because they are really christocentric. In their analysis, everything is about Jesus Christ. And from this part of reality, we are accustomed to analyzing the Bible as it applies to our spiritual lives: How do I stand in relation to the Word of the Lord? My personal behavior as a child of God? What am I doing right that he commands? Toward society? I can value my behavior toward society, but society by itself, Nicaraguan society: the politicians, businessmen, are they acting the way God wants them to? We don't carry out this analysis. We don't judge them from the focus or from a Bible perspective. From the document they sent us, at first sight they seem to be a political group, and

this causes us to be somewhat suspicious because this is like mixing the Word of the Lord with politics, but in reality the Bible questions the attitudes of people, the Bible questions us. Because of the past history of our country, we are afraid of falling into what is known as liberation theology, which is linked to social movements; therefore we do not like to mix with political positions, because of what happened in the recent past, but the truth is that the Bible asks what everyone does with the neighbor. (a Nicaraguan Pentecostal group to an Argentinean Base Ecclesial Community)

(2) We also read the text before coming together, but it was very favorable that you brought questions that would help develop the analysis. Your questions were very interesting. We answered them all, after reacting to some of the reflections you made. (Cuban group to their North-American partner group)

(2) . . . And also because of this Scottish group, we get a step further. (Dutch group to their Scottish partner group)

(2) There was a definite broadening of horizons in terms of mode of reading and paradigm. The mode of subjective engagement enabled the group to own the text, and this created the atmosphere from which barriers could be confronted to the point of repenting of our own patterns of discrimination. (Durban to Colombia)

(3) Question for the Argentinean group: Regarding the hierarchy of the Catholic church: Are you for ecumenics, or do you as a church group agree with the church hierarchy? Because the Catholic hierarchy is very hard. How do you feel in relation to the hierarchy? Are you critical of the hierarchy, which in Latin America is always on the side of people with economic success, with more economic power? With respect to the politics of the Vatican, with respect to the Protestant church, the evangelical church, how do you feel about us? (response from a Nicaraguan group to their Argentinean partner group)

(4) Your interpretation of John 4 is just like a very conventional sermon we used to hear from our senior minister. (a Korean group to their Colombian partner group)

(4) To the Chennai group, the partner group appeared to be too open. The partner group, according to the Chennai group, sees the text as mere literature, as a story and less as scripture. The text was interpreted rationally and not spiritually. They found it more as a secular reading, rather than a religious reading. (India to the Netherlands)

(4) The next point: we focused on the fact that this woman committed

adultery, but they identified her with people who are discriminated against, the colored, the afflicted, and the miserable. Maybe we did not study the background of this text too well. (Indonesia to Cuba)

(4) We don't see a confrontation with detailed reality in concrete aspects from our personal lives and as a people. We believe that the Word arose in a concrete situation and was a response to it. In the same way, we are called to question ourselves about our reality and there encounter the Lord's traces that question and reveal us. Reality is a very important moment in our exploration of the Bible, and we feel that the group in Filadelfia, at least sometimes, doesn't do so systematically. (an Argentinean group to their Nicaraguan partner)

(5) The fact that it is a biblical group of Christians from various churches also draws our attention, because this is a reality that couldn't occur on our side, where the relationships are conflicted between the groups from the Catholic church and the congregations of evangelicals and Pentecostals or the Jehovah's Witness and Mormon groups, which are the most common in our villages. (a Roman Catholic Colombian group to an ecumenical group in Huizen, the Netherlands)

(6) This allows us to assimilate the concepts of the different cultures, and also to strengthen this little link of friendship with hope for the future as a force of a deeper intercultural relationship. (El Salvador to Voorschoten, the Netherlands)

So far, the examples are of ecumenical learning and interaction. When all these responses are added together, something happens here, in all multicoloredness, at the micro level of this project, that has been described by Robert J. Schreiter as the contours of a new catholicity:

> A new catholicity, then, is marked by a wholeness of inclusion and fullness of faith in a pattern of intercultural exchange and communication. To the extent that this catholicity can be realized, it may provide a paradigm for what a universal theology might look like today, able to encompass both sameness and difference, rooted in an orthopraxis providing *teloi* for a globalized society.[58]

We turn now toward the missionary side of the project. Searching for a shared identity among reading groups, for a new unity and message to the world, must be seen as an exercise preceding the dialogue with non-Christians. The sense that God is everything in all implies that the discussion about the messianic way cannot be limited to a dialogue between Christians only. The gospel itself is transcultural and trans-border. The scripture is a product of intercultural communication. This is original data that demands a follow-up.[59] People are sensitized by intercultural Bible reading to their own cultural determination and the conditions under which a discussion about faith can be held integrally and profoundly. Those conditions—a few of which were described above—apply not only to the discussion among Christians, but also to the dialogue with non-Christians. Moreover, fundamental texts of non-Christian religions can easily be involved in the project. Why couldn't people read texts about Ibrahim, in addition to those about Abraham, and with Muslims? In that case, what happens is no longer intercultural Bible reading, but intercultural scripture reading.

From a missionary point of view, the project provides special opportunities for dialogue with non-Christians, not least because John 4 itself concerns a cross-border movement of the Messiah. Groups involved in this text get to know the manner in which Jesus himself, according to John, perpetrates trans-border intercultural communication. We find a good example in the report by a Bolivian group:

> She had spiritual thirst. She wanted to learn. Jesus had a goal, too. Both, Samaritans and Jews, were divided. God did not want that; he wanted them to be united. His objective was to eliminate hatred. To the woman he asked, and she answered with the will to learn to know more.

Many groups see that the trans-border communication in John 4 serves the elimination of barriers between nations, of inequality, discrimination, and exclusion. A few Dutch examples:

> Maybe Jesus did this to move the Samaritans "upwards." Why are there any people that feel inferior? Isn't it because they are made to feel inferior?! This was Jesus's life, too: pulling back up all that was pushed down.

> W. is very impressed with how Jesus revealed himself to that Samaritan woman. She thinks it is tremendous that Jesus is willing to accept the hospitality of the Samaritans for two days (v. 40). This is proof that Jesus is not averse to the difference in ethnicity or religion.

> But why does it have to be in Samaria? It could also have been a woman from a different people or from Canaan. Jesus wants to demonstrate that the separation between Jews and Samaritans is not valid to him. He does not stay with the woman by himself. The woman brings in her village companions, despite the fact that she was probably avoided by them. Thus, salvation also applies to non-Jews.

> But what does the story entail? On one side, in my opinion, what was being discussed is that walls are broken down. All kinds of borders and prejudices that those Samaritans are allowed to really play along, too.

Orthodox tradition ties into the legend that the Samaritan woman died as a martyr during the reign of Nero. She became a saint, called Saint Photini, the bearer of light. To argue this, one zeroes in on the final passage of the story of John 4 in which conversion of the village people and sowing and reaping are discussed. She is also regarded as the first woman evangelist. Many reading groups follow this trail and see the story especially as a mandate to evangelism and mission.

> Women must preach the good news. God's word has no limits. We have to preach the word not only in one place but everywhere. To sow good things in order to have other people reap what we have sown. (Bolivia)

> A participant from an Indian group portrays the Samaritan woman as soul winner and sees this story as a model for personal evangelism. A woman of a culture other than Jesus's communicates so effectively that she changes and was open to what he said. In turn she became an evangelist to share this news to others.

> Through the example of this woman who went to tell everyone that she met the Messiah, Jesus wants us to know that we have to preach his word to everyone, without exception, woman or man, all around the world. (Bolivia)

> Mary, a participant in an Indian group: The sower and the reaper may be separated by much more of a time gap, but let us not wait for the fruit, but do our part to sow and be ready to reap at the right time. (India)

> A Dutch participant took along seeds from her garden plot. She refers to John 4:35 about the fields that are almost ready for harvest. She is of the opinion that we all must sow the seed of the gospel, tell the people that the Messiah is about to come and the harvest is near. (Amstelveen, the Netherlands).

The discussion about differences in the world and what the task of the messianic movement is, is not confined to mutual discussions when reading John 4. Groups do not limit their longing for liberation to themselves. The project leads groups toward the perspective to which intercultural communication belongs: the unity of humankind.[60] Deference and resistance against premature types of universality are of great importance here. An Argentinean group formulates their deference in preaching the gospel in a beautiful way:

> We approach our brothers and sisters with the instrument of love; otherwise it doesn't work. Approach and proximity are created in the small, in what is near, within our possibilities, by listening attentively.

In the intercultural communication of the gospel, love is more befitting than the impulse to convert—"we approach our brothers and sisters with the instrument of love; otherwise it doesn't work"—and sensitivity and openness are more appropriate than self-righteous argument—"approach and nearness are created in the small, in what is near, within our possibilities, by listening attentively." The intercultural communication of the gospel takes place within a situation of unimaginable inequality and religious pluralism and will have to bear that in mind. The hurricane of globalization[61] brings with it a great deal of tension. The experience of the global is frequently not benign, especially in poorer countries. The questions that arise are enormous. Is the world developing with equal chances for everyone? How will there be an end to gigantic streams of refugees, increasing corruption, and economic problems? Pollution of water and air does not recognize borders. Migration is a process of a worldwide nature, with diasporas on a scale such as has rarely happened in history. What are the chances of survival for the numerous minority cultures within developing countries? When the world's major media are controlled by fewer and fewer companies, will the monopoly on communication generate a new totalitarianism? The intercultural communication within the Christian tradition cannot extract itself from the question of who the winners and the losers will be in this globalization. In order to arrive at solutions to the border-transgressing problems that humanity is confronting, ecumenical and religious treaties and conversion are necessary. Exactly here are new chances for intercultural hermeneutics that strive for liberation.

> While respect for diversity and openness to disagreement are always a requirement for serious reflection, it is equally important that both individuals and groups . . . do not seek to reach a consensus all too quickly, especially through easy compromises. What is needed is the courage to probe deeply into the material and to anticipate growth, change, and transformation in the very struggle for divine truth. One lesson to be learned from the past is that the Bible has a quality of calling forth an active response from its readers before revealing its profoundest secrets. . . . Could it be that the persistent, existential claims of the Bible are what drive a new generation forward in anticipation of genuine discovery?[62]

Empirical research

In the introduction, I formulated the central question: If (1) ordinary Bible readers from radically different situations and contexts (2) read the same Bible story and (3) enter into a conversation with each other about this reading, (4) what will happen? Research on what happens is empirical research. The purpose of the project is to contribute to a new field of research, called *empirical hermeneutics*, in which attention is focused on current ordinary readers. Whoever thought that a great deal of work had already been done in this field was mistaken. With the exception of a number of quality studies,[63] this research is still in its infancy. Even in Latin America, where a large amount of material has been published since the 1970s, with examples of "how the people read the Bible," little really systematic empirical research has been done. This lack of research undoubtedly has something to do with the multicoloredness and complexity of the research material. It has to do with the fact that new research methods must be developed.[64] But perhaps it has first of all to do with appropriate diffidence about using a scientific instrument to tackle precious material, often consisting of experiences of wounded and violated people.

Nevertheless, systematic research is necessary, if only as a tribute to the owners of this project, the ordinary readers. They have invested a great deal in this project. The story of the Samaritan woman was brought to life in a thousand different ways; many flowers were allowed to bloom here. Their interpretations are fascinating, emotional, and extremely valuable. I have seldom been so touched and overwhelmed as now by the opportunities offered by the conversation with and among ordinary readers. But the issue most deeply involved in the project also demands a great deal of scientific work. The comment is often made that Bible reading by the poor is romanticized.[65] The role of the intellectual in processes of liberating or transforming Bible reading is more problematic than Gramsci et al. thought it would be.[66] In the overall interpretation process, the exegete sometimes takes charge of a greater share than he or she is entitled to. Too often exegetes also want to determine the current meaning of the scripture. Studies by David Lehmann, B. A. Müller, et al., of Independent Churches in South Africa or Pentecostal Churches in Salvador, Bahía, Brazil, make it clear that there are also profound differences among all types of actualizing methods of dealing with the scripture. Despite the tremendous popularity of the Bible, mutual exchange, intercultural communication between ordinary readers in different continents, has as yet barely been touched on. The Bible has an effect on people's actions that can hardly be overestimated; however, we still know very little about the exact relationship between Bible reading and social transformation. For all these reasons, empirical research is necessary.

The fact that this project is international and that the researchers are dealing with precious material implies that this research must be meticulous and open. The West cannot be allowed to impose any objectives. The project may not draw to itself the suspicion that it is an attempt to revitalize Western forms of Bible reading by focusing attention on all types of "exotic" Bible reading. As a matter of fact, the project shows clearly that the situation is completely different: creative and also pale types of Bible reading can be found among all the groups! Researchers in the Southern hemisphere often act as if they were stung by a wasp when people in the Northern hemisphere want to do something with "the poor." Sometimes their response is justified, and sometimes it is the result of short-sightedness and ideological thinking. Defining the question and formulating the objective of the project has been a continuous discussion between the North and South, precisely aiming to escape this type of objection.

The raw materials of the project are made up of reading reports of small groups of Christians. Our research can be classified as qualitative research.[67] An important characteristic of this type of research is that the researcher does have a theory or intuition, but it has usually not been elaborated and consists of no more than a vision based on several central concepts. The researcher does have expectations but has not been able to test them in practice. An open research design characterizes the project, providing opportunities for different research questions. The openness to diversity appears in the results presented in this book. The research is characterized by the back-and-forth movement between developing research questions, collecting data, and carefully listening to the ordinary readers. Research questions were nourished and put on the agenda out of the empirical situation. *Qualitative* also means that researchers sought as much contact as possible with the world in which the participants in the relevant reading groups live, involving "direct examination of the empirical world."[68] The researchers attended the group sessions as often as possible and became acquainted with the world those involved live in. We strove for "a democratized research learning process with equivalent positions for researchers and those who are the object of the research." The everyday reality interpretations of those who were the objects of the research were the starting point.[69]

We tried to avoid having presumptions in the project that were too serious. The relationship between research and change is complex. Practical research in itself frequently leads to changes. Changes may function as effect and as object of empirical research. Change, as well as effect, is the object of research in the project carried out here. Facilitating a space and putting a process in motion are important results of the project. We wanted to avoid essentialisms, frequently encountered in the literature on popular reading of the Bible. Therefore, the objective of the project is not to confirm a hypothesis but is explorative. This does not mean that there was no basic intuition as the guiding principle for the structure of the project. The three phases correspond with a hoped for development. J. A. van der Ven described it as: (1) exchange (*Austausch*), (2) understanding, approach (*Verständigung*), and (3) striving for consensus (*Streben nach Konsens*). Van der Ven divides the three moments further into three aspects: cognitive, affective, and "volitive" (level of wanting to). The exchange may be cognitive (information, announcements), affective (experiences, feelings, attitudes), and standardizing (values, standards, decisions, commitments, etc.).[70] The same is true for the phase of understanding. The participants try to understand each other's points of view, emotions, and decisions. One sits in another's chair, tries to look at the text through the eyes of another, and from the text tries to look at life. One tries to adopt the perspective of the other. Striving for consensus can also be regarded under these three aspects.

Some contributions to this book are focused on the overall communicative process; others analyze material that was produced in each phase.

History

Both the participating groups and the researchers have invested a great deal in the project. It had a long incubation period. One reason for this was the conviction that such an international project could not be set up unilaterally from the Netherlands nor without a pre-exercise.

The first initiative in the Through the Eyes of Another project was taken when the Dutch Solidaridad development organization started a pilot project in 1997. Dutch groups were put in contact with a number of Latin American groups. The aim of the project was to establish more—and more direct—relationships between churches. Groups chose a biblical text on the basis of the specific experiences they had had with exclusion and reconciliation. A great deal has been learned from this pilot. The basic structure of the later international project already started to take shape here. The intended intercultural communication appears complicated from a logistics point of view. The role of the local groups appears to be of crucial importance. Groups and participants want to participate as subjects. People want information about the larger unit they are part of. Participants wish to be thoroughly informed about the project's objectives and the process in store for them. Broad support and local responsibility turned out to be important conditions for the continuation of the project.

With respect to the interaction between the groups, we were immediately confronted with an important lesson from intercultural communication: the less extensive the report, the less groups have the opportunity to get to know each other, share news, and tell each other about their own culture and context, the poorer the interaction and the encounter. Therefore, in this international project, a strong emphasis was placed on the importance of a quality report and extensive information about the group and the context. Furthermore, it appeared that we had to reflect carefully about the combination of objectives (change is effect and object; groups communicate with each other, but at the same time they are the object of scientific research); and about the group leader's and reporter's responsibilities. As far as the content was concerned, we were struck by the fact that church affiliation, often more than social status or culture, played an important role in intercultural communication. All these learning moments are included in the international project and were recorded extensively in a protocol.

After the Solidaridad experiment, a second pilot was carried out by students of the Free University theology department. A central text, Genesis 18, was introduced, and African groups were also now involved in the interaction. The process became more profound and a first set-up for an analytical framework was designed.

The result of the two experiments was sufficiently positive to risk the jump to an international project. The first project description was made in May 1999, and was discussed comprehensively in circles of both of the initiating entities (the Free University theology department and the Uniting Protestant Churches [Together on the Way churches] in the Netherlands). In the subsequent months, participants and cofinanciers were sought in the Netherlands. Both Solidaridad development organizations and ICCO (Dutch interchurch organization for development cooperation) were willing to participate as far as content was involved, as well as to cofinance the project. The Dutch Bible Society was willing to contribute to financing the project.

Because we were convinced that a project involving participation of many groups in the Southern hemisphere needed to be set up internationally, from the beginning we consulted frequently with experts outside the Netherlands. Enthusiasm for participation was great. Experts, theological centers, and nongovernmental organizations quickly became involved in the project. Contacts were established via the channels of the mission and service departments of the Together on the Way churches in the Netherlands, and scientific circles and networks of Bible scholars.

Two important moments preceded the actual start of the project: a mini-conference in Amsterdam (2–5 July 2000) with representatives from all continents, and an international conference in Utrecht (26 February–2 March 2001). At this major conference, all regional representatives who had promised to participate were present. The conference was also meant to be an opportunity for encounter. A relationship of friendship is indispensable for fruitful implementation of this kind of project. The ties of friendship contributed to the success of this project. "We are a great group of people!" was the conclusion at the end of the first day of the international conference.

The two conferences led to a consensus on the elementary components and the shape of the project: (1) the hermeneutic framework, (2) the groups, (3) logistics and implementation.

Hermeneutic framework

The three-phase structure became the starting point of the project. Groups read the text in the way they are accustomed to reading scripture; confrontation and dialogue then follow, then the sharing and the question, What now? The story of John 4 was selected carefully. All participants were asked to make suggestions for a central text. Based on a number of considerations, the following indications were given for the text selection: the text should not be too well known; the text should be open to various interpretations; the text should be narrative; the text should deal with not just religious questions. The final decision was proclaimed with full enthusiasm by the spokesman of the subgroup that was dealing with this issue: "Let's rejoice! Finally we have chosen the bride (John 4—Jesus and the Samaritan Woman). Let us feel free to refer to her!"

The discussions about scientific research were important. These discussions focused on the calibration points and other scientific queries, the text and its relationship with the empirical investigation and research queries, and the different phases in the hermeneutical process. What can calibration points, in great diversity, be in the analysis of the interpretations of John 4? The intercultural aspect of the project would be an important focus point. There is room for research of the empirical material from a group's own local research queries. Seven calibration points were proposed in the beginning phase: the way groups analyze the text itself, the world behind the text, the history of interpretation in front of the text, the spiral of appropriation and application, the contemporary context of the interpreter, the possibility of ideological distortions from a world behind each of these aspects, the interaction and dynamics within the group. These calibration points were later expanded and refined in consideration of sociological and anthropological research on intercultural communication, and of course, the reading reports themselves. It was emphasized that the empirical material (the reading reports) had to be more or less uniform to lead to sound assertions about the reading reports and the interaction between groups. A format was needed for the reports that would be produced during each phase of the process.

The groups

The question of how many groups could participate was pondered for a long time. The target number was one hundred, but eventually more than 120 groups were enlisted. Groups were recruited via regional coordinators. The continents were subdivided into regions and a central coordinator was proposed for each region.

What conditions did the groups have to meet? Did they have to have a certain profile? We decided not to set any requirements for groups other than size (preferably no more than fifteen or twenty participants). Every region was asked to have as great a diversity as possible with respect to the proportion of men and women, city and rural area, ethnic make-up, social status, church background, new and existing groups, literate and illiterate, geographic origin. Furthermore, groups had to be willing to participate in the entire process, which might stretch over a period of more than a year. Because no one set of group dynamics can apply to different sociocultural situations, and because reading methods themselves are already culturally determined, the groups had a great deal of freedom. The groups were permitted to read the text in the way they were used to. However, the possibility had to be taken into account that, while the first phase would be an open one, the role of the facilitator would be more directive in the second and third phases. Analysis of cultural differences often requires knowledge that is not immediately present in groups. Basic principles for the group's own process, as well as for interaction with the partner group, were established: equivalence (the other has the same rights), freedom (the other is not an object), and reciprocity (communication focused on response). In each group, two special roles, facilitator and reporter, were of great importance for reporting and for the group process. Therefore these are described extensively in the protocol.

How should the groups be linked to each other? This question was also pondered for a long time. Groups turned out to have so many characteristics that eventually forced links were abandoned. Ultimately, three negative criteria were used: not from the same church denomination, not from the same country, preferably also not from the same social context. It was decided not to link groups to a partner group until after the first phase was completed and the report had been sent to the central coordination in Amsterdam. A link to this or that group would not have any effect on the reading process in the first phase. In establishing the links, the wishes of the relevant groups were taken into account as much as possible. We took stock four times per year in Amsterdam, and groups were linked on the basis of reading reports that had been received.

As mentioned above, the form and content of the reading reports turned out to be crucial in the process. We had felt that intuitively in advance, and therefore their description had a prominent place in the protocol. Each phase had its own type of recording; a format was established for each report, for the sake of safeguarding uniformity. In addition to a report of the reading process, preferably verbatim, each report had to contain data about the group members and their situation. In the second phase, groups were expected to contact each other directly. They could write letters, and send gifts or photographs. Sharing experiences and knowledge from each other's context is an elementary condition for successful intercultural communication.

Implementation

After reaching consensus on the form in which the project would be carried out, we proceeded with implementation. Those involved from the Free University theology department in Amsterdam were responsible for international coordination. Regions where groups were located were clustered; there are twenty regions. A coordinator was appointed for each region. Regional coordinators were responsible for local implementation of the project and delivery of the reading reports. Translations from and into English, the language of communication, were sometimes done locally and sometimes handled by the international coordination in Amsterdam or by the team that coordinated groups in the Netherlands. A pool of translators was formed in the Netherlands, translating reading reports on a voluntary basis.

The question of ownership of the project was discussed at length. A collective was formed in order to guarantee proper progress and possible continuation of the project: The Intercultural Bible Collective. It was clear that collective ownership would be the correct form in this project: all actual participants, meaning especially all the producers of the empirical material, the ordinary readers in the groups. A consensus was reached that this material could not be handled carefully enough. To safeguard the careful handling of the material, the decision was made that only actual participants in the project would have access to the reading reports. Moreover, a code of conduct was drawn up for the use of the material, publications on the project, and financial aspects of the implementation in local situations.

In the Through the Eyes of Another project, not only the negative effects of globalization are exposed, but the project could only proceed as a result of that same globalization and its new communication technology. These were used to the full extent. Information about the project can be found on a website, (www.bible4all.org), where reading reports are made accessible to participants (one needs a password), and groups have the opportunity to contact each other directly. We hope to present the multicoloredness of the project via a television documentary.

The conference concluded with a unanimously expressed wish: we must meet again!

Pitfalls

That is how we started out, a group of involved scholars, representatives of churches and development organizations, and many hundreds of ordinary readers. We shared the desire to make a modest contribution to a more mutual understanding. We were involving an old, dangerous story in the discussion about what is in store for people in a world of bewildering inequality, never-rationed suffering, and developments that nobody appears to be in control of. We were aware of what we could not do, the pitfalls we could end up with, and the difficulties intercultural communication brings with it.

We tried to avoid the pitfall of empirical obsession in the project. Empirical research often exposes only diversity, and does not necessarily contribute to better theories, but rather tends to bring down existing theories.

Neither did we want to end up in what has sometimes been called the list-fallacy in intercultural communication: a number of attractive terms are taken from the literature and made into a list without empirical testing of the individual terms in their new connection.

From the very beginning, the researchers were very aware of the transience of reading groups and reports. A group may assert something totally different the next day, or it may consist of different participants. Reading reports were handed in in many different forms, sometimes verbatim, sometimes, to the disappointment of partner groups, as brief summaries and with no biographical information. Sometimes an almost eschatological expectation was required from reading groups. Sometimes a process took longer than two years, or stopped prematurely because a partner group ceased to exist. As is often the case in intercultural communication, the process involved disappointment, frustration, anger, miscommunication, prejudice, and colonialism. Of the 120 groups, more than half completed the process.

Development of a new interdisciplinary analytic instrument or code system was necessary for an adequate analysis of reading reports, drawing not only from hermeneutics, exegesis, or practical theology, but also from sociological and anthropological research.

Conclusion

We needed, from the beginning, to assume a modest attitude and to be willing to honor negative experiences as learning moments. The intention could not be to arrive at the ultimate reading or meaning of John 4.

While the project was developing, the world was dramatically confronted with something many had forgotten: that old texts in holy books may determine, to a considerable extent, the actions of people, for better or worse. In a paradoxical manner, this new awareness emphasized a central goal of the project. How can a process that is liberating be achieved, if people wish to draw Bible texts into the conversation about the future of the earth? Mieke Bal once expressed herself about the Bible in strong words: "The Bible, of all books, is the most dangerous one, the one that has been endowed with the power to kill."[71]

Indeed, many readings of the old book have led to death, exclusion, colonialism, discrimination, and slavery. But others have led to freedom, salvation, conversion, and new life. What we intended to achieve with the project was to design a method for Bible reading that enables one to see differences: which readings are truly life-giving, and which ones lead to exclusion and sorrow.[72] The contributions in this collection make it clear whether we are on the right path.

Notes

[1] Musa W. Dube, "Introduction," in *Other Ways of Reading: African Women and the Bible*, ed. Musa W. Dube (Geneva: WCC Publications, 2001), 5.

[2] Paul Ricoeur, "Qu'est-ce qu'un texte? Expliquer et comprendre," in *Hermeneutik und Dialektik*, ed. Rüdiger Bubner (Tübingen: Mohr Siebeck, 1970), 181–200. Also published as *Du texte à l'action: Essais d'herméneutique* 2 (Paris: Éditions du Seuil, 1986,) 137–60.

[3] Paul Ricoeur, in *Thinking Biblically: Exegetical and Hermeneutical Studies*, by André Lacocque and Paul Ricoeur (Chicago: University of Chicago Press, 1998), xi.

[4] V. Devasahayam, ed., *Frontiers of Dalit Theology* (Delhi: Indian Society for Promoting Christian Knowledge, 1997); Arvind P. Nirmal, ed., *A Reader in Dalit Theology* (Madras: Gurukul Lutheran Theological College & Research Institute for the Dept. of Dalit Theology, 1990); T. and R. L. Hnuni, "Ethnicity, Identity and Hermeneutics: An Indian Tribal Perspective," in *Ethnicity and the Bible*, ed. Mark G. Brett (Leiden, the Netherlands: E. J. Brill, 1996), 344–57; M. Gnanavaram, "'Dalit Theology' and the Parable of the Good Samaritan," *Journal for the Study of the New Testament* 50 (1993): 59–83.

[5] G. Mulrain, "Hermeneutics within a Caribbean Context," in *Vernacular Hermeneutics*, ed. R. S. Sugirtharajah (Sheffield, U.K.: Sheffield Academic Press, 1999), 116–32; Nathaniel Samuel Murrell, William David Spencer, and Adrian Anthony McFarlane, *Chanting Down Babylon: The Rastafari Reader* (Kingston, Jamaica: Ian Randle, 1998).

[6] R. A. Warrior, "A Native American Perspective: Canaanites, Cowboys, and Indians," in *Voices from the Margin: Interpreting the Bible in the Third World*, ed. R. S. Sugirtharajah (Maryknoll, N.Y.: Orbis Books, 1995), 277–88; Pablo Richard, "Religión Indígena y Biblia: 500 Años Después (Búsqueda de una Hermenéutica India)," *Biblito* 43 (1992): 4–8; Pablo Richard, "Hermenéutica Bíblica India: Revelación de Dios en las religiones indígenas y en la Biblia (Después de 500 años de dominación)," in *Revista de Interpretación Bíblica Latinoamericana* 11 (1992): 9–24. Susan Hawley, "Does God Speak Miskitu? The Bible and Ethnic Identity among The Miskitu of Nicaragua," in *Ethnicity and the Bible*, ed. Brett, 316–41.

[7] Sugirtharajah, ed., *Voices from the Margin*; Sugirtharajah, "Orientalism, Ethnonationalism and Transnationalism," in *Ethnicity and the Bible*, ed. Brett, 419–29; Sugirtharajah, "Biblical Studies in India: From Imperialistic Scholarship to

Postcolonial Interpretation," in *Teaching the Bible: The Discourses and Politics of Biblical Pedagogy*, ed. Fernando F. Segovia and Mary Ann Tolbert (Maryknoll, N.Y: Orbis Books, 1998), 283–96; Sugirtharajah, ed., *The Postcolonial Bible* (Sheffield, U.K.: Sheffield Academic Press, 1998); Sugirtharajah, "Biblical Studies after the Empire: From a Colonial to a Postcolonial Mode of Interpretation," in *The Postcolonial Bible*, 12–23.

[8] Carlos Mesters, *Por trás das palavras: Um estudo sobre a porta de entrada no mundo da Bíblia* (Petrópolis, Brazil: Vozes, 1974). Also published as *El misterioso mundo de la Biblia: Estudio sobre la puerta de entrada al mundo de la Biblia* (Buenos Aires: Editorial Bonum, 1977).

[9] Elisabeth Schüssler Fiorenza, "The Ethics of Biblical Interpretation: Decentering Biblical Scholarship," *Journal of Biblical Literature* 107 (March 1988): 3–17.

[10] Fernando F. Segovia, *Decolonizing Biblical Studies: A View from the Margins* (Maryknoll, N.Y.: Orbis Books, 2000).

[11] Elisabeth Schüssler Fiorenza, *Bread Not Stone: The Challenge of Feminist Biblical Interpretation* (Boston: Beacon Press, 1984), 141.

[12] Fernando F. Segovia, "Pedagogical Discourse and Practices in Contemporary Biblical Criticism," in *Teaching the Bible*, ed. Segovia and Tolbert, 19.

[13] J. H. de Wit, *Leerlingen van de Armen* (Amsterdam: VU Uitgeverij, 1991).

[14] Bible and Culture Collective, *The Postmodern Bible* (New Haven, Conn.: Yale University Press, 1995).

[15] Segovia, *Decolonizing,* 10ff.

[16] Craig G. Bartholomew, Colin J. D. Greene, and Karl Möller, eds., *Renewing Biblical Interpretation,* Scripture and Hermeneutics Series 1 (Carlisle, Cumbria, U.K.: Paternoster Press; Grand Rapids, Mich.: Zondervan, 2000); Brett, ed., *Ethnicity and the Bible*; Daniel Patte, *Ethics of Biblical Interpretation: A Reevaluation* (Louisville, Ky.: Westminster John Knox Press, 1995).

[17] Ingrid Rosa Kitzberger, ed., *The Personal Voice in Biblical Interpretation* (London, New York: Routledge, 1998).

[18] John Riches, "Cultural Bias in Biblical Scholarship," in *Ethnicity and the Bible*, ed. Brett, 431–48.

[19] Sugirtharajah, "Orientalism" in *Ethnicity and the Bible*, ed. Brett, 419–29.

[20] L. M. Poland, *Literary Criticism and Biblical Hermeneutics: A Critique of Formalist Approaches* (Chico, Calif.: Scholars Press, 1985), 177ff.

[21] Gerald O. West, "Local is Lekker, but Ubuntu is Best," in *Vernacular Hermeneutics*, ed. Sugirtharajah, 37–51; West, "Being Partially Constituted by Work with Others: Biblical Scholars Becoming Different," *Journal of Theology for Southern Africa* 104 (1999): 44–53; West, "Contextual Bible Study in South Africa: A Resource for Reclaiming and Regaining Land, Dignity and Identity," in *The Bible in Africa: Transactions, Trajectories and Trends*, ed. West and Musa W. Dube (Leiden, the Netherlands: E. J. Brill, 2000), 595–610.

[22] André Droogers, "The Power Dimensions of the Christian Community: An Anthropological Model," *Religion* 33 (2003): 277.

[23] J. Severino Croatto, "Hermenêutica e Lingüística: A Hermenêutica Bíblica à Luz da Semiótica e Frente aos Métodos Histórico-críticos," *Estudos Teológicos* 24, no. 3 (1984): 224.

[24] José Luis Caravias, *Temas Bíblicos para las Comunidades Cristianas* (Cuenca, Ecuador: EDICAY, Iglesia de Cuenca, 1987), 3.

[25] Carlos Mesters, "Balanço de 20 Anos," in *Suplemento do Boletím "Por trás das Palavras"* 7 (1988): 25.

[26] Itumeleng J. Mosala, "The Implications of the Text of Esther for African Women's Struggle for Liberation in South Africa," in *Voices from the Margin*, ed. Sugirtharajah, 178.

[27] This concept was popularized by Milton Schwantes.

[28] P. Richard, "La Biblia: Memoria Histórica de los Pobres," *Servir* 17 (1982): 143–50.

[29] Klaus Berger, *Hermeneutik des Neuen Testaments* (Gütersloh, Germany: Gütersloher Verlags-Haus Mohn, 1988), 75ff., 247ff.

[30] de Wit, *Leerlingen van de Armen*, 344.

[31] Gerald West, "Reading the Bible Differently: Giving Shape to the Discourses of the Dominated," *Semeia* 73 (1996): 34ff.

[32] Ibid.

[33] Carlos Mesters, "The Use of the Bible in Christian Communities of the Common People," in *The Challenge of Basic Christian Communities*, ed. Sergio Torres and John Eagleson (Maryknoll, N.Y.: Orbis Books, 1981), 197–210.

[34] John Riches, "Interpreting the Bible in African Contexts: Glasgow Consultation," *Semeia* 73 (1996): 185ff.

[35] Peter Brooks, *Reading for the Plot: Design and Intention in Narrative* (New York: Vintage, 1984), 3ff.

[36] Musa Dube, "Introduction," in *Other Ways of Reading: African Women and the Bible*, ed. Musa Dube (Geneva: WCC Publications, 2001), 7; italics added.

[37] Robert J. Schreiter, *The New Catholicity: Theology between the Global and the Local* (Maryknoll, N.Y.: Orbis Books, 1997), 131.

[38] Paul Ricoeur, "Toward a Narrative Theology," in *Figuring the Sacred* (Minneapolis: Fortress Press, 1995), 236–48; Robert McAfee Brown, "My Story and 'The Story,'" *Theology Today* 32 (1975/1976): 166–73.

[39] Hendrik M. Vroom, "Religious Hermeneutics, Culture and Narratives," *Studies in Interreligious Dialogue* 4 (1994): 195.

[40] Ricoeur, "Toward a Narrative Theology," 238.

[41] Brian K. Blount, *Cultural Interpretation: Reorienting New Testament Criticism* (Minneapolis, Minn.: Fortress Press, 1995).

[42] Brooks, *Reading for the Plot*, 4–5.

[43] J. H. de Wit, "Leyendo con Yael: Un Ejercicio en Hermenéutica Intercultural," in *Los Caminos Inexhauribles de la Palabra (Las Relecturas Creativas en la Biblia y de la Biblia): Homenaje de Colegas y Discípulos a J. Severino Croatto en sus 70 Años de Vida, 40 de Agisterio y 25 en ISEDET*, ed. Guillermo Hansen (Buenos Aires: Lumen-ISEDET, 2000), 11–65; J. H. de Wit, "'Mijn Naam Is . . .' Intercultureel Bijbellezen en Wederkerigheid," *Wereld en Zending* (2001): 18–27; Hans de Wit, "Through the Eyes of Another: A Project on Intercultural Reading of the Bible" (presentation, consultation on Intercultural Reading of the Bible, Free University, Amsterdam, the Netherlands, 2001; a version of this paper, with the same title, became the standard project handbook); J. H. de Wit, "Through the Eyes of An-

other: Towards Intercultural Reading of the Bible," in *Interkulturelle Hermeneutik und lectura popular: Neuere Konzepte in Theorie und Praxis,* Beiheft zur Ökumenischen Rundschau 72, ed. Silja Joneleit-Oesch and Miriam Neubert (Frankfurt am Main, Germany: Otto Lembeck, 2002), 19–64; J. H. de Wit, "They are drumming for compassion: Op weg naar interculturele hermeneutiek," in *De kunst van ontfermen: Studies voor Gerben Heitink,* ed. Alma Lanser (Kampen, the Netherlands: Uitgeverij Kok, 2003), 325–42.

[44] Charles Larson, "Heroic Ethnocentrism: The Idea of Universality in Literature," in *The Post-Colonial Studies Reader,* ed. Bill Ashcroft, Gareth Griffiths, and Helen Tiffin (London and New York: Routledge, 1995), 62–5.

[45] Ferdinand Deist, *The Material Culture of the Bible: An Introduction* (Sheffield, U.K.: Sheffield Academic Press, 2000), 81.

[46] Clifford Geertz, *The Interpretation of Cultures* (London: Fontana Press, 1993).

[47] L. A. Hoedemaker, ed., *Theologiseren in Context* (Kampen, the Netherlands: Uitgeverij Kok, 1997), 292.

[48] Geert Hofstede, *Allemaal Andersdenkenden: Omgaan met cultuurverschillen* (Amsterdam: Uitgeverij Contact, 1995).

[49] Walter J. Ong, *Orality and Literacy: The Technologizing of the Word* (London: Methuen, 1982), 45ff.

[50] William B. Gudykunst and Young Yun Kim, *Communicating with Strangers: An Approach to Intercultural Communication* (Boston: McGraw Hill, 2003), 18–19.

[51] Anthony C. Thiselton, *New Horizons in Hermeneutics: The Theory and Practice of Transforming Biblical Reading* (London: Zondervan, 1992).

[52] Stanley Fish, *Is There a Text in this Class? The Authority of Interpretive Communities* (Cambridge, Mass.: Harvard University Press, 1980).

[53] Hans Robert Jauss, *Toward an Aesthetic of Reception* (Minneapolis: University of Minnesota Press, 1982).

[54] David Bleich, *The Double Perspective: Language, Literacy, and Social Relations* (New York: Oxford University Press, 1988).

[55] Hans-Georg Gadamer, *Wahrheit und Methode: Ergänzungen,* Gesammelte Werke, vol. 2 (Tübingen, Germany: Mohr Siebeck, 1986), 9.

[56] Hofstede, *Allemaal Andersdenkenden,* 13.

[57] A. de Groot, "De ene Schrift en de Vele Interpretatie-Konteksten: De Hermeneutiek in de Missiologie," in *Oecumenische Inleiding in de Missiologie,* ed. Arnulf Camps and F. J. Verstraelen (Kampen, the Netherlands: Uitgeverij Kok, 1988), 155.

[58] Schreiter, *The New Catholicity,* 133.

[59] Hoedemaker, *Theologiseren in Context,* 297.

[60] Ibid., 296.

[61] Franz J. Hinkelammert, ed., *El Huracán de la Globalización* (San José, Costa Rica: Departamento Ecuménico de Investigaciones, 1999).

[62] John Riches, "Cultural Bias in Biblical Scholarship," in *Ethnicity and the Bible,* ed. Brett, 431–48.

[63] Musa W. Dube, "Reading of Semoya: Batswana Women's Interpretations of Matt 15:21–28," *Semeia* 73 (1996): 111–29. G. West, "Discerning the Contours

of Domination and Resistance in Liberation Hermeneutics: Do the Poor and Marginalized Speak?" *Bulletin for Contextual Theology* 5, no. 2 (1998): 28–35; West, "And the Dumb Do Speak: Articulating Incipient Readings of the Bible in Marginalized Communities," in *The Bible in Ethics*, ed. J. W. Rogerson, Margaret Davies, and M. Daniel Carroll R. (Sheffield, U.K.: Sheffield Academic Press, 1998), 174–92; David Lehmann, *Struggle for the Spirit, Religious Transformation and Popular Culture in Brazil and Latin America* (Cambridge, U.K.; Cambridge, Mass.: Polity Press, 1996); B. A. Müller, "Skrifgebruik in die onafhanklike Afrika Kerke: 'N Hermeneutiese ondersoek na die skrifgebruik in die inhoud en funksie van die kommunikasieproses soos gevind in 'n steekproef van vertaalde transkripsies van eredienste in die sogenaamde onafhanklike Afrika kerke" (unpublished research project, Faculty of Theology, University of Stellenbosch, Stellenbosch, South Africa, 1992); Hans A. Trein, *O evangelho no clube de mães: Análise de uma experiência de leitura popular da Bíblia* (São Leopoldo, Brazil: Editora Sinodal, 1993); Moliko Sibeko and Beverley Haddad, "Reading the Bible 'with' Women in Poor and Marginalized Communities in South Africa," *Semeia* 78 (1997): 83–92; Centro de Estudos Bíblicos (CEBI), Brazil, 1974 and the following years.

[64] We report on the analysis and coding of reading reports in chapter 22 of this volume.

[65] West, "Discerning the Contours," 28–35; Mesters, "The Use of the Bible," 197ff.; de Wit, *Leerlingen van de Armen*.

[66] de Wit, *Leerlingen van de Armen*.

[67] Fred Wester, Adri Smaling, and Lambert Mulder, eds., *Praktijkgericht Kwalitatief Onderzoek* (Bussum, the Netherlands: Uitgeverij Coutinho, 2000).

[68] Herbert Blumer, *Symbolic Interactionism: Perspective and Method* (Englewood Cliffs, N.J.: Prentice-Hall, 1969).

[69] Alma Lanser–van der Velde, *Geloven leren: Een theoretisch en empirisch onderzoek naar wederkerig geloofsleren* (Kampen, the Netherlands: Uitgeverij Kok, 2000), 129.

[70] J. A. van der Ven, *Entwurf einer empirischen Theologie* (Kampen, the Netherlands: Uitgeverij Kok, 1994), 58ff.

[71] Mieke Bal, *On Story-Telling: Essays in Narratology*, ed. David Jobling (Sonoma, Calif.: Polebridge Press, 1991), 14.

[72] John Riches, "A Response to Walter Sundberg," in *Renewing Biblical Interpretation,* ed. Bartholomew, 87.

Tableaux vivants

Hans de Wit and Marleen Kool

The project Through the Eyes of Another can be viewed from different angles. Each angle will in turn expose other aspects, because so many things can happen when people start reading the Bible together interculturally, as this collection shows in all its diversity. All around the world, people gathered around the Bible, all with their own histories, experiences, and expectations. Before we present case studies and analyses, before we explore implications of the project, we want to let their voices be fully heard, without further commentary.

We will let readers hear the participants talk about this experience themselves, in two ways. First, we will present essential moments from the reading reports that tell us something about the participants' expectations, the context in which they gathered, the way they gave shape to the meetings, and how they experienced the exchange with the partner group. Second, we asked all group coordinators to reflect on the experiences of reading groups they assisted. We conclude this contribution with a presentation of their reflections. How do coordinators from Nigeria, Ghana, Indonesia, India, Korea, Hungary, the Netherlands, and El Salvador view their experience with intercultural Bible reading?

Intercultural Bible reading through the eyes of the participants

When we peruse the participants' reports of their experiences, we feel as if we were reading a novel that is being enacted all over the world. In the blink of an eye, readers are transported to far-flung locations and meet impressive people. Together, the participants form a multicolored reading community that is interpreting and

Hans de Wit, Faculty of Theology, Free University (Amsterdam, the Netherlands); Marleen Kool, Faculty of Theology, Free University (Amsterdam, the Netherlands)

seeking its way together. They each talk about the experience in their own ways. We hear their stories and see (1) their motivations, (2) where they meet, (3) their songs and prayers, and (4) a few responses to the meeting with the partner group.

Motivation of the participants

Those of us taking the initiative have been surprised by the magnitude of the project. Many groups tackled the project with enthusiasm and sometimes eagerness. It is possible to construct an image of their motives, because the protocol asks for this information. Their enthusiasm was not because the project was initiated from the Netherlands, nor because the results will be examined scientifically—although the latter appears to have had a positive rather than a negative effect. Two motivations appear to be the most important. To put it ceremoniously, they are the joy of reading the Bible together and the expectation surrounding meeting the other.

Many reports describe collective or communal reading of the Bible as beneficial and community-building:

The Netherlands: I owe a great deal to this Bible reading group.

South Africa: The group members all have a keen interest in gaining more knowledge about the Bible, and they form a strong support group for one another. One of their major aims is to share their life experiences with one another and to pray for one another.

Philippines: In our present place, the common livelihoods are construction work and office work. Because of poverty, some have become snatchers, hostesses in nightclubs, prostitutes, or pimps. Many become household helpers or guards. As in other societies, some lord it over others. Even those who are poor still take advantage of their fellows. People are all out for themselves. Only the very poor ones really help one another. Our present group is an example. We help each other. We lend money to each other.

India: We don't know how to pray. So we repeat every sentence after the leader, who facilitates the Bible study. We come together in this church to spend time with each other and support each other with our presence.

The possibility of intercultural meeting plays an important role in participation in the project:

The Netherlands: We are very curious about the reaction of the partner group and very interested in the contact that may be created. We hope to learn from the other group's response. The reciprocity in this project really appeals to me. . . . Reading the Bible in this manner is much more intense than doing it at home alone, and I am very curious about the way the partner group experiences the readings. Are there any similarities, or are there only differences?

Indonesia: We gathered only because of this project of cross-cultural or intercultural reading of the Bible. We were motivated to take part in this project, because we are drawn to hear how Christians in other parts of the world react to our interpretation of John 4 and [to see] what we ourselves can learn from the way they read the Bible.

Nicaragua: I am very glad that we can share our Nicaraguan perspective with others. It is a privilege to be able to participate in this project. I hope this is true for both groups, for although we have a different language and culture, we are one team in Christ.

The U.S.: My background is Presbyterian and . . . my heart longs to bring people into a Bible study. When you do a Bible study, you are the one that is enriched. I have done two, and the growth was with myself. It was exciting to hear other people talk about what it means to them. My perspective is that of a little old white lady in orthopedic shoes . . . and I want to change that.

The place people gather

People left their homes and daily obligations behind to go to a place where they hoped to find each other, to read and celebrate together, to take shelter with each other. These places of gathering tell us something about who these people are, what the world they live in looks like. The descriptions show us groups that gather at the foot of the Andes, in the Brazilian province towns, under the fierce sun of the African fields, in blazing hot Nicaragua, or at a campground in a Dutch coastal town. Groups convene in venerable historic churches and under the corrugated roofs of little capillas in the slum districts of Latin American or African cities.

Bogotá, Colombia: Sixth floor of the World Vision building.

San Salvador: Colony of Sorrows neighborhood, Rose Bush Passage, no. 21.

Ghana: The Anglican Church in Abetifi.

Korea: We meet in the Songwon Condominium in Mt. Jeeri, 100 kilometers from Hanil University.

Bolivia: The Methodist church, The Messiah, is in Tembladerani on Jaime Freyre street, near the Bolívar market and facing the Bolívar Stadium, in the southeast part of the city, in the Andes region, La Paz.

Bolivia: Our group meets in the Delights district, an area located on the outside rim of the north of La Paz. People who live there are Aymaras; they are bilingual and speak Spanish and Aymara. We meet there every Thursday for three hours, starting at 7:00 in the evening.

South Africa: The women's group meets in the house of one of the members in the Dutch Reformed congregation Stellenbosch-Welgelegen in Stellenbosch, Western Cape Province. Stellenbosch is the second-oldest town (after Cape Town) in South Africa, dating back to 1679, and is well known as an excellent wine producing region.

India: This group normally meets once in a month in the CSI Weseley Church in Perambur. They use the Tamil version of the Holy Bible.

The place of meeting is more than geographical. Participants also describe their context. The differences are great.

Brazil: The group meets in the District of the Roses, an industrial district in Estância Velha. . . . District of the Roses is a neighborhood where many tanneries and shoe factories are located. Pollution is severe in this part of the city.

Colombia: The district has a bad reputation. There are criminal and violent youth gangs who fight with other gangs. That's why this district became the victim of "social cleansing" by the dark powers of the State (*las fuerzas oscuras del Estado*). A number of youths were killed in confrontations. At the moment it is fairly calm; the youth gangs are busy with dealing drugs and break-ins.

El Salvador: This past year, after our country was whipped by three earthquakes and more than 10,000 aftershocks, we extended our solidarity to the victims.

Philippines: All feel strongly for the country, and in their prayers they mentioned current situations, i.e., kidnapping, Abu-Sayyaf taking hostages for ransom, poor economy.

The Netherlands: Socially and politically there are no tensions, or barely any, in our direct living environment. We live in a peaceful village. The village has grown quite a bit in the past forty years, from a small village with some farms into a prosperous village with only a few farms and many new residents. Many residents work in other cities and villages. Only one of the group members was born in the village.

U.S.: All of the participants in this Bible study live one hour north of Seattle, Washington, in the heart of the Skagit Valley—an agricultural region threatened by rapid growth of retail stores and light industry. For more than fifty years, immigrants from Mexico have been drawn to Skagit County by the abundance of seasonal labor, harvesting strawberries, raspberries, blueberries, cucumbers, apples, and other fruits and vegetables. Many Hispanic immigrants have settled permanently in our region, making up

15,000–20,000 of the county's population of 100,000. Immigrant families struggle to feel at home in a foreign context, bringing their children up in English-speaking schools, surrounded by the dominant white culture. Many immigrants complain of being discriminated against.

South Africa: The members of the group are all members of the Xhosa ethnic group living in different townships in the Cape Peninsula, in the Western Cape province. . . . A formidable black elite arose, and through social redress through affirmative action, a considerable black middle-class has developed. But for the majority of the black population, not much has changed in terms of their economic reality and physical living conditions. Racial discrimination is still a living reality in many situations.

Indonesia: All of the members of our group name political, religious, and/or ethnic tensions in Indonesian society. P. says that the safety in Ambon still can't be guaranteed; there is much suspicion among the Ambon people, especially between religious groups. S. names the clashes between Christians and Muslims in both Poso (Central Sulawesi) and Ambon. A. adds to that the ethnic violence on her home island, Kalimantan. C. and Y. say that after the political reformations in 1998 (Suharto, the president of Indonesia was compelled to resign), violent religious and ethnic clashes broke out everywhere in Indonesia. And it still goes on. L. and A. declare that these violent outbursts have to do with the problem of a Muslim majority (more than 90 percent of Indonesians are Muslim) and a Christian minority.

Hungary: We meet in the Reformed church vestry. There are Calvinistic symbols and maps with Bible scenes on the wall, so we can look at the context of the reading. We are seated around a table that stands in the middle of the room. On the table there are candles burning, some flowers, tea, and cookies.

The liturgical setting

Interaction includes not only reading and explaining the text but also what we have called "liturgical framing." People rarely open the Bible for no reason. Readers prepare for meeting each other, for the meeting with the Living One whom they hope to track down in and through the story. Many do so by opening the meeting with a prayer, by reciting a poem or reading a text; others sing hymns or light a candle. The reports all document what was sung, prayed, and read, so it is possible to collect the songs, prayers, texts, and symbolic acts that were part of the reading process. A few examples of songs:

Cuba: We sing while holding hands in a circle: "Come, come everybody," and then, accompanied by body movements: "If we all work . . ."

Philippines: Vicky, by appointment of the group, led in the singing of two hymns found in our Filipino hymnbooks. Both were composed by Filipinos: "Dios ay Pag-ibig" (God is love) and "Makulay ang Buhay kay Cristo" (life is colorful in Christ).

Indonesia: We started our Bible study by singing a song from the official songbook of the Indonesian Churches, called Kidung Jemaat (congregational songs).

The Netherlands: At the end of the first meeting, we sang the song "Your Word comes to life inside us," by Simei Monteiro, translated by Hans Bouma.

Ghana: "Aseda yede ma Onyame" (thanks we give to God). This is a song of thanksgiving to God. It was sung slowly.

El Salvador: A new song was even composed for the occasion of the project: "La Samaritana."

India: We sing simple Tamil Christian choruses. Sad songs are a favorite in our group. Especially songs that talk about compassion and unfailing love are in demand, which only goes to explain our yearning to love and be loved. Most of us have tears in our eyes when such soul-stirring songs are sung.

A poem by a Dutch participant:

Woman at the well
I read your story
It brought me a thousand questions
Please don't try to answer
Better get more water
And yet I wonder why
you were at the well, that day
Did you know perhaps
things that we
still can't see today
It seems to me
I didn't understand it
Thought the water was just water
I'd like to think
that even so, we're part of it.

A letter from another Dutch participant written to the Samaritan woman:

Today we have read about you, and not only read; we also had a long discussion about you. Your way of talking with that man from Judah in a conversation at the well of Jacob, a discussion at first reserved, then more and more spontaneous and open, has filled us with surprise and joy—even me: a man who lives in a world quite different from yours in that story.

You were so natural in that conversation with Jesus, who is in fact not very accessible in his way of replying and asking questions. But you were without any shyness, and at the same time you stood there in a very honest and vulnerable way. How full of movement was your (re)action after your first confusion! You ran with great speed to the town, in the hottest hour of that day, without any water bottle or other ballast. And once in town, you very quickly succeeded in convincing all those Samaritans to come with you. They followed you, a woman!

You evoke in me personally many things. To say it in three statements:
Faith, for people who are inclined to lose all messianic hope.
Hope, for people who are looked down on by other people.
Love, for people who feel accepted again in the messianic community.

In my opinion you resemble Rebecca at the well a bit. Or Rachel (also at the well). Or . . . are you perhaps, over there in Samaria, so rejected by the Jews, the "daughter Zion"? That special woman about whom the nations sing in psalms and prophecies: "All my wells are in you"?

Well, perhaps I'm dreaming too much now. Thank you very much, for at any rate it is a very beautiful dream!

Groups act out the text using bibliodrama, a role-play, or a soap opera episode.

Philippines: The facilitator asked the question: If you were to produce a "telecine" (TV movie) about the passage, what would you highlight, and what title would you give it and why? (A buzz of pleasure and excitement from the group.) She divided them by twos to discuss for fifteen minutes. A report would follow. There was much animation, talking, and laughter. After fifteen minutes, the facilitator called for everybody's attention, and we listened to the group's report.

Symbols and symbolic acts:

Argentina: We put different earthenware urns on a rug (for every one of us is an urn of living water, but we are all different) and one big one. Everyone takes some water from the big urn with his own and recites a pledge.

Nigeria: The group members bring along with them such symbolic objects as bottled water, cross, candle, and pieces of white cloth. The group considers these objects symbolic of life, purity, and light, which Christ radiates in the life of Christians, etc. In addition, members of the group brought symbolic objects such as the Ikenga or Ofo, cowries, clay pots, fowl feathers, and other objects of worship believed to be accepted by the ancestors in the African cultural setting.

The Netherlands: Some members of the group brought symbolic objects: A wedding text from Isaiah 41:10, written on a framed plank. This text hangs in the room. "I strengthen you, help you, and support you with my healing right hand." It gives support in good days but especially also in bad days. . . . A *yad*, a silver pointer from Israel intended for pointing at the text from the Torah during the reading. The texts from the Torah may not be soiled by the bare hand. . . . A cut crystal, which he was given when his mother was confirmed as a preacher. The Scripture also has many facets, and thus contains a message in every context. . . . The Rembrandt Bible, containing an image of an etching from the Rembrandt Bible. Rembrandt pictures Jesus in conversation with the Samaritan woman of John 4. It is clearly visible that Rembrandt had his own outlook on the surroundings in the story. In that way, every person also has his own view and insight into the texts.

The experiences with the partner group

Is it possible to get to know one another by reading a Bible story together? The multitude of reports in which groups respond to each other speak of considerable involvement in and solidarity with the partner group. The readers would like to know who the other is, what the participants look like, and where they meet. Readers are inquisitive about each other, curious about what is different, but at the same time are focused on recognizing their individuality in the other. Despite the large differences between them, people experience a powerful degree of solidarity:

Hungary: We were very glad to hear from you again. Thank you for the introduction of your church in Komenda. We read with great interest that you have many different activities and Bible studies in your church, and that you take care of the members in need of financial support. It is always good to meet living congregations and true followers of Jesus Christ in the world. No matter where we pray, in whatever part of the world, our prayers and worship of God bring us Christians together, so we all belong to the same big family of Christian people in the world.

The Netherlands: If you read the gospel together, it is of no importance where you live, in Bolivia or here in the Netherlands. The partner group's thoughts were recognizable and could have been ours. Did we look at this story in a different way by reading the reactions from the partner group, or did we want to review something? The answer is No.

Philippines: We believe that we have helped our Dutch partners to have some understanding of what it means to be poor. They, in fact, commented and reminded us that the poor tend to be closer to the Lord. We feel we have been able to encourage them to trust God, because people whose needs are sufficiently met tend to forget God. We are glad that they acknowledged their need for God even as they enjoy what they have materially.

Ghana: We in the Elmina group like the discussions and the different rules of interpretation adopted by you and us. It gave us enlightenment. We also want to remark that women helped Jesus a lot, so it is gratifying for us that this passage was selected. Because it concerns a woman, we have seen the challenges in the text, and we would like to emulate some of them. Also in Ghana it is women who control the churches, so for us to discuss this story is very rewarding. It has helped us a lot.

South Africa: The expectation that it would be boring to read the same story one more time turned out to be incorrect. Again new elements arose that we had not thought of before. The group from El Salvador has—despite the fact that there were no significant differences—emphasized elements that the group in Stellenbosch otherwise would not have discovered. This resulted in a very interesting experience, which is why the meeting was ended with a prayer. In this prayer, the group requests God's nearness not only to their own group but also to the partner group in El Salvador.

Nicaragua: They tell the story from their point of view, from the perspective they remembered. If we had to write a Gospel, it would be the same way, and if the Dutch brothers and sisters wrote a Gospel they would write it in some other way. That is how the Bible was written, with the people's point of view and from their own experience. That is why it is interesting for me. There are many stories that are told in one Gospel, and there are others in other Gospels. Maybe John was interested in something else, as we get interested in some things and the Dutch brothers and sisters in others. I pictured that.

Brazil: We always think that our religion is the only true one. It should not be so! Only our positions should be different, but God is the same, because God expects us to follow him in our everyday life, with our heart and in spirit. That is what we learn from the exchange with our partner group.

There are also disappointments:

Korea: Our group was very disappointed because [their report] was too short [for us] to learn about them, and because it was very much like our ministers' general preaching on John 4, emphasizing evangelism. We really wanted to get to know about them and their situation and culture, etc. Although we read that the group consists of the same number of men and women, we could not hear the voice of women. I wanted to hear about how

Colombian women live in general. We just guessed about the Colombian situation a little bit. There may be serious problems of street kids or HIV patients around them in society. Then, what kinds of problems do they face because of these? We wondered about them. For example, are they treated badly, physically or emotionally? If so, how?

The Netherlands: "Well, I had actually hoped that we would be linked to an entirely different culture (somewhat laughing). Yes, to look at a Bible text from a very different angle." "Was it a bit of a disappointment in that sense, that we were linked to this group?" "Yes, for me it was."

We hope that the reader has been able to taste some of the overwhelming wealth of revealing, emotional, and special stories of the participants in this compilation.

Intercultural Bible reading through the eyes of the coordinators

Eight coordinators accepted our invitation to provide a reflection on the experiences of their reading group. We are happy to present their impressions here.

Tableau vivant from Nigeria: Jesus and the Samaritan woman
An intercultural experience

Protus O. Kemdirim, Department of Religious and Cultural Studies
University of Port Harcourt (Port Harcourt, Nigeria)

Introduction. Through the Eyes of Another, a research project on intercultural Bible reading, first caught my attention through a 2001 notice by Louis C. Jonker in the *Bulletin for Old Testament Studies in Africa*. According to Jonker, the aim of intercultural reading of the Bible is to be exposed to the reading of the Bible by people in cultural circumstances completely different from one's own. Considering, however, that the context is the story of Jesus and the Samaritan woman (John 4:1–35), I saw an opportunity to reflect on John's Gospel characterized by the theme of witness, of which the Samaritan woman is a good example. More importantly, as is the case with many other research projects, I also saw an opportunity to learn and share research experience with researchers worldwide. The fact is that I have had a long-standing thirst for intercultural and multicultural perspectives.

Methodology. In keeping with the project methodology, I constituted a very ecumenical Bible group made up of Roman Catholics, Anglicans, Presbyterians, and people from four other church traditions. Most are church leaders, military chaplains, teachers, or businessmen, or are in civil service positions. They are in positions of social influence or power. Sadly, there are no women in the group, because there are few women in theological studies in Nigeria. Elsewhere, I have observed that in Nigeria the pursuit of interpretive models in the wider field of religion or theology has yet to win the approval of women, let alone that of parents who are likely to spend their money on such studies for their daughters.

Experience and context. The experience of the group in the intercultural reading of the Bible is tremendous. As an ecumenical group, and as academics who value theology, they are challenged to engage in ecumenical Bible hermeneutics and contextual theology, interpreting the text in the light of their cultural experience and socioeconomic context. Indeed, the text opened a lively debate among members of the group about female participation in the ministerial priesthood. Thus, they engaged in a diversity of opinions and stances, which they attempted to unify. It is wonderful, too, how the group contextualized the text a good deal at group sessions, using elements of the African culture—Ikenga or Ofo, cowries, clay pots, fowl feathers, etc. These symbolic objects are acceptable to the ancestors in the African cultural setting, for worship.

Another experience is the reading of the text from the viewpoint of ancestorhood. In this angle of reflection on John 4, the ancestors are considered as the "living dead" and the Samaritan woman as the "apostle of ancestorhood." Thus, the concept of ancestorhood is related to the communion of saints in Christianity.

There is no gainsaying that interaction with the partner group in Peru was enriching for us, especially from the perspective of cultural hermeneutics. One result is that rather than talking about "laying aside all cultures," we now understand cultures to be extensive, complex, and ambiguous worldviews that need purification or elevation, but not outright rejection. Of significance also is the need for an attitude of dialogue in the context of the evangelization of cultures. Another impact is our realization that African polygamy as observed by the partner group is at least a "responsible" polygamy, in marked contrast to the infidelity and extramarital affairs in Latin America, where there is neither justice nor official recognition of the de facto polygamy practiced by some men. Indeed, looking at the partner group's interpretation of John 4, we observe how cultural differences can influence the reading and interpretation of a given biblical passage.

Conclusion. Participation in the intercultural reading of the Bible project left me and the group feeling optimistic, because the division that separated Christians for so long is in the process of being overcome. If we continue to engage in intercultural reading of the Bible, which has been needed for such a long time, then our combined strength can be used to foster ecumenical growth among Christians. The project is certainly a great one, intellectually stimulating, and culturally rewarding.

Tableau vivant from Ghana: "They start from their own environment!"
Contextual awareness as effect of intercultural exchange

Jacolien Lambregtse, Ramseyer Training Centre (Abetifi Kwahu, Ghana)

In Abetifi, Ghana, a group of local church leaders met: two Anglicans, two members of the Assembly of God, one member of the International Central Gospel Church, and five Presbyterians. Five are pastors, two lay pastors and the others lay preachers. Four are female, six male. Only one has studied theology at the university.

These leaders have been trained to explain the text in its historical context and then to find an application of it in the context of their listeners. When they read, they have in mind their congregation, and perhaps even their sermon. John 4 was read as a record of an event during Jesus's life. Initially, the core message was seen as salvation. The Samaritan woman could have lived in Abetifi. The similarities between there and here, then and now, were many: women fetching water, women and men not speaking together without being suspected by others, women left by their husbands, women living with men without being married, traditional worship (on the mountain), tribalism and conflicts about land, looking down on different cultural customs of other tribes. Only the conflict between Jews and Samaritans called for an investigation of its roots in the Old Testament.

When the exchange report from the group in Feitoria, Brazil, was read, everybody clearly saw the difference in approach of this group:

> They are putting the whole situation of the Bible text into their own cultural environment!

> They started to talk about drinking water; clean and unclean water; water from a well, a river, or a pipe. If we compare it to the way we read the Bible here, it is quite different. The Bible in Ghana is put in its situation, in Palestine. And when you hear people reading it, it does not normally come here; it is there!

Through this, the whole Abetifi group realized that they are not used to reading the Bible consciously from their own place. Though the story fits easily into the Ghanaian context, the world described in the Bible is seen as special.

The example of the Feitoria group was received with mixed feelings. Some felt that it is important to start from the historical reading, behind the text, to understand the meaning of the story clearly.

> Would starting with your own culture not make it so that people will not believe in the inspiration and special status of the Bible?

Others welcomed the approach of reading "in front of the text," to find its actual meaning within the context of our daily life.

> Is it necessary to trouble people with things that are too far away, too strange?

Thirst, according to the group in Feitoria, can also be thirst for justice, for critical understanding of political issues, for courage to address injustice. This perspective was strikingly new for the Abetifi group. Was Jesus not talking about spiritual things only? Politics was not part of his mission, was it?

> Jesus wanted the Jews to know that Christianity is universal. God is not only for the Jews, but also for the Gentiles. There should not be any discrimination.

The Word of God is more than food. You can live on the Word of God. The food and water Jesus is talking about are spiritual: eternal life and salvation.

When we talk about needs, all know that our communities are in need of good education, clean water, food, safety, good governance, fellowship, and more. But do we need Jesus for this?

Because of this question, the Abetifi group is continuing the exchange process, taking time to reflect on the relation between church and politics.

Kofi: Now that the government has raised the price of petroleum and petroleum products (nearly 100 percent), the costs of living will become too high for many of us. We will thirst for justice, and we will want to know why and how. And we as Christians will know that there is a peace even in the midst of suffering. Even in the midst of violence, we can still have a smile on our face. And people will wonder how, and it is because you know Christ. It is Christ who we finally need in everything and who is the fulfillment of our needs.

Looking back to the first discussions about John 4, the Abetifi group realized that the local context had been taken into consideration by association: discrimination between men and women, divisions between and in churches, and even colonialism was mentioned.

Second Kings 17:29 tells us that the original Israelites were exiled, and the king of Assyria brought people from his country to colonize Samaria. The Jews regarded them as colonists. And the real Israelites were exiled. And because these colonists could not worship God in the proper way, God sent some lions to come and eat them. And so they asked their king to bring them one prophet to teach them how to serve the God of Israel. And from the time the Jews returned from Babylon to Israel, they wanted to rebuild the temple of Jerusalem. These colonists had wanted to help them, but the Jews told them they had nothing to do with them, because they were not Israelites. The colonists felt that because they worship God, the God of Jacob, Isaac, and Abraham on the mountain Gerazim, they are also sons of Jacob. But in fact, they were not Israelites but colonists. The well was for Jacob, and if it was for Jacob, it was for the Jews! Then it is on the land of the Jews. They came to take the land. But because they have been on the land for a long time, they have come to consider themselves as part of Israel. But they don't regard themselves as Jews either. But it is the Jews who don't accept the Samaritans.

That the word *colonists* is contextually loaded in Ghana, with its colonial history, with its continuing dependence on foreign funds, the group did not reflect on. Because starting from our own context assumes that our mundane story is as important as the Bible story, we are not used to looking for relationships between them before explaining the text. It is in the application that examples are taken from daily life.

The group in Abetifi is very much interested in cultural issues. The story raised cultural and social associations: roles of men and women and their relationships, polygamy and marriage, and relations between different ethnic groups (north and south Ghana). Now they want to know more about these issues in Brazil.

> How is it or was it in your environment when it comes to drawing water? Was it women who do it, or girls? And other household chores? What is for the women, what for the men? And how do you feel about it? Do you have the culture of polygamy? What do you think about that? And how would you view a woman who married five times, even if it was one after the other?

They saw the theme of worship in spirit and in truth in the light of church membership. When can somebody be called a real Christian? What to do with church members who are wandering off? Worship in spirit and truth was seen as something very practical: loving God and the neighbor with all we have. Faith is something very personal, and salvation cannot be accepted collectively.

> The church is me and you, and even individual, when you try to be faithful to God. It is not the premises that are important, but you as an individual.

> This woman has heard about the gospel several times, but she ignored it. But when she sees the Messiah, she thinks, now I have to give myself to Christ. It is wrong to say: I went to this church and I never heard of Jesus Christ; that is never true. We have been hearing of it, but now that you have heard of Christ in another place, you have received Christ as your personal Savior. Which means that we don't have to look down on certain churches and say they don't preach Christ. Everyone has a time of accepting Christ, everyone their own time.

Faith is accepting Jesus as your Savior. Most group members could tell a story about the difference between the formal way they were brought up in faith, and the influence of Pentecostalism on their way of reading the Bible, praying, and worship. The mainline churches have all accepted drumming, clapping, and dancing in their worship in order not to lose members, especially the youth.

To some of the group members there is a similarity in the relationship between Orthodox and Pentecostals in Ghana and in Brazil. Some have experienced the negative judgment of Pentecostals about their faith, their being real Christians, and their place in heaven.

> Sometimes, Pentecostals think when you are Orthodox, you are not a good Christian. But if you are Pentecostal, you are more Christian than others.

On the other hand, members of mainline churches can think disapprovingly about some Pentecostal attitudes and convictions. Some saw that such statements are too general and can even bring disharmony and conflict. This type of thinking was already old at the time the Samaritan woman and Jesus met. Today we see fighting in Israel. The misunderstanding and judgments seem to be endless. But Jesus is showing a different example.

> Jesus brought liberation for the woman. He came to liberate, to break the cord of discrimination between cultures and between men and women.

Reading this passage over and over again opened our eyes to interesting details. A story we thought we knew brought new insights and viewpoints.

> You don't read anywhere that Jesus said: "Now go and preach the Word!" The woman just went by herself. She automatically did what happens when the Holy Spirit fills somebody. Most of the time, people forget that she was the first real evangelist. Even before Jesus sent the apostles, she went!

> And what she said was a question: Could this be the Messiah? And the whole town went with her to check.

> And when the woman came, it was Jesus who asked her for water, because he was thirsty. He saw the need of the woman, without her saying she was thirsty. I think this is how it should be. The poor should not have to go to the rich to ask for help. It is for the rich to see how they should help.

The group realized that the eyes of the other group helped them discover their own viewpoints, and raised questions that would not have been asked unless others did so. It is through their eyes that we see that we need more reflection. And to know sisters and brothers elsewhere, who share the same life and suffering, makes us feel less alone.

> Eunice: I appreciate so much this way of Bible reading by the Brazilian group. It reminds me of paintings from a Cameroonian artist. All the paintings show Jesus as a black. And therefore I can relate to them. He is not far away! He is a black. I even think that if the Bible would be written again, we all would do it in our own contexts, and for us it would be here in Ghana! And God would enjoy it.

> Gyeni: Paul wrote that the people in Berea were special because they discussed together everything they heard and discovered that others were nobler than they were. This is how I see it: we listen to each other, and then we learn from each other and discover nobility. And we are also noble.

> Kofi: I also am very enthusiastic about this project. I am an ecumenist, and therefore I feel it is very important that we were able to form a nucleus. If the

Holy Spirit is the water, then let us be led by this Spirit to move and talk with others. What we all share is that we are human beings. And that is a basis for talking and sharing. Even this group, we could continue by inviting anybody who is interested, irrespective of their background.

Osei: If we can't change our denomination by what we are doing, we can still do what is right. We should not let this discourage us, the fact that we cannot change our leaders. We need each other's fellowship, and then we wipe denominational barriers from our mind.

One of the questions that will accompany the discussions is how we can allow ourselves to tell our own stories in order also to listen to the stories the Bible tells. It seems there is a relation between listening to the Bible and listening to our own life.

Then we may also find the living water in our own wells.

Tableau vivant from Indonesia

Lady Paula Reveny Mandalika (Macassar, Indonesia)

From the beginning I felt excited about this intercultural Bible reading. I wanted to know how the other groups interpreted the text we discussed. In the first phase of the project, we all discussed John 4:1–42. We tried to get the message of the text. Our group, which consists of people from different places, tribes, and cultures in Indonesia, told their experience. Each of us spontaneously connected the text with our situation in Indonesia, especially our experiences related to our culture. From the discussion, we shared many stories as relevant to text. We showed interest in topics such as adultery, the exclusive attitude, and salvation. In our context, there are problems related to these topics, such as the unequal position of women and men, and an exclusive attitude in interreligious relationships and toward the people who are expelled from the community. Our stories reflected problems from our context and cultures that influenced us. We all realized that our interpretation of the text was influenced by culture, experience, and the situation in Indonesia.

The second phase was to exchange our discussion with another group in Cuba and one in the Netherlands. We had their interpretation of John 4:1–42 and discussed it in our second meeting. When we read their interpretation, we saw that they started their interpretation with analysis. For example, they started with a question about who wrote this text: When was the text written? They also looked at the map in their Bible. They didn't directly connect the text to their situation. The way they understood the text was different from how we understood it. They analyzed the text verse by verse, while we related it to our situation in Indonesia. From this exchange, we realized that we didn't do the first step that we must do to interpret the text as theology. We all realized that we should analyze the text first, then, after we get the message of the text, we should relate it to the context in Indonesia.

In the third phase, we were to comment on their reaction to our interpretation. In our discussion, we saw that some topics that were interesting to us were not relevant to their situation in the Netherlands. We expected that they would share their stories that were relevant to the text. But they couldn't do it because they didn't see any relevance with their context. Personally, from the interaction between the other groups, I started asking myself about the exclusive attitude toward people who are being expelled from our society. From the discussion, our interpretation challenged theirs as a better interpretation, which could speak to the relevance for our situation in Indonesia.

The second group in Macassar also exchanged their interpretation with the groups in the Netherlands. The groups consist of old women who were raised or born in Indonesia, but who now live in the Netherlands. In their interpretation we found some similarity. For example, we have the same interest in topics about women: they spontaneously found the relevance in their situation. The groups in the Netherlands seem to have a strong relationship with the Indonesian culture and context. It is reflected in their stories about Indonesia. And in contrast to the groups before, these groups shared a lot of stories that showed the relevance with their situation and made some comparisons with the situation in Indonesia. Actually, the groups in Indonesia expected that they would get a different interpretation. But the fact is, their idea is not different from ours. We think that although they live in the Netherlands, they are still influenced by Indonesian culture. From this interaction we learned that our culture really influenced our interpretation. The Indonesian people who live in the Netherlands can't deny that Indonesian culture still influences their interpretation of the text.

The interpretation exchange with the two groups from the Netherlands really enriched us here. The first group made us realize that we should analyze the text before looking for its relevance. And the second group convinced us that culture had a strong influence on our interpretation of the text in the Bible.

Tableau vivant from India

Sam Peedikayil Mathew, New Testament
Gurukul Lutheran Theological College and Research Institute (Chennai, India)

The Chennai group is set in India, in the context of a plurality of religions and cultures, massive poverty of the majority, and an oppressive system that discriminates against people on the basis of caste. In two lively sessions on John 4:1–42, the group saw different facets of a model for life-changing evangelism, and Jesus's inclusive approach to the lowly and the outcasts. The group members spontaneously identified mainly with the Samaritan woman, who is seen as a model for evangelism, and with Jesus as the one who crossed boundaries that separate people. The group noted Jesus's self-revelation through personal encounter with her, and his teaching of profound truths through everyday needs of water and food. His statements on worship were also commented on. The group was challenged to worship in truth, because such worship is seen as an aspect of witnessing through life. The participants found both Bible study sessions interesting, enriching, and educative, contributing to one another's viewpoint. Because of the impact of this study, the group decided to do this kind of spontaneous, participatory Bible study in their regular biweekly Bible study sessions. Some group members challenged everyone about the notion of God they have and regarding practicing what they hear. There was a challenge to get to know Jesus personally and to communicate the gospel in spite of opposition or danger.

A comparison was made between Jesus and the soothsayers/astrologers (who are very common in India), who predict the future and read the past. The group brought out the similarities and differences. The group also made reference to *Moksha*, the concept of liberation in the Hindu religious tradition, and they stressed the importance of deeds in Christian life. This reflects a positive attitude toward the understanding of salvation in Hinduism. The Samaritan woman's method of evangelism is contrasted with that of today's popular preachers of prosperity, who teach that material prosperity will come when a person believes in Christ. Unlike them, the woman brings people to Christ, and the focus is not on material benefits. The revelation of Jesus as the Messiah to the Samaritan woman is compared to Jesus's revelation as the Messiah to Peter at Caesarea Philippi (Mark 8:27–30, and parallels). In both cases, God's revelation comes to simple people and not to scholars nor to the rich and the powerful. The group was so active that the Bible study sessions often exceeded the scheduled time and continued enthusiastically. The reflections came freely, without any hesitations. There was a moment of laughter when someone referred to the Samaritan woman's past life and her attempt to hide her past.

The Chennai group agreed with the partner group in the Netherlands on the main insights of the story. However, the group was surprised at the way the partner group interpreted some statements of Jesus and the way they looked at Jesus, the Samaritan woman, and the text. The group was excited about the new information brought in about the followers of John the Baptist. The Chennai group felt that it is because of the European culture that the Dutch group interpreted differently the statement of Jesus, "Give me a drink." Whereas Euro-American culture lays stress on the formal request, in the Indian culture, as is the case in Eastern cultures, the emphasis is on the way (the tone in which) the request is made. This difference made the European partner group see this statement of Jesus negatively, expressing domination of man/Jew over woman/Samaritan. While the Indian group saw solemnity in the conversation between Jesus and the Samaritan woman, the Dutch group saw it differently. The Indians saw the secularized religion of the West as the reason the Dutch partners looked at Jesus and the text with less reverence. The attitude toward Muslims as people worshiping a God whom they do not know could be due to the predominantly monocultural context of the partner group. The identification of the partner group with the disciples may be due to the European culture that tends to shun/avoid strangers. More open relationships between men and women in Western culture may be the reason the Dutch partners have a positive attitude toward the Samaritan woman. The Chennai group wondered if the proliferation of yoga/meditation techniques in the West (a diluted and simplified version of yoga in Indian philosophy) has influenced the interpretation of true worship in "Spirit and truth" as meditation.

In the partner group's response to the Chennai group's reading, many misunderstandings of our groups were clarified. Although the partner group agreed with the Chennai group on some basic points in the story, there are marked differences in the way they looked at the Samaritan woman's past and the disciples. Our partner group had a more positive attitude toward the Samaritan woman and some cults in the Indian context.

Our experience of reading through the eyes of another has opened new ways of interpreting the text and learning to see the text differently. It has opened up meanings of the text hitherto unknown to us. It has challenged some aspects of our thinking and way of life and called for more openness to the text and to others. The way the same text is interpreted by different groups has clearly brought out the part played by the culture and the interpreter's worldview in the interpretation of the Bible. The readings of both groups have shown that the culture of the interpreter determines the main lines of interpretation of the biblical text. This is evident in the way both groups looked at Jesus, the Samaritan woman, and the disciples. When the text is seen through the eyes of another culture, one is able to transcend one's own culture and enter into a horizon of new meanings. Here we find the fusion of the horizons of the text, the Indian group, and the Dutch group, leading to an altogether new interpretation of the text. The communitarian reading process was helpful for learning from each other within the group and correcting and enriching each other. Because this process of reading provided more opportunities to contribute actively to the Bible study, the enthusiasm and the impact of the study were really great.

Tableau vivant from Korea: After ending the intercultural Bible study
Unha Chai, Hanil University and Theological Seminary (Cheonju, South Korea)

The Korean church usually does a lot of Bible study in church buildings and homes. Many Korean church members even write the Bible from the beginning to the end by hand. It takes a year or so. They love the Bible and its study. Many think that it is one of the duties of Christians to read the Bible on a regular basis. More than 99 percent of Korean churches have worship services (sometimes called "prayer service") around 5:00 every dawn, and afternoon or evening services on Sundays, in addition to Sunday morning services. One hundred percent of Korean churches have services on Wednesdays, too. Especially during every dawn service and Wednesday service, many Korean churches have Bible study; people think that they have to know what God tells us through Bible study. They read and study certain parts of the Bible—for example, Genesis or Acts—as a whole. The ministers usually explain it in detail like teachers. It is common that the minister stands at the altar, and the congregation sits in the pews. The whole congregation just listens to whatever he or she says. The minister teaches it, and they learn from him or her. In some cases, the congregation numbers in the hundreds or even more. During the study, there are usually neither questions nor any communication at all. The minister just teaches them. This is the general picture of the Korean church's Bible studies.

However, our Bible study was absolutely different from this general method of Korean Bible studies. First of all, the setting was different: the group was sitting in a circle on the floor. Everybody was equal, and the environment was so open and welcoming to all the participants. There was no actual minister or facilitator dominating the Bible study group. There was no one dominating the conversation either. Some of the participants were voluntarily quiet or silent, when they wanted to be. It was totally up to each of them. Every single person was willingly taking part in the Bible study.

In terms of content, no single person was actually teaching. The group did not have to learn from one person's instructions from the beginning to the end. They shared their feelings, emotions, and thoughts, without being judged on a moral basis or on scientific knowledge. Different ideas were also spoken of. Their personal experiences and honest thoughts were being shared. People were learning by talking or by listening to others on their own, rather than by hearing what to do from ministers or teachers. Any Bible study group, when it is well organized and led, can learn by itself and be more faithful to itself.

Through this experience, our group has learned a great deal about how to run the Bible study when they go back to their local churches. It is true that our group has advantages that groups in churches lack, because we have the same background; all are trained theological students, except one theological lecturer. They also are of a similar age. They know and understand each other well. It was quite easy for me to facilitate the group. No one was hesitant to talk. Everybody was willing to talk and listen to and learn from each other. Everybody knew one another quite well on a personal basis.

We talked about two things while we were having the meetings for the Bible study. First, we should have had more choices in the Bible text. We had only John 4. If we had alternatives, however, it would be more interesting and stimulating for us to do the Bible study. Because the text of John 4 was so well known to them and used for their Bible study in their own churches several times (for example, for their youth groups), there was not much new to be talked about, they said. They realized that they already had some fixed ideas about the text, so that it was really hard for them to get away from their former ideas on it.

Second, we did not have enough background and knowledge about our part-ner group. We had just a short summary of their Bible study, so that we had a vague idea of what they talked about and discussed. If we had had even one or two photos to know about them, we could have better understood their Bible study and their ideas about what issues they were most urgently or intensively talking about at the Bible study. It was a bit of a pity. Probably it is one of the intercultural Bible study's limits, we guessed.

All the members of our Bible study graduated from the MDiv course in our theological seminary, Hanil Jangshindae. They are no longer with me at seminary. All are working in local churches as deacons at the moment. They will be ordained sooner or later. After meeting for the Bible study, we talked a lot about how we organized the Bible study group and how it ran. Especially when we read the report our reporter wrote, we reflected a lot on it. Our reflection did not just disappear but would last a long time. We felt that we should be more responsible in our talk and more thoughtful and more concrete about our ideas. Every single word from our tongues can comfort or hurt others, because sometimes it can be very personal.

Now we talk about what culture is and what it means to our daily lives in society. However, our Korean church is so conservative and closed in general. It is still trying to keep its own identity as Christian by closing itself to the outside. This is reality in Korea and the Korean church. Thus the method of intercultural Bible study is challenging and alien in a way. However, society is changing very rapidly, and the church is also changing, although not fast enough. I do believe and want to believe that the group's members are attempting an intercultural method of Bible study at their local churches, step by step, whether consciously or unconsciously, as we experienced. It was a good experience and a challenge to all of us. I am appreciative to all of you that I had a good opportunity like this, and that I am one of you.

Tableau vivant from Hungary
Personal and communal formation and transformation
Miklos Koscev, Practical Theology
Pápa Reformed Theology Faculty (Pápa, Hungary)

Our group was linked to a group from Westmaas (the Netherlands). And before this formal connection was made, we as a group—through personal contacts and commitments—made a sort of informal first round with a Dutch group from Oostwold. In my contribution, I will try to tell about both our experiences. Right from the start, we as a group dealt with both groups in exactly the same way, using the same method, without making any distinction. Both contacts appealed to us, and because of both of these contacts we have been greatly enriched.

The group. We live along the south coast of Balaton Lake. This lake is one of the most well-known and most important tourist attractions in Hungary. The village itself is very small (some 2,000 inhabitants). As a Reformed church with 250 members, we represent only a small part of our village. Our church community is a kind of folk church. The way our Bible study group is composed, and the way we react to questions of society, religion, and church, are connected with our being a kind of folk church. The group has a higher than average education and financial situation for Hungarian Reformed church members.

Clarifying the idea of this project and the way this project should be carried out was not difficult for the eight group members. Therefore, we were able to divide the tasks among the members: one of us wrote the report, another described the group, and a third one the conversations.

This project was not really understood by the average church member in our community; it didn't mean anything to those who didn't belong to our group. This is probably because of my own failure; I didn't prepare them well enough. In practice, we had a very sympathetic and active group and hardly any commitment from the church community.

The way the reading of John 4 was carried out—in accordance with the project's expectations—was quite different from the traditional Bible study meetings.

That's why it was very good that the reading group consisted mostly of articulate church members, because of which the discussions went well—at least in my opinion. The composition of the group was largely my own choice and showed my own preferences. (In the meantime, we also started another [normal, spontaneous] reading group. The idea was to read other texts according to the same method, i.e., according to the rules set out for the project. In my opinion, this group was quite different: less qualified as far as education is concerned, more conservative in their ideas. Reading the texts was much slower.)

The group members had known each other a long time but were not familiar with Bible study activities. Not all members of this reading group attend church every Sunday.

As far as liturgy was concerned, we made a modest attempt to sing songs that were probably known to the partner group as well. In our prayers, we always remembered the other group and the whole project.

The meetings took place in a relaxed atmosphere. The room we met in was good. We always had some flowers, lit candles on the table, and at the end we almost always continued talking and drank something. In this way, these meetings were quite different from our other church meetings.

Changes and new insights. Almost half of our group had already met Dutch people or had even been to the Netherlands. Personal experiences regularly came up, yet we always experienced some surprising new thing. What became clear, for instance, was that we are not the only ones with the problem of secularization, of people leaving the church. Many saw the Netherlands as the Promised Land—and these exchanges of thoughts gave us a more realistic picture. At the same time, the voluntary activities of the partner group appealed to us. It made quite an impression and lingered on in the group members as a kind of positive example.

It was interesting to see how the partner group actualized and discovered things in John 4, often quite different from what we did or didn't do. And at the same time, it was comforting that a number of thoughts showed similarities; this always produced an effect. A spontaneous and new realization was that one could read a text in an affective/emotional and experimental/spiritual way. The group members thought these accents could not be used as much in a church service. During the meetings, some people shed tears; for others, it was strange to see people express their personal feelings in this way. It also meant a new assignment for us: we had to learn to deal with the emotions of other people.

The remarkable thing was that people were sympathetic to other people's views and tried to accept each other.

The biggest change, which was at the same time a great gain (according to many of the group members), was that they had become more mature and had learned to discuss their personal feelings and experiences in relation to a certain Bible text. This meant some growth in their faith and in their personal lives.

Cosmic vision. It is good to know the backgrounds from which the other and one's own group members are going to react. Confronting and comparing the ideas of our own group members with those of the other group, with their views of the world, religion, and church, was a good—but often demanding—task.

Maybe this was a much more honest and more direct experience, in spite of the distance and the somewhat impersonal character, of how one can think as a church member in a not very large community in the Netherlands.

Learning to know how the partner group lives and how they think differently about things, even about the same story in John 4, can be surprising and challenging. Sometimes, there was a lack of understanding in relation to the other group's opinion.

What was quite evident to us was that the partner group was able to think and express themselves more spontaneously and more freely. They gave the text less authority, whereas we didn't dare to question its authority. Their approach says something about being used to living in a more open, more democratic climate of life and thought.

We noticed that we followed a much tighter scheme and that we made more use of the provided guidelines, because of which we did our discussions in a somewhat more structured way. At least, that's how it seemed to us. This was also worth comparing.

Tableau vivant from the Netherlands
Through the eyes of another: To see and be seen
Marianne Paas, Regional Service Center Gelderland
Protestant Church in the Netherlands (Gelderland, the Netherlands)

The beginning. In the spring of 2002, thirteen people came together in a church center in Rheden, the Netherlands. The purpose of this gathering was to make a start on the intercultural Bible reading project. The initiative for this project came from the local ZWO commission (a commission involved with mission, service, and development work). One of the ministers of the church was also involved with this initiative. I was asked to attend the meeting in order to guide the process on behalf of the Regionaal Dienstencentrum (Regional Service Center) Gelderland. During this first meeting, it became clear that there was a lot of ambiguity. In order to alleviate this, we spent the entire morning extensively explaining the background, objectives, and structure of the project to the group members. By the end of the morning, everyone had become so enthusiastic that the group unanimously decided to go ahead with the project. We made an appointment for the next meeting. We also agreed that everyone would bring an object to the next meeting, which they would use to tell something about themselves.

This is the background of how we started a collective process on intercultural Bible reading in Rheden. The initial process can be characterized as careful and enthusiastic, with the participants looking for trust and confidentiality. The group tested the waters to see if we could speak openly to one another.

The first discovery we made was that we all have very different backgrounds but that it felt good to meet and to share part of our individual life stories with others. Our group is made up of six men and seven women, most of whom are older than fifty. In many cases the objects brought along to the meeting had a religious meaning: Bibles, psalm books, texts, and pictures. Other symbols were also brought along, though: a lump of clay, a wedding ring and a marriage certificate, a statue of two women, a wine glass, scales, a pair of binoculars, a diary, and a name plate. This is how we shared our life stories with each other, and it did us good.

The Bible story. During the third meeting, we finally concentrated on the text from the Gospel of St. John. Would we succeed in linking our own life stories to the story of the meeting at the well?

After reading and rereading the story, we started the discussion by asking everyone what memories, feelings, and experiences the text evoked. The purpose of this question was to create a perception of the text. It is striking that the first word said was "irritation." One of the participants stated that she found the behavior of Jesus to be quite irritating, all that twisting of words with hidden meanings. Some others shared this view. The difficulty of getting into the story (as one of the participants put it) was apparent from the repeated efforts by the discussion leader to bring the participants back to the point of the discussion: their own perception.

What does this story do to you? How does it affect you? With what or with whom can you identify or not identify? These were by no means easy questions for most of the participants: they insisted on wanting to know the exact meaning of the story. We identified different layers within the story that made it difficult to just step into it. Besides, within the group itself, various scriptural interpretations were applied to the story. At one moment, the text was looked at as a symbolic story: it does not matter whether it is a "true story." The question that is important is, what is the actual meaning of this story? At another moment, the story was discussed as if it were a report of an event that might have taken place in the distant past, and someone wondered how it could possibly have ever been written down. After all, Jesus and the Samaritan woman were alone at the well.

There was also another striking and interfering factor, though: all of us already knew the story. This text was so well known to us that it was difficult to listen to and look at the text in an open and unprejudiced manner, i.e., as if with new ears and new eyes. Everyone already had his or her own perception of this story. It became apparent within the group that the perceptions that are linked to the traditional way of explaining scriptural passages sometimes clash with a desire to look at the story from a different perspective. For example, where one person just assumed the sinful life of the Samaritan woman, another person wondered whether we had actually understood correctly what exactly was meant by "those men." We were not able to agree with each other on this. Maybe we did not always understand each other very well, although we did experience precious moments of recognition and respect. We exchanged our perceptions and feelings, and occasionally in this process something became visible of the link we made between the story and elements from our own life stories. In spite of this, generally speaking, little progress was made in the process. Our existing perceptions relating to this story seemed pretty fixed. The participants did, however, value the discussion, and everyone felt there was more to talk about.

A confrontation. We decided to meet again to discuss the story. We wanted to try to understand the story better by means of a confrontation game.

In the confrontation game, a method developed by the Vrouw en Geloof-beweging (Women and Faith Movement), the participants are divided into character groups. In our case, we divided the group into four groups representing four characters: the followers/disciples, the townspeople, Jesus, and the Samaritan woman. Each group was instructed to take on the role of their character and to formulate two questions for each of the other characters from the story. In the second phase of the game, the entire group sat together in a circle. The questions were put to the characters in turn, and the characters answered these questions. The actual confrontation demanded quite a lot of empathy and the freedom to give answers to unexpected questions. In the closing phase of the game, we jointly analyzed how we presented the different characters from the story.

Although it remained fairly difficult to really enter into the story, we experienced some tense moments during the confrontation phase. At a certain moment, the Samaritan woman asked the townswomen why they gossip about her so much. A short discussion arose, and the townswomen eventually said—in imitation of Jesus—that they would treat this woman with more respect in the future. At another moment, one of the disciples walked over to Jesus and offered him something to eat. After Jesus had accepted this food, he was immediately asked the question: "Why do you eat now, and why did you not eat at the well?" The answer given by Jesus reminded us strongly of the conversation with the Samaritan woman: this

Jesus also speaks in metaphorical language. A tense moment also arose when the tricky problem between the Jews and the Samaritans was acted out. We briefly discussed the claim within our story that salvation was to come "from the Jews," which from the perspective of the Samaritan woman entails a sense of their pride and generates a feeling of inferiority.

All in all, the game was characterized by a mixture of seriousness and humor. In concluding the discussion, we tried to summarize our experiences. How did we present the different characters from the story? We turned the disciples into ordinary people who still had a lot to learn: fishermen, people who are unreliable and therefore human, although also as people with humor who are sometimes surrounded by an atmosphere of strong group codes, characterized by a certain uncommunicativeness. They are practical, caring, and show solidarity with each other. We also hesitantly asked ourselves: Must they pass on the gospel?

The townspeople were typified as forgiving (in relation to the woman), open to something new, simple, curious, sympathetic, serious and searching, and critical. We typified Jesus differently: on the one hand, he was considered trustworthy and convincing, a good teacher. On the other hand, he was also typified as unclear, vague, irritating, and lonely. Finally, the Samaritan woman was considered brave, someone who must have been very lonely, self-confident, a deep thinker, honest, and someone who showed solidarity with the people she cared for. She was also focused on the future.

We asked ourselves whether the two meetings had changed our perspective on the story. In general, we concluded that this was not the case. However, most of us had gradually discovered a lot more details, which made the story richer and more positive. The biggest change was the attitude of individual group members toward the Samaritan woman: many indicated that their initial impression of this woman was more superficial. One of the participants stated that, throughout the centuries, attempts have been made to erase the role of women from history, but that no one will succeed in doing this. We also jointly noted that we apparently had quite fixed opinions on certain details, while in the story itself there were probably no real grounds for such opinions. Apparently, it is difficult to abandon perceptions that have been woven into a story over time.

January 2003 came, and we became increasingly curious about the reading report from the other side. We had to wait for some time for it, though.

Ghana in view: A new confrontation. The group that we had been linked to was made up of members from the Bepong Methodist New Chapel and the Bepong Presbyterian Chapel in Ghana. We came together once again, curious and full of expectation. We had all received a translation of the reading report.

We started with an exchange of general background information on Ghana. After that, we practiced singing the Ghanaian song "Oda ni oofe fee." This felt somewhat strange, but after we had sung it a couple of times, it sounded quite nice. After this, we tried to form an impression of the Ghanaian group, which proved to be quite difficult. The information provided on the group was very scant. At their first meeting, which at one time had more than ninety participants, an introduction to the Bible study was given. The participants at this meeting were mainly women. During a second meeting, two groups were formed, and the reading report that we were discussing originated from one of these groups, which consisted of eighteen people. We were aware of their professions: traders, farmers, and teachers. However, we did not know how many men and women were in this group, or their ages. We wondered whether they had introduced themselves to each other—or did they already know each other?

It was striking that, with regard to our observations on the Ghanaian reading report, we formulated so many questions to be put to the group in Ghana. However, it was not so easy to put the—probably essential—questions to ourselves. Many questions arose, and these were sometimes more statements than questions: they were full of presumptions and maybe even much prejudice. It was as if we sensed the differences but did not know how to deal with them.

The method used by our partner group raised a question about what role the Dutch person sent out to Ghana played: the Bible study questions seemed quite Western to us. We recognized them as questions that are typical for a Dutch approach.

Compared with our own experiences, it was striking that the partner group hardly spoke about the townspeople who reacted to the news of the Samaritan woman. In our group, there was a lot of appreciation for the responsiveness of the townspeople, and some members also valued their forgiveness toward the Samaritan woman.

However, most discussion in our group related to the opinions of our partner group on the concept of sin. It was through this discussion that it became more apparent than before that there were diverse opinions within our own group on this subject. Some participants stated that we, luckily, do not have such fixed views on what sin actually is. We also immediately linked a positive value judgment to this observation: we are milder (than whom?), and we do not judge so fast (as who?). Others expressed their doubts, though. Has our interpretation not gradually grown too casual? Should we not have established more clarity by now? The efforts of a number of women in our group to try to neutralize the existing area of tension was striking. They did this by expressing their opinions on the essence of the story in words: "This story tells us what is really valuable in life," and "the love of God conquers all, even evil."

There was also a clear difference in approach in the way the Ghanaian group finished their discussion. The final discussion related to the perception of how we should act in our own lives based on what the participants came across in the story. We felt that this focused very much on bad behavior and guilt/feeling of guilt (which seemed to be mirrored by the Samaritan woman), and much less on the liberating character of how Jesus acts in the story. We did not find it very easy ourselves to indicate the real meaning of this story for our daily lives. It may be precisely this absence of a simple and concrete link between biblical stories and our daily lives that has far-reaching consequences for some individual believers. We also experienced in our group, in all its vulnerability, the fear of losing everything you always believed in, the desire to finally get an answer and to know where you stand.

And now . . . We have not yet reached the final stage. The group in Rheden would like to continue meeting. There is still so much curiosity and so much need to exchange views. In addition, we have received a video made by the Ghanaian group on a theatrical adaptation of the story. We also have plans to share the experiences of the group in some way with other parishioners.

We have seen many images. We have used images to speak about ourselves, and we have heard about others through images. Gradually, we have taken on the confrontation with our old, sometimes fixed interpretations, and we have found new, surprising, and liberating perceptions in the discussions on "our Bible story." And then, at once, we were challenged to look at that same Bible story through the eyes of another. The perceptions of the group from Ghana formed a mirror for us, and so we looked—hesitantly, carefully, searchingly—at ourselves again, at our perceptions of people and cultures from what we call "the third world."

Looking through the eyes of another is not simple, but it is a very exciting and challenging search. It requires courage and openness. We are practicing this as best we can, in the footsteps of Jesus and the Samaritan woman.

Tableau vivant from El Salvador
Reading Bible, reading bodies

Larry José Madrigal Rajo, Centro Bartolomé de las Casas (San Salvador, El Savador)

Why "the body"? Many people in El Salvador have hard experiences with the body. They experience violence on the streets, in homes, in school, and between rival gangs. People in former war zones have been traumatized. Others experience oppression, daily hunger, and homelessness. People are fatigued and stressed; they run to catch the bus, and they worry about money as they watch prices rise. Eventually, we also enjoy moments of relaxation and love with friends, as we share food and hope. In suffering and in joy the body is always present, although often silent or silenced.

Biblical studies and pastoral care in Central America rarely take seriously the presence of the body and the challenges it presents. Sometimes biblical scholars and pastors in local communities offer not only a traditional reading of the Bible but an uninteresting reading that does not nurture people—who not only *have* bodies but *are* bodies. We have undergone a strict formation in historical-critical method, and more recently, one that uses contributions from literary criticism, sociology, anthropology, and feminist thought. But the body is still absent, or it appears as the object of disputation, or as a preliminary subject before serious reflection begins.

The body is key to understanding what happens with life itself, with my life and the life of others. For that reason, the body is a hermeneutical key, basic to biblical interpretation. The body points to relationships between people and with the material world, and it effectively focuses issues of power. Power is not the same for every person; how people perceive it depends on factors including gender, race, age, and religion. Can we discover power relationships behind the text by working with the body? Can we change our interpretation of the text by bringing it to the daily life of the body?

I have focused on the body because the biblical movement in El Salvador and the alternative biblical-theological training program of Centro Bartolomé de las Casas have been successful ways of working with groups who have been far from the church and from faith. They have been strong tools for empowering marginalized groups. But the body is an enormous challenge for Western epistemology with its rationalistic, male, white, well-educated, and middle-class bias. This orientation is far removed from my sisters and brothers at the periphery of Salvadoran society.

Bibliodrama is the most common way to use the body in interpreting biblical texts. This new approach, drawing on the body as hermeneutical key, combines reading the text and analysis with theatrical interpretation and various forms of corporal expression. This way of revisiting the text encourages people to involve their feelings and their bodies with a freedom that sometimes leads them to finish the narration in an unexpected way, one not contemplated in the sacred text or proposed by biblical scholars. Bibliodrama can also be an emotional meditation—using relaxation exercises or music—on corporal reactions and feelings elicited by the text. Needless to say, this approach does not pretend to be either objective or orthodox. We seek to be creative and merciful in our response to the harsh reality of life for many poor people in El Salvador.

Why is the body an intercultural experience? The handbook for the intercultural Bible reading project speaks of respect and tolerance for ways of reading the Bible within the local group, and as groups share their reading reports with one another. In light of these instructions, Bartolomé de las Casas men's and women's groups; Las Mujeres en Camino, of Colonia Los Dolores, in San Salvador; Iglesia Shekiná in Santa Ana; and BEC San Rafael in Cuscatlán[1] decided to be part of the project, to learn more about themselves and about other people around the world. No one anticipated that intercultural communication would be an occasion of not only enjoyment but also of misunderstanding and suffering.

The four groups brought their experience of working with the body as a hermeneutical key, and the facilitators are members of the Salvadoran biblical movement, represented in Biblistas Populares de El Salvador, an ecumenical network. Three of the facilitators have academic training and met to discuss method and perspective. Three groups were linked with groups unfamiliar with bibliodrama. As a result, the body became the focus of moral conflict, repentance, surprise, and happiness, when the first reactions came from partner groups. These groups did not always see all those corporal experiences as compatible with Christian faith and the respect owed to Jesus.

Some actions, reactions, and local effects. The most extreme case was that of the Bartolomé de las Casas men's group, which was linked with a Dutch group in Amstelveen. The men in this group do not meet primarily for religious reasons but as the governing assembly of the United Confederation of Salvadoran Workers, the largest labor union in the country, which was doing some special training on masculinity. Almost all are believers: Catholic (14) and Pentecostal (4), with the remaining three being atheists. They range in age from twenty-four to fifty-one, and come from the urban zone of San Salvador and from the sugar plantations of El Angel (rural San Salvador municipality), La Cabaña (San Vicente province), and several surrounding cities such as Apopa and Nejapa. All of the men took a role in the text: Samaritan woman, Jesus, disciples, Samaritan people.

The men of the masculinity program identified some of their own *machista* attitudes through the bibliodrama representation of the text. They managed to identify personal attitudes and to make commitments to change. Doing the bibliodrama brought them to see that men are educated to be sexually abusive and even rapist. Some represented the Samaritan woman, and others responded by joking. Yet playing the role of the Samaritan woman led them to understand her in a new way. They wondered, "How is it possible that they are suspicious of this poor woman who ran off and left her pitcher? She could have been violated! At moments like that, nobody remembers the work. You just think about saving your life. False men! That's what you are." Instead of interpreting the situation from the vantage point of the oppressors, the men who had analyzed their own attitudes through the bibliodrama discovered their responsibility as those who are complicit in a system that molds them to be violent males, oppressors.

The group used imagination to fill in gaps in the narration. They invented dialogue and situations, gestures and attitudes, a beginning and an ending. At first the men were at a distance from the text, watching the drama unfold. The disciples identified themselves with Jesus. Soon the majority began to express affection for, understanding of, and finally identification with the Samaritan woman and the Samaritan people. They criticized the attitude of Jesus and the disciples. A man identifying himself as a prostitute-Samaritan was particularly affected not only by the characterization but by the ridicule and insults of the men in the group. By the end of the group process, many men felt questioned and confronted by the new interpretation of the text, even to the point of proposing another representation with a different plot. Perhaps this result was possible only because of the masculinity program, but certainly the bibliodrama was essential.

The masculinity process made possible a perspective critical of Jesus. The participants asked why Jesus displays a traditional relationship based not only on cultural background of the time but also on sex/gender social structures. Suspecting that something more lies behind the text that can no longer be seen, they used corporal movement to see what they could learn of the situation in their own lives. They managed more than we can imagine: the possibility of change, because Jesus, with all his power and socialization, changed his *machista* attitude after encountering the Samaritan woman, after seeing "through the eyes of another."

The Amstelveen group is an ecumenical group of mixed gender, composed mostly of women. One might suppose that a group of this type would be an ally in deconstructing traditional images of men and masculinity. But their reaction was that the partner group's approach was terrible. They were offended by what they perceived as disrespect for Jesus, who as the Son of God has nothing to do with sin as expressed in desire, sexuality, socialization, and being a *machista* man. Then a set of questions came directly to the facilitators:

> Are we correct in assuming that your main purpose was to do something together, and that our main intention is to be engaged with what the Bible has to tell us? Does the Bible have a special value for you, or could you have used a fairy tale for your purpose, with the same effect? How do you see Jesus? Is it normal for you to accuse him of such bad things? Do you think you have changed after having involved yourselves in this way with the Bible, and if so, in what way did you change? Has it become an ongoing process for you, and in what way does that make itself felt?

Of course, we the facilitators are familiar with such loaded questions, sometimes formulated with emotion and irony, out of a kind of theological shock. They arise when you touch the basic formulations about Jesus—"one who in every respect has been tested as we are, yet without sin" (Heb. 4:15b)—particularly when the sin in question has to do with the body and sexuality. The response is not always acknowledged as emotional and subjective but is presented as objective. The facilitators faced the difficult task not just of translating the response into Spanish but of explaining it in a context of remembering that we were engaged in an intercultural exchange. The guideline concerning respect and tolerance needed to be especially prominent.

But there were more surprises to come. When men in the Salvadoran group became aware of this reaction, some wanted to convey explanations and amend or edit the report. Others were very affected and rejected the response. After a long, very deep discussion, the group agreed to send a letter to the Amstelveen group, explaining their approach.

> We have read with much respect the report you sent and also your answer based on your reading of our report. We felt that perhaps we did not study the text as you did, and we do not have the same religious commitment. Some of us are Catholic, others are Pentecostal, and some are atheistic. . . . But we have agreed among ourselves, and we have learned new things about faith, the Bible, and Jesus. We send you our apologies if there are

people who felt offended or if we have shown a disrespectful attitude. In the masculinity program, we use bibliodrama, which is a way to enter into biblical texts with our emotions and our bodies. Sometimes we act out what the text says, but other times we imagine an ending that does not appear in the text, and then we do it. Later we reflect on it, and we all speak in the first person, saying "I." We talk about what we feel before saying what we think. We do not regret what we said about our encounter with the Samaritan woman, because it was a way of seeing Jesus and later of being challenged to change ourselves.

And the message included a touch of irony: "We are so happy because our facilitators told us that a group of Dominican friars of a city in the Netherlands financed the masculinity workshops for us . . ."

Epilogue. Most men of the Bartolomé de las Casas men's group are working on gender issues in the labor union. Others rejected any "strange" approach to the Bible, such as bibliodrama. Two or three are very involved in other Bible reading experiences. We believe that the Samaritan woman touched all of us, as did the intercultural process that the project made possible. We hope that some will be thirsty and will return to the well.

Note

[1] Santa Ana is the second-largest city in El Salvador. San Rafael Cedros is a rural town in Cuscatlán, in eastern El Salvador.

PART 2

Case studies on intercultural reading and communication

CHAPTER 3

Listening with the heart

The reading experience of the Dutch groups

Arie Moolenaar

> Our partner group understood the story in a different way, so this brought
> up new material for us to discuss. Then we had to imagine ourselves in a
> different situation and a different culture to look at the story from a differ-
> ent point of view. We had to explain our own contribution better and more
> clearly, and give reasons we understood it as we did. We have learned that
> we are very involved with the Word. We have gained an insight that it is
> possible to deal with Bible stories in a different way, and this has broadened
> our outlook.

A reading group in the Netherlands used these words to describe their experience of
a reading exchange with another group. The intention of intercultural Bible reading is to put Bible readers from all over the world in contact with each other and
have them share experiences and discoveries. "Through the Eyes of Another: A
Project on Intercultural Reading of the Bible," the handbook received by all groups,
described the project with these words: "What happens if people in different cultures and situations read a Bible story together and enter into a discussion with each
other about it? Is it possible to look at the Bible, the world and yourself through the
eyes of another? Does this open new possibilities for discussion, encounter, change,
for deepening your faith?"

More than 150 groups around the world expressed an interest in participating
in the project. They were enthusiastic about the possibility of sharing the reading of
John 4 with believers from unfamiliar countries, cultures, and situations. They came
from twenty-two countries: Ghana, Nigeria, Kenya, India, South Africa, the Philippines, Korea, Indonesia, Argentina, Bolivia, Brazil, Colombia, Ecuador, Peru, Nica-

---

Arie Moolenaar, Protestant Service Center, Protestant Church in the Netherlands (Utrecht, the Netherlands)

ragua, El Salvador, Cuba, the United States of America, the Netherlands, Hungary, Scotland, and Germany.

This article will describe the experiences of reading groups in the Netherlands. First, the reading groups are described: Who expressed interest in the project, and why? Next, the steps of the process are described. The piece concludes with a discussion of the learning moments.

In order to write this article, I used group reports and reading reports. I also reviewed observations that were recorded during the meetings.[1] All participating groups received a questionnaire asking about their findings,[2] and I gratefully used the results of this survey. The experience of hundreds of participants in the Netherlands provides the basis for this essay. Their enthusiasm is contagious.

The reading groups

The interest in intercultural Bible reading in the Netherlands was very extensive. More than a hundred requests for information were received, both at the National Service Center of the Uniting Protestant Churches, and at the Regional Service Centers.[3] Those who expressed interest were sent a folder containing material defining the purpose of the project, information for finding interested people in local church communities, and articles about experiences already gained. Eventually, thirty-four reading groups decided to participate. They were pleased to turn the program into a success in their own communities.

The groups that registered received a manual describing the way to proceed. The program spelled out three phases. The first was the reading phase, in which the group discussed John 4. Group reports were translated into English. The groups also drew up a group portrait intended to introduce themselves to their partner group. In the second phase, groups were paired, and each group received a reading report from their partner group. The group discussed their partner's report and drew up a response, which they sent to the partner group. Before discussing the partner's response, group members familiarized themselves with the country and culture of the partner group. The third and last phase involved receiving and discussing the partner group's response to the primary group's initial report. They then conducted an evaluation and wrote a final letter to the partner group.

How did people in the Netherlands find out about the program? Information was provided from various sources, especially by means of the publications *Omkeer* and *Kerkinformatie*. Some read about the project in the newsletter from Kerkinactie (Church in Action) or its Regional Service Center. Almost half the reading groups indicated also receiving information through other Dutch channels, including newspapers such as *Trouw*.[4]

The reading groups formed spontaneously by many different means. Often, one person, perhaps a minister or a member of the mission committee or Zending Werelddiakonaat Ontwikkelingskerk (ZWO) committee,[5] took initiative to form a reading group. Announcements in church bulletins recruited many participants.

Inviting others in person was also a successful method. Nearly half the reading groups were made up of an existing ZWO committee or Bible study group. In some church communities, the committee for education and training included the project in its annual education programs. An existing ZWO committee sometimes added a few people for this program by one or more of these means.[6]

Many groups attended one of the training days held in the National Service Center in Utrecht, to receive information and training about the program. There the participants learned about the program, practiced reading, discussed how the manual could direct them through the entire process, and met visitors from other countries who told about their experiences. In addition, evening meetings were held or workshops were organized in the region during training days. One-third of the groups attended the training day in March 2001, one-third in May 2001, and more than one-fifth in November 2001. Thus, nearly all the participating groups attended a training day, which appeared to be important for the development of the program. The groups not only learned what they were getting into but also built enthusiasm.

> I was impressed by a one-day study meeting about intercultural Bible read-
> ing in March 2001, at the LDC [Landelijk Dienstencentrum (National
> Service Center)] in Utrecht. I wish to connect concrete Bible stories with my
> own situation and be inspired by them. It is of vital importance to read
> Bible stories in the midst of the problems one is confronted with daily.

Groups from Samen op Weg church communities[7] were particularly likely to participate. Sixty-three percent of the reading groups belonged to such a community. Other groups came from Reformed communities or belonged to a Reformed church. Ecumenical groups participated, drawing members from the grassroots ecumenical community, the Roman Catholic Church, the Perki community (of Indonesian background), and other churches.

The composition of groups varied. There were women's groups, Bible reading groups, mixed groups, groups of older people, and also a few with young people. One Bible reading group had been meeting to study together for more than thirty years. There were also house study groups and groups that registered for a course given by the education and training committee.

> I am a member of the Education and Training team. This inspired me to
> participate in this project. One of the activities of this team is Study House.
> In the Study House we read with all different types of people, and that
> already brings with it many differences. Therefore, I am curious about how
> it will be to read with people from a different cultural background. The
> Study House comes from a Jewish tradition. They have about the same rules
> as this project has: no leaders who know more than the others and listening
> to each other.

The groups came from all over the Netherlands. The largest numbers came from North Holland (nine groups), Gelderland (seven groups), Friesland, and South Holland (five groups each). Zeeland was also well represented with four groups. All of the other provinces had one group each.[8]

Motivation

All reading groups indicated enthusiasm for participating in the intercultural Bible reading program. Participants also brought their openness to learn from each other, to meet and exchange with a different reading group elsewhere in the world, to accept a faith environment from a different culture, and to actively engage in actual faith practices. They also made an effort to relate the Bible story to their own situation, to what confronts them daily.

> The Bible and faith mean so much to me that I like dealing with this in a different manner. Suddenly, intercultural Bible reading entered the picture. It is interesting how others see this, how things work for other people—especially for people in a different culture. I am curious about this.

> It is refreshing to see how others look at a Bible text and integrate this in their lives. I am also curious about the differences in interpretation.

> Reading the Bible in this way is much more intensive than reading by yourself at home. I am very curious about the experiences of the partner group. Are there any similarities or only differences?

> There is now too little discussion about faith in church communities. It seems that it is no longer possible to have a heart-to-heart conversation with one another. People are too well off; that is why they do not want to talk about faith any longer. Also, not enough young people come to church.

> I hope to find inspiration. It is of vital importance to read Bible stories in the midst of the problems you are confronted with daily.

> Our motivation for participating in the intercultural Bible reading project: challenge, becoming familiar with a different culture, learning something interesting, because people think very differently about texts. How defining is culture in interpreting the Bible text? How do our group members think about the Bible text, and how do they believe in it?

> I am curious about how others read the story of John 4. For example, it is about a well. Here in the Netherlands, that is very abstract. In other countries, that may be concrete. Will they read the story differently in that case?

> It seems to us that it is quite a challenge to experience what it might mean not only for ourselves but also our sisters and brothers, all over the world, to read this text together.

The group is very curious about what is in store for them and has great expectations about it.

Some in our group have experience abroad. Others have children abroad, or are interested in the way other peoples experience their faith. This motivates participants for our project. They have talked about the dynamics embedded in Bible texts, the meaning of faith in our lives. Participants are very curious about the response of the partner group and very interested in the contact that may possibly come about. They also brought up several times that they hope to learn something from the response of the other group.

Women in other cultures are often oppressed, while we are free. I think it will be interesting to discuss this in a group.

The first phase

The first phase began after the reading groups formed. In this phase, participants introduced themselves to each other, discussed practical matters, and made agreements about the process. They drew up the group portrait and read the Bible story together. They discussed their report together, then had it translated and sent. The first phase was the most encompassing and time consuming. In this phase, the core of the process took shape. It entailed opening up to each other, to the Bible story, and to the partner group.

Age distribution

The groups represented a cross-section of churchgoers. This range was visible in the distribution of ages, of men and women, and of educational levels. Few young people participated; six participants were between the ages of twenty and thirty (2 percent of the participants). For the rest, the age composition was thirty-four participants between thirty and forty (12 percent), forty-three participants between forty and fifty (15 percent), seventy-one readers between fifty and sixty (25 percent) and no fewer than 129 participants between sixty and eighty (45 percent). Two-thirds of the participants were female, and one-third was male.

Of course, one may ask whether the right publicity channels were used for attracting all ages. Were young people sufficiently informed and enthusiastically presented with the possibility of exchanging opinions about the story in John 4 with people across the world of the same age? Or were young people too busy with their studies, or scarcely to be found in our communities? It remains a fact that the reading groups in the Netherlands appear to have aged a great deal.

To participate in this program, participants must be accustomed to exchanging opinions in a group. They must be willing to be open to each other and trust each other. A discussion about a Bible story demands understanding the text but also requires an open attitude of faith. Do people dare to be vulnerable and show their colors as they ask questions about such a well-known Bible story?

Education and profession

All the Dutch participants were well educated, a fact that is not surprising, given that mandatory schooling was introduced already in 1901. Especially those born after 1950 were able to finish high school. Not all of the older participants had been able to do so.

> In our village, people were poor. Before World War 2, many made a living by digging peat. People had to live on a meager salary. Health care and social security were organized to a moderate extent.

> When I was thirteen, I had to leave school and begin working. Only later did I become a successful farmer.

It was precisely the well-educated older people who participated in this program. The numbers are clear: 5 percent followed a VMBO[9] education, 29 percent finished a high school education, 32 percent had higher vocational education, 21 percent had scientific academic education, and 10 percent finished some other type of education, mostly abroad. Some of the latter group were born and educated in Indonesia.

> The group has a high level of education and has a greater than average knowledge of theology.

The level of education was apparent in the diverse professions participants reported. Represented were farmers, nurses, communications specialists, a bookbinder, a personnel officer, a professional consultant, theologians, a dentist, an architect, and a chemist. Distribution into professional groups was as follows: 5 percent in the agricultural sector; 17 percent in education; 21 percent in health care; 6 percent in technology; 34 percent in services; and 17 percent employed in the church, including eighteen ministers, two priests, and one sexton.

Distribution of tasks

When groups had formed, participants began their tasks with enthusiasm. Tasks distributed among the group members included discussion leader, reporter, and translator. The secretary handled sending documents. In general, members of the group took care of the necessary logistics.

The discussion leader ensured that group members got to know each other well and that everyone had a chance to speak. Because this person managed group process, this task was usually assigned to someone accustomed to leading a group. Usually someone within the group assumed this task, although occasionally the group appointed a leader from outside the group (11 percent of the groups). If the group consisted of a ZWO committee, the chairman served as designated leader (8 percent). Often the minister or a church employee led the groups (52 percent of the groups). In 22 percent of groups, a lay member led the discussion.

The role of the group leader may have a strong effect. Some will do a bit of steering, some will provide a lot of information, and some others will, above all, let the group speak according to its own process.[10]

The reporter's task was difficult. In order to provide a quality report of the discussions held, the recorder needed to be accustomed to the work. In some groups (19 percent), the discussion was recorded on tape or video, to allow the reporter to participate. The tape was transcribed later, a time-consuming task. In three groups, the minister wrote the report (11 percent). However, groups often chose reporters based on their experience with the task (44 percent), because (for example) they write the reports for the church council, or they are professionals (11 percent). Sometimes a person from the group was designated to make the report; occasionally someone was specially invited to the group to serve as reporter.

> There is a risk that the élan gets lost at the moment when logistical and technical matters are discussed. There seems to be some tension between leisurely reading and making all the arrangements. Be wary of this. As soon as logistics come up for discussion, it is difficult to maintain motivation. Take this into account.

> Reporting takes a lot of time. This did not match up with the report we received from the partner group. Theirs was much less extensive.

Bible and liturgy

Many group members were accustomed to reading the Bible at church and at home.

> I read a chapter from the Bible every day.

> I am eighty and hope to read the whole Bible once more.

Participants used the Dutch Bible Society's new translation, as well as De Groot Nieuws Bijbel (Good News Bible), the Staten Vertaling (State Translation), and the Willibrord translation.[11]

Evening sessions usually opened and concluded by reading an article or poem, singing a hymn, saying a prayer, or reading a Bible selection.[12]

In some groups, participants brought along symbolic objects.[13] Group members were sometimes asked to bring something to establish a relation between the story and their own lives. Participants brought very different objects, each telling its own story. They gave short explanations for their choices.

> A photo of a child who was baptized last month. It is a symbol of my time.

> Rice, because the disciples return with purchases.

> A beautiful glass and a ceramic cup. The woman drank water from the well,

but she was handed living water.

An ear, because you must have ears to hear the gospel.

Well water from a bottle. Everyone drinks what Jesus gives to drink and is reborn to eternal life.

A stalk of wheat, because Jesus is the sower.

A small urn received from a Palestinian woman.

Water. The symbol of life but also of death, because you can drown in it.

Two slices of bread in a package. Disciples buy bread, but they also hand it out.

A Peruvian picture of the Last Supper. Water is very important in the story, but so is food.

Water, as a symbol of the living water, very good for our body and our spirit. Jesus gave himself to the world as living water.

Seeds from the allotment garden. This is a reference to John 4:35, about the fields that are nearly ready for reaping. We all must sow the seed of the gospel. We must preach, tell the people that the Messiah has come and the harvest is near.

A drawing of the heart. The heart symbolizes the Samaritan woman who, with all her differences from Jesus—in ethnicity (Jew-Samaritan), man-woman, tradition of faith (worshiping in Jerusalem or on Mount Gerizim)—confronts Jesus and faces him, while she dares to open her heart to the new reality in Jesus's faith, which rises above their differences.

The wedding text from Isaiah 41:10 written on a framed plank. This text is hanging in the room and provides support during good days but especially on bad days.

A *yad*, the silver pointer used to point at the text of the Torah while reading. The texts of the Torah may not be soiled with the bare hands while reading.

A cut crystal. A crystal has many facets. Likewise, the scripture also has many facets and its own message in each context.

The Rembrandt Bible. This contains a print of an etching by Rembrandt representing Jesus in conversation with the Samaritan woman. It is clearly visible that Rembrandt had his own outlook on the scene of the story. Likewise, individuals also have their own views and outlook on the texts.

A wood carving of the head of Christ made by an immigrant worker. This hangs in the living room and provides support when I am down and out and going through hard times.

A photo showing a woodcarving containing the symbolic signs of faith, hope, and love. This picture also provides support in hard times.

A photo of the Ecumenical Institute, Château de Bossey.[14] A visit to that institute taught me that one's truth does not necessarily have to be the truth of others.

A wine glass from my native country. A symbol of the good life we live here, which we wish to share.

A wedding ring. All of life is saturated with loyalty: loyalty to your parents, the church, and the people around you.

Books. Wishing to know what others think, wishing to learn from others.

Clay. Three cornerstones have become definitive in my life: nature, people, and God. I want to live together with my wife, according to the Bible as rule of life, to seek God and help my neighbor. Just as clay provides fertility, food, or beauty, depending on context, helping each other is full of blessing for people. Dealing with clay requires knowledge and patience.

A proverb characteristic of my life: "Everything pursued with more passion is enjoyed more."

A small statue of two women. Symbol for the place of women in my life.

A scale for weighing. Characteristic of a person's life, now in balance.

The Bible and a tuning fork. Courage and trust are always drawn from the Bible. I find happiness in music, among other things.

Psalm booklet, received at confirmation.

A swan, symbol of freedom but also of solidarity.

The Bible, and a book of fairy tales by Rie Kramer.

A crucifix. The sign of Christ in our midst.

A little statue of a person walking, and a rock. I like to walk and collect unusual rocks.

When the Ermelo group met, a candle, an old water jug, and a bottle of Spa water were on the table. The discussion leader opened the evening session with these words: "You see here water standing on the table in two forms, old and new. The water jug as we know it from the Bible stories, and the bottle of Spa water, which we see everywhere in our environment. Water is indispensable; that used to be so and is so now. Water means much more than its chemical formula. It frequently appears in the Bible and in modern poetry as well." Next, the leader read Psalm 23 and a poem by Willem Jan Otten:

Bwa-pl

After a trip through a dripping forest
we reached
the border lake.
It was as if a sleeping woman opened her eyes
and knew us.
You were sitting up front.
I laid my hand
on the warm coconut of your skull.
The light looked deep into your eyes.
I said: Well, so this is water.
Wa-ter.
Wa-ter.
Wa-ter I said once again.
You said: bwa-pl.
You said it once again.
It was certain, my little son,
that we didn't understand the same thing.[15]

Not all reading groups[16] brought symbolic objects.

Symbolic objects are not customary in our tradition. What we take to the meetings are the Bible, a hymnbook, and personal calendar. And everyone wears a watch. The latter two items really characterize the people in the Netherlands.

During this first meeting we noticed that we don't actually use symbolic objects. We concluded from this that we aren't very symbol-oriented people. However, one of the participants attending is. She feels the need to light a candle while reading the Bible, as the symbol of Easter. We noticed that what we bring along to such a meeting in the Netherlands does say something about our culture. Everyone has brought along a pen, a notepad, and an agenda book. The minutes are taken on a laptop. Apparently pragmatism and efficiency make us feel good.

Group process

Groups experienced reading the Bible together as something special. Often group members had been acquainted with each other for a long time. They usually had seen each other at church services. They knew one anothers' names, but did they really know each other? Writing a group portrait opened doors. This portrait provided biographical and sociocultural information to the partner group: names, ages, current or past professions, and the composition of the group. They also provided a description of their society. In addition, they brought up issues for discussion, such as any stress they were going through.

Issues that appeared to be obvious turned out to be not so obvious after all. What exactly do you wish to pass on to the other group? What changes in the church and society do you pass along? The fact most noticeable to the partner group was that young people are barely involved in church work or have even left the church.

There are few young members.

Not enough young people come to church.

Nearly all group reports mentioned concerns about increasing average age, people leaving the church, and secularization. They noted that the poverty older members experienced has entirely disappeared. Many members had been poor and had to work hard, in agriculture, industry, navigation, or land development. Only after the 1960s did the Netherlands become prosperous, with more big changes in the 1980s: mechanization of agriculture, the disappearance of the old industries, and the arrival of the service sector. Dutch people now experience living in a rich country with good social provisions.

All the participants live in a good house and have a car, and all members of the family have a bicycle (which is also used frequently).

The society of the past no longer exists. Many Dutch people have emigrated, and many new people also have immigrated into the Netherlands. Predictable tensions have resulted.

After September 11, 2001, quite a few changes occurred. Violence in the streets, although it is not terrorism, makes people feel unsafe.

One out of every fourteen inhabitants is Muslim in the Netherlands now, right?

There was plenty of material for discussion when groups attempted to describe to the partner reading group who each member was and the developments and tensions visible in the church and society. Through this discussion, group members grew closer to one another. They learned to see each other through other eyes. People of the same faith turned out to have unique histories and wanted to share them with others. In this way, trust and openness were created. People opened their hearts to each other.

Above all, we listened to each other intensively.

There is more solidarity in the group. Members are getting to know each other better.

Openness to each other is experienced as very positive. Trust is important.

By reading together, the contact became more profound.

Reading together is always a unifying factor in a group. Participants get to know each other better, because personal experiences are being discussed. Thus it is a very fine experience for the group.

It is a positive experience to read together in this way.

The group liked studying a Bible text with each other in this way. In a group, people spot more meanings and possibilities for understanding.

The group has experienced how enriching reading Bible stories together can be and that it is educational to seek possible meanings oneself.

The group process plays a significant role. Whether the group members know each other or are making new acquaintances around this exchange affects the process. In general, the reading deepens the mutual relation. The better the group members know each other, the more trust they invest in each other. They also get to know each other better by making a portrait of their own group. If someone talks about the fact that he or she is alone, this makes itself felt.

The reading process

The groups were asked to concentrate on three aspects: the story and their own life experience, understanding the text, and identification with the text. The reading groups in the Netherlands were often accustomed to discussing Bible stories with each other. This often led people to quickly jump over the first question from the manual, about the text and life experience. In one group, the first answer offered to the question, "Can you make a connection with your own life?" was, "Well, not really." Others indicated that the story as such was distant from them, and they found the question hard to answer. One participant commented, "It is not strange when someone speaks to me."

It was mainly the connection with one's own experience that was difficult. I just cannot do that. I noticed that right away I start searching for what is intended here!

The group found it difficult to connect the story with everyday reality. Group members got stuck in the Bible story.

It is not difficult to understand that connections did not come immediately. Who still could remember when women gathered around the village pump or city pump?

Water from the tap is standard in the Netherlands now. Only the older people among the participants still remembered a public pump.[17]

The reading groups all followed the Dutch tradition of reading and discussing the story one verse at a time and trying to understand what it said.

> We read the text literally and pick it apart.

> We read the story too much as spectators.

> What stands out most is that together we seek for the soul of the ancient story that is still so current.

Participants asked detailed questions, such as, "Did Jesus himself actually baptize or not?" (v. 1). "Was that sentence added to the text later? Why would this be done?" "We read nowhere else that the disciples of Jesus baptized people. What does that mean?" "There are still disciples of John the Baptist in India," one group reported. "Why did Jesus have to pass through Samaria?" "Who told him to do so?" (v. 4). "What is Jacob's well?" (v. 5). "What time is it when they say 'the third hour'?" (v. 6). "Is it normal for a woman to go the well by herself? Why is she doing this?" (v. 7). "Is a man allowed to address a woman? Is Jesus breaking with a tradition?" (v. 6). "What exactly are Samaritans? Are they still around?" "Verses 31 through 38 appear to have been added later. Why would this have been done?" In this way, questions come up one verse at a time, and possible answers are given. In other words, many groups do not first set the story in their own life situation but start looking for answers in order to understand the story in the time of Jesus himself. Then, they ask about the meaning for their own experience of faith.

Groups next tackled the question, Whom do you identify with in the text? Here are typical responses:

> With the disciples, because I wouldn't address people in a foreign city either.

> With the woman, because that woman actually does not understand what Jesus is talking about. In this conversation, it gradually becomes clear what Jesus is talking about. It is the same for me.

> She didn't think she was a good person. I also think I don't do many things right!

> With Jesus, because believing is becoming just like Jesus, just like the vine being rooted in Jesus.

In Dutch groups, the reading was characteristically meticulous and involved. People asked questions of the text rather than having the text ask them questions. The Bible story was hardly placed in the participants' social context—often not at all. Rather, it was placed in the context of the group's religious life. Questions of faith resounded abundantly. Above all, understandings about Jesus received attention. "What does it mean when the woman says that he is the Savior of the world?" "Dare we witness as the woman did, or do we have questions about Jesus himself?" Through questions such as these, the cultural context appeared to determine the reading and the understanding of the Bible story.

Other forms

Most groups followed the Bible story closely; however, a few took a different approach.[18] For example, the ecumenical working group in Zaandam retreated to a cloister community to study the story for an entire weekend, which included exegesis, bibliodrama, poetry, prose, and art. The group used a plan of twelve steps to track down the meaning of the story.[19] Group members prepared the first six steps at home. During the weekend, participants worked on the story intensively. In the meeting room, poems and artwork were placed along the walls and on the wide windowsills. To enable the transition from everyday hectic life to the calm of the weekend, they used meditation exercises. Subsequently, they read the story of John 4 in breathing units. This created a calm attention in the group. Next, smaller groups worked with the story, following the twelve steps. They commented on the process in their report:

> Amazement alternated with happy surprise, fascination, and emotion, when group members listened to each other.

Each day, morning services and vespers were held, when poems and hymns were shared. In one of these services, participants acted out the story in a bibliodrama. In acting out the story, the group members revealed a lot of themselves.

> Amazement, anger, happiness, hope, and alienation—the emotions of the characters in the Bible story—became the emotions of the actors. Acting was interspersed with laughter and tears. The bibliodrama made the insight into the story more profound. Some people recognized themselves from their own experience and their own context, in characters, expressions, or scenes from the story. Others experienced a wide gap instead.

The meeting was concluded with each person writing a personal letter to the woman at the well. An example of these letters follows.

> Woman at the well
> I have read your story
> And it brought me a thousand questions
> I will not ask you those
> You still have water to carry
> Nevertheless, I would have liked to know
> What you were doing there at the well
> Did you perhaps know then and there

What I and we
Still do not see today
But I just thought, well . . .
We didn't see through anything
Didn't recognize the water
I think that until that time
We are still known[20]

The weekend concluded with a liturgical celebration in which water played an important role. The personal letters were read to the group, and hymns that were rehearsed during the weekend were sung.

All experiences and emotions that had played a role in reading the story were clustered in the celebration.

Their report described the weekend as a quest for the meaning of the story. In their description, the group commented that the role of women was becoming more important to them. This was also true for the meaning of the water. As they studied the story in the context of the stories surrounding it, water emerged as an important theme in the Gospel according to John. By acting out the story, the participants learned that, depending on the role played, one's experience of the story changed. When a man played the role of the woman at the well, this led to a change in perspective. In this way, participants grew together near the end of the weekend, with its concluding celebration. They concluded with a water ritual in which they passed around "living" water and shared water and bread.

It was a very emotional celebration, bringing together everything we had discovered during the weekend.

The second phase

Pairing up

Next, groups entered the second phase, that of being paired with another group and exchanging experiences. A reading group did not know in advance which group it would be paired with. It was possible to express a preference, but international contact people selected the partner group based on the reports submitted at a certain time. It was decided in advance to offer four choices of time for pairing: September, March, July, and December.

The plan for the timing did not work out as anticipated. One complication was the seasonal differences. Whereas in the Netherlands church activity slows down during the summer months of June through August, the experience of groups in countries such as El Salvador and Colombia during these months is different. Groups also had differences in the resources available to them. Groups in the Netherlands had access to computers and e-mail, and often included someone willing to do the translation work. These resources were not always accessible in other countries. It sometimes took months to draw up a quality report and get it translated. The entire package then needed to be sent by mail. In one case, the package roamed around the earth for six months before the Dutch group received it. These challenges meant that some groups in the Netherlands had to wait up to six months before they were matched with a partner. For some, this led to impatience and even disappointment.

> The interim periods were too long, leading to a drop in motivation. This needn't have happened if this had been known in advance.

> The long intervals between action and response to the others' report are not so motivating, and it requires quite some energy to return to study the material.

> An essential point to consider is what to do with your group during the period after you read the story and are waiting for the report from the other group. Take a look to see if anything can be undertaken during this period to bridge the gap, to retain that motivation.

> The nicest experience was hearing that the pairing process had succeeded, especially because we had to wait fairly long.

Fortunately, long delays were the exceptions. Most groups were paired within two months after submitting their reports. Enough groups outside the Netherlands eventually took part that it became unnecessary to pair Dutch groups with each other. In time, all thirty-four Dutch groups were paired with a partner abroad. The distribution was remarkable: eighteen reading groups were paired with groups in Latin America, six with groups in Asia, eight with groups in Africa, and two with groups elsewhere in Europe.[21]

Preparation

Next came the time of preparation. Groups found it tempting to immediately begin discussing the reading report they received. However, proper preparation—learning about the partner group's country—proved to be the best approach, in order to be able to understand the reports. Group members used the Internet, visited the library, requested information from a travel agency, and invited people to come talk about their experiences. One group even had the opportunity to speak with some members of the partner group in person; in fact, they are in the Netherlands. Other groups exchanged e-mail with missionary workers of Kerkinactie in the relevant country. In some cases, a group member had been born in the country of the partner group. Some participants followed current events on television and videotaped a broadcast in order to discuss it in the group. Preparation also often included translating the partner's reading report into Dutch.

> The nicest experience was when we studied the living conditions of the partner group. Searching for information about a different culture when

you are in contact with people there can place this information in a context, which is very interesting. We also watched videos about the country.

Discussion

After groups finished preparing, they could begin discussing their partner's report. Reading groups in the Netherlands noticed that partner groups treated the manual freely. Reasons for this varied, as, for example, a Dalit group in India whose members could neither read nor write. Ghana also had a group in which the Bible story had to be read aloud. Limitations in literacy naturally had consequences for discussion and reporting. As a rule, partner groups drew up a summarizing report, not a verbatim one. One result was that the report did not always feel personal, which was disappointing. People were curious about the individuals behind the story: Who were they? What work did they do? How did they live?

It appeared that partner groups easily identified with the Bible story. They knew about the meeting place of Jesus and the Samaritan woman, the public well. Women in the partner groups' cultures often meet each other at or near the well and exchange news. This information led members of one group in the Netherlands to ask each other: What are our meeting places? Where do we talk to each other?

The possibility that a woman might go to the well by herself and meet a man there also immediately summoned images from personal experience. It could be that the woman was there as a prostitute. As an outcome of their discussion, the women's group in Ghana expressed their intention to help women in their society who are working as prostitutes because of their poverty. The story in John 4 of Jesus meeting the Samaritan woman appeared to be an excerpt from the lives of the Ghanaian group. They asked, "Can a woman just address a man, and is she allowed to do so? Are women in our society not discriminated against? What faith this woman shows! She meets Jesus and speaks about him."

The group's living situation

Dutch groups noticed that their partner groups related the Bible story to their own living situation. Participants talked about their own village and religious life:

> We were impressed by the direct way the partner group dealt with the Bible story.

> We are impressed by the way they bring the Bible texts into practice in daily life.

> We decided to devote more time to each other's story and life. This is because the partner group taught us something here.

> Directly hearing about experiencing faith in Nicaragua is meaningful. It induces us to self-reflection. This results in good contact with the partner group, as far as possible.

It is remarkable that the partner group gives the human side in the Bible a very prominent position, in contrast to our group, which sheds more light on the part of Jesus in the story.

The experiences of the various groups are that the groups in the third world relate reality and faith more to each other.

The partners read the story from the point of view of their personal life situation.

Despite their poverty, people feel they are liberated. They have a great feeling of self-respect.

The groups in the Netherlands were pleasantly surprised after receiving their partner's reports. Nevertheless, they were often at a loss to know what to do with them. They would have liked to know more. Often only the names of participants were given, and no further background was provided.

It is important that information is also provided with the reading reports about the group (background, professions, age, social questions, etc.). This is important for understanding the report and connecting it with the people who wrote it. When groups provide little or no information, the other groups experience this as a lack. After the pairing, some groups gathered information themselves about the environment of the partner group (now that they knew whom they had been paired with).

It is a pity if a group submits a summary of only a few pages. A summary is OK, but then give it in combination with an extensive report. Don't think too quickly, "We do not need to write this down, for it is irrelevant." Valuable information can be hidden right there in apparently unimportant details. It is disappointing to the other group if a very short report is handed in.

Diversity

The diversity in the reading reports received was considerable, reflecting the diversity represented in the groups with which Dutch groups were paired. There were women's groups (El Salvador, Ghana, India, Scotland), young people (Ghana), theology students (Indonesia, Cuba), a group of transsexuals (India), as well as a men's group (El Salvador). The latter group met for a weekend to exchange opinions about macho behavior in their society. The story of the man Jesus meeting the woman from Samaria turned out to be a splendid story to stimulate dialogue about macho behavior, and provided a basis for sharing the group's experience with their partner group in the Netherlands.

The living conditions of participants also varied considerably. Some lived in slums, some in rural areas, some as a minority among those practicing other religions, such as Muslims and Hindus. Most were more familiar with oral tradition than with a written one. The groups in Ghana and Indonesia wrote explicitly about this. These groups belonged to a Pentecostal community in a predominantly Catholic country. Many had deliberately opted to transfer from one church to another. This had explicit consequences for their outlook on Jesus and on faith.

Response

The reading groups in the Netherlands were happy with the reports and the contacts but often found it difficult to deal with the interpretation. The participants of one reading group expressed their perplexity in this way.

> How can you get an idea of what it means to be poor? Our partner group writes that they have no steady jobs. Everyday you have to wait and see if there is work, and if there is enough food for yourself and your family. You read it; you see it on TV or on a video. But what does it really mean to you? How does this feel? What does it eventually do to your faith? We really don't know. We can hear about it, but feeling and understanding it? Well, no!

> Participants are mainly impressed by the fact that their partners, who have to live in such difficult conditions, like the participants in Bogotá, still express their faith in a positive manner.

> We are impressed most of all by how the partner group positions itself in society with spontaneity in sharing.

Participants sometimes found themselves at a loss when encountering other cultural issues. What did they know about a society in India in which transsexuals have formed a professional group for centuries? How should one regard the macho behavior that participants in Latin America worried about? What is it like to live in a society with no formal schooling, where stories are passed on by word of mouth? How can you get an understanding of the meaning of differences in caste? In the Netherlands, men and women can exchange opinions together and are allowed to do so freely. What then was so special in this Bible story—that partner groups were amazed about?

Understanding a person from another culture from the perspective of one's own context appeared to be a difficult assignment. How can one read between the lines? Do we really understand what is being said? Could it be that the other person is holding up a mirror for us to see ourselves? Do we read from our own context, as they obviously do, and what does that consist of for us? How do we deal with our new awareness? What do faith and community of faith mean to us?

> We tend to quickly become disturbed by the other group's image of God or image of women, for example, or by the fact that the other group brings God into everything. Some in our group said, "We have a better view; we

have progressed further." Then in response: "Is that so? Why is it that you react like that? Have we really progressed further? What does that say about *us*?" What the other group says about the text and how that deviates from what we saw and heard in the story may hit hard—in a confrontational way. First we spoke about "us and them," only later about "us and us"!

The third phase

Waiting

After a group discussed the report from the partner group, they drew up, translated, and sent off a report of their discussion. When these steps were complete, the third phase began. This was the phase in which a group received the commentary from the partner on the group's own reading report. Following this exchange, the group wrote an evaluation and sent a final letter. This last phase turned out to be the most difficult. First, experience revealed that not all partners responded and sent their response. In addition, the time interval played a great role. Between the beginning of the first phase and the final phase, there were long months of waiting and expectation. In many cases, it took a year before the entire process could be wrapped up. In some cases, participants had given up hope of ever receiving a response. It sometimes took a year or even two years before the entire reading process could be brought to conclusion.

The most difficult part was waiting for the response from the partner group.

It was disappointing that no response from the partner group was received. That caused the project to get stuck.

It is also difficult to bridge the gap between the two groups in writing.

The interval between the different meetings is too long.

The response from the partner groups

When a response arrived, it acted as a mirror held up to the group. The care and effort put into making the group portrait and the reading report was usually greatly appreciated. But partners often differed in their responses to the Bible story.

Has the prosperity in which the Dutch readers live interfered with their perception of the Bible story, and especially of Jesus himself?

You read rationally and pay no attention to the emotion, to the story itself.

We are impressed by the respect with which you read the Bible.

What does it mean to you that Jesus is the Son of God? You don't pay any attention to this at all.

To you Jesus is a human being; to us he is the Son of God.

It surprises us that you do not think the conversation with the woman is nice. In our opinion, Jesus really crosses borders. He shows patience and wants to start a conversation with the woman.

For us, God is an accessible God, He is an intimate friend who sympathizes with us and shares our daily lives. That is why we can identify so well with the historical Jesus, who we always want to involve in our own lives.

It amazes us when you say that you cannot identify yourselves with anyone in the story. We all can identify ourselves with the story, for we are all sinners. Maybe not just like the Samaritan woman, but we are sinners in one way or another.

We are disciples of Jesus, and we preach and evangelize with the Word of God. Thus, in a certain way, the person who speaks is like a sower.

We agree that Jesus is a capricious character. For example, he entered the house of Zacchaeus. Zacchaeus was a robber. The disciples didn't agree with it, yet Jesus went to his house. . . . Yes, he had his own style.

I notice that they are pretty inquisitive when reading, because they want to sift out many things that actually barely interested Jesus. It is well that the people know that he is the one who is capable of doing everything, that nothing is impossible for him. So I want to say to our brothers over there that they shouldn't get so engrossed in detail but should go into the reality that Jesus represented. Jesus gave the woman life in order to change her.

We find that Jesus in a spiritual sense is more important than other issues.

The Dutch group analyzed the story more intellectually. We used our hearts and feelings more. This difference has to do with our background and situation.

Groups often discovered that their partner group used a different method for reading.

Our way of reading the Bible is influenced by the Latin American way of reading. We follow these steps: Using our reality as the starting point. Using a Bible text to shed light on this reality. Arriving at a communal agreement. Concluding the whole process with a celebration. It is never difficult for us to relate a Bible text to our daily lives.

Discussions involving society or contacts with Muslims typically generated many comments.

We do not understand why you have such a problem with Muslims. We are in contact with them daily and live in peace with them.

You write about Islam, but Islam means nothing to us.

We have become very interested in the religious and cultural world of the Netherlands. The relationship between Protestants and Catholics and references to Jews and Muslims in particular have made an impression on us. For us, this interreligious dialogue is something new, and a challenge.

We are surprised to hear that you have a queen, and not a king, and that this has been the case for three generations.

Groups sometimes found differences in the way their partner understood faith.

Faith unites people more in our world. It seems to me that it has become a point of dispute for the Netherlands.

The Dutch readers are more critical and appear to read the text more as outsiders.

We differ in opinion with you in respect to what Jesus learned from the encounter with the woman. Maybe Jesus was speaking in a parable.

Everyone is welcome in our community, not only people who confess their Christian faith, but every other person who believes one way or another. Even those who do not believe. This outlook is part of our ecumenical mentality.

Groups often made links to their own society and to the discrimination women are subjected to.

In our culture in Ghana, women are discriminated against in all kinds of ways. They are, as it were, shoved under the table. To us, this story means that Jesus liberates women when they come to him or meet him. The woman at the well was liberated from her guilt, shame, and inferiority complex. The women of Sychar were liberated from their lack of faith with respect to Jerusalem (the Jewish religion), and they declared Jesus to be the Savior of the world.

We look at the story of the Bible the way it comes to us and then look at what this means to our personal life. Then, we further reflect on how we can give shape to the good things. We are surprised that you did not make any connections with your own daily lives.

The partner's personal approach toward the text stood out in contrast to the typical Dutch approach.

We notice that you are a heterogeneous group. That means wealth in understanding the text. However, this also has an advantage. You don't just right away agree and come to a unanimous explanation. The result of this is that you also paid more attention to a literary explanation. It shows a rational and analytical approach to the text.

The age composition of the Dutch groups surprised partner groups quite a bit.

Why does your group only consist of middle-aged and older people? Where are the young people in the church? How is this possible?

Prosperity also typically elicited questions and comments.

Of course, we are similar to you in our efforts for proper health care. But for us, there is more to it. In India, we have old spiritual and cultural traditions that resist our giving attention only to the modern health care culture. Therefore, our group wants to emphasize that Western Christianity is strongly influenced by materialistic culture.

We have helped our partner group in the Netherlands to understand what it means to be poor. They reminded us of the fact that the poor merit the Lord's attention. We have the feeling that we have encouraged them to put their faith in the Lord, for people who need little tend to forget God.

The response from the Netherlands

Many of the comments made by the partner groups also applied to the groups in the Netherlands. Dutch groups were surprised by the similarity in understanding the story but also by the differences. They learn to look at themselves through other eyes.

The first thing that stood out in the Dutch responses was that people in the Netherlands dealt with the text in their own way. Is this approach the result of the education of ministers who are trained in critical Bible reading, analyzing the text, examining precisely what it says, and only then arriving at an application to religious life? Does the education of the readers play a role in making poverty disappear from their view?

We are surprised in a positive way by the differences in interpreting the Bible story.

The partner group interpreted it differently. This provided new material for discussion. We had to imagine a different situation, learn to look at the story from another point of view. We also learned that we must explain our contribution better, and make it clear why we interpret it this way.

The partner group has great difficulty with the way we, as a Dutch group, talk about this story. This got us to thinking. Don't we see Jesus too much as a human being?

The partner group provided us with new insights. We in the Netherlands have so many different church denominations. They have the heritage of oppressive discrimination.

We learned to reflect more consciously about our own way of reading and interpreting.

We learned to search to find a way to understand the Bible in our daily lives.

We learned to ask ourselves the question: Do we actually connect the Bible story to our daily lives? Don't we approach the text too much with the intellect, only cognitively and not existentially enough?

It is enriching to become acquainted with this novel way of looking at texts.

We learned to listen with the heart.

The partner's greater freedom in dealing with the Bible story also surprised many participants.

The best experience was to hear that our report from the Netherlands was acted out in a role-play.

They sent us personal letters. That was a big surprise. We answered them in turn. Then we got mail back again.

The group opted for a meditative posture; sitting, sometimes lying on the ground. People touched each other. Symbols were used such as a broken urn, a little tray of water, incense, and colored altar cloths.

We learned that we are very much preoccupied with the Word. We gained insight into the fact that you can also study a Bible story in a different way. This broadened our outlook.

The learning moments

Participating in Bible reading that includes an intercultural exchange with another group is a complicated process. Nearly all groups in the Netherlands commented on this complexity. Much more happened than people had expected or thought would happen. A number of preliminary steps are necessary. A reading group must be formed, a discussion leader and a reporter found, and a suitable room reserved before the exchange can begin. From our experience with all stages in the process, we arrived at many learning moments, summarized below.

The reading group

The group must know that a reading exchange requires a great deal of time and patience. It involves a long time period, sometimes more than one church season. An existing reading group that meets regularly and has other tasks besides the intercultural exchange has better cohesion and an ability to sustain itself during waiting.

When a group has been formed and the Bible story has been discussed, the interim periods can be spent discussing other Bible stories, practicing different ways to approach a Bible story, studying other cultures and types of Christianity. These activities can maintain excitement.

> The ZWO groups that read find it inspiring to now be together in a very different way. Usually, the emphasis has been on doing, but now it is on discussion and sharing thoughts. In the long run, this also has a positive effect on the regular ZWO work.

> We are working in a practical way and thus getting to know each other in a different way.

The discussion leader

The discussion leader's task is important. Cultivating the ambience of the group, making sure that everyone has an opportunity to talk, and monitoring but not steering the group process was quite an assignment and challenge. Groups who wanted more detailed explanations of the Bible story sometimes appealed to the leader, especially if this person was a minister. For example, participants might wish to know more about the relationship between Samaritans and Jews. For this important task, it may be advisable to invite a discussion leader trained especially for this program, a consultant from the Regional Service Center, for example.

The reporter

In practice, it turned out that the reporter is involved to the greatest extent throughout the process. This person is responsible for writing the report, translating it or having it translated,[22] mailing it, receiving and distributing the report from the partner group, etc. In short, this task requires much time. There is a great risk that readers will become detached from the entire process, primarily because of the waiting periods. Months may elapse between the initial discussion of the Bible story, the pairing of the groups, and the discussion of the partner group's report.

> The process is slow and very bureaucratic, reducing the pleasure.

> Too much time between sending and receiving a response douses the fire.

> The work of the reporter requires a great deal of time. These people spend days typing up the report.

> Too much time elapses between the various meetings.

> The most difficult thing was something practical, namely, writing down the discussion of an entire evening and translating it.

A quality reporter is vitally important to the entire process. A reporter should know thoroughly what tasks are involved. Drawing up a verbatim report is time-consuming and demands expertise. Potential reporters should not think about this enterprise too nonchalantly. The reporter is needed several times: in the group process, in drawing up the reading report, in writing up the group's response to the report of the partner group, and in drawing up a final report. The reporter is the pivot the program turns on. The time investment is substantial. This investment must be discussed among the members in advance. Inviting someone who is accustomed to making reports either as a volunteer or professionally is advisable.

The protocol

The protocol described in "Through the Eyes of Another: A Project on Intercultural Reading of the Bible" outlines the different steps of intercultural Bible reading. It provides helpful insight into the entire process and indicates how it will unfold.[23] Not only does it describe the three main phases, but it also considers how to manage the interim periods. These are the periods of waiting for the pairing to occur, for the partner's return message, and for the response from the partner group to the group's own report.

> It appears to be valuable to the process of reading and exchange that the reading groups keep to the protocol as much as possible. It is good to consider the question: What do we find more important, the content or the reading process? Keeping to the protocol and having insight into the protocol is to our advantage.

The pairing

Studying the living and faith situation of the partner group is important preparation for discussing the report. Are the group members capable of detecting the contextuality? Can they imagine the partner group? It is tempting to start discussing the report immediately after receiving it, but it is important to give preparation plenty of time. Inviting people to share who know the country and the partner group has a stimulating effect.

> It is difficult to help the participants become part of the report of the partner group. It is not easy to conjure up an image of the living and reading conditions on the other side of the world from the Netherlands.

> Experience with foster children from India, travel experience, and personal contact with a Sri Lankan woman searching for her place in society have turned out to be of importance.

The reading

Dealing with the Bible story loosens tongues and opens hearts. Not only does it have an impact on the participants in the Netherlands, but the partner group is also affected by the reports they receive. Groups report that the experience of being part of a global community of faith is an asset. Relationships begin and grow through exchanged letters, photos, songs, and poems.

> For most participants, reading with the group in the first exchange was enriching—just to experience that you don't particularly notice most of what you read. You realize that you skip over so many things. You discover the wealth of the text through the others.

> A clear learning moment is that you start looking at each other through other eyes. This experience implies that an exchange between Christians living in the group's own country can also be instructive. We also encounter different cultures and ways of believing in our own country.

Sharing beyond the reading group

In the Netherlands, church life is organized in many different groups. Groups of varying composition in the church community meet during the week. As a rule, one only meets the entire community during the weekly worship service. As a consequence, some Dutch groups shared little or nothing with others in their wider church communities about the experience they gained. The partner group, in contrast, may have been enthusiastically sharing about their contacts with a group abroad and reporting to their own community about the experience. One group even decided to turn outward and become more active in passing on the Bible message. The story of the encounter between Jesus and the Samaritan woman released so much for them. Didn't the woman, full of wonder, also go off to tell everyone about the one she had met?

The learning moment is that involving the wider community in the process is recommended. As a rule, writing an article for the church publication is not sufficient. A better idea is to hold a theme service. Many groups can be involved in the entire process and then make a contribution to the service. Every community has talented members who would love to be involved in such a theme service, and the community will appreciate it. Involving more people in the learning process and in the experience gained has a stimulating effect and gives the community a feeling of solidarity.

> Involve the community when you are involved in an exchange as a group—for example, in a service where John 4 is also discussed. This distributes the information better. It is also a good starting place to get the minister on your side. Some ministers write the church publication; others enter into discussion with the entire community on a community Sunday.

Enjoy your experiences

Participating in the project and having contact with Christians far away about a Bible story was inspiring for many participants. Although it required work—documents had to be written and mailed—happiness about the contacts with each other and with the other group predominated. Of course, the project did not go smoothly everywhere. Some groups surmounted many hurdles and practiced much patience.

An important learning moment is to take time to enjoy every step. Every step provides new opportunities to study the Bible story in poetry, art, and music. During the community worship on Sunday, people will appreciate recipes from the partner country so that they not only hear about and see but also taste the country of the partner group. Being together with one another in the community of Jesus Christ provides unprecedented chances for conversation and enrichment of life. Experiencing this community throughout the world contributes to the fascination of participating in intercultural Bible reading.

Notes

[1] The observations and focus points from the workday on 17 September 2002 at the National Service Center were particularly helpful in shaping this report.

[2] Thirty-four groups received a questionnaire; twenty-seven filled them out and returned them. The return rate enabled us to obtain a good idea of the findings.

[3] Since 1969, the Netherlands Reformed Church (NRC) and Reformed Churches in the Netherlands (RCN) have been participating in the Together on the Way (Samen op Weg) process. In 1985, the synod of the Evangelical Lutheran Church in the Kingdom of the Netherlands (ELC) decided to join the negotiations. One year later, the joint meeting of synods accepted a Declaration of Agreement, expressing agreement on all the main ecclesiological issues dividing the churches. Since the 1990s, negotiations about structure and church order have been on the agenda of the synods involved. As of 1 May 2004 the churches are united with the name Protestant Church in the Netherlands (PCN). The local congregations of the PCN are supported in their work by the National Service Center in Utrecht and the Regional Service Centers. For more information, see http://www.protestantchurch.nl/

[4] Many reading groups were informed about the program through more than one channel. The numbers are: 39 percent by *Omkeer*, 11 percent by the Kerkinactie newsletter, 19 percent by the newsletter of the Regional Service Center, 29 percent by church information, and 48 percent by other channels.

[5] ZWO committees are local church groups concerned with mission, development, and diaconal service activities.

[6] Figures on the ways participants entered the program are: 48 percent recruited through the church bulletin, 37 percent asked in person, 18 percent offered the reading program through education and training, 14 percent made up of an existing ZWO committee, 18 percent from an existing reading group, 22 percent recruited in a different manner.

[7] See note 3 above.

[8] In these provinces, the groups participated in an existing exchange contact, so they did not need to be paired with a foreign group but read with the community already established as a partner. The experiences of these last groups are not included in this article.

[9] VMBO is prevocational secondary education.

[10] This observation was made during the workday on 17 September 2002, at the National Service Center.

[11] New Translation, 88 percent; De Groot Nieuws Bijbel, 15 percent; Staten Vertaling, 15 percent; Willibrord Vertaling, 22 percent. Other translations were also used.

[12] Forty-one percent read a Bible text (sometimes the text of the day), written prayer, poem, newspaper article, service book, text for reflection, or psalm. Twenty percent sang a hymn from the hymnbook or an inspiration collection, or listened to music.

[13] Thirty-five percent of the groups brought along a symbolic object.

[14] The Ecumenical Institute is the international study and conference center owned by the World Council of Churches and based in the picturesque and historic Château de Bossey at Céligny, some ten miles from Geneva.

[15] From Willem Jan Otten, *Eindaugustuswind* (Amsterdam: G. A. van Oorschot, 1998). [This free translation of the poem was included in the English version of the original Dutch essay by Arie Moolenaar.–Ed.]

[16] Eleven percent of the groups.

[17] For example, in Batenburg the city pump disappeared in 1958. Ouddorp was only connected to the water mains in 1955.

[18] Hoofddorp worked on a bibliodrama with their partner group in Hungary and acted it out during a meeting of the two reading groups.

[19] The twelve steps are: (1) reading the text out loud; (2) writing down the text in breathing units, giving people the feel for the rhythm; (3) writing down questions and comments, feelings the story evokes, and things that stand out or are unclear; (4) looking up difficult words and names, then reading the text once more; (5) looking at the context of the story, what happens before and afterward; (6) comparing translations and noting differences that stand out; (7) studying the persons acting in the story and what they say and do; (8) noting time in the story; (9) noting location of the story; (10) outlining the scenes in the story; (11) listing key words and motifs in the story; and (12) observing basic patterns of words in the story.

[20] The poem's author is a participant named Joop.

[21] Distribution by country was: El Salvador (3), Colombia (5), Bolivia (2), Cuba (3), Nicaragua (2), Ecuador (1), Brazil (1), Peru (1), South Africa (1), Kenya (1), Ghana (6), India (3), Indonesia (2), Philippines (1), Scotland (1), and Hungary (1).

[22] One-third of the reading groups reported difficulties translating the reading reports. This was true for their own reports as well as the reports from the partner group. An appeal was made to the National Service Center to assist.

[23] Hans de Wit, "Through the Eyes of Another: A Project on Intercultural Reading of the Bible" (presentation, consultation on Intercultural Reading of the Bible, Free University, Amsterdam, the Netherlands, 2001). A version of this paper, with the same title, became the standard project handbook.

CHAPTER 4

Is God's will the same for Groningen and Nicaragua?

Saskia Ossewaarde–van Nie

Groningen, the Netherlands

A long history of Bible study

Every year a certain Reformed church in rural Groningen, the Netherlands, has a Bible study group. Most of the people who are participating in intercultural Bible reading have come to the Bible group for many years. They regret that the group is getting smaller and smaller. The number of church members is declining, and the rise in the aging population plays a role as well. Seventeen people (fourteen women and three men) between the ages of thirty-three and seventy-three participate in this series of evenings. This includes the congregation's minister, who serves as group leader. Participants come from Groningen and two neighboring villages.

Looking back at the long history this church has of studying the Bible, under the leadership of several different ministers, members believe that their views on the Bible have changed in the course of several decades. In earlier years, more emphasis was put on a punishing Old Testament God. Now members tend to view the Old Testament texts as stories. It may sound simple, but this change in their way of thinking has taken a great deal of struggling.

Participating in a Bible study group is important to these church members. The fact that they would be exchanging ideas with a Nicaraguan group was for most of them an interesting fact, but of secondary importance. It was something worthwhile, but not the deciding factor about participating.

Normally, the minister starts the Bible study with the question, "What does the story mean to you? By getting to know each other first, the group creates an atmosphere of trust. One can bring forward one's own experiences. People's life stories are

Saskia Ossewaarde–van Nie, Protestant Service Center Groningen, Protestant Church in the Netherlands (Groningen, the Netherlands)

placed alongside the Bible story. The minister values Bible study highly and thinks that exegesis in a group does more justice to the text than does exegesis in a sermon, because people engage more actively with the text. Besides, dialogue offers more opportunities for dealing with new theological developments. In dealing with questions, he can immediately explain important elements of the text as well. He thinks people contribute far more to a text's explanation than they realize, especially because they bring forward their own experiences. The leader then tries to make connections between the experiences of different members, to highlight the text's background, and to look for further meaning in the multilayered stories.

The area and the people

In this region, agriculture is the order of the day. In addition to agriculture, group members are employed in teaching, nursing, and social work, among other occupations. In addition to this work either in a paid job or at home, many have been active in church work for years. Group members have participated in an impressive list of congregational functions: elder, deacon, sexton, teacher of religion in primary school, member of the missionary committee, etc. The group carries a major concern about the decline in church membership, felt personally by many in the group because their children are leaving the church. Although good discussions are still possible, parents feel the loss that their children no longer participate in church life.

Meeting in a building next to the church

It is the end of the winter; the evenings are dark and cold. Inside it is nice and warm. A room in a simple building next to the church has been booked for these evenings. A cluster of tables forms a rectangle, cups of coffee sit on the table, and a plate of Groningen spiced cake is handed around. Because most people already know one another the atmosphere is relaxed and cheerful right away. At a quarter to eight, people are shaking hands and talking busily and cheerfully about everyday things, while someone pours coffee.

Most participants are members of the Reformed Churches in the Netherlands, but because it is understood that the evenings of intercultural Bible reading reflect movement toward church unity and are organized "on the way together," people from the Netherlands Reformed Church from a neighboring village are present as well.[1] In order to start the evening program, the group leader interrupts the lively socializing to ask for silence. He invites the group to sing several Latin American songs and leads in a short prayer.

Groningen reads John 4:1–42

The minister has copied the text of John 4 on paper, with a lot of white space around it. In this way, participants can write down their remarks and questions. The participants take turns reading aloud a couple of verses. After a short pause, a discussion of the chapter begins.

The first discussion question, "What does the story mean to you?" is not easy to answer. Initially, the Groningen group finds understanding John 4 quite problematic. When the group records its first reactions, they mainly ask questions, one after another. Why did Jesus leave Judea? What does "Jacob's well" mean? Why does Jesus tell the woman, "Go, call your husband!"? What is the meaning of "salvation is from the Jews"? What does "You worship what you do not know" mean?

Along with these questions, however, there is considerable criticism of the text. "Strange behavior by Jesus, to start a conversation with this woman," one woman argues. "That's not the way to deal with one another." "The Samaritan woman is portrayed as being stupid," another woman says. "If you don't know where to get living water, then go and get your husband. That bothers me. It's a real man's piece. Must have been written by a man, this story. Maybe that's how they dealt with one another in earlier days, but I certainly wouldn't accept it!" She talks so firmly that the others burst out laughing. A third woman is convinced that Jesus wants to test the Samaritan woman and draw her attention to something.

Jesus's reaction to the disciples who urge him to eat is perceived as confusing. The participants imagine that Jesus's disciples did not understand him. The group members try to find out whether the minister or anyone else in the group knows more about the Samaritans and the relationship between these people and the Jews.

For some time, the discussion circles around the question of whether the text has to be interpreted literally. What does John want to say in this story? Were the words supposedly said by Jesus really spoken by him? Should this chapter rather be viewed as a composition and interpretation of the evangelist? There seems to be a direct dialogue between Jesus and the woman, which is alternated with comments by the gospel writer. One of the participants has consulted a Bible commentary and shares her findings with the group.

The group talks for some time about the phrase, "worship in spirit and in truth." Is spirit related to soul? One participant thinks spirit is your innermost being, the place where you can touch God and God can touch you. Someone else hears in this verse the call to love God "with all your strength, all your mind, all your heart."

"Living water" raises a number of reactions as well. What is meant by the phrase? What image comes to mind? "Grace!" one woman [let's call her Eva] says very decisively. Someone else responds, "Grace! That doesn't mean anything to me. I find it a difficult word." Eva persists. "Grace—for me that means almost everything." A third participant offers a compromise: "You know, a gift you receive for free." One reader carries the idea of grace further to apply it to the church today. In the church, this well seems not to bubble all the time. Still, sometimes one is fortunate enough to catch a glimpse of grace. Another member gives an illustration—our being together as a group, for instance.

The discussion ends with a conclusion that John 4 invites people to open themselves to a religious revelation. At the end of the evening, the group sings a song, and soon after 10:00 p.m., members return to their homes.

Managua, Nicaragua

A beautiful old Baptist church

A Baptist church has existed for more than seventy years in a poor working-class district in Nicaragua's capital city of Managua. The church members live throughout the entire city. They are not extremely poor but belong to middle-class families who are not quite well off but are able to manage and to contribute financially to the church. The church building is strikingly beautiful and has a lovely square and water fountains with drinkable water. The Bible study group is large. Twenty-two people between the ages of twenty-eight and sixty-five are participating—thirteen men and nine women. The group is led by a Dutch minister who has been sent to Nicaragua for some years by the Together on the Way churches.[2]

The region and the people

When the Nicaraguans introduce themselves in their report to the Groningen people, they indirectly tell the Dutch about Nicaraguan society and their own place in it. One after another, the group members show their pride in their "beautiful, precious church." Not all of them have had the opportunity for a good education, and those who have had that chance are thankful. Some members mention faith as the decisive factor in successfully completing their education. Many testify to God's helping them through natural disasters or God's placing them on the right path. For instance, one mentions giving up drinking and gambling, mending of ways, and finding warmth and love among brothers and sisters within the church.

One participant gives revealing statistics. Nicaragua is one of Latin America's poorest countries. The unemployment rate is more than 50 percent. Forty percent of the population is extremely poor, and 27 percent of the adults are illiterate. Group members mention having jobs as housewife, mechanic, civil engineer, journalist, student of systems management, former bookkeeper, and shopkeeper in a spare parts shop. Although not all members of the Bible study group hold an office in the church or participate in other activities in church life, their intense commitment to church and faith resounds throughout their introductions.

Nicaragua reads John 4:1–42

After the group sings a song of praise and a member leads in prayer, the group in Managua turns its attention to John 4. The minister who leads the group has copied the chapter for everyone. Members take turns reading a couple of verses aloud. Participants then are invited to comment on what struck them in this story—and that is quite a lot! They give each person time to speak. In an elaborate report to their partner group, the Nicaraguans relate their findings.

The difficult relations between Jews and Samaritans immediately strike the eye of these readers. They note the clear goal Jesus's life reveals, when he goes out of his way to speak to this woman and thus spread his message. The group comments on the man-woman relationship dealt with in the story. The woman, who is completely honest with Jesus ("I have no man"), becomes an evangelist. God uses people we would disqualify, someone concludes. The Managua group does not doubt the bad reputation of the woman, who therefore was in great need. The woman places the burden of her heavy water jar at Jesus's feet and receives salvation and living water. Jesus preaches through the woman. The disciples are sent for bread, and Jesus speaks of living water and the kingdom of God, story elements which, according to one group member, contain a double lesson to look for food and preach Jesus as Messiah. One participant expresses the feeling that the text contains multiple stories: one about water, one about men/husbands, and one about worship.

Not only do the Nicaraguans think certain elements of the story are striking, they also feel that John 4 speaks to them personally: "We learn that the Lord stimulates us people to evangelize." "We too should take on ourselves the task to testify to people, like the woman did." They see that Jesus's message is always the same throughout all ages: "I accept you as you are. Come to me, and I will save you." For these Nicaraguans, the end of chapter 4 is the most important part. The conversion and missionary dimensions are full of meaning. They think the story is easily recognizable. It comes close to their own conversion experiences. They see the woman as a sinner, a prostitute, who repented and came to Life. For them, the John 4 story's essence is the Samaritan woman's conversion and the conversion of her fellow villagers. The people in the story listen to the Word in order to pass it on!

Groningen reads the reports from Managua

In Groningen, the reports from Nicaragua arrive. The group has been looking forward to this event! The first report alone is impressively long. For pages on end, the Groningen people read a long list of testimonies. Each of the Nicaraguan participants seems to speak to the Groningen group directly. In this way, according to the people in Groningen, the Nicaraguans are even more concerned with the brothers and sisters overseas than with each other. What strikes the Dutch group is that the Nicaraguan group is gradually growing, whereas the reverse is happening in Groningen. Bit by bit, people stop attending the Groningen church. The Nicaraguans appear to have a lot of biblical knowledge. They easily make connections between John 4 and other Bible stories. Just as easily, they make links with their own lives.

Whereas the Groningen people have emphasized the meeting of Jesus and the woman and have raised critical questions about the encounter, the Nicaraguans seem to view the conversion of the woman as the crucial element in John 4 and consider it a lesson and an admonition for themselves. The Groningen readers keep thinking it is a strange story. They notice that the Nicaraguan group is wholly unconcerned with asking critical questions. Nor do the Dutch detect any social engagement in the Nicaraguans.

Both groups have paid attention to the woman-man interaction in the story. In the Groningen group, a discussion arises about how best to interpret the scriptures.

They think the Nicaraguans read literally: "As it is written, that's how it happened." On the other hand, the Groningen people try to make a distinction between what happened and the process of writing it down at a later stage. The Groningen participants think people sometimes become stuck if they always take the Bible literally. Moreover, the Dutch group thinks a criticizing remark, such as, "This text doesn't mean anything to me," does not imply that they disregard the text. Rather, such a perspective should encourage them to dig deeper and search further for what the text does want to convey. One of the oldest participants says, "Sometimes you read certain parts of the Bible for years on end and they don't mean much to you, and then suddenly you discover and are touched by what it actually says." At such a moment, the working of the Holy Spirit is perceptible.

Nicaragua reads the reports from Groningen

The Nicaraguans' reaction to their partner's report makes apparent how disquieting the Groningen report is to the Nicaraguans. Some of their responses fall outside the scope of John 4, pertaining instead to the nature of the partner group. The Central American group is deeply shocked when they read that the minister of the Groningen group is homosexual. Although the Nicaraguan participants say, one after another, that they do not want to judge Groningen's minister ("for we are Christians"), it is clear that all of them find this very difficult. They do not understand how he was able to become a minister, and they say they will pray for him. "Just as Christ came for this Samaritan woman, so we could pray for him." The Nicaraguan's own minister, who is also Dutch, tries to clarify matters by pointing toward different cultural backgrounds. One Nicaraguan woman replies that this point has nothing to do with culture but is a matter of morality, "for it says so in the Bible." They explicitly ask the Groningen group to explain why they are so tolerant toward homosexuality, given what the Bible says about it. They do admire the minister, however, for being so open and vulnerable.

The Groningen report challenges the Nicaraguans to think about the question, "How would we receive a homosexual within our community who is looking for God at the same time?" They realize Jesus had contact with prostitutes and maybe homosexuals as well. His goal was always to renew and liberate people. He was not concerned with keeping everything the way things were.

Other aspects of the Dutch report draw the Nicaraguans' attention. They notice that the average age of the Groningen people is much higher than theirs. In spite of the fact that the partner group members are older, they do not seem to be wiser than the Nicaraguans. The Nicaraguans think, based on the first part of the Dutch report, that the Groningen people show very little biblical knowledge and ask childish questions about the texts—questions that any convert in Nicaragua would be able to answer straight away. They wonder why this is the case. Is it because people in the Netherlands at that age restrict themselves to religion as a heritage, which they do not have to study anymore? Do the Protestant churches in the

Netherlands concern themselves so little with evangelization (as little as the Roman Catholic Church does in Nicaragua) because they are an official religion?

What surprises the Nicaraguans even more is that the Dutch group's most convincing statements are made by the only Catholic woman in the group! They are troubled that the Dutch read the Bible—even Jesus's words—with such a critical eye. When the Dutch argue that the text may have been composed by John instead of being a literal account of events, the Nicaraguans respond that the Bible should be read "not according to what we think but according to what it says. Leaving out what we don't like and then arguing that that particular piece is written by a different author—that's not the way to do things." It is true that Jesus sometimes used tough words. That is one of his characteristics, always telling people the truth.

The Nicaraguans further conclude that the largest need of the church overseas seems to be for children and young people to participate; they also recognize this need in their own church. The Managuans clearly discern Dutch poverty in religious life. It seems as if the brothers and sisters in the Netherlands are not searching for God. They read the Bible mainly in an analytical way. Still, the Nicaraguans believe that the Groningen people need God as they themselves do, and they would like to hear "what the Lord does in people's lives in the Netherlands!"

Finally, the Nicaraguans wrestle with the man-woman relationships in the text. There is neither man nor woman in God's eyes, they say. Moreover, the woman in the story is apparently emancipated, because she does not immediately draw water but first says to Jesus, "You have nothing to draw with."

When the Nicaraguans turn to the second part of the report from Groningen, the comments by the Nicaraguans are different. They discover in the Dutch responses more personal, intimate reflections that are directed toward the religious aspects of the text. The Nicaraguans think they have an explanation for this change in the Groningen people. "Always, when a group starts reading God's Word, something inside opens up, so that we can open up ourselves," one of them says. The fact that some of the people in Groningen indicate that this story does not have much to say to them does not bother the Nicaraguan group. It is a fact that there are all kinds of different people in the church. Some are better at theologizing; others are better at doing practical work. More problematic is the statement from the Groningen minister who says that some parts of the story do not appeal to him very much; he is the one who has to bring the story to life in the church community.

In their prayers, the Nicaraguans ask God to inspire the Groningen group to continue their church work despite their worries about decreasing church attendance. In addition, they pray for the living water that we all need in our lives.

Looking back

Putting oneself in the place of another

On both sides of the Atlantic Ocean, the groups paid considerable attention to the empathic process. Putting oneself in another's place was somewhat easier because both groups included individuals who had experienced the other group's context firsthand. In the Nicaraguan group, this person was the Dutch minister who served as group leader. In Groningen, two women in the group who were theologians had recently spent time in Nicaragua as part of their work.

Putting oneself in another's culture and society, imagining what other people's lives are like, is extremely difficult. Although the groups clearly did their best to gather background information, the picture each developed of their partner group was only partially painted. Getting to know someone else—whether that person lives close by or far away—always takes time, energy, attention, and patience. These efforts are needed even more if one is relating to a group thousands of kilometers away, living in a very different culture. In the absence of a clear picture of the other group's experience, there is always a risk that self-developed, inaccurate pictures and prejudices will have a chance to develop. An example of such preconceptions (one the Groningen group found hilarious) appeared in the Nicaraguan report. The Nicaraguans were surprised that a Catholic participant made the most meaningful remarks in their partner's report. Without question, they had assumed that a Catholic in the Netherlands would be a passive Christian, much as they saw Catholics in Nicaragua. It is regrettable that the only reaction from Groningen was a cheerful burst of laughter.

The art of writing and studying reports

Time, energy, attention, and patience are keywords when talking about drawing up reports and dealing with the partner group's reports. Although Dutch people are used to working methodically and to dealing with texts, it took a great deal of effort for them to make a good report. The Nicaraguan reports, on the other hand, were very elaborate!

Studying and processing a report from a distance is where art is involved! There is a great risk that some issues will be simply skipped over in haste. Pages full of long testimonies seemed no more than a flood of words to the Groningen people. As they look back, they believe they did not take enough time to study the reports from Nicaragua thoroughly.

Broader social and religious horizons

Thanks to the report from Nicaragua, the Groningen group acquired an idea of their partner's cultural background. To some extent, they shared in their partner's experience of poverty in Managua and its effects on everyday life. The Dutch group received the impression that for the group overseas, church was a stronghold in a chaotic world, something the church members in the Netherlands wanted to take seriously. They concluded that different denominations can have a specific function, depending on their social context. This new understanding gave the Dutch group a broader religious horizon, which led them to the question, "Is God's will the same for Groningen and Nicaragua?" (They were not able to answer this question, although they thought there might be situations in which God would not want to work.)

In the same way that the groups increased their awareness of different religious perspectives, they also broadened their understanding of the circumstances of others' lives. Concerns prevailing in the partner group's world, which the local group had never noticed before, now received their consideration because of the participation in intercultural Bible reading. However, this awareness generally did not lead to direct consequences for personal lives. One reflection of broadened social horizons was a report from the Nicaraguans that they had a completely different idea of the Netherlands after exchanging readings than they had had before they started the reading process. As a result of the exchange, they realized that the other group has problems, just as they do.

Overcoming barriers to mutual understanding

Despite this evidence for broadening horizons, the groups learned that developing an understanding of the other (a certain degree of tolerance) did not automatically result in increased understanding (empathy) from the other group. The Groningen people certainly did not share the partner group's evangelistic interpretation of John 4. They kept the dimension of mission and conversion at a distance. One member said, "I think nothing of it; after quite some years, I finally put this vision behind me." After hearing the partner group express their concern for evangelism, the Dutch group was not able to pick up discussion where they had left off and return to the process of putting themselves in someone else's place.

The path of life and upbringing of the participants in the two groups seemed to be diametrically opposed. The Groningen people described their personal religious history as "tight" or rigid. After years of development, often with a lot of struggling, they now feel freer, more articulate, and more critical toward faith and the church. Talk about searching for God! They have managed to create space for discussing their own experiences of faith and doubt. In contrast, participants of the Nicaraguan group are often not born into the Baptist church but come to it from the Roman Catholic Church where, according to their report, hardly anything religious happened. "First I was Catholic, but I really met the Lord because of my Protestant husband." Many Nicaraguan group members find themselves in a new stage of life after their conversion, one that may cause them to be more receptive to faith than the Groningen people are.

What is remarkable is that the Groningen people tended to spare the Nicaraguans' feelings. The Dutch tried to leave options open for the Nicaraguans, in order to make it "not too difficult" for them. However, they were dealing with important elements of faith! For instance, the Nicaraguans wrote, "In great need, then you feel God. . . . I thank God for sending me this great need, so that I will not become alienated from him." "God quickly solves the problem." (This comment was about a sick child that got better without medical intervention.) "There were thieves who attacked us and wanted to kill us. But that was the hand of the Lord." Many of the Groningen participants had great difficulty with such statements. However, one responded that they needed to be careful with people who live a life full of worries, because they must take care not to take from them "the last thing they have"—their trust in God. No matter how difficult the Nicaraguans' situations are, they show that they always trust in God, fully confident of their faith, which leaves no room for doubt.

The Groningen people found this unwavering faith difficult to grasp, but they could imagine that the Nicaraguans were greatly helped by the Firm Rock. Thus, the moment in which the Dutch could have asked questions or criticized the Nicaraguan group passed. Looking back, some Groningen participants asked themselves what this joint reading process actually was about. They expressed self-criticism; the objective was not to spare one another's feelings, was it? They had rather hoped to discover what others thought of the text and how it was experienced in different environments, had they not?

Showing consideration because of poverty reflects an unwitting feeling of superiority, a feeling that also emerged when the Dutch participants expressed a desire not to be too pedantic or intellectual. In an open discussion, one group does not necessarily in advance and vicariously have to worry about the effect critical questions might have, do they? A protective attitude, even if it is well intended, does not take the other adult believer very seriously. Trying to look through someone else's eyes in all sincerity, trying to gauge the width and depth of someone else's opinions, proved to be a far more complicated exercise than they had anticipated.

The text and the believer

What is the relationship between the readers of these two reading groups and the text of John 4? The first question posed by the Groningen minister (after an elaborate introduction) was, "What does the story mean to you?" Yet what followed were questions rather than answers! Almost no one spoke of any affinity with the text (for instance, "because it's a Bible text"). In Nicaragua the first questions posed were, "Why are you a member of this church?" and "What is important to you in your faith?" The group took a lot of time to hear answers to these questions. The Nicaraguans found many "remarkable" things in the text, but those things did not raise questions for them. Instead, they heard a call to conversion, and they thought about things they could learn from the text for their own lives. They are not the only ones who can learn from this text! The way Jesus amicably met the Samaritans and engaged them in his work suggests how in modern day Israel the two nations should meet one another as well.

The images of Jesus emerging from the two groups' reports were very different. Many Groningen people thought Jesus treated the Samaritan woman discourteously. He manifested himself toward the woman as a man of his time. The Nicaraguans said that this sometimes harsh tone fit Jesus and his special message. Moreover, they seemed to recognize the divine nature in Jesus expressed in his great stamina. The long journey in the baking sun asked so much of the travelers that the disciples meanwhile went looking for food. Nevertheless, Jesus was able to walk on, despite hunger or thirst.

The expression in the Nicaraguan group that was closest to Groningen's numerous questions about the objectives and compositional choices of the evangelist happened when one Nicaraguan participant mentioned John's "theological view."

Meeting through meetings

Gradually, the Groningen group became more open with one another, partly owing to the influence of the Nicaraguan group. The Nicaraguans had responded promptly with a very clear message. They thought the partner group was childish. The partner group kept asking questions, obviously did not understand what the text was about, had wavering faith, and was too critical.

This blunt and personal approach by the Nicaraguans, straight from their hearts and addressed personally to several Groningen group members, persuaded the Groningen people to open their hearts in response. The group's conversations were no longer from the head but from the heart as well. In an atmosphere of trust, much could be discussed. The input from Nicaragua broke down barriers for the Dutch group. The Nicaraguan participants had used their life experiences as starting points for their discussions, and that helped the Groningen people do the same, although this had not been their customary practice. The Nicaraguans succeeded in bringing the Groningen people together.

The Nicaraguans in turn learned from their Dutch partners. They wrote that the Dutch had gained enough trust within the group to open up and talk without fear of criticism, and to wait for others' responses. "But now about us," they continued. "We have difficulty receiving. I think we can also learn from them." The Groningen analytical way of working and thinking appealed to them. "If we become too spiritual, we too make mistakes," the Nicaraguan report added.

Right from the beginning, one Groningen woman, "Eva," let her faith speak. Unlike the other Dutch readers, she was not full of critical questions. She had clearly heard a good message in the story of the Samaritan woman, and she was alert in giving short and pointed answers to questions formulated by others in her group. After the first meeting, she had been absent, but she did not stay away for long. The Nicaraguans had immediately identified with Eva when they read the first report, and they missed her voice when they received the second Dutch report. "Where has Eva gone?" they wondered when they received the second report from the Netherlands. When the Groningen group read this Nicaraguan question at one of their meetings, one member of the group immediately jumped in her car at eight o'clock in the evening to go and get Eva. Eva thus unexpectedly had a meeting that evening!

Recommendations

Learn about the partner's culture. It becomes obvious from the account of the Managua and Groningen exchange that it is difficult to put oneself in someone else's place. Therefore, prior to receiving the first report from the partner group, it is good to pay ample attention to the country and the people to which the partner group belongs. This task could be carried out by a staff member posted abroad or by someone who has visited the particular partner country and can give information about it (possibly with the help of films, photographs, slides, poetry and songs with translation, typical foods, recent newspaper clippings). It is also good to identify the preconceived ideas and prejudices peoples have about the country.

Pair groups in advance of sending reports. The above recommendation has implications for the process of pairing groups. A long time before the actual reading starts, a group needs to know at least what country they will be relating to, in order to be able to prepare themselves sufficiently. Experience shows that with adequate preparation an incoming report is read better and more carefully. The group reading the report will not overlook details contained in it, because they recognize and understand the context of the sending group.

Clarify expectations and invite openness. To make participants more aware of the entire process, it is important to share expectations, what members think they will be able to contribute, and how they feel about being frank and receptive. Are the participants willing to engage honestly in discussion? Do they rather want to limit themselves to the attitude, "We think this and they think that—how strange!"? What does learning from the other and learning from oneself actually mean? Are we able to express criticism toward someone and at the same time accept criticism from him or her? I suggest a preliminary phase in which such questions are frankly discussed. Although this process may be difficult in the Netherlands, time, attention, and patience can help it happen.

Select leaders with care. The role of the group leader or facilitator cannot be taken too lightly. He or she must be selected with care and needs to be able to carry out many different functions. A facilitator must have a thorough knowledge of the Bible story and keep track of subtle details in the text and in the group—details that may turn out to be important elements. The leader needs to help the group respond to reports that may contain fierce reactions. The leader needs to discover lines and themes in the discussion and to promote a discussion in which everyone present is able to contribute. A good leader will have in reserve a number of questions or remarks, in case the discussion flags. He or she may, in addition, be called on to provide information on questions, such as, "Where is Samaria situated?" Further, someone is needed who will monitor the reports and find resource people who are familiar with the partner country. Despite all these responsibilities, the facilitator must not monopolize the conversation!

Close-up of one participant. To promote empathy, a close-up introduction of one of the participants might be a good idea. After an introduction of the whole group, one of the participants might tell about her or his life in detail, describing education, living conditions, neighborhood, family situation, why he or she did or did not marry, preferred music, and many other aspects. This in-depth view could also name a biblical figure the person identifies with and explain why. By means of this written portrait, preferably accompanied by a photo, the other person becomes closer and the group's life circumstances more tangible. An alternative idea would be to pair each participant with another in the partner group.

Sharing the outcome more widely. An important question that kept bothering the Groningen people was, What do we do with the results? How do we convey these beautiful experiences to our church community? What a pity if such riches are limited to those who took part in the group! Given that intercultural exchange requires time, attention, and patience, an existing group within the community (catechism class, youth group, senior citizens club, etc.) might in the future make intercultural contact, including Bible reading, their yearly project. To entice them to do so, it could be helpful to organize a special event around a particular country. As an example, a church in Wildervank mobilized the entire church community to focus attention on a certain Latin American country, by organizing a Latin American dinner, with karaoke, group singing, a lecture, an auction, and a raffle. With such an introduction, participants in the reading group will not have to explain repeatedly what they are involved in. The church bulletin can keep the entire congregation involved, by publishing impressions of the reading and exchange experiences. Who knows—eventually a church service may center on the particular text the reading groups are discussing, which will then receive a brand new world dimension.

Notes

[1] Since 1969 the Netherlands Reformed Church (NRC) and Reformed Churches in the Netherlands (RCN) have been participating in the Together on the Way (Samen op Weg) process. In 1985 the synod of the Evangelical Lutheran Church in the Kingdom of the Netherlands (ELC) decided to join the negotiations. As of May 2004, the name of the united church is Protestant Church in the Netherlands (PCN).

[2] See note 1.

CHAPTER 5

Jesus's surprising offer of living cocaine

Contextual encounters at the well
with Latino inmates in U.S. jails

Bob Ekblad

Intercultural reading of the Bible demonstrates that reading strategies and interpretations vary widely and are relevant to reading communities to the extent that they are faithful to the text, the social context of the group, and the daily lives and concerns of individual readers. In this article, I seek to include the perspectives of Latino immigrant inmates who participated in the intercultural reading of the Bible project. How might these people identify the contemporary equivalent of the well and water in their communities and lives? Where are today's wells, where contemporary Samaritans might quench their thirst in their encounter with the Word become flesh? What is the role of the facilitator among people who are mostly first-time Bible readers, are outside the church, and often consider themselves condemned by God and unable to change?

As part-time chaplain of a jail in Washington State, I meet with Mexican and American inmates twice weekly to read and discuss our questions and the scriptures, and to pray. I met two times with two different groups to discuss the encounter between the Samaritan woman and Jesus in John 4, with hopes of forming partnerships with other reading communities through the intercultural Bible reading project. Several insurmountable difficulties made it impossible for me to fully incorporate these groups into the project through partnering with other groups. However, because of the richness of our discussions, the fruitfulness of several emphases, and the unique perspective of the men with whom I read, I will present one feature of this story that particularly engages men in jail: the symbolic function of the well as place of encounter par excellence between Jesus and the excluded.

Leading Bible studies in a jail presents special challenges to the facilitator that are similar to but also different from those encountered in more stable prison environ-

Bob Ekblad, Tierra Nueva and The People's Seminary (Burlington, Washington, USA)

ments, where people have already been sentenced and are doing their time. Our Bible study group changes from week to week as new inmates arrive and others are sent to prison, deported, or released. County jails function in the United States as maximum-security detention centers, where people arrested for crimes committed in the immediate area of the county are held until charged, tried, and sentenced. Those with financial means are able to post bail and remain free until their sentencing or acquittal. Those unable to come up with bail money are confined until they have either been acquitted of their charges or have served their time. People charged with misdemeanors can be sentenced to anything from one to 364 days in the county jail. People charged with more serious crimes can spend anywhere from two months to a year there, negotiating a plea agreement with the prosecutors or fighting to overturn their charges by trial. If the judge sentences someone to anything less than one year, the convicted person serves time there in the county jail. Any sentence over one year is served in one of Washington State's many state prisons. In addition, the jail serves as a holding facility for immigrants detained by the Department of Homeland Security for deportation or as a place to serve federal prison time for repeated illegal entry as criminal aliens.

Jail inmates are often in a state of uncertainty and crisis. In addition, many find themselves incarcerated with enemies from the streets. Inmates experience interpersonal tensions and emotional instability due to the stress of family crisis, court troubles, or detoxing from drugs or alcohol. Bible studies in this context require deliberate and often directive facilitation and a more crafted, time-limited process.

Privacy issues and jail rules limit the possibilities of verbatim recording of Bible studies. Even if recording were permitted, tape recorders would inhibit people's participation, as anything they said could be subpoenaed for use against the defendant in court. The voices of the inmate participants included in this article were written down from memory outside the jail and then translated into English.

As I prepare to facilitate a Bible study on John 4 in Skagit County jail, it is easy to notice that my own social location among Latino immigrant inmates loosely parallels Jesus's status before the Samaritan woman. As a Caucasian, English-speaking U.S. citizen, educated and male, I represent the dominant mainstream American culture in a way loosely paralleling Jesus's Jewish, male identity. My parents were both born in the United States. My grandfather on my father's side migrated from Sweden in the first decade of the twentieth century, while on my mother's side my descendants go back to some of the first English settlers in the 1700s. I grew up as a fairly privileged member of the dominant U.S. ethnicity, and benefited from many opportunities, including an undergraduate and graduate education. I now am an ordained Presbyterian pastor, jail chaplain, and director of an ecumenical ministry to immigrants called Tierra Nueva (New Earth).

My experience of passing through Samaria and sitting by the well began in 1981 with a life-changing trip to Central America. Encounters with contemporary equivalents of the Samaritan woman now consist in weekly Spanish-English Bible studies in the jail and with Latino immigrants at Tierra Nueva's Family Support Center. Every Thursday evening and Sunday afternoon, uniformed jail guards usher me through the thick steel doors into the jail's multipurpose room to meet with ten to thirty men. The guards then corral red-uniformed inmates through two steel doors to take their places in the circle of blue plastic chairs where we sit and read the Bible together.

The men with whom I read resemble Samaritan villagers more closely than I embody Jesus. Many are originally peasants from impoverished rural villages in Mexico. Pushed away by landlessness, drought, unemployment, government neglect, and global market forces, they are drawn to the perceived bounty of El Norte (the USA)—a modern-day well of sorts. Once in the United States, they find work as farm laborers or as minimum-wage restaurant, construction, or factory workers. Their willingness to work hard for low wages makes them invaluable to the U.S. economy. Many have entered the United States illegally and live on the margins of American society. Others are second-generation immigrants, identified by first-generation immigrants as *pochos* or *cholos*, if they belong to a gang. Many do not have a valid driver's license, or even identification, and they make use of counterfeit residency and social security cards. Others have had their driver's license confiscated because of driving offenses and have alias names in an attempt to escape arrest for active warrants or known illegal immigration status. Most have partners and children to support, sometimes in Mexico and in the USA. This is a nearly impossible feat if one is employed in a minimum-wage job. Many are tempted and succumb to small-scale drug dealing for extra cash. This often leads to more serious drug dealing. Theirs is a life of constant insecurity. If arrested, undocumented immigrants can be assured that they will be deported by the Department of Homeland Security back to Mexico immediately after they do their jail time.

The visible gap between me as facilitator and the immigrant inmate reading community has often provoked new insights that have proved fruitful in engaging people in reflection on particular texts. Several years before the launching of the intercultural Bible reading project, an event associated with a Bible study on John 4 inspired my later reflections on the symbolic function of the well. This event, a Thursday evening Bible study eight years or so ago, illustrates the special challenges that can require a more directive facilitation style and the urgency of coming up with contextualized interpretation, one way or another.

Some thirty inmates bustle into the jail's multipurpose room. The guards shut the doors, locking us in the room together. I have arranged the plastic chairs in a large circle. When they are seated, I invite the men to pray with me for God to send the Spirit to illuminate our reading and discussion. I notice an uneasy tension in the room as I finish the prayer invoking the Holy Spirit's presence.

I invite a volunteer to read John 4:1–15. During the reading and immediately afterward, I find myself distracted by a number of people's nervous glances and aggressive glares. Several pairs of men talk softly to each other. Pukie, a mustached gang member in his early twenties, his shoulder heavily bandaged from a gunshot wound he acquired in an attempt to rob at gunpoint the home of another drug dealer, looks especially agitated. Stimy, a heavily tattooed young white guy, on his way to six years in prison for a drive-by shooting, sits sullenly in the middle of the men to my left.

I reach into my store of methods for engaging distracted people, directing my first questions to people who are talking or glaring: "Who are the participants in this story?" When nobody answers, I invite Pukie, the most agitated in the group, to reread John 4:4–8, and then I ask the men again to identify the story's characters. After getting feeble responses, I continue with my questions, addressing this one to Stimy: "So where are they, and what's happening in this story?"

"Shit, I don't know, man. I wasn't paying attention," says Stimy, looking down at his Bible. "At some well, I guess, talking and shit."

While these questions work to some extent, people are less engaged than I can ever remember, and tensions continue to mount. I am increasingly aware that I need either more engaging questions or an attention-grabbing story to captivate their interest. In a last ditch effort to salvage a Bible study that is spinning out of control, I launch into my own contextual interpretation in a more monologuing, even preaching style.

Since I know that many of the men in the group are long-time drug dealers and/ or addicts, I invite the men to imagine that they are selling drugs out of their apartment, a quickly grasped attempt to present a contemporary equivalent to the well. I am drawing on my experience talking with hundreds of addicts about their desperation to acquire more crack cocaine, which often propels them into selling drugs to assure their own supply. Most local dealers operate out of low-income apartments or motels.

"So there you are, and Jesus comes up to your door, but you don't know who he is. He just looks like some normal *gabacho* [white person], maybe like me. He says, 'Hey, sell me some coke,' or 'Sell me some crack.'" The men all look at me, some smiling uneasily, others clearly wondering what I am going to say next.

I continue my monologue, suggesting what I imagine Latino drug dealers might be thinking. "You wonder if you can trust him, and inside you are thinking this is an undercover drug task force officer trying to make a sting. You say to him: 'No way, man. I can't help you.' And you wish he'd just go away. But he keeps insisting on talking with you.

"'Hey, listen,' he tells you, 'if you knew God's gift, and if you knew who it is who is asking you to sell him some coke, you'd ask him, and he would give you living cocaine. Because the crack that you smoke only gives you a high for a moment, and you have to keep buying more, but the coke that I will give you will give you a permanent high.'" Many of the men have raised eyebrows, and seem surprised, even shocked. I suggest at this moment that this story shows us that Jesus comes to us where we are and respects us. Many of the men are fidgeting nervously, though, and glancing across the circle and then down. Willie, a Chicano gang member I've been meeting with one-on-one, is sitting beside me. He taps me on the shoulder and insists that he wants to go back to his cell. "We need to wrap this up, Roberto—*now*," he tells me with urgency in his voice.

I tell the men that it appears we're all having a hard time getting focused, and that maybe we should end our study early. I invite them to stand and pray the Lord's Prayer together in Spanish. Everyone stands, and I close my eyes and begin the prayer. Right away I notice that only a few people are praying with me, and I hear increasing rustling around me. I speed up my prayer and race for the closing "*líbranos del mal*"—the official ending of the Roman Catholic Spanish version of the prayer.

I open my eyes to a scene of terror. The men to my left all have blue plastic chairs raised over their heads, the metal legs ready to crash down on the men on my right, whose chairs are all in different stages of being raised. A Native American man has a leaded microphone jack raised above his head like a tomahawk ready to come down on Willie's head.

I walk quickly through the middle of the crowd to the buzzer on the wall that calls the guards. Almost instantly, they are on the scene, hustling the men against the wall and out the doors into their pods. I stand there, stunned, my heart beating wildly, feeling foolish and impotent. The guards usher me out, and I drive home completely dejected.

The next morning, I call the jail and ask to speak with Willie. He immediately begins apologizing and then starts to cry. "I'm so sorry, Roberto. It was my fault. I had it all planned with my homeboys, the Norteños. We were all going to jump the others there in the group who are Sudeños. One of them had insulted Stimy, saying his girlfriend was pregnant with someone else's baby. We don't take those kinds of insults lightly. We had it all planned to fight them right at the beginning of the study, but then we didn't, out of respect for you. Man, I'm really sorry for what happened, really I am." Then he adds, "But man, I can tell you that I've been thinking about that Bible study all night. Mostly though, I've been thinking about that prayer. Man, your prayer stopped everything!" he concluded.

"Prayer? What prayer?" I ask.

"You know, that prayer right at the end."

"What do you mean, it stopped everything?" I ask, thinking back to my terror before the raised chairs and microphone jack.

Willie alerts me to the fact that nobody hit anyone. He says that everyone had their chairs raised over their heads, ready to fight, but that he felt completely paralyzed, unable to move, the moment I finished my prayer.

I think back to the night before and recall that there were in fact no blows that I could remember. I had walked right through the middle of the warring gangs to buzz for the guards. *Líbranos del mal*—"Deliver us from evil"—had been my last words. I find Willie's explanation unbelievable but intriguing. I thank him and tell him that I don't hold anything against him. After hanging up, I call Pukie, who tells me nearly the same thing: that the Bible study was in his head all night, and thanks for the prayer that stopped everything. The story spreads through the jail and then through the Latino community, about how the pastor stopped a gang confrontation with a prayer.

This event engraved on my heart both a particular way to contextualize John 4 and the power of the ending of the Lord's Prayer. At the same time, I recognize the limitations of a monologue, seeking ways to engage people that help them identify contemporary equivalents of the Bible characters, movements, and geography in their own lives and communities.

The studies I led two years ago with Latino immigrants in the jail with the intercultural Bible reading project clearly benefited from this earlier experience. There, in the face of escalating tensions, I felt an urgent need for the Bible story to somehow become more obviously relevant through some sort of immediate *relectura* or actualization. I also am convinced that there is a place for the facilitator to take the initiative in introducing contextual readings that go beyond people's natural expectations, grabbing their attention in a way that penetrates their indifference. While a contemporary rereading was not enough to stop the confrontation from erupting, it may have held it at bay until God became more fully present in response to our prayer.

In preparation for my more recent Bible studies on John 4, I pondered on the most accessible launching point in the story of Jesus and the Samaritan woman at the well. The actual location of the encounter where Jesus offers living water provides a fruitful metaphor, which I as facilitator can use to invite people to a contemplative site for possible contemporary meetings between today's Samaritans and Jesus. The deeper meaning of the well, its location outside the town, and its symbolic distance from any official religious place where "sinners" would typically expect to meet God offer surprises to people who feel unworthy of approaching God in traditional "holy" places.

Jesus's surprising presence among people in nonreligious places, who are not engaged in overtly religious behavior, is a consistent theme in the stories surrounding John 4. The reader of John's Gospel is alerted to Jesus's incognito presence right from the start, with statements such as "He was in the world, and the world came into being through him; yet the world did not know him" (1:10). John's description of the Word becoming flesh and dwelling (literally, "pitching its tent") among us (1:14) invites the reader to identify God as present and moving with humans. John goes on to describe Jesus showing up outside the traditional religious places, when people are going about their lives. The first sign, turning water into wine, takes place at a wedding (2:1–12). Nicodemus comes to Jesus at an unmentioned location by night (3:2). The official appeals to him at Cana, and his son does nothing, being healed from a distance in Jesus's absence (4:46–54). Jesus meets the paralytic who is lying beside the pool—a place symbolic of wherever people live in frustrated expectation of finding relief. He feeds the five thousand on a mountain while they are sitting passively, with no apparent faith (6:1–14). The adulterous woman is defended and pardoned outside of religious places, with no initiative on her part (8:1–11). Nor does the man born blind or Lazarus seek Jesus out (9:1–12; 11:1–46). These details are highly significant for people on the margins of society and church, who assume that their salvation depends entirely on their going to the right places and doing the right things.

In my Bible studies on John 4 with inmates and others I work with, who consider themselves excluded by the church or dominant culture, I typically begin with either a first question regarding their lives and world, or with a brief question regarding the narrative detail of the text—specifically, the characters and geography. With people who I suspect feel wary of anything religious, and who may well assume that the biblical story is irrelevant, I usually begin with a question about their lives and values. In the following composite of two different jail Bible studies with Latino inmates, the text appeared to provide an ideal jumping-off place to talk about our lives, as it introduces the well.

In both of my studies for the intercultural Bible reading project in the jail, I begin with a prayer for God to send the Holy Spirit to open our hearts and minds, and then I invite a volunteer to read John 4:1–4, before briefly commenting on Jesus's passing through Samaria. I give them a brief description of behind-the-text information about Samaria, its location outside acceptable Jewish religious places, and the religious and ethnic divisions that existed between Jews and Samaritans that do not keep Jesus from showing up.

Another volunteer reads verses 5–8, and I ask some basic questions to get people to pay attention to some of the narrative detail in this evolving story. "Who are the characters in this story, and what do we know about them up to this point?" I ask.

"There's Jesus, who has been passing through Samaria and sits by a well, tired and thirsty," someone says.

"Then who comes along?" I probe, inviting the men to look back down at their Bibles.

"There's a Samaritan woman who comes to draw water," someone responds.

I talk briefly about the importance of wells for people in the first century. "Everyone needed water to meet their most basic needs: to quench their thirst, water their animals, irrigate any crops, wash their clothes and bodies," I say. "Do any of you go to wells to meet your most basic needs?" I ask, a question that I know will acknowledge our distance from the world of the text.

They shake their heads, and someone answers the obvious: "None of us."

"So where do you go when you are thirsty for something, or when you are seeking to meet your most urgent needs?" I ask, seeking to inspire reflection on possible contemporary equivalents.

"I go to church," says a man who is a newcomer to our jail Bible study group. While this may indeed be where he would go, I suspect that he is trying to please me and God by giving the spiritually correct answer.

If people look uncertain about what I am trying to ask, or are not feeling enough trust to answer honestly, I often rephrase the question. "What do people you know do, or where do they go, to find satisfaction, to meet their needs?" Or, "If you were released right now for twenty-four hours, what are the first three places you'd go?"

"To the bar," says a Mexican farm worker in his early thirties. People smile and some nod.

"I'd go to my girlfriend's place, man," says a young Chicano gangster known as Neeners. Neeners has 666 tattooed under his lower lip and the names of past girlfriends tattooed on his neck. People laugh and nod their agreement.

"To the crack house," says a heavily tattooed Chicano man. A number of men rock back in their plastic chairs and laugh.

"Hey, wait a minute," interjects Neeners. "You may not believe this, but I go to jail to get my real needs met. This right here is the only place where I feel like I can think straight and get my shit together. Coming in here to study the Bible and shit helps me gain a new perspective," he says.

These answers loosen up the group, and men mention other places they frequent, and activities they engage in: the mall, heroin, sex, music, family, dealing drugs, cars, work, partying, dancing.

"So, do these places and activities give you total satisfaction?" I ask. "Do you feel like you are able to meet your needs?"

"No way, homes," says Ben. "Look, here we are, all of us stuck in here. I ain't satisfied by my life, not out there, not in here. None of us are." Ben's answer seems to resonate with most of the men, who nod their agreement that nothing really satisfies them.

"I've had everything money can buy—cars, women, drugs, money, jewelry. I've never been satisfied," says someone. "I know that I'm still thirsty for something." Others nod their heads in agreement.

"So, the woman from Samaria shows up at the well to get the water she needs to survive, and Jesus is already there," I summarize. "What might this mean for us?" I ask. "If this story tells us where Jesus hung out back then, what does it suggest about where we might run into Jesus now?"

The men are tentative in responding to the obvious. They look at me and down at their Bibles, awkwardly, afraid to say something blasphemous. They start with safer responses. "Could this be saying that Jesus may come to us when we are out working?" someone asks.

"Well, if that is a place where you are seeking to meet your needs, the place where you work would be a sort of well. Where else do you go to satisfy your needs, to quench your thirst?" I probe. Eyebrows are raised and I see some slow nods and slight smiles. However, at this point I am aware that I am running into serious resistance from a dominant theology deeply ingrained in the hearts and minds of Latino immigrants and most Caucasian men and women on the margins of North American society. The dominant theology envisions God as being found in Catholic or evangelical churches and other religious places, or far away in heaven, looking at the earth from a distance. Some may envision God as being near a religious shrine in the corner of their home, when candles are lit before the Virgin of Guadalupe or other saints. No one would naturally envision God as meeting them at the places they would actually frequent to meet their real physical and psychological urges.

The Bible is another place that people view as a sacred site for God's presence. However, most inmates assume that the Bible is too holy a place for them to feel welcomed into. The Bible is not viewed as containing refreshing, surprising good news for people like them. The only people who might hear good news are good people who are complying with God's infinite demands. Many Latino inmates fear that the Bible will confirm their worst fears: that they are damned because they cannot succeed at obeying the rules, or because they avoid exposing themselves to new demands. "Do this, believe that. Change, or else . . ." The Bible is not viewed as offering anything that would meet any of their most pressing needs. Consequently, whoever facilitates the Bible study is viewed as someone who invites them into a foreign, irrelevant place associated with punishment for crimes committed. People's first-time attendance at my Bible studies is often motivated by their boredom with the monotonous life in their cell blocks or by their sense of desperation, which leads them to do everything possible to comply with God's demands.

"If today's wells are places where we go to quench our thirst, like bars, crack houses, and meth labs, what do you think of Jesus's question to the woman, "Give me a drink"? I ask, inviting a direct confrontation with the dominant theology. My question, which overtly invites people to interpret Jesus's presence in a way that challenges the dominant theology, directly parallels Jesus's provocative request to the Samaritan woman: "Give me a drink" (4:7). My inmate Bible study participants are often afraid to depart from the official transcript, especially when they are detained by the state, which appears to have power that is sanctioned by the all-powerful God. Standing with Jesus, whose request shows total solidarity with them in their thirst, is a challenge to the entire system. Embracing this challenge appears risky. What if God in fact legitimates and upholds the power of the state? Their embracing of a God with them right where they are, rather than renouncing their wells in breast-beating repentance, may be perceived as leading to more sanctions in the form of more jail time or a guaranteed deportation.

The woman's response to Jesus parallels inmates' gut response to the interpretation I suggest. I ask a volunteer to read John 4:9: "The Samaritan woman said to him, 'How is it that you, a Jew, ask a drink of me, a woman of Samaria?' (Jews do not share things in common with Samaritans.)" The woman's questioning of Jesus's openness to her reflects her recognition that she is being called to ignore traditional boundaries. She reflects a hesitancy to move beyond the official transcript. At the same time, her hidden transcript apparently is not as risky as Jesus's. Jesus, a Jewish male, who would normally view himself as superior to and forever separate from an unclean Samaritan woman, is willing to receive water from her.

"Let's see how Jesus responds to the woman," I suggest, asking someone to read John 4:10. I invite the men to imagine what Jesus's offer of living water might sound like if he were to meet them at their particular wells, the places they actually go to quench their thirst. Knowing that I am inviting people to risk blasphemy, I suggest a contextual rereading of this verse, based on one man's identification of the crack house as his well. "Is it possible that Jesus's answer might sound something like this?" I ask. "'If you knew the gift of God, and who it is who says to you, "Give me some cocaine," you would have asked him, and he would have given you living cocaine'?"

The men smile hesitantly at first and then begin to see that indeed Jesus is not taking the expected sermonizing, judging tone they assume he would have adopted. Nor am I. We read on in John 4:13–14, "'Everyone who drinks of this water will be thirsty again, but those who drink of the water that I will give them will never be thirsty. The water that I will give will become in them a spring of water gushing up to eternal life,'" and the men can see that Jesus is talking about more than actual water, cocaine, or whatever the contemporary equivalent of the contents in the well might be. At the same time, to help people identify God's surprising presence there, outside the religious spaces where they would least expect God to be, I ask another question. "Have any of you experienced God as being present with you in a positive, helpful way while you were drinking or doing drugs?"

Several men start talking at the same time, feeling permission to express a hidden transcript that they have never expressed publicly to anyone. Arnold tells about how he would often drive home after drinking and doing drugs, and that he never got in an accident, even though in the morning he would have no memory of having driven his car the night before. Another man tells about how God speaks to him when he is high, making him feel a hunger for God's presence and for reading the Bible. Neeners tells about how, as a teenager, while he was stealing car stereos, he prayed to God that he would not be caught, and how he felt God's protection. Another man mentions that it is a miracle that he and many of them are alive at all. He goes on to tell the group that he is sure that if the police had not arrested him and brought him to the jail this time, he would be dead from an overdose. "God allowed me to be arrested to save my life and bring me here to get closer to God." Through these stories, the men identify God as a gracious presence who accompanies them in spite of their crimes and brokenness.

When we read together Jesus's order for the woman to return for the living water with her husband, and note that Jesus's offer is given with full knowledge that she has had five husbands, the men become more confident that this new theology may be believable. "So if Jesus reveals God's true identity, as it says in different places in John's Gospel, what is God like, according to this story?" I ask, inviting the men to summarize this positive theology for themselves.

"Jesus comes to people right where they are, no matter what they're doing or if they're messed up and shit," says Neeners.

"He offered living water to the woman even though he knew she'd lived a bad life, and without making her change first," says someone else. The men are visibly moved as we glimpse together Jesus's startling solidarity with people as apparently messed up as this Samaritan woman. Jesus seems more approachable now that they have seen his offer of living water, no strings attached, to an undeserving woman.

I ask the men how many of them feel thirsty, wanting this living water that Jesus offers. They all raise their hands or nod. An idea pops into my head that seems extreme but somehow appropriate. I invite the men to imagine a forty-ounce can of malt liquor, the stuff preferred by people on the street because it's least expensive and has the highest alcohol content; they know it as a "forty." I invite these men to imagine that this can contains the living water that Jesus offers, that unlike the old familiar malt liquor, this drink will permanently quench their thirst. At this point everyone understands clearly that the living water Jesus offers is not actual water, as the malt liquor equivalent I invite them to drink is not literal malt liquor. I invite them to pop off the top and raise their cans and drink freely together as I pray. Everyone pops the tops, and we raise our imaginary cans together over our mouths while I pray: "Jesus, we receive your gift of living water. We drink it down into our beings. Satisfy us with your loving, gracious presence."

They all cross themselves, in a way that I have come to recognize means that they have been deeply touched. I leave for home, feeling that I have shared living water at a place that functions regularly as a life-giving well for me: Skagit County jail. I return again the next Sunday, hoping that trust has grown between them and God, with each other, the Bible, and me as pastor and facilitator. My hope is that my presence, however directive or incomplete, will somehow fit within the company of Jesus and the woman, who both in their own ways bring people into authentic encounters with the source of living water.

CHAPTER 6

Intercultural Bible reading by Catholic groups of Bogotá

Edgar Antonio López

Hermeneutic approach

In recent decades, third-world theology and Bible studies have developed in a new direction, characterized by interaction between scholars and common Christian believers. This new way to produce theology has been important in Latin America, where poor communities challenge and enrich academic communities from their particular needs and desires. As a result, Latin American theology is deeply engaged with the material, economic, political, and social circumstances that surround groups of common believers (*grupos populares*), who are now also considered producers of theology.

Some years ago, the normal places to interpret the Bible were the academy and the pastorate. Scholars and pastors read and explained God's Word to common people, and it was unusual to find groups of believers reading the Bible together. The contribution these groups make in a broader way to understanding texts and ecclesial dynamics is essential in contemporary production of theology.

In addition, many people in the world have become aware of the world's multicultural nature and have begun to consider multiculturalism as an opportunity to grow together instead of a danger that must be avoided. Diversity in language, religion, ethnicity, or gender is not seen as an accidental characteristic of the world but as an elemental factor that must be reconsidered and studied.

Conflict between the interpretive tendencies of contextualism and universalism can be overcome through an intercultural perspective that allows groups with different interpretations to interact, to enrich each other, and to develop dialogue beyond each group's own horizon. With this interchange of perspectives has come

---

Edgar Antonio López, Faculty of Theology, Pontificia Universidad Javeriana (Bogotá, Colombia)

the need to establish dialogue between diverse Christian communities, in order to increase these communities' self-understanding and commitments within the multicultural world they share.

Multicultural dialogue and interconnection between theoretical and popular worlds open new horizons for Bible interpretation. In this sense, it is necessary to aim for intercultural communication that can serve to broaden a local reading with the differing perspectives other groups take before the same text. To study the differences and similarities among readings carried out in different contexts and to value the communicative experiences are important duties for theologians interested in responding to the challenges presented by our contemporary world. This is the motivation for the research discussed in this paper.

The question of what cultural factors affect the interpretation of a Bible text and how this interpretation could help different communities better understand their mission in the world can be answered by means of an empirical exercise. This exercise involves putting various groups of people into contact with one another so that they all read the same text and share their own interpretations. This experience is not only interesting for scholars but also significant for the communities that get in touch around the world to share their particular readings of the text, to learn from each other, and to better understand their function in the present world.

With this motivation, eight Catholic groups of Bogotá have read a single passage under the guidance of the Faculty of Theology at Pontificia Universidad Javeriana. They have come into contact with non-Catholic groups from different countries around the world. All these groups make up the Intercultural Bible Collective (IBC), which was established in 2001 under the auspices of the Uniting Protestant Churches in the Netherlands and the Faculty of Theology at the Free University, Amsterdam.

The experience began in January 2002, when groups of believers living in various cultural contexts had the opportunity to read a Bible text and join other groups in a valuable, strongly empirical hermeneutic experience. The theological reflection that developed thereafter can be located on a wide horizon, from which the different interpretations of a single text cannot be compared or said to be better or worse, correct or incorrect, on the basis of the extent to which they coincide with previous historical-critical or semiotic analyses.[1] Instead, differing interpretations should be appreciated insofar as they contribute to the dialogic and supportive self-understanding of communities.[2]

The empirical basis of the work is provided by the report that each group sent to a peer group. These reports include the most relevant points of a group's interpretation or the transcription of comments made during the meetings that were organized to read the text spontaneously. These first reports also include a description of group members and their context, so as to give the peer group an idea of who their interlocutors are and the environment in which they live. The communicative nature of the activity lies in the dialogue held by groups through report exchange and mutual feedback based on those reports.[3] It is worth noting that the number of participant groups, the mechanism used for gathering the groups, and the nature of the experience itself do not allow for a generalization of results to other Catholic and non-Catholic communities, because cultural and interpretation differences are considerable in each case. This fact does not invalidate the information obtained or the theological analysis made, because this is an exploratory study whose greatest value lies in the participation of community members who were willing to share the reading of the text in the light of faith.

The text chosen for the intercultural reading experience is the narration of Jesus meeting a Samaritan woman (John 4:1–42). The text has advantages for this kind of work, because it relates the encounter of two people whose communities had a long history of mutual exclusion. Gender and political differences between the two speakers make the narration even more relevant, because events do not fit into the normal habits of that particular culture and society. The conversation leads to Jesus's revelation to the woman and her transformation into a mission agent. All these elements in the text lead church communities to reflect on their particular identity and mission in the present world.

Catholic participants in Bogotá

Although all the groups that participated are Christian and are part of the IBC, there are major differences among them determined by a variety of languages, religious backgrounds, education, geographical location, social and economic status, age, and group history.

The Base Ecclesial Communities (BECs) of San Pablo, San Ignacio, San Lucas, Santiago, and Santa María de la Esperanza are members of the Catholic parish of Resurrección, located in the sector of Las Lomas, in Bogotá. The members of these groups are young people, mostly women, with a low educational level. Many of them are unemployed. Those who have a job do not earn a fair salary; the economic situation of most of them is precarious.

In spite of the fact that these groups share a history of violence, displacement, overcrowded housing, and poverty, these cheerful and hospitable communities participated enthusiastically in the activity. This same description applies to the Bible study group composed of members of different BECs from the neighborhoods of Las Lomas, Puerto Rico, Madrid, and Mirador, all from the same parish.

The other two Catholic groups in Bogotá that participated in the project have a higher social, economic, and educational level. They are the Life Project Group and a staff of teachers from the Faculty of Theology at Pontificia Universidad Javeriana.[4] The latter group was in charge of following up on the work of the other groups.

The Life Project Group is made up of professionals of various disciplines who meet periodically to reflect on important aspects of life—personal, family, and professional issues—from a socially oriented Christian perspective. The members of this group and the group of theology teachers do not live in economically depressed zones, as do members of the other six groups. Except for one case, members of the Life Project and teachers groups all have stable jobs.

Only the teachers from Javeriana University were told clearly from the beginning the purpose of this reflection. The scope of the activity was not initially explained to the other groups. It was only after they had reported on their spontaneous reading of the passage that they were asked about their interest in participating in the project. Spontaneous reading also was possible because the groups—except for the Javeriana teachers—had been meeting periodically for several years to read together and to reflect on the Bible.

These eight groups willingly and enthusiastically shared their interpretation of the text with non-Catholic groups from India, Germany, the Philippines, Brazil, and the Netherlands. The reports received from these countries and the feedback the partner groups provided about the reports sent them made possible a dialogic and supportive process of self-understanding, which had important consequences for theological reflection, as shown in the final remarks of this chapter.

Spontaneous interpretations of the text in Bogotá

The Catholic groups of the low-income sectors read the text and did their interpretations in the normal context of their meetings. These six interpretations are all similar. Their reflections have to do with elements the groups related to easily, such as various aspects of daily life and activities carried out by the church communities. Perhaps the concrete relationship established by these communities has to do with their own mind-set that is focused on material aspects of life and is therefore more sensitive to people in need, who are represented in the text by Jesus and the Samaritan woman.

For many of the members of these groups, need was the linking factor between Jesus and the Samaritan woman. The members' sensitivity to human need is combined with a traditional vision that emphasizes both human salvation through good deeds and Jesus's divinity. This combination reveals that members have received two different kinds of religious education that lead them to highlight the human aspects of Jesus in some cases, and his divine aspects in others.

The reflection on the encounter between a Jew and a Samaritan led these groups to see integration of diverse peoples as something that can be achieved when Jesus's salvation is accepted. Likewise, these communities have achieved a certain degree of integration through teamwork. For them, Jesus's love is a source of integration that extends beyond the social and religious factors that may hamper unity.

This awareness of being together around Jesus becomes a yearning for brotherly and sisterly coexistence for those who read the text in a cultural context characterized by violence. The importance given to community life is probably justified by the origin of these communities, whose members were rooted in peasant sectors and then had to migrate to Bogotá for political and economic reasons.

The openness of Jesus's attitude toward Samaritans appeals to these groups. In the reports on their spontaneous reading of the text, they see the text as an invitation to tolerance and to evangelization. This invitation makes them think about a community of faith where Jewish people and Samaritans could live together.

Prayer and total confidence in the omnipresent God characterize the interpretations of these Bogotá communities, whose work together is seen by the members as an act of God's grace and salvation. For some of the members of these groups, the encounter of Jesus with the woman is a kind of trial posed by Jesus in order to confirm her faith. The trial aspect is highly relevant for communities of common people, for whom lack of faith within their society is worrisome. In the text, they find a guide to resist skepticism; they value highly a faith that needs no evidence. The woman's total confidence in Jesus shows the clarity of her faith, in contrast to the disciples' blindness.

The daily life of these groups is tinged with the difficult political situation, notorious violence within families, and lack of safety that characterize the Colombian context. Therefore the text becomes a message of solidarity and peace, two ideals not overtly stated in the text but which can be recovered thanks to the groups' knowledge of the Bible. This knowledge has familiarized them with aspects of the social and cultural context of Israel. Commitment as citizens of the country becomes an interpretive lens for these groups who suffer violence, unemployment, and exploitation. They see in the text the life-giving God represented by water that quenches the thirst for justice.

There is a notable difference between the spontaneous interpretations of the text made by the Life Project and teachers groups, and those made by the common people's groups previously described. This difference can be explained partially by their social differences—reflected in differing educational background—but also by the atmosphere in which community readings took place. The members of the Life Project Group reflected on the content of the text during a spiritual retreat, while the theology teachers did so during a special session outside the usual academic activities in their university. As illustrated hereafter, material elements of everyday life are not so much present in the interpretations of the latter two groups. In these two groups, other aspects of the text are highlighted instead.

In the reflections of the Life Project Group, a strong emphasis on Jesus Christ himself can be observed, perhaps as a result of the meditative atmosphere in which the reading took place, and also because of the spiritual formation shared by group members. This educational background has developed in them a deep concern for the Colombian situation, as well as a commitment to put their profession at the service of the community. These two elements are evident in the group's interpretation of the text.

When addressing the woman, Jesus did not fear any criticism from his own people and was free of all prejudice against her. Such an attitude caught the Life Project Group's attention. Members also mentioned the not-so-open attitude of the

Samaritan woman at the beginning of the conversation, clearly illustrated by the questions she asked. Jesus's clever and rapid answers did not prevent the woman from going back to her own life and mission.

Jesus's calm attitude toward the woman and toward his disciples was also pointed out by Life Project Group members. To them, it became clear that Jesus is not to be found in a particular place but in one's heart, in life circumstances, and in meeting others. Openness to others' experiences is highly valued by this group, because they recognize the importance of communication in faith. This openness is emphasized by Jesus when he says that some reap what others have sown. The intention of learning God's will from the text led the group to recognize the need to give themselves over to Jesus and to do his will in their lives, that is to say, the need to drink from God's well of love that turns them into a source for others.

In their interpretation, the group of teachers at Javeriana University pointed out Jesus's wisdom and catechist attitude. Through these he leads the woman to reflect on her own life and to discover the supernatural condition of the water he offers, so that she can identify him and proclaim that he is a prophet and the Messiah. In the passage, Jesus breaks all cultural and temporal rules and guides the conversation in an unexpected direction. This disconcerting attitude suggested to the members of the group that all those who are open to Jesus's work can be saved, regardless of the cultural community to which they belong.

The theology teachers also highlighted the importance of the place and circumstances of the conversation: far from the temple, and without the disciples being present. Therefore, they concluded that the dialogue transcends institutional traditions and suggests that salvation is not exclusively intended for the people of Israel.

For this group, the impact that the conversation with Jesus has on the Samaritan woman—the expression of her faith and her becoming a witness—is important. It is one's own experience that makes the announcement authentic, not just a matter of transmitting a message but of leading to an experience of faith. This fact is reflected in the group's report through emphasis on the saving nature of water and food, represented by a needy Jesus.

According to the group of theology teachers, the text illustrates the way early Christians saw evangelization and how much they appreciated personally meeting Jesus. It also illustrates the questions believers ask as a result of encountering Jesus, and the confirmation of believers' faith in worship and proclamation experiences. Believers may find in this text their identity and the role they should play in a pagan context. As a result, for this group, underprivileged people are usually the best evangelizers.

The interpretation of the group of theology teachers was less influenced by the political, social, and economic conflicts of their context than were the interpretations of groups described earlier. Their theological background allowed them to establish relations between the text and certain biblical and theological issues rather than with material elements of life. The theoretical nature of their reflection can be explained by the academic atmosphere where teachers move daily, which is a relevant cultural difference between this and other group contexts.

Peer groups

A couple of months later, each of the groups mentioned above received the report of a non-Catholic group from a different country, giving its own interpretation of the same text. What follows is a description of characteristics of the groups that worked as peers of the Catholic communities of Bogotá. The summary also contains the most relevant elements mentioned in the partner groups' first reports.

Reading from India

The Indian community that exchanged reports with San Pablo BEC is located in Shoolagiri, where three different languages are spoken: Tamil, Telugu, and Kanarese. A division between castes marks their social context. The recent conversion to Christianity of most of the group members has meant coming to know a mind-set and a way of being that are very different from the ones they were used to. Christianity is particularly attractive to those belonging to the lower castes or to no caste at all, especially when Christian communities provide some economic help.

The presence of castes and tribal groups makes peaceful coexistence of Christians difficult. In spite of the religious freedom allowed by Indian legislation, regional authorities do not openly accept Christian conversion and initiation through baptism. This fact makes Christianity somehow clandestine. For all these reasons, the mission of proclaiming the gospel in this context becomes extremely hard and dangerous.

In the natural environment of Shoolagiri, drinkable water is scarce, and water availability is problematic, as is the availability of other public utilities. Dry seasons are long, and only upper castes have access to private wells. These circumstances make water a highly relevant topic in their interpretation of the text.

The differences between Jews and Samaritans are comparable to those between Indian castes, but they can also be compared with confrontations between Hindus, Brahmans, and Muslims. In this sense, group members openly reject fundamentalism, because they know well its negative consequences on their own communities.

This community finds a strong liberation content in the text. The Dalits (formerly untouchables) do not belong to any caste and are not allowed to participate in politics. Being marginalized by society, they identify themselves with Samaritans. Therefore, they really appreciate Jesus's open attitude toward this outside group.

Reading from Germany

The community from Marburg, Germany, who exchanged their reports with the BEC of San Ignacio, is made up mostly of young Protestant theology students who gather every month. They also hold weekly subgroup meetings where they read the Bible and analyze it from an academic, social, and daily-life perspective. Not all members of this group are German; some are from Korea and Taiwan. However, they all share the same social and economic status that allows them to live quite decently and to collect some money to help poor people living in other social conditions.

This community read the text in subgroups and focused largely on the liturgy, as can be observed by the prayers and songs that accompanied the reading of the text. Academic aspects were also taken into account through exegetical comments. This dynamic reduced the spontaneous nature of the first reading of the passage.

It was clear to the Marburg group that Jesus revealed himself to the woman through their dialogue. Also, water was connected with life and happiness. This group established a relationship between Jesus's own offering and the sacraments of baptism and Holy Communion. The situation between the Jews and the Samaritans was associated with current conflicts between Israel and Palestine. Loving God in spirit and truth is understood in this group's report to mean loving him in community with a love that surpasses all divisions between Jews and Samaritans.

An interesting point in this group's interpretation is the topic of guilt. This topic was widely discussed among them, because some see the woman as a sinner while others do not see her in such a way. The image of sowing made community members think of evangelization, and harvesting made them realize that not everyone accepts salvation by Jesus.

Reading from the Philippines

The Bogotá Bible study group, composed of members from several different BECs, exchanged reports with a group of middle-class Christian writers in the Philippines whose members work in different occupations in the city of Mandaluyong and who have certain responsibilities in their churches. Because this group of writers knew the nature of the project from the beginning of their work, their reading of the text was not entirely spontaneous. It was done in one of their ordinary monthly meetings. Their report says that they tended to analyze the passage from an intellectual point of view.

This community's report of the first reading describes the text as the narration of the woman's conversion: she was seen as a sinful person, and Jesus's comments were understood as reproaches. The enthusiasm with which the woman goes on her mission of evangelization is highlighted at the end of the report.

The disciples' astonishment when they saw their master talking to a strange woman drew this group's attention. They interpreted the disciples' silence as a natural reaction before a person like Jesus. They identified with the disciples' reaction, because in their own culture, authorities are not faced directly. In contrast, Jesus's humility and capacity to listen do not conceal his ability to face the woman.

Thirst is understood in a figurative sense, because members are not sure that Jesus was actually thirsty. The request for water seems to be an excuse to approach the woman who, just like everybody else, is thirsty for God and thirsty for others.

The group emphasized that God is not in any particular place or church. Therefore, all of us can learn from each other. This learning occurred when some group members saw new elements in the text through others' interpretation. For some of the participants, reading the Bible together is more enriching than individual reading, because they see the Holy Spirit's inspiration in everyone's comments.

Reading from Brazil

The group of theology teachers at Javeriana University exchanged reports with a group of workers and pensioners who live in Estância Velha, Brazil. The Brazilian group gathers often to read and discuss the Bible, but their meetings do not have an academic nature, because their educational level is not very high. The spontaneous reading report shows that the group's organizer had to make a big effort to get members to participate.

The meeting in which the text was read began with songs and the reading of other Bible passages that helped create an appropriate atmosphere. The aspect that first drew the group's attention was the larger number of disciples that Jesus had as compared to John. This fact led them to conclude that Jesus's message was more attractive.

Members argued that Jesus knew who the woman was; thus, it is quite interesting that he asks her—a Samaritan—for water. According to them, because life depends on water, no one can be deprived of it, not even those who belong to the people one is in conflict with.

In the report, this group states that the woman saw that Jesus did not have a container to keep the water; however, when she realized that the conversation was about a different kind of water, she did not hesitate to ask for this living water. The group maintained that evident in the text is a need to overcome eagerness for material things as opposed to spiritual things. Water is identified with God's grace, love, and salvation; food is identified with God's Word, and harvesting with the desire for eternal life.

The group pointed out that when the disciples arrived with some food, they were astonished, not only because Jesus was talking to a Samaritan woman, an attitude before which they remained silent, but also by the fact that he said he already had a different kind of food.

This group's members appreciated the dialogue in the passage because it describes finding Jesus in daily activities, and also because it illustrates how barriers between people from different religions can be overcome. The woman's condition let her see Jesus's confidence and mercy, because he does not condemn her.

For this community, Jesus is revealed to the woman through the action of the Spirit; however, Jesus's knowledge of her personality and life leads her to believe in him. The faith of the Samaritans, motivated by Jesus's words, is opposite to that of Thomas, who needed evidence in order to believe.

This group saw clearly that God is not to be worshiped in a particular place, and that true worshiping takes place in the Holy Communion. Those who sow and those who reap are equally happy, because the things harvested are communion, mutual benefit, and the very community that has been grown by others.

Reading from the Netherlands

The Life Project Group exchanged their reports with a group of Protestant Christians who live in the Dutch city of Huizen, where they enjoy a peaceful life. The Huizen group cared about having prayers and some symbolic elements that would help create an appropriate atmosphere for reading the text. Their interpretation shows their appreciation of Jesus's open and respectful attitude toward the Samaritan woman. Members of this community pointed out that Jesus did not condemn the woman and maintained that he was sent by the Father to save her personally. For some, the temporary absence of the disciples made the encounter with the woman possible, because the disciples did not accept Jesus's open attitude toward the woman. The group appreciated this openness, because they believe it would help solve many of the ethnic and cultural conflicts of today's world.

Water and food are taken in a figurative sense. For this group, lack of faith and apathy in today's societies are worrying issues. Their concern about these issues leads them to think that faith in God—as associated with the saving water that pours from Jesus himself— is probably the main point of the reading.

Some of the members of the Huizen group believe that theological knowledge could prevent texts from being interpreted according to one's own personal experience. In this sense, there is a tension between growing in faith and keeping infant transparency.

A group of middle-class Christians who live in the Dutch village of Apeldoorn also participated in this project. Its members are active workers and pensioners who meet every six weeks in order to study and discuss Bible books. Their meetings do not include any liturgical or symbolic elements. They shared their interpretation of the text with the BEC of San Lucas. The report reveals the great influence of the theological background of community members, who have studied the context in which John's Gospel was written, as well as its theological characteristics.

This group sees the water as directly related to baptism; it plays a major role in the story. They note that in Palestine's hot, dry environment, right in the middle of a hot day, Jesus asks a Samaritan woman for water, an important element for life.

Jesus's openness is recognized in the report, but members also pointed out that in the text the reference made to worshiping includes a discriminatory statement against the Jews. They highlighted the discrimination against the woman by her people because of her condition. Jesus's answers to the woman's questions are surprisingly complex. It seems as if Jesus and the woman do not understand each other. The most important point is that the text emphasizes that Jesus's salvation is not intended only for Jews.

The peer group of the BEC of Santiago was a Protestant community living in Appingedam, made up of two Calvinist churches. Members are middle-class people who meet every other week. They knew about the project by the time they first read the text, and they decided to read also the remainder of John 4.

Meetings were prepared very carefully, in terms of liturgical elements. The first meeting was dedicated to asking questions. It was only in a second meeting that members started discussing answers. The text suggested to them a question about whether there is any reason to believe that one religion holds the truth to a higher degree than the others. For this group, the very fact that Jesus goes to Samaria is an open call to overcome barriers between people and churches. This group's members acknowledged that because they have grown up in a Christian community they have difficulty understanding conversion.

The differences in gender of their interlocutors appealed to the Appingedam group. This feature reminded the members of the discrimination against women that can be observed in many cultures, not only Eastern ones. Disputes between the Jews and the Samaritans also made them think about current conflicts in the Middle East.

Another Dutch group that shared its interpretation with Colombian Catholics was that of the Protestant parish of Waarde. This group of workers has a special interest in the arts and Bible study, and they meet informally once a month. Prayers and songs reveal the warm atmosphere in their meetings.

In their first meeting, general information about the project was given to participants, who showed interest and enthusiasm. In the second meeting, each member read the text individually. After rereading the text together, a lively discussion began and extended until a third meeting. Nevertheless, participants made comments on topics not clearly related to the text, some of which made the discussion heated at times.

The first point mentioned in this group's interpretation was Jesus's openness, as contrasted with traditional Jewish discrimination against Samaritans. The group believed the encounter narrated in the text is eminently personal because Jesus knew the woman. Some members believed that, besides being a Samaritan, the woman's reputation was not good and that the story is about conversion. Others said that Jesus's affection and uncritical attitude toward the woman show that the encounter is about confirming the Samaritans' faith, particularly the woman's faith.

For this group, water is a symbol of the Holy Spirit. All of us must be sources of that Spirit through life testimony. Praying and reading the Word of God are important, but those actions must be reflected in our deeds, so that we please God and serve our neighbors. Theological and biblical knowledge are important but not as important as how one lives. Pleasing God is doing God's will, and for some members of this group, it means being one with Jesus Christ crucified. Some members of this community believe that theologians are perhaps less necessary than ordinary people who can reflect God's love.

The text led this group to think about the ethnic, cultural, and religious differences so common in Europe today. Difficult moments in family, pastoral, and personal life were also frequently mentioned after reading the passage.

Reactions to different identities and interpretations

This experience did not conclude when the groups had come to know each other and had shared access to various text interpretations. It also included a second phase. Six months after the first exchange, participant groups had the opportunity to express their own reaction to the partner group's interpretations, and in some cases, to the feedback received from them.

In the particular cases of the Bogotá BECs and Bible study group, their peers' reports were examined near the town of La Vega, one hour from Bogotá. Three of these communities had to wait until August 2003 to receive the reports. The other two Bogotá Catholic groups received them in 2002 at their regular place of meeting.

In this second phase of the project, the guide questions referred to the convergences and the divergences seen in the partner's interpretation with respect to their own spontaneous reading. Nevertheless, the groups could state any other relevant questions or commentary they considered useful to their partners.

Some groups received long and detailed reports, while other reports described briefly the interpretations and the way the meetings were carried out. The interpretations of the groups located in Bogotá always were seen as very simple by their partner groups, as if the text was very clear and no questions could arise during the meetings. Yet even the silence of some groups about aspects that appealed to others was also important to show differences among the communities and the contexts.

In some cases, the coordinator's role was important in encouraging other members to talk, but it also reduced spontaneous participation. This dynamic drew the attention of people in groups that structured the experience more freely. With no one there as coordinator, they were free to talk or be silent, in a more democratic way, depending on their own feeling.

Previous knowledge or ignorance about the final proposal and destination of the interpretation was also an influential factor when a group read the partner's report. Some groups considered that it would have been better if every group had had the same spontaneous experience. This desire for equality was common in the Colombian groups' reports, although this aspect had been left to the coordinators' judgment from the beginning of the project.

In Colombian society, contacts between Catholics and Protestants are quite contentious, so the brotherly and sisterly contact with Protestant groups was interesting for the Catholic groups in Bogotá. The influence of Spanish culture in the history of the country has shaped a Catholic society unable to recognize dialogue with Protestants as an opportunity to understand one's own society deeply. Just recently, Protestant communities are growing in Colombian society, but because they draw people away from the Catholic church, they are not much appreciated by most people.

The matching of groups for exchanging particular readings was established by looking for groups located in different countries, with different languages, denominations, and cultural backgrounds. As the groups were linked, the response to interpretations frequently introduced comments related to valuing knowledge about the partner group's particular context and situation. This factor is significant not only because of the information one can find in the reports but also because one gains self-understanding when comparing one's situation and interpretation with those of others.

The predominantly young age of members of the third-world groups called attention to the older age of those in communities located in the first world. With the exception of the German group, a community of young people, the other groups all pointed to the age difference. Members of the Colombian groups were interested to note that people from the Dutch communities in general were older than the Colombian participants.

Other differences highlighted in the reactions related to the way the text was read, the report was written, and the atmosphere was created for the meetings. Some Protestant groups opened the meetings with songs, symbols, worship, and other Bible readings, but some Catholic communities, especially the Bogotá base communities, also care about this aspect of their gatherings.

On the one hand, some Protestant groups showed surprise that Catholic people also gather to read the Bible, because they thought meeting for Bible reading was not a traditional practice among Catholics. On the other hand, Catholic groups were impressed by the intercongregational composition of their partner groups, because ecumenical experiences are uncommon in their context. Both kinds of groups expressed enjoyment at communitarian reading of the Bible, pointing out that it is more interesting than Bible reading done individually.

The reports demonstrate an important effort to establish a relationship between the text and elements of daily life, but this connection also implies important differences related to the diversity of contexts. These differences appear especially in reactions written by communities that live in precarious situations, where water and food are less plentiful.

It is important to consider the special attention paid to the different conditions communities live in. People with minimal schooling were sensitive about having to respond to interpretations coming from scholar groups, and at the beginning considered it unfair. In the process, however, these very groups were amazed to see so many correspondences with their own interpretation, less speculative but just as deep as the theoretical ones.

The same initial attitude and ultimate change were observed in groups that had a higher economic level. The reaction to interpretations that had understood the water and the food in a figurative sense pointed out the danger of spiritualizing

God's Word, a danger present also in their own interpretation. Even with the differences, these groups found common topics for dialogue, and in any case, poor communities were surprised to see the other groups show as much interest in religious questions as they themselves had shown.

Convergences and divergences among different interpretations

Group reactions to partner reading reports are important materials for analyzing the intercultural communication level reached by the participant communities in this experience. All show a richness of encounter around the text that suggests many different things from the other's perspective. Only some of the groups show evidence of an attitude open to recognizing differences as opportunities to broaden their own horizon of interpretation and to improve their self-knowledge.

These reactions reveal an important tendency to explain the interpretive differences in terms of knowledge about the partner group's characteristics and conditions. In this sense, the information a group gave its partner group about itself was the main resource used to explain the divergences between their own and the partner's interpretation.

The Indian group's reaction to the Colombian reading report was written by the coordinator, so it was not easy to see the members' reactions directly. The coordinator stated that their response came from the recognition of similarities between poor communities that suffer similar problems around the world. The report shows that the members of the Shoolagiri community responded with emotion to the partner group's reading and had many questions about the Colombian cultural situation, political problems, and social conflicts. San Pablo BEC realized that its Indian partner group also had established a strong relationship between the text and daily life elements, but found important differences between the two interpretations because of the lack of drinkable water in India and the absence of a caste system in Colombia.

Theology students at the German University of Marburg stated that San Ignacio BEC had paid attention to aspects that they hadn't considered in their own reading, which had emphasized baptism and harvest, topics ignored by the Colombian report. They pointed out that the Colombian group didn't attribute any importance to the fact that the woman had many husbands. They noted that they learned a lot about the human conditions highlighted by their Colombian partner group, because the partner group's interpretation cared more about material needs. In their reaction, San Ignacio BEC described the different meanings given by the German community to water, and also reported that they had learned a lot from the different way the German group approached the common elements of water, harvest, food, and the woman's condition.

The Christian writers group in the Philippines responded that their partners did not pay enough attention to the character of Jesus in the narrative, and they found some questions considered by the Colombian Bible study group quite child-like, possibly as a result of their different needs and conditions. Conversely, the latter found the Christian writers' report too theoretical. When the Philippine group read the reaction of the partner group, they recognized themselves in the glimpse their partners shared of their perceptions.

The Christian writers accepted their partner's observation about going deeper in Bible reflection, surely not at an intellectual level but at an existential one. This fact is significant to intercultural dialogue, because the educational background of the partner Bible study group cannot be compared to the higher educational level of the Christian writers. Through the Philippine report, the Colombian group members also recognized their own narrow interpretive horizon, in that they had considered only Catholic people worthy of including in their gathering. The Christian writers community includes people from different denominations, and the individuals' membership in several churches was important to their discussion about the text. This diversity appealed to the Colombian community.

The Brazilian reaction to the Colombian theology teachers' reading showed surprise; in spite of the cultural and educational differences, they found many convergences. The Brazilian group responded that the teachers paid more attention to Jesus's open attitude before the woman, in contrast with the tradition of discrimination. This openness presented a means to recognize their own lack of criticism of tradition. On the other hand, they thought the Colombian report did not emphasize enough Jesus's personal knowledge of the woman, an essential point for their own interpretation.

The Colombian teachers highlighted the Brazilian participants' awareness that meetings were being recorded, and noted the inhibiting effects. This inhibition was evident in the central role the coordinator played in writing the meeting report. Some elements, such as references to daily life, were common to both interpretations, but legal aspects of the well had more importance in the Brazilian report than in the Colombian one. The theologians group paid more attention to the conversation between Jesus and the woman, while the Brazilian community considered more important the material elements present in the narration.

The intercongregational composition of the Huizen group strongly appealed to its Colombian peer group. Although the Huizen community shared many of the observations pointed out by the Life Project Group, it also missed many of the individual feelings and thoughts shared in the peer spontaneous reading report. The members of this Dutch group found these aspects of the peer discussion quite interesting. Huizen people had many questions about the Colombian group's history, work, and prospects, but unfortunately did not devote much time to analyzing the Colombian group's report.

The Life Project Group's response pointed out important differences between their own interpretation and their partner group's report. The Huizen community's interpretation has a strong symbolic nature and a consciousness about the intercultural experience goals, both absent from the Colombian interpretation. However, the Life Project Group found valuable the way the Dutch peer group emphasized the unassuming character of the woman, which made her more receptive to Jesus's message than were the disciples.

Apeldoorn community noted that San Lucas BEC took God's Word as it is written, without the inquiry that characterized their own reading. They saw their partner group's reading as based on emotions and feelings and not on the rational deliberation they are accustomed to. The Colombian report suggests that the text is transparent to San Lucas BEC's members, who without any handicap or doubt see Jesus's open attitude toward people.

San Lucas community became aware that they did not ask as many things about the text as the Apeldoorn participants. Their partner group's interpretation seemed intellectual and not strong enough to impact real life. Both communities search for who Jesus is, but the Dutch group seems to go beyond the point reached by the Colombian community's reflection. In addition, in its interpretation of the text, the Colombian group recognized that it has cared less about political questions than its partner group.

Appingedam community members found Santiago BEC's report shorter than their own report. Nevertheless, it was possible for them to establish that the Dutch group read the Bible more critically, while the Colombian one looked directly for moral application of the verses. Communitarian aspects seemed to be more important for Santiago BEC than for the Appingedam group, but the report of the former emphasizes more social and political aspects, such as discrimination against women and war, especially the conflict between Israel and Palestine.

The Waarde community examined very carefully Santa María de la Esperanza's report and asked the partner community about reading details related to communion, discrimination, justification, and other topics highlighted by the Colombian interpretation. Jesus was the main reference point for the Dutch group, while the Colombian one took the common people's perspective as a reference. This perspective appealed to the Waarde community. Both communities paid attention to the relationship between Jesus and the Samaritans, but Santa María BEC members found their partners also devoted much time to discussing details Santa Maria considered worthless. These two communities appeared to have learned much from each other.

Final remarks

The experience lived by these Christian groups around the world shows the strong power of communitarian and intercultural Bible reading as well as the important influence that cultural factors have on processes of text interpretation. The analysis presented here, based on empirical evidence, has shown significant contributions these groups have given each other to enrich their own interpretation of the text but also to go deeper in understanding their mission in the present world.

In the light of faith, each community has come to know another group. In different situations, each community has discovered several elements in the text that became visible to them only through dialogue. Some partners reached an intercultural dialogue, but others went only as far as the multicultural experience led them.

The community of Marburg theology students and San Ignacio BEC, the Christian Writers group and its partner Colombian Bible study group, the Brazilian workers community and the Colombian theology teachers group, the Waarde community and Santa María de la Esperanza BEC all recognized in the other a lens to read not only the story of the Samaritan woman but also to read their own being and mission.

Differences related to geography, history, educational background, economic level, political condition, and other important factors might have kept these communities apart, but here these differences led the groups to expand their own interpretive horizon. In this way, communities reached a better comprehension of the text and also a more complete understanding of their own situation.

Other pairs of communities maintained dialogue at a superficial level, without the open attitude that led the above-mentioned groups to broaden their hermeneutic horizon. A mutual interest in knowing each other was reached, but their own interpretation of the text remained intact through the whole experience. The role taken by the coordinator and the time taken to interchange reports, among many other factors, could have been influences in these cases, but it is worth noting that all participant groups found many topics that provided opportunity to share their own vision of the text with their partner groups.

The issue of communion, represented by Jesus's attitude toward the gap between Jews and Samaritans, was very interesting for all groups. Poorer communities interpreted that convergence as a reason to fight for their rights. The same can be said about groups located in societies with strong social discrimination. For the poorer groups who received a report from a higher economic level peer group, this convergence was seen as the need to live in communion overcoming differences.

Catholic communities realized a strong relationship between the dialogue in the text and the Eucharist, maybe because this sacrament is central in their liturgical life. Protestant groups also pointed out a deep relationship between the text and sacraments, but they highlighted baptism. In general, baptism seemed to be more important for Protestant groups than for Catholic ones.

The fact that some Protestant groups saw the woman as a sinner also drew the attention of Catholic groups, in which this possibility was not discussed. Catholic groups of Bogotá did not see in the dialogue any accusation coming from Jesus concerning the woman's behavior, nor did they see in her any sinful condition. For Catholic people, it seemed quite odd that their partners paid so much attention to the woman as sinner, because the text does not suggest to them that condition at all.

Some groups learned that even when they feel their situation is the worst one possible, others face problems they do not experience, such as lack of water or food, social discrimination, and violence. This realization allowed them to think about good aspects of their own lives.

In the beginning, several questions formulated by groups addressing the text seemed simple or even crazy to peer groups, but these questions began to make sense in light of the situations in which their partner communities live. Through dialogue with their partner, some groups became aware of important details in the narrative that evidence the liberation message present in the gospel.

Communion between differing people, solidarity overcoming differences, understanding and knowing each other, confirmation of faith, and other topics arose in this worldwide reflection about a personal encounter between Jesus and the Samaritan woman. The character of a needy Jesus and the happiness of a woman who found salvation in the encounter have shown to many groups that knowledge about the other's life and needs are necessary conditions for evangelization and must guide the missionary commitment.

Differing interpretations of a single text manifest the existence of different theologies, depending on particular situations. These interpretations also show important convergences around universal questions related to quality of life that challenge believers to build a better world. The purpose of the scripture appears clear: to foster conversion and hope so that people can find a social order that corresponds to God's will. Bible reading must serve to preserve life and improve conditions for living. War, thirst, discrimination, poverty, and other kinds of injustice become lenses for reading the Bible, because groups find in the text what they most need.

This experience encouraged scholars and those without education to advance in their way of reading, understanding, and practicing God's Word, but also to overcome the traditional way the Bible is read. Furthermore, the experience shows the complementarity of popular and scholarly perspectives, and at the same time, evidences the need for biblical formation for all church members. It also advises scholars to get in touch with grassroots perspectives to better understand the message of the Word that was addressed in the first place to poor people.

It is apparent that differences in ways of thinking were overcome in this experience, as shown by the existential questions asked within the groups as well as by the feeling and care manifested in the responses. Also, prayers and blessings sent for some groups at the end of the process, wishing God's protection to their peers, display the broad human dimension of the project.

This path from a multicultural to an intercultural perspective has shown the need to accept each other as we are. Differences and convergences can improve our self-understanding through identifying ourselves with others or by contrasting ourselves with them. All of this occurs with a strong feeling of communion and an open attitude toward the differences, no matter what our denomination, religion, language, income, country, or people are.

Notes

[1] The need to examine such studies from a wide hermeneutic perspective is discussed by Paul Ricoeur, "Del conflicto a la convergencia de los métodos en exégesis

bíblica," in *Exégesis y hermenéutica,* ed. Roland Barthes (Madrid: Ediciones Cristiandad, 1976), 34–50. Originally published as: "Du conflit à convergence des méthodes en exégèse biblique," in *Exégèse et herméneutique* (Paris: Éditions du Seuil, 1971), 35–53.

[2] "A really effective solidarity among the diversity of linguistic cultures and traditions will be accomplished very slowly and with hard work. It requires the use of true language productivity so that we understand each other instead of stubbornly clinging to all those rule systems by which things are labeled as either correct or false. However, whenever we speak, we seek to understand ourselves and to be understood by others so that they can respond, confirm or correct our discourse. All this makes part of a true dialogue." Hans-Georg Gadamer, *Arte y verdad de palabra* (Barcelona: Paidós, 1998), 124.

[3] Cf. Hans de Wit, "Through the Eyes of Another: A project on Intercultural Reading of the Bible" (presentation, consultation on Intercultural Reading of the Bible, Free University, Amsterdam. 2001), 27. The contributions of Eduardo Díaz and Alfredo Escalante in data collection have been essential to the development of this research.

[4] The Javeriana theology teachers group was composed of Eduardo Diaz, José Roberto Arango, Alfredo Escalante, Ignacio Madera, Alfonso Rincón, Jorge Zureck, and Edgar Antonio López.

CHAPTER 7

Through different eyes

Indonesian experiences with an intercultural reading of John 4
Jilles de Klerk

What happens when two reading groups from different cultural backgrounds link with each other, exchange their interpretations of John 4:1–42, and then respond to the findings of the other group? That is the question behind the project Through the Eyes of Another. Beforehand, one could expect both similarities and differences in the two groups' interpretations. The more interesting questions therefore are: Will the groups be influenced by each other's interpretation, and if so, to what extent? Will a merging of horizons[1] take place, not between the cultural context of the Bible and the reader's cultural context, but between the two different cultural contexts of the reading groups, so that the groups will come to a mutual understanding? Or will a group feel alienated or even shocked by the partner group's interpretation?

One hopes that the experience of sharing will enrich the groups and that they will even feel a sense of success in reading John 4:1–42 through the eyes of the other, because this is the aim of the project. By *reading through the eyes of another*, I mean not simply taking notice of the way other people interpret the Bible story but rather letting one's own perspective on the story be widened, criticized, and changed by the other's interpretation.

This article will analyze to what extent this widening and changing of perspective happened in Indonesian reading groups that were involved in the project. I start with an outline of the Indonesian context to inform you about the groups' cultural background. Then I show how in my view their cultural context played a role in the interpretations of the different Indonesian reading groups. I next discuss the extent to which their partner groups influenced the Indonesian reading groups. I conclude with comments about obstacles and possibilities related to intercultural reading of the Bible.

Jilles de Klerk, Department of Biblical Studies, Theological Seminary of East Indonesia (Macassar, Indonesia)

The Indonesian context

Indonesia is the biggest archipelago of the Asian continent. It consists of about 13,000 islands, of which Java, Sumatra, Kalimantan, and Sulawesi are the biggest. Although these islands form one nation, the people of Indonesia show a rich diversity of ethnic groups, each with its own *adat*. Adat is an Indonesian concept that encompasses the language, traditional religion, laws, rules, and habits of Indonesia's ethnic groups. The reading group from Macassar reflected the ethnic diversity so typical for Indonesia: the ten members of this group represented six ethnic groups!

Although Christians are a majority in several regions, especially in East Indonesia (Tana Toraja, Minahasa, Timor, and Papua), in the country as a whole 90 percent of the population is Muslim. But Indonesia is not an Islamic state, nor are state and religion separated as in many Western countries. Instead, Indonesia has a political ideology that is called *Pancasila* (the Five Pillars). One of the principles of Pancasila is that every citizen must be a member of one of the five religions acknowledged by the state: Islam, Protestantism, Catholicism, Buddhism, and Hinduism. Other religions actually practiced in the society were historically excluded, such as Confucianism (now acknowledged), or are still excluded, such as the traditional religions of various ethnic groups. Despite their official exclusion, traditional religions remain influential, because in reality both Islam and Christianity are often mixed with elements of these. Examples of this influence are widespread belief in good and evil spirits, honoring of ancestors, and all kinds of rituals that have to do with life and death, health and illness, and sowing and harvesting.

After the second president, Suharto, had to step down in 1998, the idea of making Indonesia an Islamic state revived among some minor fundamentalist Islamic groups. These groups pressed for an introduction of sharia (Islamic law). Some believe that a law based on Islamic religious principles could stop widespread corruption in Indonesian society. However, many Muslims do not support the introduction of sharia. Adherents of other religions fear that introducing sharia will limit or even destroy the religious tolerance supported by Pancasila.

Indonesia has not yet recovered from the economic crisis of 1997, and many Indonesians suffer from poverty. After the fall of President Suharto, many hoped and fought for political and social reformation. Indeed, in some areas there has been improvement, in freedom of the press, for example. But corruption is still widespread and so are all kinds of violence. In the western (Aceh) and eastern (Papua) part of the country, freedom movements fight for independence against the Indonesian army. In other regions (Kalimantan, Ambon, and Poso), ethnic and religious conflicts have broken out, and thousands of people have been killed. Moreover, Indonesia has experienced its share of international terrorism, as when on 12 October 2002 a bomb in Bali killed 202 people and injured hundreds of others, mostly foreigners. Muslim extremists (possibly linked to Al Qaeda) are held responsible for this assault. They are also suspected of several bomb attacks on churches during the Christmas season in 2000 and of the bombing of a hotel in Jakarta in 2003.

Multiculturalism

The brief outline above shows that Indonesian society is characterized by racial, ethnic, and religious diversity. Therefore, one cannot speak of *the* Indonesian cultural context as if it were a single kind. The cultural context of the Toraja of South Sulawesi differs from that of the people on Java. The adat of the Batak of Sumatra differs from the adat of the Timorese or of the Papua. The multiculturalism of Indonesia does not mean that the country must be seen as a society of isolated, autonomous ethnic groups separated by the specifics of each group's identity. Such a static idea of cultures, according to Melanie Budianta, reflects an essentialist concept of culture. Budianta rejects such an essentialist definition and instead advocates a constructivist—open and fluid—definition of culture.[2] She characterizes the essentialist culture as featuring the notion of culture as (1) a holistic, unified entity, which defies heterogeneity and internal contradictions; (2) an autonomous unit with fixed boundaries with some essential, fixed nature and characteristics; and (3) as a historical product that has become static and unchanged.

In contrast to the essentialist—uniform and static—definition of culture, a constructivist definition sees culture as (1) a continuous process of becoming, occurring in different levels and dimensions; (2) a field with porous boundaries, where cross-cultural influence, interaction, and mixture takes place; and (3) a set of allusions and references that are transmitted through socialization to members, or from one generation to the next, for specific interests and according to different contexts (instead of a fixed blueprint that determines and explains group members' actions).

The constructivist view understands that there is a continuous process of interaction going on both within and between the different cultural groups of Indonesia. Furthermore, such interaction occurs between Indonesian groups and cultures from outside Indonesia. We must keep this interaction in mind when we try to sketch characteristics of the way Indonesian groups interpreted John 4. Although I think we can point to a few general characteristics, there is not one single way that can be described as *the* Indonesian way of reading the Bible. This lack of a fixed and uniform approach is partly attributable to multiculturalism within Indonesian society, which causes differences in interpretation between, for example, the reading group from Bandung on Java and the group from Macassar on Sulawesi. However, fluidity also occurs because a group and its members themselves do not possess anything resembling a fixed, static, and monocultural identity.

Groups are involved in a dynamic and continuous process that constitutes culture, and they are continually exposed to influences from outside their own culture. For example, in the case of the Macassar group, which includes members of several different ethnic groups, their reading together can already be seen as a cross-cultural event! Moreover, through surfing the Internet, some participants in the studies regularly gain knowledge of various manifestations of foreign cultures. Last but not least, the intercultural Bible reading project itself is a good example of the fluid perspective on culture. That is to say, reading through the eyes of another implies that one acknowledges the influence of cultural background, but at the same time presupposes that this cultural influence is not fixed and static. The process assumes that the reader is open and sensitive to ways of reading the Bible from another cultural perspective. With this in mind, I point to four possible Indonesian characteristics in the reading of John 4.

Four characteristics

I had access to the data of two reading groups from Indonesia. The first was a group of students from the Sekolah Tinggi Teologia di Indonesia Bagian Timur (Theological Seminary of Eastern Indonesia) in Macassar, a city in South Sulawesi. This group was linked to a group from the Evangelical Theological Seminary, Matanzas, Cuba (also students of theology). The Macassar reading group also exchanged their report with the Samen op Weg Gemeente of Warmond, a Dutch Protestant congregation in the western part of the Netherlands. The second Indonesian group was a reading group from the Catholic church of Bandung on Central Java. They had the Scottish Conversations Group from Glasgow and its surroundings as their partner group.

Approach

A striking difference between the two Indonesian groups and their respective partner groups appeared in their approach to the Bible story. Following the guidelines of the project's handbook, "Through the Eyes of Another: A Project on Intercultural Reading of the Bible," the students of theology from Macassar started by associating John 4:1–42 with daily experiences. After this they discussed the text and ended with the question, With whom in the story do we identify? In the group from Bandung, the members simply made personal remarks on the story. Instead of discussing the text of the story, they preferred a sharing of personal thoughts and experiences resulting from the reading of John 4. Thus, neither group began with an analysis of the text of the story, nor did they put forward critical questions, such as: When was this text written? What is meant by 'living water'? What was the conflict between Jews and Samaritans actually about?

Obviously, the Indonesian groups considered what John wanted to say to his readers then and now to be more or less clear. At least the groups did not feel a tension between the message of the Bible and what they as Christians believe and see as truth. Therefore, the Indonesian reading groups had no difficulty telling stories based on their own experiences that were similar to the one in John 4:1–42. In the Macassar group, several members knew women who had been expelled after committing adultery, as they understood the Samaritan woman had been. In the same way, members told several stories about ethnic and religious conflicts, similar to the conflict between Jews and Samaritans in Jesus's day.

In contrast to the Indonesian groups, the students of the Matanzas seminary started their discussion with a careful literary analysis of the text of John 4:1–42. They analyzed characters, geographical places, verbal forms, and conflicts in the text. Perhaps this could be expected from students of theology, but if so, it is even more striking that the Macassar students of theology did no exegetical analysis! Moreover, the members of the Dutch reading group, almost all of whom were lay people, had a similar analytical approach. They started their discussion of John 4 by raising all kinds of critical questions, such as: Who wrote this story, since there was no one present when Jesus talked to this Samaritan woman? Is this a story about a historical event or is it just fiction? Is the road through the city of Samaria really a shortcut? The Dutch group even checked the last question by consulting a map of ancient Israel!

The Scottish Conversations Group used an approach called Contextual Bible Study. It consists of a set of fixed open questions and aims to provide an open, reflective atmosphere that encourages and enables participants to explore the scriptures, to share their faith and insight, and to move on to some form of action in response to the group reflection. The CBS approach aims at both a close reading of the text and an exploration of the link between the text and contemporary life.

Hence the partner groups all analyzed the Bible text in a more or less thorough way, whereas the Indonesian groups did nothing like this. How can this difference in approach be explained? It is tempting to point here to Walter J. Ong's explanation of the difference between oral cultures and cultures with a high level of literacy. Ong defines a primary oral culture as a culture untouched by writing in any form.[3] Of course, Indonesia is not an oral culture in this sense, because there are newspapers, books, and magazines, and the majority of people can read and write. At the same time, there are residues of this primary oral culture in Indonesia, especially in the remote areas, but not only there. To give a few examples: When I asked a student of mine what his parents thought of his thesis, he replied that neither of them could read. When I asked my students if they had ever read novels by famous Indonesian authors, such as Pramoedya Ananta Toer or Sitor Situmorang, many said they had never heard of them. Hardly any student reads a newspaper. In general, they are neither accustomed to reading nor eager to do it. It is therefore not surprising that some of the characteristics of oral cultures that Ong outlines fit well with the way the Indonesian reading groups approached the story.

In describing oral cultures, Ong states, "Human beings in primary oral cultures . . . learn a great deal and possess and practice great wisdom, but they do not 'study.' They learn by apprenticeship, . . . by listening, by repeating what they hear, . . . not by study in the strict sense."[4] Ong notes that orally based thought and expression are aggregative rather than analytic. Traditions are preserved and passed on, but they are not questioned, nor is their truth doubted. "Once a formulary expression has crystallized, it had best be kept intact. Without a writing system, breaking up thought—that is, analysis—is a high-risk procedure."[5] Because knowledge in a primary oral culture cannot be stored and vanishes if it is not repeated over and over again, oral cultures not only are but must be "conservative and traditionalistic"; they inhibit intellectual experimentation.[6] Additionally, "writing separates the knower from the known and thus sets up conditions for 'objectivity,' in the sense of personal disengagement or distancing." In oral cultures the position of both the storyteller and audience is "empathetic and participatory, rather than objectively distanced."[7] Finally, Ong notes, oral cultures depend on sound (telling and hearing) as the most important medium for communication, whereas in cultures with a high level of literacy, vision (writing and reading) is as important as sound. "A sound-dominated verbal economy is consonant with aggregative (harmonizing) tendencies rather than with analytic, dissecting tendencies (which would come with the inscribed, visualized word: vision is a dissecting sense)."[8]

It is striking how these characteristics of an oral culture match with our observations about the approach of the Indonesian groups to the story of John 4. It is tempting to conclude that the way these groups approached the story has much to do with their cultural background, where remnants of an oral culture are still present, active, and influential.

Gospel and adat

I have already mentioned that only five religions are acknowledged in Indonesia. However, the influence of the adat, including traditional religions, is often strong, especially outside the cities. One of the participants of the Macassar group recognized this influence, noting that from the way Jesus approaches the Samaritan woman, it is clear in this story that God's grace is more powerful than human regulations. He continued, "When I compare this to my ethnic group, I must say that usually the influence of the adat is stronger than the influence of Christian faith. When there is a conflict, and a minister tries to reconcile people, he often fails, whereas an adat ritual often succeeds in ending the same conflict." The others agreed that in Indonesia the influence of ethnic traditions is often strong. Only in conflicts between people of different ethnic groups does national legislation become important. A conflict within an ethnic group will be solved through the adat, rather than through Christian ethics or national laws.

Differences between what Christian faith demands and what adat prescribes can cause much tension. For example, when someone from a higher social class orders someone from a low caste to do something, the low caste person simply has to obey, even if what is ordered violates Christian norms and values. A person who disobeys such an order will face repercussions, whereas violating Christian norms will not be punished, because such violation is not seen as a serious sin. This typical Indonesian issue, the relationship between "gospel and adat," as it is often called, became an interesting topic in the intercultural reading of John 4, as I will show.

Focus on the Samaritan as a sinful woman

Another remarkable feature in the interpretations of Indonesian reading groups was their focus on what they saw as the immorality of the Samaritan woman. She has had several husbands and is now living with a man without being legally wed.

Several identified her as someone who had committed adultery. In one group, the woman was even seen as a prostitute who tried to seduce Jesus or wanted him as her next husband! (However, others in the group objected to this interpretation.) That the Samaritan community expelled such a woman was understandable, because the reaction in Indonesian society would have been exactly the same. "If a woman committed adultery or 'behaved crazy' with another man, she would certainly be expelled, and many people would despise her," one of the Macassar students said. Although stress on the woman's immoral sexual behavior was not so apparent for the Bandung group, several members characterized the woman as someone who confesses her sins (and thus was indeed sinful).

In the Dutch partner group, the behavior of the woman was no issue at all. Neither did the Cuban group characterize the Samaritan woman as a sinner; they saw her as someone who was marginalized. When thinking about marginalized groups in their own society, they mentioned, among others, the *Jineteras* (prostitutes working in sex tourism) and homosexuals. The Cubans emphasized that these people who are often seen as sinful and immoral actually need our solidarity!

The stress on the sexual behavior of the Samaritan woman—so apparent in the Indonesian way of interpreting John 4:1–42—can be explained by noting that Asia has what sociologists call a shame culture rather than a guilt culture (which characterizes the Western world). Of course, Western people have feelings of shame as well, but for them shame is often a result of guilt. In Asian cultures (Japan, Indonesia), shame often has no direct relationship to guilt. Regarding shame, E. G. Singgih writes, "It is more than a subjective feeling conditioned by a relative cultural situation. It must be defined in terms of an ultimate authority which defines the true nature of human existence and relationship."[9] As an example of shame, Singgih tells about the case of a woman whose adolescent daughter becomes pregnant, and no one claims to be the father. This creates a situation of shame. Shame always implies social disgrace and exclusion. A Western solution would be to support the expectant mother as much as possible, so that she will be able to manage on her own. In a shame culture, however, this is not a solution at all, because "shame is related to the breakdown of interpersonal relations in the human family—both among humans and between humanity and . . . God.[10] Supporting the woman financially or morally cannot solve the social exclusion. What is needed is "to save face by performing the marriage [with any male candidate]. After that, when harmony is restored, the [husband] could start procedures for divorce."[11] The marriage will restore self-esteem and relationships.

Singgih continues, "Shame is banished when open communication is established through loving identification and the worth of each can be mutually affirmed."[12] It is exactly this that Jesus does for the Samaritan woman, according to several Indonesian readers. He gives back her dignity. In a shame culture, dignity is the counterpart and opposite of shame. According to Singgih, the good news of the gospel in the Asian context "means the lifting up of people from situations in which an individual or a group is trapped in feelings of shame."[13] In Indonesia, shame culture is particularly strong on the island of Java. It is therefore not surprising that the reading group from Bandung, Java, especially stresses that Jesus liberated the woman from feeling ashamed. One of the participants said, "This woman is liberated from the taboo of talking to a foreign man, from the taboo of talking openly about her private life. She is liberated from the feeling of shame when meeting fellow citizens and is being used in spreading the gospel to them. For me, this story is a liberation story—liberation from other people's prejudices, from shame, and from fear."

Religious and ethnic pluralism and violence

Given the ethnic and religious pluralism present in Indonesian society, it is not surprising that the Macassar group associated the ethnic and religious differences between Jews and Samaritans in Jesus's day with the sometimes problematic relationship between ethnic and religious groups in present-day Indonesia. Particularly, the relationship between Muslims and Christians was mentioned several times. However, in the Bible study of the Bandung group, the issue of ethnic and religious conflict was totally absent. Has this to do with the fact that Central Java is less stricken by ethnic and religious conflicts and violence than East Indonesia (Kalimantan, Central Sulawesi, the Moluccans)?

In the Macassar group, several remarks were made about the previously harmonic relationship between Muslims and Christians. One of the participants remembered how as a boy he often visited remote Muslim villages where people probably never had met Christians. "But I could visit these villages and was accepted as a friend and treated as if I was one of their family." A group member from Ambon, one of the regions where violent conflict between Christians and Muslims has broken out, related a similar experience. "Several of my friends were Muslims. If they were celebrating Maulid Nabi (an Islamic feast), we as Christians sang *qasida* with them. And at Christmas, Muslims sang in our choir. We had a very good relationship."

This does not mean that in earlier times there were never tensions between groups having different ethnic and religious backgrounds. Marriage between people of different religions caused problems within families, because either the man or the woman needed to change religion (mixed religious marriages are forbidden by the state). One participant told about a Christian woman who was made pregnant by her Muslim friend. They decided to get married. The husband was willing to become a Christian, but his family strongly opposed this course of action. "They threatened the church council that if they held a blessing ceremony in the church, the family would destroy and ruin the church building. But in the end, the couple married in church without anything violent taking place."

Other students mentioned an exclusivist view of Christianity or Islam as the reason for rejection and hostilities among Indonesians of different religious groups.

One said, "In the region of Kalimantan where I live, there are two ethnic groups which differ in religion. The majority of the Dayak ethnic group is Christian and the majority of the Kutai is Muslim. The Dayak consider themselves the only ones who know Christ. Moreover, they think that Christ knows only them, so there is separation between the two ethnic groups." From the way the Samaritan woman reacts to Jesus, she apparently has learned "that Jesus is known not only in Christianity, but he is working among the believers of other religions as well and is known by them."

This openness and tolerant attitude toward people of another religion is not always found. As I have mentioned, in several places in recent years, ethnic and religious violence has broken out. In these violent conflicts, religion or ethnicity is never the only—or even the most important—factor. Economic, social, and political factors are often equally important. Nevertheless, ethnicity and religion, perceived as pillars of people's identity, play their role. One participant from a violence-stricken area, when asked whom she identified with in the story, responded that before the violent conflict erupted, she would have identified herself with Jesus, not discriminating against anyone and open toward people of another religion. "But now, after the disturbances, I identify myself with the Samaritan woman. What I mean is, there are boundaries. I can't associate with you, because you are Jewish and I am a Samaritan. You are a Muslim and I am a Christian, so we can't relate to one another. If you ask me whom I identify with, that's my answer for this moment." But it was a feeling of the moment and not her last word on this issue. When asked for her opinion about the main point in the text, she replied, "Jesus is there for all nations without taking into consideration if people are Jewish or Samaritan." In fact, all the members of the Macassar group stressed this point. One said, "Salvation is for everybody even though not all people are Christians, because salvation comes from Christ and is in Christ. *In Christ* means something different than *in Christianity*. We often equate salvation and Christianity."

The Macassar group noticed that Jesus makes a breakthrough and surpasses boundaries that we as people create. One student said that this task is what they as ministers will have to do. Taking on "Jesus's attitude means that when serving as a minister, I am not allowed to look first to see if someone is a Muslim or a Christian, and then give an opinion that won't be criticized by my fellow Christians. A minister is a servant of the Lord and not a servant of the congregation. He or she has to do what God says, and not what the congregation is expecting from him or her."

It is clear that in Indonesia, the story of John 4 led to a lively discussion about ethnic and religious pluralism. How did the partner groups approach this topic? Did the issue also play a role in their discussions?

In the profile of the Cuban group, the participants described themselves as blacks or whites. They compared the Samaritans to the blacks of Cuba nowadays, who are one among many marginalized groups. Members of one religious group also sometimes exclude those of another group. In spite of the apparent presence of religious and racial divisions, ethnic and religious pluralism did not seem to have been a major issue in the Cuban group's discussion of John 4.

The Dutch group touched on the issue of exclusivism but without reference to ethnic or religious pluralism in their own society. The problem they focused on was the exclusivism in the Bible story itself: John says that Jesus is the Messiah and salvation is to be found in Jesus alone. Does this not imply that people of other religions are excluded? The Dutch group associated the conflict between Jews and Samaritans with the present-day Middle East conflict between Jews and Palestinians. The issue of ethnicity and religious pluralism in Dutch society itself (with its immigrant workers, refugees, and asylum seekers) seemingly was not an issue in the group's dealing with John 4. Nor did they make any mention of the lively political debate on multiculturalism and the "threat of Islam" that came up in the Netherlands after the terrorist attacks of 11 September 2001 in the United States. They perceived no link between the Bible story and these current topics in their own society!

Ethnic and religious pluralism did not play a major role in the discussions of the Scottish group either. The report of their meeting observed, "There was no comment about outsiders from different racial and cultural backgrounds." Like the Dutch readers, they mentioned the Palestinian-Jewish conflict as an actualization of the text. They named tolerance and the truth that salvation is for all as two important things we can learn from this story. But secularization, not religious pluralism, seems to be the real challenge for the Scottish group as Christians. They were struck by the way Jesus talks openly about religion and faith and by the way the Samaritan woman readily accepts him as the Messiah. This interaction made them wonder in what way they could witness and "live out their faith in a rapidly changing and nonsupportive social context."

Although remarks on ethnic and religious pluralism are not totally absent in the reports from the partner groups, it is clear that these groups did not discuss this issue in the lively way the Macassar group did. It is true that the focus on ethnic and religious pluralism was not apparent in the group from Bandung either, but I think that we can still see this theme as characteristic of an East Indonesian way of interpreting the story in John 4.

An intercultural reading of John 4

How did the Indonesian reading groups react after receiving the reports of their partner groups? To what extent did confronting a different interpretation influence their view of the story of John 4? Unfortunately, we can only answer this question for the exchange between the Macassar group and the Warmond group from the Netherlands. As of this writing, the Bandung group and the Scottish Conversations Group had only exchanged their respective readings of John 4 but had not reported their reaction to each other. Also, in the exchange between the Macassar and Cuban groups, the Cubans replied to the second Indonesian report (a response to the

Cuban interpretation) but neglected to say what they thought about the first report (the initial Indonesian interpretation of John 4).

Approach

A nice example of intercultural influence appears in the way the groups from Warmond and Macassar reacted to each other's approach to the Bible story (the first more analytical, the latter more associative). At first, the Dutch participants were surprised and even a bit annoyed that the Macassar group didn't try to analyze the text through some kind of close reading. "We as lay people delve into this text, whereas you would expect this [deeper analysis] from them, because they are theologians!" The Dutch readers concluded that for the Indonesian group, the story obviously converged significantly with daily experiences in life and society. "They have had so many emotions when reading this story, whereas we have read the story without much commitment," someone observed. The Dutch group admitted that by analyzing the text the way they did, they had perhaps kept it too much at a distance. They longed somehow to be touched by the story as the Macassar group had been. At the same time, they felt that the historical and cultural gap between the time of the Bible and contemporary Europe could not be easily bridged.

The Macassar group at first thought that the way the Dutch partner group approached the story was too critical, and that their approach was a sign of questioning the truth of the Bible. In an Indonesian context, a congregation would surely not appreciate such a critical attitude. A later comment recognized that the Dutch approach showed their curiosity, their desire to know the real meaning of the text. "Moreover, the risk of reading our own thoughts and opinions into the text is much greater in our approach than in theirs!" The Macassar group's reaction to the thorough way the Cuban students of theology had analyzed the text of John 4 was similar: "We must pay more attention to the historical and literary background of the text and not go straight to its application in our context."

It is clear that the partner groups enriched each other and realized both strengths and shortcomings in their own approach.

The Samaritan woman as a sinner?

On the point of the alleged sinfulness of the Samaritan woman, the mutual influence of groups across cultures was less significant. The Dutch were surprised by the focus on the woman as a sinner and were not convinced by this interpretation. They thought the Indonesians' interpretation probably had more to do with their cultural norms and values than with the Bible story. They considered this interpretation conservative and moralistic. The same difference in interpretation was seen in the report from the Cuban group, which characterized the woman as rejected and marginalized rather than sinful. But the Macassar group held to their opinion that John did indeed depict the woman as guilty of adultery, and they concluded that Dutch society no longer sees having a relationship without being legally wed as a problem. This difference of opinion did not mean that the Indonesian students did not appreciate the Dutch attitude of tolerance toward people with a different lifestyle or religion. On the contrary, some thought that the Dutch stress on individual freedom and responsibility showed that the Dutch could accept and cope with ethical pluralism in a better way than they as Indonesians could.

Gospel and adat

The issue of the influence of the adat in Indonesia needed much clarification for the partner groups. The Dutch group put forward an interesting question: "Can the adat be seen as an actualization of the Christian faith?" This question was logical, because the Macassar group itself had said that reconciliation is often realized through the adat, where Christian ethics fails. The answer from the Macassar group on this question was clear: "The adat needs to be transformed and actualized by Christian faith rather than vice versa!" Seen from a historical perspective, this discussion is interesting. In colonial times, it was Dutch missionaries, among others, who criticized the adat and often tried to abolish it or at least diminish its influence. Currently, many Dutch Christians are no longer proud of the attitude their ancestors showed toward the Indonesian cultural heritage. Many express guilt when considering the Dutch colonial past in Indonesia. Surprisingly, however, it was the Indonesian study group who rejected a too-harmonious view of the relationship between adat and gospel. It is true that a destruction of the adat will rob Indonesians of their roots, but a transformation and enlightenment of the adat is necessary, they say. For this renewal the Christian faith can be important and useful. These views reverse positions taken a century ago! History has its ironies.

Ethnic and religious pluralism

After taking in information about ethnic and religious pluralism and conflict in Indonesia, the Warmond group concluded that as Dutch people they live in a more homogeneous society than do the Indonesians, with violent incidents occurring perhaps only in the big cities. This observation probably reflects the fact that almost all Muslims in the Netherlands have a foreign background. Generally speaking, there is little contact between immigrants (and their descendants) and the native Dutch inhabitants. This fact explains why the Dutch group concluded, despite their multicultural society, that the story of John 4 is closer to the Indonesian context than to the rather peaceful situation in the Netherlands.

Not surprisingly, on the subject of pluralism, the Macassar group identified with the ethnic diversity of the Cuban society more than with the Dutch. What appealed to them was the Cuban group's stress on inclusiveness and their emphasis that Bible study must have a follow-up in the deeds of Christians and the church. "Sometimes we are good at uttering words, but actually are unwilling to do what we say," some commented. But one of the Indonesian participants said that in Indonesia, Muslims often suspect that Christian charity is an effort to Christianize people, and they reject it. "Even if we do it in a sincere way, we don't get rid of this prejudice and suspicion," she added.

Without doubt, the biggest similarity between the Dutch, Cuban, Scottish, and Indonesian interpretations of John 4 was the overall stress on Jesus breaking down and stepping across ethnic and religious barriers and boundaries. All the groups agreed that this emphasis showed the direction Christians should take in their encounter with others, when confronted with ethnic, religious, and moral differences. Although between and within the groups there were differences on what Christian witness in such an encounter should entail, they at least agreed that it had to be inclusive, inviting, and loving, rather than condemning and rejecting.

Through the eyes of another

Obstacles

More convergence in the reading procedures. As I said earlier, the way Indonesian groups approached the text differed from the approach of their partner groups in other countries. Moreover, there were differences between the Dutch, Cuban, and Scottish approaches. The Dutch did not make use of any specific method but spontaneously put forward critical questions. The Cubans used a narrative method of exegesis to analyze the text. The Scottish for their part used their customary Contextual Bible Study method. To some degree, these differences are probably attributable to cultural differences.

From a methodological point of view, however, these big differences in reading procedure generate a problem, because they make it hard to determine exactly what causes differences in interpretation. Although uniform method is perhaps not desirable, it must be possible to have the different reading procedures converge more than has been the case to date. The handbook of the project proposes a procedure for reading and discussing the text, but this procedure was obviously understood and perhaps intended only as an example, not as prescriptive. In order to thoroughly analyze the reasons behind differences in interpretation, it would be good to develop a reading procedure that is attractive and usable for reading groups from different cultural backgrounds. Perhaps the Scottish CBS method[14] could be useful, because it combines close reading of the text with commitment to the message of the text. With greater similarity in the reading procedure, it would be more evident, both to the reading groups and to those who scientifically analyze the project, to what extent differences in interpretation arise from cultural differences or are simply the result of divergent methods of reading the text.

Simultaneity in the process. In high school, I learned that in water the waves made by two objects moving with the same frequency ("in phase") will become twice as high the moment they meet, whereas the same waves will fade out when the objects move with different frequencies. I think the same is true for two groups that are involved in an intercultural project of reading the Bible. When they are not "in phase," a truly intercultural reading will probably fail. We had this experience with one of our partner groups. The time that elapsed between sending our reaction and receiving theirs turned out to be too long. The initial enthusiasm for the intercultural Bible reading gradually died away, and we had problems remembering what exactly we had written to them. However, an even greater problem was the fact that our partner group apparently did not meet between receiving our first report (our interpretation of the story) and our second (the reaction to their reading). As a result, they reacted to our remarks on their interpretation without ever having formulated a reaction to our initial report. Thus, while we were still waiting for their response to our interpretation, they had already progressed to answering our reaction to their report. You could say that as partner groups we were no longer in phase. As my high school physics teacher made clear, when this happens, the two waves extinguish each other rather than stimulating each other. This experience illustrates that simultaneity in the process of intercultural Bible reading is a necessary condition for both lasting enthusiasm and ultimate success in reading the Bible through another's eyes. The chance that such simultaneity will occur is greater when a reaction to the report of the partner group is formulated as soon as possible after receiving the report.

Many possibilities

Intercultural Bible reading can be an enriching experience, as the examples above have already shown. The practice has much potential, because it is not expensive and can be realized in a quick and easy way. There is always a risk that the project will not proceed to a true intercultural reading but will get stuck in an exchange of information and thoughts only. But the examples above show that these groups from time to time did indeed read the story through the eyes of another and were influenced by each other's interpretation. Particularly in their approach to the story, the groups experienced mutual correction and enrichment.

In regard to the characterization of the Samaritan woman, differences could not be bridged. The groups agreed, however, that these differences were perhaps more a product of their respective contexts (a Western liberal culture versus an Asian culture of shame) than a result of the way John had depicted the woman. Although looking through the eyes of the other did not cause a change in point of view regarding the woman's character, at least the exchange made the participants aware that they had always looked at the text through eyes (their own!) that were conditioned by a specific culture. Enrichment in this case did not consist in widening and correcting their own perspective but in dawning awareness that their own perspective was a limited one.

Concerning the relationship between adat and gospel, the intercultural reading had the character of informing each other. This aspect of intercultural reading is important, because a better understanding of the situation the partner group lives in can free a group from misunderstandings and prejudices. This effect became clear in the exchange pertaining to adat and gospel between the two partner groups from the Netherlands and Indonesia.

Ethnic and religious pluralism is a main political issue in countries all over the world. It is vitally important that Christians from different countries and ethnic groups share their thoughts and experiences about pluralism. Perhaps if the Dutch partner group had reflected on multiculturalism in their own society, the intercultural exchange around this topic would have been more fruitful.

Epilogue

Of course, it is not just an intercultural Bible reading project that makes us realize the great influence of our cultural background on our interpreting the Bible. But the extra value of this project is that it helps people experience this reality, instead of just thinking or reading about it. The project gives participants the opportunity not only to hear about others but also to take a look through other eyes. In that way, they see different and new things in Bible stories that may be very familiar. Of course, the eyes of Indonesians will and must remain Indonesian eyes. Nor will Dutch, Cuban, or Scottish eyes be replaced by those of others. Yet how special it is when these eyes, just for a moment, manage to look through the eyes of another and see things they would never have discovered otherwise!

Notes

[1] See, for example, the discussion of the merging of horizons in Hans-Georg Gadamer, *Truth and Method*, trans. and rev. Joel Weinsheimer and Donald G. Marshall (New York: Crossroad, 1989), 300–307, esp. 306–307.

[2] Melanie Budianta, "Multiculturalism: In Search of a Framework for Managing Diversity in Indonesia" (lecture, workshop on Multicultural Education in Asian Nations: Sharing Experiences, Jakarta, 2003), 6.

[3] Walter J. Ong, *Orality and Literacy: The Technologizing of the Word* (London and New York: Methuen, 1982), 9.

[4] Ibid., 9.

[5] Ibid., 39.

[6] Ibid., 41.

[7] Ibid., 46.

[8] Ibid., 74.

[9] E. G. Singgih, "Let Me Not Be Put to Shame: Towards an Indonesian Hermeneutics," *Asian Journal of Theology* 9 (1995): 77.

[10] Ibid., 78.

[11] Ibid., 73.

[12] Ibid., 78.

[13] Ibid., 71.

[14] The Contextual Bible Study consists of a set of fixed open questions, for example: What jumps out of the page at you from this text? What are the key issues that arise in the passage? What are the main parallels between this text and your situation in your own particular and religious context today? If Jesus is reaching out to each of us here through this encounter tonight, is there something you are being called to do when you go back to your people?

Unresolved tensions and the way forward

Eric Anum

The anticipation of the intercultural Bible reading project is set out in the initial document, "Through the Eyes of the Another: Reading the Bible Interculturally: Between Fact and Challenge: An Empirical Hermeneutical Research Project."[1] The concept envisions missionary possibilities for achieving intercultural dialogue on faith, through ordinary people from different cultures and locations reading Bible stories together and developing an empirical hermeneutic involving interculturality.

While reading through reports and responses from many linkage groups, I discovered that tensions had developed and remain unresolved. These tensions issued from queries, surprises, clarifications, shocks, and disappointments.

First, I have observed tensions with regard to facilitation styles. One senses that in some instances no one was in charge, so the reading was allowed to take its own course. Linkage groups in such situations felt that the reading ended before they were able to achieve something worth sharing with others. One group commented, for example, that "we cannot make head or tail of this reading." In other cases everything was structured, with leading questions and directives for the reading to go on. This regimentation produced a reading process that tended to stifle new movements or shifts. A third possibility also existed, one that seems to suggest a draconian facilitator who controlled the reading process, propelling it with very strong hands. I want to consider how the tension resulting from different facilitation styles affected the reading process and product, and what the implications are for the project as a whole.

The second type of unresolved tension, which I deduced from observing the interchange of readings by various groups participating in the project, is hermeneutical. These tensions related to approaches to interpreting and applying the text.

Eric Anum, Department of Religious Studies, University of Cape Coast (Cape Coast, Ghana)

They are illustrated by the reaction of one group to their counterpart. The group stated bluntly that exegesis should be differentiated from eisegesis: "If we have to analyze a text from the Bible, we should not go straight to its application. We must study the background before applying it to our situation." This group believed their counterparts had not followed this approach, which they called the "hermeneutical interpretation," and had instead applied the text to their context/experience without studying its background. For this group and others of a similar mind-set, in order to do proper interpretation of a particular text, one has "to start from Palestine . . . and bring it down to our culture," because "you can't just start to say things referring to your culture. The people will not believe the Bible." This tension surrounds how one gets into the text and begins to give meaning to its content: Do we always have to start interpreting a biblical text by reading behind the text and reading the text itself before coming to read in front of the text?

Other groups challenged this approach, characterizing it as conventional. One such group asserted that another group's report was "like a sermon written by a professional preacher for Sundays." The group wondered, "Did they have an actual discussion on it in a group?" They seemed to be making a distinction between preparing a sermon and engaging in Bible study together with others.

These diverging concerns, when they encounter each other, are likely to result in unresolved tension. Groups choose one approach or the other from their own situations and out of traditions of interpretation that they deem relevant, accessible, and capable of application in their sociocultural, religious (Christian) context. Some see conforming to a strict exegetical structure commended by one group as landing one in the situation described by the second group: preparing a well-structured message from a text in a manner normally done by preachers. But if one merely relates the text directly to one's own context without making an effort to understand its background, one risks short-circuiting. One is likely to end up with what one group termed "forced interpretation," imposing one's own views on the text.

Each approach has dangers if it is carried to an extreme. For instance, closely related to the first approach is the one that aimed at a "disengaged, informative position and not from own experience," which tried to deemphasize subjectivity and emphasize objectivity in the hermeneutical process. Some criticized this approach as too abstract and passive, saying that the best way to benefit from this text is to experience it as a group. Typical of this perspective was the comment, "They could not get into the story because they did not experience it." The tension here was with those who claim experience and context play a major role in the hermeneutical process. However, others believe that experience can impede the reading process if it is relied on too much, because the subjectivity of experience has the potential to overshadow criticality and objectivity.

In what follows, I will focus on the problem of unresolved tensions in two selected groups. I will look at their approaches to the text with regard to their tradition of interpretation, strategies of interpretation, contextualization of the text, and appropriation of the text. Then I will look at unresolved tensions arising from their differing approaches to the text, as these tensions are given expression in the reaction to the first reading report from the linkage group.

To achieve this goal, I decided to look at two groups who have completed the first two phases of the project. These groups have sent their first report and have also received a report from their linkage group; in addition, they and their linkage group have responded to the reactions from each other. This approach enables me to take note not only of the tensions but also to see the responses to them, and further, to evaluate the reasons why the tensions were expressed and what their implications are for the project as a whole.

I selected two groups from Africa: Elmina men's group in Ghana, and Port Harcourt University group in Nigeria. I also selected their partner groups: Grupo Lectura Pastoral de la Biblia in Peru, and the Matanzas group from Cuba in the Caribbean, who were linked to the Port Harcourt University group and Elmina men's group respectively. I selected these groups because I am interested in the unresolved tensions that come out of the intercultural exercise when groups in Africa link with groups from other geographical locations, and other sociocultural and political contexts. I will begin with looking at the exchange between the partner groups of Port Harcourt University in Nigeria, West Africa, and Grupo Lectura Pastoral de la Biblia, in Lima, Peru, South America.

Approaches to the text—Port Harcourt University group, Nigeria

Tradition of interpretation

In their first reading report, the Port Harcourt University group states that they read the text "from the African cultural perspective. To this end, one person is chosen to prepare the textual portion or verses that underscore aspects of African cultural values and practices." One can deduce from this statement that the group's tradition of interpretation is inculturation.

Their use of this tradition of interpretation may be attributable to their level of engagement in African theology. Indeed, these postgraduate students are likely to have insight into inculturation theology and how it works with respect to biblical interpretation. For example, the group's ritual of bringing items that are in line with ancestral worship to the meeting is related to African traditional religion. They also brought items, such as candles, that come out of Christian tradition. But what is crucial is their emphasis on life and their attempt to see concepts of the Christian life revealed symbolically and ritually within the African cultural context. The essence of these objects taken together creates the appropriate environment for the group's reading. The objects they used were items of everyday life within their cultural context, which also served to enhance their inculturation interpretive tradition.

Another factor affecting the group's tradition of interpretation was the membership of the group. Perhaps the composition of the group, which is mixed or ecumenical in nature (from different religious backgrounds and belonging to different

Christian denominations—Catholics, Anglicans, Presbyterians, and charismatics), made it easier to adopt this interpretive tradition, because no particular denomination maintained external control and expected adherence to that church's tradition of interpretation. They may also have adopted this tradition of interpretation because they are academics—open-minded intellectuals and postgraduate students from the University of Port Harcourt.

In sum, and as noted in an appreciative comment by their linkage group, the Port Harcourt group has evolved a tradition of interpretation based on cultural values within their own context.

Strategy of interpretation

A problem emerges in the relationship between the tradition of interpretation and the strategy of interpretation. The Port Harcourt group may have been conversant with the concept of inculturation, but they faced a challenge in appropriating it as an exegetical tool. Their linkage group found it strange that postgraduate students reported doing biblical exegesis for the first time; it has been easier for the inculturation movement to adopt symbols and rituals in inculturating the gospel in Africa but much more difficult for Africans to interpret the Bible using inculturation interpretive technique. So although the group had already incorporated symbolic acts into their practices, the intercultural Bible reading project likely offered an opportunity to take a step further in adopting inculturation hermeneutics,[2] through applying it to the story in John 4 concerning Jesus and the woman of Samaria.

Their linkage group regarded the Nigerian group's interpretive strategy as original, and they commended them for it. It brought to the Latin American group extra dimensions to the concept of ancestorhood, for example, for although the Peruvians prayed to their ancestors, they had not seen the concept of ancestorhood as key to the interpretation of the story of Jesus and the Samaritan woman. When the Port Harcourt group described ancestors as the "living dead," the Peruvians were enlightened about the linkage between the continuity of life and ancestorhood.

Because the Nigerian group was using inculturation hermeneutics, they identified certain cultural concepts in the Nigerian context to use as gateways into the text. They selected ancestorhood, hospitality, motherhood/womanhood, polygamy, and caste discrimination. The group therefore focused on the verses they felt were related to each of these concepts, which they termed "African values."

Contextualization of the text

The group read the text within the Nigerian context. How did they do this, and why did they decide to do so? The items that members brought to the meeting, part of their process of reading the text in their own context, were objects of ritual worship in African traditional religion. These items, such as cowries and cooking pots, were ritually presented at the beginning of the Bible study to set the tone for contextual reading of the text.

It is therefore no coincidence that one of the African values that they selected for interpretation of the text was ancestorhood, as the items of worship they presented were regarded as items acceptable to the ancestors. Specifically, seeing Christ as proto-ancestor is one of the contemporary ways that biblical interpreters working in African contexts contextualize christology. One reason this way of looking at the text appealed to the Nigerian group is the reference to Jacob as ancestor and to the well as given to the Samaritans by their ancestors. Another reason is the woman's words, "Our ancestors worshiped on this mountain" (John 4:20). These elements of the text resonate with the Nigerians' concept of ancestorhood. Because inculturation hermeneutics moves from context to text, the group capitalized on the reference to ancestors to embark on their interpretation of the text, moving to discuss Christ as ancestor of Africans.

The group was able to do this contextualization because they are African academics and theologians conversant with the concept of Christ as our ancestor, as developed in African theology. This concept is specifically articulated by Benezet Bujo in *African Theology in Its Social Context*; he argues that Christ is our proto-ancestor, our ancestor *par excellence,* the source of life, the highest order of ancestors.[3]

The five-husband aspect of the story invited the group to contextualize the text with respect to another cultural concept, polygamy. They considered the story in light of a social reality in perhaps most African contexts, the plight of women who are married into polygamous situations and who suffer a lot in their communities. The group regarded this polygamy as dehumanizing for women. Their discussion indicates awareness of current debates in their context concerning marriage. The group saw the discussion between Jesus and the woman about her husbands as a point through which they could read the text in their contemporary context.

In regard to the Nigerian cultural concept of caste discrimination, the Osu caste system in Igboland in Nigeria offered the framework for the Port Harcourt group to relate to the discrimination against Samaritans by the Jews and also to their society's discrimination against women.

Appropriation of the text

The group claimed that the text ought to be taken to indicate the mission of Christ: to bring not only men but also women to the true knowledge of God. In their estimation, women in Africa are ignorant and lack knowledge because most of them have not attended school. Such ignorance should be dealt with by empowering the women of Africa to see themselves as having the potential to influence their society as the Samaritan woman did. Through her, Samaritans were brought face to face with Christ, which led to their transformation.

Although the participants were all male, their attitude to the text was sympathetic toward the cause of the African woman. In their appropriation of the text, they stated that the Samaritan woman typifies the contemporary African woman who is marginalized by the patriarchal cultural that she operates in. The group however stressed that women in Africa have the potential to change their world if given education, resources, and opportunity. For this, the woman of Samaria provides a role model, both in what she receives from Christ and in the way she brings change to her society. The group also called for the rejection of polygamy as a cultural practice in Africa.

The group equated their rejection of the Osu caste system in Igboland with Christ's rejection of the stigmatization of Samaritans. In the story, ethnic barriers were broken, and many Samaritans came face to face with Christ. In appropriating this text, the Nigerian group suggested a need to confront the Osu caste system in Igboland. In their application of the text, they note that both the freeborn Diala and the oppressed Osu are to be seen as equal; there should be no discrimination.

The group's approach to the text seems to stem from their concept of Christ as proto-ancestor. Although this approach uses inculturation theology, its appropriation by this group is based on a kind of transcendental theology. In their economy of interpretation, Christ their ancestor transcends every culture, and therefore every cultural practice or norm has to be subjected to Christ. So, for instance, if Christ gave women education or knowledge, resources, and opportunity, when their culture withholds these things from women, they should discard that aspect of their culture. If their culture discriminates through a caste system, then Christians should do something to confront that system, because Christ does not approve of a culture that discriminates in that way.

This transcendental theology is more pronounced when it comes to the issue of polygamy. Here the group condemns polygamy; Christ's prescription of monogamy transcends the cultural practice of polygamy, so polygamy must not be practiced.

Unresolved tensions—From Lima to Port Harcourt

Regarding tradition of interpretation and interpretive strategies, the partner group in Peru, Grupo Lectura Pastoral de la Biblia, voiced no unresolved tensions. They only remarked that the other group's interpretation was different from theirs and commented that the differences were probably the result of cultural differences between them. However, the areas of contextualization and appropriation did reveal many unresolved tensions.

Contextualization of the text

The tensions that stood out were those related to the Osu caste system, to polygamy, and to womanhood/motherhood. With regard to the discussion about the Osu caste system, which evolved out of the African contextualization of marginalization, the Peruvians were not sure where to place their Port Harcourt counterparts. They wondered if the Nigerians were speaking out on behalf of the voiceless, or if some of the group were from the Osu caste. Were the Port Harcourt participants pursuing advocacy or liberation? A linkage between this caste system and discrimination might exist, but who were the sufferers, and where did the members of this particular Bible study group fit in the economy of things? What could they do from their standpoint to contend with this discrimination?

The Peruvians also picked up the issue of polygamy. They felt that the tradition of interpretation their counterparts had used here was not inculturation, but was like fundamentalism and "harsh moralizing." They found it strange that the Nigerian group completely rejected polygamy on the basis of this biblical text. They saw this conclusion as inconsistent, because earlier, when the Port Harcourt group was contextualizing ancestorhood, they had retained room for the beliefs and practices of non-Christian adherents to African traditional religion; yet the Nigerians had no room for Christians who were involved in the traditional practice of polygamy.

This issue led the Lima group to raise the fundamental question of whether the encounter between the gospel and culture results in complete rejection of the culture or in its purification or transformation. A complex interplay of considerations seemed to drive the Nigerians' contextualization of this text with reference to polygamy. These included the influence of the missionary heritage of the participants (which entails monogamy), Western theology (with which most of the participants were nurtured), and transcendental theology (dealt with above). Most of the participants belong to mainline missionary churches, so it comes as no surprise that, despite their inculturation hermeneutical stance, on certain issues they almost seemed to abandon their inculturation interpretive tradition, take up a "dogmatically correct" interpretation, and then find scriptural support to back it. As Gerald West has observed, whenever questions about issues such as polygamy are put to ordinary readers in Bible study groups, "the first response is often the 'missionary response' or the 'dogmatically correct' response."[4] Perhaps that tendency is why the Peruvians wondered whether in this case the Nigerians were not proof-texting or forcing contextualization down the throat of the Johannine text, which the Lima group thought had nothing at all to do with polygamy.

The Peruvian group detected a contradiction in the contextualization of womanhood by their counterparts in Port Harcourt. In their contextualization of the text, the Nigerian group held up the Samaritan woman as the great apostle of ancestorhood, yet later, under the discussion related to womanhood, the same readers portrayed the woman as marginalized, with a pathetic, pitiful, and inferior status. The unresolved tensions here are twofold. First, do these images reflect group members' differing perspectives on the woman, which have been thrown in together although they contradict each other? Or could these differing perspectives reflect views of the woman before and after her encounter with Christ? Second, the Peruvians wondered whether the contextualization of the woman as inferior is intrinsic in the text or rather reflects the cultural values of the participants; perhaps certain African values have influenced their interpretation of the text.

When Bible study reports provide only a summary of the discussion, one either loses some of the diversity of views that were presented, or the report contains contradictory views because the group will not agree on every point. As the Port

Harcourt report stands, we cannot deduce whether group members held differing perspectives of women that they were trying to express or whether the report just reflects incoherence in the group's portrayal of womanhood.

With respect to the second tension—whether the woman's inferiority is intrinsic to the text or reflects the values of readers—it seems to me to be a tension that the Port Harcourt people themselves raised when they indicated a concern about their partner's view of the moral status of the woman. They questioned a view of the woman as having high moral authority, as they themselves held the contrary view. Perhaps the pluriform or multifaceted nature of biblical interpretation has resulted in this tension. As they read the biblical text, the Peruvians may hear something entirely different from what the original hearers of this text heard, and the people of Port Harcourt may hear something entirely different from what the Peruvians heard. However, the question that the Peruvians raised is, How much of this difference is attributable to cultural biases of the Port Harcourt readers, and how much is not their biases but arises from the scriptures? We will revisit this question in the next section on appropriation of the text.

Appropriation of the text

Here the appropriation of motherhood for women came to the fore, an issue that called into question the Port Harcourt group's contextualization process. The Peruvians wondered how much the issue of motherhood arises from the text at stake and how much the African or Nigerian cultural perspective colored this appropriation of the text. It is interesting that the Peruvians questioned their own elevation of the status of the woman in their reading, by asking whether in their contextualization process they were not also yielding to their cultural bias, of women's emancipation and liberation. This question was appropriate, because the Port Harcourt participants also asked it, as we uncovered earlier in noting their unresolved tension concerning the social status of the Samaritan woman as possessing moral authority.

Can any reading be free of cultural bias or influence? If we grant that cultural biases inevitably exist, because the text comes to us with its own such bias, how do we ensure that our interpretation of the text is not overwhelmed by our cultural biases? Further, how do we open up our contextual readings so as to enable effective intercultural and cross-cultural dialogue through the reading of biblical texts as we together encounter such unresolved tensions in our attempt to exchange our readings?

Approaches to the text—Grupo Lectura Pastoral de la Biblia, Lima, Peru
Tradition of interpretation

The Peruvian group clearly indicated their interpretive tradition in their response to their linkage group, by saying that they were interested in the social and historical setting of the text and not necessarily in the moral and theological aspect. They used a social analytic interpretive technique. They indicated that before they start dealing with a text, they normally locate it within their own social context. Typically, biblical interpretation in a Latin American context does not overlook the sociopolitical and economic context. This tradition of interpretation may be attributable to the composition of the group; they are biblical scholars, people with reading skills who can choose any of the scholarly interpretive traditions available to them.

Strategies of interpretation

As this group approached a particular text, they used a series of questions intended to locate the text in its historical, literary, geographical, and social setting. This approach is natural, given the group's interpretive skills and sociocultural context. These historical, literary, geographical, and social elements are implied when the group talks of the world behind the text. They looked at the literary context of the text by noting key words and key themes. This approach then led to focus on the relationship between the text and God, and between the text and Christ. The group used questions to encourage the participants to discuss the issues critically, thus enabling them to identify new dimensions that the text brings to their understanding of God and Jesus Christ. These dimensions are crucial because the group needed to be sure about where God's influence and Jesus's influence could be located within the text. The influence of both with respect to the communities and people in the story was critical to interpreting the text.

However, to start off, the group made a social analysis of the place of women within their own political and sociocultural context, and of the status of women in the church. Perhaps because of their own projection, they had concluded that the text has to do with the interaction between a woman and her social context. This preliminary step served a crucial purpose, especially when it came to the appropriation of the text, because it made a connection between the strategies of interpreting and contextualizing the text.

Contextualization of the text

In bringing the text into their own context, they used the word *illumination* to indicate the aspects of their context that they might enlighten with the text. The first such aspect is the marginalization of women among theologians. The group contextualized the role played by the woman of Samaria by saying that the story brings to the fore the realization that "women can do theology." In other words, when women are given the opportunity, they do contribute to the development of theological reflection in their contexts. This realization provides illumination for the area of advocacy and emancipation of women within the context of the church hierarchy and leadership, as well as on theological faculties and commissions.

A second aspect for illumination is in the area of the relationships among Christians in their context. The example of the Samaritan woman is projected to reflect tolerance, sensitivity, and patience toward those who belong to other faiths (reflecting a pluralistic church) and also to encourage dialogue with those who belong to other churches or denominations. These ways of contextualizing the text reflect the constitution of Grupo Lectura Pastoral de la Biblia, which functions as a national coordinating group. Although they have Catholic loyalties, they need to conscientize Catholic church members toward tolerance so that they will not create problems for and will be more accommodating toward those who are not Catholic.

A third opportunity for illumination the group sees in the text is a call to evangelize. That is, the text is about creating the strong desire to undertake mission, because that is what Christ did in this text.

In analyzing these three aspects for illumination, one realizes they are directly related to a consciousness that needs to be created in the community in one way or the other. Church members need to be conscientized regarding the potentialities of women in the community, and regarding their attitude toward the people in the church and their responsibility toward those outside the church. The Lima group also brought in inculturation as one of the ways of contextualizing the text in their midst. I do not see how it fits into their general and specific ways of bringing the text home. Inculturation deals with cultural values, practices, and norms, but this interest is otherwise completely missing from the group's economy of things. However, in looking at all the ways above, I note that they all have to do with reflecting on the text at the community level within their context.

Being biblical scholars, the group then turned their attention to reflection at the critical level, returning to discuss the influence of God on them as persons who are aware of the danger of limiting faith to one's own dogmatic understanding of doctrines and excluding the individual encounter with God. Because of the separation of theological study from the church, one can be an outstanding theologian and yet have little or no direct experience of motivation from God to do certain things in behalf of the Christian community. Specifically, as biblical scholars, they recognized the challenge they feel to use their reading skills to produce "boring homilies." Critically contextualizing this text challenges biblical scholars to be certain that they can ask for "water" from each other. Here they are probably alluding to personal experience or influence of Christ as the Samaritan woman experienced him. We should be ready to share this experience with each other.

They also call for simplicity in pointing people to the living water that comes from Christ, so that others will receive their own experience of him. Here their critical reflection backs up the community consciousness that we have already talked about. The main concern of this group was not to limit themselves to being hermeneuts of the Bible but to become people who use the Bible to guide themselves as a scholarly community and perhaps also to show others the authentic and lasting source of Christianity, the living water.

Appropriation of the text

The concept of sharing became paramount to the group with respect to the appropriation of this text. The charge to go and share with others what they have learned from the intercultural Bible reading project was a good first step, because these biblical scholars have the tendency to keep what they learn among themselves and in their associations, institute, and conferences. The challenge is to go and share the product of such meetings with others and not merely to say, "It was a good meeting," "So-and-so gave a very good paper," or "We had a very good discussion." The theologians' seriousness was displayed symbolically in their sharing of fresh water with each other. Sometimes, words alone cannot communicate the import of a message. Symbols can be used effectively to carry the message home to people. This symbolic passing of fresh water had the effect of committing them as individuals and as a group to doing what they have resolved to go and do.

As a national entity, they also mentioned their commitment to participate in and collaborate with a specific body, the Commission of the Truth, which is working in their respective areas. This seems to be a specific action plan of the group.

Unresolved tensions—From Port Harcourt to Lima

The unresolved tensions in approach to the text were mainly related to the tradition of interpretation, strategies of interpretation, and the contextualization of the text.

Tradition of interpretation

According to the Port Harcourt group, the tradition of interpretation that has influenced the way their linkage group saw the text was liberation theology, while theirs has been inculturation theology. Perhaps this project has indicated that the old tension between liberation interpretive tradition and inculturation remains unresolved. Yet the Peruvians mentioned inculturation as one of the concepts they have appropriated as a result of taking part in this project. And the Port Harcourt group, in addressing identification with the text, mentioned that they were employing the liberation motif to interpret the Osu caste system with respect to their interpretation of John 4:9–10.

Could it be that both groups now understand an interpretive tradition that is not their own? Or did they just toss the other tradition in, paying lip service to it? Are liberation and inculturation interpretive traditions mutually exclusive, or can they be inclusive? I suppose most people will say the latter. As Justin Ukpong notes, the new direction in inculturation lies in the broadening of the realm of operation to include the combination of the sociological and the anthropological realms of life. Therefore "its goal [is] the transformation of the existential, social, political, economic and religious life of the people."[5] However, this tension seems to have resurfaced in this project, which means that intercultural encounters will require work to integrate inculturation and liberation.

Strategies of interpretation

The main tension in interpretive strategies between the two groups was around the social status of the Samaritan woman. The Peruvian group's strategy of interpretation gave the woman a high standing. They held that if she were not a woman of high social standing and if she did not possess moral authority, the people of Sychar would not have followed her when she went to proclaim the message to them. The Port Harcourt group felt that this thinking reflected a feminist stance, which was the outcome of their linkage group's involvement in liberation theology. The Port Harcourt group felt that women whom society has judged as prostitutes or gossips, or otherwise labeled negatively, would never be accorded moral authority. The Port Harcourt group wondered why the people of Sychar and other cultures would accord high social status to a woman who is a moral misfit. Further, the Nigerian group thought that boldness to carry information or to witness does not imply moral authority; they attribute her witness to her courage and not to high social or moral status.

This unresolved tension regarding the woman's status emerged not only between these two groups. Other groups passed moral judgment on the woman by saying she was a woman of low moral standing, branding her as a prostitute. That she was a prostitute is implied in the Port Harcourt group's placement of the woman with women whose communities have condemned them, in one way or another. Some groups also felt that the woman had high status, because one cannot prove from her having been with five men that she was a prostitute. So this tension remained unresolved not only for these two groups but also for other groups.

The second issue around strategies of interpretation was the issue of the relationship in Jesus's teaching between physical hunger and thirst, and poverty. Although the Port Harcourt group agreed with the perception of physical deprivation, they also believed that the physical need is interrelated with spiritual poverty. Their worldview looks at life as consisting of both physical and spiritual aspects that are interrelated and inseparable, because they affect each other.

The African mind-set believes that every physical occurrence has a spiritual linkage. Therefore, the two must be seen together, because they have an impact on each other. Perhaps this tension remains unresolved because people from other cultures find this mind-set difficult to take in. Where people are looking for scientific ways of explaining their predicaments, one cannot easily resort to spiritual means for answers. On the other hand, perhaps some issues for which people seek scientific answers have a spiritual linkage that could be used to solve the problem.

Contextualization and appropriation of the text

The Port Harcourt group did not have much to say about the contextualization of the text by the Peruvians, because they felt that the context of the Peruvians influenced the way they interpreted the text. The Peruvians also made this point.

In appropriation of the text, the Port Harcourt group mentioned no unresolved tensions.

Before I conclude, I turn my attention to the other two groups that I looked at, to see whether their story is different. These groups were the Elmina men's group from Ghana, West Africa, and the Matanzas group from Cuba.

Approaches to the text—Elmina men's group, Ghana

Tradition of interpretation

The tradition of reading the Bible for the Elmina men's group is one of using open questions that enable them to identify and address issues in the story that are of interest to them. The questions provide them with a semistructured guide to elicit the group's understanding of the text and to name what they feel is the text's main focus (or foci). In identifying a focus, group members are entirely free to identify any themes they choose. After identifying themes, a second question asks them to look for connections with their own context, in order to locate these themes within it. As a third step, they indicate how they as a community are going to appropriate the text directly. The questions therefore enable the group to enter the text and to progress in reading it without getting locked up at one point or another. In their approach to the text, one notices a certain spiritual and pietistic influence, reflective of their Presbyterian affiliation. This influence comes out in their responses to the key questions.

Strategies of interpretation

In the Elmina men's group, the text is read aloud by a few people who can read fluently and clearly enough for all of them to follow. After the reading, the first question is asked.

Usually, the first question draws responses that are abstract and sound "spiritual": "No matter your degree of sin, God still recognizes you." "We must do our best to seek the kingdom of God, and all other things shall be added unto you." "We have observed that the message of God is spiritual food which feeds us forever without hunger." However, when they discuss the second question, locating the text in their own context, participants make comments that are more concrete: "The passage teaches us the need to reconcile with those who are at loggerheads with us."

Contextualization of the text

The second question is related to contextualization of the text. The group related the John 4 text to marriage and specifically explored the issue of polygamy. They make concrete statements: "We realize that as Christians, we are not to marry more than one wife"; "Christian women must insist that they do not become second wives, no matter the circumstance." In this stage, the group starts narrowing their interpretation to what appeals to them. They then have more elaborate discussions on this topic.

Appropriation of the text

This tradition of interpretation develops a concrete action plan, ensuring that the reading group does not become mere talking shop. Although individuals may appropriate the text, the group as a reading community feels a need to think of ways of appropriating the text communally. The group looks at their contextualization of the text and decides what action they would like to take in appropriating the text together. In this case, because the main issue at stake for them in this text was marriage, the action plan was to promote marriage fidelity among themselves. They also decided to form a group to monitor and counsel those who are involved in adulterous relationships, which for them includes polygamy or marrying two wives, which they condemned.

Unresolved tensions—From Matanzas to Elmina

Matanzas indicated that they had no problems with the Elmina men's group's tradition of interpretation and strategies of interpretation. They indicated that this lack of tension was because they and their partner group had similar ways of handling the text. This conclusion is strange, because the two groups seem to have quite different traditions and strategies of interpretation, as one can observe in their styles. Perhaps the outcomes of the Elmina group's interpretation were agreeable to Matanzas although they arrived at these conclusions by different approaches. The only similarity of approach was that both groups used summaries in reporting their readings.

Contextualization of the text

The Matanzas group commented that the cultural differences between the two groups might have had a great influence on the differences with respect to the contextualization of the text. Matanzas indicated that the contextualization that sets monogamy against polygamy and chooses the latter was a shock to them. They commented that this choice of contextualization must be an uphill task for Elmina because, as the Matanzas group understood it, polygamy is an intrinsic part of the African culture of the Elmina group.

Appropriation of the text

In appropriation of the text, the Matanzas group again picked up on the concept of polygamy and expressed an unresolved tension. It was difficult for them to understand why the Elmina group decided to impose on themselves a commitment not to be involved in polygamy and to sanction any among them who get involved in it. The Matanzas group felt that this restriction would conflict with the real life situation of the Elmina group.

This tension concerning polygamy surfaced in other groups who linked with African groups (e.g., Port Harcourt and their Peruvian counterparts, Abetifi in Ghana and their Feitoria counterparts in Brazil). The groups outside Africa do not see how this text links to polygamy, and they cannot understand why their African counterparts introduce strong sanctions against polygamists. As one group put it, African polygamy can be understood as "responsible" when compared with illegal multiple relations in other contexts. However, for the Elmina group, the rights of the woman and the predicament of women in polygamous marriages were what drove the appropriation process with respect to women. The group, whether rightly or wrongly, seems to link polygamous men and adultery.

Approaches to the text—Matanzas group of Cuba

Tradition of interpretation

The tradition of interpretation of the Matanzas group of Cuba is a combination of historical and literary approaches to the biblical text.[6] As adherents to this tradition, the group located the text within its historical setting. Using the literary tradition, the group analyzed the literary pattern of the text, examining key words and the forms in which they occur, key themes, characters, and verbs used in the text. This process prepared the way for an analysis of the story, doing justice to almost every verse.

Strategies of interpretation

The group divided the story into sections and then reconstructed or retold the entire story as they understood it, moving through it from beginning to end. The participants seemed to be creating a running commentary on the story as it progressed. This interpretive strategy, which combines retelling or reconstructing the story in a group and at the same time interpreting it in one's own words, fits Musa Dube's description of "communal interpretation," assuming that "a story well told is a story well interpreted."[7] The interpretation depends to a large extent on effective cooperative negotiation of its meaning, summarized by the group in their report.

The main components of the story, as analyzed by the group, were Jesus as the main character and his interactions with the woman of Samaria, how Jesus handled prejudices, and how Jesus broke what the group referred to as "schemes." The minor characters in the story were the disciples, the Samaritans, and the Jews.

Contextualization of the text

The Matanzas group noted that living water, crucial for human survival, was used literally and also as a symbol for Jesus's dialogue with the woman. Because water is essential for all humankind, it provided a relevant starting point for Jesus in his conversation with the woman. The group also identified the woman (and not Philip) as the first missionary to the Samaritans but remarked that the woman's missionary work was not so acknowledged because of the prevalence of androcentric cultural values at that time.

Appropriation of the text

Although it is difficult to carry the message to remote places, the group affirmed that with the cars that we have, we should be able to reach remote parts with the message, following Jesus's example in going to difficult places with the message. The group also found in the text a call to emulate Jesus by being good listeners as well as identifying and solving people's problems. Also, the most effective way of evangelizing is by our testimony, following the example of the woman of Samaria. They noted that worshiping God is not necessarily limited to performances, music, and clapping of hands, but, as Jesus told the Samaritan woman, it involves worship in spirit and in truth.

The group identified schemes of prejudice that still exist, and they saw the woman of Samaria as a symbol of discrimination. Those affected by discrimination include people who are handicapped, old, low-income, or alcoholic. Because excluded people cannot fight for themselves, the group concluded that they have a duty to fight for equity for such people, as Jesus fought for the Samaritan woman. Lastly, they noted that marginalized and excluded people have the potential to save lives and contribute to society if empowered and given the opportunity. They can be powerful instruments of God, so Christians must give them the chance by getting closer to them, listening to them, and sharing with them.

Unresolved tensions—From Elmina to Matanzas

Tradition of interpretation

The Elmina group was not too sure about an interpretive tradition that pays so much attention to analyzing the literature of the text, to the point of identifying verbs. They would like to know what bearing that approach has on the interpretation and appropriation of the text. They seem to feel that such an approach to the text is of no use. This tension remains unresolved.

Strategies of interpretation

The Ghanaian group also did not understand why the Cuban group attempted to read the text in blocks and went through it almost verse by verse. They wanted to know how this strategy affects the reading and why the Cuban group decided to read that way. This tension also remains unresolved.

I surmise that these first two unresolved tensions have to do with the format groups adopted in reading the text. Some reading formats might be conventions of the groups to which we belong, and perhaps have been used for decades. Although these traditions seem effective and appropriate to our groups, as a result of intercultural interchange, we will need to revisit the rationale behind the adoption of a particular tradition or strategy for reading texts.

Contextualization of the text

The Elmina group challenged the Cuban group's point that Jesus was breaking barriers by talking to a woman; they wondered whether, when one has a particular status, one can decide whom to talk to and whom not to talk to. Sometimes, according to the Elmina group, one might not like speaking to a particular person, or sometimes one's society will decide for one whom one should talk to and whom one should not talk to. The group wondered whether human nature rather than culture determines whom one likes to and does not like to talk to; in that case the disciples' surprise that Jesus was talking to a woman in John 4:27 might be the result of their human nature rather than cultural differences.

The Elmina group also wondered why the Matanzas group did not comment on the woman's leaving the jar; they sense that this element is crucial to this passage. They understand that the woman leaving her jar means she has been converted. To talk about the woman becoming an evangelist, according to Elmina, one has to first talk about her conversion, about her leaving behind what she formerly used. The group's view is that without conversion, one cannot give genuine witness.

The Elmina group also felt the Matanzas group seemed to condemn the manner of worship in the Ghanaian church and specifically at their intercultural Bible reading project meetings. In particular, they condemned singing, clapping, and drumming as unacceptable ways of worship. An acceptable way of worship, as suggested by Matanzas, was to "adore God in truth." This tension is not resolved, for although the Matanzas group did contextualize John 4:23–24 as "adore God in truth," they did not indicate in practical terms how such adoration would be carried out, nor did they explain why drumming, clapping, and dancing are not adorable to God in truth.

The Ghanaian group also felt that the food and water Jesus was talking about was not literally physical food but rather spiritual food and drink: Jesus did not need food or water. He waited at the well because he was expecting the woman, not because he wanted food and water.

Appropriation of the text

The Elmina group felt that the conversation between Jesus and the woman centered on marriage. As men, they were interested in how they could in practical ways treat women properly, because men had made the life of the woman of Samaria miserable. They were surprised that marriage did not feature at all in their counterpart's reading of the text.

The way forward

As I noted at the beginning of this article, this project sets out to explore the hermeneutical gains that will accrue from a massive engagement in intercultural hermeneutics. Despite all the excitement and all the lessons learned, we also have had shocks, surprises, disappointments, misunderstandings, and disagreements. In addition, we have had what I term unresolved tension in the approaches to reading the text used by four selected groups. The question I raise now is, What suggestions can we make for the way forward in handling these kinds of unresolved tensions for the project as a whole? The remaining section outlines a few suggestions.

Continue the dialogue

The linkage program of the intercultural Bible reading project has generated dialogue between many groups, including the groups that I selected. As is characteristic of most dialogues between groups, this dialogue has included an element of suspicion and tension. This tension is especially to be expected when dialogue is intercultural, between groups from different continents, cultures, and geographical locations. I believe that this tension is just one of the steps toward developing a clear understanding of others' way of interpreting and appropriating biblical texts. Now that the project has begun and has reached the tension stage, it would be most appropriate to enable the dialogue to continue. This continued conversation would give the groups opportunity to further explore the unresolved tensions. To stop the project at this stage prematurely discontinues the linkage when it has raised pertinent questions about certain cultural practices and their relationship to this text. For instance, we have seen the exchange raise questions about the relationship of this story to the issue of marriage, and polygamy in particular. Continued dialogue could allow the counterpart groups opportunity to understand the unresolved tension concerning the strategies and traditions of interpretation.

Follow up

Although my wish is for continuation of the dialogue that has begun between the groups, some groups may not be able to continue the linkage and will discontinue conversation with each other for various reasons. Another option might be for project leaders to pick out some of these unresolved tensions and follow them up. Or researchers could perhaps pursue particular unresolved tensions through dialogue with the groups concerned. The intent would be to see whether resolution might be achieved through follow-up by intellectuals who have the capacity to interact with the tensions that have emerged.

Yet another option would be a sustained academic discussion about unresolved tensions raised in the project, between biblical scholars and other experts working in the diverse areas where groups are located. This approach would use professional competence to work with ordinary readers, in order to flesh out or reveal a group's practices, for the benefit of others.

Develop an interfaith hermeneutical approach

My first two suggestions for a way forward seem to suggest that the unresolved tensions need to be defused. It will be possible to defuse some of them, but some cannot be defused. However, these unresolved tensions could also be used as points of contact and perhaps as an excuse to continue the interaction, because unresolved tensions indicate that work remains that needs to be done and can only be done through dialogue. On the other hand, if one grants that unresolved tensions are present and have come to stay, what will be the way forward for developing the interfaith hermeneutics that is one of the goals of this project?

In this regard, T. M. Byamungu states, in "Intertextual Possibility of Interfaith Hermeneutics of Retrieval," that "interfaith hermeneutics does not aim at *agreement* but at *listening* and *understanding*." In other words, "We do not have to create a 'common ground' in other to embrace the other."[8] One gets the feeling that part of the reason for unresolved tensions is ignorance. For instance, the concept of Christ as proto-ancestor, which the Port Harcourt group of Nigeria employed, was completely new to Grupo Lectura Pastoral de la Biblia of Peru. If intercultural hermeneutics is to succeed, we have to embark on "the eradication of ignorance of each other, and the creation of an ambience where acceptance might replace unhealthy prejudice."[9] This transformation calls for open-mindedness, an accommodating spirit, and willingness to learn from those living in other contexts, whose hermeneutical practices are new and alien to us and sometimes even contradictory to our own.

Douglas Pratt proposes that the way forward in pursuing intercultural hermeneutics is to examine critically our attitude toward contemporary contextual paradigms, in our bid to relate to each other and learn from each other. Although Pratt's focus is on relating to people of other faiths, his recommendations apply to a large extent to Christians of different traditions working in an intercultural context, especially on biblical hermeneutics. Pratt argues that there seems to be a problem with seeking a common ground that will be inclusive of all the different groups that desire to work together. The problem he identifies is that the inclusive model is inhibitive and "cognitively constraining," because the inclusive model requires the dialogical interlocutors to commence from a supposed third position and reconcile the two positions they represent to that.[10] In the end, this approach does not promote the interest of any of the groups who are interacting. In the same way, I propose that despite the fact that unresolved tensions remain, the way forward is not to attempt to develop an inclusive hermeneutical model. To do so would stifle initiative and also retard the development of contextual approaches to hermeneutics.

Pratt goes on to suggest that the way forward is through facilitating "a context for interreligious engagement shaped by the paradigms of complementary holistic pluralism, dynamic parallel pluralism." Enabling dialogue is the most realistic option, where the goal "is not to reconcile perspectives and theologies . . . but to grow in mutual understanding and also deeper self-understanding."[11] In the midst of unresolved tensions, we also need to create a forum where complementary multifaceted hermeneutical approaches or dynamic parallel hermeneutical practices may develop through sustained dialogue with each other. Only through that possibility will we be able to influence each other's negativity and develop our own identity and self-understanding. These outcomes in turn may lead to more fruitful contributions to our world, as a result of our joint efforts in discovering our tensions, discussing them, and moving on.

Notes

[1] Hans de Wit, "Through the Eyes of Another: A Project on Intercultural Reading of the Bible" (presentation, consultation on Intercultural Reading of the Bible, Free University, Amsterdam, the Netherlands, 2001). A version of this paper,

with the same title, became the standard project handbook.

² Inculturation biblical hermeneutics is defined in Justin Ukpong's "The Parable of the Shrewd Manager" as "an approach that consciously and explicitly seeks to interpret the biblical text from socio-cultural perspectives of different people. This includes both their religious and secular culture as well as their social and historical experiences." In other words, it seeks to make the different sociocultural contexts the subject of interpretation. See Justin Ukpong, "The Parable of the Shrewd Manager (Luke 16:1–13): An Essay in Inculturation Biblical Hermeneutics," *Semeia* 73 (1996): 190–91.

³ Benezet Bujo, *African Theology in Its Social Context* (Maryknoll, N.Y.: Orbis Books, 1992). Christ the proto-ancestor as put forward by Bujo is, according to Nyamiti, the affirmation of "a narrative ethic that Christ is the proto–Source of life and accomplishment and a model of human conduct through the experience of his paschal mystery." C. Nyamiti, "African Christologies Today," in *Jesus in African Christianity: Experimentation and Diversity in African Christology*, ed. J. N. K. Mugambi and Laurenti Magesa (Nairobi, Kenya: Initiatives Ltd., 1989), 25.

⁴ Gerald West, "Constructing Critical and Contextual Readings with Ordinary Readers (Mark 5:21–6:1)," *Journal of Theology for South Africa* 92 (September 1995): 66.

⁵ Justin S. Ukpong, "Towards a Holistic Approach to Inculturation Theology," *Mission Studies* 16-2, no. 32 (1999): 124.

⁶ Other Cuban groups, including Santo Suárez and Evangelical Theological Seminary (Seminario Evangélico de Teología, or SET), Matanzas, used the same tradition of interpretation.

⁷ Musa Dube, "God Never Opened the Bible! Reading Matthew 15:21–28 with African Independent Churches (AICs) Batswana Women" (paper, 53rd Annual General Meeting of the *Studiorum Novi Testamenti Societas*, Copenhagen, Denmark, 1998), 17.

⁸ T. M. Byamungu, "Intertextual Possibility of Interfaith Hermeneutics of Retrieval," *Current Dialogue* 42 (2003): 10.

⁹ Ibid.

¹⁰ Douglas Pratt, "Contextual Paradigms for Interfaith Relations," *Current Dialogue* 42 (2003): 8.

¹¹ Ibid.

CHAPTER 9

The eyes of the other
as porthole and mirror

The communication between Sokhanya and Zaandam

Danie van Zyl

As part of the project for intercultural Bible reading, Through the Eyes of Another, the Sokhanya group from South Africa and the Zaandam group from the Netherlands linked with one another and exchanged their studies of John 4.

Description of the two reading groups

The Sokhanya group is a Bible school class in New Crossroads, Cape Town, South Africa. The history of South Africa is stamped by apartheid, a political system that resulted in the systematic deprivation and negation of basic human rights of all citizens who were not regarded as white. For generations, this system brought about inhuman social conditions and economic disadvantages for the black people of this country. This system resulted in innumerable hardships and oppression on both communal and individual levels. After years of struggle, majority rule was established in 1994. Despite this political change, not much has changed for the majority of the black population in their economic reality and physical living conditions. Racial discrimination is still a living reality in many situations.

The participants in the Sokhanya group are all members of the Xhosa ethnic group, which lives in exclusively black townships created by the previous government. Except for the workplace, there is not much social integration and interaction between the Xhosa ethnic group and other racial groups in the city. The Xhosas are an indigenous ethnic group consisting of different tribes who traditionally lived in the eastern part of South Africa. They form the second largest African language group in the country. Amid many hardships and disruptions, the majority of the Xhosas are very committed to their cultural traditions. Tribal and family relationships are usually very strong and are kept alive through regular visits to their "homes" in rural areas some 1,000 kilometers away, where the majority of them were born.

Danie van Zyl, Sokhanya Bible School (Cape Town, South Africa)

The members of the Sokhanya group belong to different churches. The local church scene is typical of that in many sub-Saharan African townships and is very diverse. Formally, a distinction is made between so-called mainline churches of Western origin and African Independent Churches (AICs), which were founded by Africans and have almost exclusively black members. AICs arose, among other stimuli, as a response to racial discrimination and political separation of cultural groups. In general, these churches are strongly committed to the African culture and worldview. The Zionists in particular have blended Christian and Pentecostal beliefs with African beliefs and practices. Often these churches are highly dependent on the charismatic personality of the leader. As a result, leadership conflicts within Zionist churches are common and often result in splits and the formation of new churches. A high level of prejudice, suspicion, intolerance, and favoring of relatives is prevalent in the church communities in local townships.

The Sokhanya group meets as part of Sokhanya Bible School, which offers Bible training programs for clergy and lay leaders of all denominations. Women are treated on an equal level with men, and their leadership is purposefully propagated. Teaching is based on principles of adult education, and members are accustomed to active participation in discussions. All meetings are conducted exclusively in Xhosa. The occasion of the recorded study was of historical significance, in that it occurred about a week before an international conference on racism took place in Durban, South Africa, under the auspices of the United Nations. The heated debates in the agenda of the conference made local news headlines.

The Zaandam group consists of a number of highly educated professional men and women living in the affluent suburb of Zaandam in the Dutch capital of Amsterdam. They describe their own world as one where the major values are "wealth, health, and beauty." A majority of the group belongs to the Samen-op-Weg [Together on the Way] churches, a group of Protestant churches in the Netherlands who work and worship together while in the process of merging into one. The Zaandam group formed especially to participate in this intercultural Bible reading project and has never met as group apart from these occasions.

John 4 as read by the two groups

The Sokhanya group's reading

The angle from which the Sokhanya group approached the text was introduced by the first speaker. She identified racism as an issue in the text as well as a current problem in the community. The relevance of racism was particularly heightened at the time of the reading, as indicated above. The second speaker introduced a vernacular term that incorporates the meaning of racism but also has wider connotations. This opened up avenues for the discussion to explore other aspects of the same problem. One participant offered an explanation for the phenomenon of racism, with reference to the tower of Babel in Genesis 11. His argument for why the tower was built was ingenious. He related the construction to its textual antecedent, the deluge. His conjecture was that they built the tower in an effort to escape God's judgment. According to him, the confusion of tongues is the origin of racial conflict, and thus he concluded that racism is God's judgment on sin.

Another group member stated that divisions are wrong and supported his argument by saying that believers are the bride of Christ. He thus introduced a new dimension and shifted the focus of the discussion from the issue of racism at the political level to racism within the church. He argued that preachers are sent to all nations and supported this statement with a biblical reference. Problems come, however, when recipients of the message discriminate and are prejudiced against preachers from other nations. He linked this observation to the text in John 4, referring to the Samaritan woman's prejudice against Jesus. According to this speaker, the woman's prejudice might even have come from Jacob himself, who was said in the text to have given the Samaritans this well.

According to another participant, the Samaritan woman saw something special in Jesus because of his prophetic abilities. One of the women said that the Samaritan woman discriminated only as long as she did not recognize Jesus. When she recognized him for who he was, she changed. The speaker made an application to contemporary life, remarking that we today say that we have repented and have received the Word of God, but we still keep on discriminating: "We are not like her; we keep on being jealous." Another reader remarked that Jesus's attitude brings a warning to us not to judge a stranger. Someone added that discrimination for the Samaritan woman is a sign of not yet having repented. She changed when Jesus told her about the life-giving water that he could give her. After he told her about her own life, she recognized him as Messiah. This recognition caused her to repent and to go tell others about him. The bucket that she left behind was indirectly identified with her sins (jealousy and discrimination), which she left behind.

The discussion returned to the issue of discrimination in the church, with the comment that even preachers cannot leave these buckets behind. Another aspect of discrimination in church matters was brought in, the big problem of favoring relatives. The discussion then moved to practical ways to root out discrimination.

The Zaandam group's reading

In their discussion, the Zaandam group found it strange that Jesus left the Pharisees, as if he were going in order to prevent further conflict with them. The group noted that the text states that Jesus had to pass through the land of the Samaritans. They further pointed out that there was no love lost between Samaritans and Jews. A member remarked that Jesus projected an air of superiority in the arrogant way he spoke to the Samaritan woman, an unbecoming attitude, unlike what one would expect from Jesus. While some saw the way Jesus spoke as a means to lead the woman to a discussion of her life, others found it insensitive of him.

One participant saw Jesus asking for water as a way to bring the woman to an understanding of her spiritual state. Others understood it as an ordinary request arising from his physical thirst. In making small talk with her, Jesus proved himself better than other Jews, who avoided the Samaritans. Another saw in Jesus's initiating conversation a glimpse of how human and even imperfect Jesus was. He felt disappointed and rejected and therefore tried to get sympathy from the woman. One speaker remarked that the woman actually helped Jesus remember who he really was when she asked how he could give her water.

The discussion then moved toward more spiritual aspects. The well was interpreted to be more than a literal object; it was a symbol of life within, the satisfaction of a person's spiritual needs through faith. Through this woman, Jesus discovered his mission anew, which was to connect people to God. He became the spring of living water within the woman, and she went out to become the spring to her village people. They discovered that the place of worship was no longer important. Therefore, despite the fact that she was a woman, a Samaritan, and a social outcast because of her conduct, Jesus met her as an equal and made her a person of great importance, who is remembered today.

Factors informing the readings of the two groups

Two groups who are worlds apart culturally participated in these readings. They live in worlds that differ in geographical, sociopolitical, economic, and religious/ecclesiastical realities. In order to establish the extent to which culture affects these readings, one first needs to take a close look at various factors that played a role in these respective readings. First, one must note that these readings were done by groups. Two aspects of Bible reading in a group setting seem pertinent as factors affecting the readings of the two groups: the spontaneous character of group reading and the nature and purpose of the group.

Studies of biblical texts that are available in writing and are therefore open to study, evaluation, and reflection are in most cases produced by individuals. These writers are usually academically trained in issues of interpretation and approach the text consciously from an explicit point of departure.[1] Studies of biblical texts done by groups of readers who are largely theologically or hermeneutically untrained have only started to appear in published form in the last few years.[2] By nature these studies are less coherent than those made by individuals, and participants are usually unaware of the factors that shape their particular reading. Usually, these spontaneous readings are not revised or edited. Because of group dynamics, the same group might read the same text in a completely different way on another occasion.

The purpose and tradition of the particular group play a decisive role in the way the group goes about working with the text.[3] In the present study, the Zaandam group was constituted particularly for this project, and members did not know one another well, at least in dealing with texts. This lack of familiarity contributed to their reporting that in their initial study they were holding back and were not outspoken. In contrast, the Sokhanya group is a well-established group that meets regularly. The fact that they are part of a Bible school that is conducted on the principles of adult education influenced the way they approached the study.

Biblical interpretation, particularly by groups, is always an incredibly complex process.[4] In addition to the difference already noted regarding the nature and purpose of the two groups, various other factors influencing the readings of these groups can be identified, although it should be acknowledged that identification and interpretation of these factors remain subjective to some extent.

In the Sokhanya group, the text was clearly approached "from below," that is, contextually, from the position of the reader. The first contribution, in which racism was identified as a central issue in the text, was explicitly informed by the United Nations summit on racism that was soon to be held in the country (see description of groups above). Given the history of the South African situation, naming racism as a central issue constituted an explicitly political motive. Informed by their experience as black people under the system of apartheid, the group condemned discrimination as wrong. Surprisingly, they also found in it an aspect of the judgment of God, in the link that was made to Genesis 11.

The shift in topic away from political to ecclesiastical discrimination was at least partly suggested by an earlier discussion on the problem of divisions within congregations, based on 1 Corinthians 1–2. They had discussed this text in the Bible school class during the previous session. The issue at hand was social relationships between members of a group—especially small groups within local churches. This is a widespread problem, particularly in African charismatic churches. A number of issues that were mentioned (e.g., family relations) relate to this matter. The fact that the majority of the Sokhanya participants are middle-order leaders reflects their social position and experience. That they were willing to speak openly about discrimination reflects a possible ideological motive, in the sense that it may be a veiled critique of their senior leaders. However, a critique of the attitude of more junior members was also expressed. What is significant is that group members did not use the text to justify themselves but rather were willing to have their own attitudes criticized by their reading of the text. In this openness both Jesus and the Samaritan woman served as examples for them.

The Sokhanya group's social world, which in many respects resembles that of the world of the text, served the readers well in giving them a spontaneous empathy for the text. In particular, identifying with the world of the woman came naturally to them as members of a community looked down on by certain others who regard themselves as superior. The situation of the woman who had to go to draw water was a normal life reality to many of them who had grown up in rural areas. There was therefore a substantial degree of "reading with" the woman. This identification is in one respect surprising, because they called her by a vernacular term meaning "loose woman." With such a person, they as Christians would not normally want to associate themselves. Their identification with her may be owing to the fact that she is a biblical character, which may summon religious and confessional sentiments to override other inclinations.

A high view of and strong commitment to Jesus and to the Bible as authoritative Word of God is reflected throughout the group's reading. Jesus was held in high esteem all along, and what he did was regarded as good and served as an example to be followed. The fact that he, as member of the oppressive group, did not discriminate not only shows good character but also bears witness to his divine origin. Because of their high christology, they found unacceptable the approach and comments on Jesus by the Zaandam group in their initial reading. The Zaandam group's approach to Jesus also occasioned the Sokhanya group's reflection on the mission of Jesus in their follow-up discussion. The strong evangelistic commitment of many of the Sokhanya participants is reflected in this conversation. The group's discussion also reflected the high view participants hold of Jesus's prophetic abilities, another doctrinal key prominent in their circles.

The way the Sokhanya group used the Bible to legitimize positions taken or to serve as illustration—typical approaches for many African preachers—showed the group's high esteem for the Bible as authoritative Word of God. Because of this stance, they found the partner group's looser approach to the text difficult to accept. In reading the reports, one notes that religious commitment and the influence of particular doctrinal positions obviously played a dominant role in the way the Sokhanya group appropriated the text.[5]

That the Sokhanya group performed a relevant and contextual reading of the text of John 4 in their particular situation is clear. The manner in which they moved between their own context and the text through a "spiral of interpretation"[6] is significant. In this manner, they appropriated different aspects of the text without violating the text. This approach is in line with their response to the reading of the partner group. Although the Sokhanya group expressed appreciation for their partner group's reading, they criticized them for not making concrete connections from the text to their own lives.

The Zaandam group clearly approached the text "from above," that is, with the text as point of departure and major focus. They followed a more cerebral and historical-critical approach, in which the text—and particularly the actions of Jesus—could be questioned and criticized. Neither the sociopolitical, economic, nor the ecclesiastical context of these readers appeared to influence their first reading of the text. It was only when the discussion moved toward spiritualizing the text ("the well within") that a measure of meaning for the lives of the readers dimly appeared on the horizon, but the group did not explicate this meaning at all.

Comparing the initial readings of the two groups

A wide range of diverse factors influences all biblical interpretation. Hans de Wit mentions such factors as church tradition and dogmatic position, status attributed to the text and reading attitude, economic position of the reader, and particularly issues of power, such as class and gender.[7] However, when focusing particularly on the influence of culture, de Wit suggests that Geert Hofstede's "calibration points" may offer a "metamodel" "to determine to what extent and in what manner herme-neutic formulae are culturally determined."[8] The following observations offer a comparison of the initial readings of the Sokhanya and Zaandam groups. These observations draw on Hofstede's model to analyze the groups' interpretations re-garding distance from power, collectivism versus individualism, gender relation-ships, avoidance of uncertainty, and long-term versus short-term thinking.

Distance from power

In traditional African culture, and particularly in Xhosa culture, political and reli-gious leaders are held in high regard. Still, while the community is, on the one hand, hierarchically structured, all members of the community have access to institutions of power. A level of democracy has traditionally existed in the form of meetings where governance through consensus was practiced (*iimbizo*). These traditional values have been seriously disturbed by Western political models of white supremacy, coupled with strongly authoritarian ecclesiastical structures, as modeled by Western missionaries.[9] The Sokhanya participants belong not only to a community that struggled against political domination to gain control of the country but also to black churches that have shed the burden of missionary control. Still, as working class middle-order clergy, they share very little in the benefits of either of these spheres of power. In this sense, a strong cultural influence in their reading of John 4 may be established: the Sokhanya group challenged both political domination (rac-ism) and ecclesial powers. The political powers of the day were left unnamed.[10]

In contrast to the Sokhanya group's high view of Jesus as the highest religious authority, the Zaandam group did not hesitate to question Jesus's position. Mem-bers even suggested that Jesus was uncertain about his mission and that the woman helped him in this regard. From the group's cultural background, positions of power do not seem to be an issue or are open to criticism. In a secularist and intellectualist environment, a low view of Jesus—seeing him as an ordinary per-son—comes naturally. In fact, in the third phase, the group explicitly claimed their right to hold this view despite the Sokhanya group's criticism of it. The Sokhanya group's high view of Jesus is just as natural, given that in traditional culture the realm of the spirits is sacred, and religious positions and traditions are not questioned. Their transmitted Christian religious views and dogmas are likewise above question. This inherent African religious conservatism was boosted by the fundamentalist teachings common to early missionaries and modern Pentecostalism. These teach-ings, usually in a strong evangelical mood, proclaim Jesus as the divine Savior, over against indigenous beliefs. This fundamentalist trend is typical of many present-day African churches, particularly the so-called spirit churches.

Individualism/collectivism

Enlightenment philosophy, with individualism as one of its key values, is deeply embedded in the spirit of the Western world. As Western Europeans, the Zaandam group shares in this philosophy in a profound way. They read the text in an intellectually critical way and did not initially ask what the text meant for them as a group or as individuals. Their partner group characterized the Zaandam group's manner of reading as consisting of unrelated remarks, with little group coherence.[11]

African culture is renowned for its collectivistic and holistic worldview.[12] Over against Descartes' "I think; therefore I am" stands the core African proverb, "A person is a human through other people" (Xhosa: "*Umntu ngumntu ngabantu*"). The way the Sokhanya group discussion developed reflects a communal way of reading. Repeatedly in their account, one sees participants explicitly responding to one another and moving toward consensus. Their discussion centered on racism, a social problem, and discrimination in churches, likewise a community concern, not on the issues of individuals. In their application, the Sokhanya group discussed means of solving problems of congregations.

Masculinity/femininity

Xhosa culture is traditionally patriarchal, and strong demarcations in gender roles exist even today in the community where the Sokhanya participants grew up. In most African churches, these patriarchal views are perpetuated. In South African society, active measures are being taken to counter gender prejudices and to promote the position of women.[13] Similarly, in the Sokhanya Bible School, of which the reading group is part, explicit attention is given to the position of women. Women are treated as equals to men in every aspect of the work. They partake actively in discussions, as the reading group exemplified in their study of John 4. Thus, the experience of group members has done much to modernize traditional gender roles. John 4 is the story of an encounter between a man and a woman, but the Sokhanya group tended to identify more with the woman, although the majority of the group was male. This identification was, however, more because of her social status than her gender. They focused on Jesus as their ideal. Their cultural background of gender inequality seems not to have influenced their reading of the text or the functioning of the group.

The Zaandam group belongs to a community where gender is probably not an issue any longer. Despite the fact that there were quite a number of women in the group, much of their discussion focused on the person of Jesus, the man in the story. Unlike the partner group, however, they seemed to take the woman in the story as their ideal.

Uncertainty avoidance

In the world of the Zaandam group, tolerance toward people from other cultures is a key value. The group's exposure to cultural diversity, however, differs from that of the Sokhanya group. To the Zaandam group, the "others" are minorities who are not socially included in mainstream society. The Zaandam readers were more sympathetic than their partner group toward the Samaritan woman, who belonged to the "outsider community," at least from the perspective of the text. They were also more critical of Jesus, the outsider in the story! The woman was seen as the one who initially helped him regain perspective.

An explicit case of "uncertainty avoidance" in the Sokhanya group can be seen in the high view they hold of Jesus and particularly in their strong reaction to the low view of him expressed by the partner group. The way they defended their initial interpretation in the second phase is another case in point. Perhaps one could say that the Sokhanya group is more conservative in religious matters yet more open and challenging in social issues. These responses are in line with their mostly conservative ecclesial background, over against the social dynamics in present-day South African society.

Long-term and short-term orientation

The ambiguous interplay of openness and conservatism that we have just pointed out in the interpretation of the Sokhanya group is also observable in the group's attitude toward change. In some ways, they are open to change; in others, they hold on to what is established and known. Traditional African culture is oriented toward the past, with a resulting uneasiness regarding change.[14] Changes enforced on African minds and communities by colonialization, industrialization, and more recently by globalization, have had a far-reaching impact on many of them. Often religion has offered the last stronghold of "the known." For those committed to the Christian faith, church life offers an escape from the pressures of social change. They thus react strongly against whatever threatens their core religious beliefs, such as their view of Jesus in this study.

The Zaandam group lives in a society soaked in technological progress and change, one that is constantly exploring new possibilities and easily doing away with what is outdated or traditional. In the group's initial study, they explored views of Jesus that parted with the traditional view, and in the next phases, the group held on to these views. Their reading was also much more objective, i.e., uninvolved, than that of the partner group.

Reactions of the two groups to one another's readings

The Sokhanya group seemed not to be particularly challenged by their partner group's reading of John 4. Two positions put forward by the partner group made the Sokhanya group in a sense suspicious and critical of the reading of the other. They seemed surprised that the partner group might suggest that Jesus's behavior was unexpected. The African group grappled with the ideas that Jesus might not have had a clear vision of his mission and that he might be running away. These ideas did not coincide with their view of Jesus, and a lengthy discussion on the mission of Jesus ensued, in which participants quoted examples from various scripture passages. Although this method of quoting examples is typical of this group, and to some extent typical of the way African Christians argue and even preach, the salient motive for this discussion might also be that they grappled with the partner group's view in an effort to convince themselves of the correctness of their own position.

The second position that the Sokhanya group opposed and took time to discuss was the partner group's suggestion that Jesus might have been arrogant in his confrontation with the Samaritan woman. In reaction to this position, they again reflected on the mission of Jesus, focusing on his commitment to the poor and the socially outcast. In this they were reflecting their own social location as lower-class, poor people.

The remarks by the Zaandam group on Jesus's words that whoever drinks from the water that he gives will never thirst again created some interest and sparked a contextual interpretation. It was with appreciation that the Sokhanya group noted similarities in the interpretations of both groups of the woman leaving her bucket behind and of the reaction of her townspeople when she told them of Jesus.

A level of disappointment may be sensed in the remark by one member of the Sokhanya group that the partner group did not really discuss the Samaritan woman herself. To the African group, her social position was of importance, particularly so because of their own social position. Although they did not offer clear explanations about why the groups' interpretations differed, some remarks hinted toward reasons. According to the Sokhanya group, the partner group "did not go deep into the text." The Sokhanya group experienced the partner's reported discussion as incoherent remarks by individuals instead of a thorough discussion of the meaning of the text. Related to this sensed lack of depth and coherence was the view the Sokhanya group expressed that the partner group did not ever come to apply the text to their own life situation. After looking deeply at the discussion report, the Sokhanya group later did concede that some remarks by individuals in the Zaandam group could point toward applying the text to their situation.

Reflecting on their own reading, the Sokhanya group felt that their own interpretation was thoroughly contextual. In a sense, the angle of interpretation that they took in their original study was determined by their concrete life situation (experiences of racial discrimination and tensions and divisions in their congregations). An important part of their response to the partner group's discussion centered on the mission of Jesus. In this position, once again Sokhanya's context played an important role, leading them to focus on Jesus's involvement with the poor and outcasts.

The South African group experienced differences between their own and the partner group's views of Jesus. As stated earlier, Sokhanya's position was based on a high view of Jesus, which went hand in hand with a simple faith commitment and a naïve understanding of the text. In contrast to this perspective stood the Dutch group's more open and critical approach toward the text and the person of Jesus. Although the Sokhanya group grappled with this way of reasoning, they did not show any openness toward it or any appreciation of it.

The Zaandam group felt surprised and challenged by the frank way in which the partner group used the text to speak about their own social situation of discrimination and racism. The Dutch group realized that they lacked the life experience of black South Africans, which enabled their partner group to speak openly about their own reality. From earlier experience under the past system in the South African society by a few members of their group, the Zaandam readers were able to appreciate the way the Sokhanya group appropriated the text. Their reactions reflected a measure of solidarity with the partner group's experiences.

The partner group's reading stimulated the Zaandam group to speak more openly and directly of their own situation. The Zandaam group even said that they felt empowered to liberate themselves from discrimination that others might lay on them. They also felt their partner group had challenged them to practice the love of Jesus in a concrete way.

The Zaandam group was also touched by the openness and sincerity with which their partner group spoke about problems within their churches. Their partner group's frankness challenged them to greater honesty about their own situation, particularly regarding the process of moving toward unity between the Samen-op-Weg churches. They recognized that they faced problems with leadership and attitudes similar to those the Sokhanya group described.

The Dutch group recognized that they approached the text with a low view of Jesus, primarily seeing him as an ordinary person, in contrast to the high view of Jesus held by the partner group. One member mentioned that he appreciated the way the partner group used the Bible in relating other incidents and texts in support of their arguments.

One factor that hampered the exchange, particularly for the Sokhanya group, was the fact that the second phase of discussion took place in the following year, after the group had substantially changed. Half the original group was no longer present, and more than half then present had not been part of the original discussion. The reading of the partner group did not lure the Sokhanya participants into exploring views expressed by the partners, particularly regarding Jesus, because these views were foreign to the South African readers, who regarded them as unbecoming. The Sokhanya group did express appreciation for the more spiritual aspects of their partner's interpretations, because these coincided with their own.

The Zaandam group seemed to benefit more from the exchange than did their partner group, because the line of interpretation, the focus on issues of life, and the views expressed by the partner group challenged them to look at their own situation.

The third phase exchange was, to my mind, hampered by the fact that a verbatim report of the second phase discussions was not available to the groups. This lack created a feeling of distance, particularly within the Sokhanya group.

In reporting about the third phase, the Zaandam group related that they were touched by the critical reaction of their partners. The expression of concern by their partner group helped the Zaandam group appreciate the partner's difference in approach. They attributed the divergence in approach to a difference in culture, although the critique of their view of Jesus was largely the result of differences in spirituality. The Zaandam group accepted the fact that the partner group viewed Jesus differently but confirmed that they did not find themselves taking such a view. That they had called Jesus arrogant in their first reading was to their mind not a critique of Jesus, as the Sokhanya group understood it to be. The Dutch group said that they could understand what the liberating work of Jesus meant for their partners, given the partner's situation, but reported that for them, "in the context of Western society," it was not as clear what that liberating work would mean. They seem to have been quite challenged in this regard.

The Sokhanya group felt confirmed in their interpretations by the appreciative reaction Zaandam gave to their reading. They felt that they had actually helped their partners get a better discussion going and focus on important aspects, namely, life-related social issues. Thus, the African group did not try to reconsider or change any of their former views.

Neither group was willing to let go of or even amend their core theological perspectives, particularly their interpretation of Jesus and his mission. While the Zaandam group was appreciative of the partner's alternative view, the Sokhanya group experienced the other's view as unacceptable. The exchange challenged both groups to explore the meaning of John 4 for their own contexts. In this regard, the Zaandam group managed a substantial change, while the Sokhanya group continued on their initial line of exploration. To the Sokhanya group, the intercultural exchange was a particularly affirming experience. Both groups experienced growth through the exchange. Continuing contact between the two groups and a commitment from both groups to continue to read together and exchange views witnesses to this growth.

Closing remarks

For these groups, communication across cultural boundaries occurred to only a limited degree. It is to my mind naïve to expect memorable cross-cultural communications to occur at such an early stage of reading together. From working in a cross-cultural situation for almost thiry years, I would suggest that the following conditions or factors need to be present to a greater or lesser extent for effective cross-cultural communication to take place.[15]

Time

Time is needed to establish relationships. Groups need time to build and sustain trust among themselves. The more readings and other communications that groups share with one another, the better they will be able to actually hear one another and be influenced by one another on a deeper level.

Manner of communication

The manner of communication between groups plays a decisive role. For oral communities like the Sokhanya group, written communication remains strange and creates distance. They find it difficult to have to deal with the readings of partners on paper. The human factor is very important. The more direct and personal the exchange, the more effective communication will be.

Language

Language is a major factor. Although people may be multilingual, reading the Bible and conversing on matters of faith remain most effective and meaningful when conducted in one's mother tongue. When translation is required for the sake of intercultural communication, however sensitively it may be done, many nuances cannot be transmitted. In addition, because language is a major bearer of culture and expression of values and worldview, cross-cultural communications are inevitably hampered by translations.

Choice of texts

The choice of texts for cross-cultural reading plays a role in suggesting the level of intercultural communication and mutual enrichment that will take place. The values, practices, or life situation of one cultural group may be much more in line with a particular text, or may enable them to read such a text in a culturally more meaningful way than can another group, who may not even understand what their partners find in the text.

Other factors

Other factors that may also play a role in cross-cultural readings of biblical texts include the particular purpose of a Bible reading group and the group's attitude toward their own cultural world. A negative attitude toward one's culture will probably hamper or may blur the effect of cross-cultural readings.

From personal experience, I know that it is only after a period of time and extensive engagement with members of another cultural group that the other group's values and comprehension of issues significantly influence the way one reads and appropriates biblical texts. The road from cognitive appreciation of the perspectives of others to personal change is long. Acquiring language proficiency in the other culture plays an important part. We have to be honest and modest enough to acknowledge that both our knowledge of, and the extent to which we are influenced by, a distant culture is limited and provisional.

The level of intercultural exchange made possible by this communication between the Zaandam and Sokhanya groups is like communicating through a porthole. The exchange allows participants to see a small part of the other's world, of which they had had no previous knowledge. However, it is still a distant world—a world with which the viewer has no personal experience. One glimpses only a limited part of this world. When one peers through the porthole, however, one may also see reflected an image of oneself. In the other's reactions, as in a mirror, one can be helped to see the strengths and weaknesses in one's own perspectives.

Notes

[1] This is true of traditional scholarship that has followed text-oriented approaches, from grammatical-historical through ideological-critical studies of the text (Louis C. Jonker, "Mapping the Various Factors Playing a Role in Biblical Interpretation," *Scriptura* 78 (2001): 418–21). Other authors explicitly approach the text from one or another contextual angle or ideological preference, for example, a political, feminist, or particular cultural point of departure. The contextual scholars have naturally made clear how the readings of traditional scholars are also informed by personal biases and preferences, be they ecclesial, social, gender-related, etc.

[2] This current project is a major step forward in this regard. Similar is the publication of and reflection on studies by Bible reading groups in the Cape Peninsula of South Africa, which were published in *Scriptura* 78, no. 3 (2001). The Sokhanya group, one of the partner groups in this present case study, also participated in that project.

[3] Ernst M. Conradie, "Biblical Interpretation within the Context of Established Bible Study Groups," *Scriptura* 78 (2001): 442–47.

[4] Conradie, "A Preface on Empirical Biblical Hermeneutics," *Scriptura* 78 (2001): 335.

[5] The influence of "dogmatic keys" in the reading of biblical texts is a prominent factor in many Bible reading groups. Conradie, "Preface," 335; and Conradie, "What Are Interpretative Strategies?" *Scriptura* 78 (2001): 436–38. This influence is of course also evident in the work of many scholars when they write or speak within a particular ecclesial context. When a group or tradition feels itself in a minority position, peculiar dogmatic keys are particularly emphasized. This emphasis may express itself in opposition to a stronger tradition (from within the same faith or otherwise) or simply as an affirmation of the group's own position.

[6] Jonker, "Mapping the Various Factors," 424.

[7] Hans de Wit, "Through the Eyes of Another: Toward Intercultural Reading of the Bible," in *Interkulturelle Hermeneutik und lectura popular,* Beiheft zur Ökumenischen Rundschau 72, ed. Silja Joneleit-Oesch and Miriam Neubert (Frankfurt am Main, Germany: Otto Lembeck, 2002), 19–64.

[8] Ibid., 44–54. See Geert Hofstede, *Allemaal Andersdenken: Omgaan met cultuurverschillen* (Amsterdam: Uitgeverij Contact, 1995).

[9] The way the Xhosa ethnic background interacts with Christianity has been documented in an anthropological study by B. A. Pauw, *Christianity and Xhosa Tradition* (London: Oxford University Press, 1975).

[10] The first two presidents of the new democratic South Africa both belonged to Sokhanya's cultural group, the Xhosa. On other occasions, Sokhanya group members have indeed voiced skepticism about these political leaders, because group members do not experience the economic benefits of the new order.

[11] It must be kept in mind that the initial reading was the first time that the

group met and read together. The group's approach changed to some degree in the next phases, in response to the partner group's critique.

[12] Mbiti states: "[African] traditional religions permeate all departments of life; there is no formal distinction between the sacred and the secular. . . . Traditional religions are not primarily for the individual, but for the community of which he is part." John S. Mbiti, *African Religions and Philosophy* (London: Mortis & Gibb, 1969), 2. This statement is also true of most cultures that are not rooted in Enlightenment philosophy.

[13] This effort is part of the development of a culture of human rights by the South African government, which has set up a permanent gender commission.

[14] Mbiti (ibid., 15–28) calls the concept of time "a key to the understanding and interpretation of African religion and philosophy." His exposition of the African concept of time became universally accepted; this concept is alive with a great majority of African people.

[15] Admittedly, the values named here are particularly important for African people and others of the educational and social level to which the Sokhanya group belongs.

CHAPTER 10

Artful facilitation
and creating a safe interpretive site
An analysis of aspects of a Bible study
Gerald West

The volume of material on the Through the Eyes of Another project website[1] has been overwhelming, yet our own contribution—that of the Institute for the Study of Bible & Worker Ministry project or ISB&WM—has seemed to me to be inadequate and disappointing. Indeed, it is the very awareness of the inadequacy of our work for purposes of research that has made the material on the website doubly awesome. The reports of the groups that we (the ISB&WM) facilitated find their place among many others on the website, and yet what we report there is only a partial account—partial owing to both its incompleteness and its limited perspective. Knowing the limits of our reports and recognizing that the reports of others are similarly (although also differently) limited make me wonder what it is possible to do with these reports by way of research.

It is the research element of what have been wonderfully rich processes that worries me. Our normal practice in the ISB&WM is to read biblical texts with local communities as a resource for social development and transformation. We do not do Bible reading as research. However, as a part of the action-reflection cycle, commonly referred to as *praxis*, we do reflect on our collaborative practice of Bible reading, and this reflection is a form of research, although a thoroughly secondary form. Differently put, our primary purpose in doing what we call contextual Bible study is to effect change. In order to better effect change, we reflect on our action, which in turn leads us to revise the way we work. This process continues cyclically: action, reflection, action, reflection, etc. We do not set up our reading practice for reflection; we establish it to contribute toward individual and communal development. But so that we can better serve those with whom we work, we reflect on what we do.

Gerald West, School of Theology, University of KwaZulu-Natal (Pietermaritzburg, South Africa)

On occasion, we do step outside of this praxis cycle and address another audience in the name of research proper.[2] Most of my colleagues in the ISB&WM do not do this, but I and others with an academic as well as an activist interest do regularly turn away from the action-reflection cycle to dialogue with other socially engaged scholars (and any others who may be interested). However, those of us who engage in action-reflection–related research do not usually stray far from the realities that have generated our reflection, so that in most cases, my more community-based colleagues are able to engage with what I write quite immediately; it remains close to their realities.

So I remain a bit bewildered when confronted with the massive amount of material on the intercultural Bible reading project website, wondering how to make a scholarly contribution. In the spirit of the project, I have resisted the temptation to do what I usually do, that is, to reflect on our own ISB&WM practice. Instead, I have chosen to engage with one of the participating groups, The People's Seminary in Burlington, Washington, USA. In so doing, I continue dialogue with a colleague, Bob Ekblad, and his community-based readings. The conversation with him has been growing over the past four or five years. Therefore, in the spirit of this intercultural reading project, I have given the final word to Bob Ekblad by way of a postscript to this essay.

Bob Ekblad and I began corresponding in the late 1990s, finding many resonances in the work we were doing. I visited the Tierra Nueva community of which he is the director in 2000 and again in 2002, by which time the project had grown to include The People's Seminary. Through these visits, I have been fortunate to observe Bob and his colleagues at work. In particular, I have accompanied Bob as he has facilitated Bible studies in the Skagit County jail and at The People's Seminary. Through his group's transcript of the intercultural scripture reading of John 4:1–43 posted on the intercultural Bible reading project website, I have had another opportunity to participate vicariously in their project.

I have learned much from them; indeed, in a recent article I have noted crucial ways in which our work in the ISB&WM has benefited from theirs,[3] and I reiterate these in the present essay. I want to continue with this form of respectful collaboration here by analyzing their reading of John 4:1–43. I will focus on only three aspects of their enormously rich transcript. First, I locate their transcript in what I consider to be their overall intercultural hermeneutic orientation, an orientation that I have gleaned from conversations with and observations of Ekblad and his colleagues. Second, I track the facilitation process. Ekblad is a remarkable facilitator who has developed a distinctive facilitation style that is worthy of our attention and reflection. Third, I trace the conditions that allow for the emergence of what might be called, in James Scott's vocabulary, a hidden transcript.[4]

I realize that my focus rather stretches the notion of culture that is at the heart of this intercultural reading project, but it should be noted that the intercultural Bible reading project invites this broad appropriation, drawing as it does on Geert

Hofstede's wide-ranging dimensions of culture. My particular emphasis will be on three of his five dimensions: the dimension of power and inequality, the dimension of the relationship between the individual and the group, and the dimension of the social roles expected from men and from women.[5]

The Through the Eyes of Another project has identified each of these three areas of focus as important. With respect to the first area of focus (hermeneutic orientation), context and culture clearly contribute to our orientation to the biblical text. I know this is the case on the African continent and assume that it is true elsewhere. A number of African biblical and theological scholars have commented on the difference in hermeneutic orientation between those who live north and south of the Limpopo River, which cuts across our continent. The tendency north of the Limpopo has been to adopt a hermeneutic of trust toward the Bible and to concentrate on matters of culture and religion—theologies of being; south of the Limpopo the tendency has been to adopt a hermeneutic of suspicion and to concentrate on race, class, and gender—theologies of bread.[6] So the questions I ask of the People's Seminary transcript are these: Can one detect an overarching hermeneutic orientation that is shaped by specific realities of the People's Seminary group, and what can we in the ISB&WM learn from it?

My second area of focus, the facilitation process, is of central importance to the intercultural reading project and receives considerable attention in one of the project's manuals. The document "Process Description: Manual for Groups, Facilitators and Reporters" stresses the importance of the facilitator (see section 4), and notes, "The facilitator will be continuously involved in the analysis of the development of the interpretation and group processes." Moreover, in the standard project handbook the section on theory (chapter 2) concludes with a statement of some of the research questions that the project had already (in this early phase) generated. Among these research questions are a series formulated by Bob Ekblad:

> What are intercultural reading facilitators around the world finding to be the most effective ways to help untrained readers link contextual social analysis with critical reading of diverse texts? How can one best facilitate a non-moralistic/legalistic reading of the Scriptures that still mobilizes readers to thoughtful action? How can the underlying theology of the readers best be challenged if perverse notions of God tend to unconsciously guide readings? What are some of the most helpful ways to help untrained readers link contemplative reading, social analysis and "scientific" or critical reading practices?[7]

Clearly these are the kinds of questions that Ekblad takes into the reading process of the People's Seminary group. What are his answers, in practice, to these questions, and what can we learn from this practice?

My final focus is on the areas of power, gender, and the relationship between the individual and the group. I consider this by analyzing the conditions that give rise to possible elements of the usually hidden transcript of one of the participants in the People's Seminary group, Rocío Robles.[8] My choice is especially relevant to the intercultural reading project, because it clearly represents a case of intercultural hermeneutics, in both a narrow sense of culture and in the broader sense advocated by the intercultural reading project.[9] Robles is a Mexican woman who took part in biblical study conducted in a bilingual English/Spanish group (although the dominant language in the transcript is English) in the U.S.; she is also a woman from and within a patriarchal cultural context who has been socially located by others in a particular way.

We will return to Rocío Robles and her sociocultural location later in this essay. I now turn to the first of my focus areas.

Reading the Bible as good news

The People's Seminary works among peasant immigrants from southern Mexico who are drawn to Skagit County in the state of Washington, USA, by the abundance of seasonal labor harvesting strawberries, raspberries, blueberries, cucumbers, apples, and other fruits and vegetables. Among these workers, a project similar to the ISB&WM has evolved. Facilitated by Bob Ekblad, a biblical scholar and social activist, Bible study takes place in the local jail, in immigration detention centers, in the crowded apartments and migrant labor camps in which the workers live, and on the premises of The People's Seminary in the town of Burlington, Washington.

The basic interpretive method of The People's Seminary is similar to that used in the ISB&WM, but with a number of notable differences. The most significant of these is that most of the migrant workers have a negative image of God. "People's experience of being judged, discriminated against and excluded by the dominant culture [in the USA and in their home countries] is often interpreted as synonymous with punishment and rejection by God," Ekblad observes.[10] This is not the case with most of those with whom we work in the ISB&WM, who retain a positive image of God. What Ekblad's work demonstrates, however, is that even those who have given up on the possibility of a God who is in solidarity with them have the capacity to rediscover this God through creative contextual Bible study.

Ekblad finds that among Hispanic immigrants, "a high view of providence combined with a low anthropology typifies street-level images of God and humans. God is envisioned as a distant, judging force who is both nowhere helpful and everywhere troublesome." What compounds this view of God is the immigrants' view of the Bible. "The Bible is viewed as containing the laws by which God and his law-enforcement agents judge the world. The Scriptures are often feared and avoided for the 'bad news' they are expected to contain rather than welcomed as words of comfort."[11] Yet Ekblad's experience of reading the Bible with these who believe they are damned is that they do have profound moments of recognition of another Bible and another God.[12] There are moments when they do hear the good news that Jesus came to bring; thus Ekblad and his colleagues are determined to read the Bible as good news for the poor and marginalized. No text is left to terrorize and to destroy; all texts are wrestled with until they bestow their blessing. Ekblad and his co-workers know the damage that the Bible can do in care-less hands; hence the Bible must remain a site of struggle.

Engaging with this "determinedly good news" hermeneutic of The People's Seminary has proved unexpectedly useful for our work in the ISB&WM. When I first encountered this hermeneutic orientation, I saw little resonance with our own context, in which most ordinary readers of the Bible assume that the Bible is good news and that God is on their side. However, as the HIV/AIDS pandemic has taken its toll on our society, I have begun to wonder whether this hermeneutic orientation may not be a sign to us of things to come. My sense that the work of The People's Seminary might serve as a sign to us has been given substance by the reflections of a colleague of mine in the ISB&WM.

Phumzile Zondi-Mabizela coordinates our Women and Gender Programme, a program that is increasingly involved in the interface between women, gender, and HIV/AIDS. She tells me that the resiliently positive image of God that people living with AIDS in South Africa embody is taking a battering from the relentlessly life-denying theology of the churches.[13] In South Africa, the prevailing response from the churches and local communities to AIDS is a hostile silence, and when the silence is on occasion broken, it is only by the denigrating preaching of pastors in denial. The unrelenting stigma of being HIV positive in this country damages and destroys the fragile human dignity of people usually already debilitated by the ravages of global capitalism and our own government's economic policies and their criminally tardy treatment campaign. In the words of Nelson Mandela, "Many who suffer from HIV and AIDS are not killed by the virus, but by stigma."[14] Although those living positively with HIV and AIDS in South Africa have not had centuries of erosion of their image of God in the way their Mexican brothers and sisters have had, we must not fail to read this prophetic sign of the times. Clearly, we must continue to proclaim that there is good news for those living with HIV and AIDS. We must continue to contend for the Bible as good news. We dare not ignore what is done with the Bible.

Artful facilitation

Another notable difference between the reading methods of The People's Seminary and of the ISB&WM is the role of the facilitator. We have developed a form of Bible study in which the facilitator's primary role is the formulation of questions of community and critical consciousness. Community consciousness questions draw on the vast wealth of interpretive resources the community already has, while critical consciousness questions draw from the interpretive resources of biblical scholarship.[15] These are constructed prior to the Bible study, although they are often modified during the Bible study. Within the reading group, our facilitation role is quite constrained and is limited largely to maintaining group process, that is, to enabling participation, managing conflict, promoting turn-taking, summarizing the proceedings, focusing on the questions, and keeping the time. The Bible study questions do the work. Our primary facilitation task within the group is to allow them to do their work.[16]

Having said this, however, I must also acknowledge an ongoing debate among us within the ISB&WM, and more widely among close associates of our work, about whether our roles as facilitators should be more directive. Some of us feel that the kinds of questions we construct and the agency of local communities is enough to generate contextually empowering interpretations. Others of us believe that our role needs to go further by being more directive and conscientizing. As I have argued elsewhere,[17] these different perspectives on the role of the intellectual have a lot to do with how we understand ideological hegemony. For those with a strong view of ideological hegemony, the marginalized need to be assisted by the organic intellectual to recognize the contradictions inherent in the hegemony of the dominant sectors and in so doing to discover their quiescent agency. For those with a weak view of ideological hegemony, the marginalized are already aware of their agency, but they are also realistic about the prospects of exercising their agency in contexts of domination.

My own view, as will become apparent in my analysis, leans towards the latter view. What the discussions with my colleagues have alerted me to, however, is that questions of identity also impact how we understand our roles as facilitators. Because I am a white male working with marginalized sectors that are mainly black and female, I am reluctant to be directive, tired as I am of this traditional role of white male leadership, and convinced as I am, by our apartheid history, of white male destructiveness. But because most of my colleagues are black (and many female), their perspective is different. They are organic intellectuals who come from within the very marginalized communities with which we work, and accordingly, they have the right to take a more active role in directing the transformation of their communities.[18] There are, of course, many nuances to this discussion, but I have probably said enough to indicate why I am so interested in facilitation styles, particularly when they come from contexts so different from ours.

Given the constraints of Ekblad's context, such as doing Bible study in the Skagit County jail where the group varies from week to week, where time is a factor, and where there is no opportunity to divide up into groups, Ekblad has developed a different form of facilitation. This form is more dialogical, with the socially engaged biblical scholar taking a more overt and active role in the Bible study process. To watch Ekblad in action is to watch an artist at work. His form of facilitation combines group process skills, scholarly preparation, literary sensitivity and insight, and an overall sense that the Bible is God's good news for those in the group. The questions that we in the ISB&WM formulate beforehand emerge in the dialogical reading process in Ekblad's case. As with us, he avoids giving input (although there is a place for it), allowing instead a finely honed sensitivity to group process to combine with carefully constructed questions in a dialogical format. His questions, like ours, are a combination of what I have called community consciousness and critical consciousness questions.[19] The dialogical form of interaction is his distinctive facilitation style.

Fortunately, I do not need to continue to describe and analyze Bob Ekblad's reading methodology in the abstract. The transcript from The People's Seminary of three Bible studies on John 4:1–43 provides an excellent case study, and it is to this that I now turn.[20]

The series of three Bible studies begins with "First impressions, unanswered questions, and observations." Interestingly, it is not the facilitator who makes the opening comment but another member of the group, Roger. Bob's is the third voice.[21] When he does speak, his role is primarily to summarize and sharpen the comments of the first two speakers, although there is also an element of adding scholarly input. He does this, however, in a way that indicates that he does not have the necessary expert information at hand but that it is something that could be tracked down.

Roger: What struck me first was Jesus saying to the woman, "Give me a drink." I wondered why he did not just get it himself. Was this a public or private well?

Marilynn: And some of the translations say "Please," . . . and some don't.

Bob: So this brings up the question of translation. We would have to look closer to see whether he said "Please," or whether it was just a blunt imperative—whether the translator was trying to make Jesus look like a well-mannered person.

In Bob's next contribution, he affirms what the previous speaker has said, and then goes on to support her comment with further support from the text. It is important to note that he ends his comment with a tag question, "Right?" This is a clear signal to the group that his opinion is just one opinion; it leaves his input open-ended.

Luz María: It seems that Jesus was a little rude with the woman when he said [in v. 22] that "you worship what you do not know . . ."

Bob: Yes, and it sounds exclusive. It is not like Jesus is saying that every path leads to the same place. Right?

In his next contribution, Bob continues to affirm the line of comment that the group is developing, but sharpens the line of interpretation and encourages the group to pursue it. When the group does not pursue this point—whether or not the Samaritan woman is the first person to whom Jesus reveals his true identity—probably because the point would require moving away from this particular text, Ekblad uses the opportunity to affirm Marilynn's experience that it is sometimes easier to talk to strangers, which might account for why Jesus speaks so openly to the Samaritan woman. He then adds a fairly detailed and lengthy piece of input concerning the Samaritan Pentateuch. Again, the way he concludes his input is significant in terms of facilitation: he shares the information but then goes on to show that there is related information that he does not have.

> Marilynn: But this instance is what I call a "streetcar encounter." Sometimes you just meet somebody on the street to whom you tell things that you would not be able to tell a person that was near to you. And she is one of the first people that he tells that he is the Messiah. I don't know if it was safer to tell her because he was not close to her.

> Bob: Yes, that is really interesting too. Is this the first time that Jesus is recorded as saying that he is the Messiah? It would be quite significant if the Samaritan woman would be the first person to whom Jesus tells his true identity. That brings up the question of whether or not this is the first time.

> Marilynn: Because I have a social work background, I know that it is sometimes easier to talk to strangers.

> Bob: Right. That is often true. But in this instance it is Jesus that is the one revealing, not the woman. The woman is hiding from Jesus. I also have questions regarding the Samaritan Pentateuch. You know that the Samaritans had their own separate Pentateuch from the Jews. It was an ancient Hebrew or Aramaic translation of the first five books of the Bible, which has some differences from the normal Masoretic text, or the Hebrew text that is respected by the Jews. It would be interesting to look at the story of the significance of Jacob's well in the Samaritan version to note any differences, to see if there is any additional information or notes about Jacob and his well that we don't know about. There is information that is in this reading that I don't know about.

From the transcript, it is apparent that Bob moves quite quickly into a dialogical form of facilitation. The next few exchanges in the Bible study demonstrate this clearly. After Bob's lengthy input on the Samaritan Pentateuch, Eduardo picks up on another point, having to do with the Samaritan acceptance of Jesus. Bob responds by affirming Eduardo's insight that the Samaritans do seem to accept Jesus in a way that others do not. He goes on to pose a question that probes Eduardo's insight more fully: "So what is the function of the Samaritan for John?" Marilynn, the next speaker, does not follow up this question; instead, she shifts the focus to the

Samaritan woman and how she might feel at being told by her people that their believing is not because of her. Bob now enters into dialogue with Marilynn, as he has done with Eduardo. He affirms her understanding and then again poses a question that probes her line of interpretation. Robert then comes into the discussion, but somewhat at a tangent, and comments on how the disciples were astonished that Jesus was speaking to a woman. Again, Bob is the one who takes up a dialogue with Robert, but in a way that summarizes some of the earlier points that others in the group have made. He affirms Robert's focus on the woman as a woman and asks whether gender is more of an issue in this text than ethnicity.

Eduardo: I was wondering about the acceptance of Jesus. Remember in the first chapter of John where it says that Jesus comes to his own people, yet his people don't receive him? The Samaritans were a different people, and they did accept Jesus. In many cases, Jesus used the figure of a Samaritan to let us know who accepts him. For instance, among the ten lepers that Jesus healed, the only one who came to thank Jesus was a Samaritan. This is also obvious in the parable of the Good Samaritan. So I wonder what is the significance of the Samaritan in John's Gospel.

Bob: That is right; those stories are not unique to John's Gospel. So what is the function of the Samaritan for John?

Marilynn: I don't know if this is a woman thing or not, but I always felt bad for the woman at the end when [in v. 42] they told her, "We don't believe it because *you* said it any more." That always kind of grated on me a little.

Bob: Okay, so how do we interpret this? Is that actually a slam, or is that a positive word; as if they were saying, "Okay, now we believe it not only because of what you said, but now we too have had the encounter that you have had"? How do we interpret that?

Robert: Along those same lines, [in v. 27] it says that "when the disciples came near, they were *astonished* that he was speaking with a woman." So I put this in the context of Jesus's ministry with women.

Bob: So maybe it was even more radical that he was speaking with a woman than just a Samaritan. Perhaps that was an even greater barrier, do you think?

Rocío makes her first comment as this point[22] and returns the discussion to the question of Jesus being the Messiah. Again, Bob takes up her comment, engaging in dialogue with her, just as he has with every other speaker. The very act of dialogue serves to affirm Rocío's contribution. But as is his style, Bob goes on to push her observation further in the form of a question. Roger takes up Bob's question and with it Rocío's line of interpretation, as does Marilynn, who follows Roger. In her contribution, Marilynn too shows some of the skills of a facilitator, linking up Rocío's comments to the earlier discussion about the Samaritan Pentateuch. Bob recognizes this move and uses it to bring the Bible study to a conclusion, by saying that he will follow up Marilynn's question about the Samaritan Pentateuch—signaling once again that he does not know everything, although he is a biblical scholar—and by asking whether there are any other questions "before next week."

> Rocío: In verse 29, Jesus makes a reference to himself being the Messiah, yet the woman later asks the townspeople, "He cannot be the Messiah, can he?"
>
> Bob: So it was like she was not necessarily convinced by Jesus's own proclamation or statement. Was she doubting it?
>
> Roger: Which is maybe good in a way, because it would be like today if somebody just came up and told you that he was the Messiah. [In that case] it would be good to doubt.
>
> Marilynn: This can go back to what the Samaritan Bible says. She says [in v. 25] that she knows the Messiah is coming, so maybe she knows her Pentateuch.
>
> Bob: Maybe so. And that is something that I can look up. Is there anything else? Any more questions before next week?

Eduardo uses the opportunity to say that he thinks the key issue is worship, and then provides historical information on the Samaritans and their relationship with the Jerusalem temple. Probably sensing that entering into a dialogue with Eduardo would deflect somewhat the sense of interpretive coherence that has emerged, Bob proposes that the group stop at this point. He then suggests some preparation for the next week, including identifying the characters in the story and tracing the thread and chronology of the text. From these suggestions of a way forward for the next Bible study, Bob seems to be urging the group to adopt a more narrative approach to the text, given that this first Bible study has been rather impressionistic.

> Eduardo: This is important. The real point of this was worship. The central point is worship. Here this is a historical and contextual question that the woman is still feeling. I think that this comes from the division between the northern and southern kingdoms. The Samaritans were not accepting of the Jerusalem temple, so they had to construct their own temple in Bethel.

Bob:	I suggest that we stop here. How about next week we come prepared to go through all of the identifiable characters and to go through the thread and chronology of the text, looking to go further and deeper. Maybe then we can spend five or ten minutes before getting into a more narrative read and our own impressions. Can we now close with a prayer?

Significantly, Bob ends the Bible study with a request for a closing prayer. This too is one of the tasks of the facilitator, locating the Bible study within the context of worship.

The pattern of dialogical facilitation continues in the second Bible study. After the text is read again, Luz María initiates the discussion by referring to the symbolic nature of the well. Immediately Bob takes up this suggestion, using the opportunity to contextualize and inviting all the participants to comment, by saying, "Let's think of some equivalents for Jacob's well in our own lives and community. Let's make a list." The participants, including Bob, each put forward their contextualization.

Luz María:	I think that there is something symbolic about this well. The people in the story all have [come for water], and it is accidental that they met Jesus.
Bob:	Where are some of the places that we have to go to meet our basic needs? Where do you go? Let's think of some equivalents for Jacob's well in our own lives and community. Let's make a list.
Marilynn:	I go to the store?
Roger:	To work.
Robert:	To the hospital.
Rob:	Starbucks café.

Other voices simultaneously offer "bed," "bathroom," "river," etc. When most of the group have contributed, Bob directs the discussion by noting that some of the contextual equivalents to the well are not places that a person must of necessity go, while others of these definitely are. What he is doing here, and he goes on to state this clearly, is framing the discussion in terms of the overall theological orientation of The People's Seminary (discussed in the section above). In other words, he is setting up a contrast between the predominant "bad news" theology of many of the migrant workers (and others) and the "good news" theology that The People's Seminary advocates.

Bob:	It is interesting here that the location excludes many places. We don't *have* to go to church right? The location of the well is more

like something that *we must do, that we have to do*, such as bed or the store, than something that we choose to do. Right? This goes against the type of theology that states, "It is all up to the person to make the right choices."

Eduardo interrupts this line of thought with his own observations on the story, focusing on both the Jews and the Samaritans as religious consumers. Deftly deflecting Eduardo's interjection, but in a nonconfrontational manner, Bob continues with his attempt to provide a broad theological orientation to the discussion. Again, he does this through a mixture of guiding questions and input, retaining the contextual focus.

Eduardo: I have my own observations for this story. In this story, Jesus says that both Jews and Samaritans are religious consumers. We are religious consumers right now. A religious consumer is a person that comes to stagnant water, but Jesus is the living water. He is one that challenges us to build a new story, a story of the kingdom.

Bob: But it is interesting that Jesus does not tell the woman right away who he is. He starts out saying, "Help me." So what does that tell us? What would be a modern equivalent of that? Where is a place where we all have to go and [where we might] meet a person who asks us for help? Because Jesus doesn't just come to the woman and tell her outright that he is the Messiah. But he asks for help.

Three of the group take up Bob's direction, so when he next speaks he affirms their contributions, summarizes what they have said, expands on what he sees to be the positive theological trajectory of the text, and then encourages the group to work with the text more narratively. It is worth noting that he again does his directing in a self-deprecating manner by prefacing his comments with the phrase, "Maybe I am wrong, but . . ."

Roger: It is kind of like going to work, and when you get there your boss is asking you, "What do you have for me to do today?" It is a reversal of roles.

Luz María: What else? It would be like meeting a person and having them tell you, "Oh, hello. I am the Messiah. I am the Son of God." It would seem crazy.

Eduardo: Jesus did tell her later that he really was the Son of God, but after he asked her for a drink. It was the middle of the day and he was thirsty.

Luz María: Yes, it was later.

Bob: Right. He didn't say it until way after they started talking. I think it is important to look at the chronology because we are shown . . . This is a teaching about how God shows up in our lives. God progressively shows up in our lives. Maybe I am wrong, but it could be a teaching about this. But the story— why is it organized as such? Why was it written down this way and not some other way? To me, this sort of narrative study of the Bible is very fascinating. To look at why certain details are given and when.

Robert continues the line of interpretation that has begun to emerge, by commenting at length on how Jesus "reaches out to everybody in their own context," after which Bob pushes the contextual implications of the text for the group even further (see transcript).[23] The examples he uses, however, make it clear that he is trying to sustain a reading of the story as good news for the kinds of marginalized people, such as drug addicts, alcoholics, and thieves, that they encounter in their work. The concluding question of his lengthy contribution directly invites the group to appropriate what the Bible study (so far) means to them: "How could we find God in a way similar to the way that the Samaritan woman found God?" Marilynn relates the story to the then-current anthrax scare, and Eduardo returns to his view that the text is about consumerism. In both instances, Bob engages each of them in an affirming dialogue. Bob then suggests that they conclude the Bible study here. He wraps up the discussion by affirming the progress they have made.

The third and final session of the Bible study series begins once again with a reading of the whole text. Because two new participants have joined the group, Bob begins by summarizing what the group has done so far, focusing on the previous week's Bible study. Margie immediately picks up the emphasis on personal contextualization, saying that for her the church is one of those places where she goes to have her needs met. Bob affirms her contribution and then relaxes the group by introducing a humorous comment, namely, that while the church would be a significant place for Margie, for Rob it would be Starbucks! He then invites others to speak. Rocío, Roger, Marilynn, Robert, and others contribute. As he did in the previous Bible study, when the group discussion dissolves into a general hubbub, Bob once again tries to focus the discussion, both by highlighting what the group has already acknowledged and through adding input (drawing on Paul Tillich and the Church Fathers). In other words, he uses a rather lengthy contribution, which includes summary and new input, to push the group to articulate where, and in what way, Jesus encounters each of them in their place of ultimate concern. Again, he ends this contribution with a question.

Luz María and Roger each answer Bob's question by restating it in their own words, perhaps affirming his direction but also checking to see if they have understood correctly. Bob affirms their support and query, but, as is his style, goes on to pose what for him is a key question, drawing as it does on the distinction between disempowering and empowering theologies. "Right," he affirms, and then asks, "And is this particular place in the text [in which Jesus addresses our ultimate concern] a religious place?"

Bob: So anyway, Jesus's location in this place tells us what?

Luz María: It tells us that the Lord comes to where we are.

Roger: The Lord meets us in our place of greatest need. In that physical place. And that could be anywhere.

Bob: Right, and is this particular place in the text a religious place?

Robert responds directly to Bob's question, as does Eduardo initially, although Robert then goes on to take the discussion in another direction. Bob encourages this direction, something he does not always do with Eduardo's somewhat unilateral assertions. From the transcript and cited examples, it is clear that Eduardo has a very particular reading of this text, a reading that is strongly shaped by the Centro de Estudos Bíblicos (CEBI),[24] through which he was trained in contextual Bible study. Bob nurtures Eduardo's contributions in cases where Eduardo is reading collaboratively. However, when Eduardo pursues his own particular line of interpretation in a way that excludes the contributions of the group, Bob attempts to draw him back into the group, using a range of facilitation skills. As I will show below, building communal momentum and collaboration in the reading group is an important ingredient in enabling incipient and inchoate local theologies to emerge.

Eduardo argues that the Samaritan woman is a prostitute who was offering herself to Jesus. Bob corroborates Eduardo's point of view, adding supporting arguments, and then goes on to restate the thrust of Eduardo's comments for the group. Jeremiah and Marilynn each confirm this reading but place a different emphasis on it, drawing attention to the marginal position of this woman. Once again revealing her facilitation skills,[25] Marilynn neatly links Eduardo's contribution with Bob's earlier attempt to get the group to identify their places of ultimate concern. She strongly identifies (with) the woman as someone who is marginalized.

Marilynn: I take the side of the woman. If the well stands for our ultimate concern, then she is outside of that. She comes to the well at a time when nobody else is coming. She really is an outcast. The more respectable women probably did not accept her. The most poignant part of the story for me is when she tells the townspeople that the Messiah has come. They only listen to her for a second before they need more evidence. I think that she is a very poignant person who knows why she has had so many husbands. Maybe she was forced into it economically.

Bob then encourages Marilynn to view Jesus through this marginal woman's eyes. Marilynn, Luz María, and Roger each respond, after which Bob attempts a lengthy theologizing summary of what they have said. As before, he draws on his deep conviction that Jesus is good news for the marginalized and applies this theological orientation to the case. What Bob seems to say is that the group has recognized that the truly remarkable thing about Jesus, from this woman's perspective, is that Jesus reaches out to her deepest need, knowing fully who she is.

Bob: But what impresses her? What does she tell the people?

Marilynn: Well, all of these things. First of all, who am I (a woman) that you (Jesus) would approach me? A Samaritan, a sinner. Then he said to her things that ordinary people would not know, things about her past. Then, he was approachable.

Luz María: But perhaps she was not that way. Initially, the people in her town *did* trust her, just because she told them so. She went and told them that she had met the Messiah, that she met a prophet— and everybody believed her. It seems to me that she was credible. In verse 39, it is said that they believed her at first. I don't think that you can write her off as being not credible.

Roger: I tend to agree with Luz. I don't know if she could have been totally credible, but she said, "Come and see a man who knows everything that I have ever done." I mean, who do you know who would be excited about having somebody else know about your dirty and dark past? I wonder about this. I especially would not want to go tell my friends about it. I especially would not expect a crack dealer, for instance, to go running down the street yelling, "Come and see this pastor that told me everything that I have done." People would stay away from that guy.

Bob: Although, among the people that I work with in the jail, if I were to tell them everything that they had done and still embrace them, it would be powerful. Jesus said, "If only you knew what God gives and who it is that is asking you for a drink, you would ask him and he would give you living water." Then he continued, saying, "Everybody that drinks of this water will get thirsty again, but whoever drinks of the water that I will give him will never get thirsty again. The water that I will give him will become a spring of living water and provide him with eternal life." "Sir," the woman says, "give me this water, so that I may never be thirsty again or have to keep coming here to draw water." So Jesus is offering her something. Then later, she tells him that she does not have a husband, and Jesus answers, saying, "You are right in saying this. You have been married five times, and the man you live with now is not your husband." What she sees is that Jesus offers her all of this even knowing that she had a sordid past. That is impressive. If I embrace the people and they just think that it is because I don't know them, then when they see that I do in fact know them—that is impressive to these people.

Importantly, Bob does not insist that the group follow his direction. He remains committed to engaging in dialogue with each member, no matter where they go or what they say. The remainder of this Bible study demonstrates this commitment clearly, as Bob allows the Bible study to follow several trains of thought. His primary role is to engage each member of the group in personal (but not exclusive) dialogue. Alongside this primary role, he employs the full array of facilitation skills. He continues to contextualize the study, to maintain the group's attention on the text, to ask clarifying questions, to provide relevant input from his biblical studies training, to probe responses, to summarize the discussion, to manage conflict, and to bring the fruits of the Bible study to God in prayer.

Bob is no neutral or innocent facilitator, as we have seen. He has a clear theological position, but he also has a clear respect for the text and for the voices and views of the other participants. So while he does bring his theological perspective to bear on the process, he never insists on it, always being willing to defer and to follow dialogically the interpretations of others in the group.

It is the combination of his preferential option for the marginalized (both in the text and in his context), his careful attention to the text, and the group's dialogical process that enables the local theologies of the group to emerge. Through a careful reading of the transcript, one can discern emerging local theologies. Of these, Bob's and Eduardo's are perhaps the most clearly evident, although there are signs of others. It is to one of the more marginal local theologies that I now turn.

Rocío's reading

Rocío makes only four brief comments throughout the three Bible studies, although I am sure that she responds in a variety of nonverbal ways more regularly. Having met Rocío, I recognize that this is probably in part because of her personality, although it may also have something to do with the Bible studies being substantially in English and not Spanish, her mother tongue. She is clearly more comfortable in Spanish, her biographical sketch being a translation from the Spanish. When it comes to her deepest (in my opinion) theological contribution, it is significant that she articulates it in Spanish. In this section, I will analyze the conditions that enable her final profound articulation. Let me begin by introducing Rocío to those who have not read the transcript, using her own words:

Rocío Robles, 43 years old, born in Mexico; single mother with two children; first language Spanish, originally Roman Catholic but now Commissioned Lay Pastor in the Presbyterian Church (USA) with Tierra Nueva.

My religious formation was Catholic, yet practically in an atheist family. I was the most religious of my family and always felt attracted to the church because I always chose my priest with great care. At one time I wanted to be a nun, but I wanted to study and not merely to serve the priests. When I came to Skagit County, I began coming to the Bible studies here at Tierra Nueva del Norte and found a new way of reading the scriptures. I heard some of this type of scripture reading from the priests in Mexico, but I really was not satisfied with it there. Here I began to study with Bob Ekblad and his wife, and I began to perceive another way of seeing, and I like it a lot. I continue to be attracted to it. I continue slowly, but that is how I go.

Among the factors that enable Rocío's articulation is the extended duration of the Bible study. Ongoing, prolonged participation in the process embodied in the Bible studies is, I would argue, an important factor in the articulation and owning of local theologies; for this articulation the extended involvement provides numerous resources.[26] James Scott has argued that a fundamental requirement for marginalized sectors to speak in their own voices, rather than strategically mimicking the discourse of the dominant culture, is a safe site.[27] Doing Bible study together for three weeks with a group, many of whom work together regularly and therefore know each other, must establish some sense of safety. At the very least, the duration of the Bible studies would seem to give Rocío time to decide whether it is safe to share her own deepest sense of what this text is saying. Crucially in Rocío's case, she knows that the majority of members of this group are either mother-tongue Spanish speakers or have fluency in Spanish, so should she decide to articulate her deepest discourse, she can do so in her own language.

Besides the duration of the studies and the time this provides in which to determine whether this site is safe, the dialogical style adopted by Bob is another important ingredient. Each of Rocío's contributions to the Bible study is affirmed, with two of her three contributions being overtly and directly elicited and affirmed by Bob. Early in the first Bible study, she contributes in the following group context:

Bob: So maybe it was even more radical that he was speaking with a
            woman than just a Samaritan. Perhaps that was even a greater
            barrier, do you think?

Rocío: In verse 29, Jesus makes a reference to himself being the Mes-
            siah, yet the woman later asks the townspeople, "He cannot be
            the Messiah, can he?"

Bob: So it was like she was not necessarily convinced by Jesus's own proclamation or statement. Was she doubting it?

Midway through the third Bible study, Rocío again speaks, in this group context:

Bob: Okay, I see four barriers: ethnic, moral or ethical, religious, and gender. What keeps the barriers from succeeding [at keeping Jesus distant from the woman]? These are barriers to the harvest, right? So what stops them [from being effective]? The harvest is ready, the workers are few, what is he talking about?

Rocío: Perhaps it is the very Word of God. At the moment that he is speaking, he notices that the woman is superstitious, so he approaches her and tells her about her past and meets her at that level. In this way, they begin speaking.

Bob: So it is Jesus that takes the initiative then. He insists, he pursues, even knowing all that he knows. He could have said, "You know, you're right. I am a Jew and you are a Samaritan so we cannot talk." Or he could have said, "You cannot have living water because you have had many husbands," right?

Early in the third Bible study, she makes her third response, this time a direct response to a question by Bob.

Bob: Okay, for you and for some it would be the church. . . . For Rob it would be Starbucks. What are some other examples?

Rocío: The Bible itself.

Roger: Work.

Experiencing the affirmation of the facilitator (and no doubt other members of the group nonverbally as well) and feeling herself to be a part of the group's conversation would be significant factors in making her feel a part of the group, as would the generally affirmative and encouraging style of Bob's facilitation. Indeed, it is interesting to note that Rocío always makes her comments directly after Bob has commented. His very presence, it would seem, embodies trust and safety. Although the group included a number of strong personalities with very clear views, the general atmosphere of the group must have been one in which every member felt the freedom to contribute. There were no wrong responses! Furthermore, the overall theological orientation, regularly reiterated by Bob—that the Bible is good news for the marginalized—must also have played a role in creating an environment in which someone as multiply marginalized as Rocío would feel accepted.

The enabling process I have analyzed provides the general conditions for Rocío to make her fourth and most extensive (and most personal) contribution. Once again, her contribution immediately follows input by Bob. However, this time she takes her own path, not directly responding to his comments, but clearly feeling the moment is right to risk an articulation of her ultimate concern. Again, it should be noted that duration plays a role. Rocío's contribution comes right at the end of the third Bible study. She has needed time to determine whether this is a safe enough site to share her story. Here at the end of three Bible studies, Rocío gives her answer to the questions the group has been grappling with—questions asked by Bob—namely: "Who are today's Samaritans?" and later, "Who do you associate yourself with in this story?" and "So how is this good news to you?" Deciding the moment is right, she offers the following response (translated from the Spanish).

> Rocío: I see myself within my own society; in part I would be the Samaritan. Here among my own people, it has been demonstrated that I am a Samaritan. I have two children from different men, and for the married women it is difficult for them to accept a single woman with two kids. To have married friends is difficult for me. I have seen that, because one time I lived with a married couple, and another woman asked the wife if she was afraid that I would steal her husband. It is difficult for a single mother with children; she is a Samaritan.

Besides a general sense of feeling safe, what enables Rocío to make this profound contribution? To analyze the context of Rocío's articulation, I draw on an insightful analogy from Scott's work. His discussion of the conditions that allow for the articulation of the "hidden transcript" of subordinate groups—the responses that marginalized sectors desire to articulate publicly but do not because they recognize that it is not safe to do so—underlines the importance of having enough social energy or power to enable those who share a hidden transcript to declare it openly.[28] In terms of our discussion, local theologies are not often overtly articulated, because marginalized sectors recognize that it is not usually safe to do so. However, when someone takes the risk to publicly articulate what is usually hidden, this declaration will resonate with the local theologies of others in the group—provided they are sufficiently similar—and when this resonance does take place, the power grid (Scott's image) of suppressed local theologies is activated, which enables a series of articulations and actions to take place. Something of this kind happens in this Bible study.

In analyzing the conditions that allow Rocío to articulate something of her own local theology, I pick up the group discussion at a point several contributions before hers. Here Bob summarizes the general thrust of the Bible study discussion.

> Bob: So Jesus represents a commitment to the poor very strongly by approaching the woman and revealing to the margins, to the woman, in spite of all of the divisions that could get in the way. He goes to somebody who is marginalized ethnically, marginal-

ized morally, marginalized religiously, and marginalized gender-wise . . . and those are not barriers here.

Robert confirms the absence of these barriers in the text, emphasizing the woman's "near heroic act" in accepting that these barriers do not apply in this case, given that she is such an outsider. Bob takes up the dialogue by responding, "Jesus welcomes her into the dialogue," and "He respects her and gives her a voice." This, I believe, is one of the specific resonances that results in Rocío's articulation. The idea that Jesus specifically embraces the most marginalized must have resonated with her.

Significantly, I would argue, Bob goes on to give a contextual example from his work in the jail, specifically referring to "the Mexican guys" he encounters there and their understanding of themselves as Samaritans. This is another potential resonating element. Just as the Mexicans in jail understand themselves to be Samaritans, so too, we will shortly hear, does Rocío.

Bob: Jesus welcomes her into this dialogue. He respects her and gives her a voice. His pedagogy is a liberating pedagogy. You know, the first thing that the Mexican guys in the jail said when I asked them the question about who are today's Samaritans was that they themselves were. They said, "We are." The inmates considered themselves, prisoners and criminals, Samaritans. This is interesting, because I would never say for myself that I was a Samaritan. I would associate myself with the disciples or the Jews in this story, not the Samaritan woman. So I ask now, who do you associate yourself with in this story?

Having given an example of how these Mexican inmates see themselves, he asks the group whom they associate with in the story. His invitation, echoing the invitation of Jesus to the woman, provides the opportunity for Rocío's articulation to take place, but it will only happen after more energy is inserted into the power grid. This energy, I suggest, is provided initially by Marilynn.

Marilynn is the first to respond to Bob's question, stating that she associates herself with the woman for many reasons. This statement, in my view, is a crucial contribution to the potential power grid. As we have come to expect, Bob dialogues with Marilynn, encouraging her to elaborate, "So how is this good news for you?" Marilynn responds simply but profoundly and personally, "Well, Jesus touched me." Gracie, another woman, strongly affirms Marilynn's contribution, emphasizing that this is "a real encounter." She continues, "It is so important [that it is a real encounter]. There is a spiritual dimension as well as a real dimension. It is a mystery how that happens, and you just can't understand it unless you are actually touched by it." Two women have thus added their theological energy to the emerging grid.

Robert's contribution does nothing to diminish this momentum, expressing as he does a sense of awe at this understanding: "But how cool is that? The woman goes to the well to get water, ends up leaving her jar there, and ends up leaving with something totally different." Gracie speaks again, emphasizing the mutuality of the exchange between the woman and Jesus: "And that he asks her for something and ends up giving her something." Luz María, another woman, one who is also from Mexico, keeps the focus on the Mexican perspective introduced by Bob above. She mentions how difficult it is for Mexicans to find acceptance in the United States, and how difficult it is for people to grasp the humanity of Jesus. Rocío's own experience, we are about to hear, is precisely of not feeling accepted.

Roger affirms Luz María's comments on the humanity of Jesus. Then Bob reenters the conversation. His contribution creates the final impetus to the power grid necessary for Rocío to say what this text has meant to her—that is, to articulate elements of her local theology. In his response, Bob evokes the entire context of their work at The People's Seminary, sharing his own experience of working as a white person with Mexicans. He specifically mentions that the immigrants he has worked with have even told him that they did not trust him in the beginning. What is implicit in this contribution is the reality of the trust that has developed in this intercultural reading project. It is perhaps this reminder that enables Rocío to speak now. When she does, it is in Spanish, for it is difficult to articulate the hidden transcript in someone else's language, although marginalized sectors often have no other option and therefore become adept at exploiting the dominant discourse. But here Rocío is among compatriots where she can draw on the latent energy of the grid and speak in her own voice a fragment of her lived (local) theology.

> Rocío: I see myself within my own society; in part I would be the Samaritan. Here among my own people it has been demonstrated that I am a Samaritan. I have two children from different men, and for the married women it is difficult for them to accept a single woman with two kids. To have married friends is difficult for me. I have seen that because one time I lived with a married couple, and another woman asked the wife if she was afraid that I would steal her husband. It is difficult for a single mother with children; she is a Samaritan.

Rocío derives the energy for her contribution from the factors I have mentioned, but in the same way that a spacecraft uses the centrifugal force it gains from orbiting a planet to propel it into a new direction, so Rocío uses these factors to propel her into a new articulation. Having orbited the discussions of the group, participating now and then, she has found sufficient energy to both form and articulate what she wants to say. Deriving her energy from the immediate discussion of Mexican marginality in the USA, she thrusts (and trusts) herself in her own direction, focusing not on issues of race and ethnicity, but on issues of gender—specifically the issue of being a single mother with children from different men. It is her own society, not only the wider U.S. society, that shuns her, she shares. This is what it means, she says, to be a Samaritan. Immediately, and significantly, two other women confirm and thereby affirm her insight and experience. They too know this reality.

> Marilynn: I would say that a single woman in a white church is practically shunned, because the other women would wonder who she was after. My previous husband would not come to church with me very often, and the other women would not trust me.
>
> Margie: And it happens; some women come to meet men.
>
> Marilynn: Right. But the Samaritan woman stuff is not gone from the church. It is still with us, folks.

Here is an excellent example of Bible study in which the confluence of enabling facilitation, local and scholarly interpretive resources, and a safe site generates the potential for an articulation of partially hidden perspectives and realities. And when this happens, as it does here, this local reality often becomes the intercultural property of the group.

Conclusion

I have chosen to reflect on this transcript because I know something of the work of The People's Seminary. I respect this group's work. I have entered into their Bible study in part because I sense that I am not being invasive in doing so. More importantly, I have entered into their Bible study because I believe that I can learn something from them. This is clearly intercultural learning—learning that needs to be nurtured. To use Hofstede's language, there are communal problems within our contexts and across our contexts that can only be solved by "intercultural co-operation."[29] The intercultural hermeneutics of The People's Seminary has provided resources for intercultural cooperation both within their own group and beyond.

Through the intercultural reading project, the resources of The People's Seminary have also made a contribution in other contexts faced with similar problems. Their intercultural hermeneutics have stimulated intercultural dialogue and cooperation between their project in Burlington and ours in South Africa as we struggle together to bring about God's kin-dom[30] here on earth as it is in heaven. Engaging with their reading of John 4 has changed more than my interpretation of this biblical text; it has changed my reality. This, it seems to me, is the power of intercultural readings: not that they offer us more "interesting" readings of the Bible, but that they alter and thereby transform our reality. Those of us who work with the Bible as a resource to transform our world need each other and each other's contexts; we need to cooperate. And so I stay within the action-reflection methodology with which I began this essay, reflecting on the real practices of others (in The People's Seminary) so that my colleagues and I (in the ISB&WM) might improve our practice, that we together may transform our world.

An intercultural postscript by Bob Ekblad

In response to Gerald West's generous article about my facilitation style, I would like to add some comments that I hope will clarify my context. My comments will consist primarily of observations about Tierra Nueva's ministry context, the dominant theology or official transcript, and how that context has led me to my current, but continually evolving, dialogical Bible study approach.

As a white, academically trained U.S. citizen, working with primarily Hispanic, semi-literate, undocumented people, I, like Gerald West, am reluctant to be directive. Witnessing West in action facilitating Bible studies through asking questions, and more importantly, carefully listening and documenting people's responses, has inspired all of us at Tierra Nueva. Respectful and careful listening to individual speakers, whether they are spokespeople for a small group or for themselves, does more than anything else to create a safe space for the hidden transcript to emerge. In addition to the differences between our contexts that Gerald noted related to jail Bible studies (limited time, new people coming into the group every week), I want to add several other important factors that have led me to be more directive.

The ISB&WM has determined that the best way to serve Christians at the margins of South African society is to work with organized groups who take initiative to request their services as facilitators and teachers. In contrast, my particular style of facilitating Bible studies has grown out of years of ministry to not-yet-organized people on the margins of the dominant culture and almost completely outside the church. The Bible study with Tierra Nueva's staff and volunteers depicts my facilitation style to a large extent. However, this group is atypical, consisting as it does of more trained and eager readers, most of whom already consider themselves Christians.

While the people with whom I read have often been baptized as infants and raised in Catholic families, rarely has anyone gone through first communion, participated in Bible studies, or regularly attended Mass or any other Christian worship service. Most people have avoided the church and are on the run from Christians because of perceptions that their behavior (addiction to drugs or alcohol, criminal behavior, etc.) makes them unwelcome by churchgoers and certainly by God.

Many of the people with whom I read have opened and read the Bible for the first time in a Tierra Nueva Bible study. Rarely are people organized, having arrived in our region as immigrants from many different states of Mexico and speaking different indigenous languages in addition to Spanish, and working long hours and different shifts. The only place that group Bible study takes place is when people come to bilingual studies offered twice a week in the local jail or at Tierra Nueva's Camino de Emaús (Road to Emmaus) congregation.

The group Bible studies I lead in the jail are exclusively with men incarcerated for a wide variety of possible crimes—most of which in some way involve drugs and alcohol. The negative images of God among Hispanic immigrants and inmates that

West describes are indeed present among those I serve but are not immediately apparent. They lurk covertly, under the surface, emerging most often in comments by people in crisis when they seek to interpret their negative circumstances. In ministry contexts inside the church where participation is limited to liturgical responses or worship, negative images of God are less likely to emerge. My work with offenders on the margins of or completely outside the church, whether they be men or women, Hispanic, African American, or Caucasian, has shown me a surprisingly widespread negative theology.

Careful listening to inmates uncovers a widespread assumption that God is punishing them through the agency of the police, courts, and Immigration and Naturalization Service—which regularly deports undocumented people who for whatever reason land in jail. People tend to assume a natural association between God's will and the legal and immigration consequences of their crimes. After all, when God is envisioned as all-powerful, everything is logically related to God's sovereign will. While God's demands are viewed as primarily listed in the Bible, because the state is in control most assume that God in some way stands behind the government and other powerful forces.

This official transcript is reinforced in two ways by many pastors and priests and their faithful within the immigrant community. First, some leaders closely associated with marginalized communities actually preach a facile identification between the consequences of crimes and God's judgment. They do so in part to scare parishioners into compliance that will result in social stability cherished by the immigrant community. Also, the logic of deism (speculation on God apart from God's self-revelation as suffering in solidarity through Christ's life and death on the cross) and the logic of penalties for crimes committed lead religious leaders to come to the same conclusions as inmates. Second, and as significant, is the silence from religious leaders who do not directly counter the dominant theology with a liberating alternative.

In every one of my Bible studies, people are familiar with the official transcript and assume that I as a Caucasian pastor will promote it. While many consider themselves outside any possibility of salvation from God and in revolt against religion, there are always one or more seriously "repentant" people who serve as spokespeople for the dominant theology, regardless of anything I say to the contrary. Their tendency is to read every biblical text for information regarding right behavior that would bring people into compliance with divine will, leading to forgiveness, release from jail, and success. Under such a powerful shadow of a negative theology, people are hardly free to interpret the Bible freshly for a liberating word.

The context of a jail Bible study, or any other gathering with uninitiated readers on the margins of the church, makes breaking people up into small groups to discuss questions more or less problematic, as West noted. In the jail context, there are always some people in attendance who are there to discuss their case with a co-defendant, to pass messages or drugs to inmates in another cellblock, or simply to escape the boredom of their cell.

Among the people that Tierra Nueva serves, a counter or hidden transcript has rarely if ever been considered, identified, or articulated, because people have not been exposed to preaching that emphasizes God's unconditional love and grace, nor have they read the Bible for themselves. For these reasons, I have seen my own role as a facilitator to include overtly countering the official transcript in ways that create a space for the emergence of an unexpectedly good word. Because the official transcript of the dominant theology is so strong, I have felt the need to be more active throughout Bible studies to create a space for the fragile, hidden, never-heard-before good news to be visible long enough to make an impact. As a new transcript, a counter-transcript, becomes visible and people begin to show that they are hearing something good for them in a biblical story, I find that I need to defend their reading from sabotaging comments from those more submerged in the official transcript.

As someone people assume represents the official transcript, my unexpected promotion of an alternate reading that favors the noncompliant often functions to build up emerging spokespeople of a new and liberating transcript. I have come to see, as one who is associated automatically with a punishing culture and a punishing God, that an appropriate use of my "privilege" requires that I model and encourage readings that destabilize and subvert the official transcript. When I affirm people's freer, positive readings through agreement or questions that invite them to go further in a particular direction, I observe that reactions like that of Rocío in Gerald West's article increase and become contagious. In this way, the power grid of fragile, emerging local theologies gains some desperately needed energy. While this method is more directive, perhaps it is necessary in our context so that a counter-community can emerge that eventually will become an organized alternative in the midst of oppressed, marginalized North American communities.

Notes

[1] www.bible4all.org

[2] I have discussed some of the reasons for doing this in my book, *The Academy of the Poor: Towards a Dialogical Reading of the Bible* (Sheffield, U.K.: Sheffield Academic Press, 1999), 150–57. (Reprinted in 2003 by Cluster Publications, Pietermaritzburg.)

[3] Gerald O. West, "Reading the Bible in the Light of HIV/AIDS in South Africa," *The Ecumenical Review* 55 (2003): 335–44.

[4] James Scott, *Domination and the Arts of Resistance: Hidden Transcripts* (New Haven, Conn.: Yale University Press, 1990).

[5] Hans de Wit, "Through the Eyes of Another: A Project on Intercultural Reading of the Bible" (presentation, consultation on Intercultural Reading of the Bible, The Free University, Amsterdam, the Netherlands, 2001), 21. A version of de Wit's paper, with the same title, became the standard project handbook. Geert Hofstede, *Cultures and Organizations: Software of the Mind* (London: McGraw-Hill, 1991).

[6] Anthony Balcomb, "From Liberation to Democracy: Theologies of Bread and Being in the New South Africa," *Missionalia* 26 (1998): 54–73. Knut Holter, "Old Testament Scholarship in Sub-Saharan Africa North of the Limpopo River," in *The Bible in Africa: Transactions, Trajectories, and Trends*, ed. Gerald O. West and Musa W. Dube, (Leiden, the Netherlands: E. J. Brill, 2000). Gerald O. West, "Mapping African Biblical Interpretation: A Tentative Sketch," in *The Bible in Africa*, ed. West and Dube.

[7] de Wit, "Through the Eyes of Another," 28.

[8] Names of group members are used with their permission.

[9] Hofstede refers to these as "culture one" and "culture two" respectively (Hofstede, *Cultures and Organizations*, 5).

[10] Bob Ekblad, "'I Need a Beating': Reading for Good News Among Mexican Immigrants and Inmates Submerged in the Bad News" (Intercultural Reading of the Bible lecture, Utrecht, the Netherlands, 1 March 2001), http://www.peoplesseminary.org/english/publications/120301

[11] Ibid.

[12] Ekblad, "Jacob and Esau Behind Bars: Resisting Rejection by the 'Elect' in Genesis 25–27" (lecture, 27 November 2001), http://www.peoplesseminary.org/english/publications/112701print.html

[13] West, "Reading the Bible in the Light of HIV/AIDS in South Africa."

[14] *Mail and Guardian,* 6–12 December 2002, 21.

[15] Gerald O. West, "Contextual Bible Study in South Africa: A Resource for Reclaiming and Regaining Land, Dignity and Identity," in *The Bible in Africa*, ed. West and Dube.

[16] West, *The Academy of the Poor* (2003 ed.), 110–27.

[17] Ibid., 17–39.

[18] Again, it has been in dialogue with Phumzile Zondi-Mabizela that I have begun to probe these different positions. Two other women colleagues, Beverley Haddad and Sarojini Nadar, have explored some of this complex territory in their respective PhD theses: Beverley G. Haddad, "Theologies of Survival: Intersecting Faith, Feminisms, and Development" (PhD thesis, School of Theology, University of Natal, Pietermaritzburg, 2000); Sarojini Nadar, "Power, Ideology and Interpretation/s: Womanist and Literary Perspectives on the Book of Esther as Resources for Gender-Social Transformation" (PhD thesis, School of Theology, University of Natal, Pietermaritzburg, 2003).

[19] West, "Contextual Bible Study in South Africa," in *The Bible in Africa*, ed. West and Dube.

[20] The transcript is an integral part of my essay, and I urge the reader to engage with it on the intercultural reading project website, http://www.bible4all.org/; after all, interacting with one another's Bible studies is the core of this entire intercultural reading project.

[21] I break with scholarly convention and refer to Bob Ekblad by his first name; not only does this feel more natural for me, but it is the name used in the transcript.

[22] I will return to discuss Rocío's role in the Bible study more fully later.

[23] By now the reader should have the sense of the transcript, but the detail it provides is invaluable.

[24] See Gerald O. West, *Biblical Hermeneutics of Liberation: Modes of Reading the Bible in the South African Context*, 2nd ed. (Maryknoll, N.Y.: Orbis Books; and Pietermaritzburg: Cluster Publications, 1995), 216–19.

[25] In any group there are those besides the facilitator who are sensitive to group process. Such people are a wonderful asset in any group, sustaining as they do any nascent community consciousness.

[26] Gerald O. West, "From the Bible as *bola* to Biblical Interpretation as *marabi*: Tlhaping Transactions with the Bible," in *Orality, Literacy, and Colonialism in Southern Africa*, ed. Jonathan A. Draper (Atlanta: Society of Biblical Literature; and Pietermaritzburg: Cluster Publications, 2003).

[27] Scott, *Domination and the Arts of Resistance*, 113–15.

[28] Ibid., 223–24.

[29] Hofstede, *Cultures and Organizations*, 241; see also de Wit, "Through the Eyes of Another," 19.

[30] Graham Philpott, *Jesus is Tricky and God is Undemocratic: the Kin-dom of God in Amawoti* (Pietermaritzburg: Cluster Publications, 1993).

CHAPTER 11

Continuing that miraculous conversation
Intercultural reading of John 4
Marleen Kool

An ancient story in John's Gospel about an amazing meeting at Jacob's well has brought men and women all over the world in contact with each other. This old story has brought the stories and lives of contemporary people up for discussion. What connects all these people is their faith in the living God of Abraham and Sarah, the One we encounter in the stories in the Bible, the One we search for in the lives we live together.

In this essay, I describe the reading process of two pairs of groups that were linked together to read John 4.[1] I selected these two pairs because they each show, in their own way, the possibilities and the limits of intercultural encounter through reading a Bible story together. This study also constitutes the basis for my essay, "Intercultural Bible Reading as Practical Setting for Intercultural Communication."[2]

Reading through the eyes of groups in Brazil and Ghana
The first phase: Group portraits and initial reading

In Feitoria, Brazil, a group of women of the Evangelical Lutheran Church had been meeting since the beginning of 2000 to read the Bible, to share their life stories with one another, and to support one another when necessary and possible. The group included three generations of women whose ages range from 6 to 66. They had already built up a close friendship with one another when they decided to participate in the intercultural Bible reading project. They interpreted the first phase of the process in a dynamic and individual way. Before the story of John 4 was read, the discussion leader had the group pass around two glasses of water. One glass was filled with clear water from the public water supply. This water came originally from

---

Marleen Kool, Faculty of Theology, Free University (Amsterdam, the Netherlands)

the Sinos River, which is seriously polluted by the emissions and industry of the city. It became suitable for drinking only after a complex process of chemical purification. The second glass contained water that was a bit cloudy. This water came from a natural well that produced good, pure drinking water. The glasses were passed around. The women exchanged opinions about which of the two would be life-giving, pure water. The purest, living water is not always the most transparent water, as the women discovered in this water ritual.

As they thought about the meaning of water in people's lives, the women told each other about their water sources when they were children. Although they now live in the city, they were born in rural areas and all had their own memories and experiences with water sources. Especially on this occasion, the women gradually showed more of themselves and allowed their partner group to share in their personal history. For example, Neci told the story of growing up with her family along the river. An ever-flowing source of living water provided all their needs. As she followed her thoughts of the past, however, she related that her sister drowned as a little girl in the same flow of water. The ever-flowing water that enables life also brought Neci painfully face-to-face with death.[3]

In Abetifi, a small city in eastern Ghana, a group of leaders from different churches met regularly for intercultural Bible reading in the framework of an education and training setting provided by the Ramseyer Training Centre. The group consisted of farmers, traders, pastors, teachers, housewives, unemployed people, and students. All were actively involved in the leadership of their church communities. They ranged in age from twenty-eight to sixty-five.

The Abetifi group portrait included extensive description of social, religious, and economic conditions, supported by statistical data and percentages. Abetifi is in a region that is known for its industry. The economic situation is characterized by high inflation. Their own economic position was weak, said the church leaders. They often barely had enough money to live on. "Fifty kilograms of rice is sold today at over 270,000 cedis (US$39). Last year it was 170,000 cedis (US$24). The average income of the people forming this Bible study group is around US$32 a month."[4] Group members reported that they barely earned enough to pay for food, clothing, and tuition. Therefore, women had been forced to look for paying jobs in addition to their tasks in the household. For this reason, most of them had small shops where they offered all kinds of wares for sale.

The church leaders were concerned about the political situation in Ghana. "We do not trust the big people; therefore, we suspect the politicians are there to take advantage of us." Ghana has officially been a democracy since the elections of December 2000. "But because of a bad economy the country had to join the Highly Indebted Poor Countries Initiative," they report.[5]

Not only is the country poor, but it is also plagued by ritual murders, especially of women, over the past few years. "The blood is needed to give power to the people who want to be successful as politicians but also economically."

To conclude the context and group description, the readers of the Abetifi group introduced themselves by name and gave their marital status, number of children (varying from none to ten), and their professions.

When we place the Feitoria and Abetifi interpretations of the story next to each other, great differences stand out, both in the manner of reading and in the degree of appropriation. According to the reading of the Ghanaian church leaders, the focus in John 4 is above all on the acceptance of Jesus as personal Savior. Salvation was the central concept in their reading. Jesus broke through barriers. The Ghanaian leaders recognized parallels to these barriers in the conflicts and breaches that separate church fellowships from one another in the Ghanaian context. The story called for reconciliation between churches in conflict. Moreover, the church leaders of Ghana asserted, it required a reevaluation of the position of women in the church.

The reading of the women's group in Brazil was of a very different nature. From the beginning, the women related the text to their own lives and their attitudes toward life. For example, they wondered whether they themselves would give water to someone from another culture and why is it that a woman had to fetch the water. They knew from the movies they had seen that fetching water is a woman's task but did not understand why that was so. They also saw that Jesus broke through barriers. Against all rules, he addressed a woman and in so doing crossed a gender barrier. Moreover, he was a Jew while she was Samaritan; thus he also crossed a barrier of ethnicity. These aspects of the story made the Brazilian women aware of their own isolation. "I can visit my neighbors only if I call them first, so they can tie up their dogs and switch off their alarms," said Vanda. Neci continued, "Will the world some day be without these isolating walls?"

The women expressed a thirst for peace but also for a just distribution of the nation's wealth. Gilmar said she was thirsty for knowledge so that she could be more critical and form her own opinion, for, as she said, "the politicians always mislead us with their rhetoric."

The second phase: Reading through the eyes of another

The women's group in Brazil began its response to the Ghanaian church leaders by providing additional information about their broader context. Because they were impressed by the extensive information about their partner group, they imitated their partner's introduction to some extent, presenting statistical data and background information about their country and the church.

Subsequently, the women discussed the central themes in the report from Ghana and entered into a discussion from their own social, economic, and cultural context. The observation in the Ghanaian group that walls were torn down in this story made the Brazilians look at their own situation and ask about walls. Thus, the changing position of women in the church came up. "In the past, a woman did not go to the altar during worship services; today she does. The women were always quiet, listening. Today it is changing. There are many women in the leadership of the congregation." However, they recognized that walls still exist in their own city. "There is also much separation in the city: on one side, the rich quarters with luxury houses, on the other side, much poverty. The slum is like a well that dries in a time with little rain. But God loves them, too!"

The readers in Ghana each stepped into the skin of one of the Feitoria readers as they read the report aloud together in a role-play. The Abetifi readers were very impressed with how their partner group placed the Bible story in their own context. The Ghanaians discovered a big difference between the partner's and their own reading. "If we compare it to the way we read the Bible here, it is quite different. . . . [When we read,] the Bible is put in its situation in Palestine. And when you hear people reading, it does not normally come here; it is there."

The process of reading through the eyes of the Brazilian group opened the eyes of the Abetifi participants to their own context. They discovered differences and similarities in the contexts of the two groups. The fact that the Brazilian women had learned only from movies that fetching water is a woman's task provoked a great deal of mirth for the Ghanaian church leaders. For them in Abetifi, this task is the daily reality. Women and children *always* fetch water.

A third point that the group in Ghana talked about after reading the report from Brazil was the "gossip culture" and sexual morality. They recognized the situation sketched by the Brazilians in which a pastor might speak with a woman who had already had five men. Just as in Brazil, they noted, a pastor in Ghana is not supposed to visit women alone. To prevent gossip, it is better if he brings his wife along. The church leaders wondered if this type of gossiping only occurs in the case of black people like them. However, someone in the group commented that in Brazil black and white people live together, yet the Brazilians had made no reference to racial characteristics. Therefore, it could not have much to do with the color of skin. The opinion of the church leaders was that it more likely had to do with a taboo against talking about sex. They were curious to find out if such a taboo was also a factor in Brazilian culture: "In Ghana, even if somebody abuses you, you had better not say it, because the words you will use to report will be words that have sex in it. We know that in Europe, for example, it is allowed to have sex when you want, but with us, it does not even matter if you are twenty-five or thirty: when you have not married a woman, it is still a problem. How is that in your culture?"

Eunice pointed out a striking difference in the society and culture of Brazil versus Ghana. "I see in the report from Brazil a thirst for companionship, for belonging to a group. . . . People live behind closed doors. . . . This is impossible in our African culture. People can always pop in: your family, your parents, any relative, or any other visitor." Later in my analysis, I will come back to this difference between collectivistic and individualistic societies.

Jackson, one of the Ghanaian readers, reported that exchanging readings created a great feeling of solidarity with the Brazilian group. "I have learned a lot from it. Also that we are not alone in our suffering, because I see they also suffer." Eunice expressed her happiness and noted how the reading changed her outlook on scripture. "I am also happy about this project. . . . I even think that if the Bible were written again, we all would write it in our own context, and for us, it would be here in Ghana! And God would enjoy it!"

Reading through the eyes of groups in the Netherlands and India

The following set of groups shows that an exchange can also develop very differently. We were introduced to a Dutch reading group from one of the Protestant churches of the Netherlands and an Indian group from the Syrian Church in Chennai, Tamilnadu, India.

A group of eight men and women met in Zutphen, a small provincial town in the eastern part of the Netherlands. Together these men and women form the mission and global deaconry committee of the Zutphen classis.[6] As a committee, they work with development cooperation within the Protestant Church in the Netherlands. Interest in learning about other interpretations and the desire to enter into discussion with each other about faith and inspiration motivated this group to participate in intercultural exchange. One participant described his motivation for taking part in the project: "It seems as if it is no longer possible to have a heart-to-heart talk with each other. People are too well off; that is why they don't want to talk about their faith."

The Zutphen group organized two meetings for the first phase. They always opened their meetings with a prayer and concluded with singing a hymn from the hymnbook. The participants had developed sufficient trust in each other to be able to carry out personal discussions. They also found room for expressing differing thoughts and opinions, even when they were diametrically opposed.

In Chennai, the capital of the southern state of Tamilnadu, a group of people meets weekly for Bible study. These Indian readers originally came from Kerala, one of the most developed states of India. They are members of the Syrian Christian Church. The Syrian church in India claims to have been founded by the Apostle Thomas in 52 CE. These communities are known for being closed, especially religiously and ethnically, according to the group coordinator.

The readers summarized the complex Indian context for their partner group in four points. First, there is a plurality of religions and cultures. India is blessed with a rich religious and cultural heritage that dates back to 3000 BCE. It is the country in which great religions such as Hinduism, Buddhism, and Jainism have come to blossom. Members of these different religions and people of different ethnic backgrounds live next to each other. Second, these enormous differences in culture and religion are matched by the extreme socioeconomic disparity of the people. On the one hand, there is the abject poverty of the majority, and on the other, the exceptionally great wealth of a small minority. A third characteristic of Indian society is the fact that a large percentage of people, especially in the rural areas, are illiterate. Finally, India still has discrimination based on the caste one is born into, despite having formally abolished the caste system. The so-called outcastes, who have given themselves the name Dalits, about 25 million people, are constantly oppressed and are exploited by people of higher castes. Although India is officially a democracy and despite the enormous technological, agricultural, and industrial developments that the country is also blessed with, the lot of many Dalits has not changed.

The participants in the reading group experience the tensions that exist within their society but identify themselves completely with upper-caste Hindus and are economically and politically very influential.

The reading of the Indian reading group and the response to their partner

For the readers in India, the story of the conversation between Jesus and the Samaritan woman was a model for various aspects of the life-changing gospel. The group identified with the woman, because she went to bring the good news to her people as an evangelist after the meeting with Jesus. Jesus was the one who crossed borders and revealed himself, not to priests or scholars, but to an outcast. The group talked a great deal about whether the faithful serve God in spirit and truth or whether they have the wrong idea about God, as the Samaritan woman did before her meeting with Jesus. Preaching and doing good deeds go together. Being aware of one's sins and receiving mercy ran like a red thread through this group's interpretation.

The two groups, it turned out, read the story in very different manners. The Chennai group understood that their own image of Jesus, surrounded with holiness, was severely under attack by the image of Jesus that emerged from the Dutch partner report. The idea that Jesus would be the sixth man of the Samaritan woman elicited great indignation: "Most members of this group found such a thought totally unacceptable. This comment has even put off some members from further participation in the reading. . . .They felt that the Dutch group looked at Jesus in a light manner and more as a man, with less reverence."

The Indian group dismissed the suggestions made by the Dutch group about how it happened that the townspeople of the woman believed her story. A woman reader in Zutphen suggested that maybe the woman radiated in an unusual way after the meeting with Jesus, just like Moses. "That is overblown," responded the group in India.

The interpretation of verse 8, when Jesus says to the woman, "Give me water to drink," also evoked opposite responses in the two groups. The Dutch readers thought Jesus was speaking to the woman in an anti-feminist, authoritarian manner. The Indian readers thought this not to be the case. "This is understood as a polite request in the South Indian culture. The way it is said is important. The way the woman responded also indicates that it was polite enough and not a harsh command."

In the reading of Zutphen, one reader made a comparison between the Samaritan woman and Muslims. She saw the woman as a Muslim. Just like them, the Samaritan woman supposedly does not know what she worships. "Muslims pray all the time, but they scarcely know what they are praying," the reader said. This idea not only encountered differences of opinion within the group in Zutphen itself, but the Indian readers also dismissed this depiction completely, finding it insensitive to the Muslim people with whom they live.

The positive, powerful image of the woman that emerged from the Dutch report was also not accepted by the group in India. The Indian readers suspected that this interpretation arose from the cultural point of view of the Dutch partner group: "More open relationships between men and women in the Western culture may be the reason [the partner group has] a positive attitude to the Samaritan woman." The Indian group declared that she is and remains a sinner.

The displeasure of the Indian readers with the Dutch interpretation appeared in their final statement of response. They asserted that the Dutch report was too open, too rational, and not spiritual enough. They saw it as a secular reading rather than a religious one. They felt extremely uncomfortable with the way Jesus's humanity was portrayed by the readers in Zutphen. Thus, they concluded that their own interpretation did not need to be adjusted. However, they did learn from the knowledge of their partner group on the background of the John movement.

The response by Zutphen to the reading report of their partner group

In preparation for the second phase, the readers in Zutphen collected information about India, and Chennai specifically, to get an idea of the situation in which their discussion partners lived. They were impressed by the fact that the group in India spoke so respectfully about other religions. The Indian report talked a great deal about worshiping, a term that is not so familiar to the Dutch. The fact that the partner group described itself as conservative elicited a question among the readers in Zutphen about the position of women in India. The emphasis the Indian group placed on the difference between the material and the nonmaterial was also striking. It was not clear to their partners in Zutphen whether the Indian group was criticizing the ownership cult in general, meaning also in India, or only in the West. "It is almost like a reprimand," a Zutphen reader said. "They too are well off in comparison with the rest of the world."

The emphasis placed in India on evangelization made the Zutphen group think about mission work in the past. "In the case of evangelization, we place respect for the other in the center. Evangelization as experienced in India no longer occurs in the Netherlands."

The readers in Zutphen experienced reading the report from Chennai and the exchange as very inspiring. For them, the contact is apparently not yet over. They have so many things to ask their partners in India.

How it progressed . . .

Impressed by the way the Zutphen partner group studied their reading and deepened their knowledge of their partner's context, the Indian readers carefully responded to the questions they were asked. Their initially rejecting tone and attitude gave way to more understanding and openness, when they noticed that the other side wished to know more about them. They were happy to explain why the word *worshiping* occurs so frequently in their discussion. "The word *worship* is an important word in the Indian context, where we see worship places and acts of worship everywhere (even in roadside temples and shrines). This is part of the religious and cultural heritage of India. Most of the main worship places are situated on hills where people worship the deity."

From their partner's response to their discussion about material wealth, the readers in Chennai discovered that their point did not come across very clearly: "We want to clarify that the Chennai group did not intend to accuse Western Christianity of [being a] wealth cult. In fact, Indians are also fast becoming attracted to the wealth cult and to materialism, because of globalization and the influence of the media. However, in India we have ancient spiritual and cultural traditions opposed to the wealth cult. The group only wanted to point out that Western Christianity is much influenced by materialistic culture."

The Syrian Christians also tackled the question about the position of women in India. They told their partner group that India is a patriarchal culture, but that extensive changes are taking place, especially in the big cities. Moreover, a few states in the northeast of India are matrilineal, and in certain situations women there have long had more rights than men.

In conclusion, the readers in India saw a great difference in their partner's approach to the encounter in John 4. For those in Chennai, the encounter between Jesus and the Samaritan woman was not just a meeting between humans, as the Dutch seemed to understand it. It was not significantly about an encounter between a man and a woman but much more about a meeting or conversation between a Savior and a human being. In this conversation, it turns out, the last word has not yet been spoken.

Despite the initially rejecting attitude of the Indian reading group with respect to their partner group, questions about the other group slowly began to come to the surface in the Indian group, too. "How does the Dutch group interpret the Bible?" they asked their partner group. The Indian group's question opened the door for ongoing intercultural discussion, continuing that miraculous conversation begun long ago at the well of Jacob. If we do not cease asking questions of each other and ourselves, this intercultural exchange can spread and start to flow worldwide.

Notes

[1] These reading reports are available to participants in the project at www .bible4all.org.

[2] See part three, chapter 19.

[3] First phase report of the Evangelical Lutheran reading group in Feitoria, Brazil.

[4] First phase report from Abetifi church leaders in Ghana.

[5] The HIPC Initiative applies to countries that have a GNP per capita of less

than US$865 per person per year and a deteriorating (nonsustainable) debt position. These countries must commit themselves to combating poverty and to economic reforms. Canceling debts takes place on the basis of current debt position while income from export and central government resources is omitted from consideration and thus may be used for combating poverty (and not for paying back debts). Source: www.worldbank.org/hipc/about/hipcbr/hipcbr.htm

[6] A classis is a governing body in certain Reformed churches, consisting of the minister and representative elders from each church in a district.

PART 3

Multidimensional analysis
of the project

CHAPTER 12

A Nicaraguan perspective on Jesus and the Samaritan woman

Azucena López Namoyure

Nicaragua is a Central American country with a population of five million inhabitants. Sixty percent of the active population is unemployed. Most people do not satisfy even their basic needs for education, health care, and food. Under these circumstances, the Bible has been a source of inspiration, strength, and hope for God's people in this country. The Bible has accompanied us in economic, political, and social troubles, as well as during natural disasters. The study of the Bible is a fascinating field, but among us it is still underdeveloped.

The experience of the intercultural study of the Bible has allowed us to open a new gate of exchange and to learn new interpretations. Although we do not share the same culture with our partners, we engaged in an open, dynamic, and challenging dialogue.

Five Nicaraguan groups participated in the intercultural Bible reading project: a Baptist group, two groups of theology students, a Catholic group, and a Pentecostal one. Pentecostal churches constitute 80 percent of the Protestant sector of Nicaragua and are found in the central zone as well as the Pacific zone. These churches have increased their membership and are an important evangelical presence in the country. For this reason, I chose to present the Pentecostal group in this article.

In this document, I present an intercultural Bible reading process in which a Pentecostal group from Nicaragua participated. The presentation has a qualitative character; I do not pretend that this group is representative of Pentecostals in Nicaragua. The Nicaraguan group participated with a Dutch group, but I want to deal in depth with the experience of the Nicaragua group because I have been close to it, and because I do not have all the records about the Dutch group's participation.

Azucena López Namoyure, Bible Department, Seminario Teológico Bautista (Managua, Nicaragua)

First, we will consider the doctrinal significance of the Bible in this Pentecostal church and the different times when the Bible is read and interpreted. Then, I will present the results of the intercultural Bible reading of the Nicaraguan group and the challenges of this experience.

Description of the Pentecostal group

Within the framework of the intercultural Bible reading project, we form one urban group of the Assemblies of God in Managua. The Assemblies of God in Nicaragua was founded in 1912. It has its origin in California and is the largest Pentecostal group in Nicaragua. To organize the Bible reading group, we talked to the pastor of the church to explain our purpose, project, and project objectives. Then he chose people to take part in the group and nominated a local coordinator. This particular Assemblies of God congregation was organized in 1999, and it is located in a poor neighborhood in the southern part of the capital city, Managua. This place is dangerous because there are a lot of gangs. Most of the members of the church are women. The congregation has four services during the week. The time for the Bible studies is on Thursdays during the service and also on Sundays during Sunday school. The ones in charge of teaching are the pastor and some brothers and sisters who are trained by the pastor. They do the training on Thursdays. The method they use on both Thursdays and Sundays allows brothers and sisters to ask questions. We asked the pastor if any members were studying in the biblical institute of his denomination, and he told us that they were not yet ready to study theology.

Doctrine regarding the Bible

The second article of the Assemblies of God faith statement says that we believe that the Old Testament and the New Testament constitute God's revelation to humanity, and because they were inspired by the Holy Spirit, we trust in them as our faithful faith precept, and also accept them and proclaim them as the highest authority, far above human opinions (2 Pet. 1:21; 2 Tim. 3:15–17; 1 Thess. 2:13).

The doctrinal manual explains these concepts. *Inspired* literally means "God encouraged." God worked in such a way in the minds and capacities of the writers that the words they used expressed God's will and feelings (2 Pet. 1:21; Exod. 4:10–15; Deut. 4:2; Luke 24:24; Acts 1:16; 28:25). *Bible* in Greek means "books." The Bible is a collection of books, the Word of God, the revelation of God to humans, the faithful rule of faith and conduct, much higher than conscience but not opposed to reason. The whole Bible represents the inspired efforts of at least forty men who wrote over about 1,600 years, keeping coherence, logical development, and agreement on the doctrine.

Formal education

The Bible Institute of the Assemblies of God (Instituto Bíblico de las Asambleas de Dios) was a member of the Community of Bible Institutes (Comunidad de Institutos

Bíblicos, or CIB) until 1988. Currently, it is a part of the University of the Assemblies of God (Universidad de las Asambleas de Dios). Its profile follows the denominational doctrinal line.

Outcomes of the group Bible reading. The Assemblies of God group consisted of four women and four men, aged twenty to forty-eight. The meetings were held in the temple in the evenings. The group was linked with the Dagmaat group from the Netherlands. This Dutch group has studied the Bible for many years.

Each meeting began with a prayer and some worship songs. At the beginning, people felt a little uncomfortable, perhaps because of the tape recorder, but when the group started talking about the passage they spoke fluently.

The group marked as relevant the extract from John 4:1–42, because it shows how Jesus breaks racial, social, and religious barriers. Jesus is the living water for the salvation of human beings. The Samaritan woman, who had a sinful background, was a confused prostitute to whom Jesus offered his salvation, the power of the Word of God, and the importance of preaching the Word after coming to know Jesus. In our study, we pointed out only one aspect of the historical background of the passage, the separation between Jews and Samaritans.

To explain the meaning of the passage, some participants related the story to their personal experiences. In addressing the question of why the Samaritan woman had had several husbands, one woman said:

> She just wanted to be finished with her need. She thought that in a man she could find what she needed. But Jesus, who is the king of glory, has taken us out from that lie. I am a woman whose life has been rescued by Jesus. [The Samaritan woman] felt empty, and she wanted to fill that emptiness with a man, but she could not find the source of life in men, because our Lord Jesus is the only source of life. And I say before you, I was one of those confused women, and . . . I thought that men were going to give me everything I needed. And I tell you, [I was] wrong. The only one who could fill the emptiness of my heart and stop my thirst and need was Jesus Christ. That is why today I say to everybody, to all those disoriented women, that the Christ of glory is able to set them free and rescue them, no matter what condition they are in.

What does the text tell us now? The participants based their answers to this question on God's call to his people to tell the message of salvation to the lost souls, because salvation is everywhere and Jesus loves us equally.

Some participants related John 4 to other biblical texts. A man said,

> I understood what Jesus meant when he told the Samaritan woman he could give her the water, and that she would never be thirsty. It is clearly stated that this woman caught on well to what Jesus had spoken to her. When Jesus told the woman he could give her water, he probably was

speaking in a parable, and she didn't understand. She thought Jesus was talking about the well water. But Jesus meant better water, that is, spiritual water, which is given only by Jesus when he comes into our lives through the work done by the Holy Spirit. As he said, "Let anyone who is thirsty, come to me, and . . . drink" (John 7:37).

Another man mentioned another text in the Gospel of John, in order to explain why Jesus didn't want to eat:

The disciples were very concerned because Jesus would eat food, but then he told them this food was not his, but the spiritual food was, the food that comes from the Father. In John 6:32–35, the Bible describes what the spiritual food consists of. "Jesus said to them, 'I am the bread of life. Whoever comes to me will never be hungry, and whoever believes in me will never be thirsty.'" As we see here, Jesus Christ wanted to fulfill his mission. For him, it was more necessary to obey his Father's commands than to pay attention to the things of this world.

Everybody agreed that God inspired the Bible and that it contains God's message. It touches us, makes our minds clear, and makes us change when we believe it. One of the participants said that when he reads the Bible, it shows us who we are, what we have to do, and consequently there is a change. The dialogue between the Bible and us changes everything.

The same man said also that when the Word of God enters our lives, it is a torch that lights things up: "The Word of God is alive and active, sharper than any double-edged sword. It cuts all the way through, to where soul and spirit meet, to where joints and marrow come together. It judges the desires and thoughts of man's heart." And when we share the message of the Lord, Jesus is with us.

A man noted that Jesus opened the mind of the woman:

The Lord told the woman, "Give me water." However, she did not know what water Jesus was talking about. She was confused and lost. As they continued talking, Jesus opened the eyes of her heart, and she could see differently. Everyone knows that when we talk about the Word of God, everything changes and turns into reality. Jesus used dialogue to focus on the Bible. Jesus talked about a gift that he understood very well. He was talking about something real and alive, something that the woman had to experience. In fact, this woman was religious and did not understand anything, but in the ongoing dialogue she finally caught on.

When the Word of God is spoken, it has a great impact in the lives of people. Sin and evil do not allow people to be touched. Regarding this, a man said:

Jesus never missed an opportunity to share the message he had received from his Father. He did so when he met the woman next to the well of

Jacob. He proclaimed the living and active word that touched her heart, and I am certain she was the first woman who presented the good news. She went away and told everybody that she had met a man who might be the Messiah—she was a little doubtful at first. This is what happens to many people who hear the voice of God. What is more, God reveals himself to these people, but they are blinded by their sins and don't allow the light of the gospel to shine in their spiritual eyes.

In summary, we note significant aspects of the process: (1) The group paid little attention to the historical and literary background of the passage. (2) They began with personal experience in explaining the meaning of the passage. (3) The group recognized the Bible as God's inspired Word. (4) They cited other passages from the Gospel of John to explain the meaning of some verses of the passage they were studying. (5) The group emphasized what the Bible is and noted its illuminating and changing power in the lives of people.

How did the Nicaraguan group experience the exchange with the partner group?

The Dutch group's perspective

The Dutch group linked with the Nicaraguan Pentecostal group comes from the western coast of the Netherlands. They gather weekly in order to study certain texts of a book of the Bible. They are between fifty and eighty years of age.

The members of the Dutch group used different versions of the Bible to interpret alternative translations of some words that appear in the text. They also wrote questions: Was it a well or a spring? Did they buy food or meat? Was Jesus greater or more important than . . . ? Moreover, they used other biblical stories related to the passage, in order to understand and be clear about some aspects. The group also wondered about why verse 2 is in parentheses. Do the parentheses indicate that the verse was inserted later or that it comes from another manuscript?

The Dutch report on their study of John 4:1–42 is a summary of their dialogue. It shows what aspects of the story members of the group focused on: what kind of woman the Samaritan was, why Jesus had to pass through Samaria, what the living water is, what spirit and truth are, what people in Jesus's time expected of the Messiah, what we learn about the faith of the Samaritan people in the passage and in other biblical texts, and what Jesus's role is in the passage.

What kind of person was the Samaritan woman? The group mentioned classical characterizations of the woman in commentaries and sermons, as a prostitute, as immoral. But they did not adopt these characterizations. For them, the woman is an example of growing in faith. She talked just once with Jesus and reached faith and real confidence. In contrast, the disciples took a lot of time to have faith; it came to them after the resurrection of the Lord. The woman came to faith because she opened her mind to Jesus's words. She knew what the Torah was; she came up with important questions; she was a good disciple of Jesus, a teacher of Samaritans, a sower and harvester, and a woman who witnessed as Martha and Mary did.

Why did Jesus pass through Samaria? The group said that the text does not give any answer to the question of why Jesus went through Samaria. However, someone said that from the author's point of view it was necessary for the sake of the story, so the dialogue between Jesus and the Samaritan woman could take place. The way Jesus broke with tradition and customs really stood out, because in the text he spoke to the Samaritans, and what is more, to a woman. Jewish people have no basis for complaining about Jesus; he came to save Samaritans, too. This fact prompts us to remember the question about circumcision in the book of Acts.

Living water. The living water is another important topic in the passage, because the dialogue between Jesus and the Samaritan woman brings the demand for living water. Water that is effective gives life, and so the woman will no longer be thirsty. The group asked, Is the well of eternal life our personal life? Or does it refer to the larger story and vision of the kingdom of God? The group gave no answer.

What is truth? What is spirit? Truth means sincerity, justice, the reality of God's Word, integrity, authenticity, and trustworthiness. The Spirit of God was moving over the water (Gen. 1:2) and created a living soul in the man (Gen. 2:7). In the book of Judges, the Spirit of God sent people. Jesus was also sent to the desert.

The expectation and identity of the Messiah. The group said that in Jesus's time, people had a great desire for a savior. They noted that in other Bible passages, Jesus does not want people to call him Messiah, but in this story, Jesus said to the woman: "I am he, the one who is speaking to you." They found a similar statement in Tanakh; in Genesis 16:13, Hagar calls God "the only one that speaks to her," and Isaiah 52:6 says, "In time to come you will acknowledge that I am God and that I have spoken to you." Jesus states these words about the completion of "the new earth," when God will be the king above all creatures.

The faith of the Samaritan people. The Samaritan people preserved and knew the Torah. In this story, they listened to the woman and recognized that Jesus was the Savior of the world. They became his disciples. And in Luke 17:11–19, of the ten men suffering from a dreaded skin disease, the only one who came back to Jesus to thank him was a Samaritan. It was also a Samaritan who helped the man who was beaten and robbed (Luke 10:25–37).

Jesus's role in the story. Jesus did not speak clearly in the story; he did not even say what it all was about at first. However, the group said that he assumed his listeners were aware of what the Torah was; when he spoke to the people, he used symbols people were familiar with. In that way, he gave them (and us as well) food for thought. Jesus did not condemn the woman; instead, he was pleased to talk to her and knew that what she was saying was true. Jesus asked the woman to give him water, and he wasn't thirsty at all. The disciples (who are not relevant to the story) suggested that Jesus eat, but other important things came up, including faith, inspiration, and understanding. Jesus's food was to obey his Father's commands.

Teachings of the story for our times. The group mentioned that the coming of the Messiah, the completion of "the new earth" when God will judge all creatures, makes them think they should just try to bring this world a little closer and be its spokespeople, be equal partners, be humans. Sitting together around Jacob's well, we learned this biblical story: you don't need to eat "worldly food"; you better try to be free of it. Go in that direction: respect one another, and eventually things will change.

Reactions of the Nicaraguan group to the Dagmaat group's interpretation

The Nicaraguan participants expressed some opinions that indicated differences between the groups. "The Dutch group has different knowledge," a woman said. "They know a lot about the Bible, because when they speak they take us to the book of the Kings, which is good, and moreover, they seem to know about the culture too. They say that Samaritans knew the Torah, and that is something that is not in the Bible. They mentioned the Tanakh. When people have other kinds of theological knowledge, they have other points of view and are able to interpret things differently, apart from the [point of view] the Bible has. A very prominent difference with our group is that we used only the Bible as reference, and none of us has studied in any biblical institute."

The group also expressed opinions regarding the method the Dagmaat group used. One man said, "They are very curious":

> They detailed many things Jesus didn't care about, except when he wants people to know he can do everything. I would like to tell my brother from Dagmaat not to go so deep into it, but instead to see Jesus's reality. Jesus is the one who is giving life to the woman, so that she can experience a change. We have seen that Jesus changed her life, and as a result she began to witness in a wonderful way. What I see is that they study in depth, looking for some verses in other books to find a logical base. We have a logical base: Jesus is the logic. We don't have anybody besides him; he is almighty."

Another woman agreed. "Sometimes, they question the things we consider unimportant—for instance, whether it was a well or a spring. So, the brother is emphasizing that we shouldn't go too deep in small details but in the bigger things."

One woman agreed with the way the Dagmaat group studied the Bible:

> The comparison they make is interesting. They say that out of ten men suffering from a dreaded skin disease, only one was thankful and returned to Jesus to thank him. That was really interesting, because Jesus dealt not only with Jewish people but also with ones considered non-people. If we really believe that the Bible is one of the things God works through, we can learn to appreciate it. For example, the fact that God judges people with the same standards, that he doesn't reject anybody, and that he has salvation for

everybody, has its support in these two cases. We could continue to mention other cases, such as Ruth's and that of other women, and this is nice because they are foreign women.

Interpretations the two groups did not share.

The Bible is not history. One member of the Dutch group gave his opinion and said Jesus had to pass through Samaria for the sake of the history. A Nicaraguan responded,

> I think the Lord had to pass through there, first, because he had people who were not his people, but they were going to be his, and second, because he came to seek and save the lost. And that's it. He always went to the villages where the wicked people were and always spent his time with them. The Bible isn't history; it is a living word. God isn't interested in writing history. Paul preached the truth, and the four Gospels aren't stories. The four Gospels tell me about a divine person who lived for thirty-three and a half years, who talked to the Samaritan woman, and my conception is that the Lord wanted to bring his people: "The people that didn't look for me, found me." The Lord's desire is to have his people back.

About Jesus going through Samaria, a Nicaraguan woman said, "He came to seek and save the lost in that moment. The Samaritan woman was not in communion with God, and it was necessary to stop by that place. It's easily seen that it was God's purpose, because he knew there were many people that needed the source of life that Jesus offers. Not just the woman but also the rest of the people came to Jesus. So it was not for the well-being of history."

Jesus was thirsty. The Dutch group said, "At the end of the dialogue he was not thirsty any more." A Nicaraguan woman responded, "They say that Jesus was no longer thirsty, but I think he was thirsty. What happens here is that he cared for God's plan. Remember that Jesus was human like us; he *was* thirsty and hungry, but in that moment it was more important for him to talk about God's plan, and he was doing it there. He gave living water to the Samaritan woman."

Jesus is the truth. The Dutch group wrote these questions: What is spirit? What is the truth? Truth is justice, it is sincerity, it is integrity. God's Spirit was moving over the water; it produced living soul in the man. A Nicaraguan man responded: "Spiritually speaking, Christ himself is the truth; God wants humanity to learn to love Jesus. There are two spirits, God's Spirit and the human spirit. Spirit is united to Jesus when we worship the Father: 'There is no other way to go to the Father except by me,' Jesus said. Christ Jesus is justice; when we are praying and God realizes we are outside Christ, he won't accept our offerings.

Shared interpretations. Only one man wanted to express his opinion about shared interpretations. "I agree with the brothers and sisters who said that God's plan is the salvation of humanity. Jesus is pleased with this, and we are pleased, too. It is a reciprocal well-being.

New interpretations for the Nicaraguan group.
Opinions about the Samaritan woman. One Nicaraguan sister said,

"We hardly ever mention . . . the role women play within churches. But someone [in the Dutch group] noticed the way Martha, Mary Magdalene, and other women served Jesus. These women, as well as the Samaritan woman, were the first ones to bear witness to the gospel. The Samaritan woman was the first one to say that Jesus is the Messiah. Another important thing [the Dutch group] mentioned is that Jesus told his disciples she spoke truthfully. That made us think [her words were] true, because Jesus talked not only about her dark side, but he also realized she was being sincere. It is a relief to know that Jesus sees not only the negative side of our lives but also the positive side.

One man said that the Dutch group "mentioned what we forgot to mention, that the one who proclaimed, sowed, and harvested was a woman. The other day we were discussing whether she was a sower or a harvester, when she really was planting. She was harvesting at the moment that the rest of Samaritans believed her words."

Opinions about the teachings of this passage. One man responded to the Dutch group comment, "Respect one another, and eventually things will change": "This is good, because we are supposed to live in harmony with people (relatives, spouses, brothers and sisters from the church, and neighbors); otherwise Jesus Christ is not in our lives."

Opinions about the well. One woman said: "I liked that the [Dutch group] had touched on this important passage because the place and moment that Jesus took advantage of to strike up the conversation with the woman was the right one. The woman was looking for water, and the source of 'living water' was there in front of her, Jesus Christ."

Answers to questions. The Nicaraguan group offered answers to some of the questions posed by the Dutch group. "Was it a well or a spring?" A man from the Nicaraguan group answered, "As far as I know, a well is made by people and a spring is created by God, so in the reference to well and spring we find the union between man and God." "Does this well represent our personal life?" The same man answered, "In my opinion, it represents eternal life; the one God wants us to receive." "Why is verse 2 in parentheses?" A woman responded, "I don't really think this explanation in parentheses was inserted later. Instead, I think the writer of this Gospel is the one who did it, wanting to remark that the person who baptized was not Jesus but his disciples.

Opinions about the exchange. At the end of the process, the members of the Nicaraguan group evaluated the exchange. One woman mentioned the differences:

Brother Rodolfo says that Mark, Luke, and Matthew wrote almost the same, but with differences, because they did it from their own points of view, based on what they remembered. If we had to write a new Gospel, and the brothers and sisters from the Dutch group had to do it, too, we would write completely differently. This is how the Bible was written. The writers all talked about their points of view and their personal experiences; because of this we find many stories in the Gospels of Mark, Luke, and Matthew that were not included in the Gospel of John. This looked interesting to the eyes of the Dutch group.

Another woman added, "This dialogue is very important, because despite the fact that we all say something in a different way, we don't lose our vision and focus. We all get to an agreement. That is what is happening here with the Dagmaat group."

The Dutch group said they found the experiences, life conditions, and perspectives of their Nicaraguan partners very meaningful. A Nicaraguan woman said, "I like the way [the people in the Dagmaat group] think about our group. All the members of the Dutch group are very well educated and know a lot. However, they talked to Nicaraguans in a respectful way, not looking down at us as others do. They were very impressed by our opinions and noticed we put our hearts and souls into this [process]. Moreover, I personally think that God intervened in it all, and also his Holy Spirit, who was working in both groups."

As stated before, the Nicaraguan group had different opinions regarding theological study and the use of the tools to study a passage from the Bible. Members of this group don't have theological training. They thought that referring to other biblical translations just raised more questions about the words in the text. This exercise was seen as meaningless by these members of the Nicaraguan group, and (they suggested) even for Jesus. The best thing is to get to the point, to what is real and essential, that is, to Jesus.

Another man in the group considered it unnecessary to dig so deep into the verses to find logic, because the logic is Jesus himself. However, he said that the method the Dutch group used was important, because all the theological and additional biblical knowledge they shared was in accordance with the texts. He also said that this knowledge influences the interpretation of the biblical text, because the words can be read in different ways.

Members of the Nicaraguan group did make use of other biblical verses (not stories), apart from the John 4 text, in order to reinforce their explanations of the passage. This result shows that the attitude of rejection coming from some members of the group, regarding the use of other tools and supplementary information for the study, is attributable to the kind of doctrine this denomination adheres to. But the fact that other members were more open-minded and receptive to the new way of interpreting caught everyone's attention. At least for these people, doctrine is not determinative regarding the Bible.

The Nicaraguan group articulated other concepts about the Bible. The Bible is the Word of God, and it not only touches us but it clears and changes our minds when we believe it. When people hold a dialogue with the Word of God, a change is started. The Bible is an agent of change for human beings; it has a transforming power. These characteristics are also present in the Holy Spirit and in God.

The new birth is an important experience for the Nicaraguan group, as is human transformation. Change comes throughout the communication with the Word, by the Holy Spirit, Jesus, and God. The woman's recognition of her sinful situation is coherent with it, because at the end of the story, she experienced a change that allowed her to be saved and become a gospel transmitter. One woman said, "I understand that God is calling sinners as he did the Samaritan woman. But Jesus expects these men and women to open their hearts and souls to him, so they can enjoy their salvation and be proclaimers of the gospel of salvation."

This transformational experience of the gospel of Jesus is fundamental for human being, and under this perspective, other themes are explained. For instance, about the question of what is truth, one man said, "Jesus is the truth, spiritually speaking. No one can come to the Father without Christ. Jesus is my own justice."

Another aspect is the role of life experiences and personal witness, which are important elements to explain the text. The women from the Nicaraguan group were the ones who used this method. This path joins the readers' lives with the text. Personal testimony is very important for Pentecostal believers, for it manifests and gives evidence of God's presence in their everyday life.

The two groups found different teachings in the story of Jesus and the Samaritan woman. For the Dutch group, this story evokes the realization of the new earth, where believers are partners and comrades with their equals. Everything might change if you respect one another. If we act in this way, we bring this new world closer. The story is a warning to stop using our human thinking with regard to worldly things. This teaching talks about change, but this change is just the result of human relationships established on the basis of mutual respect, fellowship, and humanism. In this perspective, human beings have a lot of initiative; their roles are determinative.

For the Nicaraguan group, the story of John 4:1–42 is a call from God to his people to share the message of salvation with lost souls. This salvation is for everybody; it has worldwide coverage. Believers now have to proclaim the good news exactly as the Samaritan woman did when she had experienced the change in her life. We have to live our salvation and not stay quiet. Prophesying means proclaiming the message of redemption. This message of salvation has to be proclaimed with the support of our personal testimony about the transformation that Christ has accomplished in our lives. While proclaiming the message of salvation, the believers are certain that Jesus speaks through them. One man said: "When we begin to talk about the Word of God, we already know that we are not the ones who do it, but Jesus does it in us."

Two women said that the differences between the Dutch group and the Nicaraguan group were the result of two different points of view and of their own personal experiences. Also, the difference was remarkable because of the high level of schooling the Dutch group had. The Nicaraguans accepted the differences between the two groups, while recognizing that there was a common message at the end. The absence of cultural, social, and religious elements caught their attention, because these factors were not mentioned as influencing their partners' interpretations.

We have to mention the participation and role of the Holy Spirit in both groups. The members of the Nicaraguan group talked about the Spirit in a general way, but one woman said that the Holy Spirit was in each of them: they were altars for the Holy Spirit. She said also that the Holy Spirit was guiding and working in both groups. That is, there were different interpretations, but the Holy Spirit was acting in each group. This perspective affirms the action of the Holy Spirit in non-Pentecostal groups (the Dutch group was not Pentecostal), specifically in interpretation of the Word of God. This statement is exceptional among Pentecostals.

We conclude that these brothers and sisters live their relationship with God day by day. God is present in their lives and in all the activities they are involved in. The Bible is God's inspired Word, and it is their faith foundation. However, when asked about the teachings of the story of the Samaritan woman and Jesus, they did not find any aspects that had to do with our everyday lives, with the struggle for survival that faces most Nicaraguan people. The biblical study of John 4:1–42 challenged the Nicaraguan group to talk about the message of the gospel, the fundamental duty of a believer, what they consider "the mission of the church." This story only teaches them how to accomplish the mission of the church. This raises a question: is not John 4:1–42 a story that reflects everyday life? Or do the ecclesiological conceptions of these Pentecostal believers influence their perspective?

We already mentioned that their personal experience was a tool to explain some aspects of the biblical text. Moreover, personal testimony is important in the Pentecostal liturgy, in the sermon or the service. Testimony is a significant moment within the community, because people talk about their experiences with God and the providence of God in their lives. But how can we relate personal testimony, which has to do with life, to the study of the Bible?

The outcomes of their process reflect the way to study the Bible in this Pentecostal group. The model of biblical study that prevails in this church is not a participatory or community reading. Doctrinal, ecclesiological, and christological elements influence their study of the Bible.

The intercultural Bible reading allowed a Nicaraguan Pentecostal group to study the Bible with a non-Pentecostal one—not something they would usually do in Nicaragua. From now on, we have to look for new ways to articulate the value Pentecostals give to the Bible, to personal testimony and the participation of the Holy Spirit in reading and interpreting the Word of God, so that we can have a liberating and contextual reading.

Shaping our lives, transforming our communities, reaching out to the world

The power of reading the Word together

Evelyn Miranda-Feliciano

Five intercultural Bible readings were conducted in the Philippines. Four were directly facilitated by this writer and one by a volunteer. One of the four was not linked with a partner. Three years into the project, only one pair is partially completed. The Samaritana (Philippine) and Wichmond (Dutch) groups have reached the "understanding, approach level."[1] At this stage, exchanges of perspectives are pursued. The ideal would have been to reach the consensus level.

The other pairs under this writer's care—Institute for Studies in Asian Church and Culture (ISACC) staff, Quezon City, and Abetifi (Ghana) Pentecostal women; Christian Writers Fellowship, Mandaluyong, and Grupo Estudio Bíblico, Bogotá, Colombia; Sambayanang Kristiyano sa Biga (Community Christian Church, SK) midlife fellowship group and El Mesías, La Paz, Bolivia—are still on the exchange level. The Samaritana staff group, although without a partner, has found the process helpful in opening new ways to read scripture with clients. Each of the three local groups has received one report from its partner and has sent its response.

Incomplete as they are, the processes and developments in the local groups still provide sufficient data on which to base a measure of tentative analysis on how intercultural Bible reading works and affects people, individually, communally, and interculturally. Using the Philippine groups as a prototype, comparisons can be made with similar groups from other parts of the world in terms of contexts, approaches, effects, or impact on individual and communal lives, as well as on intercultural widening of perspectives.

When I took on the task of organizing Bible study groups, I imagined a group of colleagues as excited as I was. Some were excited at the beginning but begged off after I explained what it would entail on their part. Thus, I found myself facilitating,

---

Evelyn Miranda-Feliciano, Institute for Studies in Asian Church and Culture (ISACC) (Quezon City, Philippines)

documenting, translating, and conveying the reports between partners through the main office in the Netherlands. Like most of the rest, I did the project on the side; my main work is something else. Although the work was "seasonal" in nature, it was labor intensive, too. In the beginning, people were volunteering to do the job, but when push came to shove, no one was there but me.

The wide gap of time in communicating with partner groups (six to eight months or more) was both a boon and a bane. It allowed the leaders/facilitators a respite to do their regular work unimpeded. But when the reports came in on top of other immediate responsibilities, chaos took over. Groups changed composition with the time lag. In three cases, those present during the meeting where a partner's report was to be discussed were (with some exceptions) no longer the members of the original group. Much time was taken for review of what had already transpired, to bring everyone up to date. The lapse of time also impeded continuity of the process, although not of learning. I therefore commend those groups from other countries that intentionally took time to go through the stages by taking retreats together. This approach made possible a more controlled environment and, perhaps, more helpful analysis. In our case, time, money, and the busyness of our day-to-day institutional affairs did not allow such leisure. The advantage for us is that the intercultural Bible reading occurred in the most natural settings, having been tucked in as part of the activities of the Philippine groups.

This analysis is written on the basis of this reality. The focus is on how their reading of John 4 has formed and transformed individuals, communities, and cultural groups. It will try to answer the following questions: How has the reading of John 4 brought about changes in those who attended the study (*personal realization*)? How has the reading of John 4 brought about changes in the group and in the communities to which the members belong (*community change*)? How have exchanges of studies on John 4 with other groups from other countries brought about depth, enrichment, new ways of looking at the Word and life (*intercultural transformation*)?

Although it is helpful to read through some fifty intercultural Bible reading reports posted on the Internet, time constraints and practical considerations dictate that I focus more on what we have discovered together on our home ground, as far as spiritual formation and transformation are concerned. Without doubt, the reports from other countries are rich, but I will leave them to the experts to mine more exhaustively, for the benefit of all. Now and then, however, I will refer to some of those reports relevant to the points of this chapter.

Spirituality, a journey of life

Personal formation and transformation, like its communal and intercultural counterparts, is a process of a lifetime. The shaping of one's life and the changes one undergoes spiritually are the results of many factors: genetics, childhood experiences, relational encounters, education, trauma, and religious encounters, among others. Growth in spirituality is therefore cumulative in nature, deepening and broadening as one allows oneself to come under the Word of God and obeys it actively in the world where one moves.

This analysis does not claim dramatic spiritual changes out of the intercultural reading of John 4 held among various groups in various places and times. It would be an exaggeration to claim that in one, two, or three Bible readings, individuals are transformed into new people. It is sufficient to say that some people did experience significant change; some were challenged to do specific actions after the study, and actually did them; others saw the need for attitudinal changes; still others were just happy to be there—affirmed, loved, and encouraged by a caring community.

The report exchanges from other parts of the world were met with excitement. As with many groups worldwide, lessons on geography and culture preceded examination of the reports. These lessons in themselves have been educational. For the first time in their lives, members have become aware of particular people with entirely different backgrounds from theirs, yet doing the same activity they were doing—studying scripture. Local groups said they felt privileged to be a partner: "We would never have met them if we were not part of this intercultural Bible reading." They were amazed that despite racial, economic, and geographical differences and distance, they were able to read the same Bible, learn much from the same passage, and more often than not, come to similar conclusions about Jesus, the woman, witness, worship, and gender and racial equality, among other things.

Contexts of study make a difference

For Bible reading to be effective—for people to be warm, open, and learning—the setting in which the study is conducted is important. *The setting* refers not only to the place (worldwide, most were conducted in churches, homes, offices, and in retreat houses), but to the emotional-psychological atmosphere surrounding the study.

Much of the responsibility for atmosphere-building rests with those who are facilitators. These leaders must be people of warmth and friendliness. But more than that, they must have prepared, so the study is participatory, dynamic, and imaginative. Beyond all these, leaders must be themselves. The subject matter must be backed up by their manner. Method cannot replace integrity; eloquence is not a substitute for truthfulness and humility.

Of the reports I have read on the Internet, the approach used with Bartolomé de las Casas men's and women's groups (El Salvador) stood out to me as effective, given the composition of the groups and the context. Meditation, music, drama, and specific focus brought out unforgettable realizations that seemed to change how some participants saw themselves and understood how they ought to relate to others.

Among the evangelical Protestant groups, whether in the Philippines or elsewhere in the world, a more creative, democratic approach to reading scriptures is important, because, as with many passages from the Bible, John 4 has become too familiar. "There's nothing much to mine there any more" is the immediate thought that comes to those steeped in biblical exposition, and is most often heard from churchmen or churchwomen.

A democratic approach means that participants are given the opportunity to read and understand scripture in their own ways, after they have a sufficient knowledge of the background and context of the passage. They are free to ask questions, engage the facilitator and one another in a discussion, and hold on to their own convictions without being seen as disrespectful or contrary. All that the communicator of the gospel can do is verbalize it, according to James Packer, as its message is a personal message from God to each hearer. And the only appropriate and effective way of communicating it is for a messenger to deliver it on God's behalf, ambassador style (2 Cor. 5:20).[2] Ambassadors come to visit and sit with the locals for dialogue, which is what happens in group Bible reading or study.

Meditation in drama

Most groups involved in the intercultural Bible reading project worldwide started their meetings with singing and prayer. Europeans usually read a poem related to the text, as preparation. Some facilitators came with objects that remind them of wells or water. A group in South America passed two bottles of water for the group to examine and guess where it came from. These imaginative approaches prepared the hearts and minds of participants to read the scripture together. They also helped foster camaraderie and warmth, as people expressed feelings and shared ideas with each other.

In the Philippines, we used a dramatic dialogue script of John 4:4–30, 34–38, with a narrator, and speaking parts for Jesus, the Samaritan woman, the disciples, and the villagers, using the Filipino translation of the Bible, Ang Mabuting Balita (the Good News). With the Samaritana group, this reading was enacted, complete with costumes and rehearsals. With the ISACC staff and the Christian Writers Fellowship, the parts were assigned prior to the meeting, and the whole script was read three times while the whole group was in silent meditation. A period of silence followed every reading. With the SK midlifers fellowship, it was read as if the group were listening to a radio drama.

The choice of a dramatic script style of presentation was made by the facilitators. The goal was to give freshness to the passage, otherwise regarded by most as worn out. Encouraging people to put themselves in the shoes of the characters, to use their imaginations, helped them greatly in understanding the story and appreciating its meaning. Jesus, the woman, the disciples, and the villagers came to life as the members identified themselves with these characters, remembering their time and context. The experience gave the passage a new face and a new feel.

Filipinos are now, more than at any other time, enthralled with radio dramas and *telenovelas* (television soap operas, both local and imported). Culturally, we are visual, musical, and artistic. Yet the evangelical Protestant wing of the church in the Philippines has yet to be weaned from sticking strictly to expository preaching. They have yet to move to telling stories, or dramatizing, dancing, or singing the good news, followed by a good biblical discussion.

Less technology, more natural interaction

After a few attempts, facilitators gave up documenting the process with the aid of a tape recorder. It hampered the natural flow of conversation. It was a distraction, as some members just like to hear their own voices. Pictures were fine, if one had an official photographer. Still, Filipinos are picture-conscious and would abandon a discussion to pose! A video was out of the question.

Responses to the dramatic approach

The ISAAC staff group found the repeat readings interspersed with silence a good way to enter into the event. Members said that they "enjoyed the process, learned much from the passage, because during the sharing time, their own understanding was enriched by other's insights." They also said they gained fresh insights from a familiar biblical incident. Giving a title to the passage, as if it were a movie to be produced today, fit well with the group's interest, because they are moviegoers and movie lovers.

If this group found listening exciting, another—the Christian Writers Fellowship—found it difficult; it was not active enough. One member did say, "Hearing the Word is easier in a group than when one is alone." Although listening is hard, reading the passage three times enabled one to get the essence of the story, and hearing had more impact than just reading it.

The difference in the groups' reception of the dramatic approach seemed, on closer analysis, to be attributable to the time of meeting and the composition of the group. Members of the Christian Writers Fellowship are professionals who work from 8:00 a.m. to 5:00 p.m. The intercultural reading was at 6:30 p.m., on a Friday, and the members came directly from their offices as an add-on activity. In contrast, the ISACC staff did the reading as part of the institutional program; thus, they looked forward to it. The institute was also more open to creative ways of handling scriptures. In contrast, the writers may have tended to be print rather than sound oriented.

Thus, there is more to becoming a Bible reading facilitator-teacher than just knowing one's Bible. One must take a sensitive and creative approach that adapts to the group's cultural and historical environment and circumstances. As Latin American theologian Rene C. Padilla points out, "It is only as the Word of God becomes flesh in the people of God, that the Gospel takes shape within a historical situation. . . . The Gospel is never to be merely a message of words, but a message incarnate in his Church and, through it, in history."[3]

Personal realization: Seeing oneself in the passage

Observation of and reflection on the text

Application to one's life follows observation of and reflection on the text. This direct correlation is common to the answers given in all the groups in the Philippines and elsewhere.[4] Examples of these answers are:

Melba of the ISACC staff was struck that the Samaritan woman makes a lot of what she has done, "Come, see a man who told me everything I did." Instead of being embarrassed or ashamed, she was only too happy with the disclosure. "Jesus is the Lord before whom I am fully disclosed and yet not afraid. He has a quality of transparency that attracts us to him. The knowledge of who I am gives me security."

Fhabi (of the Christian Writers Fellowship) was impressed by the phrase "water that will not make you thirsty again." "This is a constant reminder for me to go back again and again to Jesus, the Living Spring, so I need not thirst again."

This application is not unlike the one made by the group in Schwenger, Germany: "We are like the woman: we must come again and again to fetch water—this faith water. Like the woman, when something new started in her, there are special moments or meetings in life that change us. Our protection (or self-defense) is pulled down."

Precy of Samaritana (a group of ex-prostitutes) observed that Jesus attended to the Samaritan woman and paid her full respect. She said: "It is my honor that I am not snubbed; somebody has noticed me. I am not made to look stupid; I am a person of worth."

Vicky of SK also pointed out that Jesus was gentle. He was not embarrassed to ask for water. "Sometimes," she said, "I am hesitant to approach someone for help who may be more educated than I am. But Jesus did not have this kind of hesitation. He is always looking for opportunities at the right time."

Reflecting on the Bible drama to which the group had just given life, a man from Bartolomé de las Casas (El Salvador) confessed, "I'm quite an abusive man, because when my daughter said that she was harassed, I could not control myself [and went] to look for whoever did it. But I myself have been an abuser of women."

It is interesting to note among the Philippine groups the constant movement between objective observation of the text and personal application. It has not muddled the context of the text, nor has it led to bizarre interpretations. These people in the three-fourths world have learned to grapple with biblical truths to make them true in their own lives. For example, the Samaritana group of ex-prostitutes easily identified with the Samaritan woman's predicament of loneliness, of being excluded, and of joy in finally being accepted. This identification did not surface among the members of their partner group in the Netherlands, made up of middle-class women who have lived most of their lives in the same church and neighborhood. A number of groups, especially from Europe, expressly said that they could not easily identify with any of the characters in the passage or with the situation portrayed in it.

These differences and their various expressions may be explained by understanding the functions of culture. Culture operates as both binoculars and blinkers, as Packer puts it. It helps us see some things and keeps us from seeing others.[5] That the passage speaks to different people quite differently does not mean one is right and the other wrong. Both are right, in fact, because it is the nature of the Word to speak to us in our particular need, however culturally bounded.

Oriented to action

The device of asking, What in the story would you like to take home with you to do, to work on or to become? helped the participants focus on what is meaningful and doable for their spiritual formation. The exercise done with the ISACC staff is an effective example.

At the second meeting, participants were reminded about the action they had proposed as a response to the passage. The facilitator had written the proposed actions down, and she read them again for the group. She asked, "What happened between then and now, if something has happened?"

Armi replied immediately, "My desire to do basic evangelism as the woman did was reinforced. Surprisingly, I found myself talking to three foreign students at the Asian Theological Seminary. On reflection, I believe God sent them to me so I could help them in their struggles as they try to adjust here in the Philippines. They may not be totally non-Christian, but I felt okay about the fact that I spent quite some time with each one. Just to keep in touch with them was something important to me."

Malou, on the other hand, went home to her province aware that she should be sensitive to others, as Jesus was sensitive to the Samaritan woman. She found herself not only talking with her younger brother, the black sheep in the family—whom she did not even want to look at before—but also eating at the table with him. "I realized I have to change my approach and be more sensitive toward him."

Fabie shared that since the first meeting, she had become a more "behaved driver." "I've stopped making comments on undisciplined pedestrians, but I'm taking it out on other drivers. I have a long way to go yet, like the disciples."

Espie of the midlifers was challenged to exercise more selflessness than selfishness; *Vicky* was using the art of listening, especially in relation to her husband; and *Zeny* sought the opportunity to talk with a loose woman in her village, the one person she did not want to have anything to do with. "I thought, she does not deserve the gospel. But this passage tells me I am wrong. If Jesus himself treated the Samaritan in such a gracious manner, who am I to look down on my neighbor?"

In other words, personal and cultural contexts do condition interpretation and application of scriptures. Scriptures do not have one meaning for everybody; they are not "one size fits all." Thus, the applications are far ranging, as the passage itself remains unchanged. Furthermore, the applications are made in the context of the individual—as a neighbor, a driver, a wife, a sister, or a witness. With this cultural sensitivity and dynamism, the Bible becomes an exciting book, a source to go to as a road map for Christ-like living. Anthropologist Louis Luzbetak points out that conviction and persuasion call for the use of effective, culturally pertinent starting points of reasoning, feeling, and motivating. Persuasion to act is successful only if the motives are real—real to the receiver of the message—which presupposes a thorough acquaintance with the culture content and the value-system of the receiving group.[6]

To arrive at this outcome, Bible readings should not stop with the "we ought" and "we should" that usually end meetings. Without sounding pushy or demanding, facilitators should be more aggressive and personal, asking specific action from each one, making them accountable for whatever resolution they have made. This approach helps people actively engage with scriptures in real terms. Personal formation and transformation begin and continue here.

I am acutely aware that this style is foreign to some societies. "We are not used to expressing our personal situations as you do," wrote one partner from Europe. "We admire you for being candid and honest about your circumstances in life." In this situation, the facilitator should think of ways to encourage participants to respond more personally, without giving them the feeling that their privacy has been invaded. It is in the nature of the Word to get into our private lives, to become meaningful to us, so it can then spill out to the rest of the world.

Communal change: A widening of perspectives, a strengthening of resolve

Intercultural Bible reading opens people's eyes in a variety of ways: excitement comes in realizing that studying the Bible together can be enjoyable and relevant to life. People come to see that the Bible, and John 4 in particular, is inclusive and not exclusive. Jesus embraces not only individuals, like the woman, but whole communities, as he embraced her village. The Samaritana group, considering their circumstances, voiced this realization through one of its members: "Jesus thinks broadly. He is not narrow. He does not judge. He was kind both to the woman and to her people, staying with them for days to teach them."

The passage widened the discussion of many groups, in the Philippines and in other countries. The participants not only saw the relevance of the passage in their personal lives but also saw its impact on other issues present in their communities and in the world. Issues of gender, race, culture, religion, politics, and economics came to the fore. Some groups discussed the presence of discrimination or intolerance in their midst, in an offhand, academic manner. Others, however, such as the Shoolagiri Dalit group in India, struggle daily with the ugly and sometimes violent expressions of such religious bigotry. Some members had witnessed or suffered personally the effects of religious intolerance as Christians living among Hindu or Muslim communities. Thus, the passage had an immediate, active, and real response and application to the participants' lives and families.

Similarly and more deeply situated were the women's groups in Havana, Cuba, and San Salvador, El Salvador, whose readings of John 4 focused on the unequal relationship between men and women. The Cuban group found it liberating that Jesus broke traditional patterns and gave the woman value. That woman, as a Samaritan, brings salvation for the rest of the community. She acts as "collaborator, cooperator, creator, and transmitter of new voices." Thus, the group came to a forceful conclusion: "Gospel means No to racism, No to sexism, No to segregation and exclusion, No to rejection of alcoholics, prostitutes, homosexuals, homeless people, people of low status, and those who are mentally and physically different."

The Salvadoran group had a spirited discussion about how women are discriminated against in a machismo culture. The response of the women was to value themselves and to announce and denounce as well as to celebrate the dance of the water, the dance of freedom. They also articulated a vision of the future: "We dream of a new society, of a new man and a new woman, who are prepared to build new inroads that can give answers to the signs of the times. . . . We dream that we all will listen to the profound exchange of words between Jesus and the Samaritan woman, so that they will feed us in moments of pain and hopelessness."

While the women dreamed, men had their own realization. The Bartolomé de las Casas men's group loaded the text with their own values and prejudices during its dramatic presentation. But the men saw their own machismo. Taking the role of the Samaritan woman, they began to understand the helplessness of women and were able to identify with them and the world they inhabit. Also, they became aware of their own attitudes and condemned them. Finally, they made commitments to change.

These experiences lead us to observe that an examination of the biblical text together, a discovery of its truth in the lives of readers, and an intentional engagement of the passage with relevant issues of the day help enlarge the capacity of people to respond both individually and communally. The change on a community level may not be immediate, but the seed of response is there. Also, the bond that is formed within the group through the experience of interacting with the biblical passage makes for a closer, more cohesive community, and, most likely, a community that is changed within.

Intercultural transformation: Exchanging insights, enlarging horizons

It was a happy day when the four groups in the Philippines received their first reports from partner groups. The reports came at different times, and meetings had to be scheduled for each group to discuss them. It was important to review what had already transpired, to refresh the memory of those who were then present, and to inform new attenders about the topic at hand. What happened in these exchanges?

First, participants realized that the world is large. "I am amazed that there are Christians out there, and they are reaching out to us!" exclaimed one wife in the SK midlife fellowship, excited at the first report from their Bolivian partner. Showing the country on the map and providing basic information about the place raised participants' level of awareness of the world. Groups that were pretty much in-grown and preoccupied with their immediate environments shared this new discovery. Such new practical knowledge led to spiritual concern. Groups began praying for their partners.

Second, participants discovered that people are different. The ISACC staff entered into the lives of their partners in Ghana by pretending that they were these women. They read the way the Ghanaians introduced themselves, and they played their parts in the discussion, not to mimic them for laughter, but to feel what it meant to be Ghanaian women. They readily saw the differences in the way they lived and the manner in which they expressed themselves. They were quick to spot common concerns and issues in their religious life. In all the groups, there was an expressed desire to maintain communication and exchange pictures as much as possible with partner groups.

Third, a group initially received any kind of assessment or evaluation of their reading with anticipation but also doubts, followed by defensiveness, especially when the assessment was negative. The Christian Writers Fellowship reacted to their Bolivian partner's comment that they seemed to be "shallow" in their understanding of the passage. The Samaritana group thought their Dutch counterpart offered an unclear understanding of the passage; because they did it verse by verse, their explanation was deemed superficial. Besides, the Dutch group concentrated their discussion on the Pharisees in the first three verses rather than on the main story.

Fourth, the initial bristling at differences was muted when the groups discovered they have more things in common. I noted this response when the second exchanges occurred, as in the case of the Samaritana, when their Dutch partners tried to explain what they had meant. Most times, what seemed like value judgments passed on the partner group arose from insufficient understanding of the context of the group; sometimes they arose from translations. For example, I translated literally into Filipino the word *prostitute*, as used by the Dutch group, for their local counterpart, the Samaritana. When I asked one of the women about their response, she told me. "First, they insulted us, but then it was all right because at the end, they praised us." What the group thought was an insult was my own misunderstanding about how the word *prostitute* should be translated. "Among us, we don't use that word; it is too painful, too brutal," she explained. "We use euphemisms to describe our former work. 'Those who work at night,' will do," she continued, "or 'nightclub workers' or 'GROs' (guest relation officers). I had to apologize for my mistake to her, and through her to the group.

Although linguist-anthropologist E. A. Nida refers primarily to Bible translation, his comment applies to the mistake I committed: "Cultural differences between people will pose some barriers to communications, but these should be reduced as much as possible by an effective use of cultural equivalence, sometimes in the form of descriptive phrases."[7] And I am not even a foreigner to these women!

I am sure we have made mistakes aplenty: on the level of local documentation, in translation from the local language to English and translation from English to the language of partner groups. The manuscripts we are working on could be five times or more remote from what actually transpired. Print reports lose the dynamics and nuances of the discussion. I prefer to use verbatim reports rather than highly summarized ones from other countries. But whatever our preferences, we do what we can, guided by reasoned faith, God helping us.

Intercultural Bible reading is most needed because it opens a new world for ordinary Christians who are quite locked up in their own cultures. Diverse they may be, yet in sharing the same Christ and the Word through a communication line such as the one provided by this project, stereotypes and misunderstandings diminish while understanding and appreciation for one another grows. If we can sustain this dynamism, it will make for an eloquent Christianity and a better world at the grassroots level.

Fifth, participants rejoiced in the faith we share in Jesus Christ, despite geographical and cultural differences. "Isn't it wonderful," a member of the SK midlife group said, "that all over the world we are reading the same passage, learning similar lessons from it, and trusting our lives to the same Savior Jesus Christ, as the Samaritan woman and the villagers did? I truly feel connected. We are not alone!"

Faith in Christ apparently globalizes, in the best sense of the word *globalization*. Unlike the West's approach to homogenizing the world with its own culture, this common faith tries to understand; to grapple with what cannot be understood, by discovery and communication; to appreciate and accept differences of perspectives and contexts. It builds a consensus on common values; it reaches out toward harmony and closeness. Mediating this creation of a global reality at the core is studying the Word together in ways that are creative, participatory, and relevant to each group's situation and to the times. Also crucial is the opportunity to connect with others from other parts of the world. Without this connection, emotional and spiritual bonding would be slight and weak, even absent.

Conclusion

As seen in the Philippine three-year project of intercultural Bible reading of John 4, the Word informs, forms, and transforms people who study it together. The approach to such study varies, but it has to fire the imagination of participants enough to make them see that it is not just a story, that it could be their story. It is a story that is made lovely because it happens among neighbors—friends and enemies alike—and Christ is there to bring them together to make life full, like "a spring of water gushing up to eternal life" (John 4:14c).

From the pages of the Bible, the story leaps out to find its reality in people's lives. Exchanges of insights and learning with other groups bring an added dimension. In the exercise of exchanging notes, the intercultural Bible reading groups are once again making applications of what they have personally learned: accepting their partners as they are (as Jesus did with the Samaritan), without any imposition of their own preconceived ideas, hearing their criticisms with grace (as the Samaritan heard Jesus's gentle rebuke), treating their reports with respect and being compassionate with their lack (as Jesus demonstrated).

The project is not only a means to find out how ordinary people read the Bible; it has ingeniously provided a venue to apply the passage on a worldwide scale, bringing understanding, encouragement, and deeper faith among individuals and groups. In the process, we are making our Christian contribution to peace and understanding to this war-weary world. The truth remains:

> The law of the LORD is perfect,
> reviving the soul;
> the decrees of the LORD are sure,
> making wise the simple;
> the precepts of the LORD are right,
> rejoicing the heart;
> The commandment of the LORD is clear,
> enlightening the eyes. . . .
> Moreover by them is your servant warned;
> in keeping them there is great reward. (Psalm 19:7–8; 11)

Notes

[1] J. A. van der Ven, *Practical Theology: An Empirical Approach* (Kampen, the Netherlands: Kok Pharos, 1993).

[2] James Packer, "The Gospel: Its Content and Communication," in *Gospel and Culture: The Papers of a Consultation on the Gospel and Culture,* ed. John R. W. Stott and Robert T. Coote (Pasadena, Calif.: William Carey Library, 1979), 136.

[3] Rene C. Padilla, "Hermeneutics and Culture," in *Gospel and Culture,* ed. Stott and Coote, 104.

[4] First names of group members are used with their permission.

[5] Packer, "The Gospel," 140.

[6] Louis J. Luzbetak, *The Church and Cultures: An Applied Anthropology for the Religious Worker* (Techny, Ill.: Divine Word Publications, 1963), 17–18.

[7] Eugene Albert Nida, *Customs, Culture and Christianity* (London: Tyndale Press, 1954), 221.

CHAPTER 14

South African intercultural biblical interpretation

Toward a global postcolonial ethic of interpretation
Mark Rathbone

When people talk about South Africa, references to apartheid and the victory of democracy are usually included. What is left unsaid, most of the time, is the fact that this happy story is turning into a Jekyl and Hyde script.[1] The problem is that structural change, cosmetic as it may pan out to be, hides demons that no one wants to look in the eye. Today, the new multicultural nationalism being built and hailed by all but a few extremists on both sides of the political spectrum seems like a dream come true. It celebrates diversity, cultural tolerance, political freedom, and economic growth, producing great smiles on the faces of a select group of the previously marginalized majority of South Africans, but also on the faces of the elites of the Afrikaner apartheid empire. This situation should turn the stomach of even the most optimistic.

Speaking frankly, the proof is a matter of dollars and cents, or rather, of rand and cents. Statistics are clear: the rich are getting richer and the poor are getting poorer, as the cliché goes.[2] I do not intend to engage in a Marxist critique of capitalism, but I would like to delve deeper into the mysteries of the history of South Africa. Yes, this history is mysterious, because it is dynamic and it continues. As Edward Said has observed, "Appeals to the past are among the commonest of strategies in interpretations of the present. What animates such appeals is not only disagreement about what happened in the past and what the past was, but uncertainty about whether the past really is past, over and concluded, or whether it continues, albeit in different forms, perhaps."[3]

In this vein, J. J. Kritzinger states that apartheid racism was nothing else than the continuation of British colonialism: "The ending of British colonialism indeed did (legally speaking) establish a sovereign state, but did not put an end to colonialism,

Mark Rathbone, Department of Old and New Testament Studies, University of Stellenbosch (Stellenbosch, South Africa)

since power was transferred to a white minority, and the rights of the black majority were not enshrined in the constitution."[4] This ideological trace of the white settlers in South Africa constitutes a settler culture that continued European colonialism—separating European culture from Africa. "The white community still exhibits the typical colonial features of a threatened minority living in the midst of a black majority implementing various measures to retain their power and privileges."[5] Resistance culture existed at the same time, opposing the oppression imposed by Afrikaner nationalism, reclaiming a sense of humanity and land. These cultures did not simply vanish after the first democratic elections in South Africa; they continue. On the other hand, black nationalism grew from the black elite who were educated in the colonial education system, from which the basic ideas of liberty and freedom follow the path of Western politics.

The colonial past of South Africa and the postcolonial process did not suddenly end after 1994, but are continuing in a new form. This new form is what *The Road to Damascus: Kairos and Conversion* refers to as *global imperialism*, which is aligning with Western powers in the non-Western world to construct a powerful global network of domination.[6] Apartheid was a specific form of white settler domination. New forms of black nationalism, traced back to black elites that attended British imperial educational institutions, continue Western nationalist trends, neglecting the poor and marginalized. Thus, the benefit of globalization is limited to a small minority that have the wealth and power to effectively compete in the market. The majority of people are also affected, but as the victims of the same processes. They are losing their jobs and dying of HIV/AIDS.

Intercultural reading of the Bible will remain a pious intellectual exercise or cultural anthropological gymnastics if the ethics of interpretation are not engaged. If they are not, the benefits of global connectivity will only lead to the oppression of humanity. A global postcolonial ethics of interpretation envisions an interface between people that takes history and the geographical violence of imperialism seriously, recognizing that the other is the colonized and marginalized other, facing the reality that humanity is connected through geographical violence and that connectivity without the critique of power perpetuates oppression.

Postcolonial refers to the time colonialism and imperial subjugation began and not to a time after colonialism ended. It refers to the decolonization of texts such as the Bible, which is viewed as oppressive—the Book of the White Man. Intercultural reading of the Bible has to take this history seriously in the wake of globalization and the assault of global imperialism which aligns Western culture in the West and the non-Western metropolitan world. It will become clear that the hierarchical dichotomy of colonizer and colonized is present in the readings of the narrative of the Samaritan woman, reflecting an imperial linkage between the groups connected by the Through the Eyes of Another project.[7] The tension between Afrikaner readings of the Dutch Reformed Church in Montclair and Stellenbosch reflects imperial traces similar to those of the Western groups, while the non-Western South African groups, from the poor communities of Sokhanya and Ivory Park, have decolonial traces similar to those of non-Western groups of Colombia and of Western diasporas such as the Tierra Nueva group in the United States. Ethical issues, such as racism (Tierra Nueva and Sokhanya), geographical space (Shekiná, Sokhanya), and gender (Stellenbosch women's group, Zaandam), are all closely linked to the history of colonialism and imperial domination. Intercultural reading of the Bible that is not sensitive to the ethics of the reading process is in serious danger of unwittingly perpetuating the hierarchical bias between Western and non-Western cultures. Said warns that culture viewed as a neutral and even ahistorical concept is dangerously close to ideology.[8] The implication is that the historical and geographical tensions between cultures cannot be bracketed. These aspects are interwoven in the interpretive process, resulting in an interface between people and not a mere semiotic play. In other words, what is at stake is "overlapping territories and intertwined histories," contrapuntally linked by imperialism.[9] We must take the ideological traces of culture seriously, as well as history, and in the case of South Africa, colonialism and imperialism. In this chapter, I will refer to three dimensions of this bias located in the connections with South African groups: racism, geographical space, and gender.

Globalization, culture, and imperialism

In *Globalization and Culture*, John Tomlinson argues that globalization is not a postmodern cultural praxis but part and parcel of modernity or modern culture.[10] He views modern culture as a postnationalist phenomenon that is not linked to Western culture but rather is a development from the long history of exchange between cultures. Modernity is therefore as much at home in Japan as in the USA. It is a culture in which the link between geographical space and identity has been lost, because of the relativity of time. It is a hybrid culture.

The impact of global modernity is its potential for social consciousness and transformation.[11] The fact that people are connected through television and other communication media brings them closer together. This togetherness also increases the realization that people are dependent on each other and can affect one another, although they are geographically separated. The media can have a positive impact in creating awareness of other geographical spaces and the people who live there. The connectivity of globalization is an ethical function, not the glitz of first-class air travel and exotic vacations. Globalization is an ethics of connectivity.

Tomlinson is critical of the notion of modern European imperial culture proposed by Said. According to Tomlinson, this culture is a relic of premodernity and not global modernity.[12] At this point, Tomlinson simply negates the history and effect of colonization and imperialism on non-Western people, as if history and culture can be switched off, and we can then simply ignore them. This idealistic oversimplification does not take seriously the history of imperialism. Texts leave traces, and if the trace of the other simply evaporates, then "otherness" sounds more like an ideological strategy of silencing than like freedom. This aspect was evident in the comments of the Marburg (Germany) group about celebrating differences between people. The problem is that these differences have a history of racism and abuse, something that the Ivory Park group to which they were linked know too well from the experience of colonial racism under apartheid.

Intercultural biblical interpretation that develops a global ethic based on these notions simply connects people without taking seriously the history of colonialism and imperial power. Such a global ethic proceeds without dealing with the scars and inequalities between cultures, and it ends in more exploitation and abuse. It becomes clear that connecting is more than analyzing ethical remnants of issues; it also involves struggles that have been going on for centuries.

In *Culture and Imperialism*, Edward Said moves to a contrapuntal alternative involving colonial exploitation and resistance. Said proposes a mode of uncovering the other, or the silenced. "The point is that contrapuntal reading must take account of both processes, that of imperialism and that of resistance to it, which can be done by extending our reading of the texts to include what was forcibly excluded."[13] This contrapuntal quality points to the connectivity, but within the historical trace and exploitative dichotomous relations.[14] Said is in agreement with Tomlinson that the world is intimately connected and that a modern culture has developed. But this culture of modernity developed as a result of the exploitation of many non-Westerners, and of Korea in the case of Japan. Globalization is a function of imperialism, within which the trace of the other causes a tension in the seemingly smooth interconnectivity. Here the other has a face and history and is not simply an ambiguous other. To speak of the West as "other" is imperialist, for the center cannot be the margin, because the center is constituted by marginalization. Pretending to be the margin is deception, a strategy to terrorize.

To speak of global well-being or of "us" is not a neutral happy engagement but a place of transformation. Voices of violence must be uncovered and silences filled with dignity. Through a reading of the interpretations of the narrative about Jesus and the Samaritan woman, I will attempt to uncover these voices of the other, thus revealing connections based on history, power, and ideology. This process of uncovering is reflected in the Colombian group's connection with the Montclair group, regarding the disciples' reaction to Jesus's conversation with the Samaritan woman. "They approach the woman with prejudice, because she is a woman and a Samaritan. Jesus transforms the exclusion, instead of prejudging and pronouncing punishment on the woman. He restores her." The Montclair group had admitted that their view was colored by prejudice, which is related to the imperial linkage between Western and non-Western cultures. Racist exclusionism relegated the other to the outside, as the enemy, and linked the inside to home or security. Global connectivity is not a question of issues beyond our border but of reevaluating and possibly engaging the existing issues that connect "us." The history of interpreting the Bible in South Africa is part of this process, revealing the mode of silencing and decolonization in a process of ever-continuing negotiation, connection, and struggle.

Ethics of interpreting the Bible

The interpretation of the Bible is under negotiation in a struggle between Western and non-Western forces. Transformations in the West, from historical-critical, positivistic scientism, to semiotics and the play of signifiers in a poststructural, deconstructed world of diversity, have radically reconstituted the interpretive agenda. Non-Western hermeneutics, carrying the burden of European colonialism and imperialism, broke from its Enlightenment modes and struggled with semiotic shifts and its detachment from the world to embrace contextual modes of discourse—theology from below.[15] In the metropolitan centers of the West this negotiation stirred the fabric of establishment guilds. Elisabeth Schüssler Fiorenza's work on *Rhetoric and Ethic: The Politics of Biblical Studies* emphasizes this new historical and political consciousness.[16] The worldliness of interpretation of the oppressed, the non-West, female (the other) is firmly established as a counterculture to white, male, colonial rhetoric within biblical studies. This negotiation between Western and non-Western forces is reaching maturity in today's postcolonial writings, taking seriously the connections between the colonizer and colonized. The work of R. S. Sugirtharajah,[17] Fernando Segovia,[18] and others developed from the postcolonial trinity of Edward Said, Homi Bhabha, and Gayatri Spivak.[19]

What has become clearer is that the negotiation between West and non-Western forces has a history of its own, linking them through imperialism. This process is not a clear-cut matter of textual theory and interpretive modes but is rooted much deeper in the difference between Western culture and non-Western resistance, traced back to the time when the first white European man encountered non-Westerners. Eurocentric culture prepared the ground for colonization, constructing a white, European, Christian, civilized center in which there is no room for a non-European, un-Christian, barbaric margin that does not have the right to rule geographical space but should rather be subjugated and ruled over. At the same time, resistance culture developed—decolonization. It did not originate in the twentieth century but began with the arrival of the first Europeans. At first, violent resistance, then structural resistance and nationalism, an alternative way of conceiving human history ("the voyage in"), took shape from where an integrative or hybrid nationalism and social consciousness developed.[20] Interpreting the Bible in the world has thus become a matter of power and politics that connects the Western and non-Western world. The text excludes, silences, and oppresses, and at the same time reclaims, struggles, and liberates; it is worldly.

In the interpretation of the Bible in the South African, non-Western settler context, the role of colonialism can be traced back to the arrival of Jan van Riebeeck in 1652.[21] British imperialism intensified control of the land and the civilizing mission of the church and missionary organizations, until the first and second Anglo–South African wars led to an alliance between the British and Boers (the Afrikaner). In 1910, the union was formed. This act blatantly excluded the non-

Western populace of South Africa.[22] Colonialism continued in the developing of Afrikanerism.[23] These acts were legitimized using the narratives of Israel's conquest and seizure of the land of milk and honey from the heathen Canaanites.[24] The Enlightenment left its mark on these revelation-historical pronouncements of earlier colonialism, with its historical-critical, rationalist mode of civilized interpretation, moving beyond superstitious religion. These traditional approaches were radically challenged by the development of science that replaced superstitions with more Eurocentric rationalism, stripping biblical myths and narrative of their transcendentalist dogmatism, and moving beyond mechanical links between Israel and the Afrikaner.[25] But these scientific, value-neutral modes of interpretation were quickly revealed as just another way of controlling non-Western peoples. The scientific approach's reluctance to take the question of power seriously[26] is clear in the Stellenbosch men's group interpretation of John 4, which focuses on historical questions.

The critique of Enlightenment scientism led to a poststructuralist celebration of difference, reflected in Daniel Patte's *Ethics of Interpretation*,[27] ending in a neutral, ahistorical linkage between interpretations, traced back to the qualitative differentiations of colonialism. The Marburg group, for example, points to the importance of differences between people, and the Stellenbosch men's group focuses on reconciliation without taking into consideration the history of inequality and injustice. The remnants of imperialism and control follow in the new modes of interpretation of settler culture, silencing the colonized world, masking the agony and cruelty. Silencing cannot remove the other. The experience remains in the world, and a culture of resistance to oppression is revealed the moment people read the text.[28] The strategies and rhetoric of settler culture do not exist in a vacuum but are intimately connected to its other, against which that culture protects itself by erecting boundaries. The silenced Canaanites and barbarians have their own history, narratives, and pain, reclaiming territory, identity, and freedom.[29] They are estranged from the land that has been renamed, divided, and exploited.[30] The differentness of their place and their lives has made them objects of exotic delight and of an impulse to change, transform, and reform them into a male, Western place and people.[31]

Intercultural biblical interpretation can become a dangerous agent in the hand of globalization, but at the same time, it is a fruitful point of departure to untangle the long colonial history of the globe. The rise of the ethics of interpretation has emphasized the effect of biblical interpretation on the lives of people, and in the same way, it challenges intercultural reading regarding the effects such reading has. These effects are contextual, influencing the lives of people in time and space. In South Africa, with the growing threat of global imperialism, a global postcolonial ethic of interpretation is a responsible hermeneutical perspective. This hermeneutic is multidimensional and deconstructive, reflecting the multiple expressions of human relationships and hierarchies that exist in tension. Intercultural connections press against the boundaries of these hierarchies, revealing the tension, and breaking through the hidden cultural bias.

Unraveling the hidden connection

Racism and difference

Western colonialism is preoccupied with difference and exoticism.[32] Exploring new territory, traveling to "strange" worlds, is part of a cultural fixation on the exotic, on excitement and conquest. The racist civilizing mission of the West has a long history of exploitation and oppression, replacing "inferior" barbarian black culture with "superior" European white culture. Today, these racist remnants of the colonial past are fervently rejected in postmodern Western culture, making way for difference. But this new emphasis again follows the trace of colonial racism that extends to compartmentalized modernism and professionalism, distinguishing between I and they, what I do and what they do. A value-neutral difference conceals the hierarchical history. The analytical mode of the Stellenbosch men's group, focusing on empirical knowledge of places and people, is in stark contrast to the narratives of the Tierra Nueva group, which engaged the text on an existential level in terms of their experience of racism.[33]

The conquest and control of territories by the Spanish, Dutch, British, and others did not simply evaporate after colonies gained independence. Imperialism continues through an integrated network of relationships, attitudes, and systems that shape perceptions of the other. Although the emphasis on cultural superiority, positivism, and the civilizing mission has to an extent been left behind, the evidence of distancing and difference continues. Connecting with the other is nothing other than an exotic journey to a strange land and its people. "Through the eyes of the other" becomes a play of texts and exotic destinations. Note that the Western groups that connected with South African groups emphasized difference, while almost all the South African non-Western groups viewed differentiation as racism. According to non-Western people, this process of differentiation is a neo-racist attitude, classifying and controlling the other. European colonialism and imperialism that continued in Afrikaner nationalism and apartheid followed a historical path in which differences of race, culture, gender, etc., were not negotiated but imposed on people, affecting where they lived, where they were allowed to go, and what they could do for a living. The oppression of apartheid and its rigid legal apparatus made difference a salient motive in oppressing black South Africans.[34]

The imperial connection of racism is inherent in the connection between the Sokhanya group—located in New Crossroads, Cape Town, and consisting of pastors from African Independent Churches (AIC)—and Zaandam in the Netherlands. Sokhanya's linkage to African Independent Churches and Zaandam as part of the Western Reformed tradition is significant. The development of the AIC is largely the product of a decolonial impulse of black African Christians, who felt that their culture and identity were threatened by Western churches.[35]

The Sokhanya group focused on the issue of racism. They viewed the Samaritan woman's ethnic identification of Jesus as a Jew, as racist. The Zaandam group responded that the word *racism* "frightened us, for in our society the word *racism* is in a way taboo. It verges almost always on violent behavior." But "the Bible is a book full of richness. There is much more in it than you can discover in your own group. Take the leading thought of discrimination, for instance." Operating within a culture of difference, the Zaandam group noted that the apartheid history of South Africa justifies the focus on racism. "There is much more at stake in this text than I have been reading in it myself. It is also dealing with discrimination. It is not just a story of mission work." The encounter with another view "deepened my view of this text."

Reading through the eyes of another simply meant that the semiotic play of the text was experienced. The connection between difference and racism fell in a blind spot. Influenced by their Western cultural mode of the hermeneutics of difference, the Zaandam group responded: "We feel that you apply the words *racism* and *discrimination* to situations where we would not be inclined to do so. Instead we speak about distinctions and differences, which we try to endure in each other." The Marburg group also commented on difference: "It's brilliant, that we're all individually different." Jesus does not let the differences or prejudices stand in his way: "Jesus jumps over the barriers of such standards."

The problem is that difference can spontaneously develop in the construction of an "inside" and an "outside" space; a space of security and a place of violent boundary crossing or terror: "Human beings need friends and enemies; there will be always human beings we have problems with." Bridging this gap between the outside and inside through Christ, as the group reported, does not take into account the fact that difference constructs its own enemies and friends. It presupposes a history of violence, discriminating and disregarding. Their partner group in Ivory Park concurred with Sokhanya that the woman is racist.

This culture of difference is echoed in the settler Afrikaner culture's focus on cultural difference in the post-1994 elections. In this case, language has become a mode of retaining cultural exclusion and exclusivism. The reference to racism and discrimination bridged by Jesus is used functionally, and difference does not then hamper communication. The openness of Jesus is a functional tool in the communication of the gospel.

The "foreignness" of Jesus does not become a stumbling block, according to the Stellenbosch men's group. The fact is that difference remains intact, and openness is a mode of communication. "He used one woman to reach out to all the Samaritans" (again, the Stellenbosch men). Difference and openness go hand in hand as a means of producing the necessary effect. What is silenced in these interpretations is the link between Jesus and the Samaritan woman, the fact that racism and sexism are not only a matter of boundaries that have to be crossed for communication to be successful, but that these boundaries are constructed through a history of colonial terror. This translates to a failure to explore the impact of racism in South Africa and the particular advantages of this group of white males.

Geographical space

Apartheid dislocated people from the land, removed people, and relocated people, making them foreigners in their own land. Global modernity is a deterritorial force in which geographical location is no longer a determining factor in the formation of identity. The link to space has been transformed to a global spatial awareness; "to be in this place" is an ambiguous thing. This space is linked to other places and people. Take, for example, an airport, a space constructed to transcend this space by linking it to another space without the discomfort of traveling through geographical terrain.

In the globalizing world, there is a discomfort with space and with being linked to a particular place. If spatial boundaries enclose the self or prohibit entry into another space, one's ability to connect is limited. Refugees are a metaphor for this spatial ambiguity, but for them there is a violent dislocation or separation from space at home. Global modernity is transforming nationalist geographical locatedness toward inter-located space, in which all people are wanderers and at the same time global residents. Adhering to the nationalist myths of a particular geographical space, or clinging to borders that cut up the globe into fragmented places, creates the impression that the other space and place and person are alien and foreign, endangering our place and identity. The problem of global residency is that it ignores the marginalized position of non-Western people within the global space. The wealth and power to be a global resident remains limited to a select few in the metropolitan centers of the Western and non-Western world.[36] Everyday things like collecting firewood and water are important aspects of geographical space and socio-cultural exchange. The family and community are dependent on the same space for wood or water and one another. Most Western and settler groups emphasized the aspect of the narrative about worship not being linked to place, in their discussion of Mt. Gerizim and its historical background (see, for example, the Stellenbosch men's group). This subject is largely absent from non-Western interpretations.

Deterritorialization is rooted in the mind, thought, and imagination. The physical, vulnerable, and fallible transcend religious fundamentalism and place-ism. Rationalism, positivism, and scientism transcend the located superstitions of monsters and angels. A universal sense of reality, impatient of fundamentalist location and identification, exposes nationalist construction. Distancing and individualization prefer boundaries between texts and interpreters, uncovering principles and abstractions that are globally applicable. But this mode conceals territory, culture, history, and power, maybe even the displacement of the interpreter's own self, the demons that haunt the subconscious, the territorial fixation—voyeurism.

Non-Western resistance cultures reclaim geographical space by naming it as part of the life world of people. The voyage is one of the most prolific imperial themes—the adventure of crossing boundaries to arrive in a strange new place to explore and conquer it. For the native, this motif sounds the crisis of banishment. The decolonizing native writer "re-experiences the quest-voyage motif from which he had been banished by means of the same trope carried over from the imperial into the new culture and adopted, reused, relived."[37] In Joseph Conrad's *Heart of Darkness*, the river is functional, carrying the explorer into the mysterious new world. But Ngugi wa Thiong'o re-experiences the river by naming it in *The River Between*. It is the life of the people and a source of joy.[38] "The postimperial writers of the Third World therefore bear their past within them—as scars of humiliating wounds, as instigation for different practices, as potentially revised visions of the past tending towards a postcolonial future, as urgently reinterpretable and redeployable experiences, in which the formerly silent native speaks and acts on territory reclaimed as part of a general movement of resistance, from the colonist."[39]

In the Siyaphila group, the physicality of the well and its linkage with Jacob directed the discussion to African traditions. The engagement between Jesus and the Samaritan woman was thus a case of Jesus versus traditional beliefs. This interpretation is a stark departure from the Stellenbosch women's group, which referred to the fact that it was Jacob's well, and then entered into a discussion about the physical attributes of the well and the link between Jacob and the Samaritans, reflecting their settler deterritorialization of space. They had a merely rational discussion of the physicality and its linkage to history, but Siyaphila linked the well to their subjective experience. Geographical space is not simply objectified but is interwoven with history, culture, and religion.

The well is of far greater importance for non-Western groups, reflecting the way resistance culture personalizes geographical space. The physicality of the well is linked to daily life and not to some function. A respondent from the Durban group, consisting of white women, noted that women in poverty still have to use wells; using wells is a sign of poverty. She failed to connect the well with geographical space and dispossession that has eaten away at the social fabric of communities. Geographical elements like the well have profound importance as social space. The bucket in both the Sokhanya and the Shekiná group is viewed as a cultic element and not only as a functional item. Things have meaning and are not simply items but are personal and intimate. Life's ordinary rituals are more than simple objects and functions. The personal spaces of non-Western people that have been disregarded as backward and even demonized are reclaimed. Carrying water in a bucket is not simply a manifestation of poverty and underdevelopment but is intimately part of identity. The bucket is important because the family depends on it for water, for life. The bucket is a sacred cultic element; it contained the water that now lives in this woman.

This view of objects is in stark contrast with that of a respondent of the Zaandam group: "The well has a dual meaning: Jesus wants to say (but he speaks vaguely and slowly) that consuming water from a well is one thing, and spiritual care from the well that Jesus himself is, is another. Jesus himself is a well from which one has to draw inspiration." The well has a dual meaning. It is functional, to quench thirst, but also spiritual and existential. The woman is also regarded in this symbolic fashion as a well in her village. The Marburg group also seeks a metaphorical meaning of the well. The existential need of the woman is quenched by Jesus: "The woman in our story, she's very, very tired: tired of life." Jesus is compared to Socrates, communicating through questions until the student arrives at the "correct answer," and comes to "understand." Jesus knows her search; he wants to verbalize it. This group makes a distinction between what is written and spoken. The aim is in the "voice" or "meaning" that is verbalized.

The narrative of non-Western groups takes the location seriously. The story is of real people in a real geographical space, struggling to find their place between tradition and modernity. This story territorializes the text and the reader, with the danger of a narcissistic nationalism—emphasizing the importance of an inclusive territorialization that is not universalist but rather is an interrelated telling of the story of a history of exploitation and enslavement. Territory was controlled from abroad, alienating the inhabitants and turning it into someplace else, another place. Resistance writing is an expression of the experience of oppression. The stories of exploitation and racism are expressed. This otherness is extended into a nationalist identity or an analogical identification with the oppressed in texts like those of black theology.[40] The result is new forms of aristocracy and dictatorship, because the hybridism is lacking. The power connections and the internal traces then end in an oppressive blind spot: women, the poor, etc., are then simply forgotten.

Gender

The patriarchal structure of apartheid marginalized and dehumanized women. Women were regarded as functions of male dominance and power. The maleness of the center of discourse and history at the same time constructed a sense of gender, distancing male and female. The brutality and injustices of the male construction dislodges society's balance in order to enact the imperial impulse. The culture of silence and shame cast on the female population reinforced the patriarchal structure.[41]

A female participant in the Sokhanya group said about the Samaritan woman: "She repented from her burden when Jesus told her of the wrong things in her life. She left her bucket and went to tell about this person who could tell what she had done while it was hidden from other people. I view it that she received the gospel and went to the city to preach it." The idea of a woman preaching was met with laughter from the males in the group. The prospect of a woman preaching in public was probably unacceptable to many of these black male group members, although one member confirmed that the woman did preach. This response is ironic because AIC membership consists largely of women.[42]

Black and white women of South Africa have been relegated to a position of inferiority and silence, although white women have largely been protected by the apartheid system. The settler groups were impressed by the woman's secure manner. The Durban group noted that she was not shy or reserved. She was a liberated woman. The Stellenbosch women's group also noted that she is not shy; she is not cast in silence but is open to engage even a Jewish male. The group differs from their partner group in El Salvador, which views her as sinful and states that she even mocked Jesus. The European groups had the same appreciation for this woman's confidence, courage, and ability to communicate her experience to the people of her village against all odds (see, e.g., the Zaandam group's interpretation). This positive perspective is a far cry from the negative views of South African non-Western groups. Some thought that the woman was immoral. In the Young Christian Workers group, an argument broke out between a male and a female. The female suggested that she was not immoral but unable to find love, while the male suggested that some are immoral by nature. This patriarchal image of the shameful and seductive female was countered by the breaking of female silence in this group. The Tierra Nueva group identified more closely with the woman, whereas the white male Stellenbosch group focused on Jesus.

Western and settler groups showed the Samaritan woman as a function of male purpose, while others emphasized liberating trends. Although a more open position was held regarding women in these groups, many non-Western groups judged her more harshly. She was interpreted as the traditional shameful female, in an interpretation that clings to patriarchy. The resistance culture's emphasis on decolonization and reclaiming territory overlooks its patriarchal nationalist modes. Impatience with difference is limited to ethnic and racial tenets and is not expanded to gender.

Conclusion

Reading the Bible in the Global Village: Cape Town[43] and *The Bible in a World Context: An Experiment in Contextual Hermeneutics*[44] confirm that reading the Bible in the global context is a reality of the twenty-first century. Here intercultural biblical hermeneutics is in step with global trends of connecting people. But the danger of this process, as Musa Dube warns in her response to Justin Ukpong's approach (which includes ordinary readers and the process of inculturation), is that without a firm ethical sensitivity, reading in the global village will perpetuate inequalities.[45] The questions of racism, geographical space, and gender are three dimensions of intercultural hermeneutics that have to be addressed if this project is to free itself from an ominous entanglement with the forces of global imperialism.

Notes

[1] This can be seen in the failure of government to respond to the HIV/AIDS pandemic in South Africa. More than 11.6 percent of the total population (according to a South African Department of Health HIV report in 2001) of South Africa is infected with HIV, and thus far, antiretroviral treatment is only available to a minority that can afford this expensive treatment. Once again, it is the poorest of the poor who are most affected.

[2] Comparison of the official unemployment rate between Census 1996 and 2001 shows that unemployment of black South Africans rose more sharply than

that of whites: black Africans from 42.5 percent to 50.2 percent; coloured 20.9 percent to 27 percent; Asian 12.2 percent to 16.9 percent; while in the white sector unemployment only rose from 4.6 percent to 6.3 percent (Statistics South Africa 2003). All information from Statistics South Africa 2003 is taken from the webpage www.statsa.gov.za

[3] Edward W. Said, *Culture and Imperialism* (London: Vintage, 1993), 1.

[4] J. J. Kritzinger, *A Theological Perspective on White Liberation* (Stellenbosch, South Africa: Centre for Contextual Hermeneutics, University of Stellenbosch, 1990), 3.

[5] Ibid.

[6] Catholic Institute for International Relations, *The Road to Damascus: Kairos and Conversion* (Johannesburg: Skotaville Publishers, 1989).

[7] The interpretations of the South African groups and their partners are based on reading reports found on the official website of this project, Through the Eyes of Another, at www.bible4all.org

[8] Said, *Culture and Imperialism*, xiv.

[9] Ibid., ix.

[10] John Tomlinson, *Globalization and Culture* (Cambridge, U.K.: Polity Press, 1999), 32–70.

[11] Ibid., 205–207.

[12] Ibid., 74.

[13] Said, *Culture and Imperialism*, 79.

[14] Ibid., 36.

[15] Liberation hermeneutics from Latin America; African theology; Minjung, Dalit, and other contextual theologies moved beyond a theology located in the mind, detached from the experiences of suffering and injustice, and have developed a firm nationalist mode of discourse, located in the experience of the people struggling for liberation from oppression (Christopher Rowland, ed., "Introduction: The Theology of Liberation," in *The Cambridge Companion to Liberation Theology* [Cambridge, U.K.: Cambridge University Press, 1999]); R. S. Sugirtharajah, *Asian Biblical Hermeneutics and Postcolonialism: Contesting the Interpretations* (Maryknoll, N.Y.: Orbis Books, 1999); Edward W. Said, *The World, the Text and the Critic* (Cambridge, Mass.: Harvard University Press, 1983), 31–35.

[16] Elisabeth Schüssler Fiorenza, *Rhetoric and Ethic: The Politics of Biblical Studies* (Minneapolis, Minn.: Fortress Press, 1999).

[17] See R. S. Sugirtharajah, ed., *The Postcolonial Bible* (Sheffield, U.K.: Sheffield Academic Press, 1998); and Sugirtharajah, *Asian Biblical Hermeneutics*.

[18] Fernando F. Segovia and Mary Ann Tolbert, ed., *Reading from this Place*, vol. 2, *Social Location and Biblical Interpretation in Global Perspective* (Minneapolis, Minn.: Fortress Press, 1995); and Fernando F. Segovia, *Decolonizing Biblical Studies: A View from the Margins* (Maryknoll, N.Y.: Orbis Books, 2000).

[19] See Madan Sarup and Tasneem Raja, *Identity, Culture and the Postmodern World* (Edinburgh: Edinburgh University Press, 1996), 147–70, for an introduction to the work of these authors.

[20] Said, *Culture and Imperialism*, 260–61.

[21] This Dutch settlement enclosed from the uncivilized heathen populace at the

Cape soon spread to the inland, making geographical advances (J. A. Loubser, *The Apartheid Bible: A Critical Review of Racial Theology in South Africa* [Cape Town: Maskew Miller Longman, 1987], 3–6). With the Bible in hand, these settlers were convinced of the lowly status of the people of the land and that their uncivilized culture was unfit to rule the land. Thus, they took control of that land, constructing a European enclave in the midst of darkest Africa.

[22] T. R. H. Davenport and Christopher C. Saunders, *South Africa: A Modern History* (Hampshire [U.K.]: Macmillan Press Ltd., 2000).

[23] From 1948 and the victory of the Afrikaner nationalist party, the imperial trace laid down by the British through apartheid continued. Segregation and later apartheid, claiming heaven and earth, ensured that the European enclave would remain a beacon of Christianity and capitalism against the communist threat. This settler culture continued the geographical control of earlier forms of colonialism by the Dutch and the British.

[24] Michael Prior, *The Bible and Colonialism: A Moral Critique* (Sheffield, U.K.: Sheffield Academic Press, 1997), 43.

[25] Ferdinand Deist, *Ervaring, rede en methode in skrifuitleg: 'n Wetenskapshistoriese ondersoek na skrifuitleg in die Ned. Geref. Kerk 1840–1990* (Pretoria: Raad vir Geesteswetenskaplike Navorsing, 1994), 31–75.

[26] Gerald O. West, *Biblical Hermeneutics of Liberation: Modes of Reading the Bible in the South African Context* (Pietermaritzburg: Cluster Publications, 1994), 32–34.

[27] Daniel Patte, *Ethics of Biblical Interpretation: A Reevaluation* (Louisville, Ky.: Westminster John Knox Press, 1995).

[28] Musa W. Dube, "Reading of Semoya: Batswana Women's Interpretations of Matt 15:21–28," *Semeia* 73 (1996): 111–29.

[29] R. A. Warrior, "A Native American Perspective: Canaanites, Cowboys, and Indians," in *Voices from the Margin: Interpreting the Bible in the Third World,* ed. R. S. Sugirtharajah (Maryknoll, N.Y.: Orbis Books, 1995), 277–88.

[30] Said, *Culture and Imperialism*, 252–65.

[31] Ibid., 159–96.

[32] Ibid., 130.

[33] Racism and difference influence every aspect of life and the modes of interpretation of text. The modes of analysis and criticism of texts separate the text from the world, creating distance between text and interpreters and their differences. What we are left with is play and diversity, without recognizing the connections—overlapping territories. Geography, narrative, and dialogue are reduced to functions and principles of the text and differences of interpretations.

[34] The effects can still be seen in the fact that the 2001 census shows that 22 percent of black Africans aged twenty years have received no formal education, and less than 5 percent have received tertiary education, while 1.4 percent of whites received no education, and more than 29 percent have received tertiary education (Statistics South Africa 2003 [see n. 2, above]).

[35] Z. J. Nthamburi, "Ecclesiology of African Independent Churches," in *The Church in African Christianity: Innovative Essays in Ecclesiology*, ed. J. N. Kanyua Mugambi and Laurenti Magesa (Nairobi, Kenya: Initiatives, 1990), 43–44.

[36] The luxury of accessing other spaces is problematic when only 39 percent of black South Africans use electricity for cooking food (Statistics South Africa 2003).

[37] Said, *Culture and Imperialism*, 254.

[38] Ibid.

[39] Ibid., 256.

[40] See James H. Cone, *A Black Theology of Liberation*, 20th anniv. ed. (Maryknoll, N.Y.: Orbis Books, 1990).

[41] This patriarchal structure is clearly reflected in the unemployment rates of the 2001 census. Black African males showed an unemployment rate of 43.3 percent versus 57.8 percent of the black African females, while white males only had 6.1 percent unemployment versus 6.6 of females, a decrease of nearly 0.5 percent from 1996 (Statistics South Africa 2003). Although gender discrimination affected all population groups, it is specifically black African women who also carry the burden of differentialism.

[42] N. H. Ngada and Kenosi Mofokeng, *African Christian Witness: The Movement of the Spirit in African Indigenous Churches* (Pietermaritzburg: Cluster Publications, 2001).

[43] Justin S. Ukpong, ed., *Reading the Bible in the Global Village: Cape Town* (Atlanta, Ga.: Society of Biblical Literature, 2002).

[44] Walter Dietrich and Ulrich Luz, *The Bible in a World Context: An Experiment in Contextual Hermeneutics* (Grand Rapids, Mich.: Eerdmans, 2002).

[45] Musa W. Dube, "Villagizing, Globalizing, and Biblical Studies," in *Reading the Bible in the Global Village: Cape Town*, ed. Ukpong, 55.

CHAPTER 15

Making things in common
The group dynamics dimension of the hermeneutic process
Alma Lanser–van der Velde

The group as context

The intercultural Bible reading project Through the Eyes of Another presupposes that culture determines the way we read. Factors that contribute to how one reads a Bible story include the country where one lives and the social class to which one belongs. Bible reading is inevitably a contextual event. This book describes from many different perspectives the way this reading happens and the effect the context has on the interpretation process.

By using the adjective *contextual,* biblical scholars and hermeneuts initially refer to the cultural influence on the reading and interpretation process. The big cultural differences dealt with are those between continents and related to the influence of social position, prosperity, safety, and perspective. In addition to the big cultural influences, the context of the smallness of the group also influences the reading process. This "smallness context" and the group dynamics aspects and their effects are described and analyzed in this article.

The hypothesis of this article is that in addition to culture, the dynamics in the group play a role in the hermeneutic process. Each group, consisting of these special people—women, men, or women and men; with certain ages; in this number; meeting at a specific time in a specific place—creates the context of that one unique reading process. Reading and communicating, the group collectively gives a meaning to the story of the woman at the well. Their meanings come into existence in that specific group. Only these unique people, with their own backgrounds and irreplaceable experiences of life, can put together these meanings in one unique process.[1]

Alma Lanser–van der Velde, Faculty of Theology, Free University (Amsterdam, the Netherlands)

The title of this essay, "Making Things in Common," was taken from John Dewey. This American educator observed that learning and communication processes are always contextual and time-related events. People who read together and talk to each other about their reading participate in a mutual practice for the duration of the situation. People were made to be together, and in their intersubjectivity they develop relationships of mutuality and collectively give new meanings to the texts.[2] People complement each other in the dynamics of conversation and the mutual search for meanings. All reading processes are context-related, which means that a reading process cannot be repeated, not even by the same people at another time. This fact shows that the group, and the communicative dynamics in the group, influence the reading practice and therefore are aspects in the hermeneutic process. It is not only the continent, the country, and the culture that affect the way meaning is attributed to Bible stories; the sociopsychological and educational aspects of the group process are also important dimensions of hermeneutics. This article aims to provide an insight into the aspects that play a role and to indicate the way group dynamics influence the reading process.

Method of analysis

The reading reports of the intercultural Bible reading project formed the research material for this article. Those who have been privileged to read all the reports will agree that the material is incredibly diverse in form and content. Some reports are verbatim transcriptions of an entire meeting. Sometimes, a report was written by someone observing from the sideline, who added appreciative and critical comments. Some accounts are limited to short summaries of what was said and done in a group. The variety is increased because some reading groups on different continents received different instructions about reading methods. The South American groups used a different list of questions and points for attention than the Dutch groups had, and apparently the instructions given by the project coordinators in Asia were still different.

The great diversity in material is an expression of the richness of the project. That is our first and joyful conclusion. The second conclusion, directly related to the first, is that this richness makes analysis of the reading reports very complex. The great differences in form and content make it impossible to conduct a comparative analysis of the group dynamics factors. One report details the conversations among the group members, and it traces the participants' thought processes, while another report offers only a summary of the group's conclusions. Because the instruction material that the groups followed was very different, it is difficult to trace with any certainty where the groups followed their own path and where they adopted the project coordinator's recommendations. This great diversity makes it difficult to properly assess the data and to compare the processes that took place in the groups.

A third observation is that fewer than half of the groups incorporated in their reporting information on the methods they used. Approximately 60 percent of the groups did not provide useful information on the method followed or the group dynamics process. The groups that did report on their methods and group processes did so in very different ways and reported on very diverse topics with respect to the group dynamics and social interaction. For these reasons, this article is based on only a portion of the reports and on non-uniform data. It is impossible to express a broadly valid opinion on the role of the group dynamics in the hermeneutic process on the basis of the material provided.

Because of the richness and the limitations of the material, I have chosen a qualitative approach and exploratory method for this research.[3] I read all the available material and made a selection of the parts in which group dynamics information was provided. These texts were gathered, labeled, grouped, and placed in a theoretical framework. The non-uniform reporting provided insufficient information to establish a complete theory, but the material induced me to study further certain aspects of the functioning of a group, including its leadership and the way facilitators organized and guided the meeting. The result of this study was the establishment of the influence of a number of specific factors on the reading process.

In analyzing the material, I applied an inductive method.[4] For readability and clarity, I have presented the research results in reverse order. First, I will briefly outline a theoretical framework. Second, I will provide an elaboration on the two leadership types, using information derived from the analysis. Both facilitation styles have a number of characteristics that are illustrated using quotations from the research material. The quotations indicate the empirical data on the basis of which the conclusions have been made. By focusing on the differences in facilitation styles and their characteristics, I have described the influence on the interpretation process of the various working methods in the groups.

Task and relationships

In the study of group dynamics, a distinction is made between task and relationships, according to the communication theory of Paul Watzlawick and company.[5] These two dimensions are actually closely connected. If things are clear and circumstances ideal, the relationships in a group will develop while people work collectively on the task. In discussing, working, and praying, the group members get to know each other better and begin relating to each other more openly. Conversely, working on a task goes more smoothly and better when the relationships in a group are good and when people trust and feel safe with one another. Both dimensions undeniably influence each other, although for the purpose of analysis a distinction can be made.

An important aspect of the functioning of a group is leadership. The way the leader takes up his or her task has a profound effect on the way the group functions. Leading a group can be differentiated into the same two dimensions: task-oriented and relationship-oriented aspects.[6] In the task-oriented part, the leader works toward achieving the external group goal. The characteristics of this formal functioning are: the leader monitors the continuity of the group; makes sure that the goal is achieved; keeps the group focused on the task; takes care of the formalities of a meeting, such as opening, closing, and implementing the intended program; monitors output; and emphasizes production. In short, a group leader steers group process that is focused on the group's task.

In the intercultural Bible reading project, the members of the reading groups were invited to meet and read John 4 together. Their task was clear and univocal for all the groups: they read the story of the woman at the well. They reported on their reading processes. Each group was linked to a partner group from another culture. These groups studied each other's reading reports, looking for differences and similarities, and reported back to each other and to us. The result achieved by the group leaders in the project Through the Eyes of Another, by working on their external group goal, could be established on the basis of the material, the reading reports on the website. The execution of the task-oriented function by the group leaders is shown in the large numbers of reports from groups throughout the world.

It is difficult to make visible the relational skills of the group leader, but these skills nonetheless play a significant role in the whole process. The relationships are based on interactions, feelings, and activities that arise from the internal functioning of the group. To guide this process, qualities of social-emotional and psychological leadership are required, which are demonstrated in the ability to maintain a group as a group. The group leader performs this role by paying attention to the internal system of the group, i.e., to the interactions between the group members. A facilitator must have developed an interactional sensitivity and know what is important in relationships between people. A relationally skilled group leader is sensitive, is focused on the members of the group in their uniqueness and subjectivity, supports people where possible, and monitors the level of satisfaction of the group members. A good group leader has an antenna for the psychological and personal functioning of the members and knows how the group can meet the needs of the members.

The group leader's task was more extensive in the groups that were formed specifically for the reading project than in groups that were already in place. If people already know each other and if they have together developed a reading method over time, their group is in a different, more stable phase of group development. The members of the group are then better able to work through the process together. They share responsibility for their task and relationships, and work more democratically. As a group of Korean students said: "Our Bible study was good in that we do not have to worry about what others think. We know each other quite well. Therefore, we did not have to hide our present situation and were able to be honest in expressing our ideas. We felt relieved in a way by doing so. It was very democratic, because everybody could take part in the Bible study freely."

People in groups that meet for the first time have to get to know each other. They are unsure about the way the group will work. They do not yet know what is expected of them, although they come to the first meeting with more or less awareness of their own expectations. In occasional groups, group development is in a less stable phase. However, in such groups a safe atmosphere and a good exchange of information can also develop: "While we were talking, there was a very pleasant atmosphere. We listened to what the others were saying, which often led to new ideas." In these groups, the role, and therefore the responsibility, of the leader is more extensive. The group members will be more dependent on the group leader, and the guidance of the process will demand better skills on the part of the leader.

Facilitator

The instructions to the reading groups refer to the group leader as the facilitator. The facilitator is the person who creates the conditions that enable the group members to read together and collectively search for the meaning of the scriptural passage. The facilitator's task is described by Gerald O. West in the project handbook:

> The primary role of the facilitator is to enable "group process" to take place, to manage group dynamics, to promote turn taking, to keep time, to summarize and systematize the reading results, to find creative and empowering ways of reporting back to plenary the findings of the group, and to move on the group from reflection into action. Besides the more general group process concerns, the facilitator's task in the contextual Bible study process is to stimulate the use of local reading resources and to introduce critical reading resources—in the specific sense that this term is used within biblical studies—into the reading process as they are requested and required.[7]

In brief, a facilitator needs knowledge and skills to be able to guide the group process effectively. As indicated in the first sentence of the task description, the facilitator should know all aspects of group dynamics and be able to implement them as needed. A facilitator should also motivate the group members to act: the group should move from reflection to action. The facilitator must be also able to apply more than one reading method: in addition to the reading method the group is used to, the leader may introduce a critical reading in order to help the readers better understand the story. Group leaders can only offer an alternative reading perspective if they have at least two perspectives at their disposal; they can help others further if they can offer a new critical perspective as the situation and the needs of the group members require.

The project Through the Eyes of Another focuses on the ordinary reader, both in implementation and in scientific research. The organizers encourage ordinary readers "to read as they usually do." Elsewhere, group members are called on to follow a process of "spontaneous reading," and they are appointed co-actors and co-owners of the project. The power lies within the group,[8] although with this statement not everything has been said. Facilitation is a function of the group, and a skilled facilitator will use all available knowledge and skills to serve the functioning of the group. In order to carry out this task of group guidance with an attitude of service, facilitators should possess the aforementioned skills and should be aware of the way their power influences the group process. A facilitator has the "power of leadership" and should also have the "power of expertise" (see West's description of the facilitator). Group leadership is not concerned with the presence or absence of power but with the skills and the awareness of the responsibility to place everything in the service of the functioning of the group.[9] How facilitators dealt with this responsibility, and whether they valued the group members as competent actors,[10] is evident in the way they followed the project instructions or modified them with a view to their own group.

Speaking in very general terms, in the project Through the Eyes of Another, two styles of facilitation could be recognized. Some facilitators worked in both task- and relationship-oriented ways, and some led the groups with their main focus on implementing the task. As explained above, both dimensions—task and relationship—are present in each group. The distinction between these two styles was therefore a relative difference. Some facilitators attended mainly to the task aspect, and other facilitators clearly worked on task and relationships. A number of characteristics of both styles can be recognized in the material, giving more meaning to the difference between the task- and relationship-oriented styles.

Task- and relationship-oriented facilitation

Harmonization between the group and the project

To give participants in the project a working method, instructions for possible procedures were incorporated in the project description. The handbook for the functioning of the group gave six group rules and some reading questions. The reports show that different reading methods were used on different continents. It was crucial for the group dynamics and for research that the facilitators dealt with these instructions in very different ways.

Relationship- and task-oriented facilitators took seriously their own skills and the instructions for the project and the group. This type of facilitator incorporated the project instructions into a working method uniquely appropriate for the group. One such facilitator gave account of the considerations on which the group's reconstruction was based: "Question 4: Are there any questions/clarifications people wish to put forward about this text? Approach: This question was designed to allow participants to share their knowledge of the issues within and background to this passage. It was led in the full group. This question took about 15 minutes." The group leader harmonized the different group dynamics aspects, giving appropriate attention to both the task and the relationship. The facilitators who applied this kind of working method made use of their freedom and bore their responsibility in relation to the framework offered. They used the questions provided insofar as these were relevant to the reading process of their own group.

A group of seven women in Colombia had been meeting for many years to study the Bible together. The women used to begin their meetings with prayer. From the questions provided they chose the question for identification. Of all the people in the story they could identify themselves most with ... the disciples. They identified themselves with [the behavior of] the disciples because they found they also tended to exclude other people. "Very few times we learn from the other one because we have a fixed idea of what you want. The dialogue goes around the woman. The knowledge takes us away from people, and the challenge is that it brings them near."

Instead of following all questions provided, the women searched for the story that was *not* told in John 4 in order to broaden their knowledge. They filled in the "gaps in the text" by telling each other what else happened. They put words to what went on in the woman's mind when she was speaking to Jesus. They spoke for Peter in order to know what he thought when he saw what was happening at the well. They told each other what happened that afternoon after the conversation at the well in the village of Sychar: What did the woman tell her fellow-villagers?

Activating learning methods and creative arts

Task- and relationship-oriented facilitators translate their own educational preparation in activating learning methods, and they prefer to use creative arts. Activating learning methods and creative arts encourage the group members to read, study, and interpret topics by themselves. These methods create space, inspiring stimulating dynamics with creative actualization. In the above example, the women chose a simple narrative form and adopted an unexpected approach. They broadened their knowledge of the story by searching for the "gaps in the text." They may have adopted this approach from feminist Bible scholar Elisabeth Schüssler Fiorenza.[11] Opting for creative arts—such as drawing, drama and bibliodrama, music, and storytelling—and working with symbols rather than methods in which conversation was dominant, are remarkable characteristics of the groups that used a free working method.

As a closing act at the end of the third meeting, the facilitator asked the participants to represent what had affected them most during the process. The group leader took along large sheets of paper, crayons, and colored pencils. While the group was drawing, they listened to classical music. The participants drew, for instance, a well, a stream, and themselves with their feet in the water streaming from the well, or a meeting of two "people with stamina"—Jesus and the woman—causing a fire in the course of their meeting.

This example shows that creative arts stimulate the design of unexpected new and in-depth interpretations and images. Singing songs and voicing prayers involve imaginative activity. In some groups, participants spontaneously expressed their perception of the text in a prayer or song. The participants also used imagination in these expressions and created space to connect with the text.

Reflectiveness and exchange of perspective

Gerald West notes in his description of the facilitator that this leader should be capable of offering the group an alternative reading perspective, if necessary. It would be ideal if the group itself had reflected on the diversity of reading methods in the group. Looking "through the eyes of another" does not only occur when views are exchanged with a group from another continent, but such an exchange of perspective may also occur in one's own group. Within the group, the readings and interpretations are also determined by individual life experiences, and the different members will use different perspectives. In some groups, the difference was related to gender. In a South American group, a woman said that she wished to discuss the position of the woman in the story, but the men in the group considered that interest to be the woman's "personal problem." Naming this diversity can be an exercise in exchange of perspective and may therefore function as preparation for the exchange of information with the partner group in the second phase: "The facilitator asked the participants a question regarding the aspects that played a role for each of them in their interpretation process. The participants talked to each other about this question. They mentioned 'a need to search for a well in your life' and 'you see the story through your own eyes, but learn from the interpretation of others which you have not read in the story yourself.'"

A facilitator may encourage the exchange of perspective in the reading process by asking the participants this kind of reflective question. Putting reflective questions to the group members invites them to think just a little deeper, and that is where the skill of the facilitator comes in.[12]

This process is explained in more detail in Gerald West's contribution, "Artful Facilitation and the Process of Creating a Safe Interpretive Site: An Analysis of an Actual Bible Study," chapter 10 in the present volume.

The world in the group

The fourth characteristic of the task- and relationship-oriented facilitation style is the presence of the world in the group. There are two moments in a group meeting when the social environment outside the group specifically comes up for discussion, i.e., at the beginning and at the closing of a meeting. Relationship-oriented group leaders tried to connect to the social environment of the participants. In groups that paid close attention to relationships, personal questions were asked, sometimes even very specific questions, such as these posed by a Colombian group:

> What has been my personal story, and who am I now? How am I as a person? What about my current condition, my ambitions, my qualities, my experiences? What is my relation with others like, regarding paternal aspects (giv-

ing life and guiding others), fraternity (receiving life and guiding others), nuptial relations (personal relations with others, administration of my body and my sexuality). [What are] ways [I participate] in my community: my strengths and weaknesses regarding planning, execution, and evaluation of personal and group actions.

Some also found creative ways to make a link to the outside social environment. One facilitator introduced the scripture passage by relating to participants' daily life experiences in a very concrete and visual manner.

> The pastor took along two bottles of water, one holding water from the river and one holding water from a well. The water from the river was highly polluted but became clear through artificial purification. The water from the well was less clear but pure. The symbolic message was: It is not always the more transparent water that is the water of life. After this activity the coordinator suggested that the members of the group speak about the wells of their childhood, because many were born in the rural area.

The second specific moment when the world was present in the group was at the end of the reading process. A few groups moved from reflecting to acting.

> The women considered how they could move from their reading, thinking, and discussing into acting. What could they do with what they had learned from the scriptural passage? They filled in this step very concretely and personally. They mentioned examples from their lives of places and times they had excluded others: the shoeshine boy in the street, because he was from another culture and another people, and a family member leading a life that the rest of the family did not appreciate. Finally, they expressed ways they intended to change their attitudes and behavior. "What should I do before excluding the other one?" They gave the following answers: "to ask and to speak," "to come closer and to dialogue" and "not to take the things in a very personal way, this is selfish."

During the reading process these women not only developed new meanings but they linked concrete intentions to their development in order to fulfill the meaning of the story—Jesus does not exclude people as the disciples and they themselves did—in their own lives. This report showed that approaching the text together, freely and creatively, using activating learning methods and creative arts, enabled group members to develop new meanings and new opportunities to act.

Task-oriented facilitation

The discussion leader follows the scheme provided

The following description of a group made by the group is characteristic of a task orientation: We concluded that we aren't very symbol-oriented people. . . . We noticed that what we bring along to such a meeting in the Netherlands does say something about our culture. Everyone has brought along a pen, a notepad, and an agenda book. The minutes are taken on a laptop. Apparently, pragmatism and efficiency make us feel good."

Task-oriented facilitators were indeed characterized by a certain degree of efficiency. They mainly focused on the external group goal: it was important to participate in the project, and as a result, a report must be made. Because of their efficient, task-oriented approach, they chose to follow the questions provided by the project without making many adjustments. In a number of cases, this efficiency had its price. In cases where a facilitator kept too strictly to the role laid down by the project organizers, the project organizers became the authority. The questions were regarded as rules "from above": the protocol says that we should do it like this, so we will do it this way. In those groups, an external authority—the project organizers—existed, who steered the reading process, instead of the readers themselves guiding it, supported by their facilitator.

There seems to be a relationship between the term identifying the group leader and the method followed by a group. In some reports, the group leader had a first name, and in others this person was identified functionally, as the pastor or the minister. In the report of the objective and efficient group mentioned above, the leader was called "chairman"; in other reports, the leader was referred to as "discussion leader." These names say something about the way the leaders fulfilled their roles. A chairman leads a business meeting, while a discussion leader has to try to align different opinions. In any case, the interpretation of the role is more businesslike and task-oriented than in the description of a facilitator given by Gerald West.

In task-oriented groups, the leader had the central role, and one infers that the leader was the most active person during the group meetings. When this type of group made a verbatim report, this activity is evident in the discussion leader's frequency of speaking and duration of speaking time. A leader who exerted strong control over the discussion may create a kind of safety for the participants, but they engaged in less discussion among themselves. In some sessions, readers only reacted one by one to a text, after which the next question was dealt with.

On the other hand, there were group leaders who deliberately limited their own contributions to the group. These group leaders may not have been very familiar with the role of facilitator. On a few occasions, I came across an explicit announcement that the facilitator would be saying little. One pastor notes, "I said as little as possible; it is difficult to say little. . . . I should have said even less." Another report comments, "The task of the chairman has to be reserved; everybody is responsible."

But a leader who takes too modest a role is not always helpful: "The second evening we ended with only questions and no answers. The guide did not add much of his theological knowledge to the conversation among the participants. The idea was that they would search for their own solutions to their questions about the text. But as they are not accustomed to doing so, they concluded without understanding the meaning of this text." This facilitator aimed to play a modest role but forgot that his role was to facilitate the reading process of the participants. Group members need to be given a structure, in order for authentic exchange to take place. If a group leader does not deliberately provide a suitable method, participants will miss opportunities to learn from one another.

Discussion method

In groups with a task-oriented facilitator, the method used was, in fact, only discussion. The facilitators followed the questions provided, and for leaders with little training in group dynamics, discussion was a logical choice. For most groups, this was the case. This approach is, of course, based on a wide theological tradition: one talks and thinks about texts. Words ask for even more words. The choice to stick to talking will in most cases have been made subconsciously; the facilitators will not have considered an alternative possibility.

The advantage of discussion as a method is that participants feel comfortable with it. They are used to talking about texts. The fact that this form is common is also a disadvantage, however. The participants told each other what they already knew and did not easily come to read the scriptural passage in an alternative way. Listening to each other, understanding each other, and connecting with each other was not easy. Participants often followed their own flow of thought. A tendency to rationalize and pose problems about the text may go hand in hand with this approach. They were less likely to use imagination or to spontaneously follow intuition.

Text-oriented

The method of discussion is linked to text orientation. In the groups that paid most attention to the task and where words dominated, people had difficulty giving a meaning to the text. The task-orientation became clear in the cognitive text-centered reading method; groups using it tended to pose problems regarding the scripture passage. They particularly wondered what the passage meant; I read more than once that people found the Bible difficult to read: "We could not have known this, because we need a theologian or theological knowledge here." "We conclude that we are not very much touched by this passage as believers. It is vague; it does not tell us what the will of God is or how you must worship God and what the living water is. It is abstract—no manual." "We concluded that our Western way of looking at the Bible—rational, explanatory—is hindering us. We believe with our heads and not with our hearts. We want to understand."

Task-oriented facilitators who followed the project handbook posed the question of which person in the story one identifies with. This question is intended to bring the story of the woman at the well closer to the readers of today. In a task-oriented group, the participants found this personal question difficult. A number of groups, particularly the Dutch groups, were unable to deal with it. In one group, the participants responded to the question by explaining what was difficult for them in this story.

Sometimes, one can observe a link between the position of not understanding the text and identifying with the disciples. This result was remarkable, displaying self-knowledge and a subtle understanding for the behavior of the disciples. In the story in John 4, the disciples were not involved in the communication between Jesus and the woman. They did not really understand what took place, as the participants felt they did not understand the scripture passage.

The world in the group

Task-oriented facilitators and groups brought in their social environment in a different way than those working in more relationship-oriented groups. In relationship-oriented groups, the text and faith were strongly linked to personal questions and circumstances. In the task-oriented groups, social and community problems were more frequently discussed, and the tone of such discussions was somewhat distant. Many reports from all over the world reflect discussion of tensions between population groups in the participants' countries. They compared these tensions with the problematic relationship between the Jews and the Samaritans. The reports mention relationships between Muslims and Christians, Catholics and Protestants, immigrants and indigenous peoples, caste and tribe differences, and differences between hardliners and "softies" in their own communities.

Because task-oriented facilitators usually followed the project's list of questions, they rarely moved on from reflecting to acting. When they were asked for the significance of the text for their own lives, they referred again to the tensions between groups. Sometimes, however, the tension in the world turned out to be present in the group, and then it was harder to talk about it.

> It was clearly difficult for the group to move away from this discussion, touching as it did a deep tension within most of them between their faith and culture. However, the discussion did move on when one of the group said that they also felt that the text was about how in talking to the woman, "Jesus was trying to destroy the [racial] segregation." This shifted the discussion to racism, with the group wondering whether it would ever end. Though there was not a lot of hope that it would, the group argued that the only way to destroy racism was to "really know a person."

The effect of the facilitation styles on the hermeneutic process

Each of the two facilitation styles described above —task- *and* relationship-oriented, and *only* task-oriented—has four characteristics. Before we can say anything about the influence of the different styles on the hermeneutic process, we should note that all four characteristics were found in only a few groups. More often, the reports mentioned one, two, or three characteristics of a facilitator's style. The conclusions about the relationship between the facilitation style and the hermeneutic process should be read with this observation in mind.

In the reports from the groups in which the facilitators displayed characteristics of both the task- and relationship-oriented styles, one finds many remarks expressing the joy participants experienced in reading together. They explicitly state that reading the Bible together was an enriching experience. The participants in task-oriented groups also stated that they valued reading the Bible together, but the reports express this appreciation less frequently and in a more reserved manner.

The groups that gave more attention to relationships created more space for the individual members to put a meaning to the text. They did not tend to try to reach a consensus on the meanings within the group. The differences in interpretation were accepted, and it was not necessary to reach unanimity among the participants. In those groups, participants experienced their diversity and differences in meanings as enriching. The groups led by task-oriented facilitators more often came to a uniform conclusion on the meaning: the core of the story for us is . . .; the message of this story is . . .

In the groups that paid attention to relationships within the group, the individual social environment was deemed important. In these groups, the meanings given to the scriptural passage were more often explicitly linked to the members' own lives: my life is like this, and that is why this text means . . . to me. With this movement, the message of the story takes its place in a network of meanings. The meaning that is given to it in the hermeneutic process is included in and integrated into daily life. In these groups, the members seemed more often to make the story their own.

Only a limited number of groups moved on from reflecting to acting; the groups where this occurred were led by a task- and relationship-oriented facilitator. In the groups where visual art forms were used, participants gave the most contemporary expressions of the meaning of the story. Apparently, creative art creates space to explain the text in one's own words.

On the basis of this analysis of the reports on the group dynamics aspects, I offer this conclusion: Task-oriented leadership leads to the formulation of more uniform and objective meanings, while task- and relationship-oriented leadership leads to more differentiation and more personal interpretations.

Learning from the group process of the partner group

As a final step in the analysis of group dynamics as part of the hermeneutic process, I compared the difference in facilitation styles with the exchange of information between the partner groups. Did the more task-oriented groups respond differently to the exchange with the partner group than did the task- and relationship-oriented groups?

In general, the groups responded to each other very sympathetically and with much interest, but it turned out that it was not easy to look through the eyes of another. On the basis of the group dynamic analysis, an explanation for the reactions from the groups to the partner groups can be found in the way the groups themselves worked. Groups with a task-oriented style tended to continue their more businesslike, rational, and text-oriented approach in their comments on the reading of the partner group. These groups read the partner group's report in the way they read the John 4 story: with great interest but mainly in a text-oriented and analytical way.

> In contradistinction to our group, they don't discuss very much what they read in the Bible, what the rationale is, but they take the word as it is written.

> In relation to their way of believing, we see many differences, i.e., because we are accustomed to ask for the meaning of a Bible text and we discuss the meaning of saying a prayer. We have less or no open-mindedness in relation to matters of faith. We don't know what is meant if somebody says "to calculate with God." Our belief is more a matter of rationality and deliberation than of emotions and feelings.

They described and paraphrased their partner group's report; they spoke of "we" and "they" and mainly identified the differences in approach. Because of this approach, they stuck to their more rational text-orientation, even now that the text was the report of their partner group. The tendency to pose problems of the text (problematize), which goes with this approach, was often implicit in the questions they put to their partner group. A genuine exchange of perspective—if we read the passage in their way, what would we get from it?—happened only with difficulty and only for small parts of the text.

The third characteristic identified in the description of the more task- and relationship-oriented facilitation style was that some facilitators of these groups demonstrated the ability to encourage their group participants to an exchange of perspective. In task- and relationship-oriented groups the facilitators did not take expression of differences in opinion, religious vision, or interpretation as threatening or as an incident that needed to be resolved. They seized appreciatively on differences in interpretation and in participants' subjectivity, as opportunities to learn together and from each other. This openness, which had already been practiced in their own group, was continued in the contacts with the partner group.

> You have a very different view than we have. You see the Bible stories much more practically. You take it more directly into your daily life. The story that is read is more spontaneously involved in your daily life. You work more practically, while we work more cognitively, and on other occasions more emotionally. All in all: we sympathize with your approach, and we acknowledge the need to imitate this from you, which means that our attitude that determines the way we read the Bible will have to change gradually.

It is striking that the writer formulates the response relationally. He does not say "they" and "we" but speaks to the partner group: "you" and "we." This group paid attention to the relationships, and this communication style was continued in the contact with the partner group.

The members of the task- and relationship-oriented groups have already gained more experience in looking through the eyes of another. The facilitators of these groups showed them how to do this, and the participants were given space for subjectivity and diversity. People are not naturally able to copy the reading perspective of someone else. An exchange of perspective can and must be learned. Before they exchanged reading reports, relationship-oriented groups had already practiced this skill more than the task-oriented groups had. As the report quoted above rightly states, change is a gradual process. Learning to look through the eyes of another takes time and a skilled facilitator's careful guidance.

For some groups, the way the partner group combined attention to the task and the relationships was a revelation. These groups immediately saw what they could learn from their partners. They were touched by the warmth and attention to the relationships in their partner group.

> The fact that our partner group shows more warmth when they meet could be the result of the fact that they know each other well. If we understood it correctly, they have been meeting each other for Bible study over a couple of years.

> Reading the interim report, we realized that we actually never ask each other how things are going, personally. Because of this, we decided to do so in future.

This example shows that partner groups learn not only from each other's differences in interpretation but also from the way people in the group interrelate. This Western "businesslike" group realized that a combination of a task- and relationship-oriented approach will inspire the mutual Bible reading process even more. The exchange with the partner group showed them that the context of their own group, the personal attention people paid to each other and to them, made a difference. More importantly, they not only realized this but indicated in one short sentence that they would move from reflection to action: "We decided to do so in future."

In the vastly enriching process of the project Through the Eyes of Another, this exchange of perspective is something to be treasured. The many women and men who read, discussed, sang, and played together shared their experiences with each other and with us. We found very valuable treasures in what they shared with us.

Notes

[1] Alma Lanser–van der Velde, *Geloven leren: Een theoretisch en empirisch onderzoek naar wederkerig geloofsleren* (Kampen, the Netherlands: Uitgeverij Kok, 2000), 39.

² Raymond D. Boisvert, *John Dewey: Rethinking Our Time* (Albany, N.Y.: State University of New York Press, 1998), 135.

³ Fred Wester, *Strategieën voor kwalitatief onderzoek* (Muiderberg, the Netherlands: Coutinho, 1991).

⁴ Gerben Heitink, *Practical Theology: History, Theory, Action Domains: Manual for Practical Theology* (Grand Rapids, Mich.: Eerdmans, 1999), 228ff.

⁵ Paul Watzlawick, Janet Beavin Bavelas, and Don D. Jackson, *Pragmatics of Human Communication: A Study of Interactional Patterns, Pathologies, and Paradoxes* (London: Faber, 1968).

⁶ Jan Remmerswaal, *Handboek groepsdynamica: Een nieuwe inleiding op theorie en praktijk* (Soest, the Netherlands: Uitgeverij Nelissen, 2003), 267.

⁷ Cited in Hans de Wit, "Through the Eyes of Another: A Project on Intercultural Reading of the Bible" (presentation, consultation on Intercultural Reading of the Bible, Free University, Amsterdam, the Netherlands, 2001), 45. A version of this paper, with the same title, became the standard project handbook.

⁸ J. H. de Wit, "Intercultureel bijbellezen," *Gereformeerd Theologisch Tijdschrift, Tijdschrift voor theologen op het grensgebied van wetenschap en praktijk* 3 (2003): 188.

⁹ Lanser–van der Velde, *Geloven leren*, 318.

¹⁰ Harry Coenen, "On the foundations of a relationship based on equality between the researcher and the researched party in Exemplarian Action Research," in *The Complexity of Relationships in Action Research*, ed. Ben Boog, Harry Coenen, Lou Keune, and Rob Lammerts (Tilburg, the Netherlands: Tilburg University Press, 1998), 23.

¹¹ Elisabeth Schüssler Fiorenza, *In Memory of Her: A Feminist Theological Reconstruction of Christian Origins* (New York: Crossroad, 1983).

¹² This process is explained in more detail in Gerald West's contribution, "Artful Facilitation and the Process of Creating a Safe Interpretive Site: An Analysis of an Actual Bible Study," chapter 10 in the present volume.

CHAPTER 16

Biblical scholars and ordinary readers dialoguing about living water

Hans Snoek

Over the past decades, hermeneutics worldwide has undergone a fascinating development. In Western Europe, the theoretical studies of Hans-Georg Gadamer and Paul Ricoeur have served to place the role of the reader high on the hermeneutical agenda. Partly as an extension of this development, millions of believers in the third world—usually under the supervision of scholars—began reading the Bible in the light of their own context. This "irruption of the reader" has resulted in a stream of literature describing the way ordinary people interpret the scriptures. By extension, many exegetes have emphasized that the way poor, black, and other marginalized groups read the Bible constitutes an important contribution to the science.

The exchange between ordinary readers and involved biblical scholars has been very productive over the past decades. At the same time, however, it is clear that the seemingly organic relationship between ordinary people and academic exegetes covers up some methodological areas of tension. A first fundamental issue, in my view, is precisely how the contribution of the scientific supervisor relates to the input of the ordinary people. Is the exegete merely a glorified secretary, who compiles a report of the Bible study? Or is he or she an expert who feeds the ordinary people information and corrects them when they say wrong or foolish things about the text? If I'm not mistaken, many exegetes play—consciously or not—the second role, which implies that in the final report it is unclear where the views of the ordinary people end and the vision of the exegete begins.

A second fundamental question raised by the interest in "reading from the grassroots" is in what sense the insights of ordinary people are of interest for the scholarly study of the Bible. Much Latin American liberation theology contends

Hans Snoek, Southern Africa department, Protestant Church in the Netherlands; Nederlands Bijbel Instituut, Hogeschool voor Theologie (Utrecht, the Netherlands)

that because the Bible was originally written for the poor, biblical scholars can benefit from the keen intuition with which these people read the text.[1] But this line of argument raises the question of how ordinary and scholarly readings are related. Is a fruitful discussion between intuitive and schooled readings really possible? Or should one admit that, however valuable ordinary readings might be, academic approaches to the Bible are fundamentally different?

The problem areas sketched above are closely related. Precisely because the role of the scholar engaged in conversation with ordinary readers is not always clear, it remains uncertain how naïve readings might make a contribution to biblical scholarship. Beginning with the understanding that it is important to drive back confusion on both scores, the intercultural Bible reading project has emphatically opted for an empirical approach. To put it differently: the reports of the conversations are to be as objective and detailed as possible, so that it is easy to distinguish between how ordinary readers view the text and what role the supervising scholar plays.[2] This approach gives rise to the possibility—in the second phase, using the reports as a basis—of doing research in an objective and sober way on how naïve views relate to scholarly readings of the text, and what their contribution might be.

This chapter will focus—as objectively as possible—on the question of how a number of selected reading reports from Latin America, Africa, Asia, and Western Europe (in this case the Netherlands) relate to the scholarly literature.[3] I propose to limit the field of research from two directions. First, it seems prudent, in view of the fact that John 4 is a relatively long chapter, to concentrate our attention on one pericope. I propose to focus on the metaphor of living water in John 4:7–15. An important consideration in this regard is that metaphors generally have a great surplus of meaning and are therefore interesting from an intercultural viewpoint. Second, I want to limit the discussion of scholarly views, for the simple reason that in the framework of this article it is not possible to cover the contributions of biblical scholars from four continents. A further consideration is that in the Netherlands, where I live, there is insufficient scholarly literature from the third world. On balance, I will concentrate on eight Western European and four North American academic publications that enjoy a certain status.[4] In the course of this small study, we will have to see if a discussion between North Atlantic scholarly perspectives on John 4:7–15 and those of ordinary readers from four continents proves fruitful. I begin by mapping the way the consulted literature deals with John 4 and the metaphor of living water. Subsequently, on the basis of excerpts of a number of intercultural Bible reading reports, I will investigate the extent to which points of contact exist, in this specific case, for a fruitful dialogue between scholars and ordinary readers.

Visions of North Atlantic biblical scholars

A quick overview of the literature leads to three insights. To begin with, it is striking that practically all the consulted scholars are concerned with the structure of John 4.

Some exegetes emphasize that the chapter is made up of an introduction, followed by two or possibly three scenes.[5] Others point to the concentric structure of John 4 and argue that John 4:19–26 constitutes the heart of the chapter.[6] An important observation, within the context of our inquiry, is that none of the biblical scholars consulted is of the opinion that the metaphor of living water in verses 7–15 forms the heart of the chapter.

A second point that strikes one in reading the literature is that practically all the exegetes consulted raise the question of the meaning of living water. In this discussion, too, a number of main streams can be distinguished. Josef Blank states, partly on the grounds of an appeal to the Song of Solomon, that living water in John 4 refers to the eschatological nature of Jesus's revelation.[7] Rudolf Schnackenburg, using, for example, a reference to John 6:35, contends that living water in John 4 can mean both the Holy Spirit and godly living.[8] Craig Koester links living water to revelation and the Spirit.[9] James Montgomery Boice emphasizes, on the grounds of diverse texts from the Old Testament, that living water is narrowly linked to God.[10] And Rupert von Deutz pleads for a synthesis by stating that living water refers to the Holy Spirit and therefore to God.[11] A remarkable similarity among almost all the biblical scholars is that they try to support their interpretation of the metaphor with intertextual arguments, drawing on references from the Old Testament, New Testament, and/or extra-biblical texts.

A last point of interest is that in their explanation of John 4:7–15, almost all the biblical scholars consulted focus on the world behind the text and/or the world of the text. Only two exegetes attempt to trace what the meaning of John 4 might be for readers today. Ben Witherington makes a plea for reading the story from the perspective of evangelization techniques and results.[12] He criticizes the ease with which North American churches shut themselves up in their own ethnic and racial subcultures. "The Sunday morning worship hour in most churches is still one of the most segregated hours spent by any large number of people during the week. . . . The story of Jesus and the Samaritan woman is extremely potent to use as a tool both for sharing the Gospel across socio-economic, ethnic and racial barriers and for exhorting Christians to get on with doing so."

Boice, also a North American, concentrates especially on the image of the spring in John 4.[13] He points out that a spring, even when covered up with soil, will always prove to be stronger. He considers it a beautiful image to illustrate that God will never let go of those who turn to him in faith. "This spring will be eternal, free, joyous, and self-dependent. But He is also warning you that you will never be able to bulldoze anything over it!" Whatever one might think of these attempts to bring John 4 up to date, it is a striking fact that only two of the twelve scholarly publications consulted devote attention to the dialogue with contemporary readers. Further, it is striking that these two exegetes are both from the U.S. None of the consulted biblical scholars from Western Europe incorporate the world of the reader in their discourse.

Readings from the "third world"

All in all, this short exploration of the North Atlantic scholarly literature has evoked a relatively pluriform impression of the way John 4 is interpreted. There is no consensus about the structure and heart of John 4. Neither is there agreement about the meaning of living water. There is, however, an implicit consensus among most of the exegetes that a scholarly approach to John 4 implies that one will focus on the world behind the text and/or the world of the text, leaving the world of the reader out of the picture. The section that follows will review how these views of North Atlantic scientists correspond to twenty-two reports from Latin America, Africa, Asia, and Western Europe.

An initial reading of the reports reveals that twelve of the fifteen groups from the third world go into a more or less detailed discussion of John 4:7–15.[14] Members of a Pentecostal congregation in Nicaragua make a connection between living water and eternal life. Groups from Bolivia, Ghana, and the Philippines emphasize that the metaphor symbolizes spirituality. Participants from Bolivia and El Salvador associate living water with the Word of God. And one group from Colombia relates the metaphor to the Holy Spirit. All in all, these reports offer a varied picture. At the same time, it is striking that practically all the reading groups from the third world—independently of each other—interpret John 4:7–15 as a mandate to evangelize.[15] A Baptist from Nicaragua expresses it as follows:

> I am not surprised about the fact that he chooses water for a symbol, because it is the vital element everywhere in the world. There can be shortage of water, but the biggest shortage is of spiritual water. As there were people who were thirsty in terms of spiritual needs in that time, we are now even more thirsty, and we should satiate the current needs, the necessity of Christ coming inside each heart. All people have the opportunity . . . to sow the Word of the Lord wherever they go, so all can reap the benefits.

Only three of the third world reading groups paid no attention to John 4:7–15. Two groups from South Africa discuss at length the ethnic tensions between Jesus and the Samaritan woman and go on to relate this friction to the conflicts between black and white in their own country. In a report from an ecumenical diaconal organization in the Philippines called Samaritana, John 4:7–15 is also absent. The staff members of this organization, who offer support to prostitutes, identify strongly with the Samaritan woman. They regard her as a prototype of a fallen woman and are particularly drawn to the way she deals with her social isolation.

Dialogue with biblical scholars

Although a comparison between North Atlantic exegetes, on the one hand, and Latin American, African, and Asian reading reports, on the other hand, is in a certain sense incongruent, it may still be interesting to investigate how they relate to each other. None of the reports from the third world seem to indicate that participants raised the question of what the heart of John 4 might be. Neither do the reports contain signs that these groups wanted to provide scholarly support for their interest in a particular fragment of the text. To put it differently, the interest in John 4:7–15 (or the lack thereof, in some reports) was evidently not determined by textual arguments but by the intuitive feeling that this fragment connects to their own context.

On the subject of explaining the metaphor, it is evident that the various groups participating in the project interpret living water very differently, just as the North Atlantic scholars surveyed above did. In most of the reports, no exegetical arguments are given to support their particular view. The only exception is the report from Colombia, where a participant relates living water, by means of an intertextual argument, to John 7:37–39—verses in which living water is associated with the Holy Spirit.

To conclude, it appears from the reports that most participants from the third world are primarily interested in the question of what living water might mean in our day. There is significantly less interest in the world of the text. On balance, their approach is very different from that of the European biblical scholars cited, who, in their exegesis of John 4:7–15, do not go into the world of the actual reader(s). There is, however, an interesting resemblance between Witherington and Boice (the two North American exegetes) and the various reading groups in the third world, in their (direct or indirect) association of living water with evangelization and/or spirituality.

This short exploration seems to lead to the conclusion that the scholarly approach to John 4:7–15 is generally at right angles to the more associative reading style of the believers in the third world. Perhaps the underlying differences in approach to the metaphor are so great that a dialogue between the parties is simply not possible. But theoretically, precisely the differences might offer points of contact for a fruitful dialogue. Biblical scholars might show ordinary readers how interesting it can be to concentrate on the world behind the text and the world of the text. Ordinary readers, in turn, could pose to the consulted scholars the question of why they so emphatically leave the world of the actual reader(s) out of consideration. On what scholarly theoretical concept is this implicit choice based? And how does this blind spot relate to insights in modern hermeneutics?

Readings from the Netherlands

While the third world groups devoted considerable attention, relatively speaking, to the metaphor of living water, of the Dutch groups, only the one in the village of Lisse goes into it in detail.[16] The conversation leads to a discussion about the precise meaning of the metaphor of living water in John 4:7–15. One person associates it with faith, another with eternal life. The conversation moves on to consideration of the extent to which eternal life also applies to believers today. One participant underlines the fact that she relates the living water to herself. Another doubts if the metaphor is applicable to her. They do not reach a consensus. Then, some of the participants attempt to approach John 4:7–15 from a different angle, by looking for an intertextual interpretation of the metaphor. In Jeremiah 2:13, God says: "They have forsaken me, the spring of living water." When one relates this text to John 4, it leads to the view that Jesus uses the metaphor of living water to refer to himself as in the image of God. Developing this application further, one person comments that people are also created in the image of God and that the metaphor therefore contains a command to be a source of living water.

The remaining six reports from the Netherlands address the metaphor only a little or not at all. Nevertheless, from a methodological standpoint, there are various similarities to the report from Lisse. The focus is on the text, and people are divided about the logic of the story. A few salient examples: In Geldrop, the participants find that the story would flow better if verse 21 were scrapped altogether. In Amstelveen, a participant comments that the strange transition between verse 31 and 32 is detrimental to the logical development. In Zaandam, one participant remarks that Jesus appears arrogant and talkative, while a woman in Geldrop finds Jesus too long-winded.

Only a few reports contain a brief reference to living water. Someone from Geldrop notices that in John 4 "the spring" and "eternal life" symbolize comfort, but adds that she does not know how one might apply this symbolism in practice. A participant from Amstelveen mentions that she drinks a glass of water each day and follows this act with prayer—a habit she associates with God's presence and protection. Someone else, also from Geldrop, comments:

> It is difficult because so many things in the text are vague. It gives me the impression of . . . an evangelizing story with a quick answer in verse 25, where a woman says, I know that the Messiah is coming. I think the biblical story turns a corner too quickly. . . . John gets tired of telling a lot in a nutshell, and that's why it becomes unclear, obscure, vague.

These fragmentary and rather brief comments do not give us many clues for determining why the different reading groups devote so little attention to John 4:7–15. Still, the Dutch responses to the reading reports from partner groups overseas offer some possibilities for an explanation. The most significant quotation comes from the report of the Apeldoorn reading group, in response to the report from Bolivia: "Within this situation their faith is a very practical one. They don't discuss the basic principles very much. Their problem is to live from inspiration of the Bible in the midst of the problems of each day. . . . Our belief is more a matter of rationality and deliberation than of emotions and feeling." This insight does not, however, lead the Apeldoorn group to reflect on their own rather rational approach. Neither do the participants decide to review their own reading report to determine whether they had perhaps overlooked certain parts of John 4.

The group from Ermelo has a different emphasis in their correspondence with the partner group. Several participants note that their Colombian partners are more concerned than the Dutch group is with the question of how John 4 relates to everyday life. The group discusses this point at length. Various participants indicate that they do not generally explore the meaning of biblical texts for their daily lives. At one point, the discussion leader intervenes and reminds the participants of World War 2:

> Our country was occupied then by Germany, and when a psalm about God who would punish his enemies was being sung, then everybody in church immediately knew who the enemy was. Now that we are living in peace we don't make this connection any more.

Dialogue with biblical scholars

The analysis of the relationship between North Atlantic biblical scholars and ordinary readers from the third world is in a certain sense incongruous. In contrast, one might expect that the relationship between the consulted biblical scholars and the Dutch reading groups might be significantly easier to map out. With a certain amount of care, it is possible to establish that the methodological approach of the consulted biblical scholars corresponds, on various points, with the way Dutch readers approach John 4. Both concentrate heavily on the world of the text and use exegetical methods in this process, which are—at first sight—more rational than associative. One notes several similarities, such as an interest in close reading, sensitivity to irregularities in the text, the use of intertextual arguments, and a lack of attention to the world of the actual reader(s). The abundance of similarities might almost give the impression that, methodologically speaking, the observations of the consulted biblical scholars and the Dutch participants in the intercultural Bible reading project coincide. This conclusion is perhaps just a little too facile.

On reading most of the Dutch reports, one might conclude that participants were rather satisfied with their own rational way of reading the Bible. They seem to give the impression that they have proceeded through the text in an almost scholarly manner. But is this so? In any case, six of the seven reading groups did not address the metaphor of living water. A trained exegete would have had difficulties with this neglect and would have indicated to the Dutch participants that John 4 is a carefully structured whole, in which each pericope contributes to the unity of the text. On balance, precisely because they bypass John 4:7–15, the relationship between the consulted biblical scholars and the Dutch reading groups is, despite many similarities, more complicated than one might suppose at first glance.

What then are the possibilities for fruitful dialogue between exegetes and ordinary readers? It is difficult to imagine that the consulted Western European biblical scholars would be interested in the outcome of the reading exercises of Dutch participants in the intercultural Bible reading project. Measured against the prevailing academic standards, the ordinary readers' views on John 4 seem rather deficient. Conversely, it might well be interesting for project participants to learn from exegetes how their close-reading techniques could be improved. But whether the dialogue could extend beyond this specific point is doubtful. In the last part of this article, I would like to explore this opinion in more depth.

Fundamental differences between scholarly and faith-oriented approaches

Judging from the reports, it appears that the Dutch participants in the intercultural Bible reading project were strongly influenced—consciously or unconsciously—by the way Western European biblical scholars analyze texts with an exegetical scalpel. This approach is a good way of protecting oneself against superficial or fundamentalistic readings of the text. But at the same time, it appears obvious that believers are not able to read the Bible in a truly scholarly way; they are simply not trained in this method. I am not implying that believers are exempt from the task of reading the texts as accurately as possible. I do mean, however, that the project participants would be wise to realize that there are—and should be—differences between an academic and a faith-oriented approach to the scriptures.[17]

The differences operate on at least two levels. First, believers, at least when compared to Western European academic biblical scholars, have much more freedom to question the text from within their own sociocultural setting. More specifically, many of the Dutch believers live in a world characterized by a declining role for Christian faith in society and a growing timidity when it comes to expressing one's own spirituality. Believers have complete freedom to introduce questions arising from this secularized environment into the dialogue they, as readers, engage in with the Bible.

Second, believers read the Bible with a different purpose than that of exegetes, as they are not obliged to pursue a scholarly analysis of the text. Ordinary readers may well make use of scholarly instruments in studying a biblical text. But, also by virtue of the contrasting premises, applying these instruments is not an end in itself. It is merely a means to achieve, in as responsible a way as possible, a process of appropriation that strives to use the text to reach a deeper understanding of one's environment and spirituality.

Applied to our case: the Dutch reading groups would have benefited greatly from focusing more attention on one of the crucial premises of the intercultural Bible reading project, namely, that Bible reading is, by definition, culturally determined. If in the initial phase of the project the groups had been more sharply aware of their own sociocultural context, they might have posed more faith-oriented questions to John 4. In the process, they undoubtedly would have noted their ambiguous stance toward the metaphor of living water, and perhaps John 4:7–15 might have challenged them to explore in greater depth their own spirituality (including all the forms of timidity associated with it).

It is striking that in the case of the Dutch groups, this exploration hardly happened, or did not happen at all, while both the format of the project (which required a description of the group's sociocultural context) and the reactions of the partner groups called for exactly this response. There is every indication that in the groups investigated, the tradition of reading the text from a (semi)scholarly point of view is apparently so strong that even powerful pressures from the project and the partner to take another course yielded very few results.

What does this analysis imply for the possibility of fruitful dialogue between project participants and exegetes? Based on the considerations sketched above, believers are advised to be aware of the specific modality—initial premises and ultimate goal—with which they read the Bible. A possible discussion with scholars would have to help the clarification of these junctions. Within Europe, one might consider as discussion partners modern hermeneuts such as Gadamer and Ricoeur, who have reflected on, among other things, the initial questions one might pose to a text, the role of the reader, and the importance of the context. Beyond Europe, one might consult the many exegetes in Africa, Asia, and North and South America who are seeking ways to integrate hermeneutics and biblical scholarship, and have gained much experience in working with ordinary readers. Such a discussion with scholars from Europe and beyond is no guarantee, however, that the metaphor of living water will suddenly spring to life. But it might stimulate Dutch believers to become more aware of the contextual dimension of their own faith and so find a better balance between the world of the text and the world around them.

Associations with *living water*: An overview

Africa

Ghana	Presbyterian	spirituality
South Africa	Reformed	none
South Africa	Reformed	none

Asia

Philippines	Roman Catholic	spirituality
Philippines	ecumenical	none

Latin America

Bolivia	Methodist	spirituality
Bolivia	Lutheran	Word of God
Brazil	Protestant	love of neighbor
Colombia	Roman Catholic BEC[18]	love of neighbor
Colombia	Roman Catholic BEC	love of neighbor
Colombia	Roman Catholic	spirituality
Colombia	Protestant	Holy Spirit
El Salvador	Baptist	Word of God
Nicaragua	Pentecostal	everlasting life
Nicaragua	Baptist	spirituality

the Netherlands

Amstelveen	PCN,[19] Roman Catholic, Perki[20]	none
Apeldoorn	PCN	none
Ermelo	PCN	none
Geldrop	PCN	none
Huizen	PCN	none
Lisse	ecumenical	faith [eternal life?]
Zaandam	PCN	none

Notes

[1] J. Severino Croatto, "Hermenêutica e Lingüística: A Hermenêutica Bíblica à Luz da Semiótica e Frente aos Métodos Histórico-críticos," *Estudos Teológicos* 24, no. 3 (1984): 69; Carlos Mesters, "The Use of the Bible in Christian Communities of the Common People," in *The Challenge of Basic Christian Communities*, ed. Sergio Torres and John Eagleson (Maryknoll, N.Y.: Orbis Books, 1981), 205.

[2] Although the various reading groups all used the same project handbook, the reporting was not uniform in nature. Some reports offer an integral reproduction of the discussion; others offer more of a summary. Most of the reporters, for understandable reasons, left matters such as body language, tone, and underlying emotions out of the picture. All of this implies that it is wise to realize that, no matter how empirical the reports may be, it is in fact impossible to get a complete picture of what actually took place in the various reading groups.

[3] For this article, I focus on the twenty-two reports that came in first. The reports originate from Latin America (10), the Netherlands (7), Africa (3), and Asia (2). Protestants are especially well represented (16). Roman Catholic (4) and ecumenical (2) groups are in the minority. For an overview, see the table at the end of this article.

[4] Diverse criteria were used in the selection, including regional spread (Germany, Great Britain, the United States), chronological spread (over the past forty years), and methodological spread (commentaries and thematic studies). A unifying factor is that all books consulted are to be found in theological libraries, suggesting that they enjoy some influence.

[5] See George Raymond Beasley-Murray, *John*, Word Biblical Commentary, vol. 36, 2nd ed. (Nashville, Tenn.: Thomas Nelson Publishers, 1999), 59; Thomas L. Brodie, *The Gospel According to John: A Literary and Theological Commentary* (New York: Oxford University Press, 1993), 215–16.

[6] See Frédéric Manns, *L'Evangile de Jean, à la lumière du Judaïsme* (Jerusalem: Franciscan Printing Press, 1991), 124, for example.

[7] Josef Blank, *Das Evangelium nach Johannes* (Düsseldorf: Patmos Verlag, 1977), 288ff.

[8] Rudolf Schnackenburg, *Das Johannesevangelium* (Freiburg im Breisgau, Germany: Herder, 1965), 467.

[9] Craig R. Koester, *Symbolism in the Fourth Gospel: Meaning, Mystery, Community* (Minneapolis, Minn.: Fortress Press, 1995), 171.

[10] James Montgomery Boice, *The Gospel of John: An Expositional Commentary*

(Grand Rapids, Mich.: Zondervan Publishing House, 1975), 344ff.

[11] Rupert von Deutz, *Lesungen über Johannes: Der geistige Sinn seines Evangeliums* (Trier, Germany: Spee-Verlag, 1977), 211.

[12] Ben Witherington, *John's Wisdom: A Commentary on the Fourth Gospel* (Louisville, Ky.: Westminster John Knox Press, 1995), 123–24.

[13] Boice, *The Gospel of John*, 346.

[14] By "more or less detailed," I mean that in the reading reports two or more sentences are devoted to the explanation and/or interpretation of *living water*. However, it is not always possible to determine, on the basis of the reports, to what extent a specific interpretation of *living water* can claim to represent a consensus in the group.

[15] Exceptions are a group from Brazil and two Catholic Base Ecclesial Communities from Colombia who associate living water with love of neighbor.

[16] The report from Lisse that appears on the project website is a summary of the Dutch report. For the sake of completeness, in what follows I draw from the full report.

[17] For a further analysis of the methodological differences between scholars and "ordinary believers," see Clodovis Boff, *Teología de lo político: Sus mediaciones* (Salamanca, Spain: Ediciones Sígueme, 1980), 55ff.

[18] Base Ecclesial Community.

[19] Protestant Church in the Netherlands.

[20] Indonesian Church in the Netherlands.

CHAPTER 17

Jesus among the ancestors
Continuity and discontinuity
Louis Jonker

Names of people and places in biblical narratives are normally not "innocent." They usually serve as devices for characterization and geographical orientation. However, they often also serve a wider purpose, to construct worlds of association. Using names as ports of entry into wide worlds of association, narrators subtly or explicitly provide the horizon against which they want their stories to be understood.

This perspective on personal and place names in narratives has been accounted for in various scholarly approaches to biblical interpretation. For example, in approaches that analyze the Bible according to the conventions of the literary sciences,[1] various scholars have indicated that names (personal names, in particular) often serve as devices for providing information that is vital for understanding the narrative plot. However, in these approaches the methodological reflection on the use of names in biblical narratives does not always give account for the pragmatic-rhetorical function of these names in the communication process of which the narratives form a part. Other approaches[2] indicate that the use of names in literary texts (especially narratives) not only serves the inner dynamics of the narrative but also situates it in a wider sociocultural context of communication. Mentioning personal and place names is then seen as a device that forms part of the textual strategy to convince or influence an audience.

This article will particularly attend to the occurrence of the personal name Jacob and the place name Sychar in the narrative in John 4. In verses 5–6 the narrator of this story provides the following geographical information:

> [5] So he came to a Samaritan city called Sychar, near the plot of ground that Jacob had given to his son Joseph. [6] Jacob's well was there, and Jesus, tired

Louis Jonker, Department of Old and New Testament, University of Stellenbosch (Stellenbosch, South Africa) out by his journey, was sitting by the well. It was about noon.

In verse 12, the narrator of the story tells us that the Samaritan woman refers to her ancestor, Jacob:

> [12] Are you greater than our ancestor Jacob, who gave us the well, and with his sons and his flocks drank from it?

Although the ancestors are not mentioned by name in verse 20, this verse is closely associated with the verses cited above:

> [20] Our ancestors worshiped on this mountain, but you say that the place where people must worship is in Jerusalem.

After exploring how discontinuity and continuity between the patriarchal context and the life and meaning of Jesus are created by this rhetorical setting of the narrative in John 4, I will examine how various Bible study groups interpreted this patriarchal/ancestral setting when they read this narrative as part of their participation in the intercultural Bible reading project.

Jesus in (dis)continuity with patriarchal history

Jesus at Jacob's well near Sychar

John 4 starts by indicating that Jesus left Judea for Galilee.[3] On his way to Galilee he had[4] to pass through Samaria where he came to the town of Sychar. The town is immediately specified in the text, and it is even qualified as being "near the plot of ground that Jacob had given to his son Joseph"; "Jacob's well was there." The town of Sychar is identified by many scholars with the modern-day village of Askar at the foot of Mount Ebal near Nablus.[5] Hendrikus Boers is correct, however, when he argues that "the geographical information has no significance in itself. Its significance is that it spatializes the narrative, placing it in a setting which affects almost everything that is about to transpire."[6] In the unfolding of the conversation between Jesus and the Samaritan woman, it will become clear that what it is all about is "living water" and "a place of worship." Boers therefore continues, "The village itself is not significant for the story. Its importance is that it is located close to the well and the mountain."[7] That conviction also motivates Friedhelm Wessel's statement that "the topography of the narrative is presented to us as a *theological* topography."[8]

The location at Sychar is rich in patriarchal history. Genesis 33:18–22 mentions the following:

> [18] Jacob came safely to the city of Shechem, which is in the land of Canaan, on his way from Paddan-aram; and he camped before the city. [19] And from the sons of Hamor, Shechem's father, he bought for one hundred pieces of money the plot of land on which he had pitched his tent. [20] There he erected an altar and called it El-Elohe-Israel.

According to Genesis 48:22, Jacob gave some land to his son Joseph in this region:

> ²² I now give to you one portion more than to your brothers, the portion that I took from the hand of the Amorites with my sword and with my bow.

The Hebrew word translated as "portion" in this verse is *Shechem* (with the literal meaning "shoulder," but referring here to "mountain slope"). Scholars often see in this text an allusion to the piece of land that Jacob bought near Shechem (according to Gen. 33:18ff.). Another significant reference in the Hebrew Bible is Joshua 24:32.

> ³² The bones of Joseph, which the Israelites had brought up from Egypt, were buried at Shechem, in the portion of ground that Jacob had bought from the children of Hamor, the father of Shechem, for one hundred pieces of money; it became an inheritance of the descendants of Joseph.

It is, however, interesting that there is no Old Testament reference to the digging of a well by Jacob or the other ancestors on this piece of land. Boers is of the opinion that the Palestinian Targum of Genesis 28:10 may provide a clue to our story.[9] This Targum mentions five signs performed by Jacob; the fifth is: "After our father Jacob had lifted the stone from the mouth of the well, the well rose to its surface and overflowed and was overflowing twenty years: all the days that our father dwelt in Haran."

The author of the Gospel of John was certainly aware of the rich world of tradition associated with mention of this geographical setting. This awareness is made explicit in the narrative by means of the question the woman asks Jesus: "Are you greater than our ancestor Jacob, who gave us the well, and with his sons and his flocks drank from it?" (v. 12).[10] Leon Morris indicates that "there can be no doubt that the Old Testament played a large part in the author's thinking.[11] He had obviously read it well and pondered it long." The prominent place of Old Testament traditions in the Gospel of John is therefore related by many commentators to its rhetorical purpose. Herman Ridderbos, for example, writes:

> Not only early church tradition but also the content of the Gospel itself clearly point to a historical development in which the Gospel has its *Sitz im Leben* and to which in a sense it responds. Especially relevant is the continual confrontation with "the Jews," a theme that completely governs the conversations about Jesus' identity. . . . This sharp confrontation with "the Jews" has to be seen also in the context of the position of the later Christian church as it was confronted by the resurgent synagogue after the destruction of Jerusalem. . . . For in that confrontation people were divided over the core question that kept (and keeps!) the church and the synagogue at arm's length: Was Jesus the Christ? And how could he be the Christ, he who, in his (supposed) descent, conduct, and death on the cross in no

respect conformed to what the Jews pictured to themselves, and could picture to themselves, as the Messiah? . . . This historical position of the church vis-à-vis the synagogue may have been one reason that the Evangelist focused his story entirely on the meaning of the person of Jesus, and it may have been for him an important criterion in the selection of his materials and the construction of his Gospel.[12]

This perspective on the use of the Old Testament in the Gospel of John (and therefore on the patriarchal context mentioned in the narrative in John 4) emphasizes that one should not limit the pragmatic-rhetorical analysis only to the inner dynamics of these narratives, but that one should also focus this analysis on the interaction of the narratives with their supposed original contexts of interpretation. Or to put it in another way, one should not only ask the question, What influence do the patriarchal/ancestral references have on the *dynamics of the conversation* between Jesus and the Samaritan woman? but also, What function did this narrative about the conversation between Jesus and the Samaritan woman perform *within the communication process* with an intended audience of interpretation?[13]

The next two sections will try to answer both of these questions with reference to the concepts of discontinuity and continuity.

Worlds apart, but with common ancestors! From discontinuity to continuity

After the introduction by the narrator in verses 1–6 of the narrative,[14] the conversation between Jesus and the Samaritan woman starts in verse 7. The theme around which the initial part of the conversation is built is that of water. When Jesus asks for a drink, the geographical setting of the narrative, namely, the well of Jacob, is interpreted by the reader in a physical sense. The initial expectation created by the narrative is that the woman will be in a position to quench the thirst of the exhausted Jesus.

However, the response of the Samaritan woman immediately complicates this expectation. Her reaction in verse 9 is negative, and she immediately points out the sociocultural problems involved in this interaction. Jesus retaliates in verse 10 by returning to the theme of water, but already it is clear that *water* becomes a metaphor for something else, namely, the new life that Jesus is able to give. Again, in verse 11, the woman refers to the sociocultural sphere within which the conversation takes place. But, as is the case with the reaction of Jesus, where a deepening in meaning can be seen between his initial question in verse 7 and his retaliatory statement in verse 10, one can also see a deepening of meaning in the woman's sociocultural references. Her reaction in verse 9 points out the difference between them, while the reaction in verse 12 asks for a proof of authority.

Many commentators have indicated that the Greek construction of the question in verse 12 is significant. The question starts with μή (*mē*), a negative interrogative that normally introduces a rhetorical question expecting a negative answer. The woman's question in verse 12 can be paraphrased: "You are not greater than our ancestor Jacob, are you?" The question already implies a lack of authority. She does not regard the water that Jesus promises as more valuable than the water that their ancestor Jacob provided by means of the well at Sychar.

The majority of commentators on John's Gospel refer to this dynamic in the story when they state that the contrast between Jew and Samaritan is highlighted by the reactions of the woman. The history of tension between Jews and Samaritans would certainly have been well known to the audience of John's Gospel.[15] It is not necessary to spell out the well-known history of animosity between Jews and Samaritans here. However, it is necessary to emphasize that the woman, in her reactions, wants to focus on the sociocultural contrast between her and Jesus. She wants to focus on discontinuity and difference.[16] Later in the conversation, in verse 20, she takes up the place of worship[17] as another attempt to emphasize discontinuity. That reaction serves the purpose in the conversation not only to emphasize the sociocultural discontinuity but also its religious and spiritual implications.

The irony is, of course, that the reader or hearer of this conversation (having been introduced to the setting at Jacob's well near Sychar) is fully aware of the fact that Jews and Samaritans have a common history.[18] By mentioning the names of the ancestors Jacob and Joseph, as well as indicating the geographical setting, the narrator has prepared the reader to evaluate the woman's reaction as a nonargument. Although she is protesting against the difference and discontinuity between Jesus and herself, the narrative setting speaks more loudly about continuity.

It is interesting that Jesus does not react to her attempt to focus on discontinuity. He rather refocuses the conversation by metaphorically referring to living water. That is probably why the woman realizes that she will not get very far with her remarks on their sociocultural differences. Her reaction in verse 11 initially follows the line introduced by Jesus (namely, the theme of living water), but she then reformulates her viewpoint on their *discontinuity* by raising the issue of authority in verse 12. It is significant, however, that she does this now with explicit reference to the symbols of their *continuity*, namely, the ancestral origin of the well of Sychar.

In the tradition of the ancestors, but different! From continuity to discontinuity

It is clear from the above explanation that the narrative thrust leading up to the woman's question in verse 12 is a movement from discontinuity to continuity. Jesus's reaction (v. 10) to the woman's emphasis on discontinuity (v. 9) shows that he does not want to focus on the sociocultural differences, but that he would like her to focus instead on who he is, and on the living water he is able to give her. He brings her to the point where she wants to evaluate him in a common context, namely, the ancestral heritage.

However, at this point in the conversation, Jesus starts referring to another discontinuity. In his reaction in verses 13–14 to the woman's question on his authority, he indicates that there is a qualitative difference between the water that the ancestors were able to provide and the water that he is giving.[19] Ridderbos describes Jesus's reaction as follows:

> He . . . contrasts the water from Jacob's well ("this water") with his gift. He does not condemn the first as though there was something wrong with it. He had, indeed, begun by asking for it. But it has only a limited effect. It only temporarily quenches one's thirst. In the nature of the case, this is as far as the gift of father Jacob goes. Over against it Jesus sets the water—described with repeated emphasis as *his* gift—that will forever assuage a person's thirst, water one does not over and over have to go and get but that becomes a spring of living, self-replenishing water *within*. Not that a single drink will satisfy, but as the gift of God it is an everlasting, self-renewing spring of refreshment and life.[20]

By using water as theme for this conversation, Jesus succeeds in identifying himself to the woman as somebody in the tradition of Jacob who wants to provide means of life. However, by indicating that the water that he provides is living water, he identifies himself as a *new* Jacob. He is bringing life for his people like the ancestors did with their provision of land and water, but then in a completely different way. Although he stands in continuity with the ancestral traditions, he is also different—in discontinuity.

More than one listener!

The progress in the conversation so far is of the utmost significance for those who hear or read the Gospel of John. Eugene Botha states: "In 4:13–14, the author again makes sure that the readers do not follow the woman by emphatically explaining via the word of Jesus what was meant earlier. The readers are supposed to pick that up, not the character of the woman."[21] The manipulative character of the Gospel presentation of the conversation should not be overlooked at this point. By means of an intricate interplay between continuity and discontinuity, the implied author leads the implied reader to come to certain conclusions about the identity of Jesus. The woman's role in this presentation is to emphasize difference. The discontinuity between her and Jesus is formulated in sociocultural categories: he is a Jew and she a Samaritan, he is a man and she a woman. The well of Jacob is for her the meeting point between these two cultures. At this meeting point, she emphasizes contrast, difference, and discontinuity.

But Jesus's reaction does not latch onto this emphasis. In both of his reactions (vv. 10, 13), he indicates that the water he is offering is not of the same kind as that presupposed by the woman. As Botha puts it: "Because this water is of a different nature, her questions regarding his ability and relative authority compared with Jacob are no longer valid."[22] Jesus's reactions use the setting at the well of Jacob differently. He also emphasizes discontinuity, but not the sociocultural discontinuity between the two of them. In his reactions, he focuses on the discontinuity between the role of their common ancestor Jacob as the provider of physical means for life, and himself as the provider of spiritual means for life. The well of Jacob, in Jesus's reactions, is the meeting point between the old covenant and the new, between traditions that prepared the way for the salvation of God to be fulfilled, and the fulfillment of this salvation in Jesus.

Within the context of the first hearers/readers of John's Gospel, this ironic twist[23] to Jesus's story would certainly have been of great significance. With this presentation of the interaction between Jesus and the Samaritan woman in the patriarchal context at Sychar's well, the hearer/reader is not led to provide new answers with regard to Jesus but rather to ask new questions.[24] The rhetorical force of this narrative is summarized by Botha as follows: "By using the concept of water from the immediate context, the mission and identity of Jesus are summarized for the sake of the readers. Although no new information regarding Jesus' mission is offered, these utterances serve to throw the whole dialogue into a different light in the perception of the reader. Whereas Jesus' approaching the woman felt completely wrong at first, the situation is now rectified to some extent."[25] The progress in the narrative (from the discontinuity that the woman emphasizes, to the discontinuity that Jesus indicates) leads the reader to realize that Jesus does not fit into a picture of sociocultural difference. Who he is and what he does are not functions of sociocultural discontinuity. His identity should rather be sought on the level of fulfillment of the promise of life to the ancestors, but in a radical way. He is indeed a new *Jacob*, but in a *new* way.

This message would certainly have been of great significance for the early Christian church in the latter quarter of the first century CE. After the fall of Jerusalem to the Romans, and with the expansion of the church into non-Jewish Mediterranean societies, it would have been an important part of the process of identity formation within the Christian community to reflect on the identity of Jesus. As many commentators indicate, the Gospel of John played an important role in this process. The meaning of Jesus for the early Christian community, existing in a multicultural environment, is certainly formulated in a creative way by means of the Gospel's narrative about Jesus's encounter with the Samaritan woman at Jacob's well. It would have become clear from this story that it is part of the Christian identity to override sociocultural discontinuities in order to proclaim the life-giving power of Jesus, who is the fulfillment of God's gifts to the ancestors. The Christian religion is therefore defined both in continuity as well as in discontinuity with Judaism. The early Christians, whether they were from Jewish or Gentile origin, had to realize that Jesus stands in the same tradition as the patriarchs, but then in a radical new way. The water that he gives is radically different from the water of the well of Jacob. "Everyone who drinks of this water will be thirsty again, but those who drink of the water that I will give them will never be thirsty. The water that I will give will become in them a spring of water gushing up to eternal life" (vv. 13–14).

Reading from different contexts

Interculturality and Bible reading

The early Christians were, of course, not the last readers of this conversation and of John's Gospel. After the canonization of this Gospel and the New Testament, various traditions of interpretation began to flourish, traditions that continue to our day. Without implying that these longstanding traditions[26] are of no importance for contemporary interpretation,[27] the discussion will now provide certain examples of contemporary interpretation. The focus will be on how the dynamics of continuity and discontinuity resonate in different contemporary sociocultural contexts.

The examples are taken from reading reports prepared by various Bible study groups in the international project on intercultural Bible reading, Through the Eyes of Another.[28] One should distinguish in this regard between different levels of intercultural reading: (1) When contemporary readers of the Bible, from their modern sociocultural environments, read the Bible, they often feel estranged, because of the sociocultural distance between the ancient and modern contexts. The reading of the Bible in contemporary contexts is therefore, by implication, an intercultural encounter. (2) However, when contemporary readers from different sociocultural contexts read the Bible *together*, it creates another level of intercultural encounter. There is then a double estrangement: because of the distance described in the first point, as well as because of the sociocultural distance between different contemporary environments and traditions of interpretation. The project Through the Eyes of Another focuses mainly on this second type of intercultural Bible reading.

The chosen text in the above-mentioned project was John 4. Before analyzing some of the interpretations of this text, it is important to reflect explicitly on the network of interculturality that influences the reading process. With the above distinction in mind, at least the following intercultural relationships are present in this reading exercise: (1) the intercultural contact between Jesus and the woman (Jew || Samaritan; man || woman),[29] (2) the intercultural contact between the world of origin of John 4 and the world of contemporary interpreters (early Christian society || various sociocultural modern Christian contexts), and (3) the intercultural contact between the sociocultural worlds of different contemporary interpreters.

The next section will indicate how different aspects of the interaction described in (1) are emphasized in various contemporary readings. I will argue that these differences can often be accounted for with reference to difference in (2), namely, the sociocultural distance between the world of the Bible and the world of the contemporary readers. In the next section, one example of the interaction described in (3) will be discussed in order to determine the dynamics of that interaction.

Intercultural encounter between text and contemporary readers

The patriarchal/ancestral setting of the conversation in John 4 serves as point of departure for several trends in the reading reports that were available[30] on the website of the project Through the Eyes of Another. Although it is possible (and even necessary) to reflect thoroughly on each of these angles, the focus of the discussion within the limited scope of this article will mainly be on the interpretations of the two last-mentioned groups.

Discontinuity between Jew and Samaritan. In their interpretations, the majority of the groups referred to the sociocultural discontinuity between Jew and Samaritan (alluded to in the question of the woman in verse 9). Generally, this aspect of the conversation is interpreted (along the lines of traditional scholarship) as the background for accentuating the identity of Jesus. However, in only a few groups (of which the Sokhanya Bible School, Cape Town, South Africa, is a good example),[31] the discontinuity between Jew and Samaritan was appropriated politically and racially in their own contexts. In some of these readings, the well of Jacob is then interpreted as a symbolic point of reconciliation.[32]

Gender discontinuity. In many other groups (of which the Macassar group, Indonesia, is a good example),[33] the man-woman discontinuity present in the conversation of John 4 was taken as point of departure for gender sensitive appropriations in their own contexts.

Ancestor setting. In a minority of the reading reports, a third angle was taken on the sociocultural discontinuity between Jesus and the woman. In these reports, the ancestor setting and explicit mention of the patriarchs formed the point of departure for their appropriation. The two examples of this type of interpretation are the groups from Port Harcourt, Nigeria, and Siyaphila Bible Study, South Africa.

In the description provided by the Port Harcourt group, Nigeria,[34] the following is reported about their context and their method of Bible reading:

> The text of John 4 is read contextually, i.e., from the African cultural perspective. To this end, one person is chosen to prepare the textual portion or verses that underscore aspects of African cultural values and practices such as hospitality, ancestorhood, motherhood/womanhood, polygamy, and the Osu caste system in Igboland or elsewhere in Africa. The group later discusses this. The group members bring along with them symbolic objects such as bottled water, a cross, a candle, and pieces of white cloth. The group considers these objects symbolic of life, purity, and light, which Christ radiates in the life of Christians. In addition, members of the group brought symbolic objects such as the Ikenga or Ofo, cowries, clay pots, fowl feathers, and other objects of worship believed to be accepted by the ancestors in the African cultural setting. The group had an atmosphere of thinking, laughter, and emotional sympathy with the woman of Samaria, when she portrayed her strong belief in the traditions of her ancestors and their place of worship. . . . The reading of the text (John 4) evoked interesting thoughts, memories, and experiences in the individual lives of the members of this group. The verses remind the members of diverse aspects of African cultural

values and practices, namely ancestorhood, the problem of the Osu caste system in Igboland, polygamy, hospitality, and womanhood/motherhood.

With reference to verses 10 and 22, the group reports the following:

> It is undoubtedly clear that in both biblical and African traditions, people lay hold of their ancestral heritage. Thus, the Samaritan woman minced no words in presenting to Jesus the Samaritans' belief in their ancestors whose deeds and benevolence are worthy of remembrance: "Are you greater than our father Jacob, who gave us this well?" Further in verse 20, the woman says: "Our fathers worshiped on this mountain." These words particularly reminded the group members about the tenacity of ancestorhood in our own localities. The fact is that ancestors hold a key position in African traditional religion and culture. Hence, they are thought of and venerated as the living dead. Here in the text, the woman of Samaria is fittingly seen as an apostle of ancestorhood. The group therefore sees the text of John 4 as significant for the Christian understanding of the communion of saints. Second, the text is far more crucial for the portrait of Jesus as ancestor. Indeed, just as ancestors are mediators of the *élan vital*, the life-flow, to their communities, Jesus too is the living water (4:14). No doubt the portrait of Jesus as ancestor resonates more with the portrait of Jesus in the Gospel of John than in the synoptic [Gospels]. Consequently, African Christians would hold on to Christ as ancestor whose words and deeds must be the guide for their daily living. Just as the woman claimed Jacob as their father (ancestor), Christians today in Africa would hold on to Christ as their proto-ancestor. This is very significant.

Ancestorhood is taken up here in a twofold way: On the one hand, the Samaritan woman is evaluated positively, because she shows an awareness of the ancestors and their influence on her life as the "living dead." The Nigerian group members find themselves in continuity with the Samaritan woman, exactly because of this. On the other hand, they evaluate Jesus very positively. He, being the living water, is the one who provides "the life-flow." Again they find themselves in continuity with this narrative about Jesus, because he is their "proto-ancestor."

When this group reflects on their interpretation, they are quite aware of the fact that their African sociocultural background plays a determining role in their interpretations. It is even part of their method to explicitly reflect on the question, What does this mean for us in our African context?

It is clear that this group's view of the intercultural exchange between Jesus and the Samaritan woman (type 1 mentioned above) is determined by the continuity that they experience between their sociocultural world and the sociocultural world embodied in the text (type 2 mentioned above).[35] The main feature of the conversation, for them, is the fact that ancestorhood creates the possibility of contact between Jesus and the woman—even amid other complicating factors that emphasizes their difference.

Another example of a group that used ancestorhood as interpretive key to the narrative in John 4 is the Siyaphila group, South Africa. It is significant, however, that this key was treated differently here. The Siyaphila group reports the following:

> The view that the text was about belief in the ancestors generated a long and intense discussion. The well was associated with the ancestor Jacob, and so symbolized their cultural heritage. The text, seen from this perspective, then seemed to be about the tensions between Jesus and traditional (African) beliefs in ancestors and the veneration of ancestors by slaughtering an animal. However, some of the group seemed to feel that Christian things and traditional things were not so much in tension as they were belonging to two separate and parallel realities in their lives. A lengthy discussion on these points resulted, with some arguing that most cultural practices were problematic for a Christian, while others were more nuanced and held that there are good and bad cultural practices.

> A member of the group wanted to know, in the light of this discussion, whether it was a sin to slaughter. The response of the group was again mixed, with some seeming to imply that it was a sin if one knew the (Christian) truth, while others now openly admitted that they slaughtered and would never stop doing it. Gradually, there seemed to be agreement that these were difficult matters to decide on as individuals, and that there needed to be some respect for one's family and its traditions.

> Among some of the other traditions mentioned was the tradition of virginity testing and other traditions associated with young men and women becoming adults and entering into marriage.

> The discussion then turned to the implications of this discussion for the group itself, and it was agreed that it was important for the group to recognize that although there were differences among them, there were also important things about which they agreed. They felt that it was important for them to be patient with and understanding about their differences, and in so doing to support and respect one another.

> It was clearly difficult for the group to move away from this discussion, touching as it did a deep tension within most of them between their faith and culture.

The dynamics in this group discussion were different from those in the Port Harcourt group. It is clear that a part of the Siyaphila group saw in the ancestorhood background of the text a confirmation of their own cultural practices, while another part emphasized the fact that Jesus condemns ancestorhood by not latching on to that part of the woman's reaction. This second part of the group saw in the text a basis for warning against syncretism.

It is interesting to find that continuity and discontinuity with the biblical intercultural dynamics exist in a single group. The biographical information of this group, compared with the Nigerian group, does not provide any obvious clues to account for this interesting difference between the groups. Both groups exist in urban or semi-urban environments, and both groups draw their members from African cultural backgrounds. This difference seems to be attributable to the fact that the Port Harcourt group is probably a more homogeneous group than the Siyaphila group.

Intercultural encounter among contemporary readers

How did the partner groups react to these interpretations? Or, to put the question more theoretically, how did these interpretations influence the intercultural exchange in contemporary contexts (type 3 above)? In answering this question, the intercultural interaction between the Port Harcourt group, Nigeria, and their Peruvian partner group is significant.[36] With reference to the interpretive key of ancestorhood that the Nigerian group employed, the Peruvian group responded:

> We found this a totally novel element for our group: It never would have occurred to us to have this angle of reflection on John 4. This was a very original contribution for our group, enriching for us, from your contextual theology and cultural hermeneutics, from your social setting in Nigeria.

> Considering one's ancestors as the "living dead" was very interesting to us, as were the Samaritan woman as the "apostle of ancestorhood" and the relation of this theme to the "communion of saints."

> We asked ourselves if there was anything comparable to this in the ancient or indigenous Peruvian cultures. . . . Today, in the occidentalized Peruvian culture, you don't find this sense of reverence for ancestors as the "living dead." There *is* a great deal of reverence and prayers offered for the dead, but it doesn't seem to have the same nuances as the matter has for you in Africa.

> On the other hand, we are in agreement with you in the recognition that women tend to be the "apostles" who transmit the history, traditions, wisdom, and culture. Perhaps in the majority of cases, it is women who also transmit the faith.

> We would like to highlight the importance of *life* in your vision of things: thanks to the ancestors, life continues to be transmitted.

The Port Harcourt group, after considering the interpretation of the Peruvian group, returned this response:

We therefore concluded that the differences in our interpretations are due to the new insights or ways of doing theology in our respective regions, viz. liberation theology in Latin America and inculturation theology in Africa.

From these reactions, it seems as if the intercultural exchange between these groups functioned constructively, at least on the following levels:

Both these groups seem to have a high tolerance for diversity. They do not limit the meaning of the biblical text to their own understanding but rather leave open the possibility of diverse interpretations and a multiplicity of meanings. The intercultural exchange strengthened this value.

Exposure to the other group's interpretation of John 4 made them aware of discontinuity and difference between them, without letting this influence their exchange destructively. They rather were sensitized by the intercultural interaction to identify reasons for the uniqueness of their respective interpretations.

Conclusion

In the first part of this chapter, I indicated the following: (1) The patriarchal/ancestral setting of the narrative in John 4 plays a central role in the communicative dynamics of the story. (2) In the exchange between Jesus and the Samaritan woman, it becomes clear that an interesting interplay with continuity and discontinuity brings about progress in the narrative. (3) Exactly this progress was determinative for the understanding of the narrative in the context of the early church in which John's Gospel originated.

In the second part of the chapter, I distinguished different levels of interculturality. We have seen how two groups (both from the African continent) found in their own sociocultural context continuity (although in different ways) with the sociocultural context of the Biblical text.

In conclusion, it could be said that this study created an awareness of the intricate and dynamic nature of intercultural exchange in Bible reading. The project Through the Eyes of Another seems to be only the beginning of the great venture of describing and analyzing this exchange. At least the following desiderata should be indicated at this stage: (1) More empirical studies on this aspect are needed before any clear patterns and structures can be described. (2) Biblical hermeneuts should reflect more consciously on the role of culture in biblical interpretation.[37]

Notes

[1] There are a few standard works normally referred to in this context: the works of Robert Alter, *The Art of Biblical Narrative* (New York: Basic Books, 1981), and *The World of Biblical Literature* ([New York]: Basic Books, 1992); Robert Alter and Frank Kermode, *The Literary Guide to the Bible* (Cambridge, Mass.: Belknap Press of Harvard University Press, 1987); Shimeon Bar-Efrat, *Narrative Art in the Bible* (Sheffield, U.K.: Almond Press, 1989); Adele Berlin, *Poetics and Interpretation of Biblical Narrative* (Sheffield, U.K.: Almond Press, 1983); J. Cheryl Exum and

David J. A. Clines, *The New Literary Criticism and the Hebrew Bible* (Sheffield, U.K.: JSOT Press, 1993); Mark Allan Powell, Cecile G. Gray, and Melissa C. Curtis, *The Bible and Modern Literary Criticism: A Critical Assessment and Annotated Bibliography* (New York: Greenwood Press, 1992); and Meir Sternberg, *The Poetics of Biblical Narrative: Ideological Literature and the Drama of Reading* (Bloomington, Ind.: Indiana University Press, 1985).

[2] It is particularly approaches interested in the rhetorical or pragmatic function of textual communication that attend to this aspect. Many of these approaches take their theoretical point of departure from speech-act theory. See, e.g., the work of the Old Testament scholar Hardmeier (summarized in Christof Hardmeier, *Textwelten der Bibel entdecken: Grundlagen und Verfahren einer textpragmatischen Literaturwissenschaft der Bibel*, Textpragmatische Studien zur Literatur- und Kulturgeschichte der Hebräischen Bibel, vol. 1, no. 1 [Gütersloh: Gütersloher Verlagshaus, 2003]); as well as the New Testament scholar Botha (J. Eugene Botha, *Jesus and the Samaritan Woman: A Speech Act Reading of John 4:1-42* [Leiden, the Netherlands: E. J. Brill, 1991]; and J. Eugene Botha, "John 4.16a: A Difficult Text Speech Act Theoretically Revisited," in *The Gospel of John as Literature: An Anthology of Twentieth-Century Perspectives*, ed. Mark W. G. Stibbe [Leiden, the Netherlands: E. J. Brill, 1993]), who has illustrated his approach with reference to John 4.

[3] Many commentators (e.g., Leon Morris, *The Gospel According to John: The English Text with Introduction, Exposition and Notes* [Grand Rapids, Mich.: Eerdmans, 1971], 53ff.; and Siegfried Schulz, *Das Evangelium nach Johannes* [Göttingen, Germany: Vandenhoeck & Ruprecht, 1976], 82), accept the literary-critical view that the order of chapters 5 and 6 should be reversed because of the geographical indications. Chapter 5 is again located in Jerusalem, while chapter 6 has Galilee as setting. Many scholars argue that a confusion of the order of the manuscript pages seems to be a probable explanation. A more recent commentator (Herman N. Ridderbos, *The Gospel According to John: A Theological Commentary* [Grand Rapids, Mich.: Eerdmans, 1997], 181ff.) argues, however, that the lack of a proper transition between chapters 5 and 6 can also be explained differently, with reference to matters of content, theme, and narrative strategy, and that they should not necessarily be switched around. The discussion of this issue shows that the geographical indications in the Gospel of John should be studied in close connection with the theological content. These place names do not merely serve as local indications; they are part of the strategy of the author to construct a world of association.

[4] Commentators have provided mainly two explanations for this expression in the text. Some interpret it theologically, i.e., with the connotation of divine providence, while others see in the indication nothing more than a geographical focus. The main road from Judea to Galilee actually ran through Samaria.

[5] However, other scholars argue that Sychar was really the biblical Shechem (modern-day Balata, near Nablus). See the discussions in Morris, *The Gospel According to John*, 257, n. 19; Hendrikus Boers, *Neither on this Mountain nor in Jerusalem: A Study of John 4* (Atlanta, Ga.: Scholars Press, 1988), 155, n. 18; F. F. Bruce, *The Gospel of John* (Grand Rapids, Mich.: Eerdmans, 1983), 104; and Ridderbos, *The Gospel According to John*, 153.

[6] Boers, *Neither on this Mountain nor in Jerusalem*, 155.

[7] Ibid., 156.

[8] Friedhelm Wessel, "Die fünf Männer der Samaritanerin: Jesus und die Tora nach Joh 4,16-19," *Biblische Notizen* 68 (1993): 27; my translation, Wessel's italics.

[9] Boers, *Neither on this Mountain nor in Jerusalem*, 156.

[10] Some scholars (see, e.g., Botha, *Jesus and the Samaritan Woman*, 117ff.) indicate that "the request of the lone figure by the well also recalls the Old Testament betrothal scenes vividly—with the difference that while the usual scene takes place in a foreign territory amid friendly people, this scene takes place in the midst of the territory of Israel among hostile people. While it is expected of the protagonist in the Old Testament type–scene to ask for water, here it is exactly the opposite." This is another strong indication of the author's purposeful association of what is narrated in John 4 with the Hebrew Bible traditions. See also Lyle Eslinger, "The Wooing of the Woman at the Well: Jesus, the Reader, and Reader-Response in John 4," in *The Gospel of John as Literature*, ed. Stibbe, 178ff.

[11] Morris, *The Gospel According to John*, 60.

[12] Ridderbos, *The Gospel According to John*, 10.

[13] Robert Gordon Maccini, "A Reassessment of the Woman at the Well in John 4 in Light of the Samaritan Context," *Journal for the Study of the New Testament* 53 (March 2001): 37, mentions that "various proposals have been made that the author of John was a Samaritan, or employed Samaritan sources and theology, or directed the Gospel to a Samaritan audience. The theory of Samaritan influence in John has gained ground but remains unproven. . . . Still, whatever John's background(s) and target audience(s) may have been, his Gospel was read by both Jews and Samaritans. R. Bultmann points out that the Samaritan episode of John 4 evidently assumes local knowledge in its hearers. Both Jewish and Samaritan readers therefore must be considered."

[14] Compare Botha's speech-act analysis of this introductory part (Botha, *Jesus and the Samaritan Woman*, 97ff.). He sees verses 1–4 as a more general introduction, while verses 5–6 serve as specific introduction to the story.

[15] The fact that the parenthetical sentence in verse 9—which should be seen as the narrator's voice rather than the woman's speech—namely, "(Jews do not share things in common with Samaritans.)," is missing in certain manuscripts, may be an indication that this knowledge was not presupposed in later stages of reception, and that later redactors added this note as explanation. The common view among commentators is, however, that this sentence is an addition to the conversation by the evangelist.

[16] It should be noted that her self-identification as "a woman of Samaria" emphasizes that she defines the discontinuity between herself and Jesus not only on the level of his being a Jew and she a Samaritan but also that she is a woman and he a man. It is well known that women were regarded as being of inferior status in the patriarchal society of the time of origin of John's Gospel.

[17] The history of division on the issue of a place of worship is summarized by Ridderbos (*The Gospel According to John*, 161): "From of old the Samaritans had worshiped Yahweh alongside their idols (2 Kg. 17:26f., 32, 41). In distinction from the Jews who, according to Dt. 27:4 (MT), brought their sacrifices to Mount Ebal, the Samaritans, in their Pentateuch, gave this significance to Mount Gerizim, which

was situated adjacent to Jacob's well ('this mountain') and worshiped Yahweh there. In the course of time they built a temple there (with permission from Alexander the Great, according to Josephus), but it was destroyed by John Hyrcanus I, a Jewish king, in 128 B.C. But the Samaritan worship of Yahweh was continued on Mount Gerizim and remained the great religious bone of contention (cf. Luke 9:53)."

[18] See Wessel, "Die fünf Männer der Samaritanerin," 26: "Die Ortsangabe 'Quelle Jakobs' (4,6) deutet schon diesen Hintergrund an: sie weist nämlich hin auf den gemeinsamen Ursprung von Samaritanern und Juden in ihrem Stammvater Jakob (=Israel). Dort, in diesem Quell Jakobs, begann die Geschichte der zwölf Stämme Israels. Und trotz der späteren Verzweigung ihres Weges durch Eroberung, Verbannung, Exil und Rückkehr bleibt der Ursprung das Verbindende zwischen Juda, dem israelitischen Südreich, und Samaria, dem Zehn-Stämme-Reich im Norden. Die Begegnung zwischen Jesus und der Samaritanerin an diesem Ort ist also eine Begegnung an der gemeinsamen religiösen und geschichtlichen Wurzel."

[19] Many scholars have commented on the different Greek terminology used for "well" in this conversation: πηγή *(pēgē)* in verses 6, 14 and θρέαρ *(threar)* in verse 11. Botha's view (*Jesus and the Samaritan Woman*, 108) seems to reflect the consensus: "One could of course argue that πηγή perhaps has the connotation of running water, and that the author uses πηγή in connection with the name of Jacob (4:6) to indicate or correlate the true religion of the Jews as running or living water, whereas θρέαρ is used in (4:11) by the Samaritan woman. Whether this is a significant distinction here, is hard to decide. The decision can only be based on the interpretation of the context here, and not on the meanings of the Greek words. It is also possible that the variation could, of course, be a purely 'stylistic' variation to avoid monotony, with no allusions to anything else."

[20] Ridderbos, *The Gospel According to John*, 156.

[21] Botha, *Jesus and the Samaritan Woman*, 134.

[22] Ibid., 135.

[23] Botha (ibid., 132) indicates how the strategy of irony is used in the Gospel to manipulate the hearers/readers into associating with certain characters in the story: "At this stage the readers and Jesus, as an 'insider' group are contrasted with the Samaritans as an 'outsider' group. The effect of this use of language is that the Samaritans are seen rather negatively. This is also necessary because of the effect of the utterances in the previous section where the woman is pictured rather favorably in the sense that she acts politely, and adheres to the required socio-cultural modes of conduct, while Jesus is actually criticized by the implied author. This situation has to be rectified and this explains the use of such a powerful literary device as irony."

[24] Ridderbos, *The Gospel According to John*, 152, also indicates that the focus is on Jesus rather than on the woman. Different characters are portrayed by the evangelist in order to "serve as mirrors in which, each time in a different way, the image of Christ is reflected." He also warns that the "focus is not on their (the different characters') histories or their psychological makeup. They appear on stage too briefly and too fragmentarily for that. Their stories have quite another focus. It is not the task of the exegete—as has been all too often attempted with much imagination and skill—to supplement the profile sketched by the Evangelist with historical and psychological detail." In reaction to Ridderbos's point of view, one should, however,

mention that this is exactly the reason why many exegetes with a gender hermeneutic associate with the woman in this narrative. In traditional (male, Western) scholarship, the role of the woman is often interpreted as being a function of the narrative about Jesus; she is not a character in her own right. The experience of marginalization of many women causes exegetes with a gender hermeneutic to focus on this facet of the text, and to emphasize the role of the woman as interpretive key to this text.

[25] Botha, *Jesus and the Samaritan Woman*, 136.

[26] Biblical hermeneuts should take notice of the warning expressed by certain church history and systematic theology colleagues, that one should not ignore the sixteen centuries since the final canonization of the Bible when interpreting the Bible in contemporary societies. Modern interpreters are the products of these diverse traditions of interpretation. The interaction with biblical texts in new contexts does not take place in isolation but is part of the continuous spiral of interpretation since the early Christian church.

[27] It could, for example, make an interesting study to analyze Calvin's interpretation and application of the narrative in John 4. He evaluates the Samaritan woman very negatively and applies the narrative directly to the controversy in his day with the Roman Catholic Church. "As the Samaritans were despised by the Jews, so the Samaritans, on the other hand, held the Jews in contempt. Accordingly, this woman at first not only disdains Christ but even mocks at him. She understands quite well that Christ is speaking figuratively, but she throws out a jibe by a different figure, intending to say, that he promises more than he can accomplish. She proceeds to charge him with arrogance in exalting himself above the holy patriarch Jacob. . . . It ought also to be observed that the Samaritans falsely boasted of being descended from the holy Fathers. In like manner do the Papists, though they are a bastard seed, arrogantly boast of the Fathers, and despise the true children of God. Although the Samaritans had been descended from Jacob according to the flesh, yet, as they were altogether degenerated and estranged from true godliness, this boasting would have been ridiculous" (Jean Calvin, *Commentary on the Gospel According to John*, trans. William Pringle [Grand Rapids, Mich.: Baker Book House, 1989, 1847]).

[28] The reports were available to the author on the project website www.bible4all .org. References in this part will only contain the names of the respective groups, as well as their origin.

[29] The text of John 4 was chosen, among other criteria, because of its explicit mention of sociocultural differences. See chapter one of this volume, Hans de Wit, "Through the Eyes of Another: Objectives and Backgrounds," for a description of how the text for the reading exercise was selected.

[30] The reports from the first phase that were available in June 2003 were scrutinized for this analysis. See the description of the project methodology in chapter one of this volume.

[31] The Sokhanya Bible School group saw in the Jew-Samaritan discontinuity a reflection of the South African history of racism, of which all of them were victims (see the biographical information about this group on the project website). Of significance is the reaction of their partner group, Zaandam (the Netherlands), to this interpretation. The Dutch group reacted with surprise, almost with shock, to this interpretation. Another South African group that paid attention to the political

implications of the text is the Siyaphila group. They report that "one of the group members said that they also felt that the text was about how in talking to the woman, 'Jesus was trying to destroy the [racial] segregation.' This shifted the discussion to racism, with the group wondering whether it would ever end. Although there was not a lot of hope that it would, the group argued that the only way to destroy racism was to 'really know a person.' Other types of segregation besides racial segregation were then mentioned, including the discrimination felt by single mothers."

[32] See, e.g., the interpretation of the Sancti Spiritus group, Cuba: "His passing through Samaria is an inclusion gesture which is aimed at the establishment of links in a context full of differences. These are ethnic, religious, geographic, and generic links. Jacob's well is a special and chronological reference that brings to mind the historical times of the patriarchs, in which there was no difference between northern and southern communities. . . . That is why the well is the ideal place for meeting and reconciling; from a symbolic point of view it is the 'source of life'–place for the community."

[33] See the reactions of some of the group members: "Perhaps it has already been said by other members, but some people, when reading the Bible, have a tendency to overlook the interest of women. That irritates me as a woman. I have my questions, and I even oppose the Bible when women are often depicted as the root of all problems. I myself try to be more objective on this point. I thank God that Jesus is not taking up the gender issue here and even makes a new breakthrough on this point. He doesn't look at her from a patriarchal point of view but approaches women and talks with them. So the gender issue is not of influence here." "As a woman I feel a little irritated when so many times in the Bible it is said that a woman committed adultery, like in this text. . . . This issue never comes up when Jesus is talking with men. . . . Perhaps this reflects the patriarchal background of the Bible. I'm a little irritated when the Bible often talks about adulterous women and about women having several men. . . . Why does the Bible not mention the men who committed adultery as well? It shows the patriarchal society which so often comes to the fore in biblical stories." Cf. also the reactions of the Hanil University group, South Korea, and the Centro Intereclesial de Estudios Teológicos y Sociales (CIEETS) student group, Nicaragua. It should be pointed out here that the reactions from a gender perspective vary from a positive evaluation of Jesus's interaction with the woman (e.g., the first response above) to a negative evaluation of the patriarchal perspective that can be detected in biblical texts (e.g., the second response above). It should furthermore be noticed that the term *patriarchal* in this context bears a negative connotation. Patriarchal societies, according to this view, are societies where men form the center of power and in which women are oppressed and relegated to a lower status. This should be distinguished from the reference to the "patriarchal background" of the conversation between Jesus and the Samaritan woman. In the conversation in John 4, the woman evaluates her patriarchal background positively, and this background even becomes the measure according to which she evaluates Jesus.

[34] Although the main emphasis in this discussion will be on the ancestorhood-interpretation of John 4 by the Port Harcourt group, this is not the only angle that

they take. They also pay attention to the second type, namely the continuity between the Samaritan woman and women in their society. Note the following remark: "The woman of Samaria typifies the image and status of women in Africa. They are denied the right to formal education, which in turn impairs their vision. They suffer from an inferiority complex that is a product of patriarchal culture. They are condemned to polygamous life—thus they are left with an unending, helpless struggle to make a living. For instance, at the death of the husband, they may become prostitutes."

[35] This identification could probably be explained with reference to three of the depth-dimensions that Hofstede (Geert Hofstede, *Allemaal Andersdenkenden: Omgaan met cultuurverschillen* [Amsterdam: Uitgeverij Contact, 1995]) identifies: individualism vs. collectivism (the "living dead" as active part of the community); uncertainty avoidance (the ancestors as life force in dealing with the challenges of life); long term–short term awareness (an orientation in the present with a strong awareness of the past).

[36] At completion of this article, the second phase reports of the Siyaphila group were not yet available. This interaction cannot therefore be considered here.

[37] The works of Brian K. Blount, *Cultural Interpretation: Reorienting New Testament Criticism* (Minneapolis, Minn.: Fortress Press, 1995); Randall C. Bailey, "The Danger of Ignoring One's Own Cultural Bias in Interpreting the Text," in *The Postcolonial Bible* (Sheffield, U.K.: Sheffield Academic Press, 1998); and J. H. de Wit, "Through the Eyes of Another: Towards Intercultural Reading of the Bible," in *Interkulturelle Hermeneutik und lectura popular: Neuere Konzepte in Theorie und Praxis,* Beiheft zur Ökumenischen Rundschau 72, ed. Silja Joneleit-Oesch and Miriam Neubert (Frankfurt am Main, Germany: Otto Lembeck, 2002), 19–64, are attempts in this direction.

CHAPTER 18

Reading John 4 in the interface between ordinary and scholarly interpretation

Néstor Míguez

Jesus and the Samaritan woman, the scholar and the ordinary reader

He is a Jew from Galilee, coming back home after being in Jerusalem, where he debated with one of the best scholars of the council. She is a Samaritan living in Sychar, a small town, where people worry about the rains, the crops, the Roman tax collectors. He is a teacher and has disciples. She is an ordinary village woman accustomed to heavy chores. He is used to profound, subtle discussions with priests and Pharisees. She has to deal with pails of water from the deep well. He wanders through the country according to the requirements of his ministry and becomes known in many places. She stays in the one village she knows, probably the only place where she is known. He has been pointed out by the prophet as the Lamb of God. She has been pointed out by commentators as an adulterous woman. People will learn more about him and his doings for centuries to come; what he says and does will be studied in many places and will give rise to many books. She will only be remembered—not even by name, and with a certain slander—through the telling of this little story, because she encountered him and they had this dialogue.

They meet, closer to her world than to his. He is sitting by the well, resting; she comes under the heavy midday sun to fetch some water. Unexpectedly, he starts a dialogue. Disrespectful, she answers with a certain irony (when thirsty, even a Jewish rabbi has to talk to a Samaritan woman!). He talks with heavenly wisdom; she speaks from practical realities. He speaks about eternal life; she talks about everyday duties. He talks about lively water, coming up from his presence; she speaks about the traditions received from her people. He speaks the spiritual truth; she talks the earthly existence. Really, it is not a dialogue but two monologues in parallel. We say,

Néstor Míguez, Department of Bible Studies, Instituto Superior Evangélico de Estudios Teológicos (Buenos Aires, Argentina)

"She does not understand, because she is unable to see beyond the material appearance." She says, "They are talking foolish nonsense because they have time to spare but are unable to lift a bucket full of water."

We know nothing about him being married or having a family of his own. Yet he asks her about her family life. At first, she refuses to engage in talk about that subject. He goes on, "For you have had five husbands, and the one you have now is not your husband. What you have said is true!" He is able to recognize the truth in her life. "Now he is hitting hard ground," she thinks. "Now he is talking about what I can really relate to: my own life."

Hearing this statement from Jesus, we say, "Five husbands! An adulterous woman. A wavering person." We think of fickle Hollywood starlets and their quest for promotion, or an unsatisfied Cinderella searching for the true prince, or even a village whore running from one house to another. Commentaries wonder whether "for you have had five husbands . . ." is a factual statement about the woman's life or a symbolic reflection about Samaritan people and theology.

She may not know anything about who is the gift from God, but she knows about rejection. Women could not divorce, but they could be dismissed and expelled from their homes. Five times she has had to leave behind her house and security, or perhaps she has mourned the death of a supportive partner. Five times she had been put out on the street, the target of many malicious commentaries (including some that continue to attack her twenty centuries later). Five times (and many more) the victim of gossip and ridicule, of prejudice and defamation. Now she has found a man who offers her shelter, but he wants no fixed obligations. Once again, in her time and ours, she is under the uncharitable scrutiny of the politically correct, of the legal sages, and of the righteous religious. "The ignorant, adulterous woman of Sychar," the "ordinary person." From a historical point of view, she is the epitome of dark existence, of the marginal people constrained to the lesser cultures, the no-person. Until she meets Jesus.

She wonders: What do they know about this affliction? How can people who ponder about life, safe behind the walls of temples and schools, aloof from the griefs and trials of a rejected rural woman, distant from the everyday struggles for survival—how can such people ever come near to the meaningless routine imposed on me? How can they make sense of my sufferings? But this man seems to know something more. He ventured through the countryside. And now he speaks to my real life. I know such people exist. I have heard about them: they are prophets. Maybe he is one. Let's see whether he is a prophet or just another proud Jew.

"Not here, nor in Jerusalem . . ." He is able to go beyond, to make God closer. I will share this with the other people of the village. But she does not talk about finding the water that springs up for life eternal. She says nothing about the true worshiper or about God as Spirit. "Come and see a man who told me everything I have ever done! He cannot be the Messiah, can he?" He might be her Messiah, because he is able to talk about her life, her doings, what is happening to her.

Let those who have ears, hear how the interaction between Jesus and the Samaritan woman is an allegory of the interface between the scholar and the ordinary reader.

The experience of transcultural reading

The quantity of readings, the variety of views, and the diversity of experiences conveyed in the reading reports of the intercultural Bible reading project make it impossible to summarize in a brief essay the many facets seen in them. It would be a substantial task just to put together the many expressions about a single verse or image. I will nonetheless try to bring an overall view of some issues involved in the experience, with the awareness that I am not doing justice to the nuances and details in many of the reports, or to the shrewd perspectives that come out when a text is depicted against the multifaceted world of such a wide range of reading experiences. I will intentionally skip some of the high points, where the views of most of the readers coincide (e.g., that Jesus is someone who crosses boundaries). I do so not because these views are unimportant. On the contrary, the possibility that a text can communicate similar things, can create concurring images of Jesus's ministry in such different locations, also merits inquiry. Yet, given the limits of this presentation, I will point out only some contrasting aspects of the reports, to be deepened in a more detailed work. I will not analyze any specific report, although here and there I may make indirect reference to some; my aim is to paint a more general picture instead.

Culture and metaphors: the diversity of connotations

As I read the different reports, the most salient feature that I saw at first glance was the way the metaphors and images of the passage produced such a wide range of different—contrasting and even contradictory—connotations for the readers. This variety is also discernible when we see, in many reports, the use of so many different symbols and metaphors to explain, evoke, or relate to the text. Also, one can perceive the different ways of approaching the text, and how this variety results in dissimilar understandings of the same words. Methodology is culturally related, and the use of one approach or another in reading the Bible is already indicative of the mentality with which we approach the text. Some groups were quite conscious of this, while others engaged in discussions with their partner group without taking clear notice of how much the method, as well as the context, was part of the contrasting views.

Let us take, for example, the case of the metaphors. Such issues as water, vessel, food, harvest, even when they suppose a similar material object or activity, relate, in the minds of the interpreters, to different experiences and concepts, culturally forged, when they are mentioned as metaphors. Take, for example, the case of water, to name the most salient item and the one most often mentioned. One report from Brazil establishes: "Jesus asks for water. . . . I think water one cannot deny to anybody. I came to that conclusion. Jesus asks that woman for water. She cannot deny it. You can't deny water. . . . This is what I think, that water cannot be denied to anyone." These sentences begin an important part of that report. A strikingly similar phrase comes in the report of another group from the same region: "I've learned since I was a child that you can't deny water to anyone." A similar line of expressions can be found in other parts of the world where the scarcity of fresh water plays a major role in culture.

Eventually, water that cannot be denied is also a metaphor for other things: love (even of the enemy), eternal life, salvation, a link to God. One of these reports contrasts the polluted water of the nearby river and its "purification" with the "pure water" of an artesian well. Another says that the living water is a river, in contrast to the still water of the pit. Again, the concern for the purity of the water becomes an issue for congregations of rural origins. The material object of the metaphor is a matter of serious consideration in these and other reports. Yet, many other reports bypass the "real" water in the related metaphors ("Water is not such an important matter here," says one Dutch report), or easily jump to the *living water* concept and in some cases to baptismal rites.

These differences illustrate the dissimilar degrees of importance of the issue of water in the cultures and regions represented. The contrasts illustrate how the degree of importance of the issue influences the reading of the text, because the word *water* has different connotations in different environments. In the dialogue between the groups, these contrasts became evident, and were so signaled by some of the participants. The weight of the water metaphor differs according to traditions, geography, and ritual practices involving water in the diverse settings. The text has a different impact on readers, because access to water in their living situation conditions the associations of this image.

While the water metaphor is, in one way or another, directly grasped in every culture, other elements of the text require more detailed explanation and depend on the information received. Therefore, the information available molds the projection of an analogous situation in the local situation. Thus, it is notable how, in the task of bringing the passage to today, the same feature can recall different and even contradictory identifications, according to theological backgrounds, cultural constructions, and social sensitivity. Take, for example, the case of "the Samaritan." Most of the reports show that groups needed some explanation about who the Samaritans were. This information was provided by the group leaders, or came out of the memory of some previous teaching, or from the reading of another biblical text (2 Kings 17).

The image they had of the Samaritan people was mostly the projection of the Jewish conception of the Samaritans: a "mixed" people, lacking Jewish purity, a syncretistic religious group. We do not find any understanding of Samaritans as the true Israel, which was their self-understanding. Some reading groups even regarded them as Gentiles and pagan, ignoring their Abrahamic origin shown in the phrase "our ancestor Jacob." So, for some, Samaritans are idolaters and sinners who have to be redeemed, while others identify Samaritans with the destitute of society, the despised that are to be restored of their dignity, which was stripped by prejudice or subjugation. Some even identify themselves with the Samaritan people as despised and rejected, victims of prejudice (Dalit group in India). In more than one report, the issue of Samaritans is related with Islam. Obviously, the question of Islam (a religion that did not yet exist in the times of Jesus) is an urgent concern for many today, and thus it is introduced into the text. From these associations also flow different attitudes. For those who consider Samaritans as sinners and idolatrous, there is the need to "evangelize" the Samaritans of today. However, those who identify with Samaritans, or consider them marginal and destitute, advocate acceptance, love, and working with them in solidarity. Similarly, in keeping with the local reality in South Africa, the problem of racial discrimination was seen as a major issue in the text. In Bolivia, syncretism in culture was an issue related to the Samaritan. So one can see how a certain figure of speech can be filled with different connotations, in accordance with the pressing themes of the local agenda.

A word should be said about the idea of the Jews as oppressors, which is a matter of debate in some groups. Here the local history is very strong. As one group notes, for western Europeans who are close to the Holocaust, it seems unfair to name Jews as oppressors. Yet, for those who feel themselves close to the Palestinians, because of their political stand or experience of imperialist expansion of the West, the idea that Jews are part of a system of oppression is also historically very close. These differences are a clear example of how cultural issues are often, and sometimes decisively, political. Along similar lines, many side remarks in the reports about food, development, differences between Western and Oriental cultures and personalities, and so on, reflect the influence of ideologies, hegemonic discourse, images of others created by the media or even by so-called scientific (anthropological) investigation, all of which are vehicles of the strategies of political powers. Some of these images recede as a result of the contact with the partner groups. But one also notices that some of the expressions of the partner group are seen through the deforming lenses of popularized concepts about Africa, "the South," or, "the affluent world."

Gender is also a strong feature in many reports. For many readers, the woman represents the sinner *par excellence*. In other reports, her attitude appears as a vindication of a struggle for equity in gender relations. In some cases, the Samaritan woman is thought to be, at least at the first part of the dialogue, a little bit dumb, unable to understand the subtle offer of living water in Jesus's words. She is a vulgar village woman, unsuited for a dialogue with "the Christ." Jesus seems to treat her, according to those interpretations, with a certain superiority not bereft of compassion, as he does the adulterous woman in John 8, a passage some groups brought into the picture. In some readings, the "dumb woman" who does not understand Jesus, the adulterous prostitute, prototype of sin and infidelity, suddenly becomes the alert true disciple. An almost miraculous conversion not only arouses her faith but also changes her intelligence, personality, moral character, and social standing. But other reports see her as a daring woman who takes the risk of engaging in a witty conversation with a Jewish rabbi. References to other biblical women (Martha, Mary Magdalene) support a more positive approach, making her the exemplary apostle who evangelizes her community, the same village out of which the other (male) disciples were only able to get ordinary food. It is worth noting that this more positive approach prevails in groups of women. This important issue shows the different degrees of gender consciousness developed in different communities and cultures.

As for the methodological questions, much depends not only on a given cultural (regional) environment but also on the leadership and constituency of the group. The nature of that leadership depends on another set of cultural conditions. For example, some groups, organized from more culturally sophisticated circles (university, long church tradition), even in very different parts of the world, expect a more scholarly introduction to the text and rely on historical and exegetical information, elaborated input coming from biblical scholars, and a theological framework that requires previous study of John's Gospel, christology, or other theological knowledge. Other groups are more "spontaneous" and work with a methodological approach that tends to encourage more direct associations with everyday life. Yet, as will be noted below, sometimes this "spontaneity" conceals previous implicit theological approaches, which already interpret the text in one way or another.

The bias embedded in interpretation

The project title, Through the Eyes of Another, struck me in a new way as I read some of the reports that came from "third world" groups. In many reports from Asia, Africa, or Latin America, we see the influence of the missionary tradition, the continuance of the cultural bias of the theological schools that introduced the Bible for the first time in those places. In many respects, they read with the lenses imposed by the initial notions seeded when the Christian faith was introduced in that location. Extensive parts of the reading focused on items that one can easily recognize as part of the theological and cultural framework established by the authoritative interpretation of European and North American missionaries who "taught the natives" how to read the Bible and what to find in it. It is apparent that those lessons were learned. Although one can see local nuances in the examples brought to elucidate the passage, when boiled down to its essence the message was more or less what one would expect to come out of missionary preaching and teaching.

Certainly the kind of Christianity that was introduced on the mission field was not innocent, and the consequences of colonization are still present in the theology of many groups. This theology laid emphasis on the superiority of Christianity; the divinity of Jesus; the priority of the spiritual; the moral critique of sexual behavior, living habits, and cultural practices of "the natives"; and evangelizing as the fundamental activity expected of true believers. These emphases came out quite distinctly as the core message in some reports, representative of this trend. For example, it is noteworthy how much the dialogue about the "husbands" of the Samaritan woman turned, through interpretation, into a question of moral sexual behavior. Some reports identify the woman as a prostitute, causing surprise to the "first world" partner group. In societies that had polygamic customs, the "multiple husbands" of the woman become a question about monogamy, one of the crucial issues brought into the local culture by western evangelizing. In that sense, there is a repeated reference to the need of the woman to "repent of her sin" (something which is not in the text at all). Sin is always interpreted in moral terms. In popular religion, in many places of the world, this interpretation predominates, but the question remains: Why does that interpretation of sin prevail? Is it not the consequence of previous teaching, mostly by missionaries in the third world, who used that understanding of sin to establish a "moral control" over the local population?

A similar conclusion can be drawn about the divinity of Jesus. Most groups reading the text take Jesus's divinity as a given. One can find in some of the readings a note about Jesus's humanity, with stress on the fact that he is tired or thirsty. But the humanity of Jesus disappears in the interpretation of the dialogue that follows. There Jesus is a divine revealer, and the fact that there are problems of human communication is left aside or attributed to the woman's lack of comprehension. It is never attributed to Jesus, who speaks in images that the woman, using her experience of everyday life, cannot but interpret in the way she does. In that sense, the humanity of Jesus is not part of the picture. Perhaps Jesus is not interpreting the world of the Samaritan counterpart until he strikes the hard ground of her everyday life, the question of her frustrated marriages.

The question is not only about the content of the message in this interpretation but also about the mind-set that produces this approach. People are conditioned from previous guided experiences of what the Bible is about, and what we should expect to glean from reading it. And with that conditioning in the back of one's mind, one's ways of reading and perceiving have been narrowed from the beginning. The basic orientation of the missionaries and of the denominational origins persists, more than people realize, beyond their presence and through various experiences. Sunday school lessons, catechism, preaching, rituals, and the like create a reading environment that conditions what the people read in scripture. Some reports stress the fact that the group has origins in this kind of missionary work. Even if the environment changes, the reading habits and a particular understanding of the mission of believers established by missionaries tend to persist. In many cases, the action suggested by the reading of the text is related to evangelizing and moralizing, the thrust imposed by the missionary movement. We will not develop this in depth here, but it would be worthwhile to study how the doctrinal conception brought into a given context persists in a more cohesive manner than in its place of origin. Looking at the reports, one can find a more traditional Calvinist view in churches in Africa than in Calvinist groups in the Netherlands.

Sometimes academic scholarship, using another kind of approach, imposes its prejudices on the text. Through normative Bible study, standard Bible commentaries for lay leaders, and the like, this scholarship creates a "canonical interpretation" that limits the freedom of ordinary readers, and thus tends to line up the more spontaneous approaches behind its own paradigm. One finds, in some of the reports, a "popularized scholarship" in the rendering of the "ordinary reader." By the way, these occasionally include some erroneous data, held to be "scientific." In more than one report, Samaritans were spoken of as Palestinians, non-Israelites, or even pagans. One report, for example, states that "their fathers worshiped on top of mountains. They worshiped idols. They did not like worshiping God." Yet the text makes no reference to this problem: on the contrary, the problem is *where* to worship the same God.

This misinformation may be the consequence of an oversimplified popularizing of scholarship, or of the fragile understanding and memory of the people. In my experience, it is a combination of both: the intention and expression of the academy are so self-centered (in what it supposes to be common knowledge and in learning habits) that ordinary people find its findings difficult to integrate into their own worldview, in which knowledge and wisdom are acquired in other ways. So people grasp what they can from the information provided by scholarly circles and integrate it as they are able into their own preexisting schemes, many times generating some confusion.

Along similar lines, one can easily see in some of the reports that the Bible study leader channeled, through his or her interventions and comments, more "learned" information that created a certain bias in the interpretation, directing it toward certain results or perspectives. In that sense, many ordinary readers are already reading "through the eyes of another." Although the local culture comes to the fore in some examples and expressions, one can observe that the hermeneutical framework has been provided by an imported tradition, a foreign interest, even an intellectual and methodological practice, or a kind of expertise that differs from the local wisdom. In fact, the real challenge for these readers would be to learn to read with their own eyes again.

When the local is already global

This missionary theology was not necessarily the way the gospel was preached in the sending churches of the time, nor was it always theological thought that prevailed on the North Atlantic scene. The contrast is evident in some interactions between groups. And that contrast is highlighted in some of the responses. For example, the idea that the woman is a sinner is not so much present in the North Atlantic groups as in some of the groups from the South. A group expressed surprise that the issue of sin appeared at all in the report of its counterpart. The question of the existence and the idea of sin was only introduced into the discussion of the second (Northern) group by its central place in the report of the partner (Southern) group. This dynamic reflects how and with what emphases biblical interpretations evolved in different contexts.

Many reading communities of the "first world" were more aware of the cultural conditioning of their own reading, and made efforts to bring forward methodological alternatives to make possible a more creative interpretation, with fewer ties to the traditional ecclesiological renderings. This may also be a sign of the times. In poor countries, the population tends to be more homogeneous, and the churches include people of the same area and normally of the same cultural milieu and economic level. Therefore, they tend to repeat what they already know, and to feel with less intensity the challenge to consider alternative ways. Some reports show that they already consider themselves an alternative (spiritually, culturally) to the surrounding society. People who come from outside, especially missionaries, visiting pastors, or representatives of an agency, are vested with a degree of authority (although that authority is not always free of certain distrust), because they represent a world of power. So the people one could expect to be more critical and to propose a different reading, because of their position in the world or their experience of suffering and exclusion, are in a sense more uniform as a reading community and follow a more or less traditional path. Nevertheless, changes in society inevitably occur, and the traditional order is disrupted. But religion (even the religion learned from the missionaries, or its values reshaped in new forms) tends to become a refuge. It is a way to maintain order and stability in the midst of the storm, or a place where one steps aside to regard changes as part of the illness of "the world."

But in our globalized world, the disruption of the traditional order, in culture and in church life, tends to be evident in the affluent countries. These counties attract immigrants from many places who sometimes find, in the churches, communities to which they can relate. These newcomers confront congregations, generally of variegated origins, that meet in large cities of the Northern world. The immigrants bring their difficulties and cultural diversity as challenges to the ethical integrity and doctrinal coherence of the church. And sooner or later, their presence affects these congregations in their reading of the Bible. Unlike the missionaries, the immigrants are not in a position of authority, yet their presence compels congregations to think in different ways. So the churches in Northern countries that receive immigrants and are challenged to act in the presence of "the other" become more aware of the differences and intercultural challenges than do groups in the countries that produce emigration, although the latter usually suffer to a greater degree the consequences of globalization.

Many reports (from the North as well as from the South) show a conscious effort to overcome the logocentric tendency that predominates in traditional Bible study. Some groups achieve this shift through the use of alternative forms for presenting the story, the stimulus of nonverbal and symbolic communication, and the use of techniques of group dynamics. The results reveal a wider range of possibilities in the text. They introduce other approaches and draw out different understandings, avoiding the usual shortcomings created by normative reading. The results produce a more variegated and rich approach to the diverse items that the story proposes, allowing for other emphases generally ignored or concealed. This effect is very positive. Yet the diversity sometimes puts at risk the identity of the text. If openness to new forms can justify all interpretations of the text, the text itself can become only an incitement to personal communication or subjective expression, losing its own message. This sometimes produces erratic interpretations and allows for a debasement of the original story, which relaxes its meaning and becomes an occasional point of reference for cultural or political interests that were present before the readers took up the text. Some of those concerns or contentions may well be legitimate in themselves, although they may have no necessary connection to that particular text but are introduced into the reading because of other concerns.

The challenge posed by this experience is twofold. On one side is a need to overcome the established ways of reading the Bible. Certain crystallizations of traditional knowledge can impede or hinder the expression of the world of the (real) reader, imposing on the text and the reader a certain method, worldview, frame of reference, set content. Here the challenge is to liberate the text from the conditioning of the so-called learned approach, displaying the prejudices and unfounded assumptions that inform even what is supposed to be objective scholarship. Scholarship must deal not only with anachronisms and cultural bias but also with the religious slant introduced by previous interpretations, which is sometimes very rigid and has its own assumptions. The scholar's work here is to recover a certain freshness in the text, to wipe off the dust accumulated during centuries of Christian reading and missionary theology, in order to offer a text that can provoke the interpretive activity of the new reader, without the charge of a canonized result. Yet the scholarly approach must be aware of its own bias, its propensity to introduce its own concerns in place of the life concerns of the ordinary reader.

Something that looks like the opposite sometimes happens. The reader's world takes such precedence that the text is little more than an excuse to uncover other expressions. The Bible study is the occasion to highlight prior agendas. The concerns that the modern world creates—which do need to be addressed by the Christian faith—are brought into the reading in such a way that the gospel loses its cutting edge, its vocation to make a difference in the prevailing cultural ethos. Or, as we also see in some reports, a certain goodwill ethics is present that wants to keep its distance from the more destructive features of today's culture but fails to uncover the roots of those evils. Once again, we find in the text what we are intent on finding from the start. The issue is, How is the text able to modify, enrich, or challenge our previous assumptions, so that the practice of interpretation becomes also a praxis of critical hermeneutics? How can it become not only a critical understanding of the text, but also a critical understanding of the reader's preconceptions rooted in the standard cultural and ideological patterns? In this case, a more academic approach has to bring in a certain methodological rigor that will allow the text to function as an external critique of any previously assumed understanding.

Traditional reading, ordinary reading, and biblical scholarship

Many biblical texts, including the story of Jesus and the Samaritan woman in John 4, are short "life stories" that narrate perceptions of the presence of the divine in everyday life. This awareness of divine presence is mediated through the story of Jesus's meeting with the Samaritan woman and the people of the village, as a consequence of certain identifications readers make with some of the characters in the story. This reading tends to facilitate review of the reader's own life story and relating the experience of the biblical witness to the reader's own religious and everyday life. In the process, readers open and interpret the text in ways that are relevant to their own faith, world, and situation. This way of "reading with" is present in some of the reports.

Yet, many times, what happens is an inversion. The model of the biblical narratives shapes their account in such a way that their own life, in some way or other, is revisited through a paradigmatic understanding of the biblical narrative. And an optimistic concordance or parallelism ignores the cultural and historical gap. In some examples, the historical setting is bypassed with an "updating" that totally detaches the text from its original world and forces it into the present. That kind of interpretation entails the danger of a hidden fundamentalism. I will not engage in a criticism of that kind of reading here, but only point out that it is present in some reports, of the South as well as of the North, although in contrasting forms. In some cases, an afterthought reflecting on their methods made groups aware that they had proceeded this way.

Along these lines, it is necessary to distinguish between "ordinary" and "traditional" reading. "Ordinary reading" is seldom a first-time encounter with the biblical text. Most Bible readers have been introduced, in some way or other, to the Bible as scripture. That is, they acknowledge that they are reading an authoritative text, which conveys a revealed message from the divine, however they interpret that claim. We can go even further: the core of this message has been already spelled out for most readers. A "traditional" reading (one established through a practice of centuries, which thus becomes natural for a given society or group) must be presumed as the standard interpretation of most readers. Even if they have never been confronted with this particular passage, they already have an overall understanding of what the biblical message is. This preconception resulted in shock for some people when they saw Jesus reacting in a way different from how they expected him to react, out of step with their previous image of him.

People tend to read not what the text says but what they think they are expected to read. Obviously, traditional readings carry with them vested ecclesiastical interests, cultural and social prejudices, and superimposed power struggles, previous and current. A first chore, then, is to discern this traditional reading, identifying how the history of interpretation, and the successive hegemonic ideologies inbred in it, have already established the frame, conditioned the minds, imposed the methods, and dictated the expected outcome for the reading of any biblical text. In that sense, *tradition* describes not only the reading but also the cultural environment, which values some conducts and practices more than others. For example, the issue of homosexuality, which came up in some reports, is valued in contrasting ways, depending not only on the ecclesial tradition but on the ways traditions of social morality are in force today in one society or another.

Traditional reading tends to skip some elements of the text, add by association others that are not really there, emphasize some sentences and ignore others, according to the needs of the previously accorded or encoded message. Yet different traditions highlight different aspects of the message. A cross-cultural reading of the Bible must be considered a contribution to clear off the charge of traditional reading, or at least to make explicit its impositions on the text, and sometimes also to confirm some understandings as coherent with the text. Looking at what others see that we have overlooked, or (on the other hand) reflecting on what others did not bring into the text because of their reading location, is a good way to analyze how much of our reading was brought in by the context, how much by a creative application of our own experiences, and how much was inserted simply by traditional reading.

Interpretation then becomes a serious task. It is bridge building, and a bridge that has feeble foundations or carries a burden larger than it can support, may fall and cause a disaster and serious harm. Reading the Bible is a process that entails crossing a gap between centuries, cultures, worldviews, and life experiences. Interpretation gives an account of a particular kind of text, a text that for many carries the weight of a sacred book and is a needed resource for asserting their own true selves. But it is also the book of endless controversies, the center of unbounded conflicts (even wars), which has been used to justify conquest and genocide. Biblical scholarship and transdisciplinary studies about the Bible, if they are true scholarship, cannot ignore this significance. If interpretation is to contribute to building bridges, if it is to give meaning to the text as a way of giving meaning to the life of the people, it must work to overcome the prejudices already installed in Bible reading. It must also replace them with a larger wisdom, both in the knowledge of objective facts that shape the text, as well as in the historical facts that surround it. In that sense, in the interface with "ordinary readers" in different locations, the scholar's hermeneutical contribution will include providing reflection that will serve as support for the bridge. In bridge construction, the end is not the bridge itself, but the people whom it will help to communicate across a gap. In our case, the scholar may assist ordinary readers in overcoming distances between their cultural contexts and between themselves and the people in the Bible. In this process, interpretation introduces the possibility of combining stories to make life more meaningful and abundant.

Contributions and shortcomings from the reader's world

Most of the reports indicate the presence of some kind of biblical expertise as part of the groups' reading process. If correctly applied, the data provided by a more scholarly approach can help overcome the breach between the text and the present. Yet, as we can see in some examples from the reports, it also creates bias in the way the so-called ordinary reader handles the text. Information provided by biblical research helps provide a point of reference for comparing different life situations. But only when readers break through the world of the text and read the words in their own world is the text opened once again, so that it becomes not just the vehicle that conveys a message from ancient times but the occasion of an enriching dialogue that will furnish the text with new meaning. In a sense, that new meaning is already in the text, but in another sense it can only be created by the questions and challenges brought about by the distant reader. The readers are challenged by other readers viewing it from another angle, who see different lights and shades, perceive meanings that were hidden and obscure even for the people that generated the narrative. Other readers approach the text from another perspective, posing different questions, inquiring with new methods, from diverse wisdoms. These readings "shake" the text in hopes of dislodging new meanings that can match the worries and hopes of today. The act of reading the Bible is in itself an exercise in transcultural hermeneutics. Distance is an obstacle but also a source of creative alternatives. As anyone knows, looking from a distance offers the possibility of a wider horizon, a larger landscape. It can allow one to grasp an overall picture that someone standing too close to the object will never able to observe.

The question that motivates our studies, then, is not only, What does the text say? as most biblical scholars inquire, or, What does the text says *to me* (*to us*)? but fundamentally, What does the text say to others, thus communicating beyond my limited horizon? In this case, a critical approach to the text is provided, not only by academic research, but also—mostly—from the interface of different cultural settings.

Three questions remain: First, as laid open above, how can these diverse forms of knowledge be integrated with the readers' world (especially if they are outside Western culture), without that knowledge imposing its own dynamics and thus closing off the possibility of new meaning?

Second, what are the elements in the world of the readers that allow them to lay hold in a creative way of the elements brought in by other readers?

Third, what are the elements in the world of the reader that tend to prevent the emergence of more daring aspects of the text and of the other readers' approaches to it? The world of the reader, as many reports in our project show, is not devoid of its own problems and prejudices, originating in the readers' culture itself or imported as a result of the ways the Bible reached the people.

Cross-cultural reading and interpretation of the Bible may become a good occasion, then, for "ordinary readers" to take a look at their own world and see through the text the potential it offers for a more abundant life as well as the problems and hegemonic ideologies seeded in that worldview, and in the text. The text and the contribution of other (real, situated, demanding) readers then becomes a critical witness to the readers' world. Some reports from the groups are clear about this dynamic. Sometimes, the comparison also shows the patriarchal bias or the power bent that exists in the text, and how it is also present in the readers' society.

Some of the exchange letters reveal that these (and many other interesting things) did happen, even in the ways the exchange took place. One can see the different kinds of reactions as another example of how diverse cultures are, and yet how people in them can become sympathetic to one another. In some cases, we find simple reactions that concentrated on the content of the textual interpretation, but we also find others that emphasize the possibility of personal relations, of mutual help, of global solidarity. And in one case, people even tried a role-play in an effort to understand the others (or to realize how difficult it is to understand certain reactions and concepts from another cultural milieu). If the distant reader brings new questions to the text, it is also true that the distant text brings new questions to the reader. If this last step does not happen, readers will only reproduce their culture and prejudices, and the gospel loses its cutting edge. A more sensitive approach can pick up the suggestions of the "ordinary" hermeneutics of multiple readers and work them through critical lenses in order to construct new meanings, more closely connected with the life and faith of the believers. And along with those new meanings, such an approach has potential to create new community. Putting the narratives of the Bible side-by-side with the narratives of ordinary interpreters can throw new light on the text, but also on the situation of the readers. And the gospel will be performing its life-giving purpose.

CHAPTER 19

"When people discuss the Word of God with one another, everything becomes real"[1]

Jan Hartman

Introduction

Solidaridad is a Dutch cofinancing organization with almost forty years of experience in development work. Begun as an ecumenical fundraising organization, it has been focusing almost exclusively on Latin America, where we have developed an extensive network of partners dedicated to issues such as fair trade, human rights (truth-finding processes and universal jurisdiction), culture, and the strengthening of civil society. Our approach—and that of many of our partners—is based, from a theological point of view, on liberation theology. Meanwhile, a lot has changed in the world, and in Latin America in particular, and old paradigms no longer offer the ideological clarity and consolation they once did. For example, the concept of the poor as relatively free, abnegated, and revolutionary subjects, willing to take over power as soon as conditions are ripe, has given way to a much more complicated picture of people with faces, specific histories, ethnic profiles, and genders, who are not always keen on radically changing their lives. Many more factors than were considered before have to be taken into account before a person or a group of people starts to change their lives and their society.

While recognizing that we live in a changing, globalizing world, in which huge transnational business corporations seem to be in charge, we believe that subjects and groups of subjects matter and can represent a countervailing power in a process of globalization from below. One of our most visible contributions to this process is our effort to link groups of European consumers with Latin American producers. As a result, European consumers buy coffee, bananas, and fashion items in common supermarkets and stores, paying a fair price for these articles and thus contributing to sustainable agriculture and to reasonable wages for farmers and factory workers.

Jan Hartman, Solidaridad (Utrecht, the Netherlands)

Spirituality

Spirituality plays an important role in our work, in the sense that both of the core groups in and for which we organize our fundraising and consciousness-raising activities—our Latin American partners, and the Dutch (mainly Catholic) churches—are aware of the motivating and stimulating power of religious traditions. Rather than looking at the matter from a sociological point of view, we feel that for us as members of Solidaridad, spirituality (in the broadest sense of the word) and the spiritual practices that are derived from it are vital assets on the tortuous road to freedom.

In more specific terms, we support quite a few indigenous nongovernmental organizations (NGOs) in Latin America that explicitly stimulate projects where the reversion to indigenous knowledge systems and beliefs constitutes an integral part of the development strategy. In the Netherlands, we try to provide our church-related target groups with liturgical materials to be used in church services, in an attempt to link spiritual resources from one continent to those of another. In doing so, we hope to stimulate people to rethink the relationship between liturgy and engagement, between their context and the world around them.

Spirituality is, in other words, a concept that we feel at ease with. At the same time, we realize that the word is ambiguous and that it is used by a whole range of organizations and networks that we do not necessarily sympathize with.

Bible reading

As a Solidaridad staff member, I had the privilege a couple of years ago of executing the first intercultural Bible-reading experiment, a spiritual practice *par excellence*. Its outcome helped with conceptualizing the framework for the present research project, Through the Eyes of Another. The first project was set up to explore the possibilities of dialogue, not the dialogue of the institutions, but dialogue as an encounter on paper between grassroots groups in two totally different contexts.[2] We expected that this kind of communication would contribute to democratizing existing relationships between missionary and other church-related institutions. I do not deny that we also conceived of the experiment as a kind of romantic date between ordinary people at a grassroots level, whom the aforementioned institutions claim to represent, but who are virtually absent in the discussions between the institutions, discussions that—one way or another—are always about money.

Of course, the twenty or so groups that participated could not meet the high expectations to which we aspired. However, apart from the frustrations the project entailed at a logistical level, I can still remember the thrill and even embarrassment of finding myself reading very personal reports on the meaning of a biblical text, and listening in on the dialogue that developed from it between individuals in totally different worlds. Where the groups actually responded to each other's contributions, something happened.

Relevance of the project for us?

It is on this *something* that our hopes are centered. It is also this something that we want to come to grips with. It is what this book is about in the first place. What exactly happens when people from different social and cultural contexts come together to read the Bible? What is the potential of this kind of intercultural communication? What exactly is it contributing to? To put it more bluntly, and considering it from a more organizational point of view: What is in it for us? Does intercultural and intercontinental Bible reading have any specific relevance for the kind of work we are doing?

Given the background and the identity of Solidaridad, these questions may sound preposterous, as though we doubted the relevance of spirituality. This, of course, is not the case. Spiritual beliefs and practices are widely recognized as having an impact on developmental processes. Moreover, we are convinced that we know that they have an impact on our work. However, the question is whether it is possible to identify empirically a positive relationship or a *trait d'union* between the specific spiritual practice of intercultural Bible reading and the kinds of activities Solidaridad, as a cofinancing organization, sympathizes with and supports in financial and other terms. We did not seek a link in the sense that one practice could generate or cause the other, but rather in the sense of an internal logic that connects the world of biblical reflection with the processes we as a development organization find ourselves immersed in.[3]

Analysis of the context parameters

As an NGO specializing in Latin America, we tend to perceive our work as a contribution to the process of globalization from below: "People at the grassroots around the world link up to impose their own needs and interests on the process of globalization."[4] We believe that the Through the Eyes of Another Bible reading project has the potential to link up grassroots faith communities. We would therefore like to know whether it is possible to identify a growing awareness of interconnectedness in the reports of the participating groups. If such an awareness is discernible, we want to know if it leads to a more practical recognition of having some kind of common social agenda. The parameter we think is indicative of the awareness of interconnectedness is the extent to which the *context*, the world of the participants, becomes more or less transparent in the reports, assuming that awareness of one's own context, and in general of the world we live in, is a prerequisite for awareness of interconnectedness.

When we use the term *context* in the following paragraphs, we do so in a nontheoretical and nonphilosophical way. It refers simply to the world as it appears in the biblical text, in the (written) reflections on this text, and in the reflections on how the other group followed the same or similar procedures. As a theologian and as an exegete, I would have been inclined to focus on what happened with and within the biblical text. However, as a staff member of Solidaridad, I want to concentrate on how and where groups' reports make reference to the "real" world.

Selection of the material

When I started working with the material, not all of the groups had brought the Bible reading experiment to an end. Only four or five had actually reached the third phase. It would have been nice to be able to choose from a broad range of completed reading experiences, but that was impossible. I therefore decided to select ten pairs of partners of which at least one had accomplished the second phase. The ten pairs are:

South Africa: Stellenbosch women	El Salvador: Shekiná Baptists, Santa Ana
Ghana: Abetifi Pentecostal women	Philippines: ISACC[5] staff
Brazil: Bairro das Rosas, Estância Velha	Colombia: Javeriana University[6] staff
Nicaragua: Novio del Cordero, Managua	the Netherlands: Dagmaat Lisse
the Netherlands: Huizen Adventists	Colombia: Project of Life, Bogotá
the Netherlands: Westmaas PCN[7]	Hungary: Balatonszárszó
Nicaragua: Filadelfia Baptist Church, Masaya	Argentina: Santa Cruz BEC[8], Buenos Aires
Philippines: Christian Writers Fellowship, Mandaluyong	Colombia: Grupo Estudio BEC Bíblico, Bogotá
the Netherlands: Wichmond PCN	Philippines: Samaritana, Quezon City
Cuba: Matanzas[9]	Indonesia: Macassar[10]

I wanted the majority of pairs to have either a Latin American or a Dutch component, or both, for obvious reasons. On the other hand, I felt I should include a number of pairs representing the South-South axis. I could not avoid the majority of these pairs being Latin American in at least one component, for the simple reason that I found only one Africa-Asia combination that had actually read and commented on each other's reports.[11]

Reading the material

Again, it was a thrilling experience to read the material. The experience was different from what I had done in the past, because the material was more diverse, and the excitement about participating in something big and interesting was palpable. There were a number of impressively extensive reports on what members had said and on what they had felt during the process of reading and rereading the text of John, reading the interpretation of the other group, and commenting on it. In some cases, the final comment was presented in a warm good-bye letter, in which the second and third phases of the project were combined.

Context indicators in the first reading

The individual context. Although the instruction guide asked participants to present themselves and the world they live in, there are interesting differences in the ways the participants did so. Some of the Dutch groups (Huizen, Westmaas, and Lisse) were thorough and detailed in their self-presentation, as was the South African women's group from Stellenbosch. In the reading reports by these groups, the names of the participating individuals are explicitly linked to their respective comments on the text. As a whole, this linking suggests that there might be some relationship between the social (and intellectual?) status of the participants and the willingness to come out as an individual in the report. An illustration is the case of the partnership between Bairro das Rosas and the Catholic University of Colombia. The first group underlined the fact that in terms of formal education most of the members "had only attended elementary school," and they invited the members of the partner group (Colombian academics) to identify themselves (*pedindo uma apresentacão mas detalhada dos componentes do grupo*) without offering a presentation of the composition of their own group. Another example of the same phenomenon, i.e., that of the individual fading away in the group, is the somewhat paradoxical case of the Abetifi women's group from Ghana. Although the individual members of the group did provide a presentation of themselves, they showed a striking tendency to underestimate their value as individuals. At least that is how I interpreted the repeated comment, "I am just a . . ." in the presentation section.[12]

On the other hand, some Latin American groups (Santa Ana, Colombia Grupo Estudio Bíblico, Colombia Project of Life, and Buenos Aires) did offer a brief list of participants and their respective professions and marital status, but the names do not reappear in the report itself.

Some groups, especially Latin American groups that adhere to liberation theology (e.g., Buenos Aires, Colombia Grupo Estudio Bíblico, and Santa Ana), gave a description of the general socioeconomic context of poverty, corruption, and violence, or made allusions to this legacy using "liberational" concepts, such as *excluded* when talking about the subjects of evangelization (Javeriana University, Santa Ana).

One gets the general impression that very few groups actually offered a clear-cut description of the context they are immersed in, let alone that they were conscious of the mission of the group in that particular context. This lack of contextual clarity was perhaps to some extent a result of the fact that several groups consisted of interested individuals with no clear connection to one specific community (e.g., Stellenbosch, Philippines ISACC, Javeriana University, Lisse, Philippines Christian Writers, Colombia Grupo Estudio Bíblico, and Macassar). In other cases, groups did seem to belong to and form part of the community, but did not have an idea of what joint Bible reading could contribute to community life.

Awareness of context of John and revision of the group's own context. In the majority of cases, there seemed to be some basic sociological knowledge of the conflict and tensions between Jews and Samaritans. When talking about the equivalent of these tensions in the group's context in today's world, some referred to tensions between Protestants and Catholics, both in the past (Wichmond) and in the present (Bairro das Rosas, Colombia Grupo Estudio Bíblico); one group mentioned the conflict between Israel and the Palestinians (Wichmond); and one group alluded to Muslim-Christian relationships (Ghana). The most eloquent case of applying the cultural scheme of John 4 to the individual context (in combination with the gender theme of the next paragraph) was that of Macassar, where theology students discussed the way adultery is treated in Indonesia's different cultural settings. Finally, two Dutch groups emphasized the importance of communication between antagonistic groups who consider the other as "different" (a clear allusion to growing tensions between Muslim immigrants and the Dutch population).

Another level of application is made from a gender perspective. Several groups (mainly from the South) focused on the position of women, both in ancient Jewish society and in modern times. In most of these cases, groups saw Jesus as the great communicator (Christian Writers and Javeriana University), or the gentle Savior (Samaritana group of ex-prostitutes in Quezon City, and to some extent, Stellenbosch), thus epitomizing God's defense of the dignity of women. In one interesting report, Jesus was presented (unintentionally, I am sure) as a negative role model, in the sense that according to this Philippine group (ISACC), Philippine women are uncritical admirers and worshipers of their husbands.

On a third level, the idea of solidarity in a violent and poverty-stricken context was put forward as the modern equivalent of the meeting between a thirsty Jewish man and a Samaritan women. According to the groups from Buenos Aires and Colombia Grupo Estudio Bíblico, the poor in their societies are thirsty for social recognition.

One general conclusion of this section could be that the basic awareness of some social and cultural parameters of John 4 (i.e., antagonism between Jews and Samaritans and the position of women) in most cases leads to the recognition of similar tensions and problems in one's own context.

Context indicators in the second reading

The context of the other. In the second phase of the reading process, groups were confronted with visions of the text that originated from a context other than their own. We suppose that most of the groups implicitly or explicitly approved of the idea of intercultural Bible reading. In the reading reports, however, only a few groups actually showed their enthusiasm for or adherence to the idea of exchanging views on the text of John 4 (Masaya, Philippines ISACC, and Huizen). To others, the project was simply presented and subsequently accepted without much discussion: "This could be interesting" (Christian Writers and Hungary). There is no reason to jump to conclusions on this matter, because much of what actually happened in the groups could not be or was not registered. But in the light of what has been written in the last years on themes such as globalization, global civil society, etc., and in the light of what happened on September 11, 2001, and in its aftermath, one would perhaps have expected a greater eagerness and awareness of the necessity to meet. Almost all reports of the reading process were written after September 11. In very few reports (Westmaas, Christian Writers,[13] and Lisse), we find explicit references to this event that had, and continues to have, global repercussions. In a sense, this is an amazing phenomenon, especially when you realize that John 4 contains elements that evoke the theme of different cultures meeting each other.

In the reports of the second phase of the reading process, we wanted to trace the extent to which the social context of the other group is perceived and interpreted. Not all the groups responded to each other's readings (no second phase material had been received from Santa Ana, Javeriana University, Ghana, and Cuba Matanzas). In the reports of the groups that did respond, people tended, in the first place, to emphasize the striking differences with their own context. "They are Catholics!" (Masaya about Buenos Aires). "They are upper-class people, whereas we belong to the lower strata of society" (Colombia Grupo Estudio Bíblico about Christian Writers). "They are simple folk. . . . They are very productive, have lots of kids" (Philippines ISACC about Ghana). "Very few people are married" (Stellenbosch about Santa Ana).

In some reports, feelings that came close to embarrassment about the other group's context were expressed. One group (Wichmond) was shocked both by the hard life reflected in the report of the ex-prostitutes group from the Philippines, and perhaps by the rather harsh recommendation they received in response to their own report: "I wish they could be challenged to read like we did." In the case of the Stellenbosch group's receipt of the report from Santa Ana, the participants could hardly believe people could be that poor. "They assume [says the coordinator/reporter] that although the partner group lives in a poor community, most of the members have (had) jobs, and because of that might be a bit more prosperous." Another case of denial was that of Hungary, when confronted with Westmaas's interpretation of John 4. Whereas Westmaas regarded it as impossible to read the story of Jesus and the Samaritan women without taking into account what happened on September 11, the Hungarians responded by stating that there are no Muslims in Hungary.

At first sight, it seemed to be difficult for groups to really understand the context of the other group. Were there any signs indicating that, in spite of this difficulty, knowledge and information about the context of the other group somehow affected the way groups looked at themselves and their own context? To some extent, the way the other group looked at and interpreted John 4 did seem to have some influence. Thus, Masaya sounded impressed with the verdict of the Argentine group on corrupt leaders, and acknowledged that the biblical prophets assumed very critical positions toward those in power. Why then was there no criticism of the corrupt Nicaraguan leaders? The Wichmond group started reflecting on the changes that even their stable rural community is facing in modern society, as did Hungary when it realized that other faith communities in the Hungarian context are expanding at their expense. The Stellenbosch group remembered the fact that in times of institutionalized apartheid it was unimaginable that a white man would publicly address a black woman. The Brazilians from Estância Velha reflected on their German background and the power of tradition, and wondered whether this background is an obstacle to the success of their evangelization practices.

At face value, these examples may seem to offer proof of the power of communication between groups from different cultural contexts. That is not the whole story, however. Reading through the material could provide examples to make an equally strong case for the opposite conclusion. The Masaya group, for instance, stuck to its principle that the gospel has to be read from a spiritual perspective (i.e., non-politically) and that this is best done in an evangelical (i.e., not Catholic) setting. The Argentinians thought the Nicaraguans remained too spiritual. The Stellenbosch group felt that it is easier for them to identify with Jesus than with the Samaritan woman, because "he plays a more dominant and powerful role in the story."

The general impression of this section is that there seemed to be a very human and understandable tendency to see one's own convictions positively or negatively confirmed in the position of the partner group (so Brazil, Philippines Samaritana, Philippines Christian Writers). This tendency does not indicate that people did not appreciate the exchange: there were heart-warming comments on how, in spite of all the differences, it was beautiful to see Christians from all over the world communicating about the gospel. The group from Lisse, for example, underwent a Pentecost experience: they felt as though they were sitting at the well and talking with the other group. The Filipino ISACC group explained that they shared with the group from Ghana in their common search for integrity and honesty. The group from Huizen emphasized the fact that having been able to "talk" with Colombia had led to mutual understanding, which in turn qualified as a small step on the road to world peace. The group from Westmaas expressed their empathy with the group from Hungary by dedicating a church service to this country and by remarking that meeting the other group through the biblical text was like meeting God.

Some conclusions

On general and specific relevance of the project

In the sections above, I have tried to analyze several aspects of the intercultural Bible reading project. In the limited number of reading reports I decided to work with, we were able to have a closer look at the extent to which people were capable of critically assessing their own context. Then, we assessed the extent of their perception of the context of John and their subsequent reinterpretation or application of this knowledge to their individual context. Finally, we considered the extent of their susceptibility to the ways other groups described their surroundings, and of their creativity in linking the other's context with their own. We asked ourselves if intercultural Bible reading between different groups would have a growing effect on the awareness of interconnectedness and the subsequent establishment of a common social agenda, produced by the meeting of reading partners.

I believe that, given the very specific criteria of relevance to our work, it was not possible to identify such effects in the reports we studied. In other words: the criteria for a process of "globalization from below" were not met in the sense described above, "that people at grassroots level around the world link up to impose their own needs and interests on the process."

It is, however, undeniable that *something* happened in the encounters between reading groups from socially and culturally different backgrounds, and that this something in itself justifies continuation of the project or similar projects. People are actually listening to each other and exchanging visions of biblical texts that many consider of vital importance when coping with daily life. The idea of intercultural communication on Bible reading is in this sense a promising one.

We are convinced that religious traditions and movements that are open to dialogue and discussion can play an important role in "enhancing the normative underpinning of civil global society."[14] Although tensions may arise between the presumed exclusivity of religious communities and the requirements of inclusion, civility, and freedom of choice of civil society, the mediation of these tensions can happen through an internal discourse within religious communities and a simultaneous dialogue with other movements and communities.[15]

Our understanding is that our intercultural Bible reading experiments would fit in these kinds of processes. The Through the Eyes of Another project has proved that an open attitude is not necessarily and exclusively found among those congregations and communities that consider themselves liberal or liberationist. A broad range of communities is able to comply with these criteria.

However, regarding the suggested simultaneity of internal discourse *and* dialogue with other movements and communities, I think that in the actual intercultural reading process this latter aspect is missing, at least from the point of view of a developmental organization such as Solidaridad. In other words, as long as faith communities embark on projects like this out of sheer curiosity about meeting another group from a totally different context, the outcome will be sympathetic, pleasant, and even inspiring, but the effects of this encounter will rapidly fade away. However, when a specific issue—a prior concern about something that bothers us as believers and citizens in the world we live in, or that even threatens our very existence—serves as the starting point for dialogue and the exchange of visions on biblical texts, something with more specific relevance to development organizations such as Solidaridad might emerge.

On differentiating exchange methodologies for the future

Solidaridad supports several Bible-reading initiatives in Latin America. The method they use can be traced back to the community Bible reading sessions developed by Carlos Mesters from Brazil. In these sessions the meaning of a biblical text is established by reading the text together and by linking it to the context people find themselves living in. The method has convinced thousands and thousands of people, and the fact that some groups still experience reading the Bible together as a kind of voyage of discovery shows that Mesters has struck a vital chord in Christian spirituality. Meanwhile, however, times in Latin America have changed, as we have already noted. In previous decades, people marvelled at the idea of being a poor subject, as long as this meant that in the eyes of God and the community you were entitled to throw off the yoke of the oppressors. Now, it has turned out, you are no longer exclusively a poor subject; you are also black, female, urban, peasant, Indian, member of church, and member of civil society. This is the new reality Bible reading groups are confronting, and it challenges them to rethink their ways of reading the Bible and their identity as a group: Who are we? What do we want? What is our mission? I think we are in the middle of a process of redefining visions of the function of Bible reading. To judge from the somewhat petrified and obligatory descriptions of the context provided by the classical base communities that participated in the project, there is still a lot of work to be done.

Consequently, for intercultural Bible reading projects to meet the standards of relevance for our kind of development work, the methodology will have to be differentiated. It is not within the scope of this article to elaborate detailed proposals, but given the nature of our work, it would be interesting to explore the possibility of organizing similar Bible reading experiments with faith communities that are confronted with or consciously focus on similar topics. What would be the outcome of, for example, linking faith communities in Guatemala with their equals in Peru, considering that in both countries they have to cope with the consequences and traumas of genocide? Can the spiritual practice of joint Bible reading contribute to a strengthening and deepening of their voices in the human rights movement and in civil society? Another question that could be examined is whether intercultural Bible reading could prove to be a useful tool in the communication between Dutch faith communities who wish to improve contacts with their Muslim neighbors, and Indonesian communities used to living together with Muslims, while at the same time being aware of growing tensions at a national and international level in Muslim-Christian relationships.

As an ecumenical organization specializing in development projects, Solidaridad has no reason to doubt the motivating power of religious traditions and the spiritual practices (such as reading the Bible) that spring from them. In that sense, we sympathize with the joyful exclamation of Rodolfo from Managua: "When people discuss the Word of God with one another, everything becomes real." We are convinced that for us, given the specific and concrete nature of our activities, it is absolutely essential to make our point of departure a specific mission rooted in the real world where this promise can come true.

Notes

¹ "Cuando hay diálogo acerca de la palabra del Señor, todo viene transformándose en una realidad" (Rodolfo Munguía, Managua, Nicaragua).

² In fact, a considerable number of contexts participated, in the sense that approximately ten different Latin American groups communicated with the same number of groups in the Netherlands.

³ We do not feel tempted to hope that the participation of groups in intercultural Bible reading processes would eventually lead to their engagement in the aforementioned kinds of activities. Given the complexity of, for instance, the fair trade concept, and our efforts in building up and sustaining a fair trade praxis in several commodities, it would even be cruel to suggest that grassroots faith communities could embark on a project such as this only if they became, so to speak, biblically aware of the necessity of fair trade. Apart from this, what would we be looking for in the vast reported material we had at our disposal? If the Bible text under discussion had been John 2:13–22, we might have expected to find some hints at the unfair trade conditions third world countries face when they want to export their products. But even then, we might wonder whether that would have been convincing evidence for the positive relationship we are looking for.

⁴ Jeremy Brecher, Tim Costello, and Brendan Smith, *Globalization from Below: The Power of Solidarity* (Cambridge, Mass.: South End Press, 2000), ix.

⁵ Institute for Studies in Asian Church and Culture, Quezon City, Philippines.

⁶ School of Theology, Pontificia Universidad Javeriana, Bogotá, Colombia.

⁷ Protestant Church in the Netherlands.

⁸ Base Ecclesial Community.

⁹ Student group, Seminario Evangélico de Teología (SET), Matanzas, Cuba.

¹⁰ Student group, Sekolah Tinggi Teologia di Indonesia Bagian Timur, Macassar, South Sulawesi, Indonesia.

¹¹ I realize that, given the vast amount of material in the reading reports, presentations of groups, photographs, prayers, and other texts, the selection represents only a fragment and does not pretend to be scientifically representative of the rest.

¹² Two other examples of a possible relationship between intellectual background and more or less extensive self-presentation are Sekolah Tinggi Teologia di Indonesia Bagian Timur student group (Indonesia) and the Christian Writers Fellowship (Philippines). An exception to this supposition was represented by the groups from Nicaragua, where the individual contributions were highlighted in the reports. One of the groups (Masaya) even criticized the partner group for not offering a detailed description of the participants.

¹³ In the latter case, we read about a participant in the Open Doors organization, who speaks about one of the leaders of the organization, Brother Andrew, inviting people to convert as many Muslims as possible, in order to prevent them from carrying out airborne suicide attacks!

14 In the yearbook of the Centre for the Study of Global Governance (Helmut K. Anheier, Marlies Glasius, and Mary Kaldor, eds., *Global Civil Society Yearbook 2002* [Oxford, U.K.: Oxford University Press, 2002]), Abdullahi AnNa'im writes about the possible synergy and interdependence of religions and global civil society, focusing on three historical and empirical cases: the Ghandi vision on religion and society, liberal Islam as expressed in thousands of Islamic associations and initiatives in Europe and the United States, and the experiences of liberation theology in Latin America (Abdullahi AnNa'im, "Religion and Global Civil Society: Inherent Incompatibility or Synergy and Interdependence?" in *Global Civil Society Yearbook 2002* [http://www.lse.ac.uk/Depts/global/Yearbook/outline2002.htm]).

15 Ibid., 58.

CHAPTER 20

Intercultural Bible reading as a practical setting for intercultural communication

Marleen Kool

Economic progress is blossoming in many parts of the world. Since the middle of the twentieth century, democratic governments that respect human rights and freedom have been instituted in many countries. On average, people live longer than before. Ours is an age of unprecedented wealth and possibilities in the area of communication. The various regions of the earth are now more linked together, or in any case, are more aware of one another's existence than ever before.

And yet, roughly a quarter of the world's population still lives in great poverty; the daily lives of millions of people are determined by structural forms of repression, armed conflict, and terror.

In spite of all the means of communication, differences in the way people live and their living together lead to conflict and even polarization. Ethnic, religious, and cultural differences set people against each other, instead of side by side. The September 11, 2001, attacks on New York and Washington have made particularly apparent the urgency of communication between different religions and peoples. The awareness of estrangement, the lack of interest in and information about one another, has led since September 11 to a breach of trust between the South and West, the poor and the rich, Muslims and Christians. The U.S. invasion of Iraq reinforces these developments, and the holy books and God are used in an ever more refined fashion to authorize terrorist acts and warfare. Therefore, it comes as no surprise that many consider religion the source of evil, and the Bible and the Quran as dangerous books, reinforcing polarization in communication. In this global context, the intercultural Bible reading project has a special role. It explores whether the Bible can be a factor for binding different cultures together, an instrument and a catalyst for intercultural communication.

Marleen Kool, Faculty of Theology, Free University (Amsterdam, the Netherlands)

One of the participants involved in the intercultural Bible reading project in the Netherlands is ICCO (Interchurch organization for development cooperation). With respect to content, ICCO's interest is focused on research on the relevance for development of the intercultural Bible reading project. The project addresses the question, To what extent can an intercultural exchange via communitarian Bible reading contribute to deepening insight into the relationship between religion and development? This question is central to this chapter.

Religion is inextricably bound to communication. The word *religion* is derived from the Latin word *religio*. *Religio* is primarily considered a derivative of the verb *religare*, meaning "tying up" or "attaching"; religion as faith refers to "the service of people to God in order to confirm the relationship between God and people." However, religion is derived not only from *religare* but also from the verb *relegere*, which means "rethinking, rereading." It is a continual process of reflecting on and interpreting one's relationship to God and with others each time anew. To remain credible and vital, religious people must continuously reinterpret their religion and its sources. In this process of interpreting and coming to new understandings, cultural, social, and psychological factors, and—as an extension of these—the values and standards that people recognize, all play a role. Together, these factors ensure that people living in different times, in different cultural contexts, can attribute different meanings to the same Bible story. This recognition that faith is context- and time-specific gives rise to multiple understandings of scripture. At the same time, Bible stories contain universal aspects, aspects that are beyond culture. Stories about life experiences and problems transcend culture and the time the stories were created. The stories appeal to basic experiences, experiences that have to do with human existence in the world. Sharing these Bible stories and sharing human experience enable Christians to communicate globally. Communication, participation, and dialogue form the original shape of human contact and development.

To explore the relationship between religion and development, and to portray the possible deepening of that relationship through the intercultural Bible reading project method, this article is structured as follows. First, I will attempt to differentiate aspects to test the relevance of this project for development. I will approach this relevance by considering the capacity to change perspective and the capacity for inclusive thought. These two main themes are outlined in a process of development and transformation that can be the result of the intercultural Bible reading project. In conclusion, I will return to the question of whether this project can give more profound insight into the relationship between religion and development. In this final section, I will demonstrate how and under what conditions a communitarian intercultural reading and reflection on Bible stories can give added value to development cooperation.

The theoretical reflection on the query formulated above is based on a thorough analysis of the reading reports (available on the project website: www.bible4all.org). From the multitude of reading experiences, I have selected two for further analysis, support, and illustration for the formation of my theory. These are described in my essay, "Continuing that miraculous conversation: Intercultural reading of John 4," in part two of this volume.

Reading together as a source for living together?

An important theme in current programs for development cooperation is "creating involvement" among people. How can the basis for development cooperation be reinforced and broadened? This question has everything to do with the possibility of portraying the situation and the people involved. Can we put ourselves in the situation of another person? Does the other person have a face for us? Or can we hardly imagine their situation? Do we perhaps hardly even want to? The way we look at other people is inextricably bound to how we look at ourselves and constitutes the central question of human development. Development is much more than combating poverty. Development is determined by factors such as self-awareness, critical consciousness of one's own context, access to interaction with others, freedom of opinion and expression, freedom of communication, and experiencing faith. Development, in the broad sense of the word, is the all-encompassing process of liberation from oppressive bonds. It involves removing structural sources of injustice, exclusion, and violence, as well as mental transformation of repressed awareness toward an internal form of freedom. This assignment is vast. And what role is reserved for religion in this process? Can the intercultural Bible reading project contribute to deepening insight into the relationship between religion and development?

The reading experiences demonstrate that the method of intercultural Bible reading forms a special practice ground, a unique practical setting, for intercultural communication. Participants enter into communication with each other via a Bible story they share. This organized communication through sharing a Bible story elicits the question, important to this chapter, of whether intercultural Bible reading could be a catalyst for sustainable involvement among people who live in different socioeconomic, political, and cultural contexts. Is there a transformation in this reading process that causes people to look at themselves and others in a different way? If there is, what does that transformation consist of? What factors contribute to it and which ones impede such a process of change?

The overwhelming treasure of reading experiences exposes not only what reading together does to readers (first phase) but also, especially, what the exchange with Christians worldwide means to participants (second phase).

Experience shows that the second phase of the reading process is more arduous than the first. Waiting a long time for a response, or receiving a disappointing response from the partner group, has a negative effect on the motivation and effort of reading groups. In a few instances, a group fell apart for unknown reasons and is thus no longer capable of continuing the contact. Another delaying factor that must be taken into account is the limited access participants and their coordinators have to the Internet in some areas. A large percentage of the participating reading groups are enthusiastically and devotedly involved in the second phase, reading through the eyes of another. The responses to the other are as colorful and diverse as the participants themselves. There are splendid examples of groups that, despite great differences between them, discover common ground and ask each other for information. Other groups make it strikingly visible in their responses that it is difficult to bridge gaps in culture, faith, communication, or socioeconomic background.

On the basis of two central concepts, namely, change of perspective and inclusiveness, I would like to show how this project can change the views and experiences of the participants of others and of themselves.

Conditions for change of perspective in intercultural communication

In mutual relationships between people, and certainly in the case of intercultural relations, the capacity to change perspective is of great importance. This capacity enables you to put yourself in the situation of another person, to look through the eyes of another, and thus to look at the other person—but also at yourself—through the eyes of another person, arriving at a different perspective. Time and again, changing perspective turns out to be a huge task.

Case studies described in part two of this volume are representative of the treasure of reading experiences in the intercultural Bible reading project, providing insight into factors that stimulate intercultural communication as well as exposing factors that impede this communication or even block it entirely. These experiences elicit the question of what instruments are necessary to understand each other, and as an extension, to arrive at a change of perspective. What is the reason that one set of groups manages to hold a dialogue and another set does not? I identify two main factors in the process of changing perspective and elaborate them below.

Attitude toward the partner group. The most important condition for successful intercultural communication is the attitude people have when they enter the process. This attitude can make or break the process, as the following two examples demonstrate.

The response of a group of readers in India is characterized by tenacious adherence to the group's own reading and rejection of other, different (i.e., new) points of view, as they emerge from the interpretation of John 4 in the Netherlands. The readers in India are painfully affected by the deconstruction of Jesus they encounter in the report from Zutphen: The idea that Jesus is the woman's sixth man is unacceptable; the woman may not be correlated with Moses; praying in spirit and truth is very different from meditation and must especially not be interpreted interreligiously. Any differences are negated in forceful and sharp terms. The readers in India put the reading of their partner group in the context of Western culture. But what, in fact, is their own position toward the West? Looking through the eyes of these readers in India, the West is secular (confirmed by the deconstruction of Jesus), rational (focused on increasing knowledge), monocultural (not used to living together with

Muslims and foreigners), free in relationships between men and women (resulting in a positive image of the Samaritan woman). Moreover, the readers in India observe a spiritual hype in the West, an attitude inspired by the Indian philosophy's rich tradition of yoga and meditation. As it is reflected in their report, the attitude of these readers in India toward the reading group in the Netherlands, as well as toward the West as a whole, is closed. The group's outlook is more or less fixed, and they appear to be unwilling to pry open the images and interpretation frames formulated by the group.

A very different attitude is displayed in the exchange between Ghanaian and Brazilian reading groups. The first thing one notices is that both groups assume each other's language and method in their responses. This strategy forms a bridge between two initially very different ways of reading the text and presenting themselves. Here, what takes place in all forms of communication becomes apparent, namely, a subconscious or conscious process of mutual influence.[1] For example, the Brazilians copy the way the Ghanaian group presents its context, using statistics to clarify their socioeconomic situation. The effect on the Ghanaians of the Brazilian group's way of reading is noticeable. The way the Brazilians reveal themselves in the light of the story they read liberates the Ghanaian group from their dogmatic reading and clears the way for an open dialogue between the text and the group. The frank and personal reading from Brazil is experienced by the readers in Ghana as an invitation to show themselves. First, they crawl into the skin of the other group, and then they look at themselves with other eyes. A basis of trust is created. Because of this mutual frankness, space for meeting each other is created. A feeling of being connected to and curious about the partner group grows. The willingness to learn from each other and share problems—with discrimination, suffering, and poverty—stimulates the communication between these two reading groups. They recognize each other as people who share basic experiences.

The brief analysis above makes it clear that changing perspective demands an open and uninhibited attitude in which participants take into consideration possible differences and misunderstandings. Respect for the other as different is important in this process, but more than anything, it is vital to develop skills that people can use to consider themselves and each other as carriers and designers of culture, where difference and dynamics are seen as normal, as facts of life.

An important concept in the formation of theories on intercultural communication is *mindfulness*, awareness of a group's own manner of communicating.[2] As an extension of this concept, Brian Spitzberg and William Cupach differentiate three conditions that must be met in order to have a fertile intercultural exchange: knowledge, motivation, and skills.[3] Analysis of the reading reports in the first and second phases of the intercultural Bible reading shows the relevance of these conditions.

Knowledge refers to the awareness of one's own cultural positiveness, the insight that one must gain knowledge of one's own cultural positiveness if one is to understand someone else to some degree. This condition becomes visible in part in the response by partner groups when they ask the other group questions about their customs and habits, about their cultural and religious context, and about their expectations with respect to the mutual exchange. To gain the necessary knowledge, a certain sensitivity to the outlook and experience of the other is required. Participants need a flexible attitude, suspending, and if necessary, adjusting prejudices about the other context.

Motivation consists of the entirety of feelings, intentions, needs, and factors that move people to participate in this form of intercultural Bible reading. For all participants in the project, this motivation initially entails curiosity toward others and a great intercultural interest. Participants want to hear from others about how they deal with their faith and what role and significance the Bible has in their lives. Moreover, they really look forward to the contact that may be created and hope to learn from each other and be challenged. Factors such as fear of alienation, uncertainty, and ethnocentrism may also dominate the motivation of a group. These factors are usually not made explicit, but they may implicitly play a role and stand in the way of real exchange and dialogue between groups. In such a situation, authentic change requires the capacity of one of the two partners to gain the trust of the other group and to break the other group open by, for example, asking questions. This approach may reduce the group's own insecurity as well as that of the other group. As the motivation is determined by more positive factors, such as interest in and involvement with others, and a longing for new insights, knowledge, and experiences, these impulses will stimulate the interaction between groups.

The third condition, as formulated by Spitzberg and Cupach, consists of *skills*, the capacity to communicate effectively and appropriately with the other group. This condition involves the awareness of how the group presents itself to the partner group, as well as of the content being communicated. Experiences gained through intercultural communication appear to play an important role in the exchange between reading groups. Those who are confronted for the first time with a different culture may experience shock and shrink back from the images evoked by the other group, or rather read very selectively and concentrate unilaterally on similarities with and recognition of the other group (premature assimilation).

An open attitude, involving mindfulness, a certain intercultural adroitness, and the willingness to reveal oneself, as well as flexibility and a capacity to deal with uncertainty, appear to be conditions for coming to a change in perspective in an intercultural exchange using a biblical text.[4]

Cultural background of the readers. From the analysis above, it is clear that culture has an important effect on the attitude of the readers. But what is culture? And what relationship exists between culture, interpretation, and communication?

There are many definitions of culture, and one notices that in recent decades the emphasis has shifted more and more to culture as a dynamic process, as the following description by Clifford Geertz demonstrates: "Culture is not a static entity of values or habits, but a permanent process of constructing meaning."[5]

In the handbook for participants, the Intercultural Bible Collective (IBC) bases its approach on the definition of Geert Hofstede, who describes culture, along the lines of Geertz, as "the collective mental programming that differentiates the members of one group or category of people from those of others."[6] Cultures have universal aspects, which Hofstede calls "cultural depth dimensions," that make it possible to compare cultures with each other. "The five dimensions Hofstede identifies are the systematic differences among cultures in relation to power and inequality (1), to the relation between the individual and the group (2), to the social roles that are expected from men and women (3), to the manner of dealing with the uncertainties of existence (4) and to the way people are dealing or focusing on the future, the past or the present (5)."[7]

In this chapter, I will limit my analysis to the first three factors, insofar as they play a role in intercultural communication and the process of changing perspective.

Power and inequality. Along with the question of instruments necessary to understand one another, we cannot avoid the question of differences in power and conflicts of interest between the various participants. This question arose at the project's inception, and at that time it especially focused on the issue of ownership of the project. Because the introduction discusses this subject extensively, I will not do so here. I will instead address the issue of how power and interests play a role in the intercultural communication between reading groups.

Every society harbors inequality. There are always people everywhere who are bigger, stronger, or smarter than others. Subsequently, some gain more power than others. In the communication with another reading group, what role does a reading group's socioeconomic position, average level of education, and larger religious context play?

Because of the broad diversity of reading experiences, it is not easy to answer this question. Contrasts between reading groups paired with one another are sometimes considerable. Participants who feel they are relatively powerful, because they can express their opinions in freedom and have sufficient means of subsistence, are brought into contact with participants who consider themselves powerless, because they cannot or can barely exert any effect on the way their lives are lived or on their environment. Poor and rich, educated and uneducated participants read the same Bible together. One group is situated at the margin in a multireligious context, another group is part of the dominant mainstream, and a third is somewhere in the middle.

Only by linking up these groups are communication channels opened and relationships formed, and a process of democratization takes place. In principle, every group contributes the same amount to the intercultural discussion, and everyone carries the same amount of responsibility for the contents and the development of the contact with the partner group. Despite this democratic principle, power and inequality always play a role within the group as well as in the communication with a different group. The question is, How do they play a role, and when?

When the socioeconomic position of a reading group is explicitly or implicitly introduced into the discussion, it can have various effects on communication between people. A Cuban reader (who gives us no information about his background) feels alienation when reading a response from someone in an American partner group to the question about what they are thirsting for.[8] The thirst of one of these readers is directed toward "security" and "safety." His biggest fear is that he will have to live without money and without a car. The Cuban's response is extreme astonishment: "The insecurity you show about 'losing the car' sounds strange to us. Our insecurities are related to survival: What to eat? How to support our children? We don't even think about having a car here."[9]

Difference in socioeconomic outlook may summon out a feeling of bashfulness and lack. Especially in the Netherlands, readers notice that they are preoccupied with material goals, often in contrast with groups from a low socioeconomic background. They lack spontaneity and rarely surrender to faith, because so many things have to be done from the mind and so many less from the heart, and so much has to be arranged. The difference between rich and poor confronts participants and calls out a sense of responsibility. A group in the Netherlands responds to a group of Dalit women in a small village in the south of India: "They described a situation that does not apply to us. . . . We belong to what they call the upper class. . . . Is there any way we can give these women material help?"[10]

Poverty and repression acquire a face, because partners are confronted with stories about the lives of participants who live in such circumstances. The unequal distribution of the world's wealth comes closer in the encounter between participants who read a Bible story together. The Dutch readers show their need to give money, from their feeling of being involved with and responsible for their partner group, but perhaps also from their shyness about their own material wealth.[11] There is also concern on the part of economically unendowed readers for their partner groups in a better economic position. A group of former street prostitutes from the Philippines, for example, is concerned about the large gap that exists between their rich Western partner group and God. The women in the Philippines are convinced that trust in God has everything to do with your social origin. "God is nearer to us because we are poor. The rich, they don't pay much attention to God, because they don't need him." Their evaluation of the exchange with their partner group documents their realization that they have something to offer, spiritually, to their partners in the West. "We believe that we have helped our Dutch partners to have some understanding of what it means to be poor. They, in fact, commented and reminded us that the poor tend to be closer to the Lord. We feel we have been able to encourage them to trust God, because people whose needs are sufficiently met tend to forget God. We are glad that they acknowledged their need for God even as they enjoy what they have materially."

Socioeconomic position is often closely tied to participants' level of education. This inequality often hampers intercultural communication between participants.

Understanding the situation of the other person becomes easier as participants have more information about the world and are familiar with the fact that people think and live differently elsewhere in the world. Not only is there a difference in level; groups also notice a cultural difference as a result of education.[12] Participants from Western or individualistically oriented societies learn how to analyze and reflect from a young age. This tendency becomes apparent in the way groups deal with the Bible and their faith: "In contrast to our group, they don't discuss what they read in the Bible very much; instead they take the words as they are written. . . . We discuss the meaning of saying a prayer. . . . We don't know what is meant if someone says 'to calculate with' God. Our belief is more a matter of rationality and deliberation than of emotions and feelings."[13] For readers living in poverty, a story such as the one in John 4 often has a very immediate meaning: they recognize themselves in the narrative. The liberating power of the story appeals strongly to the needs of participants who live in situations of exclusion or repression. Many reading groups in a strong socioeconomic position experience the confrontation with their partner group's more personal reading as deepening their own reading. They are challenged to put their own life situation into the context of the story. In this way, differences can be fertile ground, and people can learn from each other.

A third factor is the position of the reading groups within their own religious context. In my opinion, there is a correlation between this position and the intercultural communication. To clarify this correlation, I refer once again to the exchange described above, between the Syrian Christians in India and the Zutphen Protestant Christians in the Netherlands. The reading of a group that is a minority within their own context, as the Syrian Christians in India are, appears to be more homogeneous than that of a "dominant" group like the Christians in the Netherlands. Members of the nondominant group have to present themselves as united toward the outside, in order to maintain themselves. Formation of individual opinion may be experienced as a threat to solidarity. To minority groups, dividedness—or better expressed, pluriformity—may seem to be a sign of weakness relative to the ruling order, and therefore may be combated. In general, the greater the familiarity with the existence of different values and standards, the greater will be the intercultural competence, and the better the chance of developing and maintaining intercultural relations.

Individualism versus collectivism. Many—especially Dutch—readers are astonished by the unanimity in interpretation of their partner groups. They notice that while they spend their time formulating their own opinions about the story, their partner group in Nicaragua or Colombia, for example, tries to reach a consensus on the meaning of the story.

This phenomenon has to do with the degree to which societies are oriented more individualistically or more collectivistically. A society is individualistic if the ties between individuals are loose: people are expected to take care of themselves and their immediate families. A society is collectivist if individuals are included from

birth in strong, tight groups that offer lifelong protection in exchange for unconditional loyalty.[14] In collectivist societies, people learn at a young age to form their
opinion on the basis of others'. Little value is attached to "personal" opinions: opinions are derived from the group. In individualistic societies, people are instead
encouraged to form their own opinions: you gain respect if you can express what
you yourself stand for. In communication between people from these different
types of societies, the differences may result in misunderstandings and problems. A
Colombian reading group (in a collectivist-oriented country) points out the wealth
of the heterogeneity of their Dutch partner's reading report, but notes that still it
lacks a certain consensus: " It is a brainstorm that shows various ways of interpreting
the text. We can see that inside that heterogeneity everyone expresses their visions
without having to make deals or agreements." The Dutch group finds the Colombians' report a bit dull, on the other hand: "Everyone agrees so much with each
other. . . . We do like a bit of variation."[15]

Both types of societies display certain behaviors and follow certain standards
and values that may play a big role in communication between them. Hofstede
states that "differences in Individualism and Collectivism may be the largest source
of cultural misunderstandings in our world."[16] For example, the direct manner of
responding and asking critical questions, as is customary for people in an individualistic society, may come across as very strange and even offensive to people from a
collectivist society. For that matter, in collectivist societies people are, in principle,
not used to expressing criticism: for them, maintaining harmony is an important
virtue. In collectivist societies, a much stronger communal standard prevails, so it is
also less natural in such a context to be open to new situations and perspectives. In
individualistic societies, from the beginning there is, in general, a range of standards
and values allowing for more openness to new angles.

In order to estimate the value of each other's method of interpretation, participants need to be sensitized to this difference regarding individualism and collectivism in their two societies. If people are aware of the consequences for mutual communication of this cultural dimension, they are able not only to put themselves in
each other's situations and lives but also to become more aware of the limits and the
eventual "enslavement" of this cultural dimension. This insight could stimulate
them to a careful formulation of observations and questions, and could prompt the
intercultural discussion, the change of perspective.

Man/woman. A third cultural dimension involves the division of roles between
men and women. I concentrate the analysis of this dimension on the gender query
insofar as this plays a role in the exchange between participants in the intercultural
Bible reading project.

The majority of the participating groups consist of mixed groups of men and
women. A mixed composition does not guarantee equal participation in the group
process. Equal participation of women and men in the discussion is determined by
a variety of factors, such as the degree to which a society's orientation is more

masculine or feminine,[17] the church affiliation, and local conditions and the group dynamics. Groups that present themselves as a mixed group, but in which women's voices are not heard, are often questioned by their partner group. "Where are the women in your story? What is their outlook on the meeting between the Samaritan woman and Jesus? What do they think about that miraculous conversation at the well?" critical students in Korea ask their partner group.[18]

Church groups worldwide consist mainly of women. The number of exclusively women's groups within this project is therefore much higher than the number of men's groups. Another thing that strikes one is that women's groups, especially from the South, deal differently with the Bible and faith than do people in the North. This difference becomes apparent in intercultural Bible reading in the fact that certain women's groups—for example, the Dalit women in India, women in El Salvador, and the group of former prostitutes in the Philippines—feel they are addressed much more directly by the Bible story than groups in a country such as the Netherlands. Especially for women whose living conditions give them reason to identify themselves with the Samaritan woman, this story has an enormously liberating force. Women who are weighed down by the patriarchal structures of their society draw strength from the conversation between Jesus and the woman. For them, it is important that Jesus addresses her, a woman. But it is more that: this woman does not listen to what Jesus has to say in a submissive way. She has the courage to enter into discussion with Jesus, to question *him*. The rehabilitation of the Samaritan woman manifest in this story is also an important stimulus for their own rehabilitation; it gives them courage to stand up for themselves and to resist repressive patriarchal structures.[19]

In the intercultural exchange, these women not only reinforce themselves with these points of identification but they also help others move the story closer to their own lives and their own context. A good example is the response by the Philippine women who used to work in street prostitution, to a group in Wichmond, the Netherlands.[20] The Philippine women, who are going through a profound process of social transformation, challenge the Dutch readers to read the story from their hearts and not from their minds. They comment that the readers in Wichmond cannot identify themselves at all with anyone in the story, and that as a result they cannot make the story their own. They remain at a distance. The readers in Wichmond say, in their response to the Filipino women, that they have much to learn from the huge faith these women have: "They see things in life more as miracles. Because we have it all, we sometimes have difficulty believing in God. We do not depend on God for everything. By everything, we mean the primary necessities of life: food and a roof over our head, school, work, or a pension. In a nonmaterial sense, we don't have everything, either: we also have disease, sorrow, and death. And there are many poor people in the Netherlands, too."

Using the same insistent tone and feeling the same affinity for the Samaritan woman, a women's group in El Salvador opens the eyes of their partner group of

Dutch women. The Salvadoran women ask the readers in Voorschoten to go find the Samaritan woman in their village. Who are the people in your village who are avoided? Who are the broken and the outcasts in your country? Conversely, the women in El Salvador are impressed by the way the group in Voorschoten thinks and speaks from the equivalence of different denominations: "They have religious freedom, but it's not real in every country. They don't differentiate that some are Catholic and others are from the Reformed church—a beautiful example for us in our reflection."

From the perspective of development, this type of intercultural exchange definitely involves reciprocal learning. For ages, the Bible has supported women and consoled them, but it has also been misused to justify their repression and subordination. In places where women themselves take the Bible in hand, especially in situations of poverty in the broadest sense of the word, their readings are often remarkable for making a direct link between spirituality and their concrete daily life. They experience the liberating power of this special holy book and allow others to share in it, in a personal and creative way.

Inclusiveness

In the extension of the capacity to change perspective lies the capacity for inclusive thinking. Inclusive thinking means that one experiences and approaches another as someone with the same human dreams and longings for a safe, happy, and full life. The question that surfaces here is whether a communitarian intercultural reflection on Bible stories can contribute to reinforcement of inclusive thinking. In all modesty, I think that the method of the project can make a valuable contribution to this inclusive thinking. The force of that contribution naturally depends on the duration and intensity of the contact with the partner group. However, what is striking is that many participants in this project are surprised by the alliance they feel they have with their partner group from the moment they read each other's reports, and sometimes even receive photos or gifts. For many people, especially in countries where communitarian Bible reading has become less matter-of-course, it is enormously stimulating to begin to read the Bible again in the knowledge that participants all over the world are studying the same story. In many participants, this creates a strong feeling of solidarity with the global Christian community.

Communitarian Bible reading mediates in making a confidential contact. The participants don't just do something "at random"; they read the Bible together, a book that inspires the community of the faithful and gives it orientation. This inspiration happens to everyone in a different way. In the great multicoloredness of the communitarian intercultural Bible reading, it is apparent that the Bible story brings the story of the participants' lives up for discussion, too. And in that very connection between Bible story and life story, the participants recognize each other, without obscuring their differences, first of all as fellow humans, as beings made in God's image. "I see that everybody is in the first place a human being. And after that a Christian, or a Muslim. . . . What we all share is that we are human beings. And that is the basis for talking and sharing. . . . We could continue this group by inviting anybody who is interested, irrespective of their background."[21]

In spite of the often huge differences in cultural, religious, and socioeconomic context, the story being read appeals to experiences that transcend the context of the reader. The story of the encounter between Jesus and the Samaritan woman at the well contains for almost all participants the liberating message that salvation is for everyone, regardless of race, gender, or status. The story stimulates everyone to some form of reflection about barriers in personal faith and life; it summons people to reconciliation and breaking down prejudices.

Openness and respect are necessary for reading the Bible with this vision of reconciliation in mind. Such reading demands that readers see each other as fellow humans searching for truth and righteousness. An important condition for seeing each other truly as brothers and sisters is the capacity and the desire to live with differences. In principle, we all are equal but we are not all alike, and this very multicoloredness makes intercultural Bible reading such an enriching experience.

Intercultural Bible reading sets in motion a process of internal awareness, as the analysis above demonstrates. Participants become aware of the limits of their own perspective and sometimes even formulate what is referred to as "Third Culture perspective." For example, a theology student in Macassar (Indonesia) looks at Cuban society through totally different eyes after reading the partner's report from Cuba: "Regarding Cuba's background as a communist country: I suspected that maybe its people would tend to be stubborn, rigid, and with not too much concern for their surroundings. I don't mean to label communist countries as evil, but I always thought that these kinds of countries had a tendency in that direction. But obviously the reality is totally different from what I thought, because those involved in the discussion are actually very concerned for the social reality in Cuba."[22] This confession is only one of many beautiful examples of a Third Culture perspective, in which the readers' own standards and values and the prejudices toward the "foreign" culture are broken open, giving rise to a new outlook on both the other and oneself.

Reading the scripture together forms a unique and valuable practice ground for intercultural communication. Around a shared story and from a common belief, participants have the opportunity to question, criticize, and compliment not only each other but also themselves. As a result of the confrontation with others, participants can be lifted above their own local community and can broaden their horizons. Through the eyes of another, not only does the other's face emerge, but participants also encounter themselves anew.

This internal transformation sets participants in motion. The Bible as a source of inspiration, read in a global community of the faithful, challenges participants to expand their borders. It challenges them to no longer always walk the well-marked paths, to no longer see themselves as inferior, to no longer judge others and avoid them because they are different. Plans are made: women in Ghana decide to set up an action committee to visit street prostitutes in their villages and read the Bible with them. "We do not have money . . . but we don't need money to visit these people regularly and encourage them. We can help them in some practical ways. . . . Some of us have skills. . . . For instance, we can teach them certain handcrafts—tie-dye, how to make jam, . . . which in the end will address the issue of poverty."[23]

Another Ghanaian woman wants to help people with HIV/AIDS, for these are often the ones in her setting that people would rather avoid. In El Salvador as well as in South Africa, participants attempt to bring about a dialogue between different groups in their own country using the intercultural Bible reading method. They hope in this way to contribute to reconciliation and tolerance in their own context.

It is difficult to measure the effect of the actions in this project, but the reports testify—implicitly as well as explicitly—that reflecting on the Bible together has an effect on behavior, as the examples cited here show. Especially to the faithful in third world countries, the Bible is a book that participants relate directly to their own lives and in particular to their own actions. What is read is almost always converted into action or plans. Readers in the West are often blamed for reading too distantly, too rationally. But at the same time, there are plenty of examples of readers in the Southern hemisphere who are amazed by reading the Bible in light of the world's problems, an approach many readers in the West demonstrate. Problems between religions, a growing fear of terrorism, being involved in development cooperation— these are all brought to light by means of an ancient Bible story that draws together people all over the world.

Conclusions

We return to the question of whether this project can provide a more profound insight into the relationship between religion and development. I approached the relevance for development in terms of the capacity to change perspective and the capacity for thinking inclusively. These two constitute aspects of a transformation process that is created and can be stimulated by an intercultural, communitarian reading of the Bible. I formulated the conditions for arriving at a change in perspective with regard to the attitude and cultural background of readers. The attitude required from participants can be summarized in terms of openness and respect for the other's differences. I concentrated the role of the cultural background in intercultural communication on the role of power and inequality, the degree of individualism versus collectivism, and the man/woman relationship within the participants' own society. Awareness of the effect of culture on self-image as well as on how one understands one's faith appears to enrich intercultural communication.

Involvement between participants is often determined by a certain functionality and purposefulness. Intercultural relations are usually determined by economic interests. Consider the large American telecommunication companies that hire young students in India to do their administration, at low wages. Or large multinationals have their products made in third world countries as cheaply as possible and sell them at the largest profit possible. The involvement that is created between participants engaging in intercultural Bible reading is of an entirely different order. No financial interests play any role whatsoever. Out of a purely content-based motivation, mutual ties are created between groups in the Southern hemisphere and the West. From the beginning, the project's intention has been to break through asymmetric relations. No one has more to contribute to the process of understanding the Bible and one's own context than anyone else. In this regard, the project ties in with the need for deconstruction of the dominant paradigm of development, which maintains the inequality that has been created, and where all too often thoughts and actions are conveyed in the context of a subject-object relationship.

Ideally, in the dialogue that is created, participants discover new points of view on the contents of their faith; their outlook changes with respect to the Bible in relation to the rest of the world. In the contact with other Christians, ideas on themes such as gender, homosexuality, and ethnicity are exchanged between groups of people who would otherwise never—or not so easily—talk about these subjects with others in their own circles. Contact with others allows participants to shake themselves loose from their rigid framework of thought and makes them go search again for their own sources of inspiration. Christians in the West are often caught off guard by the enthusiasm and the urge for conversion expressed by Christians in the Southern hemisphere. "Things here aren't bubbling so strongly," says a woman reader in the Netherlands. At the same time, Christians in the Southern hemisphere are amazed by the frank discussion in many Western groups, by the way many questions are asked and different opinions are shared. Quite a few groups that were paired up, however, show in turn that stereotypes of South and West do not automatically hold: Langezwaag (the Netherlands) responds to Cuba: "We find your approach more analytical and theological: you apparently have more knowledge of the Bible than our group. We find your approach partly more detached. . . . Our approach is much more fed by personal experiences and visions."

Participants discover that their self-understanding and their worldview are created not only by interaction with others in their immediate surroundings but also by interaction with a more extensive community of the faithful. This transformative interaction does not involve exchange of knowledge so much as commitment between participants. They share together what they find important to their lives and to those around them. They can practice carrying on an intercultural dialogue, gradually, through their ups and downs, discovering each other as full-fledged partners. To use the words of Paulo Freire, they can develop a dialogic attitude toward life: "Being dialogic is not invading, not manipulating, not imposing orders. Being dialogic is pledging oneself to the constant transformation of reality."[24]

This may be the hardest task for participants: to be able and willing to meet the other as the other. In this development, people in the North and South, East and West can all assist one another.

In this article, the relevance for development of the method of the intercultural Bible reading project was described, using a definition of development as a multidimensional process. The added value of the method of this project, beyond other, traditional types of development cooperation, becomes apparent in various factors that I will summarize in conclusion.

The relationships established among participants are characterized by a fundamental reciprocity. A reciprocal process of empowerment replaces the unilateralism that occurs in development projects in which the essence is material development. Participants, regardless of their social, economic, or cultural background, are enabled to get to know one another and one another's context on a basis of equality.

There is no encounter with the other that is not also an encounter with oneself. Because participants introduce themselves to the other by name and by telling about their life situation, they are challenged to look at themselves once again. In the confrontation with the other, this process of becoming self-aware is stimulated even further. If one truly arrives at a change in perspective, no one remains out of range. In a true dialogue and confrontation with participants who live in a totally different socioeconomic and cultural context, no one remains free of obligation; the exchange will irrevocably set in motion a process of growing awareness with respect to the relationships among participants.

The method of intercultural Bible reading stimulates a democratic process of developing faith. In group discussions, participants are invited to share their own sources of inspiration and faith. That there is space for everyone's outlook on faith and the Bible is emphasized as much as possible. This method is not focused on examining the "correct" meaning of Bible stories but on setting in motion a dialogue between the traditional stories about experiences people had with God in those days and the life stories of participants today.

Notes

[1] Some use the term *recursivity of communication* to identify the process of continuously holding up mirrors in front of each other (unaware and without being asked), showing how the other person's message was received. See Edwin Hoffmann, *Het TOPOI-model: Een pluralistische systeemtheoretische benadering van interculturele communicatie* (Houten/Diegem, the Netherlands: Bohn Stafleu Van Loghum, 1999), 49.

[2] Ellen Langer differentiates three aspect in mindfulness: (1) creation of new categories, (2) openness to new information, and (3) awareness of more than one perspective (Ellen J. Langer, *The Power of Mindful Learning* (Reading, Mass.: Adison-Wesley, 1997).

[3] Brian H. Spitzberg and William R. Cupach, *Interpersonal Communication Competence* (Beverly Hills, Calif.: Sage Publications, 1984).

[4] For further background information on intercultural competence, see Richard L. Wiseman, "Intercultural Communication Competence," in *Handbook of International and Intercultural Communication*, ed. William B. Gudykunst and Bella

Mody (Thousand Oaks, Calif.: Sage Publications, 2002), 207–24.

[5] Clifford Geertz, "Thick Description: Toward an Interpretive Theory of Culture," in *The Interpretation of Cultures: Selected Essays by Clifford Geertz* (New York: Basic Books, 1973), 3–30.

[6] Geert Hofstede, *Allemaal Andersdenkenden: Omgaan met cultuurverschillen*, 10th ed. (Amsterdam: Uitgeverij Contact, 1998).

[7] Hans de Wit, "Through the Eyes of Another: A Project on Intercultural Reading of the Bible" (presentation, consultation on Intercultural Reading of the Bible, Free University, Amsterdam, the Netherlands, 2001; a version of this paper, with the same title, became the standard project handbook).

[8] This question comes up in reference to John 4:10–15, the discussion on living water.

[9] Exchange between the Cuban Presbyterian Reformed reading group from Sancti Spiritus city and Belmont Mennonite Serendipity group, Elkhart, Indiana (USA).

[10] Exchange between the Dutch Protestant group from Vlissingen and the Indian Dalit women's group.

[11] This is the only case where a group has indicated that they are willing to help financially. The Vlissingen group was referred with their offer to current projects of Kerkinactie [Church in Action] in India to assist Dalits.

[12] B. Gras, "Taking a Critical Look at *Through the Eyes of Another: A Provisional Evaluation of a Project on Intercultural Bible Reading*" (doctoral thesis, University of Groningen, Groningen, the Netherlands, 2002), 57.

[13] A Dutch Protestant group from Apeldoorn reacts to the Roman Catholic San Lucas group from Bogotá, Colombia.

[14] Hofstede, *Allemaal Andersdenkenden*, 71.

[15] Exchange between the Project of Life group from Colombia and the Protestant Huizen group from the Netherlands.

[16] Hofstede, *Allemaal Andersdenkenden*, 104.

[17] A society is masculine if social sex roles are clearly separate: men are supposed to be assertive and hard, focused on success; women ought to be modest and sweet and especially focused on the quality of existence. A society is feminine if social sex roles overlap; both men and women are supposed to be modest and sweet and focused on the quality of existence (Hofstede, *Allemaal Andersdenkenden*, 108).

[18] Exchange between Hanil theology students from Korea and the reading group Comunidad Cristiana de Crecimiento Integral from Colombia.

[19] This becomes apparent in, among others, Dalit women's groups in India, and in groups in the Philippines, El Salvador, Korea, Colombia, and West Africa.

[20] Exchange between the Samaritana women's group from the Philippines and the Dutch Wichmond group.

[21] Quotation by Kofi, a participant in a Ghanaian reading group.

[22] Exchange between a student group from Macassar, Indonesia, and the Matanzas group from Cuba.

[23] First reading report from the Elmina Presbyterian women's group in Ghana.

[24] Paulo Freire, *¿Extensión o Comunicación?* (Buenos Aires: Tierra Nueva, 1973), 46.

CHAPTER 21

Living water

Wonderful words of life

Janet W. Dyk

One intriguing element in the story of Jesus's encounter with the Samaritan woman at the well is the mention of water in the conversation. Given the situation, this theme would seem to be an obvious one: Jesus had journeyed and was tired and sat down at the well where the woman came to draw water. From these simple, everyday ingredients, a conversation develops containing a whole spectrum of associations. In the reports of the readings of this story, many facets of this theme are mentioned and discussed.

The reading reports made clear that water is universally significant. Thus, it was possible for readers to identify elements in the story with aspects of their own experience. The comments about water can be roughly divided into those discussing water as physical and tangible, and those discussing it as a metaphor for something else. Both tangible water and metaphorical associations of water can be described in a static manner—this is equivalent to that—or in a dynamic way, with movement and development—with life. In the readings, we find both static and dynamic interpretations, although there is often a natural overlap between the two aspects.

The fact that water was requested precipitated comments on the dynamics of this encounter. The thirst that apparently motivated the request for water gave rise to comments on what generates thirst. The question about whether Jesus and the woman received an answer to their thirst intrigued a number of the participating groups. To further fill in the picture, the role of the well and the water pot extend in an interesting way the image being brought forward.

The comments having to do with water have been abstracted from a selection of the reading reports and arranged under the headings mentioned. The danger is that

Janet W. Dyk, Faculty of the Arts and Faculty of Theology, Free University (Amsterdam, the Netherlands)

in abstracting, essential information may be omitted, and that in the arrangement, comments may be taken out of context. In spite of my attempts to treat the material with care, some misrepresentations may have occurred. For this I apologize.

In this approach, I am seeking explicitly for the many facets of the interpretation of water. No attempt is made to identify a particular geographical area, socioeconomic group, or church affiliation as tending toward a specific understanding of water in this passage. Unavoidably, in such a collection the comments are at times contradictory, but that fact makes the whole more fascinating.

Reports from fifty-seven groups have been used for the analysis that follows. They exhibit the following geographical distribution:

area	countries surveyed	participating groups
South America	6	21
Africa	3	15
Asia & Far East	3	7
Europe & North America	4	14
total	16	57

The selection of the groups was arbitrary, except that I aimed at a broad geographical scope. When I selected a country, I decided to use all reading groups within that country, except in the case of the Netherlands. Because of the large number of groups from the Netherlands, I used only an arbitrary selection of groups. As the focus here is on the richness of meaning brought out by the groups around the world, I have kept the connection of a particular comment to the group from which the comment came in the background although not entirely obscured. The remarks taken from the reading reports are rendered much as encountered in the reports, with minimal editing. After each comment, the group or groups making the comment are identified using parenthetical numbers; these numbers correspond to a listing of the groups that appears at the end of the article. Interspersed between these comments from the reading reports are sentences that I wrote to serve as transitions.

Let us immerse ourselves in the semantic richness of our theme as read by the worldwide community of those represented in this project.

Physical, tangible water: Static

In a newscast about its search for life on Mars, a representative of the European Space Agency noted that where there is water there is life—at least on earth. Water and life are indivisible for earthlings. Not only is water a prerequisite for maintaining life, but the presence of water indicates that life is present. This intimate bond between water and life is expressed in many ways in the discussions on John 4.

The reading reports give much attention to water as a physical and tangible element. One group compared samples of heavily polluted water that had been chemically treated to make it drinkable with pure water from an artesian well, which was less transparent than the chemically treated water (8). Universally, the image of water refers to something pure, although the local water may not be uncontaminated (12). Water brings up associations with transparency and cleanliness (12).

Jesus's request for water is related directly to his tiredness and thirst after journeying (2, 5, 6, 8, 14, 33, 45, 56). In a hot, dry country such as Palestine, water is an essential condition for life itself (38, 49). It is then important to meet somebody who can give you some water (38). Water must have been one of the best drinks in such a dry area (53). Our bodies are made up of water to a large degree (6). Drought is life-threatening (49). Unquenched thirst is painful; the thirst of children is even more painful (27).

Jesus's thirst is seen as proof of or emphasis on his humanity (3, 6, 11, 23, 31, 45, 46, 47, 53). Jesus requested water at noon, when it was very hot (41). This means he did not present himself as a rabbi but as a tired and thirsty human being (41). Water cannot be denied to anybody, not even to an enemy (Jew versus Samaritan) or a stranger (6).

Jesus was not arrogant (41). He belonged to the common people and made a humble request (6, 24). The water was not offered to him; he had to ask for it (41). He needed a helping hand when he begged for water (46). He never said thank you for the water (41).

On the contrary, some were of the opinion that because Jesus is God he should not have asked something from the woman; he could not have been in need of anything a human can give (23).

Because Jesus said that those who drink will be thirsty again, he must also have been referring to physical water at least part of the time (57). The woman, expecting a material solution, was confused and surprised, and the conversation ran for a while on different levels (1, 2, 4, 14, 23, 30, 42, 44, 47, 53). Clearly, the Samaritan woman thought the living water was ordinary water (23).

Physical, tangible water: Dynamic

Many reports gave physical water an extra dimension in their discussions. A Dutch nature magazine characterized living water as water with life in it. That water can be dynamic—full of movement and life giving—often surfaces in the reading reports. Living water is contrasted to still, dead water in which things begin to rot (36). Living water does not dry up (36); it cannot be staunched (11). It is a fountain that continues to flow (36); it bubbles (35), is fresh and flowing (9, 26, 36), babbles, and sparkles (36, 44). Flowing, living water in a river in South Africa makes the pebbles lying in it look beautiful (35).

When he spoke of living water, Jesus was referring to rolling water (35), which moves and flows and gives life (36). It is a vital and necessary fluid (12), without which life is not possible (36). Water is life! (1, 6, 8).

The woman responded to the offer of living water as though it were an impossible offer in a fairy tale (40). The woman understood Jesus to be speaking of some source of flowing, living water, by means of which she would never again physically need to drink (9), because it would be like a spring within her (57). If there would be such water that could quench thirst forever—what a boon that would be! (27). Who would not snatch at the offer of such water? (27).

Under this heading we insert another—to some, unexpected—explanation of water, related to the concept of living water being water with life in it. Jesus's request for water is interpreted as a hidden language, a code, as when a man proposes something to a woman in indirect language (15). The worst part is that the woman answers him as if she wants what he has—water with life in it (15). Who knows whether she wanted a man to take away her economic predicament or just wanted to make out with him (15). The disciples left Jesus alone because they did not want to cramp his style (15). The proof that the disciples already knew Jesus's intentions is that when they returned, they did not ask him anything when they caught him having this conversation with her (15). Jesus, seen as the common or contemporary man, wanted to score with the girl (15). Although he knew the Samaritans to be an impure people, when meeting her alone he still made advances to her (15).

Spiritual, metaphorical water: Static

That the water being spoken of has more than one dimension makes the conversation between Jesus and the Samaritan woman intriguing. As with some groups' comments on physical water, when speaking of water's metaphorical significance, some made comments that express a rather static equivalence, as though an in-group were conversing in terms they assumed all would understand. The tendency then is to express oneself in terms resembling a declaration of faith. Others bring out a more dynamic aspect which is not predefined but open-ended, to be filled in perhaps more individually, according to the personal situation. Quite often, a reading group reports both types of comments. In this section, we present the more static explanations, expressing a packaged equivalent. Although the equivalents in themselves may be understood to be dynamic, they are presented in the discussion as boxed truths. This being the case, it remains true that the distinction between the two cannot always be clearly drawn. Overall, a broad range of possible metaphorical significances of living water is presented.

Water in itself is a symbol of life and death: one can drown in it (35).

Living water is a message: the Word (56, 57), Jesus's words (1, 2, 4, 57), God's Word (3, 5, 19, 25), the message that God gave (57), the Word of everlasting life (3), whose essence is salvation (57). It is good news (12). There is no better news than that of having received Jesus Christ (45). The water Jesus gives is locked up in his words which quench thirst (43). The message of God is spiritual food which feeds us forever (21). The Word must flow in us to affect others (19).

Living water represents the Holy Ghost (44, 46), something rising above everything else (44). It is the touch of the Spirit (9); it is Jesus in our lives through his Holy Spirit (47). This presence is achieved by confessing Christ as our Lord and

Savior (47). The living water is spiritual satisfaction, being filled with God, by the joy of the Spirit which is Christ himself (47).

Living water is salvation (20, 30, 45, 46) for poor people (4), redemption for the world (13). The water Jesus offered her was the water of salvation, of eternal life, a link to God (6). Eternal life can be received through the Word of God and not through water (23). Living water is life everlasting (1); it is the gift of God (33). Jesus used water as a symbol of eternal life (54, 57). He offered to give eternal life, the spring of eternal water (5, 57). Only Jesus can give living water; to have some of it, we must read the Bible and do his will (23).

Living water is an image of personal faith (44). It is a source of inspiration: living water must be ingested; it gives inspiration to live on (44). The living water that Jesus Christ offers is spiritual; it saves, and sets us free (4). It is Jesus himself (1, 44, 46). Jesus gave himself to the world as living water (23, 35). He is the spring of life; whoever takes it will never be thirsty (24). He showed that he is the Savior the world is expecting (24). The spiritual water Jesus offered is meeting him in an encounter with the living God who comes and shows him to be the Messiah (56). When the woman made a turnabout and went back to her village to share the good news, the living water with which she quenched her thirst was the revelation that Jesus is the Messiah (29). Living water is the secret of the Messiah and God's kingdom, which is not revealed to everyone (35). It is an expression of the values of the kingdom (1), a symbol of the kingdom of God (36), Jesus's announcement of the kingdom (1).

The material, flowing water the woman thought Jesus was offering her is compared to a superficial knowledge of Christ, to looking for him in churches, looking for wonderful healings, for something supernatural to believe in instead of real life, the well of living water (9). Going to church to request help when you are having problems is like the Samaritan woman wanting the water so she would not have to carry water anymore (5). Activities on important days in the church can quench spiritual thirst, but Jesus was talking of spiritual salvation (20).

Stagnant water is like consumerism (56); it is unsatisfying. You need to go back to it over and over again, because you are dependent on it (56). The water the woman came to draw is the daily grind—sleeping, eating, consuming. Jesus offered her a way out of this routine (56). Living water is a metaphor for spiritual sustenance versus material preoccupation (49). That woman was materialistic, and we too are interested in material things much more than in the will of the Lord (5). The woman was looking for worldly things: riches, fame, and health (20).

In the dialogue, Jesus unites two cultures (Jewish and Samaritan), using as a symbol the water that is life (17).

The conversation between Jesus and the woman was about living a better life (20). The story was about salvation and the work of God (22)—that she should stop sinning and start life afresh (30).

By saying that "he whom you now have is not your husband," Jesus told her in no uncertain terms that he is God and she could not fool around with him, trying to have a relationship with him at that moment (30).

Water is shorthand for sexual morality. The well was the place where men and women meet. Fetching water was an excuse for other things (55).

Spiritual, metaphorical water: Dynamic

In John 4, the interaction between Jesus and the Samaritan woman is dynamic, moving swiftly from physical attributes to spiritual dimensions. In this section, we gather comments that indicate change and movement—a dynamic development taking us to God knows where.

Living water is a spring which is Jesus's presence within us and is always alive (1). Jesus adopts symbolic language, because what is inside is unutterable and can only be made known through symbols (1). The woman passed from the basic need for water, to a desire for an unfathomable fountain of water, and finally to water that springs up to life eternal (1). Jesus offered a fountain of fresh, living water to fill the soul and life, which flows and overflows—fresh water expressed in all our being (47).

Living water is the substance of God that enters believers; this water comes forth from the power of Christ, that excellent power of God that is given us (47). It is like a fountain that flows and fills us and quenches our thirst; it is a fountain that flows like a river of living water (46).

With the living water, we are to be together, living as brothers and sisters, to calm this thirst which only he can satisfy (1). One must satiate one's thirst and then give the water to others (1). To do the will of the Father is to calm thirst and hunger (1).

The issue here is happiness: the well continues nourishing you, and you continue drinking from it until the end of life (41). In time, you understand more and more, but you will continue to be thirsty and long for more (41). We must always ask ourselves what it is that flows from our rivers of "long life" water: is it love, comprehension, and solidarity with others, or something else entirely? (18).

Jesus is the spring of life (2). Jesus speaks of drinking water from the spring of everlasting life (4). We are never far from the well of eternity that God offers us (4). There is a thirst that can be filled with living water, and it is offered only by Jesus (4).

Jesus's conversation with the woman was aimed at causing her to know the truth about life (1). Although at first she was suspicious, she began to ask questions, called him "Lord" three times, asked for the living water, and called him a prophet (1). She felt special when she noticed that she was not wanted as a woman, as an object, but as a person, as a human, thirsty not only for water but also for the knowledge of how to change her life (45). The Lord captivated her; she was completely new (45).

Jesus was showing the woman that the water he was talking about purifies from every sin; when we drink that water, we no longer have to seek for solutions in ourselves or in material things (9).

Living water is a confrontation with a certain way of life; it is conversion, change, a possibility for cultural exchange, a challenge (12). The adjective *living* gives an important nuance to the phrase (12). It means renovation, cleanliness, movement, durability, dynamism, happiness, and liveliness (12).

The deepest meaning of the story is that a change of identity took place: the one who drinks what Jesus gives to drink will be reborn into everlasting life (35). This change is symbolized by drawing water from the well (35). Why do we strangely always try to keep our feet dry? (35).

Jesus offers what the woman finds unbelievable—a spring of water welling up to eternal life (33). Eternity is the source of everlasting life: a promise is implied; temporal becomes eternal (35). The whole story tells how one changes from stranger into friend; the stranger turns out to be the source, the living water (35).

This exchange is about spiritual matters, about the water of life, an inner fountain (26). It is about the way to God: Jesus finds us and approaches us (26). He is the one who arouses the longing for living water (26). He reveals our existence (26). Jesus himself is the well from which one has to draw inspiration (41).

The dialogue between Jesus and the woman is about spiritual matters of a different dimension—spirit and truth (36). It is about water, about worshiping (42). The well of eternal life means worshiping God in spirit and in truth (56). Then the divided families will no longer discriminate but will be united (56). Maybe "spirit and truth" describes the means by which these barriers no longer signify anything (56). The water Jesus offered was in contrast to the division he encountered between the Jews and Samaritans, between men and women (8). Living water is the Holy Spirit through which Jesus condemned the segregation between Samaritans and Jews; the Spirit breaks through the bonds of discrimination (49). We must act as Jesus did: he sat down at the well to break down walls (2).

When Jesus began to speak of living water, the woman understood that he was referring to something "greater" than the water from the well that Jacob had dug for them (36). He takes her a step further: first from a well to a spring, then from a spring to something by which you never thirst again—step by step (36). The Lord took her little by little to the kingdom of God (45); he persisted with her until eternal life (54). He took her to a spiritual level, pushed her to raise her consciousness, her human state; he took her toward repenting (47). In this way, he wanted her to receive the living water that he is (47). He was opening her mind, giving her a new vision (47). The change came when Jesus told her of the life-giving water that he could give her, the water that would be like a bubbling fountain that gives eternal life (54).

The woman was confronted with something that was not perishable: Jesus conducted her to the source, to something that would be transcendent in her life—Jesus himself, who is that living water which does not stagnate, but flows like a stream and is within our being (46).

The woman did not go back and announce that there was living water at the well, but that there was somebody who told her everything about herself, who knew all about her (54). Jesus makes unknown things known, using something tangible to illustrate things unseen: life everlasting (55). Jesus is revealed as Christ through the interaction—water to living water (29). She came to draw water but went back to share the person she had met (29). The Samaritan woman returned to the village carrying the fresh and true message of the gospel of Jesus (12).

This story is a universal story with a deeper meaning, a different story underneath (42). What you are looking for outside yourself, you have to find within yourself (37). The message of the story lies underneath and is not apparent at first (37). There is a deeper level to this story—you have to drill a well within yourself; do not wait for others to do it (37).

Understanding Jesus's use of symbols is not so much a matter of catching on to riddles as a question of feeling, of experiencing how he comes to you, in a relationship (40). Jesus wanted to go above and beyond water to the real essence of what life is really all about (40). If you are fed by the Spirit, you will have no desire for everyday matters (40).

Jesus speaks about the fountain of spiritual water that comes from within a person, that sustains people to eternal life (49). The living water Jesus provides gives life even in the midst of physical drought (49). Jesus as living water is an eternal spiritual truth (49).

The living water that Jesus offers is good for us, body and spirit; it makes us whole (35). It is the spiritual peace the woman needed at that moment (45). It is the gift of God to a needy heart, to a life that yearns for peace and calmness (46). Jesus offered what refreshes the soul of the spirit, what the Samaritan woman wanted to learn (32). She was thirsty and open to something new (7). In general, humankind hungers after spiritual, inner peace (26).

Water represents gratefulness; it is a life devoted to another person (6). It is the water of the love for our neighbors, which gives eternal life (6). It has everything to do with happiness, a kind of perpetual feeling of well-being (37, 47), because he is living within us (47). You know you are not alone; there is a God who cares for you (37). You feel good about yourself; you feel things are going well for you in your life (37). When you are not really happy, you are always looking for something in your life; you are always thirsty (37). Living water is about where to find happiness (37).

The core of faith is full of movement; it moves with what occurs about you in society and does not remain the same from one generation to another (36). Living water babbles and sparkles and is thus a picture of faith (36). When there is dialogue about the Word of the Lord, everything changes and transforms into a new reality: the dialogue breaks all obstacles (47).

Jesus challenges us to build a new story, a story of the kingdom (56). It is a mystery how that happens; it is incomprehensible, unless you are actually touched by it (56). The woman goes to the well to get water and ends up leaving with something totally different (56). He asks her for something and ends up giving her something (56).

Living water in the Old Testament

When Jesus spoke of "living water," he did not coin a new term. Images of thirst as longing and water as satisfaction and fulfillment are to be found throughout the Old Testament. "To those who are thirsty I will give from the spring of the living water, without any cost" (4); (cf. Isa. 55:1). There is the promise that people will take joyfully from the spring of salvation (4); (Isa. 12:3).

Old Testament passages compare the longing for God to the thirst for water; the woman did not have access to the source where that was written (54). The longing for God is compared to a hart panting for a water brook (Ps. 42:1).

Isaiah 55:1 says, "All who are thirsty, come to me and drink water." God is speaking through the prophet Isaiah, but the water is not just a liquid, because Isaiah does not talk about food, or about money, or about a whole lot of material things (46).

The exact expression "living water" occurs nine times in the Old Testament, and many of the shades of meaning contained in the intercultural reading reports are also present in these texts.

In Genesis 26:19, we read that Isaac's servants dug a well in a wadi and found there a spring or well of living water. In Leviticus and Numbers, we read of various offerings that are to be made over living water, and of purification rituals in which one is to wash in living water (Lev. 14:5, 50; 15:13; Num. 19:17). In Jeremiah, we read of the Lord complaining that his people had left him, the fountain or source of living water (Jer. 2:13; 17:13). In Zechariah 14:8, the prophet speaks of a future time when living waters will flow out of Jerusalem, half of them flowing to the eastern sea and half to the western sea. Finally, in Song of Solomon 4:15, living water is part of the description of the bride: a fountain of gardens, a well of living waters, streams from Lebanon.

These Old Testament references provide the background for Jesus's use of the term in his conversation with the Samaritan woman. In these references, living water refers to water with movement in it, which bubbles up and provides drink to the thirsty (Gen. 26:19), and flows plentifully (Zech. 14:8). Living water in its ritual usage refers to its purity and cleanliness (Lev. 14:5, 50; 15:13; Num. 19:17). In Jeremiah (2:13; 17:13), living water is clearly metaphorical, referring to a lasting source of what is essential to spiritual well-being. In Song of Solomon 4:15, the reference can hardly be understood otherwise than sexually, referring to the physical response to lovemaking. Thus, all the references to living water in the Old Testament contain a dynamic dimension (living), and can be divided between the physical and the metaphorical dynamic aspects.

To some reading groups, it was surprising that the partner group made reference to possible sexual connotations in the water imagery of John 4, yet in the Old Testament the term *living water* is used exactly in this way. This is perhaps something to think about.

Extra dimensions

A number of comments in the reading reports are so vitally connected to the theme of water that it would be a pity to miss the extra relief they bring to the whole. These are dealt with consecutively and are not necessarily interrelated.

Thirst

The way these groups translate the meaning into current existential terms reveals that there is no cut-and-dried formula for understanding what satisfies. They voice longings relating both to personal needs and to the needs of others.

We thirst to be known and accepted and received (57). We thirst for time for one another, for discovering all that one is receiving, for giving thanks (1). We thirst that all days would be worth living, that we might be called to action, that we might be a church more dedicated to the people and to the poor (1).

Jesus talks of "long life water" that goes beyond natural thirst and refers to satisfying a primal need, keenly felt by people of that era, just as in our days (16). The Word of God is a stream of living water (19). It can quench our thirst and answer many of our perennial needs (29). The Word of God is like water that calms thirst—the personal problems—and gives rest (5). To be spiritually nourished in this way would answer our basic problems (29).

There is a thirst that those in power might find living water to be able to attain justice for those who are hungry, oppressed, humiliated, marginalized; there is a thirst for bread for the tables, roofs for homes (1). There is a thirst for love, solidarity with the needy a thirst for human values (1), for justice (1, 2), for respect and dignity; a thirst to have peace and to not suffer any more (1). Thirst is the troubles people have (2).

Jesus offers water that soothes the thirst for justice and love so that the Father's plan may be fulfilled (17). The greatest thirst is the necessity of Christ coming inside each heart (45).

If we take the conversation as an illustration of prayer, then thirst is the longing for what is true, for love (36). There is an inner awareness that there is something we will never fully know, but for which we long; we thirst to know more and more, and we experience a kind of homesickness (36).

Living water is the only thing that can satiate our thirst (1).

The interaction

Although it may seem logical that Jesus's request for water be related to his thirst, his request evoked a whole spectrum of associations relating to the question of what type of interpersonal transaction was involved. His request is seen as an opening to make contact, to establish a relationship (36), a means of linking up with the woman's situation (18, 45, 47, 54, 56). Asking for something that was in her power to grant created an opening (45).

This was an authentic request for a drink, not just a ploy to get her to do something (56). Jesus did not just drop the term *living water* on her (56). It was a real encounter, not just God being patronizing (56). In contrast, one group said that if his intention was to start a conversation, the request for water delayed matters, because water had to be given before a conversation could be begun (41).

The authenticity and power lay in the relationship (56). Jesus and the woman both shared with each other about themselves (22). He was seeking congeniality and acknowledgement by this woman: she was someone who did not fit in, and he also did not fit in (41).

When he asked for water, she was only preoccupied with the prejudice she had against the Jews (45). The woman initially treated Jesus with hostility, as a stranger; she was furious at the start (23). Although Jews and Samaritans did not associate, Jesus had to associate with the woman because he had no bucket (41). Petitioning her for a service was an approach that revealed Jesus to be unprejudiced toward the Samaritans (47). Jesus loves everybody the same—he does not look at differences in sex or color (45). Jesus was aware that Samarians and Jews were not on good terms, yet he asked for water in order to help remove the bad relations between them (20).

The woman was suspicious because this stranger was talking to her (15). She was at first taken aback (1, 4, 6, 36, 52) and responded rather mockingly: "You, a Jew, speak to me? And you ask me for water?" (57). By mentioning the issue of discrimination, she was confirming whether it was really his intention to make this request (27). She was used to being on the defensive; the hour at which she went to the well shows that she did not want dealings with anyone, that she was tired of being accosted and criticized (18).

The Samaritan woman's explicit confrontation of Jesus as a Jew enabled Jesus to think, "Yes, that is who I am" (41). Actually he was not engaged in conversation with her, but her response helped him rediscover himself (41). By her reaction, Jesus regained himself and could continue his mission (41). He really needed her (41).

The woman felt unworthy to give Jesus a drink, because of her way of life and because of being a Samaritan (40). Jesus may have had a historical bias against Samaria, but he was a quiet and open person, brave in a way to cross over this boundary (34). Jesus asked for water to break the silence (33).

Some groups found Jesus brusque and demanding in saying, "Give me a drink" (42). As a stranger, he could have asked her: "Could I have something to drink, please?" or: "Can you get some water for me?" (43). The words used are interpreted as a display of power and authority, talking down to a woman, and a Samaritan at that (43).

Other participants found this interpretation of the question disturbing; the suggestion was made that the phrasing is the result of a less than adequate translation (43). Some countries, such as France, would use the imperative in this way, but in some languages another translation would have been better (42). It was also pointed out that the Lord's Prayer speaks in imperatives (42). Still others, presuming Jesus to be kind, interpret the manner of speaking as mere directness of approach, not meant sternly (43). The masterful tone Jesus used was intended to make the woman understand that he had a lot to say: He was no ordinary male (43). He wanted her to listen to him (43).

By means of the request, Jesus sought an opportunity to speak of nonmaterial things, to progress on to talking about the kingdom, about invisible things (36). He asked for a drink in order to initiate a dialogue with her and to carry her along the paths that he desired (1). It is a serious conversation, in which Jesus told the woman her secrets and introduced himself as the spring of life (24). The woman wanted water badly and came at an odd hour to get it (29). Jesus addressed her need (29). If one is to reach others, needs must be addressed (29). Jesus, being God, knew who she was and wanted to minister to her (33). He wanted to show her who he was (40). Because the Lord initiated the contact, the woman had the right to ask him to give her some of the water (19).

Her confusion was intensified when he asked about her husband. Because of the social structure, her husband would properly be the one to give permission to grant Jesus's request for water (54). It was a patriarchal society, so it was necessary for Jesus to ask to speak to the head of the family (46).

We do not know whether the woman was mocking Jesus, or whether she saw the possibility of liberating herself from returning to the place that only reminded her that she was marginalized and criticized by her people, when she said to Jesus: "Sir, give me this water, so I may never be thirsty or have to keep coming here to draw water" (18). The response of the woman is described by some as sarcastic, as though Jesus's offer were a joke: "Yeah, right. Give me that living water, so I don't need to go to the well" (4).

Others thought her interest in the living water was primarily related to saving herself the trouble of going the distance to the well at noon and having to draw and carry the water pots. It was a shortcut for getting her water supply (6, 33, 40, 43, 47), so she would not be thirsty (29, 47). She looked for a favor from God to make a profit (47).

Not all associations that groups saw in the relationship between Jesus and the woman were platonic. Perhaps Jesus was using the excuse of wanting water to enter into some kind of relationship with the woman (55). He behaved suspiciously (55). He might have been waiting at the well while the disciples went into town because he wanted to propose love to the woman (the well or the river are places for proposing love) (55).

The well

To many groups, a well brought back memories from childhood and anecdotes from more recent times. When traveling and in need of water, one goes to rest by a well, because there water is not bought or sold but is given freely (5). Where there are no water pipes, one can see passers-by coming to a well and asking for water (40).

Wells are still used for water supply, but in some areas the water needs to be checked, because of the heavy infiltration of chemicals from industry (8).

Some translations of this story in John refer both to a well and to a spring. A well, fed by ground water, has less movement than a spring does, but it is not like a swamp, where things rot (36). The water in a spring bubbles up of its own accord, but water has to be drawn up from a well (42). A well often has negative connotations, while a spring is positive, although both have to do with underground water and water pressure (42). Most of the time, wells have walls and are man-made (42).

Within the passage, the well was where the story took place, the central spot in the story (14, 42). The well is important as a source of water, where physical thirst can be quenched, and in this story spiritual thirst as well (12, 57).

A well is a place where people meet one another (3, 8, 12, 35, 41, 42), where dialogues are begun (8). The well in the story was a sacred place where he met her (3); it was placed there by God as a meeting point for the Samaritan woman and Jesus (57). The well was a place where men and women met (55). It is one of the few places in early times where boys and girls could meet each other (42). It is a place where you can find your bride-to-be (42). This association leads to the suggestion that the woman in this story is the bride of Jesus (42).

The identity of the well as Jacob's well merited some attention. A group that consulted the story of Jacob in Genesis found no reference to this well (8). The reference is perhaps to the patriarchs in general, because Jacob himself does not seem to have dug the well (54). It was on a piece of land that was owned by Jacob (54). Reference is made to the fact that while in Egypt, Jacob gave a piece of land in Canaan to Joseph, but Joseph never occupied that land himself, because he died in Egypt (36).

The mention of Jacob and Joseph indicates the importance of the relationship to the tradition of the people there (14, 34, 43). The fact that the well was associated with the ancestor Jacob—and thus symbolized the cultural heritage of that time and place—provided occasion for a discussion about the confrontation between the culture of Jesus and traditional African beliefs (51).

We also have a well, but it is deep and dry, and the fountain is already old: we have water that is left behind, a dry well, because we do not look for the true living water that Christ has (47). We get to know the gospel and after a while take it for granted (47). Then we have that deep, dry, old well inside (47).

This well is symbolic: the people in the story all have needs, and the well is a place to meet basic needs, things that are not optional (56). The well was the place to look for the solution (2). Some equivalents to Jacob's well in our own lives are a bed, a job, or a store, a bar or a crack house, a help center that provides basics to the needy (56). It is different for everyone (56). What is your ultimate concern, the thing to which you give most of your attention? (56). Jesus came to that place: the Lord comes where we are, and meets us in our place of greatest need (56). That physical place could be anywhere (56).

The water jar

The water jar enters the story as an obstacle that the woman perceives as standing in the way of Jesus's offer of water: how could he draw water to give to her if he did not have a bucket? (23, 47, 57).

The woman's objection is explained as an illustration of how excuses are presented when the possibility of a new challenge or an opportunity for change presents itself (6). She was suspicious of his offer (1). She was quite right in asking how Jesus would provide living water if he himself had nothing with which to draw water (27). The fact of the matter is, she—not he—had a water pot in her hands (57). She had the tools for drawing water out of the well (45). There is no doubt that his disciples had a bucket of water and had taken it with them; that is why the woman noted that he did not have anything with which to draw water out of the deep well (4). Her question about the water jar could also be an indication that she was already wondering about what type of water he could be referring to (57).

The task of going to fetch water in an earthen pot is one with which not a few communities could identify: the scene is culturally so evident as to be taken as a matter of fact (52). This chore is traditionally one assigned to women (45, 49). The task is felt to be an expression of poverty, something shaming, from which they should be freed (49).

As the story progresses, the woman leaves her water jar behind. The water jar is seen as a symbol of the things from which the woman needed to be liberated (45). The change began when she faced her own reality, i.e., the immorality and the complete lack of dignity in her life (4). The woman left behind her water jar and her sins (46, 52), from which she repented (26, 52); she was converted (26). The water jar symbolized the burden of existence, the wrong things in her life (52). She left her jealousy and discrimination behind (52). This act of leaving the decanter behind invites us to leave behind the concrete reality in our life that prevents us from proclaiming: "You are my Lord" (16).

When she left the vessel, she liberated herself from all that oppressed and marginalized her, all that reminded her of her sadness (18). Now free and without bonds, she goes to share the good news (18). The woman believed she would find what she needed with men, but she could not find the fountain of life there (47). Only Christ could cure and satiate her thirst (47). She left her jar and ran to tell the men, who supposedly were her lovers: "There is a man . . . ," the only one who can fulfill the emptiness, quench that thirst, and satisfy that need (47).

Her act is interpreted as positive, a new beginning. The woman no longer needed her water jar: she was satisfied, she had received living water—Jesus himself (26). Now that Jesus had told her that he had living sustenance, the jar was no longer important (37). She left it as the apostles had left their nets (1). This symbolic act refers to the satisfaction of receiving water in more than the direct and material sense of the word (12, 45).

She returned to her house without her water pot, because she wanted to share her extraordinary experience as quickly as possible (4). The menial task of carrying water became secondary to her new calling of proclaiming the gospel (49). The woman left her bucket and went to tell about the Messiah: "He has told me everything I have ever done!" (52). The turning point is when the woman left her jar (42). The woman did not draw water; she even left her jar (42). She had become a well herself—Jesus, as the living water was sufficient for her (42). The woman forgot her urn (44). She who first looked for solitude made a turnabout and went to visit the other women in the village to tell of meeting Jesus (44).

A more pragmatic approach remarks: it seems this woman was a vagrant, because she roamed the streets talking to men, leaving the decanters cast aside—and decanters were expensive (15).

Did Jesus or the woman actually get a drink?

A final aspect that surfaced in the discussions is the question of whether Jesus or the woman actually got something to drink. It is interesting that of those that mention the matter, most of the reports surveyed agree that Jesus did not get something to drink, while the majority agree that the woman did partake of the living water offered to her. Although we are told that Jesus asked for water, it is not mentioned whether he really got some (38, 56). She does not give him water, and he does not give her living water (41). They are talking about it, but an exchange of water never took place (41). The fact that the woman left her water pot behind indicates that Jesus had not yet drunk (35), perhaps inferring that the woman left the water pot so he could draw some water.

One clear reason given for why Jesus did not get water had to do with discrimination. The woman did not give Jesus a drink because Jewish people do not have dealings with Samaritans (4). The fact that Jews as the dominant, oppressing class were intimidating meant that she was not willing to give Jesus water (30, 31). Jesus met a woman at the well and begged her for some water, but the woman refused to give it to him (25). The woman's refusal to give Jesus a drink did not, however, hinder him from going on to talk about the gift of God (33).

Christ did not receive the water (46). The most urgent priority at that moment for Jesus was to spread the gospel (46). Although there was a true physical necessity—he had swallowed dust and it was summer—his first priority was to bring salvation (46). He was thirsty to execute the plan of salvation for her life (47). During the dialogue with the Samaritan, Christ did not drink the water, but he probably did after his disciples arrived (46).

If this woman had known who was asking her for a drink, she would have given it to him, but because she did not know, she withheld it from him (45).

A minority concluded the opposite: Jesus asked the Samaritan woman for a drink, and she did not deny him the water (16). The woman gave Jesus water, but she also accepted him as the one who could truly free her from her predicament: she accepted the spiritual dimension of life (24). The same report stated that because the woman refused him water, Jesus wanted her to know the sort of person he is—that he is the Savior and works through the Spirit (24).

Did the woman drink the spiritual water? Except for the comment mentioned above that no exchange of water took place, the reports are unanimous: Yes! She put down her vessel, the inference being that she had no more need of it, and left (56). The simple fact that she went back to town to tell what had happened to her meant that she had already drunk the living water: she had come for water, indispensable to life, and she left her water jar behind (57).

Conclusions

This has been only a partial survey of a selection from the reading reports. Relatively, the most attention was devoted to the request for physical water and to the dynamic metaphorical significances of living water. A bridge between these two is provided by the term *living,* which in the Old Testament was used to refer both to physical water and to its metaphorical dimensions.

In this collage of insights and impressions, the degree of identification that some groups have with the physical context of the story of John 4 is noteworthy. We mention two aspects: the fact that the woman came to draw water, and the water source as a place of encounter for men and women. These points of identification lead to interpreting the story in direct relation to the situation known to the readers. The chore of having to draw and carry water is seen as degrading, something from which she (and all women) should be liberated. The water source as a meeting place for men and women led to more than one comment on what the implications are for the contact between Jesus and the Samaritan woman.

The most extensive treatment of water was in its metaphorical, dynamic aspect. It is here that faith takes wings. Clearly, symbols enable one to speak of dimensions beyond the physical. In this area, metaphors are essential, to help express what is unutterable. The comments of the groups reflect being lifted by faith beyond the daily run-of-the-mill existence.

It has not been the intention of this contribution to trace the various insights offered by the reading groups to socioeconomic, geographical, or political factors, or to church affiliation. Rather, we aimed at collecting a broad sampling and collating the comments under the headings as here presented, in an attempt to bring forward the complementary potential of the worldwide reading community.

We are blessed indeed with the wealth of insights shared from around the world. No single group could have captured the breadth and depth brought forward in the worldwide effort.

List of reading reports included

1. Argentina: Santa Cruz BEC, Buenos Aires
2. Bolivia: Comunidad Bet-El, La Paz

3. Bolivia: El Mesías Methodist women's group, La Paz
4. Bolivia: Aymara/Quechua group Jerusalem, La Paz
5. Bolivia: Los Amigos, La Paz
6. Brazil: Bairro das Rosas, Estância Velha
7. Brazil: Centro de Estudos Bíblicos, or CEBI (Ecumenical Center of Biblical Studies), Mato Grosso do Sul
8. Brazil: Feitoria Evangelical Lutheran Congregation, São Leopoldo
9. Brazil: Second Presbyterian Church of Porto Alegre, Rio Grande do Sul
10. Cuba: Alamar group, outskirts of Havana
11. Cuba: Matanzas group
12. Cuba: Sancti Spiritus group
13. Cuba: Santo Suárez group, Havana
14. Cuba: Seminario Evangélico de Teología, or SET (Evangelical Theological Seminary), Matanzas
15. El Salvador: Bartolomé de las Casas men, San Salvador
16. El Salvador: Dolores neighborhood, San Salvador
17. El Salvador: San Rafael Cedros group
18. El Salvador: Shekiná Baptist Church, Santa Ana
19. Ghana: Ashiyie Presbyterian Church group
20. Ghana: Elmina Presbyterian Church women's group
21. Ghana: Elmina Presbyterian Church men's group
22. Ghana: Victory Presbyterian Church English group, Frafraha, suburb of Accra
23. Ghana: Komenda Presbyterian group
24. Ghana: Victory Presbyterian Church Twi group, Frafraha, suburb of Accra
25. Ghana: Abetifi youth group
26. Hungary: Balatonszárszó group
27. India: Dalit women's group, prisoner families
28. India: Shoolagiri Dalit group
29. India: Syrian Christian group, Chennai (Madras)
30. India: Perambur transsexuals group, Chennai (Madras)
31. India: Uthiramerur group, near Chennai (Madras)
32. Indonesia: students of the Theological Seminary of Eastern Indonesia Macassar (Sekolah Tinggi Teologia di Indonesia Bagian Timur, STT INTIM), Macassar, South Sulawesi
33. Kenya: New Seventh Day Adventists, Kisii
34. Korea: Hanil University theology students
35. Netherlands: Amstelveen
36. Netherlands: Amsterdam Johannes Groep
37. Netherlands: Andijk

38. Netherlands: Apeldoorn
39. Netherlands: Appingedam
40. Netherlands: Arnhem
41. Netherlands: Zaandam
42. Netherlands: Zaandam ecumenical base community (Oekumenische Werkplaats Zaandam, OWZ)
43. Netherlands: Zutphen
44. Netherlands: Zwijndrecht
45. Nicaragua: Filadelfia Baptist Church, Masaya
46. Nicaragua: Centro Intereclesial de Estudios Teológicos y Sociales, or CIEETS (Interchurch Center for Theological and Social Studies) students
47. Nicaragua: Novia del Cordero, Managua
48. Scotland: Craigend group, Glasgow
49. South Africa: Durban group
50. South Africa: Ivory Park Methodist young people, township near Midrand (Gauteng)
51. South Africa: Siyaphila Bible Study, a support group for people living with HIV/AIDS, near Pietermaritzburg
52. South Africa: Sokhanya Bible School, near Cape Town
53. South Africa: Stellenbosch men
54. South Africa: Stellenbosch women
55. South Africa: Young Christian Workers group, near Pietermaritzburg
56. USA: The People's Seminary lay pastor training program, Burlington, Washington
57. USA: The People's Seminary Mexican women, Burlington, Washington

Codes and coding

Hans de Wit

Biblical scholars are trained in the analysis of biblical texts. Empirical research on how contemporary readers deal with Bible texts demonstrates affinity with exegesis in some components. Careful analysis of texts by means of questions is also essential in this research. The reception-critical empirical research that has to be carried out in the Through the Eyes of Another project is different in that the list of questions that must be asked about the texts at hand must be expanded. Another new aspect is the comparative component, the interaction between groups, and the fact that contemporary readers are involved.

One of the objectives of the project was to check whether it was possible to find significant correlations between a certain group profile, the interpretation of John 4, and the subsequent interaction with the partner group. Would it be possible to make a statement based on this process about factors that could lead to success or failure in intercultural communication? To be able to answer this question, a new analytical instrument had to be designed.

The difficulties that present themselves are legion. In addition to the fact that this type of research is undeveloped terrain for exegetes, the research material at hand—reading reports of groups from different cultures—is exceptionally diverse. The composition of groups changes; reports are not of a uniform nature; groups have different styles of leadership; the issue of translation plays a role; the level of education and the social position of participants in the interpretation process are different. Therefore, every conclusion must be modest and provisional.

That reading reports could actually be analyzed—coded—and compared has to do with the fact that reporters were asked to maintain a certain format. In this sense, the material to be analyzed also has a certain uniformity. A number of ques-

Hans de Wit, Faculty of Theology, Free University (Amsterdam, the Netherlands)

tions were answered, and it was possible to draw some cautious conclusions. Reading reports could be tested for color, as it were. The questions to which they were subjected helped. These questions were intended to expose the salient features of the reading reports. They helped create a relief map revealing certain constants and characteristics of the reading reports. Sensitivity for what was actually written, how groups dealt with the text, and how they subsequently related to each other, was intensified.

In this contribution, I intend to discuss the research methods we used. In spite of all the difficulties, it is vital that we take steps in the area of empirical research. Many biblical scholars who read the Bible "with the people" scarcely recognize the importance of this type of research. Yet careful systematic analysis of the material is the only way to find answers to hermeneutic and theological questions that are essential to the Through the Eyes of Another project. These questions include: What is the effect of reading the Bible on social transformation? What is the relationship between culture and interpretation? Is there a close correlation between church affiliation and reading attitude? How is change in perspective affected? What leads groups to "freeze" or "unfreeze" their own religious insights?

I will discuss the following elements. First, I will present the format the reading reports had to comply with. Next, I will discuss the background and application of the method of reading report analyses used, and I will give some examples. In conclusion, I will discuss the code lists used for coding the texts. Examples of these will also be presented.

The format

Participating groups could make use of prepared models—formats—for making the meeting reports. I will limit myself to describing the formats of the reports that were used as empirical material for the researchers. I will begin by describing the first phase—specifically, the place of the research in the first phase—and the formats of the reports. Then, I will do the same for the second phase.

The first phase

The place of research in the first phase of the project. The first phase can be designated by a number of concepts from empirical research. It can be called the *theme phase*, the phase of *exploring territory*, or the *formulating phase*. In this phase, the researcher and the co-actors collect the materials and observe the situation. The researcher is searching for the right categories to use for subdividing the multitude of phenomena, and discovery is the focus. The participants bring up (partial) themes. The theme phase or formulating phase is mainly inductive and exploratory and is characterized by an open method of approach.

The formats for the first phase. The project protocol requested a report of the actual interpretation of John 4, as well as other information that would be of interest to the partner group and to the researchers. The requested information consisted of two parts: a specific description of the sociocultural location of the group and a presentation of the group meeting (report A), with as extensive as possible a report of the interpretation of John 4 (report B).[1]

The project handbook describes the format of report A as follows:

A protocol describes the sociocultural context of the group (length: 3–4 pages). This report will have two focus points and will, as much as possible, include an answer to the following questions:

Biographical information. Where do the members of the group live (country, region, city/village)? How many members does the group have? What are the names of the group members? How many are women/how many are men? How many are married/single? What jobs do the members have? (Are they paid or unpaid?) Where do they meet? How often? How are meetings usually organized? What translation of the Bible do they use? What songs do they sing? (Add examples to report.) How do they pray? What symbolic objects do they bring along? Why do they participate in the Bible study? Can the group send a picture along?

Sociocultural information. To what church or theological tradition do they belong? What is the social position of the members of the group? The location, context, or situation in which the reading process takes place is important. A short historical picture, and politico-socioeconomic information could be considered. How do the members of the group describe their situation? Do the members of the group experience tensions in the social reality they live in? Are there tensions in the church? Are the members among those in power or the powerless? What cultural information do they find important for the partner group? What language/dialect do they speak? What ethnic group do they belong to? What characterizes this group? What historical information does the partner group need access to in order to understand them? (Provide as much information as possible to characterize the group.)

Actual information about the *group process*. Was there a liturgical opening? Were symbolic objects or candles used? Was information about the project given? Were the roles and responsibilities of participants explained? Did the participants begin to trust each other more? Did the group have to be stimulated? Did the group find the process educational, enriching, laborious?

The *interpretation process* is also briefly described in this report: brief reproduction of moments that were theologically charged (associations, God images, questions) and hermeneutically charged (confrontation, conflict, change, choice); the development of the process (the text became more important, people learned from each other). Discussions are summarized in a sentence, moments of uncertainty in a word. Moments of meaningful group dynamics are indicated briefly (laughing, emotion, etc.).

The following text was included for the description of the format of report B, or the group's interpretation of John 4:

The ideal format of a comprehensive report is without doubt a video recording. However, in most cases video recording will not be possible or desirable. An unprejudiced report on the basis of a tape recording (transcript) will in most cases be the best way to reproduce the interpretation process for further analysis.

The reporter will be responsible for the audio recording (verbatim report) and will send this verbatim report to the regional coordination and the regional research team. However, it will not be possible to make both a tape recording and a transcript from it in every case.

Names of participants are only recorded with permission; anonymity is safeguarded.

It is important to add the songs, poems, or stories to the report as supplements.

It is important to add a copy of the Bible translation used (with "back translation" in English or Spanish, if possible).

If the partner group so desires (and it is possible), a copy of the tape recording can be sent along. It may be important for interaction that group A can hear the voices and responses of group B.

The second phase

The research in the second phase of the project. In this phase the theoretical framework must be nourished and refined by analysis of the material obtained from the practical research. What factors play a role when ordinary readers read a Bible text in their own context? What role is played by the culture factor? What differences are there? What factors allow for comparative research? Can a taxonomy of factors be determined? Can factors be subdivided or related to categories (theological, church, social, cultural, gender)? Can they be related to interaction-promoting or interaction-inhibiting factors?

In this phase, the analysis focuses on the intercultural encounter. Now that the groups are talking to each other, the objective of the analysis will shift and be more focused on the question of what the intercultural communication has yielded and whether it has succeeded. A number of guiding questions can be: What factors appeared to obstruct interaction? What factors promoted interaction? What differences are there in response pattern (cognitive, affective, and normative)? What perception does the group have of the differences with the partner group? Is it dealing with these differences in a standard manner? Can we detect any broadening of horizons, or are the groups just hanging on to what is their own? Did the insights of the partner group have any effect, according to the group? Is the text better understood now? Can we detect exchanges and learning? If so, at what level: cognitive, affective, normative?

In the overall research process, this second phase can be characterized as the phase of *exchange* and *approach*. Participants exchange places, trying to look at the text and reality through the eyes of the other group.

From the perspective of practical research this phase can be defined as the *crystallization* or *specification phase*. A conversation is held with the participants (groups) involved, about the factors that appear to be important for intercultural communication. The multitude of components is reduced to workable proportions.

In this phase, the researcher focuses on the structure shown by the differences, on what further potential for interaction is offered by the process. Researchers identify the components in the reading reports that continue to play a role, and consider the place they occupy in the intercultural communication (*sensitizing concepts*). The regional researchers may decide, in consultation with the participants, to select one theme as the principal theme. Research questions and hypotheses that took shape out of the theory are tested against the material obtained. In this phase, a conversation is held about the accuracy of the questions researchers collected during the previous phases. Because of the progress of the research and learning process, this is the time when the researcher concludes open data collection as the principal activity and concentrates on the material now available.

The formats for the second phase. The information requested in the second phase also consisted of two parts: a *summary* of the confrontation with the partner group's interpretation (report A; length 2–3 pages) and a *verbatim reproduction* of the confrontation with the interpretation of the partner group (if possible)—in writing (transcript), or in audio or video format (report B; length not defined).

Report A of the second phase could be structured around the following questions: How did the group respond to the partner group's interpretation? Were people open, surprised, curious, disappointed, interested, etc.? What answer was given to the question of why the partner group read the text differently or in the same way? How did the group respond to questions such as, Are you of the opinion that you must adapt, expand, change your original interpretation of John 4? How? Why?

Report B is a verbatim report of the interpretation of John 4. The instructions for the verbatim report of the first phase applied here as well. For a number of reasons, the verbatim report was not sent to the partner group, but only to regional and central coordination and research teams.

Grounded Theory

The texts that constitute the basic materials of our project demand careful analysis. Texts in the first phase were doubly stratified, as it were. The text in question is a *corporate personality* text—a text produced by several readers—that provides interpretation of a Bible text. The stratification is even more distinct in the second phase: the text is an interpretation of an interpretation of John 4. A new analytical instrument had to be designed. The process uses a method of empirical research that leaves room for the researcher's initial questions and hypotheses but is more inductive than anything else, meaning that it would do justice to the material obtained.

To this end, researchers used a number of insights and methods developed by Barney Glaser and Anselm Strauss and recorded in their Grounded Theory model.[2] The basic assumption of Grounded Theory is summarized as follows: "One does not begin with a theory, then prove it. Rather, one begins with an area of study and what is relevant to that area is allowed to emerge." Grounded Theory opposes the "prevailing dogmatic approach to theory testing." Grounded Theory research begins by focusing on an area of study and gathers data from a variety of sources, including interviews and field observations. Once gathered, the data are analyzed using coding and theoretical sampling procedures. In their work, Glaser and Strauss have argued for the inductive discovery of theory grounded in systematically analyzed data. Their inductive perspective has stemmed in part from their dissatisfaction with the prevalent hypothetico-deductive practice of testing "great man" sociological theories (Brian Haig).

The first phase of this type of qualitative analysis reduces the overwhelming amount of text data by identifying the content of more or less encompassing text segments. Then a code—an abbreviation or name—is attached to this text segment. In what follows, these codes are used as representants of text segments or units of meaning in the text. Fundamentally, this is a process of categorization, where the categories may emerge during text interpretation or may be taken from an already existing category system, depending on the researcher's epistemological orientation. During the second phase, researchers try to reconstruct the text producer's subjective meaning system from the units of meaning in their text data. In the third and final phase, researchers try to infer invariants or general commonalities by comparing individual systems of meaning. Thus, the researcher moves back and forth between theory formation and collecting and revising data. Individual data are conceptualized and processed into categories and propositions (hypotheses) from there.

The reading reports have been coded by means of Atlasti software, especially developed for qualitative text research. One or more codes are attached to the semantic units the texts consist of. The scores on specific codes are the carriers of the main features of the reading report. The report can now be compared with other reports, and correlations can be detected among, for example, the interpretation of

John 4 and extra-linguistic factors such as culture or gender that (co)determine these. Researchers designed a code list for each phase. In the spirit of qualitative research, an attempt was made to preserve a balance between codes (categories) that originate from theory and hypothesis and those based on what is found in the actual reading reports. The issue of dissimilarities in reading reports and groups creates extraordinary complexity. This complexity will naturally have an immediate effect on the coding system. Coded segments of a summary of a reading report have a degree of importance that is different from the importance of coded segments of extensive verbatim reading reports. Therefore, quantitative results must first be validated via careful assessment.

I will clarify how some of this process functions, with the help of a few illustrations. When the code list has been composed, the text of the reading report can be coded. The text and code list are set next to each other (see fig. 1).

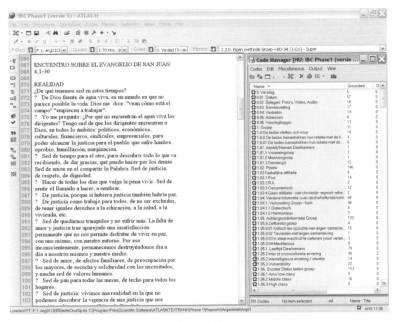

Fig. 1. A Reading report text and a code list.

The researcher goes through the text of the reading report using different research queries each time. Thus, a text segment may be assigned many codes (see fig. 2).

A text segment (*quotation*) can be assigned different codes, because it contains more than one component. This segment may be a combination of question and answer, or a combination of semantic fields, or a segment that requires coding under several categories. Take a simple segment, such as this one from a Bolivian report:

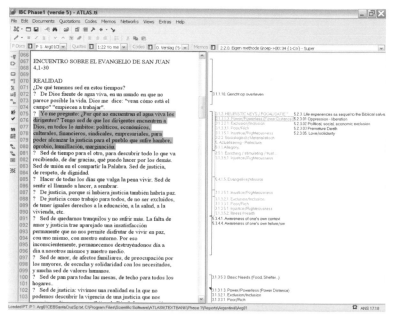

Fig. 2. Coded text.

"'Jews and Samaritans do not deal with one another,' and the woman in that time was rejected. The woman felt afraid. In our society there is social discrimination between woman and man. Jesus paid attention to the woman because she knew the patriarchy very well." It can be coded several times, specifically, under the main category EXPLANATION STRATEGIES by the code *Social-ethnic*; under the category EXPLANATION OF THE TEXT ITSELF under the code *Central concepts/characters in the text*; under the category EXPLANATION OF THE TEXT ITSELF by the code *Relationship between Jews-Samaritans*; under the category EXPLANATION STRATEGIES under *Historical (world behind text), Circumstances of origin, M/F*; and then a few other times under the main category ACTUALIZATION. The result of this process of polysemic coding can also be visually presented as a network. On the left, the quoted phrase from John 4 ("Jews and Samaritans do not deal with one another") can be found, while the attached codes are posted in the spectrum on the right (see fig. 3).

After coding, a reading report or parts of it can be graphically represented and the features of it can be mapped. The frequency of coding of a reading report can be visually represented, and thus a picture, a relief map, can be made that displays the semantic richness of the text. The icon on the left in figure 4 represents a reading report from Argentina; the spectrum consists of all *quotations*, all coded text segments.

Things get interesting when individual or group reading reports can be compared with one another. The software provides the possibility of clustering separate

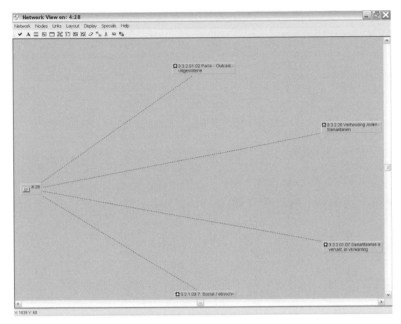

Fig. 3. Network view of coded text.

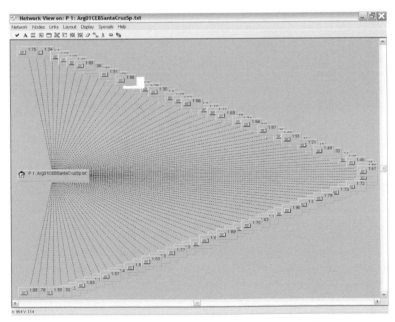

Fig. 4. Network view of a semantically rich Argentinian reading report.

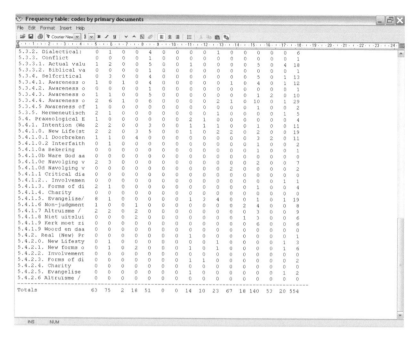

Fig. 5. Comparison of families displaying differences in ACTUALIZATION scores of randomly selected African, Latin American, and Dutch groups.

reading reports into families and of comparing families with one another using certain research queries. Are there any significant differences between African and European groups in scores on the codes (or code families) of culture, actualization (*applicatio*), reading attitude, or focalization? Figure 5 lists five African, five Latin American, and five Dutch groups (randomly selected) next to each other. The horizontal rows represent how groups scored on the codes on the left side of the screen in the main category of ACTUALIZATION. The result has hermeneutic and theological significance. Some groups were very sober; others spent a great deal of time on the question of how the Bible text could be actualized.

Groups may be of the opinion that they brought the process to a good conclusion. In other words, successful ecumenical interaction and intercultural communication took place. We can trace our way back now from the final result; scores of the two groups can be analyzed and compared. We can discover *sensitizing concepts*, factors that have led in a particular way to quality interaction. Next, the process can be repeated with groups that are of the opinion that the interaction with the partner group failed. Comparison of the two processes may result in identification of a number of factors or conditions that may obstruct or stimulate successful intercultural communication. A visual presentation can be made of how groups that are linked scored on certain codes. Differences can be investigated using the query for

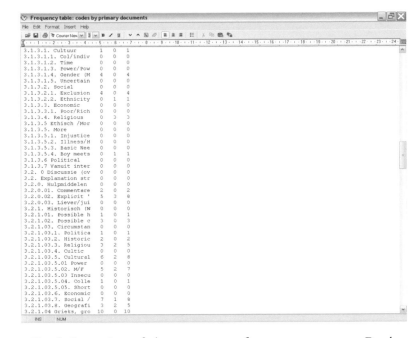

Fig. 6. Comparison of phase one scores of two partner groups, a Dutch group and a Nicaraguan group.

the final result of the interaction. This tool allows the researcher to study all sorts of hermeneutic and theological aspects of interpretations of John 4. Did the perception of what happens in John 4 change after the interaction with the partner group? Does this change in perception have any consequences for the insight into faith or praxis?

Figure 6 presents a score list for two partner groups, a Dutch ecumenical group and a Nicaraguan Pentecostal group. The scores in the first phase diverge a great deal. The Dutch group (column on the far left) spent a lot of time on the text, its historical background, the basic language, and the narrative and rhetorical structure of John 4. This group scores many times higher than the partner group on these components.

Differences in approach to a text and ways of dealing with it can also be expressed in network views.

Figures 7a and 7b show how the Dutch and the Nicaraguan group scored in the EXPLANATION STRATEGIES categories. The differences are immediately obvious. Both groups' reports are about the same length and have the same number of code quotations.

When we look at the actualization of the text, the situation is exactly reversed (see fig. 8). The Nicaraguan group (middle column) now scores the highest.

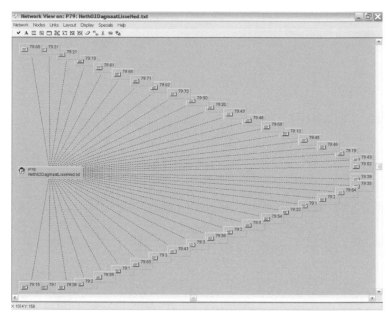

Fig. 7a. Network view of Dutch group's score on EXPLANATION STRATEGIES.

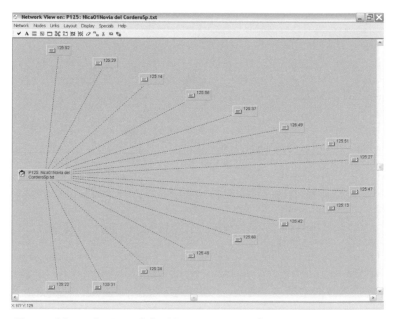

Fig. 7a. Network view of the Nicaraguan group's score on EXPLANATION STRATEGIES.

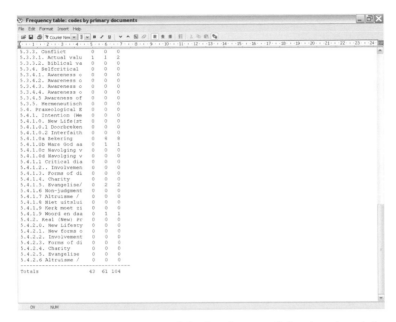

```
File  Edit  Format  Insert  Help
```

```
5.3.3. Conflict          0   0    0
5.3.3.1. Actual valu     1   1    2
5.3.3.2. Biblical va     0   0    0
5.3.4. Selfcritical      0   0    0
5.3.4.1. Awareness o     0   0    0
5.3.4.2. Awareness o     0   0    0
5.3.4.3. Awareness c     0   0    0
5.3.4.4. Awareness o     0   0    0
5.3.4.5 Awareness of     0   0    0
5.3.5. Hermeneutisch     0   0    0
5.4. Praxeological E     0   0    0
5.4.1. Intention (We     0   0    0
5.4.1.0. New Life(st     0   0    0
5.4.1.0.1 Doorbreken     0   0    0
5.4.1.0.2 Interfaith     0   0    0
5.4.1.0a Bekering        0   8    8
5.4.1.0b Ware God aa     0   1    1
5.4.1.0c Navolging v     0   0    0
5.4.1.0d Navolging v     0   0    0
5.4.1.1 Critical dia     0   0    0
5.4.1.2.. Involvemen     0   0    0
5.4.1.3. Forms of di     0   0    0
5.4.1.4. Charity         0   0    0
5.4.1.5. Evangelise/     0   2    2
5.4.1.6 Non-judgment     0   0    0
5.4.1.7 Altruisme /      0   0    0
5.4.1.8 Niet uitslui     0   0    0
5.4.1.9 Kerk moet zi     0   0    0
5.4.1.9 Woord en daa     0   1    1
5.4.2. Real (New) Pr     0   0    0
5.4.2.0. New Lifesty     0   0    0
5.4.2.1. New forms o     0   0    0
5.4.2.2. Involvement     0   0    0
5.4.2.3. Forms of di     0   0    0
5.4.2.4. Charity         0   0    0
5.4.2.5. Evangelise      0   0    0
5.4.2.6 Altruisme /      0   0    0
-----------------------------------
Totals                  43  61  104
```

Fig. 8. ACTUALIZATION scores of the Dutch group (left column) and the Nicaraguan group (middle column).

In the second phase, the groups approach each other, expressing great appreciation for each other. Looking through the eyes of another, the groups become aware of their own way of reading and discover the method and interpretation of the partner group as complementary to their own reading. The Dutch group expresses this as follows:

Many thanks for your report about the reading of John 4. First, all of us read through your discussions at home. Then, we came together on two evenings in order to talk about your experiences with the text. And we were touched by your enthusiasm!

Although we read the same biblical pericope, the meeting at the well evoked different associations and questions in your group and ours. Isn't that like what happened in the story of that first Pentecost? "We hear, each of us, in our own native language." It is not only our way of speaking but also our social and ecclesiastical situations that are not the same. And speaking honestly, we in Lisse, in the Netherlands, realize the reserve we used to have in speaking with each other about our feelings and about what biblical stories stir up in us.

A personal comment by one of the Dutch participants:

Many thanks for letting me take part in your faithful Bible reading, in particular, of the Gospel of John. I experienced and tasted what great significance the Bible has in your day-to-day life. Am I right, when I observe, modestly and carefully, that you read the biblical texts literally and try to realize them in your everyday life? I, here, read the Bible more as poetic, as an old Jewish narrative-style book of that period. Beside what is concretely and literally written, I also look for the symbolic and metaphorical message of the Bible.

For me, too, the Bible is the evangelical way for my daily life, the message of Jesus of Nazareth. Just like one of you says: it is a wonderful and unique book. The Bible is of all times, for all people, for all nations and cultures. I became aware of this during this reading. Wonderful, that we understand each other, without seeing and knowing each other. Isn't that Pentecost? It's worthwhile to continue it.

God be blessed and thanked. May he bless you and be close all your days.

The Nicaraguan group is fascinated by the knowledge and questions of the partner group, and the information in the Dutch report teaches them a lot:

I think the Dutch group knows a lot about the Bible and especially follows the historical lines. They even take us to the book of Kings. This is very good. Moreover, they appear to know something about the culture. . . . This knowledge helps us understand the message of the text better.

The group in the Netherlands emphasizes something that we hadn't thought about, namely, that the Samaritan, a woman, is the one preaching the gospel, sowing, reaping. . . . Our brothers and sisters showed us what the Samaritan woman managed to attain.

These and many other encounters that took place in the framework of the project are models for profound discussions held in the world of ecumenism, where churches are seeking ways to approach each other. Analysis of factors and attitudes that lead to an approach as outlined above is of great importance. In the example above, an approach is made because group members become convinced of the fact of the complementarity of interpretations. Somebody in the Nicaraguan group comments: "I think that if we were to write the gospel, we would do it in our way, and the Dutch in a different way. In both cases it is about the gospel." What takes place here is a damping of differences to achieve a higher goal: loving Jesus and following his example.

Code lists

What questions were posed to the reading reports? How was the color of the reading reports determined? As is suitable in the case of qualitative, open research, the researcher tackled the texts with a number of initial questions. At the same time, the reading reports themselves became a source that again resulted in a number of orientation and calibration points. Thus, the code lists were drawn up, corrected, supplemented, and refined until they were saturated and the reading reports no longer introduced any important components. The value of this exercise is that the researcher reads through the reading reports extremely carefully, each time anew. Just as in the case of the exegesis of Bible texts, one continually discovers new things here.

I will discuss the code lists as they were initially developed for the first and second phases of the project. A number of main categories that correspond with elementary aspects of the hermeneutic process can be discerned among the multitude of codes. The text below was included in the protocol of the project;[3] it contains the main categories of the code system for the first phase and partially also for part of the second one. The basis for this list came from a set of questions developed within the framework of the research project "Determining Relative Adequacy in Biblical Interpretation," under the leadership of Louis Jonker (University of Stellenbosch) and Ernst Conradie (University of the Western Cape).[4]

1. Did the group give any indication that they took notice of the textual features (e.g., genre, narrative or poetic structure, wider literary context, intratextual parallels or references, rhetorical structure, etc.)? [ATTENTION TO TEXT ITSELF]. 2. Did the group give any indication that they took notice of the possible history of origin of the text, its possible compositeness, or the circumstances (political, historical, cultic, cultural, economic, social, etc.) from which it originated? [ATTENTION TO THE WORLD BEHIND THE TEXT]. 3. Did the group pay attention to the different ways the text has already been interpreted by other individuals/traditions/theologies? [ATTENTION TO THE TRADITION OF INTERPRETATION]. 4. How did the group link the text to contemporary life/experience/worldview? What status does the text have for them? Do they regard the text as having an influence on their lives, behavior, etc., or is the Bible an "object of study"? Did they associate with the characters in the narratives (where applicable), and did they allow the plot of the narrative to change them? Which interpretive strategies did they use to bridge the gap between the text and their life? Did they perhaps try to identify eternal values/truths which can comfort them/assist them/strengthen them in their own earthly struggle? Or did they see their life/experiences/ suppression/political, social, economic exclusion as sequel to the biblical salvation history? Or did they find fulfillment of God's promises in their life/experience? [INTERPRETATIONAL STRATEGIES]. 5. How did the group fill in the gaps of the narrative? [STRATEGIES OF IMAGINATION]. 6. Which actor did the members of the group identify with? ["READING WITH"]. 7. What model was used for the appropriation of the meaning of the text (e.g., allegory,

typology, correspondence of terms, correspondence of relationships, *Dialog der Verhältnisse*)? [APPROPRIATION STRATEGIES]. 8. Did the groups develop new praxes out of their understanding of the text (e.g., new forms of social or political action, involvement in resistance movements, forms of diakonia, assistance)? [PRAXEOLOGICAL EFFECT]. 9. Which heuristic keys or codes did they use to unlock this meaning from the text? Are there specific themes/concepts, etc., which originated in their experiences of life that provided them with mechanisms to unlock meaning from the text (e.g., poverty, feelings of exclusion, richness, injustice, etc.)? [CODES/HEURISTIC KEYS]. 10. Which reading attitude does the group have (e.g., literary, dogmatic, liberative, contemplative, psychologizing, pietistic, transformative, with suspicion, to retrieve something, as a means of survival, resistance, productive, reproductive, etc.)? [READING ATTITUDE]. 11. Did the group give any indication of a self-awareness, of an understanding of who they are, and what the contexts and cultural settings are in which they live? Did they give any indication that they are aware of how these contexts influence their reading? Did their reading influence their way of thinking about their contexts/cultural settings? [ATTENTION TO THE CONTEMPORARY CONTEXT OF INTERPRETATION]. 12. Did the group show any awareness of ideologies or power relations that may orient, influence, guide, distort their interpretation of the text? [ATTENTION TO THE WORLD BEHIND THE INTERPRETATION PROCESS]. 13. Describe the interaction in the group. Was there a strong leader, different factions, outsiders, insiders in the group? What rhetorical purpose does their interpretation serve in terms of the group's self-understanding, self-esteem, convictions, faith, values? Could a process of development (in terms of trust, intimacy, nearness, solidarity) be witnessed in the group? Or just the opposite? Was the communitarian character of the reading process experienced as enriching, or rather deconstructive? [ATTENTION TO GROUP DYNAMICS].

As the project developed further, and reading reports became available, this list was refined and enriched from empirical practice. The main categories have been maintained. Many codes were added for the second phase. The essence here was the interaction between groups, a new and complicated component. I lack sufficient space here to discuss all the codes that were included. Almost 250 codes were used for coding the reports in the first phase and 671 for the analysis of reading reports in the second phase.

The number of codes makes clear how diverse the material is, how broad is the range of questions that can be developed, and from how many angles the research can be done. The use of many codes does not imply that the project was based on the statement, The more codes, the better the resulting theory. Rather, the inductive method and the wealth of the material have led to the inclusion of many codes.

We have defined codes as abstractions or labels that can be attached to text segments of reading reports. Codes arrange basic data of texts into categories. These categories can subsequently be used again as queries posed to new material, depending on the research questions. Codes may in that case play an important role in the dialectics between the interests of the researcher and those of the texts. They can be considered as an agency that defends the interests of the texts. An extensive code instrument forces the researcher to pay attention to the semantic richness of reading reports and to the great care observed in the reading.

A summary of the codes is attached as a supplement. At this point, I will discuss the main categories of the code lists as well as codes that require explanation. I will limit myself to discussing the code lists of the first two phases.

First phase

The code instrument for the first phase consists of three main categories. In the first block, data about the groups and group-dynamic aspects of the interpretation process are recorded. In the second block, researchers examined the reading attitude of the group, the status of the text (for the group), focalization and the question of the extent to which it is culturally determined, explanation strategies, the central message of the story as formulated by the group, and patterns of identification with characters or actors in the text ("reading with"). The third block examines whether and how groups actualize the text. Does identification and appropriation take place? With whom? How? What appropriation model is used? Does a certain praxeological effect take place?

First block: Group composition and dynamics. We focus on the first block of the first phase: data about the groups. All sorts of data are collected here on the composition of the group—participants' church background, intercultural experience, social status—and on the group process. The motivation cluster (1.12–1.12.2.5) is important, as are certain group-dynamic aspects of the interpretation process (2.6–2.6.3).

Motivation (1.12–1.12.5). Why did groups participate in the project, and what are implications of this motivation for the development of interaction with the partner group? What motives led the group to participate? A differentiation can be made between *affective and cognitive motivation.* Affective motivation leads groups to participate because they wish to help, intend to improve the world, wish to reduce asymmetry, etc. A great deal of research has been done—on the interaction between Palestinian and Jewish groups—to identify the connection between cognitive motivation and possibilities for change in beliefs. When a set of beliefs of one group is incompatible with a set of beliefs of the other group, this situation is defined as cognitive discrepancy.[5] In a conflict situation, the cognitive discrepancy involves incompatibility of beliefs regarding solutions, incompatibility in the accounts of the background or the course of the conflict, and other contents. A certain type of motivation leads to *freezing* of belief based on knowledge, and a different type of motivation leads to *unfreezing* them. One can analyze the factors that lead to rigidity (freezing) or softening (unfreezing) in the event of large discrepancies in insights and convictions, in the case of epistemic or cognitive discrepancy. Analysis differentiates between (1) motivation for validity, (2) motivation for structure, and (3) motivation for specific content.[6] Motivation for validity is the factor that leads most to growth from discrepancy to consensus. Motivation for specific content is the factor that leads most to a freezing of convictions or beliefs based on knowledge.

Groups characterized by *motivation for validity* are looking for a challenge. New knowledge (e.g., how the partner group reads the story) serves to expose "being right" to criticism, and complete or nuance one's reading. These groups are willing to exchange perspectives. They expected differences to emerge in discussion with the partner. As a group in Hungary reports:

> We were motivated to take part in the group work by the following: curiosity (how the same part of the Bible is explained and read in different countries in the world); the new and modern way of reading the Bible (we are not only listeners but active participants); we think this story is very current in our world, which is full of conflicts; a new possibility for talking about belief.

Groups characterized by *motivation for structure* and safety desire knowledge on a given topic. They express no preference for specific knowledge, and they seek any knowledge that allows closure on a given belief. Under the influence of this motivation, individuals commit themselves to a belief and refrain from critical challenge of it. They do not generate alternative hypotheses but settle with the beliefs they have. In this situation, the individual's preference is for structure as opposed to the ambiguity, confusion, and uncertainty that result from entertaining alternative hypotheses and collecting inconsistent information. A group in India reports:

> The participants found both of the Bible study sessions so interesting, enriching, and educative that they decided to do this kind of spontaneous, participatory Bible study in their regular biweekly Bible study sessions. All the members participated in the discussion spontaneously and freely.

Groups who display *motivation for specific content* are looking for more of the same. They want to hold a given belief as truth and refrain from entertaining alternative hypotheses. Rival hypotheses are rejected as undesirable, while the desired one is accepted. Individuals in this situation are sensitive to evidence and ideas consistent with the desired belief. They collect these ideas, but disregard and/or interpret subjectively any information inconsistent with it. This motivation is a result of wishes that individuals try to fulfill and/or fears they try to avoid. In contrast to motivation for structure, which motivates the person to close on *any* belief, the motivation for specific conclusion motivates the person to close on a *specific* belief. In the former case, the directing mechanism is avoidance of ambiguity and/or confusion, while in the latter case, the directing mechanism is personal wishes and/or fears.[7]

In the second phase of the project, researchers can verify factors that had an effect on freezing or unfreezing of beliefs. In the code instrument for the second phase, freezing is also called *Return to the group's own repertoire*. The main category is *stagnation*.

A group characterized by freezing considers a given belief to be fact and does not generate alternative hypotheses. Freezing can be a consequence of factors such as incapacity to produce alternative hypotheses, lack of information, and inability to collect information. The epistemic process that can be used to incorporate new ideas in the cognitive system, to actualize old insights and collect new information, is, to a great extent, guided by needs. In turn, needs are strongly connected to fears and wishes that strongly determine the epistemic process. Certain needs often cause freezing under the conditions of motivation for specific content. Examples are ideological exegeses, or exegeses strongly determined by culture or tradition of faith, the outcome of which is important for identifying the ideological framework of which the method is part (e.g., sociological or Marxist, certain types of feminist, black, Pentecostal, or sectarian Bible readings).

In the code instrument of the second phase, *Unfreezing* is coded in the main category Growth. Unfreezing involves a process that leads from cognitive discrepancy to cognitive consensus. Daniel Bar-Tal names four factors that may play a role in this process: (1) recognition of relativism; (2) satisfaction of needs; (3) salient and significant information; (4) third party intervention.

Recognition of relativism is awareness of the relativity or subjectivity of all knowledge. An unfreezing occurs when both parties realize that neither of them has a monopoly on truth and objectivity, that knowledge is subjective, and that each of the parties grasps its own truth, latching on to facts that reflect only its own reality constructed on the basis of its own history and experience.

On the basis of the analysis of the needs of the parties involved, it is possible to infer that *satisfaction of needs*, the removal of fears and the fulfillment of wishes, may change the epistemic motivation of the two parties.

Salient and significant information may sometimes be absorbed and processed, even if it is inconsistent with the desired beliefs, when that information is so striking that it cannot be disregarded.

In many cases of international conflicts, the unfreezing process comes as a consequence of *third party intervention*, where the third party plays the role of an epistemic authority. Epistemic authority is defined as a source from which a given proposition or information may exert a determinative influence on the tendency to accept inconsistent information and/or entertain and generate rival alternative solutions.[8]

Group dynamic aspects of the process of semiosis (2.6–2.6.3). Attention to group dynamics involves examining the question of whether any culture specific patterns can be found. Sometimes, meetings have a strictly *collectivist* nature. Conversation and discussion are specific for hierarchic patterns; those in authority and experts determine the development of the conversation and the meaning of the text; the conversation serves the collective; opinions are not exchanged freely; members associate with the previous speaker and do not discuss the text. Little confrontation or discrepancy is involved, and few audacious questions are asked.

Individualistic reading patterns exhibit a lot of discussion. There is often an open attitude with respect to the text; individual opinions do not come to a consensus; the group is not focused on appropriation but more on the meaning of the text for their own lives, personal development, engagement, or enrichment. This dynamic involves few experts or authorities.

Some readings are very repetitive and remind one of "interpretation of *listening readers.*" Walter Ong summarizes characteristics of this interpretation process:

> It is additive rather than subordinative. It is aggregative rather than analytic. Clichés serve an important function in stabilizing the recitation in memory. It is redundant or "copious." Since there is no possibility of backward reference as there is in a text, effectiveness in oral communication depends on constant repetition, summary, reduplication. It is conservative or traditionalist. Knowledge is hard-won and preserved by repetition. Experimentation is not encouraged and age becomes a form of status, since the old are the guardians of tradition.[9]

Second block: The interpretation process. In the second block of the code instrument for the first phase, the actual interpretation process of John 4 is coded in three steps. First, hermeneutic aspects are analyzed in two steps: What is the reading attitude of the group? (3.1.1–3.1.1.20). What heuristic keys are used by the group? (3.1.3–3.1.3.7). Subsequently, in an extensive third step, the exegesis or explanation of the text as such is coded (3.2.0–4.2).

Reading attitude (3.1.1–3.1.1.20). Reading attitude may mean the result of the combination of the status of the text for the readers, the result expected from the interpretation, and the methods to be used for it. As many central concepts as possible from different hermeneutics are brought to bear here. The connection is very tight between the status of the text for the reader, the problems detected by readers in their own society or their own lives, and the relevance the text may have for solving these problems. I will explain the following codes in more detail:

Liberating is used here in the classic meaning in liberation hermeneutics, thus also as a polemic term against hierarchical structures in church or society, against other "alienating" current religious movements or insights.

The code *With suspicion* is strongly linked to the previous one. Suspicion is a concept that has played a role in liberative/liberation exegesis and is directed there—in the first phase of this movement and as coined by theologians such as Juan Luis Segundo—to the question of whether "classical" exegesis actually analyzed all components of the text and did not spirit anything away. Has the "dangerous memory" been silenced by the way the church hierarchy dealt with the text? In some reading reports, we also encountered suspicion as a critical attitude toward the moral preached by the text. It is to these kinds of suspicion that this code refers.

Some reports show evidence of interpretation *With an eye to life*. The immediate hermeneutic circulations are from the text to life, and from life to the text. The text is read with no historical distance and is focused on the readers' own social or existential problems.

The attitude *Full of confidence* stands in contrast to *With suspicion*. Some liberation exegetes also approach the encounter with the text full of confidence. However, nowadays the opinion that the text must be reconstructed plays a role: all types of layers must be scratched away from existing texts, and only then they will be able to be liberative. The code *Full of confidence* indicates the opposite of the suspicious reading attitude. This reading attitude is encountered for the most part in more pietistic or Pentecostal groups.

The difficult concept *Pentecostal* refers to reading done with the thought that all has been predestined, all is subordinate to Christ. Narrative changes or questions are solved by means of the theological scheme of predestination or by appeal to the omniscience of God or Jesus. For example, one report addressed the question of why Jesus had to pass through Samaria as follows: "He was told (by God) to go to Samaria; it was predestined, because a people thirsting for God lived there."

The reading attitude *Critical/deconstructive/reconstructive* is frequently encountered among Western groups. It intends to deconstruct characters in the text: "Wasn't Jesus a coward?" "Isn't Jesus very arrogant here?"

Focalization (3.1.3–3.1.3.7). This important category connects heuristic keys and focalization. By *heuristic keys,* we refer to the question of which components from the reader's own context/experience are constitutive for the interpretation process as a selection process. Our use of *focalization* is a variant on Mieke Bal's: We refer to the relationship between the components presented in the story and the outlook the readers have on it. Storytelling theory, as developed over the course of the past century, uses various terms for the concept referred to here. The term used most is *perspective* or *storytelling perspective*. Others include *storytelling situations, storytelling points of view, methods of telling stories, point of view*.[10] However, none are clear on one item. They do not make an explicit distinction between the outlook from which the components are presented and the identity of the agency that operationalizes that outlook. In this category, we especially examine the cultural components that help determine the interpretation as a selection process.

Interpretation of the text as such (3.2.0–4.2). In this extensive category, we examine the more exegetical aspects of the reading process. How does the group explain the text? What methods do they use? Do the readers pay attention to the world behind the text? If so, how? Is a particular identifiable method being used (literary, rhetorical, historical-critical, sociological, etc.)? What central components or characters in the text are reflected on by the group? With whom do readers identify? What, according to the group, is the central message? Are there any text problems that weren't solved? How are the gaps in the text filled in (imagination strategies)? I will explain several codes in more detail:

The code *Discussion (about methods)* refers to discussion among readers about the limits of the exegesis. For example: What methods are allowed or not allowed? What is the relationship between imagination and the text?

The code *Genre (symbolic-literal, etc.)* is used if the group wrestles with the question of whether the text (or parts of it) is (are) intended literally or symbolically.

Interpretations that place the text or parts of it within the context of the John movement or the theology according to John are coded with the label *Theological/ theology of John*.

If the group regarded John 4 as the product of the John community that strove for a certain ideological or theological goal, the code *Literary fiction* was used.

The code *Symbolic* includes references in a number of reading reports to the (patristic) opinion that the five men represent five Assyrian gods.

If narrative twists in the story are attributed to or solved from God's omnipotence, predestination, fate, predilection, etc., these segments were coded *God/God's providence/God knew.* . . . This deals with the role of God in the story. Some—especially Pentecostal—readings place a great deal of emphasis on the "character" of God, while in the story itself this subject does not actually play any significant role.

Along the line of the previous code, some groups introduce themes or concepts—the Holy Spirit, for example—that play no overt role in the text. Report segments that address such subjects are coded CENTRAL CONCEPTS IN INTERPRETATION THAT ARE NOT CENTRAL IN THE TEXT.

A question in the protocol asks, "Whom are you reading with?" The essence of the code "READING WITH" is the question of which character or actor in the story the group identifies with.

How do readers deal with the elliptical nature of the text? Are the things not said or things not made explicit in the text filled in via intertextual parallels, or from the reader's own experience and imagination? The code STRATEGIES/CONTENT OF IMAGINATION applies to segments addressing this subject.

Third block: Actualization. In the third block, we examine how groups actualize the text. Is actualization or recontextualization problematized? What characters do readers identify with? Does the reading become a place to practice developing a new praxis, a new project? This block includes four main categories: REREADING OF CHARACTERS IN THE TEXT (5.0–5.0.22), APPROPRIATION STRATEGIES (5.1–5.2.3.07), APPROPRIATION DYNAMICS (5.3.–5.3.5), PRAXEOLOGICAL EFFECT (5.4–5.4.2.6).

REREADING OF CHARACTERS IN THE TEXT (5.0–5.0.22). In this category, we examine which characters or actions readers especially focus on in the process of actualization. How does the text get a new context, a new reference? Do Jesus, the Samaritan woman, or the villagers become models for how group members themselves act?

How? Is there a general message that readers think will provide the stimulus to action or reflection: evangelism, sowing, reconciliation, meeting Jesus now, mission, conversion, breaking through barriers, preventing discrimination?

APPROPRIATION STRATEGIES (5.1–5.2.3.07). The central question here is, How, by means of what *strategy*, is the text actualized? If actualizing texts is the process in which the original reference of a text is replaced by a new one (Ricoeur), how does this process develop for the reading groups? For categorizing this process, we use classical models from hermeneutics that can all be found in the reading reports: allegorical, typological, model of the parallelism of terms—also called the tracing paper model, model of the correspondence of relations,[11] model of a *Dialog der Verhältnisse*. This last model is described by J. A. van der Ven and assumes a critical relation to the mode of correspondence of relations used by Boff. The concept of correspondence is based too much on agreement; there must also be room for criticism and confrontation. "Der Begriff Dialog bietet . . . diesen Raum, weil Dialog zwar auf Übereinstimmung gerichtet ist, aber nicht von ihr ausgeht."[12]

APPROPRIATION DYNAMICS (5.3–5.3.5). What happens to the perspective and self-image of the readers? The power of the story is measured here. Does the story have a critical function? Is the confrontation between the story and the reader's own life distinct? Do the readers see their own life as a fulfillment of the story they read (In my life God's promises are fulfilled)? Has the story led to new insights? Do readers have a different self-image? Have they become more sensitive to their own prejudices, cultural bias, ideological positiveness, their own failings?

PRAXEOLOGICAL EFFECT (5.4–5.4.2.6). This important category contains codes related to the question of what the praxeological effect of the reading exercise actually was. Is there any empowerment toward others ("The story empowers me to conquer my own problems, uncertainty, failure, false interaction with people"), or empowerment of the self ("The story empowers me to find more balance, peace, self-acceptance in my life")? Is there a *Critical dialogue with alienating contemporary religious movements*? Is there a display of *Nonjudgmentalness*, an attitude that will be extremely important for the second phase and that will be coded there again ("Jesus does not judge, so we won't either. Treat others with compassion")? Can any significant correlations be pointed out between reading the Bible and social transformation? Will it remain an effect at the level of "we should" or is there actually talk of a new lifestyle, an action?

Second phase

Interaction with the partner group takes place in the second phase. Are development and growth involved, or rather stagnation and freezing? The code instrument is now strictly focused on the analysis of the interaction with the partner group. How does the group deal with the partner group as such, and what is the effect of the interaction? The three main categories are: CIRCUMSTANTIAL (1–1.04.11.2), CONFRONTATION (2–2.04.8.7.4), and EFFECT (3–3.2).

First main category: Meetings and characteristics. Just as in the first phase, information is collected on the group and partner group. Changes in participants can be recorded. Once again, motivation, intercultural experience, and expectations of the group are examined. All this is continually related to the partner group, now a known quantity, whose data can also be coded. Much will have to be referred back to the results and information from the first phase. Only two codes need explaining.

Exploratory affective exchange (1.04.08.2.3) is a concept from sociology. It symbolizes an interaction based on affective components. "This exchange of experiences of faith enriches us; it encourages and it strengthens in the search for the truth," writes a Salvadorian group to a partner group in the Netherlands.

Sometimes financial relations are created between groups, or groups enter the process with financial expectations. These can be coded *One wants to help* or *One wants to be helped* (1.04.09.2.4 or 1.04.09.2.5).

Second main category: Contact with the partner group. This exceptionally important main category maps contact with the partner group. Does the group acquire knowledge from the context of the partner group? Does it address the partner group directly ("Dear partner group")? Are culture–co-culture (e.g., poor-rich; powerless-powerful) communication patterns involved, along the lines Paulo Freire describes? Is there any interest in the profile of the partner group? Do certain issues of the partner group stand out (vulnerability, experience of suffering, ethnic background, openness, etc.)? What attitude does the group assume: critical, mindful, nonjudgmental, open, vulnerable, tolerant of ambiguity? Or does the group wish to convert? Is there need for control?

The hermeneutic-exegetical aspect of the interaction is also coded here: What differences or similarities does the group itself (and subsequently, the researcher) discover in method, focalization, identification patterns, appropriation, and actualization of the partner group? How does the group deal with these similarities and differences? Do similarities lead to an *ecumenical honeymoon*? Does the group deal with differences in a way anthropology calls *graceful fighting*? Are differences *damped* (e.g., "We are, after all, all brothers and sisters, and there is one God"), or do they lead to breach and rejection? The first part of this main category consists of the inquiry into the interaction with the partner group. The following codes require explanation.

INTERACTION WITH THE PARTNER GROUP (2.02 etc.). How group A and partner group B interact is coded here, bypassing the confrontation with the partner group's interpretation of John 4. Does the group pay attention to the profile—the composition, age, education, church background, etc.—of the partner group? Are participants individualized?

ATTITUDE TOWARD THE PARTNER GROUP (2.02.3). The attitude can be specified further as mindful, critical, tolerant, sensitive, pedantic, proselytizing, open, etc.

Mindful (2.02.3.0). This important concept in intercultural communication is defined by William Gudykunst as a cognitive concept, having to do with conquering tendencies to interpret strangers' behavior on the basis of our own frames of reference.[13] Mindfulness requires concentrated attention, openness, and sensitivity. Mindfulness involves openness to new information and the insight that more than one perspective is possible. As a partner group writes to a South African group: "Fear and violence are part of the life world of the group. The South African group associated with this." "The topic I would like to discuss—and this will probably not be so easy, in the sense that we cannot point it out precisely, but we should also be wondering about this—is, To what extent do a number of the differences we just ran into have anything to do with the difference in background between our group and the one in Scotland?" says a participant in a Dutch group.

Critical (2.02.3.1). Participants want explanations, do not understand what is being said, or find the report disconnected. "Well, on the one hand, they dug deep. That is very nice, but haven't they done it a little bit too arduously?" says someone to the partner group. "The Indian group felt that the solemnity of the conversation between Jesus and the Samaritan woman in John 4 is not recognized by the partner group."

Tolerance for ambiguity (2.02.3.4). What is the degree of tolerance for theological inconsistencies in the partner report?

Vulnerability 2.02.3.5. This fundamental concept in intercultural and ecumenical communication refers to members of a community taking off their masks. M. Scott Peck contends that the development of community requires that we expose our inner selves to strangers and that we be affected by strangers when they expose their inner selves to us.[14] Vulnerability is connected to two universal conditions for intercultural interaction: being willing to not exclude and being prepared to interact.[15] "There are many personal additions that make the reading more realistic" (Durban to Colombia). "Inclusions of prayers were appreciated" (Durban to Colombia). "We don't want our partner group to get the wrong impression of us. . . . We cannot help it that we are white, of average age, well-to-do, etc." (Dutch to Scottish group). A "little old lady from the U.S.": "My background is Presbyterian and . . . my heart longs to bring people into a Bible study. When you do a Bible study, you are the one that is enriched, and I have done two. I have done Ephesians, and last year I did Jeremiah. And the growth was with myself. It was exciting to hear other people talk about what it means to them, but my perspective is that of an Anglo, a little old white lady in orthopedic shoes . . . and I want to change that."

Direct expressions of admiration (2.02.4.1.1). An important condition for successful communication, expressing admiration is related to discoveries the group makes in the text, solidarity with the partner group, human rights, ecology, asymmetry, etc. It also applies to comments on the partner group process, the care with which they read the text. A Cuban group responds to their partner in the U.S.: "We also read the text before coming together, but it was very favorable that you brought questions that would help develop the analysis. Your questions were very interesting. We answered them all, after reacting to some of the reflections you made."

Pairs are formed (2.02.4.2). In this special mode of communication, individual members of a group choose one person from the partner group and follow him or her during the entire report. Then, they write this ally a personal letter of response.

Power/asymmetry in communication (2.02.4.5). What patterns can be discovered in the communication with the partner group that have to do with power, power inequality, social asymmetry, etc.? This code alludes to James Scott's theories of hidden and public transcripts[16] and Paulo Freire's *Pedagogy of the Oppressed*. An entire chapter is devoted to the subject in Gudykunst's handbook for intercultural communication.[17]

The three patterns defined in culture–co-cultural interaction are assimilation, accommodation, separation (or resistance). Assimilation implies the desire to become part of the mainstream culture. Accommodation strategies try to get dominant group members to accept co-cultural group members. Separation is rejection of the possibility of common bonds with dominant group members.

Co-cultural group members are marginalized in the dominant societal structures, and they use certain communication styles to achieve success when confronting the oppressive dominant structures. Culture–co-cultural communication refers to interactions among underrepresented and dominant group members. The focus of culture–co-cultural theory is on providing a framework "by which co-cultural group members negotiate attempts by others to render their voices muted within dominant societal structures."[18] A Cuban group that considers itself part of a poor and restricted co-culture writes to its U.S. partner: "What are you thirsty for? The insecurity you show about 'losing the car' sounds strange to us. Our insecurities are related to survival: What to eat? How to support our children? We don't even think about having a car here."

Development–underdevelopment patterns (2.02.4.5.4). This code is linked to the previous one. When groups in the Northern hemisphere are linked with groups in the Southern hemisphere, some communication patterns in reading reports stem from readers' perception of the first world–third world relationship. In this code and the following one, the two most extreme aspects in the spectrum of "communication in development situations" theories and practices are applied. On one side is the modernization paradigm, and on the other is the empowerment paradigm. The empowerment paradigm is actually not a useful concept here, but the modernization paradigm is. The *modernization paradigm* is an Enlightenment paradigm and is economically and socially charged. Growth, knowledge, and development are central concepts. We refer to it as conscious or subconscious assumption of a hierarchical relationship between North and South. This general assumption has a hermeneutic variant. According to this opinion, readers in the North are "further advanced," have more (biblical) knowledge available, and are better capable of completing the interpretation process, because they have resources (commentaries, etc.) available. This way of thinking is often nurtured by a concentration on the more exegetical side of the reading process. Exactly at the point of appropriation of the text, significant differences between Southern and non-Southern groups can be observed. An example of this contrast is shown in figures 6, 7a, and 7b above. Southern groups often concentrate more on the significance of the text for the current moment. Sometimes the non-Southern partner groups understand the differences in terms of development. They may speak in terms of *head start* and *disadvantage*. The Southern partner group is seen as being in a primitive stage of Bible reading. The communication model is often asymmetric here: subject versus object.

A second component of the main category CONFRONTATION is devoted to the more hermeneutic-exegetical aspects of the interaction. Several codes in this category merit discussion here.

Analysis of the method of the interpretation (2.04.4 etc.). Is group A paying attention to the method used by partner group B in the explanation (exegesis) of the text? Are any differences in reading attitude discovered? Are any differences in focalization and concentration on text segments observed? Are the appropriation strategies of the partner group analyzed? Is the process of appropriation submitted to analysis? How are the differences and the similarities evaluated? If differences are found to be enriching and positive, can we use the term *ecumenical honeymoon*? Will the result be continuing contact?

Imagination strategies (2.04.8.3.4). How does a group respond if the partner group fills in gaps in the text from their imagination? A Dutch group thinks that the fast conversion of the villagers may have something to do with the fact that the woman, after having met Jesus, is "radiating" when she returns to the village (as Moses did in Exodus 34). The partner group finds this nonsense and fills in this gap in the text by pointing out the sociocultural setting of the story: "She just changed, and this is the reason the villagers follow her to Jesus." This case sets one group's imagination against the other's.

Jesus is too human (2.04.8.3.6.04.01). The outlook or vision of Jesus appears to be extremely important for groups and is frequently a breaking point. Groups that have a "low" outlook on Jesus find it difficult to understand a "high" outlook, and vice versa. Groups with a low outlook find a high outlook often too abstract, too little involved with life and with the people's struggles. Groups with a high outlook find Jesus in the low one too worldly, too human, not godly, and not mighty enough. The impasse can be broken when components from both outlooks, for example, representing exclusion and struggle on one hand, and Jesus is God on the other, are linked to each other. A South African group reported to a Dutch group that without exception they identified with the Samaritan woman and read John 4 as an apartheid story. They considered it a sign of mercy that Jesus, God himself, had turned to her and begun a conversation with her. *This* Jesus, condescending to start a conversation with an outcast woman, may not be deconstructed! This perspective made a great impression on the Dutch group. An Indian group of Dalit women (outcasts, untouchables) presents from their own situation how a high image of Jesus can still be charged and cherished from the point of view of exclusion and discrimination. The group talks about the conversation between Jesus and the Samaritan woman. "From the viewpoint of the high-class person, *Conversation* with the downtrodden means 'Command and demand' and 'Hire and fire'; whereas for the unprivileged the meaning of the word *Conversation* is urging or pleading or begging. How differently this Son of God interacts with this untouchable woman!"

PERCEIVED DIFFERENCES (2.04.8.4 etc.). The way a group deals with differences is unusually important. Is the group capable of putting into perspective differences in interpretation with their partner group and attributing them to differences in background, culture, church involvement? Does the group detect consistencies in differences? In the same way that difference A is a result of this connection, so also is difference B. Differences can be dealt with very differently.

Graceful fighting (2.04.8.5.1). Graceful fighting is a certain way of dealing with differences and is nourished by the conviction that if we can live together in community, then someday we will be able to resolve our conflicts. The outlook here is that conflict is associated with community. As Martin Buber contends, community is not a group in complete harmony; rather, "Community is that group that can deal with conflicts."

Damping (2.04.8.5.2). Differences are put into perspective to benefit a higher purpose. Damping or dimming can happen by appeal to cultural universals, such as the ideal of preserving human life; looking to the well-being of close relatives; prohibiting murder and theft; valuing affection and companionship; reciprocity in helping and being helped; hospitality; responsible conduct, which requires virtues of truthfulness, courage, fidelity, and respect.

Damping can also take place because religious universals are appealed to, or when components are discovered in John 4 that are metacultural. Faith is more than culture. Cultural codes are cracked in John 4. Boundaries are moved. Among all the differences, there are also a couple universal aspects in the story. From a biblical-theological point of view, the Pauline thought of the "one body with many members" can be argued; "Despite all differences, we all do believe in the same God." The essence is that ethical consequences of differences are categorized in a hierarchic structure that leads to damping, because it is a condition for the survival of the group.

Third main category: Effects of the interaction. In the third main category, the code instrument is directed toward measuring the effect of the interaction. What happened to the group's own opinion of the text? Is there any growth? Why, and based on what factors? Is there any rejection of the reading of the partner group? Why, and based on what factors? Has the intercultural competence (insight into the cultural positiveness of the group's own values and those of the partner group) increased? Were the group's own insights put into perspective? Has a so-called Third Culture perspective developed, or is there instead culture shock and a return to the group's own repertoire? The reading reports and insights from sociological research were used once again for defining these codes. The result is a large, but mixed main category. Growth and stagnation are coded here and are subdivided under the same subcategories. The following codes need further explanation.

New focalization (3.1.1.1.2 etc.). Characters/actors who were not recognized by the group as important ones are brought into the picture via the reading of the partner group. There is disclosure. The partner group supplied new knowledge related to the world behind the text. The group wants to study the text once again, after the partner group has gotten them to think some more about it. All these effects are categorized under Growth.

Rejection of the partner group's point of view (3.1.1.1.4 etc.). The point of view, the outlook (on the central message, for example) of the partner group is rejected as untenable. The group's own outlook is reinforced. There is a clash or conflict of interpretations. The interaction with the text, the partner group's interpretation process (manner of appropriation, or rather, the lack of it) is rejected by the group and is considered to be illegitimate, incorrect, inadequate, or improper. The group's own interpretation remains intact and is regarded as adequate, legitimate, and proper, compared to the partner group. There is no clash involved. No culture shock, but faith shock. These effects are categorized under stagnation and return to the group's own repertoire.

More intercultural competence (3.1.2.4 etc.). The "big three" of intercultural communication are coded under this subcategory: knowledge, motivation, and skills.[19]

Knowledge (3.1.2.4.1). Knowledge is fundamental for intercultural competence. Gudykunst et al. define knowledge in this context as "the information necessary to interact appropriately and effectively, and the requisite cognitive orientation to facilitate the acquisition of such information."[20] Important conditions for acquiring intercultural knowledge are open-mindedness and nonjudgmentalness.

Motivation (3.1.2.4.2). Motivation was written about in the discussion of the code list for the first phase. A certain motivation is also basic for acquiring intercultural competence. Intercultural sensitivity, a positive attitude toward a different culture, and empathy are positive factors, while ethnocentrism or religious fundamentalism are negative ones.

Skills (3.1.2.4.3). Skills have to do with behavior. Skill reflects the needed behaviors to interact appropriately and effectively with members of different cultures: being mindful, interaction involvement, appropriate self-disclosure, uncertainty reduction strategies, appropriate display of respect.

More awareness and/or comprehension of ideology of partner group (3.1.3.3). Has the group acquired more understanding for ideologically determined expressions, outlooks, convictions of the partner group? Did any self-criticism by either group play a role?

Description of process by group at the end of process (3.1.4). How does the group itself describe its development during the process? Were any stages observed? Did something like culture shock or self-shock occur? Is the U or W figure involved? Was there any development of honeymoon-like interaction with the partner group toward a stable exchange?

Affective growth: from orientation to stable exchange (3.1.4.1). The stages mentioned here are often from orientation via exploratory affective exchange and affective exchange to stable exchange. There is development and growth. Moments of relapse and miscommunication are sometimes described via the U or W model. The U or W figures represent cultural/self/religious shock. The figure describes the experience of taking one step forward, two steps back, characteristic of culture/self/religious shock. The process concerns disintegration during transition, in situations such as divorce, death, changes in values.

A loss of a familiar framework of reference often occurs in intercultural meetings. "Everyone requires the ongoing validation of his or her experiences, and being unable to meet this basic human need can lead to symptoms of mental, emotional, and physical disturbance. . . . The shifting of the self-world relationship brings about heightened levels of inner conflict through an increased awareness of the split between internal, subjective experiences and external, objective circumstances."[21] Culture shock is a form of self shock, an existential dilemma as a consequence of a large and painful discrepancy between what is and what should be. Something we could call a religious or faith shock, with all the characteristics of culture shock or self shock, may occur in the interaction between groups that read the Bible together and end up in a conversation about fundamental outlooks on faith.

Assessment of process by group at the end of process (3.1.5 etc.). How does the group view the overall process? Does it see it as growth, or does the group wish to return to its own repertoire? Gudykunst et al. understand growth to be the process in which a person becomes a new kind of person at a higher level of integration. Within the framework of the intercultural Bible reading project, we can define growth as the eventual result of a process of confrontation, relapse, and progress, leading to new insights (in faith), an increase in intercultural competence, being able to put differences in perspective, a reinforced engagement and effort for a better world, and willingness to continue participating.

Third Culture perspective (3.1.5.1.2). The process was enriching, horizon-broadening to the group itself. A new perspective developed. The culture of the partner group is no longer assessed from the group's own culture, nor vice versa, but a perspective is being developed that is fed by the desire for a new culture, a third culture. The person who develops a Third Culture perspective is "open-minded toward new ideas and experiences"; feels "empathy toward people from other cultures"; has a "more accurate perception of differences and similarities between the host culture and our own"; is more capable "of describing behavior we don't understand than evaluating unfamiliar behavior as bad, nonsensical, or meaningless"; is better capable "of detecting role behaviors"; is better equipped "to establish meaningful relationships with people from the other cultures"; is "less ethnocentric."[22] The special role of the theologian is coming into view here. When central themes of the Christian tradition and Bible testimony are involved in the intercultural discussion, other words—theological words—such as justice, love, reciprocity, liberation, and deliverance, will determine the color of this Third Culture perspective. It will become then a Third Church perspective.

Main factors responsible for return to one's own repertoire (3.1.5.2.3). What causes stagnation? According to the group, why does it hold on to its own repertoire? Is it the result of breaking with the opinions (of faith) of the partner group? Causes could be theological motives (outlook on Jesus), ethical motives (the Samaritan woman as a whore or victim), the method of the partner group, or the conviction that the culture of the partner group (Western secularized culture, for example) can only lead to incorrect interpretation of the text. "Our culture looks more like the one in the Bible." Another example is a "brazen," too pious, or too politically charged appropriation of the text.

Conclusion

Hermeneutics must not become *Herrschaftswissenschaft*, an imperialistic theoretical practice, pretending to be able to dominate and understand exhaustively processes of interpretation. What we have tried to do in this contribution is to take the reader along the road of the development of a new analytical instrument in the field of empirical hermeneutics. The multicolored, complex character of intercultural Bible reading is clearly demonstrated. Time and again, it appears to be a fascinating process, the richness of which can scarcely be recorded. Should professionals wish to participate in this process with a contribution of their own, they may do so by developing instruments that enable people to taste that richness. The tracks of many ordinary readers who participated in the project can be found nowhere but in the reading reports. Careful reading of these texts is a tribute to their efforts and creativity.

Codes for the first phase

1. REPORT; 0.01 Date; 0.02 Appendixes: Photos/video/audio; 0.03 Summary; 0.04 Verbatim; 0.05 Addresses; 0.06 Reporter; 1 Group; 1.0 The members introduce themselves; 1.0.0 The members emphasize their relation to the church/faith/the Lord; 1.0.01 The members emphasize their relationship to society; 1.01 Number/names of participants; 1.01.1 Women's group; 1.01.2 Men's group; 1.01.3 Mixed; 1.02 City; 1.03 Church affiliation; 1.03.1 Protestant; 1.03.2 Roman Catholic; 1.03.3 Ecumenical; 1.03.4 No affiliation–non-Christian–agnostic–atheist; 1.04 Further information with respect to church; 1.04.1 Group–church relation; 1.04.1.1 Dialectic; 1.04.1.2 Harmonious; 1.05 Background information of the group; 1.05.0 Group self-image; 1.05.0.01 Critical toward group's own society (established standards and values); 1.05.0.02 Satisfied with group's own society; 1.05.0.03 Capable of exercising power (for change); 1.05.0.04 Powerless; 1.05.1 Age of participants; 1.05.2 Intercultural or crosscultural experience; 1.05.2 Interreligious experience/situation; 1.05.3 Vulnerability; 1.06 Social status of group members; 1.06.1 Poor/low class; 1.06.2 Middle class; 1.06.3 Upper class; 1.07 Cultural information of the group; 1.08 Ethnic background of group members; 1.09 Language of group members; 1.10 Context description; 1.11 Important current events; 1.12 Motivation; 1.12.1 Cognitive; 1.12.1.1 One wishes to be challenged (motivation for validity/

acquiring new knowledge (also with respect to the Bible); 1.12.1.2 One seeks structure/safety (motivation for structure); 1.12.1.3 One seeks more of the same (motivation for specific content); 1.12.1.4 More understanding for each other; 1.12.1.5 One wishes to share insight into faith with others; 1.12.2 Affective; 1.12.2.1 Empathy/emotionality/solidarity; 1.12.2.2 Longing for a better/different world; 1.12.2.3 Curious/exploratory affective exchange; 1.12.2.4 One wishes to help; 1.12.2.5 One wishes to be helped; 1.13 Project included by local organization

2 GROUP PROCESS; 2.0 Description of the group process with respect to the protocol; 2.1 Liturgical framework; 2.1.0 Reading is celebrating; 2.1.01 Hymns; 2.1.02 Prayers; 2.1.03 Symbols; 2.1.04 Other; 2.2 Reading dynamics; 2.2.0 Group's own method; 2.2.1 Everyone one verse; 2.2.2 Everyone for himself; 2.2.3 One for all; 2.2.4 Roles/bibliodrama/soap; 2.2.5 Familiar with IBC project yes/no; 2.2.5.1 Protocol translated and/or used; 2.2.5.2 Introduction in process and project; 2.2.5.2 Partner group preference; 2.3 Facilitator: name/role; 2.3.1 Focus questions/intervention, 2.4 Interaction in the group, 2.4.1 Existing group, 2.4.2 New group, 2.4.3 Different factions/Opinions, 2.4.4 Outsiders/insiders, 2.4.5 Mutual trust, 2.5 Communitarian reading process, 2.5.0 Horizon broadening, 2.5.1 Enriching/stimulating/ trust . . . ; 2.5.2 Threatening . . . ; 2.5.3 Results in a "second" reading; 2.6 Group dynamic aspects of the semiosis process; 2.6.1 Collectivistic; 2.6.2 Individualistic; 2.6.3 Oral tradition/ illiterate; 2.7 Commentary on the group events

3 INTERPRETATION PROCESS; 3.1 HERMENEUTIC ASPECTS; 3.1.0 Reading process; 3.1.0.1 Associative; 3.1.0.2 Systematic; 3.1.0.3 What touches us; 3.1.1 Reading attitude; 3.1.1.0 Open/questioning/problematizing; 3.1.1.01 Literal; 3.1.1.02 Dogmatic; 3.1.1.03 Liberating; 3.1.1.04 Contemplative; 3.1.1.05 Psychologizing; 3.1.1.06 Pietistic/Spiritual; 3.1.1.07 With an eye to social transformation; 3.1.1.08 With suspicion; 3.1.1.09 To retrieve something; 3.1.1.10 Focused on survival; 3.1.1.11 Productive; 3.1.1.12 Reproductive; 3.1.1.13 Contextual; 3.1.1.14 With an eye to life; 3.1.1.15 Full of confidence; 3.1.1.16 Prophetic; 3.1.1.17 Focused on personal faith (individual/individualistic); 3.1.1.18 Scientific; 3.1.1.19 Pentecostal; 3.1.1.20 Critical/deconstructive/reconstructive; 3.1.2 Status of the text; 3.1.2.01 Effect on life; 3.1.2.02 Object of analysis; 3.1.2.03 Reliable; 3.1.3 HEURISTIC KEYS/FOCALIZATION; 3.1.3.1 Culture; 3.1.3.1.1 Collective/individualized; 3.1.3.1.2 Time; 3.1.3.1.3 Power/Powerless (Power Distance); 3.1.3.1.4 Gender (M/F); 3.1.3.1.5 Uncertainty Avoidance; 3.1.3.2 Social; 3.1.3.2.1 Exclusion/inclusion; 3.1.3.2.2 Ethnicity; 3.1.3.3 Economic; 3.1.3.3.1 Poor/rich; 3.1.3.4 Religious; 3.1.3.5 Ethical/morality (also sexual morality); 3.1.3.5 More; 3.1.3.5.1 Injustice/ righteousness; 3.1.3.5.2 Illness/health; 3.1.3.5.3 Basic needs (food/shelter . . .); 3.1.3.5.4 Boy meets girl/erotic/sexual; 3.1.3.6 Political; 3.1.3.7 From an interfaith point of view or interreligious dialogue; 3.2.0 Discussion (about methods); 3.2 EXPLANATION STRATEGIES; 3.2.0 Resources; 3.2.0.01 Commentaries; 3.2.0.02 Explicit "exegetical" input by facilitator or other person of group; 3.2.0.03 Rather/rather not; 3.2.1 Historical (world behind text); 3.2.1.01 Possible history of origin of the text; 3.2.1.02 Possible compositeness of text; 3.2.1.03 Circumstances of origin; 3.2.1.03.1 Political; 3.2.1.03.2 Historical; 3.2.1.03.3 Religious; 3.2.1.03.4 Cultic; 3.2.1.03.5 Cultural; 3.2.1.03.5.01 Power distance; 3.2.1.03.5.02 M/F; 3.2.1.03.5.03 Uncertainty avoidance; 3.2.1.03.5.04 Collective/individual; 3.2.1.03.5.05 Short/long term; 3.2.1.03.6 Economic; 3.2.1.03.7 Social/ethnic; 3.2.1.03.8 Geography; 3.2.1.04 Greek/source language; 3.2.2 Literary; 3.2.2.01 Genre (symbolic-literal, etc.); 3.2.2.02 Narrative; 3.2.2.03 Rhetoric structure; 3.2.2.04 Broader literary context; 3.2.2.04.1 Intratextual parallels or references; 3.2.2.04.2 Intertextual parallels; 3.2.2.04.2 Thematic parallels; 3.2.2.04.3 Word parallels; 3.2.3 Sociological/materialistic; 3.2.4 Psychological; 3.2.5 Structuralistic/semiotic; 3.2.6 Theological/theology of John; 3.2.6.1 Literary fiction/story of John's community with certain ideological goal; 3.2.7 Symbolic; 3.3 EXPLANATION OF THE TEXT ITSELF; 3.3.1 Text segments; 3.3.1.01 vv. 01–03; 3.3.1.02 vv. 04–06; 3.3.1.03 vv. 07–08; 3.3.1.04 vv. 09–10; 3.3.1.05 vv. 10–14; 3.3.1.06 vv. 15–19; 3.3.1.07 vv. 20–26; 3.3.1.08 vv. 27–30; 3.3.1.09 vv. 31–

5.0.13 Contemporary well (as meeting place or the like); 5.0.14 Living water; 5.0.15 Discrimination/exclusion/untouchability/etc.; 5.0.16 The Jews; 5.0.17 Five men/husband–faithful/unfaithful; 5.0.18 "If you knew who it is that . . ." (v. 10); 5.0.19 Differences among groups/peoples/religions; 5.0.20 Getting water then/now; 5.0.21 Worship in spirit and truth; 5.0.22 Healing/disease/miracles; 5.1 Appropriation strategies; 5.1.1 Allegory; 5.1.2 Typology; 5.1.3 Parallelism of terms (tracing paper); 5.1.4 Parallelism of relations; 5.1.5 *Dialog der Verhältnisse*; 5.2 Appropriation content; 5.2.1 Eternal values; 5.2.2 Truth as strength for their own earthly struggle? 5.2.3 Life experiences as sequel to the biblical salvation history?; 5.2.3.01 Oppression-liberation; 5.2.3.02 Political/social/economic exclusion; 5.2.3.03 Premature death; 5.2.3.04 Guilt/grace/redemption; 5.2.3.05 Love/solidarity; 5.2.3.06 Empowerment toward others; 5.2.3.07 Empowerment of the self; 5.3 Appropriation dynamics; 5.3.1 Harmony: in my life God's promises are fulfilled; 5.3.2 Dialectical: the narrative changed my perspective; 5.3.3 Conflict; 5.3.3.1 Actual values have to change; 5.3.3.2 Biblical values overruled; 5.3.4 Self-critical; 5.3.4.1 Awareness of one's own context; 5.3.4.2 Awareness of one's own ideology; 5.3.4.3 Awareness of one's own cultural bias; 5.3.4.4 Awareness of one's own failure/sin; 5.3.4.5 Awareness of one's own prejudices; 5.3.5 Hermeneutic circulation: context-text-context; 5.4 Praxeological effect; 5.4.1 Intention (we should . . .); 5.4.1.0 New life(style); 5.4.1.0.1 Breaking through cultural barriers; 5.4.1.0.2 Interfaith dialogue; 5.4.1.0a Conversion; 5.4.1.0b Worshiping the true God; 5.4.1.0c Imitating Jesus; 5.4.1.0d Imitating the Samaritan woman; 5.4.1.1 Critical dialogue with alienating contemporary religious movements; 5.4.1.2. Involvement in resistance movements; 5.4.1.3 Forms of diakonia; 5.4.1.4 Charity; 5.4.1.5 Evangelize/mission; 5.4.1.6 Nonjudgmentalness; 5.4.1.7 Altruism/love for the other(s); 5.4.1.8 Nonexclusion; 5.4.1.9 Church must renew itself (worship, building, style, location, etc.); 5.4.1.9 Word and deed (personal faith and good deeds); 5.4.2 Real (new) praxis; 5.4.2.0 New lifestyle; 5.4.2.1 New forms of social or political action; 5.4.2.2 Involvement in resistance movements; 5.4.2.3 Forms of diakonia; 5.4.2.4 Charity; 5.4.2.5 Evangelism; 5.4.2.6 Altruism/love for others

Codes for the second phase

1 CIRCUMSTANTIAL; 1.01 Meeting; 1.01.1 Location; 1.01.2 Date; 1.01.3 Number of sessions; 1.01.4 Date first phase concluded; 1.01.4.1 A few months ago; 1.01.4.2 Half a year ago; 1.01.4.3 Longer ago; 1.01.5 Date first phase of the partner group concluded; 1.01.5.1 A few months ago; 1.01.5.2 Half a year ago; 1.01.5.3 Longer ago; 1.02 Report; 1.02.1 Type; 1.02.1.1 Verbatim; 1.02.1.2 Summary; 1.02.1.3 Other; 1.02.2 Date of report; 1.02.3 Appendixes; 1.02.3.1 Photos; 1.02.3.2 Video; 1.02.3.3 Audio; 1.02.3.3.1 Group discussion; 1.02.3.3.2 Hymns, etc.; 1.02.3.3.3 Other; 1.02.3.4 Other; 1.02.3.4.1 Letters; 1.02.3.4.2 Gifts; 1.02.3.4.3 Personal expressions; 1.02.3.4.4 Other; 1.03 Group characteristics; 1.03.1 Composition; 1.03.1.1 The same; 1.03.1.2 Partially new; 1.03.2 Names/number; 1.03.2.1 5–10; 1.03.2.2 10–20; 1.03.3.4 >60; 1.03.4 M/F; 1.03.4.1 50/50; 1.03.4.2 >50% M; 1.03.4.3 >50% F; 1.03.5 Church affiliation; 1.03.5.1 Ecumenically composed; 1.03.5.2.1 Pentecostal tradition; 1.03.5.2.2 Reformation tradition (Lutheran/Presbyterian/etc.); 1.03.5.2.3 Baptist; 1.03.5.2.4 Quaker; 1.03.5.2.5 Mennonite; 1.03.5.2.6 Other; 1.03.5.2 Protestant; 1.03.5.3 Roman Catholic; 1.03.5.4 Roman Catholic revival movement (charismatic); 1.03.5.5 BEC; 1.03.5.6 Order; 1.03.5.7 Other; 1.03.6 Group's "place"; 1.03.6.1 Social; 1.03.6.1.1 Status/class; 1.03.6.1.1.1 Upper class; 1.03.6.1.1.2 Middle class; 1.03.6.1.1.3 Low(er) class; 1.03.6.1.2 Work; 1.03.6.1.2.1 Type; 1.03.6.1.3 Unemployed; 1.03.6.2 Politics; 1.03.6.2.1 Liberal; 1.03.6.2.2 Social Democrat; 1.03.6.2.3 Middle–Christian Democrat; 1.03.6.2.4 None; 1.03.6.3 Ethnicity; 1.03.6.3.1 Minority; 1.03.6.3.2 Majority; 1.03.6.3.3 Caste; 1.03.6.3.4 Caste; 1.03.6.4.5 Outcasts; 1.03.7 Intercultural experience; 1.03.7.1 Own context; 1.03.7.2 Traveled; 1.03.7.3 Lived in a different culture/abroad; 1.03.7.4 School/education; 1.03.7.5 Friends; 1.03.7.6 Work; 1.03.7.7 Other; 1.04 Partner group characteristics; 1.04.01 Composition; 1.04.01.1 The same; 1.04.01.2 Partially new; 1.04.02 Names/num-

ber; 1.04.02.1 5–10; 1.04.02.2 10–20; 1.04.02.3 >20; 1.04.03 Age of participants; 1.04.03.1
15–20; 1.04.03.2 20–40; 1.04.03.3 40–60; 1.04.03.4 >60; 1.04.04 M/F; 1.04.04.1 50/
50; 1.04.04.2 >50% M; 1.04.04.3 >50% F; 1.04.04.4 Only M.; 1.04.04.5 Only F; 1.04.05
Church affiliation; 1.04.05.1 Ecumenically composed; 1.04.05.2.1 Pentecostal tradition;
1.04.05.2.2 Reformation tradition (Lutheran/Presbyterian/etc.); 1.04.05.2.3 Baptist;
1.04.05.2.4 Quaker; 1.04.05.2.5 Mennonite; 1.04.05.2.6 Other; 1.04.05.2 Protestant;
1.04.05.3 Roman Catholic; 1.04.05.4 Roman Catholic revival movement (charismatic);
1.04.05.5 BEC; 1.04.05.6 Order; 1.04.05.7 Other; 1.04.06 Partner group's "place"; 1.04.06.1
Social; 1.04.06.1.1 Status/class; 1.04.06.1.1.1 Upper class; 1.04.06.1.1.2 Middle class;
1.04.06.1.1.3 Low(er) class; 1.04.06.1.2 Work; 1.04.06.1.2.1 Type; 1.04.06.1.3 Unemployed; 1.04.06.2 Politics; 1.04.06.2.1 Social Democrat; 1.04.06.2.2 Liberal; 1.04.06.2.3
Middle (Christian Democrat); 1.04.06.2.4 None; 1.04.06.3 Ethnicity; 1.04.06.3.1 Minority; 1.04.06.3.2 Majority; 1.04.06.3.3 Castes 1.04.07 Intercultural experience; 1.04.07.1
Own context; 1.04.07.2 Traveled; 1.04.07.3 Lived (outside own culture); 1.04.07.4 School/
education; 1.04.07.5 Friends; 1.04.07.6 Work; 1.04.07.7 Other; 1.04.08 Motivation of
the group; 1.04.08.1 Cognitive; 1.04.08.1.1 One wishes to be challenged (motivation for validity); 1.04.08.1.2 One seeks structure/safety (motivation for structure); 1.04.08.1.3 One seeks
more of the same (motivation for specific content); 1.04.08.2 Affective; 1.04.08.2.1 Empathy/
emotionality/solidarity; 1.04.08.2.2.Longing for a better/different world; 1.04.08.2.3 Exploratory affective exchange; 1.04.08.2.4 One wants to help; 1.04.08.2.5 One wants to be helped;
1.04.09 Motivation of the partner group; 1.04.09.1 Cognitive; 1.04.09.1.1 One wishes to be
challenged (motivation for validity); 1.04.09.1.2 One seeks structure/safety (motivation for
structure); 1.04.09.1.3 One seeks more of the same (motivation for specific content); 1.04.09.2
Affective; 1.04.09.2.1 Empathy/emotionality/solidarity; 1.04.09.2.2 Longing for a better/
different world; 1.04.09.2.3 Exploratory affective exchange; 1.04.09.2.4 One wants to help;
1.04.09.2.5 One wants to be helped; 1.04.10 Expectations on the part of the group; 1.04.10.1
Of the process and its effect; 1.04.10.2 Of the partner group; 1.04.11 Expectations on the part
of the partner group; 1.04.11.1 Of the process and its effect; 1.04.11.2 Of the partner group

2 THE CONFRONTATION; 2.01 PROFILE SESSION(S); 2.01.1 Liturgical; 2.01.1.1 Prayers;
2.01.1.2 Hymns; 2.01.1.3 Other; 2.01.2 Convivencia; 2.01.2.1 Eating/celebrating together;
2.01.2.2 Game; 2.01.2.3 Other; 2.02 INTERACTION WITH THE PARTNER GROUP; 2.02.0 Linking
process; 2.02.0.1 Satisfied; 2.02.0.2 Not satisfied; 2.02.1 One gets acquainted with the context
of the partner group; 2.02.1.1 In separate preparatory session; 2.02.1.2 During the reading
process; 2.02.1.3 Via expert who knows the country of the partner group; 2.02.1.4 Via photos/
video of partner group; 2.02.2 Attention to/analysis of profile of the partner group; 2.02.2.1
Partner group issues that stand out; 2.02.2.1.1 Personal experiences/vulnerability/disclosure;
2.02.2.1.2 Information determined by context; 2.02.2.1.2.1 Socioeconomic; 2.02.2.1.2.2
Politics; 2.02.2.1.2.3 Cultural; 2.02.2.1.2.3 Age/composition; M/F proportion; 2.02.2.1.2.4
Ethnic; 2.02.2.1.2.5 Ecclesiastical; 2.02.2.1.3 Aspects of the interpretation process of the
partner group; 2.02.2.2 Perceived similarities; 2.02.2.2.1 Age and composition of the group;
2.02.2.2.2 M/F proportion; 2.02.2.2.2 Religious/exegetic professionals; 2.02.2.2.3 Relationship work-church; 2.02.2.2.4 Social status; 2.02.2.2.5 Level of education; 2.02.2.2.6 "Place"
where one reads; 2.02.2.2.7 Information determined by context; 2.02.2.2.8 Culturally determined information; 2.02.2.2.9 Information determined by church tradition; 2.02.2.2.9a
Aspects of the interpretation process at the partner group; 2.02.2.3 Perceived differences; 2.02.2.3.1
Age and composition of the group; 2.02.2.3.2 M/F proportion; 2.02.2.3.3 Relationship work-
church; 2.02.2.3.4 Social status; 2.02.2.3.5 Level of education; 2.02.2.3.6 "Place" where one
reads; 2.02.2.3.7 Information determined by context; 2.02.2.3.8 Culturally determined information; 2.02.2.3.9 Information determined by church tradition; 2.02.2.3.9a Aspects of the
interpretation process at the partner group; 2.02.2.3.9b Religious/exegetic professionals; 2.02.3
ATTITUDE TOWARD PARTNER GROUP; 2.02.3.0 Mindful; 2.02.3.1 Critical; 2.02.3.2 Nonjudgmental;

2.02.3.3 Openness; 2.02.3.4 Tolerance for ambiguity; 2.02.3.4a No tolerance for ambiguity; 2.02.3.5 Vulnerability/sensitivity to disclosure of the partner group/reading "out of wound"; 2.02.3.6 The need to convert/pedantic; 2.02.3.7 The need to control; 2.02.3.8 Admiration; 2.02.3.9 Extremely biased; 2.02.4 Communication with the partner group via report second phase; 2.02.4.1 Direct ("Hello, Tom, Dick, and Harry. It is a privilege to . . ."); 2.02.4.1.1 Direct expressions of admiration/gratitude/trust; 2.02.4.2 Pairs are formed; 2.02.4.3 Indirect: "they," "their"; 2.02.4.4 None; 2.02.4.5 Power/asymmetry in communication; 2.02.4.5.1 Hidden/public transcript; 2.02.4.5.2 Patterns of Freire; 2.02.4.5.3 Culture–co-culture communication patterns; 2.02.4.5.3.1 Assimilation patterns; 2.02.4.5.3.2 Accommodation patterns; 2.02.4.5.3.3 Separation patterns; 2.02.4.5.4 Development-underdevelopment patterns; 2.02.4.5.4.1 Modernity paradigm; 2.02.4.5.4.2 Empowerment paradigm; 2.02.5 Expectation of result of confrontation with partner group report in relation to own report; 2.02.5.1 One expects a universal unambiguous meaning; 2.02.5.2 One expects and accepts diversity; 2.02.6 Overall judgment of the interpretation by the partner group; 2.03 ANALYSIS OF THE PARTNER GROUP'S READING REPORT; 2.03.1 METHOD OF ANALYSIS OF THE PARTNER GROUP REPORT; 2.03.1.1 In everyone's possession/read by everyone; 2.03.1.2 Not in everyone's possession/a summary is given; 2.03.1.3 The order of the partner group report is maintained; 2.03.1.4 Pairs are formed; 2.03.1.5 One associates freely/operates eclectically/no system; 2.03.1.6 The previous session(s) is/are referred to; 2.03.1.7 The group rereads its own reading report; 2.03.1.8 The text of John 4 is reread; 2.03.1.8a One is absorbed by issues in the partner group's reading report that are not understood; 2.03.1.9 One visits the website; 2.03.1.9a One is concerned about the translation; 2.03.2 GROUP DYNAMIC DEVELOPMENT ANALYSIS OF THE PARTNER GROUP REPORT; 2.03.2.1 Nobody is boss; 2.03.2.2 Dominant voices; 2.03.2.2.1 M/F; 2.03.2.3 Silent group members—due to: 2.03.2.3.1 Internal factors; 2.03.2.3.1.1 Dominants in group; 2.03.2.3.1.2 Not accustomed to speaking; 2.03.2.3.1.3 Other; 2.03.2.3.2 External factors; 2.03.2.3.2.1 Due to opinions of partner group; 2.03.2.3.2.2 Asymmetry between groups; 2.03.2.3.2.3 Other; 2.04 ANALYSIS OF THE INTERPRETATION PROCESS BY THE PARTNER GROUP; 2.04.1 Analysis of the development of the process of the partner group's interpretation; 2.04.1.1 Number of sessions of partner group first phase; 2.04.1.2 Content and development of sessions; 2.04.2 Analysis of available exegetic resources to the partner group; 2.04.2.1 Commentaries; 2.04.2.2 Knowledge of languages; 2.04.2.3 Experts; 2.04.3 Translation of the partner group; 2.04.4 ANALYSIS OF THE METHOD OF THE INTERPRETATION ("EXEGESIS") OF THE TEXT BY THE PARTNER GROUP; 2.04.4.1 Classification is done technically—according to "type"; 2.04.4.1.1 Historical-critical; 2.04.4.1.2 Sociological; 2.04.4.1.3 Literary; 2.04.4.1.4 Cultural dimensions (Hofstede); 2.04.4.2 Classification is done intuitively; 2.04.4.2.1 Cerebrally/distant/scientifically; 2.04.4.2.2 Historical/historicalized; 2.04.4.2.3 Focused on appropriation/life/actuality; 2.04.4.2.4 Other; 2.04.4.3 Perceived similarities; 2.04.4.3.1 They read just the way we do; 2.04.4.3.2 Other; 2.04.4.3.2a ASSESSMENT SIMILARITIES; 2.04.4.4 Perceived differences; 2.04.4.4.1 They are more focused on the text (technical, historical, objectifying); 2.04.4.4.2 We are more focused on the text . . . ; 2.04.4.4.3 They are more disconnected/associative; 2.04.4.4.4 We are more disconnected/associative; 2.04.4.5 ASSESSMENT DIFFERENCES; 2.04.4.5.1 Complementary/enriching; 2.04.4.5.2 Disagreement (incorrect, nothing to learn); 2.04.4.5.3 Irritation; 2.04.4.5.4 Don't understand what they are talking about; 2.04.5 ANALYSIS OF THE STATUS OF THE TEXT FOR PARTNER GROUP IN RELATION TO OWN; 2.04.5.1 They: Holy Scripture; 2.04.5.2 They: historical text; 2.04.5.3 They: object of scientific analysis/no actualization; 2.04.5.4 We: Holy Scripture; 2.04.5.5 We: historical text; 2.04.5.6 We: object of scientific analysis/no actualization; 2.04.6 Analysis of the reading attitude of the text by the partner group in relation to own attitude (first they, then we); 2.04.6.1 Literal; 2.04.6.2 Dogmatic; 2.04.6.2 Focused on life; 2.04.6.2.3 Other; 2.04.6.3 Liberating; 2.04.6.4 Contemplative; 2.04.6.5 Psychologizing; 2.04.6.6 Pietistic/spiritual; 2.04.6.7 With suspicion; 2.04.6.8 Productive; 2.04.6.9 Reproductive; 2.04.6.9a Contextual; 2.04.6.9b Individual/individualistic; 2.04.6.9c Communitarian/collective; 2.04.6.9d Scientific; 2.04.7 Analysis of the result hoped for or intended/effect of the interpretation of text by

430 Hans de Wit

partner group in relation to own one (first they, then we); 2.04.7.1 Effect for today (relevant); 2.04.7.1.1 Social transformation; 2.04.7.1.2 To retrieve something; 2.04.7.1.3 Focused on survival; 2.04.7.2 More information of (the world of) the text (pertinent); 2.04.8 ANALYSIS OF THE RESULT OF INTERPRETATION OF JOHN 4 BY PARTNER GROUP IN RELATION TO OWN INTERPRETATION; 2.04.8.1 PERCEIVED SIMILARITIES; 2.04.8.1.1 Central message; 2.04.8.1.2 Centrality/role of characters; 2.04.8.1.3 Broader literary context (Intra/intertextual parallels; 2.04.8.1.3.1 Thematic parallels; 2.04.8.1.3.2 Word parallels; 2.04.8.1.4 Imagination strategies; 2.04.8.1.4a Conflicts in the text; 2.04.8.1.5 Heuristic keys/focalization; 2.04.8.1.5.1 Culture; 2.04.8.1.5.2 Socioeconomic; 2.04.8.1.5.3 Religious; 2.04.8.1.5.4 Ethical; 2.04.8.1.5.5 Other; 2.04.8.1.6 Specific themes; 2.04.8.1.6.01 (Living) water; 2.04.8.1.6.02 Quick conversion of Samaritan woman; 2.04.8.1.6.03 Passing through Samaria; 2.04.8.1.6.04 Image of Jesus (in the text); 2.04.8.1.6.04.1 Godly figure (looks through people, knows all); 2.04.8.1.6.04.2 Jesus breaks through barriers; 2.04.8.1.6.04.3 Jesus method (pastoral, pedagogic); 2.04.8.1.6.05 Identification with Jews and their conflict; 2.04.8.1.6.06 Sixth man; 2.04.8.1.6.07 Samaritan woman; 2.04.8.1.6.08 The meeting; 2.04.8.1.6.08 Sixth hour; 2.04.8.1.6.09 Father Jacob; 2.04.8.1.6.10 Conflict between Jews-Samaritans; 2.04.8.1.7 Text segments (first they, then we); 2.04.8.1.7.1 vv. 01–03; 2.04.8.1.7.2 vv. 04–06; 2.04.8.1.7.3 vv. 07–08; 2.04.8.1.7.4 vv. 09–10; 2.04.8.1.7.5 vv. 10–14; 2.04.8.1.7.6 vv. 15–19; 2.04.8.1.7.7 vv. 20–26; 2.04.8.1.7.8 vv. 27–30; 2.04.8.1.7.9 vv. 31–38; 2.04.8.1.7.9a vv. 39–42; 2.04.8.1.8 Actualization; 2.04.8.1.8.1 Appropriation strategies; 2.04.8.1.8.1.1 Allegory; 2.04.8.1.8.1.2 Typology; 2.04.8.1.8.1.3 Parallelism of themes (tracing paper); 2.04.8.1.8.1.4 Parallelism of relations; 2.04.8.1.8.1.5 *Dialog der Verhältnisse*; 2.04.8.1.8.2 Appropriation content/praxeological; 2.04.8.1.8.2.1 Difficult to be a disciple; 2.04.8.2 ASSESSMENT SIMILARITIES; 2.04.8.2.1 Positive/ecumenical honeymoon; 2.04.8.2.2 Negative/it's a pity—disappointed/not exciting; 2.04.8.2.3 Other; 2.04.8.3 PERCEIVED DIFFERENCES; 2.04.8.3.0 Information on/perception of the world behind the text; 2.04.8.3.1 Central message; 2.04.8.3.2 Centrality/role of characters; 2.04.8.3.2a "Reading with"; 2.04.8.3.3 Broader literary context (intra/intertextual parallels); 2.04.8.3.3.1 Thematic parallels; 2.04.8.3.3.2 Word parallels; 2.04.8.3.4 Imagination strategies; 2.04.8.3.4a Conflicts in the text; 2.04.8.3.5 Heuristic keys/focalization; 2.04.8.3.5.1 Culture; 2.04.8.3.5.2 Socioeconomic; 2.04.8.3.5.3 Religious; 2.04.8.3.5.4 Ethnic; 2.04.8.3.5.5 Other; 2.04.8.3.6 Read/discussed sections of John 4; 2.04.8.3.6 Specific themes; 2.04.8.3.6.01 (Living) water; 2.04.8.3.6.02 Quick conversion of Samaritan woman; 2.04.8.3.6.02 Father Jacob/ancestors/ancestors; 2.04.8.3.6.03 Passing through Samaria; 2.04.8.3.6.04 Perception of Jesus; 2.04.8.3.6.04.01 Jesus too human; 2.04.8.3.6.04.02 Jesus too exalted/divine/not human enough (looks through people, knows all, etc.); 2.04.8.3.6.04.10 The meeting too human; 2.04.8.3.6.04.2 Jesus breaks through barriers; 2.04.8.3.6.04.3 Jesus's method (pastoral, pedagogic); 2.04.8.3.6.05 Identification with Jews and their conflict; 2.04.8.3.6.06 Sixth man; 2.04.8.3.6.07 Samaritan woman; 2.04.8.3.6.08 Five men; 2.04.8.3.6.09 Worship in spirit and truth; 2.04.8.3.7 Text segments; 2.04.8.3.7.1 vv. 01–03; 2.04.8.3.7.2 vv. 04–06; 2.04.8.3.7.3 vv. 07–08; 2.04.8.3.7.4 vv. 09–10; 2.04.8.3.7.5 vv. 10–14; 2.04.8.3.7.6 vv. 15–19; 2.04.8.3.7.7 vv. 20–26; 2.04.8.3.7.8 vv. 27–30; 2.04.8.3.7.9 vv. 31–38; 2.04.8.3.7.9a vv. 39–42; 2.04.8.3.8 Actualization; 2.04.8.3.8.1 Analysis of appropriation strategies (first they, then we); 2.04.8.3.8.1.0 One is touched by the actualization of the partner group; 2.04.8.3.8.1.1 Allegory; 2.04.8.3.8.1.2 Typology; 2.04.8.3.8.1.3 Parallelism of terms (tracing paper); 2.04.8.3.8.1.4 Parallelism of relations; 2.04.8.3.8.1.5 *Dialog der Verhältnisse*; 2.04.8.3.8.2 Analysis of contents of appropriation (first they, then we); 2.04.8.3.8.2.0 Interfaith dialogue (e.g., Christian-Islam); 2.04.8.3.8.2.1 Eternal values; 2.04.8.3.8.2.1 Difficult to be a disciple; 2.04.8.3.8.2.2 Other; 2.04.8.3.8.2.2 Truth as strength for their own earthly struggle; 2.04.8.3.8.2.3 Life experiences as sequel to the biblical salvation history? 2.04.8.3.8.2.4 Oppression-liberation; 2.04.8.3.8.2.5 Political/social/economic exclusion; 2.04.8.3.8.2.6 Premature death; 2.04.8.3.8.2.7 Guilt/grace/redemption; 2.04.8.3.8.2.8 Love/solidarity; 2.04.8.3.8.2.9 Other; 2.04.8.3.8.3 Analysis of the praxeological effect of appropriation (first they, then we); 2.04.8.3.8.3.1 Difficult to be a disciple; 2.04.8.3.8.3.2 Other; 2.04.8.4 ASSESSMENT DIFFERENCES; 2.04.8.4.0 One looks for correlation between differences and backgrounds of both groups, respectively; 2.04.8.4.0.01 Church background; 2.04.8.4.0.02 Context; 2.04.8.4.0.03 Group converts difference with the partner group to connection of culture and text interpretation at the p group; 2.04.8.4.1 Positive: ecumenical honeymoon—diversity leads to growth; 2.04.8.4.2 Negative: diversity is dividedness; 2.04.8.4.3 Other; 2.04.8.5 Dealing with the differences; 2.04.8.5.1 Graceful fighting; 2.04.8.5.1.1 Group arguments using proof from the text; 2.04.8.5.1.2 The group's own interpretation is supported by new arguments; 2.04.8.5.1.3 Group solves questions by the partner group by means of interpreting the text; 2.04.8.5.1.4 Other imagination strategy; 2.04.8.5.2 Damping; 2.04.8.5.2.1 Appeal to: Cultural universals; 2.04.8.5.2.1.1 The ideal of preserving human life; 2.04.8.5.2.1.2 Looking to the well-being of close relatives; 2.04.8.5.2.1.3 Prohibiting murder and theft; 2.04.8.5.2.1.4 Valuing affection and companionship; 2.04.8.5.2.1.5 Reciprocity in helping and being helped; 2.04.8.5.2.2 Appeal to religious universals; 2.04.8.5.2.2.1 Metacultural aspects of the story; 2.04.8.5.2.2.2 One body and many members; 2.04.8.5.3 Rupture/withdrawal; 2.04.8.5.3.1 Group arguments using proof from the text; 2.04.8.5.3.2 Group solves questions by the partner group by means of interpreting the text; 2.04.8.5.3.3 The group's own interpretation is supported by new arguments; 2.04.8.5.3.4 Questions/shyness of the partner group are answered and regarded as a sign of incorrect or incomplete interpretation; 2.04.8.5.3.5 Other imagination strategy; 2.04.8.5.3.6 Other; 2.04.8.6 Nonperceived similarities; 2.04.8.6.1 Culture; 2.04.8.6.2 Social status; 2.04.8.6.3 Knowledge; 2.04.8.6.4 Hermeneutic; 2.04.8.7 Nonperceived differences; 2.04.8.7.1 Culture; 2.04.8.7.2 Social status; 2.04.8.7.3 Knowledge; 2.04.8.7.4 Hermeneutic

3 EFFECT; 3.1 Perceived effects; 3.1.1 Interpretation process John 4 (partner group reading related to own reading); 3.1.1.1 Understanding the text; 3.1.1.1.1 New outlook on the text; 3.1.1.1.1.a No new outlook on the text; 3.1.1.1.2 New focalization; 3.1.1.1.3 New information on (historical background of) the text; 3.1.1.1.3 Challenged to new study; 3.1.1.1.4 Rejection of the partner group's point of view/reinforcing own group's point of view; 3.1.1.1.5 New outlook on central characters in the text; 3.1.1.1.5.01 Samaritan woman; 3.1.1.2 Method; 3.1.1.2.1 New information/group imitates method of partner group; 3.1.1.2.2 Rejection of the method of the partner group/not necessary to learn new ways; 3.1.1.3 Hermeneutic 3.1.1.3.1 Horizon broadening; 3.1.1.3.2 Clash/conflict of interpretations; 3.1.1.4 Theology-faith-church-ecumenism; 3.1.1.4.1 New insights into faith; 3.1.1.4.2 Reinforce own interpretation/nothing learned; 3.1.2 Self image of group after (as effect of) process; 3.1.2.1 More awareness of one's own culture; 3.1.2.2 More awareness of one's own bias/prejudices; 3.1.2.3 More awareness of one's own ideological framework; 3.1.2.4 More intercultural competence; 3.1.2.4.1 Knowledge; 3.1.2.4.2 Motivation; 3.1.2.4.3 Skills; 3.1.3 Relation to the partner group; 3.1.3.1 More awareness of context of partner group; 3.1.3.2 More awareness of relationship/problems partner group to/with its society/church/etc.; 3.1.3.3 More awareness and/or comprehension of ideology of partner group; 3.1.3.4 More awareness of cultural bias of partner group; 3.1.3.5 Self-criticism of the partner group serves for self-criticism of the group; 3.1.4 Description of process by group at the end of process; 3.1.4.1 Affective growth: from orientation to stable exchange; 3.1.4.2 Cognitive growth: from cognitive discrepancy to cognitive consensus; 3.1.4.3 U or W figure Cultural/self/religious shock; 3.1.5 Assessment of process by group at the end of process; 3.1.5.1 Growth; 3.1.5.1.1 Acknowledged augmented competence in intercultural communication; 3.1.5.1.2 Enriching for group itself (Third Culture perspective); 3.1.5.1.3 More critical attitude toward the group's own interpretation of the text or actuation in the context; 3.1.5.1.3 Main factors responsible for growth/change; 3.1.5.1.3.1 Interpretation of partner group of John 4; 3.1.5.1.3.1.1 Reading method of the partner group; 3.1.5.1.3.2 Faith of the partner group; 3.1.5.1.3.3 Appropriation and actualization of the text by the partner group; 3.1.5.1.3.4

Vulnerability of the partner group; 3.1.5.1.3.5 Knowledge of context of the partner group; 3.1.5.1.3.6 Motivation of the partner group; 3.1.5.2 Return to the group's own repertoire (stagnation); 3.1.5.2.1 Freezing: closure on a given belief; 3.1.5.2.2 No Third Culture perspective; 3.1.5.2.3 Main factors responsible for return to one's own repertoire; 3.1.5.2.3.01 Culture; 3.1.5.2.3.02 Secularization of partner group context; 3.1.5.2.3.03 Appropriation (*applicatio*); 3.1.6 Praxeological effect–behavior; 3.2 Nonperceived effects

Notes

[1] Hans de Wit, "Through the Eyes of Another: A Project on Intercultural Reading of the Bible" (presentation, consultation on Intercultural Reading of the Bible, Free University, Amsterdam, the Netherlands, 2001; a version of this paper, with the same title, became the standard project handbook).

[2] Barney G. Glaser and Anselm L. Strauss, *The Discovery of Grounded Theory: Strategies for Qualitative Research* (Chicago, Ill.: Aldine Publishing Co., 1967).

[3] De Wit, "Through the Eyes of Another."

[4] Louis C. Jonker and Ernst M. Conradie, "Determining Relative Adequacy in Biblical Interpretation: Biblical Interpretation in Established Bible Study Groups in the Western Cape, South Africa," *Scriptura* 78 (2001): 448–55.

[5] Daniel Bar-Tal, "Israeli-Palestinian Conflict: A Cognitive Analysis," *International Journal of Intercultural Relations* 14 (1990): 7–29.

[6] E. Tory Higgins and Arie W. Kruglanski, *Social Psychology: Handbook of Basic Principles* (New York: Guilford Press, 1996).

[7] Bar-Tal, "Israeli-Palestinian Conflict."

[8] Ibid.

[9] Walter J. Ong, *Orality and Literacy: The Technologizing of the Word* (London: Methuen, 1982), 45ff.

[10] Mieke Bal, *De Theorie van Vertellen En Verhalen: Inleiding in de Narratologie* (Muiderberg, the Netherlands: Coutinho, 1978).

[11] Clodovis Boff, *Teología de lo Político: Sus Mediaciones* (Salamanca, Spain: Ediciones Sígueme, 1980).

[12] J. A. van der Ven, *Entwurf einer empirischen Theologie* (Kampen, the Netherlands: Kok, 1990).

[13] William B. Gudykunst and Young Yun Kim, *Communicating with Strangers: An Approach to Intercultural Communication* (Boston, Mass.: McGraw Hill, 2003), 285.

[14] M. Scott Peck, *The Different Drum: Community-Making and Peace* (New York: Simon & Schuster, 1987); cited in Gudykunst and Kim, *Communicating with Strangers*.

[15] Henk Procee, *Over de Grenzen van Culturen: Voorbij Universalisme en Relativisme* (Amsterdam: Boom, 1991).

[16] James Scott, *Domination and the Arts of Resistance: Hidden Transcripts* (New Haven, Conn.: Yale University Press, 1990).

[17] William B. Gudykunst and Bella Mody, eds. *Handbook of International and Intercultural Communication* (Thousand Oaks, Calif.: Sage Publications, 2002).

[18] Mark P. Orbe, *Constructing Co-cultural Theory: An Explication of Culture, Power, and Communication* (Thousand Oaks, Calif.: Sage Publications, 1998).

[19] Richard L. Wiseman, "Intercultural Communication Competence," in *Handbook of International and Intercultural Communication*, ed. Gudykunst and Mody, 207–24.

[20] Ibid.

[21] Gudykunst and Kim, *Communicating with Strangers*, 377–78.

[22] Ibid., 384ff.

PART 4

Further implications of the project

CHAPTER 23

Through the eyes of practical theology and theological education

Daniel Schipani and Mary Schertz

This essay consists of two parts, as suggested by the title. The first part, of which Daniel Schipani is the primary writer, starts with a section discussing how the intercultural Bible reading project Through the Eyes of Another can be envisioned in light of practical theology as a discipline. It also considers how intercultural Bible studies and practical theology can enrich each other. The second part of this chapter, written mainly by Mary Schertz, consists of a reflective report on the pertinence of the project for theological education and ministerial formation. The chapter ends with the Greek text of John 4 and the English translation Mary prepared for the seminary class on teaching the Bible in the congregation that we teach as a team.

Through the eyes of practical theology

The last several decades have seen the development of a new disciplinary understanding of practical theology understood as a theory of action with descriptive-empirical, interpretive, normative, and pragmatic-strategic dimensions and tasks.[1] Indeed, the uniqueness of practical theology can be stated first of all in terms of its contextual engagement, that is, its focus on the realities of concrete human beings in given historical and cultural situations. Second, practical theology is empirically grounded, involved in systematic observation of actual experiences of people, using tools normally associated with the behavioral and social sciences, such as survey and interview instruments. Third, practical theology is a hermeneutically constructed theological endeavor always necessitating interdisciplinary work, especially the careful interfacing of theological and human science perspectives and contributions. Finally, practical theology is strategically committed, in the sense of including open-ended guidelines in the form of "rules of art"[2] meant to help those who participate

Daniel Schipani, Church and Ministry Department, and Mary Schertz, Bible Department, Associated Mennonite Biblical Seminary (Elkhart, Indiana, USA)

in or lead certain faith practices or ministry arts, such as reading the Bible and leading and teaching Bible study groups.

Practical theologians dream about participating in research that is inherently interdisciplinary, international in scope, ecumenical in character, and jointly sponsored by academic and ecclesial bodies. So several years ago, I welcomed the invitation to join a small number of practitioners and scholars to evaluate a recently completed program designed to foster intercontextual Bible reading and communication across cultures, and to explore the possibility of launching a much larger project.[3] I then became involved in the implementation of the Intercultural Reading of the Bible project as a consultant, regional coordinator, and researcher. The following observations stem from that participation.

Intercultural Bible reading in light of four practical-theological dimensions

In the following paragraphs, the practical theological nature of the project will become evident. I will thus illustrate those interrelated dimensions and tasks pertaining to the structure of practical theology viewed as a unique theological endeavor in its own right and aimed at constructing contextualized action-guiding theories of ecclesial and faith practices.[4]

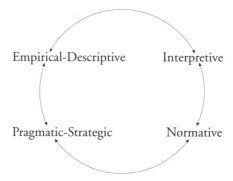

Empirical-Descriptive   Interpretive

Pragmatic-Strategic   Normative

The empirical-descriptive dimension. As documented throughout this book, the research was focused on the real life situation of numerous Bible reading groups in a variety of sociocultural contexts. Reporters and researchers, in consultation with the group members themselves, needed to engage in the task of describing as fully and accurately as possible the particular nature of those sociocultural contexts and the unique characteristics of the groups. They also needed to describe thoroughly what went on in each session (that is, not only the actual practices of reading, discussing, interpreting the text, and responding to the partner groups' reading, but also the activities involved in gathering and dispersing, rituals and other faith practices, group dynamics and ways of relating and communicating, etc.). The more complete the observation and description—the more detailed the response to the question, What is going on?"—the better founded the task of interpretation having to do with the question, Why is that going on? which is the focus of the task briefly discussed below.

The interpretive dimension. Local researchers were also in charge of doing a hermeneutical analysis of the groups' readings of the John 4 text. The purpose was to situate the empirical research within a more comprehensive explanatory framework. It became apparent, however, that description and interpretation are a two-way street. The hermeneutical task interpreted the descriptions, yet those descriptions often opened up and even corrected the interpretations. The resulting reports included a rich variety of hermeneutical-theoretical analyses of the readings. Special attention was given to diverse sets of criteria, having to do with categories such as the following: (1) modes of reading with which the text was interpreted (through study, music, art, other?); (2) attention to the text itself and to the world behind the text (Were the groups aware of particular textual features? Which aspects of the text informed and shaped their reading?); (3) heuristic keys and codes and interpretation strategies (How did the groups link the text to present life and experience?); (4) strategies of imagination (How did the groups develop meaning from the text? How did they fill in the gaps in the narrative?); (5) interculturality and intertextuality (What features of the text were related to their local culture, and how? What other biblical texts played a role in their reading?); (6) overall reading attitude (Was it literalistic, pietistic, dogmatic, contemplative, psychologizing, liberating, other?); (7) self-awareness (Were participants aware of their own interpretive contexts, and of the biases, ideologies, and power relationships that tend to influence Bible reading?); (8) praxeological effect (Did the groups seek to develop new forms of relating, acting, and serving in the larger society?).

The normative dimension. The tasks involved in this dimension of the practical theological work point to the question, What forms ought the practices of Bible reading, leading and teaching study groups, and intercultural communication take in each particular social context? So the primary focus is on the construction, affirmation, or revision of theological and ethical norms. This dimension is directly connected to the descriptive and interpretive tasks previously noted. Researchers needed to ponder a number of practical issues, such as how to identify and foster leadership and group dynamics more conducive to better ways of communicating and relating, and better ways of reading the Bible and interpreting other people's reading of the John 4 text. Again, practitioners and researchers alike were required to engage in a multiway conversation involving sources and contributions stemming from the Christian tradition (e.g., biblically grounded and theologically articulated guidelines, and established church practices), and those available in the human sciences and in the practical wisdom of the participants themselves, including the rich reservoirs of their own cultural settings.

It is worth noting that attention to this normative dimension did not simply follow from consideration of the empirical-descriptive and hermeneutical tasks. In fact, it was present from the beginning and contributed to shaping those tasks, even as it was in turn reshaped by the work of observation and interpretation. Further, normative considerations were also influenced by the pragmatic and strategic interests that normally inspire and guide practical theological endeavors.

The pragmatic-strategic dimension. As indicated earlier, one of the unique features of practical theology as a theological discipline is its strategic commitment and its orientation to action and change. For example, practical theology plays a crucial role in efforts to sponsor formation and transformation in the life of the faithful, to improve ministry practices and develop new ones, and to foster the integrity and effectiveness of the church's witness in the world. In the same manner, far from being a narrowly academic and scientific exercise, one that is supposedly neutrally conceived, this intercultural Bible reading project was designed with pragmatic and strategic considerations in mind. Researchers sought to identify factors as well as specific practices that would potentially encourage holistic growth in the life of faith on the part of individuals and communities. They were also interested in possible ramifications related to interchurch communication and collaboration, and to missiological concerns in particular.

Seen through the eyes of practical theology, therefore, the project appears as an integrated whole, whose four dimensions and tasks are closely interrelated and interdependent. Thus, pragmatic and strategic concerns (stemming from the church, the academy, and development agencies) oriented the empirical research. Interpretive analyses of the actual experience of the Bible reading groups were influenced by theological and ethical norms and by empirical investigation, which in turn further shaped the tasks of interpretation. The circulation process thus continued and was eventually completed.

How intercultural Bible studies and practical theology can enrich each other

It is possible to summarize this discussion by pointing to a triple analogy at work. The unique structure of practical theology, with its fourfold pattern of dimensions and sets of tasks, has been replicated in a rich variety of contexts. That replication happened both in the multiple settings of Bible study groups around the world that participated in the project, and also in the overall design of the research project as such. Simply put, a special kind of inductive process took place, not unlike the well-known method of Bible reading popularized by Latin American Base Ecclesial Communities, involving *seeing, judging,* and *acting.*

Intercultural Bible study significantly enriches the discipline of practical theology, and this particular study has provided a wealth of experience and materials waiting to be mined. Not only is practical theology an inherently hermeneutical theological discipline, it also necessitates a strong biblical and hermeneutical foundation for its interdisciplinary work. In turn, practical theology can enrich intercultural Bible studies. A good example is the question of "perspective transformation"[5] as a possible result of reading the Bible intercontextually and interculturally. Practical theology can illumine the issue by integrating and applying resources from the human sciences (especially psychology of cognition and personality, social psychology, and anthropology) as well as from a number of biblical-theological sources, in order to identify conditions that make such transformation possible. Indeed, among other possibilities, practical theological analyses can help identify diverse ways of knowing and learning in intercultural Bible reading, and it is also indispensable for adequate processing of pertinent ecclesiological and other theological concerns.

I have also experienced that kind of mutual enrichment on a professional and personal level in the context of theological education, and especially in collaborative work with my colleague Mary Schertz, as we teach a seminary course on teaching the Bible in the congregation. In the framework of the interdisciplinary and interdepartmental cooperation normally involved in that effort, our decision to make the Through the Eyes of Another project a significant part of the course agenda has sharpened our vision and enhanced our vocational horizon, as documented in the second part of this chapter.

Through the eyes of theological education

We are theological educators and teachers of teachers. Our primary purpose for incorporating the perspectives acquired by our association with this intercultural Bible reading project was to grow in our own competence as seminary teachers. We wanted to work with a group of students committed to the relationships valued by the project—the relationship between Bible and church, the relationship between reading and culture, the relationship between different cultures. We wanted to think about the implications of the project for theological education and to assess our own methods of teaching in light of the values of the project.

We approach the task of theological education from our different disciplines—New Testament and practical theology. We also approach the task of theological education from our own experiences and ideologies—American feminist hermeneutics and Latin American liberation theology, as well as from a shared Anabaptist practice of faith. We have been team teaching a class on teaching the Bible in the congregation for nearly a decade, in a small, denominational seminary situated in the Indiana heartland, but with a disproportionate number of international students. The classes have generally attracted ten to twelve students ranging across the curriculum, enrolled in both MDiv and MA programs.

In preparing for the session in which we were studying John 4 along with the other groups in the intercultural Bible reading project, we considered a number of goals. The overall objectives for the class included assessing congregational attitudes toward and current approaches to the Bible, bridging the real or perceived gap between scholarship and the church, constructing effective teaching modules for various congregational settings, addressing biblical illiteracy and biblical irrelevancy, discerning the role of the pastor and other congregational educators in teaching the Bible. We had designed the class for those who want to nurture spiritual maturity by helping a congregation encounter the Living Word both informationally and formationally. Underlying these objectives, and influencing the pedagogy of the class, is a commitment to an Anabaptist ecclesiology and its assumptions about every member's responsibility to participate in the communal interpretation of scripture.[6]

Within these shared goals, I as a biblical scholar also wanted to address a problem that North American Christians often have in reading the biblical text. We are apt to fall into a trap, a type of colonization, in which we assume that we know what the text says, and we assume that it accords with our own dominant worldview. As Jon Paulien notes, we at times "tune out and reinterpret threatening biblical concepts. . . . It is easy for us to avoid the truth and deceive ourselves, even as we study the Bible."[7] In my own experience, the study of the biblical texts in their original languages is, as Paulien suggests, the "best safeguard against self-deception."[8] No other kind of study with the text, no matter how heartfelt or hard-headed, can so powerfully disabuse me of my preconceived Western notions of what the text says. No other kind of study can so expose my tendencies to domesticate the text, my prideful standing over the text, as simply reading it in Greek or Hebrew.

The problem is that the ability to read the text in its original language is, in itself, not always available, even to seminary students. Given that reality, we wanted our students to have the next best experience—a disorientation from their normal way of reading the text that would enable them to see it through other eyes.[9] The starting point of the classroom work with the text would be an English translation of the Greek clauses, organized in the simple format of a list—one clause, or basic unit of meaning, on a line. The Greek clause layout and my English translation are available at the end of this chapter. I did some additional preparation of the text. The story of the Samaritan woman at the well is a long text. I divided it into its "regions," since a "passage is normally composed of a series of segments that show internal organization."[10] In this case, the divisions fell along the lines of two simple observations—dialogue, who was talking to whom; and movement, who came and who went. These divisions are indicated with headings in the clause layout.

When the class met, Daniel Schipani led us in a short meditation, and we made some announcements and conducted other business. Then, we moved rapidly into the Bible study of John 4. I made some comments about the text—mainly some historical and cultural comments about the New Testament setting. I reminded the students of some basic information about the Pharisees, the Samaritans, and about women in the ministry of Jesus. My objective here was twofold. I wanted them to be able to imagine the cultural, historical, religious, and linguistic setting of the story. I also wanted them to move beyond stereotypical thinking about the political factions and parties of first-century Judaism. I wanted to direct them away from the tendency some of us have to deconstruct a text for gender bias only to fall into the pit of anti-Semitism. These were seminary students, most of them in their second or third year of study, and this information would not have been new to them. But in my experience, such a reminder at the beginning of a study session is often helpful and lends depth and nuance to the discussion.

After these introductory comments, we read the text, with students taking the parts of the different characters in the story. It is a simple device, but with a dialogical story such as this one, it is often surprisingly effective and moving. Then, the students gathered in small groups of three or four to work with the text on questions. I gave them these instructions:

> Work through the questions. They are designed to help you read the text in sections. I think it will be fairly obvious which question goes with each section. Don't try to be too profound—just list your hunches or suppositions and go on to the next question. Someone should act as the recorder and jot down a few phrases, without trying to get everything down verbatim.
>
> I'll give you a signal when it's time to change focus: For the last 5–7 minutes, you should stop wherever you are, even if you have not finished all the questions, to ask yourself what insights you've gained about this text. It's all right to be profound at this point!
>
> At the bottom of the page, you might want to list the questions and insights that you come up with.

The questions were as follows:

For small group discussion:

What social, ethnic, or cultural tensions are assumed or established by the narrator in the introduction and in the conversation between Jesus and the woman?

What is going on behind the Samaritan woman's initial response to Jesus's request for water? Why does she give him questions instead of water?

As John portrays Jesus, this is the first time in the Gospel that Jesus himself is quite so transparent about his identity. Why do you think he chooses this rather unlikely stranger for his self-revelation?

What social, ethnic, or cultural assumptions does Jesus make about the woman? How are these assumptions the same as and how are they different from the assumptions that the disciples make about her when they return?

In the conversation with the disciples, Jesus uses a variety of metaphors for what he is about—food, harvest, doing God's will, completing God's work. Do you think these metaphors have anything to do with the rather vivid portrayal of social, ethnic, and cultural tensions in which the story is framed?

What is the content of the salvation claimed by the Samaritans in the last line?

For plenary discussion:

What does the conversation between Jesus and the woman suggest for teaching the Bible in the congregation?

Because this class is a class in teaching, we use a variety of methods and are as transparent as possible in our use and modeling of methods. In this session, as in many of our sessions, the general structure of the class was a variation of the movements suggested by Thomas Groome.[11] The flow from meditation, shared experience, interaction with the biblical tradition and its contexts, to implications for faith in action is an example of Groome's shared praxis approach to Christian education. Reflecting on present Christian action and the Christian faith tradition as the two relate to each other is a large part of what we try to model in each session. The actual list of questions we composed uses insights and techniques drawn from Walter Wink's *Transforming Bible Study*.[12] Wink encourages the careful development of questions that are balanced between the personal and the social, that raise critical questions as well as open-ended ones, and that include profound questions of meaning.

The discussions in both the small groups and the plenary sessions were lively and engaging. One of the realities that quickly became evident is that the men and women in the class read the text differently. That realization led to a discussion of other barriers of social location—race and class. In the week between the class sessions, the students were encouraged to access the data available from the project.[13] The discussion and the reading then led into an additional discussion in the following class session on how reading the Bible with others and as "other" in itself is a part of how our salvation evolves. We talked about the evidence in both biblical testaments that complacency and self-satisfaction are among the major impediments to what God wants to do with people. Although these sins never make it into the Ten Commandments, time after time what separates people from God is personal (and national) self-satisfaction. Often, the way God brings the people back into relationship, back into position to be the people they were created to be, is through cross-cultural experience. The sojourn in Egypt, the exile in Babylon, learning to sing the Lord's song in a strange land, table fellowship that includes all sorts of marginalized people, and at last, the nations gathering in Revelation to sing the Lord's praises—are all images and motifs of cross-cultural interaction. We concluded with a question: Is it only when God's people are reading the history of how God has acted among us with multiple perspectives, or at least not just from our own parochial perspective, that we come close to fulfilling our mission to live in and extend the reign of God? We also noted, and lamented, that imperialistic readings of the biblical texts are fueling the political rhetoric we are hearing in such a devastating way in the United States in our own time.

In assessing our first experience using the values and objectives of the intercultural Bible reading project in the context of theological education, we find ourselves feeling excited about how the project enhanced our classroom work, and intrigued with the implications and possibilities for our future teaching. We noted that the project gave students a sense of reading in a world context—a firsthand acquaintance with difference and an awareness of the importance of testing readings of scripture with the insights of others around the world. The project gave the students the sense that this testing is important for everyone, but absolutely crucial for those of us who are privileged and rich. We also noted that the project provided us, as teachers in different disciplines and academic departments, a way to deepen our commitment to teach an integrated approach to teaching the Bible in the congregation. We look forward to teaching the class again and using the essays in this book to develop more fully a unit that helps our students become world-sensitive readers and teachers of scripture.

John 4:1–42

¹Ὡς οὖν ἔγνω ὁ Ἰησοῦς
ὅτι ἤκουσαν οἱ Φαρισαῖοι
ὅτι Ἰησοῦς πλείονας μαθητὰς ποιεῖ
   καὶ βαπτίζει ἢ Ἰωάννης
²-καίτοιγε Ἰησοῦς αὐτὸς οὐκ
   ἐβάπτιζεν ἀλλ᾽ οἱ μαθηταὶ
   αὐτοῦ-
³ἀφῆκεν τὴν Ἰουδαίαν
καὶ ἀπῆλθεν πάλιν εἰς τὴν
   Γαλιλαίαν.
⁴ἔδει δὲ αὐτὸν διέρχεσθαι διὰ τῆς
   Σαμαρείας.
⁵ἔρχεται οὖν εἰς πόλιν τῆς
   Σαμαρείας
   λεγομένην Συχὰρ
   πλησίον τοῦ χωρίου
   ὃ ἔδωκεν Ἰακὼβ [τῷ] Ἰωσὴφ τῷ
   υἱῷ αὐτοῦ·
⁶ἦν δὲ ἐκεῖ πηγὴ τοῦ Ἰακώβ.

ὁ οὖν Ἰησοῦς κεκοπιακὼς ἐκ τῆς
   ὁδοιπορίας ἐκαθέζετο οὕτως ἐπὶ
   τῇ πηγῇ·
ὥρα ἦν ὡς ἕκτη.
⁷Ἔρχεται γυνὴ ἐκ τῆς Σαμαρείας
   ἀντλῆσαι ὕδωρ.
λέγει αὐτῇ ὁ Ἰησοῦς,
Δός μοι πεῖν·
⁸οἱ γὰρ μαθηταὶ αὐτοῦ
   ἀπεληλύθεισαν εἰς τὴν πόλιν

Introduction

When Jesus learned
that the Pharisees heard
that he was making and baptizing
   more disciples than John
(although Jesus himself was not
   baptizing, rather his disciples),

he left Judea
and went away again into Galilee.

And he had to go through Samaria.

He came then into a city of Samaria

   called Sychar,
   near the field
   that Jacob gave to Joseph his son.

Jacob's spring was there.

Conversation with a woman

Then Jesus, wearied from the
   laborious journey, was simply
   sitting there by the spring.
It was noon.
A woman from the Samaritans came
   to draw water.
Jesus says to her:
Give me (water) to drink.
[For his disciples had gone into the
   city

ἵνα τροφὰς ἀγοράσωσιν.
⁹λέγει οὖν αὐτῷ ἡ γυνὴ ἡ
  Σαμαρῖτις,
Πῶς σὺ Ἰουδαῖος ὢν παρ' ἐμοῦ
  πεῖν αἰτεῖς γυναικὸς
  Σαμαρίτιδος οὔσης;
οὐ γὰρ συγχρῶνται Ἰουδαῖοι
  Σαμαρίταις.
¹⁰ἀπεκρίθη Ἰησοῦς καὶ εἶπεν αὐτῇ,
Εἰ ᾔδεις τὴν δωρεὰν τοῦ θεοῦ
καὶ τίς ἐστιν ὁ λέγων σοι,
Δός μοι πεῖν,
σὺ ἂν ᾔτησας αὐτὸν
καὶ ἔδωκεν ἄν σοι ὕδωρ ζῶν.

¹¹λέγει αὐτῷ [ἡ γυνή],
Κύριε, οὔτε ἄντλημα ἔχεις
καὶ τὸ φρέαρ ἐστὶν βαθύ·
πόθεν οὖν ἔχεις τὸ ὕδωρ τὸ ζῶν;
¹²μὴ σὺ μείζων εἶ τοῦ πατρὸς
  ἡμῶν Ἰακώβ,
ὃς ἔδωκεν ἡμῖν τὸ φρέαρ

καὶ αὐτὸς ἐξ αὐτοῦ ἔπιεν καὶ οἱ
  υἱοὶ αὐτοῦ καὶ τὰ θρέμματα
  αὐτοῦ;
¹³ἀπεκρίθη Ἰησοῦς καὶ εἶπεν αὐτῇ,
Πᾶς ὁ πίνων ἐκ τοῦ ὕδατος τούτου
  διψήσει πάλιν·
¹⁴ὃς δ' ἂν πίῃ ἐκ τοῦ ὕδατος
οὗ ἐγὼ δώσω αὐτῷ,
οὐ μὴ διψήσει εἰς τὸν αἰῶνα,
ἀλλὰ τὸ ὕδωρ ὃ δώσω αὐτῷ
  γενήσεται ἐν αὐτῷ πηγὴ
  ὕδατος
    ἁλλομένου εἰς ζωὴν αἰώνιον.
¹⁵λέγει πρὸς αὐτὸν ἡ γυνή,
Κύριε, δός μοι τοῦτο τὸ ὕδωρ,
ἵνα μὴ διψῶ
μηδὲ διέρχωμαι ἐνθάδε ἀντλεῖν.
¹⁶Λέγει αὐτῇ,
Ὕπαγε φώνησον τὸν ἄνδρα σου
καὶ ἐλθὲ ἐνθάδε.
¹⁷ἀπεκρίθη ἡ γυνὴ καὶ εἶπεν αὐτῷ,
Οὐκ ἔχω ἄνδρα.
λέγει αὐτῇ ὁ Ἰησοῦς,

in order to buy food.]
The Samaritan woman said to him:

How (is it that) you being a Jew ask
  from me being a Samaritan
  woman?
For Jews do not have dealings with
  Samaritans.
Jesus said to her:
If you knew the gift of God
and who it is that is saying to you:
"Give me a drink,"
You would have asked him
and he would have given you living
  water.

The woman said to him
Mister, you do not have a bucket
and the ground water well is deep.
How then do you have living water?
You are not greater than our father
  Jacob, are you?
—the one who gave us the ground
  water well,
who drank from it and his sons and
  his livestock.

Jesus said to her:
Everyone who drinks from this water
  will thirst again.
But whoever drinks from water
that I will give her
will never ever thirst—for eternity!
Rather the water which I give to her
  will become in her a spring of
  water
    leaping up into everlasting life.
The woman said to him:
Mister, give me this water
that I might not thirst
nor come through here to draw.
He said to her:
Go call your husband
and come back here.
The woman said to him:
I do not have a husband.
Jesus says to her:

Καλῶς εἶπας
ὅτι "Ανδρα οὐκ ἔχω·
[18] πέντε γὰρ ἄνδρας ἔσχες
καὶ νῦν ὃν ἔχεις
οὐκ ἔστιν σου ἀνήρ·
τοῦτο ἀληθὲς εἴρηκας.
[19] λέγει αὐτῷ ἡ γυνή,
Κύριε, θεωρῶ
ὅτι προφήτης εἶ σύ.
[20] οἱ πατέρες ἡμῶν ἐν τῷ ὄρει
    τούτῳ προσεκύνησαν·
καὶ ὑμεῖς λέγετε
ὅτι ἐν Ἰεροσολύμοις ἐστὶν ὁ τόπος
ὅπου προσκυνεῖν δεῖ.
[21] λέγει αὐτῇ ὁ Ἰησοῦς,
Πίστευέ μοι, γύναι,
ὅτι ἔρχεται ὥρα
ὅτε οὔτε ἐν τῷ ὄρει τούτῳ οὔτε ἐν
    Ἰεροσολύμοις προσκυνήσετε τῷ
    πατρί.
[22] ὑμεῖς προσκυνεῖτε
ὃ οὐκ οἴδατε·
ἡμεῖς προσκυνοῦμεν
ὃ οἴδαμεν,
ὅτι ἡ σωτηρία ἐκ τῶν Ἰουδαίων
    ἐστίν.
[23] ἀλλὰ ἔρχεται ὥρα
καὶ νῦν ἐστιν,
ὅτε οἱ ἀληθινοὶ προσκυνηταὶ
    προσκυνήσουσιν τῷ πατρὶ ἐν
    πνεύματι καὶ ἀληθείᾳ·
καὶ γὰρ ὁ πατὴρ τοιούτους ζητεῖ
    τοὺς προσκυνοῦντας αὐτόν.
[24] πνεῦμα ὁ θεός,
καὶ τοὺς προσκυνοῦντας αὐτὸν ἐν
    πνεύματι καὶ ἀληθείᾳ δεῖ
    προσκυνεῖν.
[25] λέγει αὐτῷ ἡ γυνή,
Οἶδα
ὅτι Μεσσίας ἔρχεται
ὁ λεγόμενος Χριστός·
ὅταν ἔλθῃ ἐκεῖνος,
ἀναγγελεῖ ἡμῖν ἅπαντα.
[26] λέγει αὐτῇ ὁ Ἰησοῦς,
Ἐγώ εἰμι,
ὁ λαλῶν σοι.

You spoke well (when you said)
"I do not have a husband,"
for you have had five husbands
and the man you are with now
is not your husband.
This you have spoken truly.
The woman says to him
Mister, I see
that you are a prophet.
Our fathers worshiped on this
    mountain,
and you all say
that Jerusalem is the place
where we have to worship.
Jesus said to her:
Believe me, woman,
the hour is coming
when you all will worship the Father
    neither on the mountain nor in
    Jerusalem.
You all worship
what you do not know.
We worship
what we know,
because salvation is out of the Jews.

But the hour comes
and is here now
when true worshipers will worship
    the Father in spirit and truth,

for the Father also seeks such to
    worship him.
God (is) spirit
and it is necessary for the ones
    worshiping him to worship in
    spirit and truth.
The woman said to him,
I know
that the Messiah is coming,
the one called Christ.
Whenever that one comes
he will report to us all things.
Jesus says to her
I am (that one),
the one speaking to you.

Through the eyes of practical theology and theological education **447**

²⁷Καὶ ἐπὶ τούτῳ ἦλθαν οἱ μαθηταὶ
αὐτοῦ
καὶ ἐθαύμαζον
ὅτι μετὰ γυναικὸς ἐλάλει·
οὐδεὶς μέντοι εἶπεν,
Τί ζητεῖς
ἢ Τί λαλεῖς μετ’ αὐτῆς;
²⁸ἀφῆκεν οὖν τὴν ὑδρίαν αὐτῆς ἡ
γυνὴ
καὶ ἀπῆλθεν εἰς τὴν πόλιν
καὶ λέγει τοῖς ἀνθρώποις,
²⁹Δεῦτε ἴδετε ἄνθρωπον
ὃς εἶπέν μοι πάντα
ὅσα ἐποίησα,
μήτι οὗτός ἐστιν ὁ Χριστός;
³⁰ἐξῆλθον ἐκ τῆς πόλεως
καὶ ἤρχοντο πρὸς αὐτόν.

And at this his disciples came

and they were marveling
because he was speaking to a woman.
However no one said:
What are you wanting?
or Why are you talking with her?
Then she left her water jar

and went away into the city,
and said to the people:
Come see a man
who said to me all the things,
whatever I have done.
Could this be the Christ?
They came out of the city
and went to him.

Conversation with the disciples

³¹Ἐν τῷ μεταξὺ ἠρώτων αὐτὸν οἱ
μαθηταὶ λέγοντες,
Ῥαββί, φάγε.
³²ὁ δὲ εἶπεν αὐτοῖς,
Ἐγὼ βρῶσιν ἔχω φαγεῖν
ἣν ὑμεῖς οὐκ οἴδατε.
³³ἔλεγον οὖν οἱ μαθηταὶ πρὸς
ἀλλήλους,
Μή τις ἤνεγκεν αὐτῷ φαγεῖν;

In the meantime, the disciples were
asking him:
Rabbi, eat.
But he said to them:
I have food to eat
which you do not know.
At that, the disciples were saying to
one another:
No one brought him anything to eat,
did they?

³⁴λέγει αὐτοῖς ὁ Ἰησοῦς,
Ἐμὸν βρῶμά ἐστιν
ἵνα ποιήσω τὸ θέλημα τοῦ
πέμψαντός με
καὶ τελειώσω αὐτοῦ τὸ ἔργον.
³⁵οὐχ ὑμεῖς λέγετε
ὅτι Ἔτι τετράμηνός ἐστιν
καὶ ὁ θερισμὸς ἔρχεται;
ἰδοὺ λέγω ὑμῖν,
ἐπάρατε τοὺς ὀφθαλμοὺς ὑμῶν
καὶ θεάσασθε τὰς χώρας
ὅτι λευκαί εἰσιν πρὸς θερισμόν.

Jesus said to them:
My food is
that I do the will of the one having
sent me,
and that I complete his work.
Do not you all say
that it is still four months
until the harvest comes?
Look, I say to you all,
raise your eyes
and see the fields,
that they are white for harvest
already.

ἤδη ³⁶ὁ θερίζων μισθὸν λαμβάνει

The reaper receives a wage

καὶ συνάγει καρπὸν εἰς ζωὴν
αἰώνιον,

and gathers fruit for eternal life,

ἵνα ὁ σπείρων ὁμοῦ χαίρῃ καὶ ὁ
θερίζων.

so that the sower and the reaper
might rejoice together.

[37] ἐν γὰρ τούτῳ ὁ λόγος ἐστὶν
ἀληθινὸς

In this respect the saying is true

ὅτι "Ἄλλος ἐστὶν ὁ σπείρων καὶ
ἄλλος ὁ θερίζων.

that "one is the sower and another
the reaper."

[38] ἐγὼ ἀπέστειλα ὑμᾶς θερίζειν

I sent you to reap

ὃ οὐχ ὑμεῖς κεκοπιάκατε·

what you have not labored over.

ἄλλοι κεκοπιάκασιν

Others have labored

καὶ ὑμεῖς εἰς τὸν κόπον αὐτῶν
εἰσεληλύθατε.

and you all have entered into their
labor.

The Samaritans arrive

[39] Ἐκ δὲ τῆς πόλεως ἐκείνης πολλοὶ
ἐπίστευσαν εἰς αὐτὸν τῶν
Σαμαριτῶν

Out of that city many of the
Samaritans believed in him

διὰ τὸν λόγον τῆς γυναικὸς
μαρτυρούσης

because of the word of the
woman witnessing:

ὅτι Εἶπέν μοι πάντα

"He told me all the things

ἃ ἐποίησα.

that I did."

[40] ὡς οὖν ἦλθον πρὸς αὐτὸν οἱ
Σαμαρῖται,

Then as the Samaritans came to him

ἠρώτων αὐτὸν μεῖναι παρ' αὐτοῖς·

they were asking him to stay with
them.

καὶ ἔμεινεν ἐκεῖ δύο ἡμέρας.

And he was staying there two days

[41] καὶ πολλῷ πλείους ἐπίστευσαν
διὰ τὸν λόγον αὐτοῦ,

and many more believed on account
of his word.

[42] τῇ τε γυναικὶ ἔλεγον

And they were saying to the woman:

ὅτι Οὐκέτι διὰ τὴν σὴν λαλιὰν
πιστεύομεν·

"No longer do we believe because of
your word,

αὐτοὶ γὰρ ἀκηκόαμεν

for we ourselves have heard

καὶ οἴδαμεν

and we know

ὅτι οὗτός ἐστιν ἀληθῶς ὁ σωτὴρ
τοῦ κόσμου.

that this one is truly the savior of the
world."

Notes

[1] For a comprehensive theory of practical theology, see Gerben Heitink, *Practical Theology: History, Theory, Action Domains,* trans. Reinder Bruinsma (Grand Rapids, Mich.: Eerdmans, 1999). Heitink defines practical theology as "the empirically oriented theological theory of the mediation of Christian faith in the praxis of modern society" (6).

[2] The concept *rule of art* was introduced by Friedrich Schleiermacher in his original discussion of practical theology in *Brief Outline on the Study of Theology,* trans. Terrence Tice (Richmond, Va.: John Knox Press, 1966), par. 265ff.

³ The meeting took place 3–5 July 2000, at the Free University, Amsterdam (the Netherlands), and included fifteen participants. The main decision made was to hold a conference the following year in Utrecht, with representatives of five continents. In that conference, 28 February–2 March 2001, the Intercultural Reading of the Bible project was unanimously endorsed and officially begun by a network of people and institutions who became the Intercultural Bible Collective.

⁴ The following figure is a modified version of one presented by Richard R. Osmer and Friedrich L. Schweitzer in the introduction of the book they edited, *Developing a Public Faith: New Directions in Practical Theology* (St. Louis, Mo.: Chalice Press, 2003), 1–11. Osmer and Schweitzer propose that attention to all four distinguishable but mutually influential tasks of practical theology allows practical theologians to construct *action-guiding theories of contemporary religious practice.* Further, they helpfully conceptualize the mutually influential relationship of those four tasks, along the lines of a hermeneutical circle that can be entered at any point, provided that all four tasks are attended to in a comprehensive program of practical theological reflection.

⁵ Understood holistically, *perspective transformation* denotes significant change in viewpoint and perception (sometimes even paradigm change) that happens together with attitudinal change and dispositions for certain kinds of actions. From a liberationist perspective, the notion of perspective transformation is analogous to the meaning of *conscientization* associated with Paulo Freire's pedagogy and philosophy of education, that is, "a process of cultural action in which women and men are awakened to their sociocultural reality, move beyond the constraints and alienations to which they are subjected, and affirm themselves as conscious subjects and co-creators of their historical future." Daniel S. Schipani, *Religious Education Encounters Liberation Theology* (Birmingham, Ala.: Religious Education Press, 1988), 13.

⁶ See Lake Lambert, "Active Learning for the Kingdom of God," *Teaching Theology and Religion* 3, no. 2 (2000): 71–80, for an interesting discussion on the relationship between ecclesiology and pedagogy.

⁷ Jon Paulien, "Why Biblical Authority Rarely Impacts the Local Church," *Ministry* 71, no. 5 (May, 1998): 6.

⁸ Ibid.

⁹ For a more detailed description of this method of Bible study, see Mary H. Schertz and Perry B. Yoder, *Seeing the Text: Exegesis for Students of Greek and Hebrew* (Nashville, Tenn.: Abingdon Press, 2001).

¹⁰ Schertz and Yoder, *Seeing the Text,* 67.

¹¹ Thomas H. Groome, *Christian Religious Education: Sharing Our Story and Vision,* (New York: Harper and Row, 1980); and *Sharing Faith: A Comprehensive Approach to Religious Education and Pastoral Ministry* (San Francisco: Harper, 1991).

¹² Walter Wink, *Transforming Bible Study: A Leader's Guide* (Nashville, Tenn.: Abingdon, 1980).

¹³ In addition to hearing oral presentations, and reading the manual prepared by Hans de Wit, our students were encouraged to become acquainted with the project via the Internet. Further, they had access to the reports generated for the local Mennonite group and its partner Bible study group from Cuba, including the

interchange of responses to the respective readings. We requested special permission from both groups to use those materials exclusively for the purposes of our class. This encounter with the project was facilitated by the fact that Daniel Schipani had been an observer and research participant directly involved in the process.

From bipolar to multipolar understanding

Hermeneutical consequences of intercultural Bible reading
Rainer Kessler

Participants in the intercultural Bible reading project had different motives and aims. Many people in the Bible reading groups simply wanted to record their experience of reading and discussing a biblical text and share it with others who live under different conditions. Perhaps they also were eager to learn from other readers. Those who initiated the project also had a variety of motives and aims. One aim was to bring people together in order to expose them to different ways of reading the Bible. A second aim was to do research on the material compiled by the project. This might be research on different ways of understanding a given text or on the influence of national, cultural, ethnic, denominational, or social factors on understanding. What I want to do in the following pages goes a step further. I am not so much interested in understanding the concrete text of John 4, although I will take examples from the reading of this text. What I am most interested in is the hermeneutical implications and consequences of the process of intercultural reading.

The traditional hermeneutical model

The traditional hermeneutical model may be called bipolar. The center of this model is always the text, which may be written or spoken, although biblical texts are, of course, written texts. One pole of the bipolar model represents the text's author (speaker, writer, or sender). The author of the text may be either an individual or a group. A committee, for example, might formulate a political statement or a liturgical agenda and thus function as author in the model. Many biblical texts have a history (which might span centuries) of writing, rewriting, redaction, and editing. All of the writers, redactors, and editors over this time span constitute the

Rainer Kessler, Faculty of Theology, University of Marburg (Marburg, Germany)

author of the text. The second pole of the bipolar model represents the receiver of the text. She or he might listen to an oral text or read a written text. The receiver might be an individual or a collective entity—an audience, for example, or a group that reads and discusses a text, as in the case of the Bible reading project.

Understanding of the text is influenced or conditioned not only by the author but also by the hearer or reader of the text. The author puts his or her intentions into the text as the author's contribution to understanding it. Readers of the text, however, have their own ideas that they bring with them when they read the text. In the understanding of the text, these ideas are as important as those of the author. Opinions differ on how much stress to place on one or the other of these two poles. In the classical hermeneutic of the nineteenth century, the main aim of understanding was to grasp the author's intention. In the late twentieth century, there arose an opposite tendency to negate the author's role entirely. "The author is dead" was the watchword. For our present discussion, it is not necessary to take sides. Even if one pole is negated, the structure of the model remains bipolar.

Here is a rough sketch of the bipolar model of understanding:

Multiple factors influence all parts of the model. The author or sender lives in a specific cultural world, as does the reader or receiver. The author uses a certain language. In the case of biblical Hebrew or New Testament Greek, this is a language that modern readers do not have as their primary language but must learn. The formation of a text may follow special rules, as is the case in poetry. Modern readers need to know these rules in order to understand the meaning of the text. The form of the text depends on the language in which it is written. For example, Hebrew narratives normally use very short sentences, while Greek narratives love long ones.

Two hundred years of historical-critical reading of the Old and New Testaments have been directed to better understanding of biblical texts using the frame of the bipolar model. It has been generally accepted that the pole represented by the reader/receiver is historically determined in the same measure as that of the author/sender. In reality, however, the reader or receiver in this model is an abstraction. Traditionally, scholars have engaged in little reflection on the historical conditions of concrete readers. For modern interpreters of biblical texts, the "normal" reader has been a white European or North American male.

In summary, the traditional bipolar model of historical-critical exegesis has generated much reflection on the position of the author of the text, on the text itself, and on the rules of the functioning of texts. However, reflection on the concrete reader or readers of the text has been neglected.

Challenging the traditional model

Since the late 1960s, biblical scholarship has seen a manifold challenge to the traditional model of understanding. All of these debates take their starting point from the position of the reader and assert that it is hardly normal to assume the white European or North American male as the reader of the biblical text.

Critical and liberal movements in the late 1960s recognized that human beings have highly diverse social and political positions and interests. With this awareness of human diversity in mind, the biblical scholar may ask, Is there a difference between the understandings of poor, middle-class, or wealthy readers who read the same text? In his famous *History of Israel*, the German scholar Herbert Donner describes the general release of debts and restitution of land to former owners, ordered by Nehemiah (Neh. 5:1–13). Then Donner comments, "These were certainly not very popular measures" (*Das waren sicherlich keine sehr populären Maßnahmen*).[1] For the German professor, it was natural to side with the rich, who by the release of debts and the restitution of the land lost money and land they had obtained from poor and indebted peasants. For the wealthy, Nehemiah's measures were unpopular indeed. For the poor reader who was indebted, the same text is a gospel message—truly good news! Understanding of the text depends deeply on the social position of the reader.

The year 1968, when the Latin American Bishops Conference was held in Medellín, Colombia, marks the birth of liberation theology. Liberation theology recognized that just as societies are divided into classes with different interests, the whole world is divided between a few rich countries and many poor ones. The "option for the poor" proclaimed by the Medellín conference pertains not only to the poor within nations but also to the poor on an international scale.

An example of the impact of social position on biblical interpretation is found in the writing of George Pixley from Nicaragua. In the first issue of *Revista de Interpretación Bíblica Latinoamericana*, Pixley drew an analogy between the circumstances of Central America and those of ancient Israel. For him, the Assyrian empire of Hosea's time that threatens the small nation Israel is the North American empire that threatens the peoples of Central America. The rich Israelites, including the ruling class who cooperated with the Assyrians, are the upper class of the Central American countries who are closely tied to the interests of North American companies.[2] George Pixley is not an abstract or neutral reader of the text. He is a reader with a clearly formulated political position. Other readers will read the same texts in a very different way.

The final two decades of the twentieth century also brought a new wave of feminism. With this wave came an awareness that the subject who reads a text is not "man" as a genderless being but is either male or female. Understanding of the biblical text differs, depending on whether a man or a woman is reading the text, particularly for texts such as Ezekiel 16 and 23, which portray God as violating his "wife" Jerusalem. Feminism also raised the question of whether all biblical texts were written by male authors, as has been generally assumed. Why not suppose that there are also texts with female authors? The gender issue depends not only on the reader or author of the text but also on the text itself. As Fokkelien van Dijk Hemmes and Athalya Brenner describe it, texts may have male or female voices.[3] They refer not to the question of who wrote or who will read the text but to a quality of the text itself.

The experience of the Holocaust gave new impetus to Jewish-Christian dialogue. This dialogue also had great influence on the reading of biblical texts. Especially when reading Old Testament texts that speak of Israel and the nations, Christian commentators have often identified with Israel. The nations then are assumed to be non-Christian nations, a definite distortion of the text. Even worse, when commenting on texts where God threatens Israel with punishment, writers may identify Israel with the Jewish people, but when they move to texts where God is gracious and merciful, they may identify Israel with humankind or even with the church. Jewish-Christian dialogue has taught us first, that *Israel* in the texts really does mean Israel, and second, that the term *the nations* means non-Israelite nations—including Christian nations.[4]

In many ways, these twentieth-century developments have challenged the traditional model for understanding scripture. Yet these different approaches to scripture are not always compatible with one another. For example, Latin American liberation theology readily identifies the people of Israel with the poor people of Latin America, a move that within the Jewish-Christian approach would be considered inappropriate. In the late 1960s, the main categories that interpreters used had a social character, and gender differences were not an issue. In contrast, some feminist authors have stressed the gender category in such a way that questions of social position or race no longer played any role. Of course, there were also many combinations of the different approaches.

All of these newer approaches to interpretation have continued to fit within the frame of the bipolar model. They have brought new aspects to each part of the model but have left the model as a whole largely intact. I believe that intercultural Bible reading continues in the direction established by the newer approaches but takes them a step further.

Consequences of intercultural Bible reading

So what is new about interpretation in the intercultural Bible reading process? In the traditional model, the reader is understood to be singular—one reader. This does not mean that only one person reads (or hears, or receives) the text; the reader might be a group. Even when a group discusses the text, however, it is a single group that discusses. In contrast, within the process of intercultural Bible reading, the position of the reader becomes plural. By definition, the reader is no longer an individual or a single group but multiple readers who are linked together. The receiver of the text is not a single pole in this hermeneutic model; it is a plurality of poles. That is what I call the multipolar model.

The following sketch tries to visualize the multipolar model.

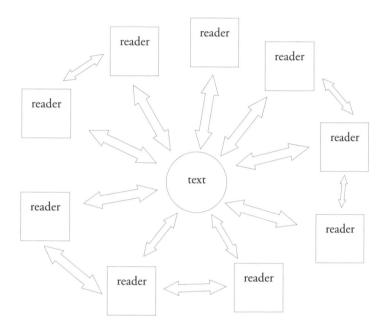

The sketch needs some explanation:

1. One must imagine a third dimension, because the position of the author is missing in the sketch. The author should lie behind the text.

2. The model stresses the position of the reader. The influence of the text on the reader is marked by the arrows that run from reader to text and then back from text to reader. For every hermeneutical model, it is crucial to define the role of the reader in front of the text. A merely reader-oriented model might make the text disappear, as interpretation becomes an arbitrary act. This is not my intent. As in the classical bipolar models—with the exception of the extreme reader-oriented positions—there is interaction between reader and text.[5] What is new in the proposed model is that the single abstract reader is replaced by a plurality of concrete readers.

3. These readers do not simply have the text as the object of interpretation; they have other readers with whom they communicate. Reading the text thus becomes a double communication. It is communication with the text, as in the traditional bipolar model. And by means of the text, it is communication with the author. However, reading also includes communication with other readers. This

communication forms a constitutive part of the process of understanding. Understanding the text is no longer possible without this communication with other readers.

Through intercultural Bible reading, these other readers are no longer readers who come from the same context. They may be academic groups, Base Ecclesial Communities, feminist meetings, etc. These readers are different from one another, and they are global. In intercultural Bible reading, I am no longer merely confirmed in my thinking by my group; I am also challenged by readers who are, by definition, different.

What are the consequences of the new approach? We now have plenty of material—the reports from the reading groups—that shows the practical consequences. One person does not have time to study the abundance of material. I will draw on the experiences of groups I worked with personally. One group was composed of students from my university. What they discussed in John 4 was the question of how the water in this text is linked with baptism. No hint of the word *baptism* appears in the reports from the groups in South Africa and Colombia with whom they were linked. These groups instead discussed issues of interracial contacts (between Jesus the Jew and the Samaritan woman) or simply of decent behavior toward people in need.

When we compare the discussions of these three reading groups—from Germany, South Africa, and Colombia—with the discussions that we find in scholarly books, the result is astonishing. One might think that the discussion of the German students, most of whom have studied theology and are able to read the New Testament in the original Greek, would be closest to the results of historical-critical research. However, this was not the case. I consulted seven commentaries by German, English, and Spanish authors that have appeared in the last hundred years or so. Only one mentioned the possibility that the combination of John 4 with John 3 might be an allusion to baptism.[6] Other authors discussed the significance of water in the Old Testament, in ancient Judaism, in the Greek world, and in the religions in general.[7] However, neither these commentaries nor several others[8] even mention the word *baptism*.

The scholarly discussion of John 4 has as one focus the relationships between Jews and Samaritans. Scholars have treated this as an issue of relationships between religious groups. This is surely true in the historical sense. Does it have any additional meaning in the modern world? Readers from South Africa transfer it to their postapartheid situation, which is still marked by racial conflict. Surely the text does not contain the concept of race, which is a modern notion. However, it seems to me that these readers are closer to the meaning of the text than the scholar Rudolf Bultmann. Bultmann writes about the Jewish-Samaritan conflict, yet he does not even mention racial conflicts, even though the first edition of his commentary appeared in 1941, just when the extermination of Jews in Nazi Germany for racial reasons had begun to accelerate.

The Colombian readers gave special stress to the simple matter that the story tells about a thirsty man who wants something to drink. For their situation in a Bogotá suburb, questions of survival in everyday life are crucial. The Colombians' perspective runs counter to that of Bultmann and other historical-critical authors. For Bultmann, Jesus's request for water is simply a pretext for theological discussion. The real water is not water one can drink but "the water of life." For the scholar who may never in his life have lacked water, the physical substance of water is not "true water." He sees an opposition between real water and the water of life.[9] People who must work hard every day to obtain water read the text in a very different way.

The question is not, Who is right? There are many aspects to be discovered in the text. By the process of intercultural Bible reading, we learn that our own reading is only one reading among many others. When the German students heard the reports of the readers from South Africa and Colombia, they were astonished, but they received a new perspective on the text. A triangle—or better, a quadrangle—came into being: the text—one's own group—partner group A—partner group B. The process of multipolar reading not only revealed new aspects of the text but also brought a new self-understanding to the group. It caused them to ask, Why do we read the text in the way we do? And why do others read it in another way?

The approach of the intercultural Bible reading process has consequences for the academic treatment of texts that occupy me as a university teacher. In the traditional model, the ideal was to read the text without any prejudice—*sine ira et studio*. We have since learned that this ideal is not attainable: the supposedly neutral reader is in reality the European or North American professor. (To be honest, I think that most European and North American academics have still not learned that an objective reading is not possible.) The lesson is that the subject who engages in academic reading must acknowledge his or her position—male or female, black or white, rich or poor, from the center or from the periphery—and bring it into the reading process. The new lesson taught by intercultural Bible reading is that it is not enough to say who I am as a reader of the text. I must also listen to other readers from different contexts. Without their voices, I will not be able to listen to the full voice of the text that I wish to understand.

A lot of work lies before us. The intercultural Bible reading project is a starting point—no more. But it is the starting point for a very new way of reading the Bible.

Notes

[1] Herbert Donner, *Geschichte des Volkes Israel und seiner Nachbarn in Grundzügen* (Göttingen, Germany: Vandenhoeck & Ruprecht, 1995), 459.

[2] Jorge Pixley, "Oseas: Una nueva propuesta de lectura desde América Latina," *Revista de Interpretación Bíblica Latinoamericana* 1 (1989): 67–86.

[3] Athalya Brenner and Fokkelien van Dijk Hemmes, *On Gendering Texts: Female and Male Voices in the Hebrew Bible*, Biblical Interpretation Series, vol. 1 (Leiden, the Netherlands: E. J. Brill, 1993).

⁴ See my commentary on Micah: Rainer Kessler, *Micha*, Herders Theologischer Kommentar zum Alten Testament (Freiburg, Germany: Herder, 2000).

⁵ This issue is emphasized by Johannes Taschner, "Orientierende Kanon-Lese: Rezeptionsgeschichte als Kultivierung des Streits um eine angemessene Interpretation," *Wort und Dienst* 27 (2003): 161–78.

⁶ Walter Bauer, *Das Johannesevangelium*, Handbuch zum Neuen Testament 6 (Tübingen, Germany: J. C. B. Mohr [Paul Siebeck], 1925), 65.

⁷ Heinrich Julius Holtzmann, *Evangelium, Briefe und Offenbarung des Johannes*: Hand-Commentar zum Neuen Testament 4 (Freiburg im Breisgau, Germany: J. C. B. Mohr [Paul Siebeck], 1983), 83; Bauer, *Das Johannesevangelium*; Rudolf Karl Bultmann, *Das Evangelium des Johannes*: Kritisch-exegetischer Kommentar über das Neue Testament 11 (Göttingen, Germany: Vandenhoeck & Ruprecht, 1956), 133–36; C. K. Barrett, *Das Evangelium nach Johannes*: Kritisch-exegetischer Kommentar über das Neue Testament (Göttingen, Germany: Vandenhoeck & Ruprecht, 1990), 251–52.

⁸ Wilhelm Heitmüller, *Das Evangelium des Johannes,* Studien zum Neuen Testament 2 (Göttingen, Germany, 1908), 685–861; Siegfried Schulz, *Das Evangelium nach Johannes*: Das Neue Testament Deutsch 4 (Göttingen, Germany: Vandenhoeck & Ruprecht, 1987); José Luis Espinel Marcos, *Evangelio según San Juan: Introducción, traducción y comentario*, Horizonte dos mil. (Salamanca: San Esteban: 1998).

⁹ Rudolf Bultmann, *The Gospel of John: A Commentary* (Philadelphia, Pa.: The Westminster Press, 1971), 185–86: "When he [man] hungers and thirsts, then fundamentally he does not desire this or that thing, but he wants to *live*. The real object of his desire is not water and bread, but something which will give him life and will rescue him from death, something which might therefore be called real water, real bread."

CHAPTER 25

Intercultural hermeneutics
Conversations across cultural and contextual divides
John Riches

One of the intriguing features of the Through the Eyes of Another project is the striking appropriateness of the text chosen for study to the wider aims of the project. This is a text whose central moment is a first-century conversation between a Jewish man and a Samaritan woman. At its heart, our project is an attempt to explore the possibility and understanding of conversations across cultural boundaries comparable to the one in the text, whether between contemporary readers and this ancient text, between members in any given group, or between various partner groups who have exchanged their readings and reactions.

Diverse groups read the conversation in John 4 very differently. Among the groups in which I have participated, the nature, dynamic, and outcomes of the exchange between Jesus and the woman have been very differently perceived. Some have focused on the misunderstandings that occur, on the seemingly disjointed and unrelated nature of the discourses that the account of their exchange contains. Others have seen the account as a model conversation, leading to a genuine exchange and interaction between the two parties, enabling both the woman and Jesus to grow and move on. Some have emphasized Jesus's control of the dialogue and the way he leads the woman beyond her misunderstanding of his opening remarks to a deeper understanding of her needs and condition. Others have read her remarks as spiced with irony—seeing her as able to hold her own as she challenged Jesus's sense of cultural superiority, yet also as vulnerable and open to his probing of her personal life and circumstances. Some have seen the conversation as instrumental to Jesus's mission to the Samaritans, a means of his imparting truth and life to those outside Israel. Others have seen the conversation as a model for interchange, demonstrating dialogue as a life-enhancing vehicle for the discovery of truth by

John Riches, Theology and Religious Studies Department, University of Glasgow (Glasgow, Scotland)

those who engage in it. Still others have seen the point of the story in the overcoming of social and cultural boundaries that lie between the participants, bringing liberation and thereby transformation.

Such varied views of the story in John 4 both support and cut across the various goals that underlie the search for intercultural reading of the Bible that is at the heart of our project. A broad consensus among those who planned the project outlines a central aim of enabling participants to "read with" others. In this process, participants allow their understanding of the text to be enlarged by looking at it through the eyes of others whose readings, like their own, arise from the exchange between experience and the biblical texts. Through this encounter with others' readings of the text,[1] participants allow their subjectivity, understanding, and sense of identity to be enlarged, informed, and transformed.

While this conviction about the importance of communitarian reading of the Bible was generally held among the preparatory group—arising out of personal experiences of Bible study—the group articulated more specific goals that led to the project formulation. Specifically, the project intended, first, to explore the relationship between scholarly and popular, ordinary readings of the Bible, and second, to gain a better understanding of the nature of intercultural Bible study.[2] The project is an exercise in practical hermeneutics, designed to generate specific examples of work, which "an international group of scientists"[3] will study from a hermeneutical point of view, seeking to understand the nature of the cognitive, group dynamics, and praxeological processes at work. In simple terms, the project set out to organize large numbers of conversations between groups in their local settings and the text of John 4. Based on the reports of these studies, the project further sought to promote dialogue between pairs of groups across cultural boundaries.

In practice, the goal of studying the relationships between scholarly and ordinary readers has somewhat slipped from view in the structuring of the project (although such relationships have certainly played their part in the conversations themselves), which has become far more a case of scholars studying the readings of ordinary readers. Even the second goal has been realized less clearly than was hoped. One reason is that the exchanges between partner groups, where they have occurred, were perfunctory in many cases. Another factor is that it proved difficult to have serious dialogue with a group from a different culture and context, when all one had was a brief report on a Bible study. The disparities in form and style of the reports of the local groups' conversations, and of the conversations that have occurred between groups from different countries, make clear how difficult the medium is in which participants have attempted to communicate with each other. Nevertheless, memorable encounters have taken place, just as failure to transcend cultural boundaries has also occurred. Both are instructive in their different ways.

It is on intercultural exchange and its hermeneutical implications that I shall concentrate in this paper. The preparatory documents locate this part of the project quite clearly within the contemporary political (secular and ecclesiastical) context and within debates in theological hermeneutics. The project concerns itself with the increasing globalization of the world, on the one hand, and the growing diversity of local cultures, on the other. How can Christianity survive in the face of this diversity? What new forms of Christian catholicity might emerge, if there were to be genuine dialogue?[4] These questions are posed in the context of the emergence in Latin America of a Bible movement whose vigor, creativity, and political engagement have inspired many involved with this project. Is it possible that a dialogue between Western and non-Western readings of the text can breathe new life into the churches in the West? Is it possible that out of this intercultural dialogue, life and hope can come for those who suffer in our globalized world?

What then are the hermeneutical strategies that underlie the project? First, an understanding of culture is required in order to evaluate the cultural formation of the different reading groups who engage in dialogue, as well as to evaluate the contribution of culture to the groups' readings. This understanding is largely provided by the Dutch scholar Geert Hofstede, who defines culture as "the collective mental programming that differentiates the members of one group or category of people from those of other ones." What interests the project are the underlying "cultural depth dimensions, the basic questions about power and inequality, the relation of the individual and the group, the social roles ascribed to men and women, the manner of dealing with the uncertainties of existence, and the way people are focused on the future, the past or the present."[5] These concepts certainly provide tools for attempting to discern common concerns. However, they do little to analyze how the "mental programming" that people have received within their cultural setting affects their use of cultural tools from an alien (first-century Mediterranean) culture—albeit one that has been assimilated variously in their own culture—to make sense of their life experiences and to address the deep concerns that they hold in common with their unfamiliar dialogue partners.

Second, across this concern for the cultural dimensions of a given reading runs a different classification derived from Paul Ricoeur, which in practice contributed greatly to the program as it was eventually set up. Ricoeur distinguishes between different kinds of readings. He contrasts naïve, spontaneous readings with the "analytical exploration of a text and the examination or validation of the naïve reading." From such analysis emerges a third stage of "knowing understanding." The first of these distinctions is directed toward a particular way of reading a text, based on an attitude "which is not focused on scientific analysis or distantiation."[6] As we shall see, this distinction is clearly useful in analyzing the results of this process. What is more difficult to see is how precisely these distinctions relate to the Through the Eyes of Another project as it was devised.

The project falls into three phases: the initial reading by a given group, which the preparatory documents describe as "naïve/spontaneous." "Confrontation and dialogue with the reading of the partner group," is next, followed by "sharing the results of the confrontations."[7] This description raises critical questions. Can only the first reading be properly understood as naïve/spontaneous? Does the process of intercultural exchange initiate the reflective moment and introduce an element of self-awareness, possibly even of self-criticism, comparable to the element of criticism that scholars trained in biblical criticism brought into popular readings in Latin America? How does scholarly analysis of these exchanges relate to the intercultural dialogue?

The project's use of Ricoeur's threefold distinction of forms of reading is confusing. On the one hand, we have essentially a two-stage process of intercultural reading: first, the individual groups read independently of each other; then, they exchange readings and reactions to each other's readings. The second stage is openended, although the project does not track what happens if groups develop longterm relationships with each other. On the other hand, we have a two-stage process of scholarly analysis: first, the data is generated (in two stages), and then, the data is analyzed by scholars, again in two stages. It is not clear how scholarly analysis is to inform or relate to the intercultural relationships of the reading groups. Is this an independent process, in which scholars can work with the data (once it is collected) without any interaction with or acknowledgement of those whose conversations generated them?

Before turning to reflect on some of the exchanges that took place, I raise one last set of considerations. Can we be more precise about the purpose of enabling intercultural dialogue? Is it to promote international peace and justice and to work toward the individual and social transformation of the lives and societies of the various groups represented? Or is it to create a particular quality of dialogue—the kind of dialogue between people of different cultures and social and economic power and status that will bring about the catholicity of which Robert Schreiter speaks?

These two aims are not incompatible. Indeed, it may be that without the creation of the "dominance-free discourse" of which Jürgen Habermas speaks, it will be impossible to tackle global questions of justice and peace. The two aims do however correspond to the readings of the conversation in John 4 that I introduced at the beginning of this essay. Some saw the importance of the conversation as lying in the quality of the exchange, which permitted it to be life transforming; others saw the significance of the story as lying primarily in its account of the woman's acceptance and change of status in relation to both Jesus and her village. Despite the different emphases that readers placed on aspects of the story, the story makes it clear that the two readings are intrinsically related. There is, however, a greater gulf between these two types of readings and a third that sees the direction of the conversation as essentially one-way, with Jesus knowing precisely what he wants to tell the woman and what he wants to achieve through her agency. However, even in such an overtly evangelistic reading of the story (not without support in the text), there are connections in the story to the two readings already described.

An account of what happened

At this point, we need to give some account, however one-sided and partial, of what actually happened. To what extent did the project achieve intercultural dialogue? To what extent did dialogue occur within the individual reading groups, whose views then became the object of scrutiny, and beyond that, of further dialogue? How appropriate are the categories of "naïve/spontaneous," on the one hand, and "analytical exploration of a text and the examination or validation of the naïve reading," on the other?

Let me start with the known and work toward the less well-known. Proceeding in this direction is not so much a matter of convenience as an attempt to demonstrate how difficult the process of understanding becomes when one no longer has direct contact with and knowledge of the group itself. This is not to say that understanding what happens in familiar groups is without difficulty.

One of the groups in the Glasgow area of Scotland was centered around the Roman Catholic parish of St. Dominic's in Craigend, located in a peripheral housing estate with a reputation for gang violence and sectarian tensions. Glasgow is home to deep-seated tensions between Catholics and Protestants that go back to the nineteenth century, when Catholic and Protestant migrant laborers came to Scotland to meet the demand for labor in mining and heavy industry. The composition of the Craigend group was certainly diverse. The local contextual Bible study (CBS) group had worked with this group for several years and facilitated the discussions for this project. Most of the members of the CBS group had theological qualifications, as did the parish priest. The other members of the group had no formal academic training in theology, although they had participated in various forms of parish education and engaged easily in discussion. They also had a wide range of intellectual, reading, and personal skills. Above all, there was a strong sense of loyalty within the group, which made it possible for people to discuss their experiences with unusual freedom and trust.

The reading of John 4 in Craigend focused on the conversation between Jesus and the Samaritan woman and saw it primarily as a conversation that led to change in both participants. The group recognized this exchange, which addressed deep issues of cultural difference and personal concern, as life enhancing and leading toward individual and social transformation. When the group was asked to point to experiences in their own lives that had resonance with the story, one member named a time of crisis when he had been entrusted to the care of a member of the Orange Order (a Protestant organization with strong links to Protestantism in Northern Ireland). He described how this man had been available for support day and night for years. "He was," he said, "the embodiment of Christianity, the epitome of kindness. He opened my eyes, which had been closed by instruction." The man taught him basic values of honesty and decency, which enabled him to overcome his problems. This member's account opened the way to a wider discussion, where group members shared their experiences of Catholic-Protestant relationships, expressed their dismay at the lack of genuine communication in much talk within their local community, and discussed ways of finding other opportunities for such life-giving converse.

There is no doubt that what occurred at this meeting was spontaneous. The group's discussion evinced openness to the text and readiness to make connections between the narrative and their life experiences that could in a quite specific sense be understood as naïve. On the other hand, this naïve response does not mean that group members were unaware of the distance between their own situation and that of Jesus and the Samaritan woman. At a certain point, the group asked for information about the Samaritans in order to make better sense of the story. They certainly expected to make creative connections between their experience and the text. They also, on occasion, expressed a strong sense that some biblical passages speak a "foreign language."

The processes of appropriation, distantiation, critique, and reappropriation for this group may not be as formalized as they are within the discourses of the academy, but they still may be understood as analogous to the progress to a second naïveté of which Ricoeur speaks. To note a lack of formal progression is not to deny the presence of the various elements that Ricoeur has identified. Rather, I mean to point out that such elements may be present more or less simultaneously within "ordinary" readings—that is, in readings where the critical, reflective moment arises more or less spontaneously out of a group where academically trained readers (who were certainly present)[8] are largely confined to a role of facilitation.[9]

In this case, a close reading of the text led to a certain distance, as points of conflict in the conversation between Jesus and the woman were located within their first-century Mediterranean context. The connection between the gospel story and the story of the encounter with the member of the Orange Lodge opened up a new stage of dialogue with the text and between members of the group. Moreover, that dialogue was formulated in such a way that it challenged some of the deeply held official views of the Craigend community (just as the Samaritan woman challenged Jesus's sense of cultural superiority).[10] People recounted their experiences of a Catholic upbringing and the limits and checks that had been imposed on their relations with Protestants, even within "mixed" families. In this way, the underlying doctrinal position (*extra ecclesiam nulla salus*) was exposed and challenged (an informal kind of *Ideologiekritik*) and the way opened up for a new appropriation of the original text. Thus, it is possible to identify all the various elements of Ricoeur's account of the appropriation of the meaning of biblical texts within "ordinary readings." This identification is, I take it, what "empirical hermeneutics" is intended to do. Such analysis also opens the way for a revision of the importance to the church of such popular, ordinary readings, a matter I will take up in the final section.

Such analysis also opens up questions about the nature of the communication that may or may not occur between contemporary groups from different cultures.

To take us further into this discussion, we will look at two examples of such encounters that will illustrate different aspects of this kind of exchange. The first encounter was between two groups that differed greatly in cultural context and theological stance. The two groups concerned were a group of students in the masters of divinity program of Hanil University in Korea and a group from the Comunidad Cristiana de Crecimiento Integral from Soacha Township, Colombia. The latter group reported about its members only that they "come from different ages, occupations, genders (in equal proportions), and regions of the country, and all attend the same church."

The Korean group was one of the few groups who submitted a full report according to the format that the organizers had requested. This group was clearly conscious of the conservative nature of most of the Korean churches and explicitly critical of it. The members had all filled in a questionnaire distributed by their facilitator, a female professor, and many of the responses show a well-formed understanding of the respondents' place in society and culture.[11] The reading itself started by focusing on the woman and her position in her village and culture. The group clearly distanced itself from standard interpretations of the woman as a prostitute and the type of a sinner. Instead, she was seen as someone with greater initiative and understanding than the disciples, a woman who, like the Syrophoenician woman, is able to "awaken Jesus, who has a certain kind of cultural bias. She advises Jesus on this matter." The number of her husbands was explained (tentatively) in terms of Jewish laws requiring a woman to marry her brother-in-law on the death of her husband. Meeting Jesus changes a woman who was already personally courageous into an equally courageous social activist. The group speculated about what she might have become after the encounter and suggested that she became very independent (and therefore may not have married again), proclaiming the coming of the Messiah. This led then into more explicit discussion of the present place of women in the church in Korea—specifically, of the church's change from employing single women as evangelists to now wishing "to employ married women because it thinks that experience is the most important qualification and that married life gives a lot of experience."

In addition to discussing the woman's position as a woman, the group discussed the relevance of the story for cultural and political divisions in Korea between North and South and between the Youngnam and Honam areas. Some saw similar cultural divides between Christians and those whom they judge, that is, those using alcohol and tobacco and not attending church. The church should be a community, not a closed circle. The church needs, said the professor, "a protestant and reforming spirit to be a community." They noted divisions within the church between those who are rich and who observe all the church's rules and those who are poor and have to work on Sundays to survive. This led into further discussion of the church's concern with holiness and its inability to acknowledge that Christians have "good things and bad things" in them. This focus on holiness engenders guilt. The group recognized a need to set practical and achievable goals. "We have to be more specific and practical rather than just to dream noble ideals. We have to change our attitude and our life, starting from my life." To this, one member added, "We need to encourage each other, not to judge. Then we can change ourselves more easily."

In general, the Korean group was well informed and critically aware, socially, politically, and theologically. Group members had clear views about the cultural situation of the Samaritan woman and were able to relate her situation to their own condition. They were familiar with historical-critical and feminist readings of the text, so that their reading was far from being a spontaneous and uncritical reading. As the hermeneutical analysis of the discussion notes, the text was well known to the female students and was therefore not very exciting and did not arouse much curiosity. The report gives the impression that the group may have been casting about for a new direction in which to take the text and was beginning to touch on an important question in relation to perfectionism/holiness in the church and the refusal to recognize human failure among Christians.

The account of the Colombian group's reading was much briefer and combined a straightforwardly socioeconomic account of the woman's plight with a charismatic view of salvation. They saw the woman as an outcast whose isolation brings tragic consequences: "low self-esteem, criticism, rejection, negative perception of herself, culpability, social resentment, disappointments, frustrations, complexes, and so on. The situation she lives in is the product of a society that rejects her; that is to say, it sickens and isolates her." This account is far from a traditional view of human sinfulness. Jesus overcomes all these barriers to meet her and offer her health and salvation. He does so by making her face up to her own situation. It is this confrontation with the reality of her situation that is the key moment in the conversation. In the woman's confrontation with reality the group identified a link with their experience: "In Colombia, we have lost the capability to face our problems. We ignore or do not want to remember them, worsening our crises in all areas: social, economic, and cultural." What Jesus offers the woman as a solution to all these problems is the gift of the Spirit springing up within her (John 7:37–39). This gift restores her to her place in society, and from this restoration and transformation springs the obligation to tell others about the source of such restoration. "We are workers with a mission: to preach the gospel, to demonstrate that we have been restored and transformed, that our society needs to meet the one who gives the water (as the Samaritans met him), so that we have a spring of water welling up to eternal life."

There are considerable difficulties involved in interpreting the report of the Colombian reading, not least because they give little information about the nature of the group and of the church of which they are a part. It seems likely that it is broadly charismatic/Pentecostal and that their reading of the text is naïve and spontaneous in that it reflects clearly the views of the church. The gift of the Spirit, which one may conjecture is central to the worship and life of the church, enables people of every walk of life to face the problems of daily life. "God is present in our daily life, helping us to live it and to make it better." This is not a revolutionary reading of the gospel, one looking for a radical change in the position of women in society or for radical reform that will bring justice to the poor, but rather one that helps people cope and better themselves in a world and society where change and the overcoming of poverty come only slowly. If this interpretation is right, then there was little critical reflection in this group. Rather, the group reported on an unconscious reading of the text in light of its own core convictions. There was no distancing or experience of alienation from the text. The text was there as a mirror for the views and experiences of the group. As such, it was very effective and gave us a moving view of the group's situation and of the strength that they receive from such stories.

It is fascinating to observe the reaction of the Korean group to the report (just summarized) that they received from Colombia. It triggered strongly negative reactions from the Koreans. They thought the report was "just like a very conventional sermon we used to hear from our senior minister." They recognized that the "participants are not theologically trained but lay people with a different background," but then were faced with the problem that they knew nothing about the other group's background and situation. They noticed the partner group's lack of discussion about the Samaritan woman's situation in society as a woman. The Colombian group, they objected, had not thought about the woman's personal experience; "they have not thought of her as a subject" but "as a model to do some work for the gospel." They wondered what the Colombians thought about the usual views of the woman as a prostitute. They regretted that the Colombians did not discuss social and economic issues more closely or indicate how they might tackle them. Instead, their partner's "solution seems to be that they have to preach them the gospel to prevent such problems." Like the church everywhere, "we concentrate on just the soul's salvation rather than on social problems and their causes." In the end, there was no real dialogue or possibility of interchange. "We do not see new insight from the report."

To date, there has been no response from the Colombian group to the Korean report.

It is perhaps hardly surprising that there was such a negative response to what is in many ways a very moving and transparent reading of the text. It is, of course, quite correct to say that it is difficult to respond, in light of the lack of information about the Colombian group's situation. It is also true that the modes of reading of the two groups are strikingly different; the Korean group's reading is reflective and analytical, probing the social and cultural setting of the Samaritan woman and analyzing their own social and ecclesial situation. It is critical of conventional theologies that focus on the conversion of the individual and do not attempt to address the causes of the social problems with which they struggle. One may conjecture that their own experience (or at least the experience of many in the group) was of the transformative potential of a critical analysis of their position and the liberating effects of a similarly critical reading of this and other texts. There are grounds for thinking, however, that they may have read the Colombians' report too hastily. (We would need more information to check this out.)

For the Colombians, the salvation that Jesus offers is not salvation of the individual soul from its sins, but restoration of oppressed people weighted down by the pressures of life on the margins of society. The Spirit gives them strength to surmount their problems, to reenter society, and to better themselves. The gospel provides a way of coping rather than a way of transforming the whole of society, but in situations where radical change is a distant hope, coping strategies offer a less exciting but perhaps more realistic hope. At the least, there would have been a basis for dialogue here, challenging both sides to think through their own received or achieved positions. Such a dialogue, had it occurred, might have provoked the Colombian group to move beyond its first naïve acceptance of the harmony between their received beliefs and the text. On the other hand, it might have prompted the Korean group to continue the process of critical reflection on their own strongly held beliefs and their harmony with the Johannine text.

If this is a case where intercultural dialogue was refused, there are other cases where it led to creative exchange. A group of women led by their male minister from an Afrikaans-speaking church in Durban, Natal, South Africa, was paired with a group of women from the Unidad Cristiana Universitaria (UCU) in Bogotá, Colombia. The Afrikaans group was "a homogenous group and were brought up in a European Afrikaans culture." Their ages ranged from fifty to seventy-four; they had no university experience. They described the situation in their country as follows: "The tensions in our country have their origin mostly in political changes that have been brought about in the country since the democratic elections of 1994 and the legacy of the previous apartheid regime. Sudden changes in areas such as education, technology, government, health, transport, communication, etc., have created an uncertain climate. The high crime rate and a feeling of vulnerability among ordinary citizens bring about tensions." Their church was primarily Afrikaans-speaking but had recently introduced an English service. Members of all nationalities were now accepted (not formerly the case), but "because of our 'Rainbow Society' (many ethnic and cultural groups), the natural tendency is still for people to cluster to their own groups. This has nothing to do with discrimination, but reflects a spontaneous feeling of being with those who share the same interest and the same cultural background." (Quotations are taken from a report compiled by two of the women.)

The Colombian partner group was also all women, mostly single, around thirty years of age, and from evangelical churches. They had spent anywhere from six to thirteen years studying the Bible. They were conscious of living in a society that promotes machismo (taught in a matriarchy by women to their sons) and is very class conscious. They came from middle- and lower-middle-class families and had all studied at university and been part of the ministry of the Unidad Christiana Universitaria. They represented all the different regions of Colombia "and therefore different cultural contexts." They had studied a wide range of topics, but not theology as such.

The Afrikaans-speaking group (like the Korean group) identified the Samaritan woman as a model of courageous action. She was not shy about going to tell others. "Carrying water, the duty women were socially prescribed to perform, became secondary to the proclamation of the gospel." This identification linked with their own experience of widowhood, to the fact that they have to perform both male and female roles and have found this "to an extent liberating." They were also aware of similarities between the Samaritan woman and "the many women in Africa who also have to collect water." "In this regard, it is our responsibility to help relieve their poverty." More specifically, they were challenged by the crossing of ethnic/racial and gender boundaries described in the text. Some felt that these were important issues for church and society and that it is good that such boundaries should come down, but there was clearly not unanimity here. "In government and church, more and more women are in leadership positions. In church, this move is justified and empowering, because more women than men actively participate in church programs and functions." We are not told whether they felt this empowerment of women was also good in government. However, we are told that the group had a difference of opinion about whether the church should be engaging in "political" matters or should focus on spiritual matters instead. Nevertheless, the group "concluded that the church has to raise its voice about these issues to be responsible and credible in her proclamation of the Word." The group agreed on the following action points: "Believers are called to proclaim the gospel of Christ in boldness, like the woman, and many will come to know him. Following Jesus's example, we must engage one another without discriminating on grounds of race, sex, etc. His style of love, humility, and compassion is the power of the gospel for credible evangelism."

The Colombian women focused with remarkable concentration on one aspect of the story. They saw the story as a "meeting of a person who is excluded with the excluding one." They continued through a series of prayers, meditations, stories, and reflections to consider how they should appropriate the message of this story about Jesus. For them, to encounter those who are excluded in their society can be dangerous, and the prospect inspired fear. "To speak with a street person could be dangerous, because they can attack us and steal from us." They saw this avoidance as exclusion at work—the exclusion of those who are lower in the social hierarchy. But if one breaks through these fears and barriers, "we will discover that the excluded one has a lot to give." They saw Jesus as a model of how to relate to the excluded. "Jesus transforms the exclusion into inclusion." "Instead of prejudging and pronouncing punishment on the woman, Jesus restores her. Jesus doesn't reject the person but the behavior." The group reflected on how such inclusion of the excluded can occur in practice. They also reflected on the more negative experiences of active exclusion, not the least of which is exclusion within the church. One member related a story about being shunned by a shoe cleaner who came into her office. She excluded him, and it took seven years before he was willing to polish her shoes.

The South African group's reception of the Colombian report was deeply appreciative and picked up many details with great attention. They noted the point made "that the water is also in us, and therefore we have to give of ourselves. The South African group only saw the water and bread as objects of salvation that had to be handed out. This leaves the person detached and neutral or unaffected." They agreed that they should not be fearful of others. They acknowledged that "the collective history of apartheid formed them, and this history of pride had to be dealt with."

The South Africans reflected that a culture with many dos and don'ts is crippling. "We need to interact with others for self-knowledge. We know ourselves through others." The awareness that self-knowledge comes from engagement with the other and through what one may learn from the other was crucial and it led to a remarkable judgment on the South African group's own reading. "Our group did not include themselves when referring to discrimination in the text. We did not become the subject of the text and could therefore not be confronted by our prejudices. We spoke about racism and sexism as something that did not include us." In particular, they related this observation to their remarks about rural women in South Africa carrying water. "We cut ourselves off, but maybe we need to be more creative in bridging the boundaries we set for ourselves when we think we have nothing to learn from the Samaritan woman, as the disciples thought. We were acting on instinct and learned patterns of thought. Even the comment on how sorry we feel for rural women who have to carry water is a sign of this. We can learn from this woman because we are all women of Africa."

This remarkable response provides another intriguing example of how received patterns of reading can be challenged and lead to a reappropriation of the text in a reading that is genuinely liberating. It is clear that the South Africans come out of a culture where boundary crossing was strongly discouraged, and that this culture has now been strongly (and successfully) challenged within the politics of their country. Equally clearly, they as a group were still grappling with these questions and coming to resolution of them in their first reading. They concluded, "The church has to raise its voice about these issues to be responsible and credible in her proclamation of the Word." This, in light of their reaction to the Colombian report, is already an interesting formulation. It remains in a certain sense at a distance from them: "*The church* has to raise its voice." However, they did also draw practical conclusions for themselves: "Following Jesus's example, we must engage one another without discriminating on grounds of race, sex, etc." The question that their subsequent reaction to the Colombian reading raises is how far that action point was imaginatively appropriated.[12] What the imaginative and prayerful rehearsal of these beliefs in the Colombian group achieved was precisely the rooting of them in the minds and wills of their South African dialogue partners. Boundary crossing, reaching out to the downtrodden in society, was no longer an abstract duty but an invitation to a liberated and enriching new way of existence, to a new set of dialogues with those whose prescribed absence in their inherited culture had diminished and impoverished them.

Concluding thoughts

These three brief studies show, if nothing else, the extraordinary richness of the readings that the text inspires and the complexity of the process of its reception. Certainly, what we have seen confirms the broad outlines of Ricoeur's schema whereby readers move from a first to a second naïveté via a process of distantiation, confrontation, and dialogue. What is equally clear is that the diverse elements in this process are present at all stages of the present project and that the critical reflective moment may just as well have its roots in the conflict of cultures and prior beliefs within a group or between groups as it does in the encounter with specifically scholarly readings. Scholarly readings may foster a critical openness to the text, but so may conflicts or overlaps between different popular readings. Such readings may sit more or less easily with inherited or "official" readings of the church community from which the group comes.[13] Again, the complexity of these matters is illustrated by the Afrikaans-speaking group. This group was clearly still working through inherited attitudes and beliefs. They voiced divergent views about the current situation in South Africa regarding the role of the church and whether they should be pursuing "a strategy with a strong socioethical consciousness" or one "searching for eternal truths." An interesting middle way through this difference was found in the suggestion that "Jesus's loving and open style of engagement with others in a nonracist and nonsexist way is an essential message of the eternal truth of God's love for all people."

The preceding quotation came from the hermeneutical analysis by Mark Rathbone, the group's facilitator. He described his role as follows: "The group is facilitated to share openly and freely with each other. The facilitator's function is to let this process flow, answer problematic questions raised by the group, and provide summaries of discussions." There is little reason to quibble with this description of the process. If the minister shows his hand at all in the hermeneutical analysis, it was when he said of the group that it was "engaged in a process of social consciousness raising for a just society." Then, he immediately noted that because the process was open-ended and nonthreatening it allowed for a tension between those who "welcome this focus and others who are still reluctant." Nevertheless, one cannot help but feel that the fact that the minister of the Dutch Reformed Church could describe the process as he does must have added an interesting dimension to the dialogue. If the one to whom respect was owed in the apartheid church now challenges those former teachings, however nondirectively, what effect does this challenge have on those who still wish to hold on to as much of their inherited tradition as possible? One can see how unsettling this change must be and how it prepares the way for a significant personal and social reorientation on the part of the group. What is extraordinary is that this moment of real transformation grew out of interaction with a group of unknown women on a different continent with quite different cultural traditions.

To what extent can this interaction be seen as an intercultural exchange? Clearly, we are concerned here with the struggle of groups of women with powerful ideologies that have had and continue to have great influence in their societies. In the case of the Colombians, the hierarchical class structure and machismo, which are promoted precisely by the women who adopt the role of matriarchs within that society, provide the codes that determine the ways people think, the "mental programming," so to speak. For the Afrikaners, it was the doctrines of apartheid that underlay many of their attitudes. These were doctrines that specifically forbade cross-boundary encounters, as evidenced in legislation such as the Group Areas Act and the Immorality Act (forbidding marriage and sexual relations across ethnic divides). I once listened to an account of an early mixed-group Christian conference, a striking example of crossing these boundaries, where an Afrikaner minister had for the first time engaged in dialogue with a member of another racial group. The conversation came as a surprise, he said, because he had been brought up never to speak to blacks except in commands or questions.

It is clear that, while the cultural codes in Colombia and the old South Africa were significantly different, as were their manifestation in societal and political terms, both cultures were dealing in similar ways with "basic questions about power and inequality, the relation of the individual and the group, the social roles ascribed to men and women." At certain points, it is hard for an outsider to pick up what is going on (the incident with the shoe cleaner puzzled the South African women), but the South African women identified easily with the fear that results from sharply drawn boundaries and the sense of danger associated with those who are excluded. Both groups had no difficultly in seeing the analogies between their situations and the situations of the woman and Jesus in John's story. Here the Johannine narrative functioned as a kind of cultural intermediary. Before they came to exchange their own views, both groups had already engaged in a cross-cultural reading of a text, translating cultural codes from first-century Mediterranean cultures. It is their understandings of this text that formed the basis for their conversations. The verification of this exchange, that they indeed correctly understood each other's codes, lay in the moments of identification of analogous experience: the fear of the other and the loss of identity that results from this denial of the other.

One last set of reflections. The focus of this project has been on intercultural exchange. What we have seen is that such interchange is fraught with difficulty but at its best can be transformative and renewing. We have also seen that the local studies contain within themselves, *in nuce* at least, those elements that the project planners anticipated the exchange between cultures would add. In the same way, we have seen that such intercultural exchanges can be either productive or unproductive of further reevaluation and transformation. The fact is, most people who live in a metropolitan environment are constantly confronted with different modes of discourse and different cultural codes. Therefore, opportunities for such intercultural exchange grow all the time. Further investigation might look more closely at the kinds of intercultural exchange that occur within such urban environments, allowing for much closer documentation and investigation than is possible when groups are at a great distance from one another.

A final point of interest arises out of the observation that what occurs in "local" studies contains, potentially at least, all the elements that Ricoeur identified as contributing to a fully reflective apprehension of the text. If that is so, then what is the relationship of this kind of discourse to more self-consciously reflective theologies articulated by scholars in the academy or in official positions in the church? Can we speak here of "incipient theologies"[14] in the sense that what is articulated, however informally, however unsystematically, is indeed a reflection on the church's traditions in the light of often very raw experience and read against the background of scripture? Is its claim to be called theology—to express the wisdom of those in the church—precisely this mixture of honest striving for a reconciliation of biblical text, church tradition, and the experience of those at the margins of our society? Or would it be more fair to see this as a creative form of religious language, a dialogical kind of prayer that enriches the language of faith, on which theologians need to reflect, seeking, where possible, to clarify, while resisting all attempts at totalization?[15] At stake here is the extent to which the church and academy and their theologians may learn from such discourse, and the extent to which such discourse may renew the church and its wisdom.

Notes

[1] See, e.g., Gerald West and Musa W. Dube, eds., "'Reading with': An Exploration of the Interface between Critical and Ordinary Readings of the Bible: African Overtures," *Semeia* 73 (1996); and Gerald O. West, *The Academy of the Poor: Towards a Dialogical Reading of the Bible* (Sheffield, U.K.: Sheffield Academic Press, 1999), especially 34–62.

[2] "The project will be concerned with two issues: the interaction between the scientific and the ordinary reading of the Bible and the intercultural reading of the Bible" ("Intercultural Reading of the Bible" [report of a conference held at the Free University, Amsterdam, the Netherlands, 3–5 July 2000], 5). The second issue is more fully formulated in Hans de Wit, "Through the Eyes of Another: A Project on Intercultural Reading of the Bible" (presentation, consultation on Intercultural Reading of the Bible, Free University, Amsterdam, the Netherlands, 2001), 8: "Can the reading of the Bible by Christians in diverse social and cultural situations become an instrument for enriching and deepening missionary and diaconal relations, particularly at the grass-roots level of the churches?" The planned exchanges of readings by different groups "will also serve to intensify the dialogue between rank and file Christians from different cultures." The second aim, "the question of to

what extent the widespread 'non-Western' Bible movement has led to dialogue with the 'Western' interpretation of the Bible," is again addressed on page 14.

³ Ibid., 7.

⁴ This comes out particularly strongly in the reference to Geert Hofstede's parable of the twelve jurors, who have to resolve their differences and come to a common mind before they are allowed to leave, and in the citation from Robert Schreiter, who looks for a new catholicity, "marked by a wholeness of inclusion and fullness of faith in a pattern of intercultural exchange and communication. To the extent that this catholicity can be realized, it may provide a paradigm for what a universal theology may look like today, able to encompass both sameness and difference, rooted in an orthopraxis providing *teloi* for a globalized society" (ibid., 19).

⁵ "Intercultural Reading of the Bible," 7.

⁶ de Wit, "Through the Eyes," 26.

⁷ Ibid., 27.

⁸ I do not wish to underplay the role that academic theologians have had in the development of the Craigend group. They have had regular lecture series on matters of theology, ethics, and philosophy. The Craigend group's meetings over the years with the contextual Bible study group have certainly encouraged critical reflection and discussion on their part; this has not, in my perception, imported a wholly new element into the group. The influence of the CBS group may well have allowed the Craigend group to develop critical elements in its discussions.

⁹ I realize that all these judgments are open to question and that an independent observer might have assessed the contribution of academically trained readers differently.

¹⁰ In this sense, this particular connection posed a critical moment in the group's dialogue, which enabled a movement from a "first naïveté" where the text was read within a given theological understanding of canon and doctrinal teaching as mutually reinforcing, to one where the text was freed to become a source of creative theological reflection, a "second naïveté" where what is "appropriated is the meaning of the text itself, conceived in a dynamic way as the direction of thought opened up by the text" (Paul Ricoeur, *Interpretation Theory: Discourse and the Surplus of Meaning* [Fort Worth, Tex.: Texas Christian University Press, 1976], 92; quoted in Lewis S. Mudge, "Paul Ricoeur on Biblical Interpretation," introduction to *Essays on Biblical Interpretation*, by Paul Ricoeur, ed. Lewis S. Mudge [Philadelphia, Pa.: Fortress Press, 1980], 16).

¹¹ One example: "(1) I am economically unstable and poor. I am politically very open and liberal. (2) I am deeply thinking about the problem of the necessity of church in the future. As a student, I have difficulties in getting regular incomes and in considering future work. (3) Our church is based on neo-classism, the extremity of secular and sacred and people's oppression by church in the name of God. This is a big problem, I think. (4) I think that I belong to a marginalized class because I am not well off and I can have no voice in church. (5) I am interested in the reformation of Korean church and society and Koreanized theology (contextualized theology)."

¹² John Henry Newman in *An Essay in Aid of a Grammar of Assent* (New York: Longmans, Green & Co., 1947), 67, distinguishes between "notional" and "real apprehension and assents." The former are abstract: as, for example, in the notional

apprehension of the proposition that slavery is wrong. The idea is grasped, but not the full reality of the phenomenon to which it refers. Where the apprehension is real, where the full reality of the phenomenon is grasped and seen in all its brutality, a different kind of assent to the proposition occurs. Such assents have a powerful effect on molding the will and the personality of those who make them. They "form the mind out of which they grow, and impart to it a seriousness and manliness [!] which inspires in other minds a confidence in its views, and is one secret of persuasiveness and influence in the public stage. . . . They kindle sympathies between man and man [or in our case: woman and woman] and knit together the innumerable units which constitute a race and nation. . . . They impart to it homogeneity of thought and fellowship of purpose." Newman's distinction provides a remarkable commentary on this moment of turning from an older, deeply held set of national beliefs to a cultural openness inspired by a group of women from the other side of the Atlantic.

[13] There is an important discussion here about the ways in which official ideologies/hegemonies are undermined or overturned by subalterns, which has its roots in the work of James C. Scott, *Domination and the Arts of Resistance: Hidden Transcripts* (New Haven, Conn.: Yale University Press, 1990). See particularly West, *The Academy of the Poor*. For a helpful discussion of the notions of culture, hegemony, and ideology, see Jean Comaroff and John L. Comaroff, *Of Revelation and Revolution: Christianity, Colonialism, and Consciousness in South Africa*, vol. 1 (Chicago: University of Chicago Press, 1991).

[14] See James R. Cochrane, *Circles of Dignity: Community Wisdom and Theological Reflection* (Minneapolis, Minn.: Fortress Press, 1999). In pointing to the importance of popular theologies, Cochrane stresses the creativity of local theologies that come from the margins of society, and indeed of the church, and which thus articulate a perspective from below, from those without power.

[15] Rowan Williams, "Theological Integrity," in *On Christian Theology* (Oxford, U.K.: Blackwell Publishers, 2000), 3–15.

Intercultural Bible reading and hermeneutics

Hans de Wit

In this chapter, we will cast a quick glance at a few hermeneutic aspects of the Through the Eyes of Another project. I will focus on the following issues: (1) Intercultural hermeneutics is intended to be descriptive, to describe what happens when interpretation of Bible texts takes place within the framework of intercultural dialogue. Are there also normative principles that apply? Where do these normative criteria originate? (2) The project ties in to flesh and blood readers and to their culture and situation. At the same time, the project intends to stimulate a discussion that rises above the local situation. How does the project deal with the relationship between the local and the global? (3) How can intercultural hermeneutics be defined, and on what levels can it be made operative?

Normative criteria: Non-exclusion and willingness to interact

Hermeneutics may be defined as the theoretical practice that reflects critically on how interpretation processes of texts develop. Hermeneutics is not hermeneusis, the interpretation itself, but rather the scientific reflection on how those processes work. What instruments must be available? What factors play a role? Who are the players in this field, and what are their roles? Biblical hermeneutics then concerns the interpretation of Bible texts. By the word *process* in my opening definition I mean to indicate that more than the scholarly explanation is at stake in reading and understanding Bible texts. Hermeneutics also engages in actualization processes. Exegesis, focused on the question of what Bible texts might have meant in their historical setting, is one phase of a more encompassing process, in which actualization and praxes of current readers also play a role. Hermeneutics may focus on certain aspects of the process, or certain readers, or certain hoped for results. For example, one may

---

Hans de Wit, Faculty of Theology, Free University (Amsterdam, the Netherlands)

use the term *liberation hermeneutics* to work with the question of how reading Bible texts can serve processes of change. Thus, in hermeneutics, one formulates and analyzes the rules of proper reading. But what is proper reading? Are there a few basic rules among the multitude of hermeneutical designs that could apply to all? Is there a normative minimum that could be decisive here?

Anthony Thiselton has demonstrated that there is a development in two directions among the multitude of opinions and topics in modern hermeneutics.[1] One is a more contextual or sociopragmatic current, and the other is a more universalistic one. A similar development is also apparent in culture studies, in which universalism and relativism are especially important. *Universalism* is the system of unity, the understanding that there is one reality, one method to gain knowledge about it, and one proper system of moral judgment. One looks for a coherence in all diversity that can serve as a guideline for human existence. In *relativism* the contextual and the diverse is the central theme. There are many realities, many ways to obtain insight into them, and various systems of morality.[2] Developments in hermeneutics parallel those in culture studies. The image of universalistic hermeneutics is also visible, in contrast to a more contextually determined approach. One might say that sociopragmatic or contextual hermeneutics asserts that nothing can be said about a Bible interpretation outside of the context, while the more universalistic approach asserts that a universal framework is available that fits any situation, and that every interpretation process can only derive its legitimacy from this framework. Thus, Eurocentric hermeneutics has long had universal pretensions. In protest against and as proof of the incompleteness of the Eurocentric approach, a more relativistically and contextually determined approach, termed *genitive hermeneutics*, has arisen.

In the current hermeneutic situation, sometimes described using the metaphor of the battlefield, every interpretation, every approach to the scripture, appears to be worth as little or as much as any other. Where can external standards be found that could pass an independent judgment? After all, both ways are problematic when formulated to an extreme. The contextual approach pins people down to cultural values—the social and political situation they just happen to be in. Sometimes, this approach involves a strong reductionism, for in it readers coincide with their context. The universalistic way provides every interpretation, every reading, with the right to express itself, as long as it stays within the universally applicable framework this way has defined. This procedure often involves excluding groups of people, declaring inferior those forms of interpretation that are perceived as foreign, and promoting an idealism that bypasses the pain of the historical moment.

How can intercultural hermeneutics offer a solution here? It can connect with two central concepts in culture studies: eccentricity and interactive diversity. *Interactive diversity* makes cultural diversity operative and visible as a factor in the way people read the Bible. Sometimes, confrontation is necessary for growth and change in perspective. Confrontation may occur (or may be intentionally organized) when discussion about the meaning of Bible texts involves diverse perspectives.

A more profound question would be why interaction is included as a quality of the hermeneutic process. To address this question, I tie in to the concept of eccentricity as used by Henk Procee in his study on transcultural morality. The philosophical concept of *eccentricity* has to do with an attribute that is specific to the psychological makeup of human beings. It refers to "the insight that a human being is not only a body, but also has a body, is master and plaything of his psyche, product and producer of his culture."[3] One is—and is related to—that being. One never totally coincides with oneself. Eccentricity leads to polymorphism of human individuals, as well as to the great diversity of cultural patterns. Some cultures are strongly focused on interactions; others are just the opposite. Based on this attribute, it is possible to be both open to new influences and to exclude oneself from them. Eccentricity as a general human peculiarity means that interactions are essential for human beings.[4]

Procee develops two "(meta) standards for transcultural morality": the principle of non-exclusion and the principle of stimulating interactions. "The standard of non-exclusion originates from the idea of 'human dignity' that is present on the abstract level of eccentricity in which all people are, in principle, equal. This means that people have the right to a minimum existence and have equal basic rights to their interactions. It also means that when power and making decisions is involved, everyone must have the right to participate. Prohibiting this on the basis of race, culture, gender, social position is not permitted." The second standard is willingness to stimulate interactions; it is "linked to the actual differences between people on an empirical level and has a more content-based character as an addition to the previous one—promoting interaction. It qualifies inter-human relations, policy measures, social processes, cultural convictions on the basis of their contribution, positive or otherwise, to the interactive possibilities of groups and individuals."[5]

The theme of eccentricity can also yield insight for intercultural hermeneutics. One is not only a product of one's Bible interpretation, but also the producer of it. One can also examine other interpretations. However closed or reproductive interpretations of scripture may be, those who interpret never totally coincide with the interpretations. Readers can objectify their own interpretation. Thus, the concept of eccentricity applied to hermeneutics also leads to formulating normative hermeneutical criteria: the avoidance of exclusion and the willingness to stimulate interaction. These criteria offer two minimal normative components that may apply to hermeneutics as well as to exegetical activity. I say *normative*, because these components indicate where the quality of interpretations lies, namely, in the possibility for continuing discussion—in the willingness to not exclude, to be vulnerable, and to strive for consensus.

Local versus global

The most important conclusion regarding normative criteria is that when one critically researches the much-cherished idea of equality of interpretations, one arrives at an unexpected result: Taking this value seriously has the consequence that interpretations are not equal. Interpretations differ in the degree in which they are open to learn from "foreign" interpretations. The more they learn from other interpretations, the more valuable they are. When non-exclusion and willingness to stimulate interaction are normative criteria for assessment of hermeneutics, then it is clear that intercultural hermeneutics, which strongly desires to be determined by these values, may also have a testing and critical function. Intercultural hermeneutics would like to bring universalistic hermeneutical designs and more contextually defined approaches into discussion with each other. In this way, the critical function can be practiced in two directions.

The local

Is it necessary to confront contextual hermeneutics with the normative criteria of non-exclusion and willingness to interact? Contextual hermeneutic models seek to graft the interpretation process of the scriptures onto their own situation; they want to bestow the Word on a new subject, drawing attention to new problems and experiences. Contextual hermeneutics has obviously proved to be a very fertile movement. These hermeneutic models have only recently emerged, yet we are already asking them to look across their borders and be self-critical! Why, therefore, are we underlining the need for *inter*cultural hermeneutics?

Hermeneutics seeks to formulate the essence of the interpretation process, an assessment of the depth of the understanding generated, how text and context are related to each other and how the old text can be used in the new situation, which roles the actors are playing, and who must have ample space as privileged readers. Further, the choices made in hermeneutics are determined by cultural values and take place in situations that are constantly subject to change. This implies that no hermeneutic model escapes from cultural bias or from the dialectic between being open and being closed.[6] When one group or situation is privileged, another is excluded or invisible as a result. The discussion with postmodernism has made us sensitive to how explicitly interpretation and power are interwoven. Each reading process is likewise always a "grab for power." If one neglects one's own cultural bias, something similar to the phenomenon Randall Bailey observes in black faith communities is likely to occur. "We in the black church have been prepared to be somewhat progressive on the question of race, but on the issue of gender we have been most oppressive. That list of oppressive variables could be extended. It appears that we are only prepared to massage our own pain and ignore that of others. We seem to want to be more than conquerors, such that we will join other oppressors, as long as the oppression is not geared toward us."[7]

The question emerges: How can one arrive at hermeneutical models that, on the one hand, have an open eye for the personal context, but that, on the other, are less excluding, ideologically determined, and closed? This question indicates a problem for which intercultural hermeneutics can offer a solution. Genitive hermeneutics by definition understands itself as an alternative to ruling hermeneutics. The position represented by genitive hermeneutics makes genuine, profound interaction difficult. Interaction, certainly when it results in critical self-reflection, is easily interpreted as a betrayal of the issue of justice or liberation.[8] For this reason, genitive hermeneutics often ends up maintaining a ghetto position. People from the outside cannot get into the insiders' interpretation. Sometimes, a significant reductionism is visible in genitive hermeneutics: Bible readers are reduced to flat categories. Precisely because one encounters one's own reductionism and thus loses openness, it becomes necessary to specify one's position in greater and greater detail.

This process has been exposed clearly in different locations in the Latin American region. There has been a development from hermeneutics of the poor to feminist or womanist hermeneutics, to the Indian readers, to Afro-Brazilian readers, to readers from Pentecostal churches, to "urban" readers, etc. If one wishes to do justice to specific subjects, one must always continue to specify further. In this process, one runs the risk of being left all by oneself. The fact that empirical research is rarely or never carried out on the specific "hermeneutic" characteristics of the Pentecostal, the black, the Indian, or the poor in the slums of the city also avenges itself. Bypassing the principle of eccentricity, one allows readers to coincide with just one characteristic in their existence: poor, woman, Indian, etc. That this involves different categories is not problematized. However, the matter becomes urgent when one is dealing with readers who belong simultaneously to different categories—and what reader does not belong to more than one category at the same time? What category does a person belong to who is a woman, black, poor, divorced, and a member of a Pentecostal church? Besides that, concentrating on one type of reader, with the wish to contribute to alleviating that type's need by means of reading the Bible, often makes these interpretation processes, in cases where new methods are being generated, dependent on what is developing elsewhere in academia.[9]

In summary: intercultural hermeneutics does not demand that genitive hermeneutics give up what belongs to its specificity, namely, the attention to the local situation. Rather, intercultural hermeneutics invites genitive hermeneutics to take a critical look at its expressions of exclusion and unwillingness for real interaction. Here, interaction and self-criticism will have a complementary relationship: true interaction will also expose possible ways of exclusion.

The "other" local

For universalistic hermeneutics, the implications of the normative criteria of non-exclusion and willingness to stimulate interaction are perhaps even more important than they are for contextual hermeneutics. I have argued that ordinary readers belong to a neglected category of readers. This is particularly true for the North Atlantic situation. Here biblical scholars involve ordinary readers in the discussion of the meaning of Bible texts to a much lesser extent than in the Southern hemisphere. Although one must be acutely aware of caricatures, it is not an exaggeration to say that Western exegetes also largely neglect the great number of professional readers in the Southern hemisphere.

Mechanisms of exclusion, limited interaction, and the effect of culture on hermeneutic designs and exegetical practices in the Northern hemisphere become clear via confrontation and comparison with others. Elsewhere I have attempted to compare recent North Atlantic interpretations of the book of Judges with interpretations from the Latin American region.[10] In that work, I focused on results of exegetical work. Within the framework of this article, it is useful to briefly focus our attention on the results of such an exercise in intercultural hermeneutics. No matter how much one wishes to avoid caricatures and generalizations, it must be said that the differences are enormous and concern almost all aspects of the exegetical process: the method, the target group, what readers regard as the fundamental theme and message of the book of Judges, the style of argumentation. Many of these disparities are determined by cultural differences. Most North Atlantic researchers do not carry out contextual exegesis and do not focus on actualization processes; their aims are more universalistic, in the sense that they do not wish their exegesis to serve a specific context. Nevertheless, current Western culture has left deep and ubiquitous tracks. Let me give a few examples.

Objective of interpretation and method. Among Latin American authors, the interpretation of the book of Judges serves two purposes: reconstructing the historical context hidden behind the text and creating possibilities for actualization. Judges is important because the book can shed light on the current Latin American situation. The sociological method rules because interpreters think it may serve the liberation project. The liberation project understands the world in terms of contrasts: oppressors are against the oppressed. An exegetical method that tracks social contrasts in ancient Israel may give results that help in constructing analogies. A search for sociological approaches among European and North American Bible scholars is in vain, for they use literary, rhetorical, and narratological methods instead; the Gottwald school has had a lot more impact on Latin American biblical scholars than on North Atlantic exegetes. North American and European scholars are interested in literary style and narrative patterns. The accent lies on gathering knowledge about the historical text, not on its actualization. Interpreters who are oriented to the classic historical-critical approach are also active. They are especially interested in a book's final edition.

Central message. Latin American researchers find portraits of the liberated Israel in the book of Judges. They read stories from the book as a welcome contribution to their own liberation project. They recognize the situation of oppression, empathize with heroes and liberators, and perceive the religious and social aspects of the book as closely bound. An important role is reserved for the people (*el pueblo*). Western interpreters see tragedy everywhere in the book of Judges; they perceive within it criticism of ethnocentrism and nationalism and think that any liberation is attributable largely to YHWH, not to human effort. According to them, Judges is a critical, nonpolitical, anti-ideological book. Many of its stories are considered "humorous adventure tales" and must be regarded as literary fiction. There is no question of a liberation project. Project Israel is tainted by evil, violence, death, and complacency from the very beginning. Irony is an integral part of the essence of the book. Judges is not a political book but instead shows antipolitical tendencies. It is not about a new, social, national project; the reader is rather led into the private sphere. Relationships between father and daughter, mother and son, man and woman, and between brothers are recurrent themes; these are profoundly personal issues.

Latin American exegetes see a profound confrontation with "other" systems in the book of Judges, systems that have negative and oppressive relations with the new Israel. The "other" is the one who must be distantiated, the one from whom people must liberate themselves. The new Israel only takes shape when a break is made from the oppressing Canaanite social system. Western interpreters agree that the relationship to the other is a major theme in the book of Judges. However, the presentation of the other is not only negative. It is also a mirror. Sometimes, the liberation of Israel depends on a person who is not an Israelite. Not all generals in Israel are heroic (Judges 4); not all tribes have solidarity (Judges 5); not all leaders are reliable, honest, or steadfast (Jephthah, Samson); Israel has its dictatorial leaders (Gideon, Abimelech). Through these depictions, Judges is criticizing complacency and nationalism.

Latin American interpreters see a tight connection between the social system, politics, and religion of the new project. Conversely, some European researchers are of the opinion that the story of Jephthah, who is a model for all of Israel, is rather intended to be a plea for depoliticization of religion. The account expresses profound criticism of the tendency toward adapting religion to political standards. The book of Judges can be regarded as exposing political abuse of religion.

Many Western exegetes contend that liberation in the book of Judges only comes from YHWH, as opposed to the Latin American interpretation of the book as a "big story" in which participation of the people is important. The liberators in the book of Judges are an important identification point for Latin American interpreters. Western authors primarily see anti-heroes in the book of Judges.

North Atlantic commentaries and articles do not seek models for a new society in the book of Judges. Almost nowhere is there any mention of the liberated Israel. Israel is considered from a more individual perspective and understood as fragmented and nearly tragic. There is no search for images from the new, liberated society but for portraits with which individuals can identify. The Latin American longing for a new big story and their trust in the possibilities of the people participating in it are confronted by a deep mistrust of big stories and by attention to the small steps and the large problems in the private sphere of existence.

Relevance. Latin American authors are eager to involve ordinary readers and common believers in their interpretation process. They find that the results of their own work are relevant to these groups and to the society they live in. This interest is scarcely found in Western exegesis, and certainly not so explicitly. Generally Western biblical scholars do not aim to produce relevant research in the sense that it would serve the immediate solution of current problems. In contrast to what can be found in the work of their Latin American counterparts, Western scholars rarely refer to present-day believers or churches. Actualization is not a fixed component of the work process. Direct actualizations are thus the exception to the rule.

Culture. There is no room in this article for an extensive analysis of the cultural definitions of the exegetical treatises discussed. However, the five cultural depth dimensions of Hofstede can all be found. Let the following observations suffice.

Western interpreters have a strong tendency to avoid insecurity. They formulate carefully, are often vague on the exact historical background, and insist on ample time frames. But this hedging does not result in even the beginning of a consensus. The historical period in which the final edition of the book of Judges would best fit, according to interpreters, varies from the early monarchy to the late post-exilic period. Latin American authors display little inclination toward insecurity avoidance. Without a care, they jump back to the beginning, although the book of Judges clearly contains texts from a later period.

The Latin American interpretation of the book of Judges is strongly collectivist and nationalistic. It concerns the new Israel, a collective project, and political liberation. A collectivistic dimension can further be detected in the results obtained by various interpreters, which are marked by uniformity. Something is at stake that is shared by all interpreters. Interpretation of the book of Judges is done out of the interests of a collective that has a certain (liberation) project in mind. Western contributions, conversely, breathe the atmosphere of individualism, of debate and dispute. Their work concerns schools, not a project, and certainly not a collectivistic project. Difference is important and means progress. Consensus—on anything whatsoever—is barely found. Updating and interaction are important but take place within the limits established by the guild. Disparate schools continue to exist without many cross-connections, and ruling paradigms only are problematized as an exception to the rule.

Male/female. Latin American authors detect many masculine values in the stories. They enjoy the action of the heroes and liberators. The enemy is defeated; a new road is paved forcefully to a liberated, different society. There is optimism about the effort of the individual; history can be changed. Western contributions are critical of this emphasis on masculine values, and are in that sense more postmodern. To them, the book of Judges is defined by the small story at the level of the tent and the family; fragmentation is part of the message. Women play an essential role; they are also the victims. The chief actors are anti-heroes, who are unmasked. They do not contribute to liberation but are instead responsible for the failure of the project.

Time. Western authors are focused on producing long-term results. They want to contribute to the development of research on the book of Judges, not to solving current social problems. Therefore, they rarely actualize explicitly. Latin American authors want short-term results. They focus on relevant research. For them, the book of Judges can be a mirror and can provide models for liberation for the present.

Non-exclusion? Exclusion occurs in every exegetical practice. It is simply impossible to have seen or read everything. This is also true for Western practices. What makes exclusion special here is that large groups are excluded even as scholars cherish the pretence of completeness. Exclusion involves two groups here. There is no conversation with ordinary readers, nor any interaction with professional readers from groups other than those of the North Atlantic. Bartelmus provides a summary of all that has been published about the book of Judges since the days of Martin Noth, and his article illustrates what I mean.[11] Of the hundreds of works on the book of Judges published in the Latin American region during the period discussed by Bartelmus, he mentions only two. That would not necessarily be bad, were it not for the fact that this is a summary and that the author claims to be complete. The conclusion appears thus justified that among Western interpreters, interaction with non-Western interpretations is not in the least one of the rules of the game.

Complementary angles

Thus far in our exercise in intercultural hermeneutics, we have encountered great differences that are partially culturally defined. More important than continuing to point out the differences and the exclusion, though, is showing what the fruits of interaction might be. In the case of the book of Judges, the question of which liberating and collectivistic components of the book are not exposed by the anti-utopian, anti-ideological, and individualistic approach can be put to Western exegetes. Latin American interpreters in turn can be asked if they are prepared to discount the tragedy of many stories in their actualization processes.

However one intends to value the differences, confrontation and interaction may contribute to new insights. Interaction among exegetes appears to be limited to their own cultural circles. Precisely because of this narrowness, the Through the Eyes of Another project views interactive diversity broadly, as an encounter between readers from radically different situations and equipped with radically different skills. For Western exegesis, this encounter not only requires a far more generous or interested attitude toward non-Western interpretations of scripture than has been the case up to now, but also the development of new *hermeneutical* attitudes and insights. It is, of course, not sufficient for Western exegesis to be interested in non-Western interpretations of the Bible only because they are exotic. What is needed is a critical, open confrontation of interpretations of the Bible that come from different cultural circumstances. It is urgent that biblical scholars be present at the heart of this interaction and that we analyze what happens there.

Local plus local is global

How does the Through the Eyes of Another project deal with the relationship between local and global? Much has been written lately about the tension between tribalism and universality. There is a widespread belief that this new interaction should be seen as a new opportunity. In his book on globalization, Robert Schreiter affirms that "the fact of globalization is a challenge and a new opportunity for the church to reach a new wholeness, a new catholicity. Faced with the diversity of cultures and the implications of taking them seriously and the challenge of maintaining the unity and integrity of the Church worldwide, the eschatological sense of catholicity, so important to the Orthodox and many Protestant churches . . . takes on new salience at the interface of the global and the local."[12]

The project shares with Schreiter the insight that globalization is not only negative. Globalization also offers possibilities for a project such as Through the Eyes of Another. On the other hand, the project provides opportunities to identify the noxious effects of globalization at the very modest level of the local community of faith, and to make the process somewhat more humane. I refer to the following: the project connects the global and local aspects to one another in a simple and surprising manner. The objective of the project is not to put the burden of the world's suffering on the shoulders of the local community of faith. Who is capable of taking hold of the ends of the earth, that "the wicked be shaken out of it?" (Job 38:13). No, participants are asked instead to make contact with another small, local community of faith.

In the interaction between "local" and "local," participants first enter into a discussion about each other's context. They talk about legitimate differences, about contextual expressions of faith, about their own interpretation of the Bible text. However, they also speak about what goes beyond their own context and situation, about influences from the outside, about problems caused by global differences in wealth, power, and resources. This means that the discussion about "the global village" or "international relations" can be stripped of mystifying tendencies and become very concrete. After all, the discussion is fed from the participants' own experience. Thus, groups undertake concrete actions at the micro-level of this specific encounter, which is much more meaningful than general struggles against globalization in the abstract. In this manner, groups are able to determine together which differences are legitimate and may continue to exist next to each other, and where communal action for transformation is appropriate.

It is obviously essential that what was said in the gospel provide the basis, contents, and result of the communal assignment of Christians. I think especially of the statement in Ephesians 4, that every person is given a gift to use in behalf of the whole, and of the comment that the task of the church is to help fan into flames the gifts God has given (2 Tim. 1:6). At the modest level of the Through the Eyes of Another project, groups are invited to participate in a process of interaction and dialogue by sitting quietly together in the presence of God, reflecting on their stories and the biblical story, listening to one another's deepest longings, considering the great needs of the world, and (as Bob Ekblad suggests) perhaps gaining discernment about where their passion might intersect with some specific people or group

or need in a way that moves toward lifting up, healing, reconciling, making whole—
for us, and for those we serve. This leads participants to heed what was expressed so
nicely in Ephesians 4:2–16:

> . . . with all humility and gentleness, with patience, bearing with one an-
> other in love, making every effort to maintain the unity of the Spirit in the
> bond of peace. There is one body and one Spirit, just as you were called to
> the one hope of your calling, one Lord, one faith, one baptism, one God
> and Father of all, who is above all and through all and in all. But each of us
> was given grace according to the measure of Christ's gift. . . . The gifts he
> gave were that some would be apostles, some prophets, some evangelists,
> some pastors and teachers, to equip the saints for the work of ministry, for
> building up the body of Christ, until all of us come to the unity of the faith
> and of the knowledge of the Son of God, to maturity, to the measure of the
> full stature of Christ. We must no longer be children, tossed to and fro and
> blown about by every wind of doctrine, by people's trickery, by their crafti-
> ness and deceitful scheming. But speaking the truth in love, we must grow
> up in every way into him who is the head, into Christ, through whom the
> whole body, joined and knit together by every ligament with which it is
> equipped, as each part is working properly, promotes the body's growth in
> building itself up in love.

Intercultural hermeneutics and liberation

A word is in order about the relationship between intercultural hermeneutics and a
keyword of the gospel: salvation or liberation. Intercultural hermeneutics attempts
to bring the inculturation of biblical stories within one culture into relationship
with their inculturation in another context, not for the sake of intercultural discussion itself, but to make it serve the quest for truth, justice, and life. For this reason,
we speak about intercultural hermeneutics of liberation. Intercultural hermeneutics
of liberation would go a step further than regionally determined liberation hermeneutics. It would learn from postmodernism that violence and repression take place
more on the everyday level and are more culturally determined than some liberation
theologians believe. Intercultural hermeneutics of liberation would widen the area,
as it were, in which liberation, justice, and wholeness of existence are searched for.
Intercultural hermeneutics would involve not just social and political structures in
its analysis but also those areas in which people are sacrificed to cultural values.

We agree with those who say that raising the matter of justice and the praxis of
the liberation struggle as a starting point for theology—characteristic of liberation
theology in the narrow sense—marks a point to which no one single theology that
would be globally and ecumenically credible can return. In our opinion, the same
applies to intercultural hermeneutics. The concept of liberation can continue to
perform a meaningful function in intercultural hermeneutics as critical reflection on

the transformative power of the word of the gospel. This can happen, however, only if the concept is made fruitful in the broader context of human life itself and is enabled to also criticize theological models and interpretations of biblical texts that define themselves sometimes too hastily as liberative. In this way, the longing that the liberating God will be everything in everyone is the touchstone for the quality of the intercultural interaction.

The challenge for those who engage in cultural readings of the Bible lies precisely here: to so read the texts that we may discern the reality of the infinite God of life in the concrete situations of our culture, yet at the same time to always be ready to hear the voices of others who from their culture, their situation of difference, of suffering and oppression, may criticize and enlarge that understanding of God.[13]

Intercultural hermeneutics: a definition

What is culturally determined in biblical interpretation—in context and method—in one cultural context can be specified by comparison with interpretations in other cultural contexts. Subsequently, scripture can be brought into the intercultural discussion about Christian faith and its meaning in the world. Thus intercultural hermeneutics is not only concerned with what is in the text, but also, especially, with analysis of how we have read the text.[14]

Intercultural hermeneutics concerns itself with the inculturation of biblical stories and the opportunities these stories offer for intercultural communication that is oriented by the gospel. Intercultural hermeneutics thematizes the border-transgressing nature of the scriptures and is aware of the performative—even transformative—nature of religious narratives. Inculturation of the gospel is more than the distillation of the biblical story in a certain culture. Inculturation is a process where a double movement can be observed. Not only is the story read via certain cultural codes, the story also emits a power that inspires, changes, liberates, and evangelizes this culture. Intercultural hermeneutics analyzes this interaction and compares it with the same process in different cultures. Thus, intercultural hermeneutics introduces the interpretation of the scriptures into the broader context of border-transgressing cultural communication. Exactly because biblical stories have become values, the intercultural discussion is of fundamental importance. What has become value in one culture is brought up for discussion with values from other cultures, thus doing justice to the integrating and border-crossing nature of the gospel as expressed in scripture.

Intercultural hermeneutics can then be defined as consisting of the following elements: (1) Intercultural hermeneutics concerns itself with the analysis of the interaction between culture and the process of interpreting biblical texts, within the setting of intercultural confrontation and dialogue. (2) Intercultural hermeneutics explores the conditions that make communication of the meaning of biblical texts possible across cultural boundaries. (3) Intercultural hermeneutics also presses questions of liberation and of truth across cultural boundaries.

In relation to the interaction between culture and the process of interpreting biblical texts, intercultural hermeneutics can operate and contribute on three levels: on the level of the biblical texts themselves, on the level of hermeneusis, and on the level of analysis of the role of culture in determining the hermeneutics that is valid in a given context.

At the level of the text

The presence of cultural dimensions in every culture offers a framework for checking which position biblical texts themselves select with regard to power and distance from power, man-woman relationships, I and the other, fear and uncertainty, and time. The fact that the Bible is read in so many different cultural contexts is also indubitably the result of what one can call its metacultural dimension. Much research will have to be done on the manner in which the cultural codes prevailing in the ancient Mediterranean culture are "cracked" in the stories of the Bible. One can consider in this case relationships between old-young, powerful-powerless, man-woman, tradition–new revelation, dealing with time (kairos versus chronos), among others.

At the level of hermeneusis

How culturally determined are exegetical methods? Which methods are used and why? Can we speak of complementarity? Who are the members of the group, the *civitas disputantium,* that the interpreter considers himself or herself to belong to? Can we speak of a systematic discussion with interpreters from contexts other than Western ones? How are loyalty to the group and the individual interest of the interpreter related? What roles do the historical context and the history of the reception of the text play? What insight is provided by the method chosen for obtaining exegetical results? What is the style of argument? What is the relationship between result and method? What is the relationship between the perception of current reality and the perception of historical context?

Cultural determination of hermeneutical models

A hermeneutic is a construction that describes and analyzes the way the interpretive process of historical texts is realized. Intercultural hermeneutics asks questions about the way this process is established and about what factors in this process play certain cultural roles. Hofstede's description of the depth-dimensions of cultures is one instrument that can help us become more sensitive to the relationship between hermeneutics and the interpretation of the Bible and culture. One might consider the following questions when analyzing the cultural specificity of hermeneutic designs.

Power distance. Who declares an interpretation valid? How much space do exegetes require? How are the concepts *exegete* and *exegesis* defined? How are exegete and community of faith related? What role does the exegete play in giving the text topicality? Can we speak of privileged readers? If so, why are these particular readers privileged? Is the relationship between ordinary reading and exegesis defined hierarchically? Why? How vulnerable does the exegete make himself or herself? How is the competence of nonprofessional readers seen by professional exegetes, and vice versa?

Man/woman. What role does gender play in the community of interpreters? How do the interpreters deal with the elliptic nature of the texts? How do they deal with what is inexplicable in the text? What goes against the plot or makes it impossible? Are the great biblical-theological themes clung to in the interpretation, perhaps too hastily, omitting the small stories of the excluded? What position does praxis take on? Because "the meaning of a text is discovered not only through reflection on it, but also in concrete social action based upon it,"[15] what type of praxis is considered an essential component of the interpretation process? Is the interpretation process directed toward resistance? Against whom?

Collectivist/individualistic. What position may other actors in the interpretation process acquire, and how are the various reader categories—professional versus nonprofessional readers—related? Where does the primary loyalty of the readers lie? Does the interpretation process take an individualistic form, or a more collectivist one?

Uncertainty avoidance. Which methods are used? How long do prevailing paradigms remain valid? How are old and new interpreters and methods dealt with? How does one deal with innovation? How is methodological innovation dealt with? How long are methodological paradigms maintained? How exclusive is the interpreting community's claim with regard to the meaning they have discovered in the biblical text they have encountered? Who is engaged in a polemic with whom, in what way, and why? What role do political and ideological presuppositions play? Which opportunities for falsification are offered here?

Long term/short term. What is the relationship between relevance (short term) and pertinence (long term) of the results of an exegetical practice?[16] What does this relationship mean for the development of the profession of hermeneutics, for the contribution of exegesis to giving the text current meaning?

Conclusion

Intercultural hermeneutics does not aim to control or freeze hermeneutic processes by mapping cultural differences. Intercultural hermeneutics would rather set in motion reading processes showing gastronomic (Umberto Eco) or fundamentalist traits. Taking plurality seriously is intercultural hermeneutics' essential characteristic; it lives on interactive diversity. It subscribes to the notion that the interpretation of scripture involves a rich, never-ending process, a continuous interaction. The basic given for eccentricity—no one coincides with himself or herself—can also be made fertile hermeneutically. This reflection leads to two basic normative principles: commitment to non-exclusion and willingness to stimulate interaction. Authentic interaction requires vulnerability and a willingness to arrive at new insight. Intercultural Bible reading takes place in a world in which the blood of the innocent is shed by other people. Fundamentalism and its cruel sister terrorism are expressions of the opposite: a lack of willingness to interact or change perspective.

Sometimes—and only sometimes—vulnerability and new, small-scale ties of friendship will be able to lead to new sensitivity and to the insight that the capacity to love is not reserved to one's own group. In order to love, it is not necessary that everyone know what kissing is. However, in order to know that other people also love, one must have knowledge of and insight into the codes and forms of expression of love that exist in other cultures. In one of his stories, Father Brown remarks, "When will people understand that it is useless for a man to read his Bible unless he also reads everybody else's?"[17] What makes reading the Bible especially worthwhile is that we read it together. Intercultural hermeneutics is above all interested in that process. Intercultural reading of the Bible can teach us that the Bible is an interpretive means rather than an interpretive end.

Notes

[1] Anthony C. Thiselton, *New Horizons in Hermeneutics* (London: Harper Collins, 1992).

[2] Henk Procee, *Over de Grenzen van Culturen: Voorbij Universalisme en Relativisme* (Meppel, the Netherlands: Boom, 1991).

[3] Ibid.

[4] Ibid.

[5] Ibid.

[6] John Riches, "Cultural Bias in Biblical Scholarship," in *Ethnicity and the Bible*, ed. Mark G. Brett (Leiden, the Netherlands: E. J. Brill, 1996), 431–48.

[7] Randall C. Bailey, "The Danger of Ignoring One's Own Cultural Bias in Interpreting the Text," in *The Postcolonial Bible*, ed. R. S. Sugirtharajah (Sheffield, U.K.: Sheffield Academic Press, 1998), 83.

[8] Hans de Wit, *En la Dispersión el Texto es Patria: Introducción a la Hermenéutica Clásica, Moderna y Postmoderna* (San José, Costa Rica: Universidad Bíblica Latinoamericana, 2002).

[9] Hans de Wit, "Leyendo con Yael: Un Ejercicio en Hermenéutica Intercultural," in *Los Caminos Inexhauribles de la Palabra (Las Relecturas Creativas en la Biblia y de la Biblia): Homenaje de Colegas y Discípulos a J. Severino Croatto en sus 70 Años de Vida, 40 de Magisterio y 25 en ISEDET*, ed. Guillermo Hansen (Buenos Aires: Lumen-ISEDET, 2000), 11–65; de Wit, *En la Dispersión el Texto es Patria*.

[10] de Wit, "Leyendo con Yael"; and J. H. de Wit, "Lezen met Jael: Op weg naar interculturele hermeneutiek," *Amsterdamse Cahiers voor Exegese van de Bijbel en zijn Tradities* 19 (2001): 71–96.

[11] Rüdiger Bartelmus, "Forschung am Richterbuch seit Martin Noth," *Theologische Rundschau* 56 (1991): 221–59.

[12] Robert J. Schreiter, *The New Catholicity. Theology between the Global and the Local* (Maryknoll, N.Y.: Orbis Books, 1998), 127–28.

[13] Riches, "Cultural Bias in Biblical Scholarship," 447–48.

[14] Bailey, "The Danger of Ignoring One's Own Cultural Bias."

[15] R. S. Sugirtharajah, "Inter-faith Hermeneutics: An Example and Some Implications," in *The Postcolonial Bible*, ed. Sugirtharajah, 317.

[16] J. H. de Wit, *Leerlingen van de Armen* (Amsterdam: VU Uitgeverij, 1991), 236ff.

[17] Sugirtharajah, "Inter-faith Hermeneutics," 316.

The ecumenical relevance of intercultural Bible reading

Theo Witvliet

The events of September 11, 2001, shook the world. They revealed the vulnerability of the astonishing economic and technological achievements of modern times. As a theologian, I was especially shocked by the revelation of the dark side of religion. September 11 exposed the extreme violence of certain religious beliefs. It would be far too easy to attribute the violent, demonic side of religion exclusively to Muslim fundamentalism. The reactions from Christians also showed the violence of self-righteousness. Everywhere in the turbulence of those days people claimed God was on their side. The story is ancient indeed: religion used as a means of self-justification, religion used to escape any kind of self-critical reflection, religion as a means to divide the world into the good and the bad, religion as a justification for identifying the other as the source of evil.

The period after September 11 exposed something else. From beneath the surface of our rationally organized societies, feelings of anxiety, insecurity, and uncertainty emerged. A frantic search for identity is going on at personal, political, and religious levels. The loss of traditional social structures in the name of boundless freedom and progress causes a feeling of instability.

No wonder that restoration of norms and values is high on the political agenda! In a world of globalization and media culture, however, the restoration of faith in values that are durable stands little chance of succeeding. Sociologist Zygmunt Bauman speaks of an erosion of basic, daily trust in the durability of things toward which human life may be oriented. "The promotion of competitiveness, and of a 'free for all' pursuit of the highest gain, to the rank of the main (even a monopolistic) criterion to distinguish between proper and improper, right and wrong actions, is

Theo Witvliet, Theology and Religious Studies Department (emeritus), University of Amsterdam (Amsterdam, the Netherlands); Ecumenical Institute, Château de Bossey (Céligny, Switzerland)

the factor that bears the ultimate responsibility for the 'ambient fear' which permeates the life of most contemporary men and women, for their widespread, perhaps universally shared, feeling of insecurity."[1]

If there is some truth in Bauman's observation, then it becomes clear why there is so much "uncertainty avoidance"[2] in our societies. The extent to which people nowadays feel threatened by uncertain and unknown situations fosters an attitude of maintaining distance from whoever represents "the other." What is different seems dangerous. In order for us to feel at home, we accept people of other cultures only as long as they do not interfere in "our" culture. It cannot be denied that after September 11 the crossing of boundaries between people of different cultures has become increasingly difficult. Face-to-face encounters that would expose us to people from other cultures are replaced by what we learn from watching television. Nowadays, the images we have of people of other cultures and religions are frequently determined by media culture.

When we lack personal encounters with those who are different from us, media culture shapes our image of the other. This influence encourages stereotyping, which is in turn reinforced by other psychological processes. Those who lose self-identity need somehow to compensate for what is lost. The compensation may come through fixation of the identity of the other, especially when the one experiencing the crisis of identity does not recognize it as such and the crisis remains unconscious. If one feels uncertain and anxious at a deep level, then one has a need to create fixed images of the supposed causes of one's fears, the enemies. Creating fixed images becomes a way of smoothing over fears. To put it briefly: stigmatization of the other is the reverse side of the disintegration of identity.

Christian churches do not escape these dynamics. The spirit of ecumenism, prevalent during the 1960s and the 1970s, has nearly disappeared. Churches are becoming increasingly aware of the different and very diverse inculturations in which Christian faith takes shape. They also realize that Christianity is moving away from Europe and becoming more and more a religion of the Southern hemisphere. The gospel and Western culture are no longer identical. It is widely accepted that Christianity has become a multicultural and pluralistic phenomenon. These insights, however, have not promoted the crossing of boundaries between Christians of different cultures. Inculturation in different contexts all over the world has seldom become *inter*culturation. "Christians of other cultures are accepted as long as they do things in their own way *on their own*."[3] Making acquaintance with churches of different cultures is often limited to sightseeing, and, for churches that are poor, to offering practical financial assistance.

By and large, church members share the attitude of uncertainty avoidance evident in most people. There is a tendency toward segregation in churches at present.[4] Church people want to feel safe. They therefore stick to their own confession and to the familiar religious culture they feel comfortable with.

Intercultural reading of the Bible as an ecumenical endeavor

These tendencies explain sufficiently why the spirit of ecumenism has faded. An ecumenical attitude demands the courage to cross borders. Ecumenism is in fact essentially the art of transgressing boundaries. In a world of globalization and media culture, ecumenism understood in this way is of utmost importance. It is a way of counteracting the fateful God-on-our-side ideologies that divide the world into "us" and "them."

The experiment of the Through the Eyes of Another project takes part in this ecumenical endeavor of transgressing boundaries. It tries to bridge not only the gap between Christians from different cultures and confessions but also the gap between scholarly reading of the Bible and the spontaneous *lecturas populares* of the great majority of ordinary Christians in different parts of the world. Because the project invites all of the groups involved to deal with communal and intercultural reading of the sources of their religious traditions, inevitably members of the groups are exposed to fundamental questions regarding their faith. They cannot limit themselves to mutual sightseeing. On the contrary, exposure to one another's thinking challenges them to wrestle with readings of biblical texts that are unfamiliar.

In the present global context, this process of mutual exchange is a sign of hope. It is fascinating to read the project's reports, with all of their different views on the story of Jesus and the Samaritan woman; with their creative and sometimes surprising insights and reflections; and with all the prayers, songs, and symbolic acts that were part of the reading process. The differences between European groups and the groups of the Southern hemisphere are, generally speaking, great. While Europeans tend to focus on the text itself and its historical context, the spontaneous readers from groups all over the world are able to relate the biblical story directly to their own lives. While academically trained readers are inclined to strive for objectivity in their explanation of the biblical text, common people concentrate on those features of the text that appeal to their own situation.

African women or Dalits from India study the Bible with their life experiences as the starting point. Biblical stories are reread within the totality of life experience. This rereading creates space for their own experience, just as their own experience creates space for hearing the familiar biblical stories in a new way. In the process of identification with biblical figures and motifs, historical distance falls away. The Samaritan woman comes to life in the history of present-day African or Asian women.

But there is a risk involved here. Is there still space for the alien, surprising, even disruptive character of biblical stories? Is there still space for seeking criteria, which in the confusing diversity of biblical interpretations can help distinguish a legitimate interpretation of biblical texts from one that is not acceptable? Is there any room left for the achievements of scholarly exegesis? What should be done to prevent the biblical texts from being used to prop up a God-on-our-side ideology that excludes others?

The same risk is, in a different way, also involved in the reading of European groups. Their first interest is understanding the text. By trying to understand the text in a historical way, they experience the gap between their present situation and the ancient biblical story. Their major concern is to bridge the distance by considering what this remote story "still" has to say to us modern men and women. The danger here is that, perhaps without our being aware of the fact, modernity functions as a criterion, a center, a normative authority to which the biblical narratives must be adapted. This adaptation of biblical interpretation to modern self-awareness could easily lead to an ideology of self-righteousness in which "God" functions as a transcendent guardian of our powerful image of the world and of ourselves. The adaptation of biblical interpretation to modern self-awareness could then be a subtle way of uncertainty avoidance, of avoiding God as the wholly Other.

At this point, intercultural communication becomes critically important, however tentative and complex such a process might be. In my view, serious intercultural reading of biblical texts could be the most effective way to avoid the pitfalls of biblical fundamentalism, on the one hand, and postmodern relativism where anything goes, on the other hand. Only if we are willing to put ourselves at risk by carefully listening to interpretations and experiences from other cultures, only if we are ready to let the sources of scriptures speak for themselves, will there be a chance for a vital hermeneutical circulation. Otherwise, the hermeneutical enterprise runs every risk of remaining a closed circle.

After studying some of the precious reports of the Through the Eyes of Another project, I cannot avoid drawing an obvious conclusion. It is clear—at least in my experience—that the process of intercultural reading needs to meet certain conditions if it in fact is going to open new horizons for understanding a living God who has made all things new.

In a tentative and provisional way, I would like to offer three propositions that could be of assistance in meeting these conditions for a vital hermeneutical circulation. I will first mention all three propositions, and then I will try to briefly clarify each one of them. They are as follows: (1) The basic form of biblical interpretation is dialogue (commentary, dispute). This form is operative in the biblical scriptures themselves: they comment on each other. (2) Biblical stories cannot be pinned down to one meaning; they point beyond themselves to a historical "surplus." This eschatological dimension, intrinsic to biblical texts, allows for the possibility of various readings. (3) Being familiar with biblical stories means becoming aware at all times of their strangeness.

The freedom of communal reading

My first proposition underlines the importance of communal reading, or reading in dialogue. By now scholars generally acknowledge that interpretations of biblical texts cannot be abstracted from their cultural context. Always appearing within a specific tradition or at the crossroads of diverse cultural and religious traditions, interpretations somehow take part in the vicissitudes of a tradition. Every interpretation, however faithful to the sources, is a commentary on the original text, from within a certain context. The same is true for Bible translations, even for the famous *Verdeutschung* by Martin Buber and Franz Rosenzweig, which stays as close as possible to the Hebrew text.[5]

Buber and Rosenzweig themselves were very much aware of the role of context. They used the term *commentary*, in the Midrashic sense, to describe their work. Living in the Weimar Republic, these men thought the time had come for a mating of the Jewish and the German spirit. They sought, as Klaus Reichert explains in an instructive article, "to invent a language that is at one and the same time thoroughly Hebrew and the embodiment of a German that never existed, but might come into existence, be revealed, in the act of creation."[6] The aim of their translation is "to draw the reader into the world of the Hebrew Bible through the power of its language."[7] In their view, the internal coherence of the "large conversation" that is going on in this world of texts is represented by *Leitwörter* (leading words) that point to thematic connections within and between the different stories.

It is a misunderstanding to think that tradition begins where scripture stops. Scripture, too, represents tradition, in which texts constantly refer to one another and clarify one another by use of a great variety of stylistic means (repetition of words, word-plays, allusions, quotations). The friends of Job correspond to different positions represented in the Five Books of Moses. The small story of Jonah is full of allusions to the story of creation, the Exodus, the Psalms, Lamentations, Jeremiah, Hosea, and so on. Luke is concerned to correct the clumsy language of Mark. Many similar examples can be given to illustrate how, already in the books of the Bible themselves, a dialogue is carried on, a commentary is given, and tradition is constructed and reconstructed in a permanent but provisional way.

The rational, scholarly interpretation of biblical texts sometimes suffers from a fixation on written texts. It tends to forget that its work depends on the collective memory of a living community. Written texts create a distance that may be healthy (see my third proposition), but what has been set down in writing also has an irrevocable quality; it can no longer be changed. There are no longer possibilities of enriching or correcting written texts; the reader can only say yes or no. This quality can make written texts alienating. They tend to produce splits in the community, as opposed to free, oral discussion in which conflicts can still be settled. Therefore, it is encouraging, especially as a result of the contributions of feminist and African theologians, that the ecumenical movement presently pays more attention than it once did to the value of oral traditions, which as a rule remain close to everyday life.[8]

Intercultural communal Bible reading, whether on a local, regional, or global level, may prove to be an important way of helping us understand that God's revelation needs dialogue, exchange, and dispute in order to be grasped. For it is not doctrine but ongoing free commentary within the community of God's people that is the characteristic form in which something like truth can be brought to light.

The eschatological dimension

The reports of the groups involved in the Through the Eyes of Another project show abundantly that the story of John 4:1–42 cannot be pinned down to one clear meaning. A consensus about a single meaning of the text is impossible. Of course, certain common elements in the story are discovered by nearly all groups: the transgressing of cultural, social, and religious boundaries in what happens between Jesus and the Samaritan woman; the message that the gospel is for all people, especially for the excluded. Nevertheless, however important these common insights are, diversity dominates.

For the members of the Sokhanya Bible School class group in South Africa, the story of John 4 deals with discrimination and racism. Yet for their Dutch partner group from Zaandam, this reading came as a great surprise. Some groups consider Jesus's behavior toward the woman a model of how to relate to the excluded; other groups detected in Jesus's approach a degree of paternalistic arrogance. Some groups see the Samaritan woman as a prostitute and sinner; for other groups she is the victim of sexism and racism. Some groups discussed at length the time of day of the encounter; for other groups this element had no significance. Factors such as situation, culture, historical knowledge, and church affiliation influence to a large extent the moments of the text that are selected for discussion.

The confusing diversity of all these readings raises questions. Do hermeneutical criteria exist that might distinguish legitimate diversity from illegitimate aberrations from the biblical truth? Can scholarly exegesis provide these criteria? Beyond doubt, the historical-critical exegesis that has developed since the Enlightenment has produced insights and methods that cannot be discarded. Nevertheless, contextual readings from different cultures—and above all, feminist readings—have brought out the one-sidedness of this scholarly tradition.

Readings from the common people challenge the rationality of historical-critical investigations. These readings remind us that the history of God's covenant with the people of Israel and its Messiah comes to us in the context of Hebrew narrative art, and calls for a communal commemoration that uses not only rational means but also fantasy and imagination. Without a bit of fantasy and imagination, the letter of the text remains dead. Intercultural reading of the Bible is therefore asking for a revaluation and a rediscovery of other ways of dealing with biblical texts, ways that were used for centuries in the church. I am thinking of the allegorical, analogical, and moral sense of biblical texts. These point to a historical "surplus" that meets human hope and suffering, longing and despair. By this recollection and harvesting of meaning, the faith of the church through the ages recognizes the eschatological dimension of the *res gesta*, of God's *debarim* (words/deeds).

But the question remains: Are there clear criteria by which it is possible to separate the grain from the chaff? In my view, the discovery of intercultural communication in Bible reading is of abiding ecumenical significance only if the diversity of cultures does not lead to an arbitrary pluralism. Certain hermeneutical rules may be helpful for avoiding the ideology of postmodern relativism.

What rules might these be? A first rule could be the recognition in principle that in the diversity of cultures, different approaches to the text are possible and desirable. This rule would then have to find its counterpoint in a second rule, which states that every local reading community must be able and willing to show responsibility to the church as a whole; it must be open to critical questions and prepared for dialogue. A third rule might be that the community's praxis—which consists not only of action but also of reflection on action—should also be brought into the dialogue.

These rules might help bring out the eschatological dimension that is at the heart of the Jewish and Christian heritage. However difficult intercultural communication on a local or global level might be (examples of failed communication abound), intercultural communication nevertheless expresses a messianic yearning for wholeness and justice. "Just when groups try to look through the eyes of another, an *eschatological perspective* unfolds. People are deeply affected by the pain of the other and the inequality in the world. But one also corrects the other and exposes the mechanisms of exclusion that are present in each group."[9] However provisional and confusing the interaction between communities from different cultures might be, in struggling together the communities point to the mysterious world of God's kingdom.

The liberating distancing of biblical narratives

The ecumenical significance of intercultural Bible reading ultimately depends on the quality of the interaction. In this respect, intercultural communication on a local level might offer even more possibilities than does global exchange, because regular face-to-face meetings in a local setting increase the chance that the communication will be intense and lasting.

However, the quality of the confrontation and interaction between partner groups depends on the willingness of each group to be open to an exchange of perspective. When people become familiar with a biblical narrative, they are in danger of appropriating the story for their own needs and desires. People easily consider themselves the owners of the text.[10] Their domestication of the narrative leaves no room for other perspectives. A different outlook on the message of the text is perceived as threatening.

But if groups are willing to learn from the way partner groups detect other meanings and messages in the same narrative, then a new openness toward the text and toward one another may come into being. Horizons are widened and people become more aware of their own prejudices and cultural bias. A salutary space opens between text and readers, which leaves room for the otherness of the text.

In my view, it is essential that space be left between the text and its readers. This space or distance is of great hermeneutical significance. We need to realize that texts and narratives confront us with distance. All texts do that; even if they are autobiographical, they are about something or someone, which we are *not* at that moment. My view is that only if we can resist the pressure toward premature appropriation, only if we dare to maintain the distance, can stories have the power to create space and open up new, liberating perspectives.

Precisely by preserving a certain distance, a fundamental relationship can develop between the understanding of texts and self-understanding. As Paul Ricoeur demonstrates in his hermeneutics, the reading and interpretation of texts is not about a hidden truth in or behind the text but about clarifying one's own existence before (*devant*) the text. The text puts us at a distance; it represents otherness—and that can be salutary.

An awareness of distance recognizes differences, without making them absolute. The presence of the other is still felt in the distancing. Ricoeur, in his polemics with Gadamer, rightly refuses the opposition between participation in the world of the text and distantiation. He puts it this way: "For me the text is much more than a particular case of inter-human communication, it is the paradigm of the distanciation in all communication. As such it reveals a fundamental character of the historicity of human experience, communication within and by means of distance."[11]

In the interaction between text, context, and reader, everything depends on the dynamics of the open space between the three. We have to remind ourselves continually that the Bible is a collection of writings from the ancient Near East. All attempts to do away with this alien character, by means of modern translations, for example, amount to a misuse of these texts. The emphasis by liberation theologians on the correspondence between the situation of the poor who produced the biblical texts and the Latin American poor of the present time is in this respect in danger of domesticating "the poor" as well as the biblical narratives.

It seems such a paradox: distancing as an *attitude*, a way of creating space for otherness and diversity, so as to make authentic communication possible in our world of globalization and media culture. This attitude, however, might prove to be the best way to avoid the violence of religious self-righteousness and to resist the deep-seated desire for self-justification.

Notes

[1] Zygmunt Bauman, *The Individualized Society* (Cambridge, U.K.: Polity Press, 2001), 159.

[2] Geert H. Hofstede, *Culture's Consequences: International Differences in Work-Related Values* (Beverly Hills, Calif.: Sage Publications, 1984), 110–47.

[3] Abraham van de Beek, "Christians in the Clash of Civilizations," in *Christian Identity in Cross-Cultural Perspective*, ed. Martien E. Brinkman, Dirk van Keulen, and Abraham van de Beek, Studies in Reformed Theology 8 (Zoetermeer: Meinema, 2003), 97.

[4] Ibid., 97–99.

⁵ Martin Buber and Franz Rosenzweig, *Die Schrift und ihre Verdeutschung* (Berlin: Schocken, 1936).

⁶ Klaus Reichert, "'It is Time': The Buber-Rosenzweig Bible Translation in Context," in *The Translatability of Cultures: Figurations of the Space Between,* ed. Sanford Budick and Wolfgang Iser (Stanford, Calif.: Stanford University Press, 1996), 173–74.

⁷ Everett Fox, *The Five Books of Moses: Genesis, Exodus, Leviticus, Numbers, Deuteronomy* (London: Harvill, 1995), ix.

⁸ "Towards a Hermeneutics for a Growing Koinonia," in *Faith and Order in Moshi: The 1996 Commission Meeting,* ed. Alan Falconer (Geneva: World Council of Churches, 1998), 132–35, 280–81.

⁹ J. H. de Wit, "Through the Eyes of Another: Towards Intercultural Reading of the Bible," in *Interkulturelle Hermeneutik und lectura popular: Neuere Konzepte in Theorie und Praxis,* ed. Silja Joneleit-Oesch and Miriam Neubert, Beiheft zur Ökumenischen Rundschau 72 (Frankfurt am Main, Germany: Otto Lembeck, 2002), 27.

¹⁰ Ibid., 59.

¹¹ Paul Ricoeur, "The Hermeneutical Function of Distanciation," *Philosophy Today* 17 (1973): 130.

Epilogue
Hans de Wit

Let us take stock. What fruit has the intercultural Bible reading project produced? When we review the contributions collected here, what more general conclusions can we draw? What challenges lie ahead for us?

Results

If we ask ourselves what kept the initiators and implementers of the project going during the past few years, through an unimaginable quantity of logistical and administrative work—meetings, reports, protocols, committees, publicity, contacts with groups and coordinators all over the world—we come first of all to the devotion, the creativity, and the effort of the owners of this project. These owners are the ordinary readers whose tracks can be found in the reading reports. Every reading report presented new discoveries, new methods, new songs. We have been astonished to see how one well-known Bible story has created endless possibilities for actualization and interaction. The theological and hermeneutic implications are profound and overwhelming. In the second place, we must mention the cooperation with colleagues all over the world. They shared the sense that we were dealing with an unusual project here.

That this is an unusual project is expressed in this book in many ways. There appears to be cause to speak about this project's mystical qualities. Intercultural Bible reading appears to awaken a longing in Christians, an opportunity that faith itself creates. People want to share the story of the gospel with one another, to learn from one another. Participants meet one another in the unguarded everyday aspects of their existence. Reflection on the Bible story is almost always also reflection on their own life stories. The conversations make participants visible to one another.

Hans de Wit, Faculty of Theology, Free University (Amsterdam, the Netherlands)

They see the others' worries and pain, and at the same time, their merriment and courage. In the intimate space of the meeting, they tell their story, they sing, they celebrate, they point to the places where they see God and to the places where God seems absent. They surrender themselves to others and become vulnerable. We can sense the devotion they display in reading the text. We see how and why the story works, what Holy Scripture actually is. More than a collection of stories, it brings people in touch with transcendence.[1] Reflecting on the story of the gospel brings out the best in many people: their helpfulness, their willingness to listen and change, their love. Thus, the reading reports show people groping for God, how they behave in the shadow of the Almighty, in the encounter with an old and venerable story.

Statistics

We received first phase reading reports from about 120 groups. About ninety groups also went through the second phase, the phase of interaction. A much smaller number have also finished the third phase. Some groups decided to repeat the process with the partner group, with a different text. A number of groups are still in the process of concluding the third phase of the project. Participants came from more than twenty-five countries and more than a hundred denominations. Their churches have exquisite names: *Novia del Cordero* (Bride of the Lamb), Base Ecclesial Community *Santa María de la Esperanza* (Holy Mary of Hope), *Ethiopian Kush Church, Reform Zion Apostolic Church.* In addition to participants from the Presbyterian-Reformed tradition, many Roman Catholics participated, including a considerable number from Base Ecclesial Communities and others from the charismatic renewal movement. Other participants are members of Pentecostal churches, independent churches, and Zionist churches. Baptists, Anglicans, Lutherans, Quakers, and Mennonites participated.

Some groups that described themselves as poor and powerless participated, and other groups said they were part of the powerful, and considered themselves middle or upper class. Some participants could not read; many only attended school for a few years, at the primary level. Other participants received higher education, and some have advanced degrees. Shoemakers and masons participated, lorry drivers and concrete workers, theology teachers, preachers and priests, managers and cleaners, secretaries and artists, nurses and musicians. There were also unemployed and retired participants. One of the Cuban groups reported participation by a number of people who are deaf and mute.

All or part of the protocol and other written materials were translated into more than twenty languages, including Spanish, Aymara, Quechua, Quichue, Tagalog, Taglish, Ilokano, Hiligaynon, Fanti, Twi, Afrikaans, English, Zulu, Xhosa, Indonesian, Telugu, Hindi, Tamil, Malayalam, Hungarian, Portuguese, German, and French. The interaction was often most successful in places where the protocol was used carefully and supplemented by people's own creative methods. In those cases, there was a certain uniformity in the reading reports and the group processes.

Measured statistically, the number of interactions is exceptionally high. There is reason to take this as confirmation that this model offers a new, attractive method of reading the Bible. Yet the fact that interaction is established does not mean that the intercultural communication is successful. There were interactions in which insights were frozen in both directions. In these cases, participants were only critical toward the partner group, and they held to their own repertoire. Prejudices were not readjusted, and profound differences continued on next to each other. However, this type of interaction cannot just be considered a failure. Negative learning moments are also valuable. And always *something happened* between the groups. Interactions never ended in a complete split with the partner group; negative experiences in the initial phase were often readjusted later. Where interaction was not established—in about 30 percent of cases, primarily because of insufficient motivation and logistical problems—groups expressed great disappointment. They invested a great deal in the process and were frustrated when the partner group did not respond.

Through the eyes of the participants

Motivation. Why did groups participate? What did they sing? How did they respond to their partner group? Their reports indicate that groups participated because they were motivated by the communitarian and intercultural aspects of the project. They were drawn by the prospect of reading the Bible with others in their own group and by the possibility of encounter with a group on the other side of the world. A Dutch participant describes this combination: "I love sharing things with others. Being a congregation also means doing these things outside of the Sunday service. There is the additional dimension of doing this with foreign cultures." Another Dutch group reports: "The motivation for participating in this project is described this way: People are curious about and interested in how the other thinks about stories in the Bible, how others read and understand the Bible in an entirely different culture. We wish to go to the Well together, to gain inspiration from the other's point of view."

Liturgical setting. People rarely open the Bible for no reason. Readers prepare for meeting one another, for meeting the Living One whom they hope to track down in and through the story. Many prepare by opening the meeting with a prayer, by reciting a poem or a text; others sing hymns or light a candle. In the reading reports, groups present their songs, their ways of celebrating the reading process, their prayers, their symbolic objects and acts. In Ghana and El Salvador, participants composed new songs for the occasion of the project.

Methods. Groups were allowed to use their own method for reading John 4. A large number of very different methods are registered in the reading reports. We see the method of the Base Ecclesial Communities; the systematic reading of the text, one verse at a time; spontaneous and associative reading of groups that use no particular method. Some groups used bibliodrama, role-plays, or other ways of dramatizing the text.

Ramifications

The project has also shown its effects beyond the level of the groups. The project was taken up by a number of organizations and churches (nongovernmental organizations, theological seminaries and faculties, local and national churches) and integrated as part of their own activities. Some groups that already had a partner group somewhere else used the method to deepen existing contacts. In El Salvador, the project was taken up by the Roman Catholic Church to see whether this method could contribute to reconciliation and to healing the traumas of their civil war. A local follow-up project was started between migrant and nonmigrant churches in a large Dutch city with many migrant churches. A number of scholars are undertaking further scholarly reflection on the results of the project.

Learnings

Have the objectives of the project been met? Did we find a new method of reading the Bible, relevant to the academy and churches? Did what we were hoping would happen actually happen? Did the project create interactions involving culture, context, asymmetry in the world, and faith to the fullest extent, where discussion about differences in these aspects would lead to processes of change and to changes in perspective? We can only answer this question with a heartfelt Yes, with all the subjectivity from which we who took initiative in this project can scarcely escape.

What conclusions can we draw? On the basis of this book, readers can judge for themselves what the gain of the project has been in the specific areas of formation and transformation, exegesis and ecumenism, theological education and the churches and—in the first place—in the groups themselves. I will limit myself to stating the most important learnings and will do so from the perspective of the interaction, a central feature of the project.

Format

The format for the interaction as described in the protocol has proved successful. Retaining a two or three phase structure is essential. The format is suited to simplification and adaptation to special situations, including local settings where racial, ethnic, sociopolitical, or religious conflicts play a role. Quality reporting is vital to quality interaction.

Conditions for successful interaction

In addition to conditions such as proper preparation, patience, and effort, we found a number of other basic conditions for successful intercultural Bible reading. I will present a brief summary.

Attitude. Successful interaction requires a basic attitude of openness, trust, vulnerability, and willingness to criticize oneself and to see one's own faith insights as relative. This attitude applies to the reading process of the group itself as well as to the interaction with the partner group. Confrontation is allowed, but it must be based on trust. Not every type of motivation is productive. Motivation especially focused on acquiring new knowledge, focused on challenges, turns out to be enriching. Expressing admiration for the partner group and exchanging good or even bad news can greatly stimulate the interaction. Including recognizable stories about life in the group process can stimulate the transition from spectator to participant.

Knowledge. The group needs basic knowledge of how cultures operate. Differences between groups soon become apparent, but it requires knowledge to see how these cultural differences can be identified and understood. The analysis of the partner group report will proceed more satisfactorily if this knowledge is available, and if participants are sensitive to the limits of the importance of culture so they are able to involve noncultural factors in the discussion as well.

Insight. Insight into the group's own reading attitude and interpretation method is also important. This insight enables participants to discover the connection between the method and the results of their interpretation and that of the partner group.

Leadership. A combination of task-oriented and relationship-oriented leadership turns out to be fertile. Encounters focusing on reading the text have better results if they are supplemented by other types of interpretation, e.g., creative or dramatic processing of the text. The safe space of the small group must be cherished.

Results and learning moments of interactions

The summary above corresponds to an important degree with general conditions that apply to satisfactory intercultural intercourse. What makes intercultural Bible reading different now?

Culture. First, we observe that culture turns out to play an important role in interpretation of the gospel in the project, too. There are vast differences between Western and non-Western groups in the interpretation of John 4. These are often culturally determined. Those differences can be mapped via culture analysis. Cultural sensitivity is a great asset in hermeneutics and exegesis. The same is true for spontaneous understanding.

Not everything is culture. However, great differences in interpretation can occur within a culture. Church background and theological insights, and moral views stemming from these sources also appear to play an important role. Differences become visible when groups enter into discussion with each other about a Bible text. "High" or "low" views of Jesus are not immediately culturally determined and may form a breaking point. The view that the Samaritan woman was a prostitute or that she was widowed five times can only be partially attributed to the interpreters' cultural setting.

Evangelical competence. The added value of the project becomes clear when one sees that participants are not merely intent on acquiring intercultural competence. They do not read John 4 to be better prepared for emigration to or functioning in a different culture; instead, they desire to be better Christians within their own culture, with a broader, global perspective. Participants are not interested in acquiring the status of the ideal intercultural person; they want to acquire more evangelical competence. This desire leads them to look for depth that goes beyond culture. As a result, the relationship between the gospel and culture is often full of tension. Almost all reading reports give occasion to take into account the special weight of religion in human communication. In the intercultural encounter between Christians who read the same Bible story, components become operative that can break culture. In this project, this element is exaggerated in part because people read a story about crossing cultural borders and about radical changes in situations where people have been sacrificed to cultural values. Evangelical values acquire a special importance; these include taking care of others, following the Lamb, prophetic indictment against poverty and oppression, and liberation.

Interaction. More obstinate than certain merely culturally determined values are insights introduced from church traditions. For example, the way one understands salvation, how one sees the Samaritan woman, and what the praxeological effect of the text is are largely determined by the combination of church background and reading method. To shake up this process, interaction is necessary that meets the conditions of vulnerability and willingness to relativize one's own insight and one's own method of interpretation.

Consensus. The disparities between groups are vast, and they often involve legitimate differences. When one can survey the entire field, that perspective is enriching. Only when one appraises the whole can one see the wealth of the text. Fortunately, diversity is not all that one sees; that would lead to inaction and paralysis. When we look over the process and ask whether, among all differences, something was also shared, we can draw a conclusion that is typically evangelical: A consensus could be found among all groups that a determining factor breaks through barriers among all ethnic and religious differences, and that factor is Jesus. The text was capable of offering a meaning that was seen by all groups, one that implied a program of action for many of them. Every single group signals that the encounter between this man and this woman at the well was of a special nature. It is remarkable how many groups reflect on the "method of Jesus" that cracks a multitude of cultural codes, delivering people from pressure from their culture, and making them want to follow him along this path. In general, the groups had the feeling that what they shared was greater than the differences between them.

Exegesis—spontaneous reading. The project made it clear how important spontaneous, precritical understanding of the Bible is. Spontaneous interpretations bring out meanings of the text that cannot be found in the commentaries. They bring out material that may subject exegetic schools and methods to severe criticism, because scholars have not noticed meanings and relationships because these meanings were not asked for. On the other hand, many groups wrestled with the narrative development of the text, the curious sequence of question, answer, and counter-question, concepts they do not understand, the broader literary context, the basic language.

Appropriation. We discovered an important learning moment at the intersection of understanding the text in its historical setting and its actualization. In addition to culture, one important difference between Western and non-Western groups is the issue of actualization of the text. The struggle to connect the text to people's own lives is visible as a red thread in all analyses of Western reading reports. Many reasons for this difficulty can be proposed: the effects of the Enlightenment and secularization, caution about exercising faith in pluralistic and multireligious societies of the West, the consequences of the way biblical disciplines are taught in Western academies. Pastors and priests, who often lead the group process, are hardly trained in dealing with the foreground of the texts. This deficiency poses a tremendous challenge to theological education. Actualization is essential to interpretation as such, and especially to the interaction between ordinary readers. The interaction is poor in cases where life stories are not shared. Non-Western groups are often impressed by the more technical, historicizing method of reading, which their Western partner groups engage in. They consider this approach a good supplement to their own method. At the same time, they often justifiably ask their partner group, "Where can the Samaritan woman actually be found in your village?"

Variables. Researchers have analyzed interactions between groups. The code system provides the possibility of making visible the profiles of reading reports. A number of significant correlations between culture and interpretation, church background and interpretation, successful interaction and underlying factors have been mapped. We have analyzed enough material to be able to differentiate between dominant and less dominant factors, to indicate approaches that inhibit successful intercultural communication. Steering this process with mathematical precision is something we cannot do and would not want to do. That would take the Spirit out of the process. The case studies collected here show that in every new group, at every new pairing, new variables loom up that lead to new interpretations and different types of interaction. In that sense, the result of this project is also a tremendous warning to all essentialist judgments on the reading of the poor, Africans, Latin Americans, Asians, Europeans. What we have developed above all is sensitivity. The expertise accumulated permits the project to make an important contribution to groups that can render the process as rich as possible.

A look ahead

Intercultural Bible reading is fascinating. In all modesty, we acknowledge that we are standing at the beginning of a path that can lead to new impulses to church life in the local congregation, to new scientific research, to ecumenical and missionary relationships. But in order to realize these results, a lot more work lies ahead of us.

Local churches would be able to use the methods to intensify relationships with churches elsewhere, and to provide new impetus for the discussion on faith in their own local communities of faith. The method could be used to bring different groups within a church or between different churches into conversation with each other. Communitarian Bible reading is a great benefit to the congregation, as has been proved many times over.

Agencies working with ecumenism, mission, and development cooperation could simplify the method and adapt it to special circumstances such as situations of ethnic conflict or religious tensions, for example. Acquaintance with the learning moments of this project could be a stimulus to a new policy. Intercultural Bible reading is an excellent method for democratizing missionary and ecumenical relationships, for bringing them back to their core.

Theology and theological education should grapple with a number of issues arising from this project. Curricula in these areas could be much more inductive, and could give a great deal more attention to how "the people" live, read, and believe. To accomplish this end, the empirical research must be more profound. Interaction between spontaneous understanding and scholarly exegesis is essential for the health of both. Exegetes who wish to read "with the people" too often lack time for careful analysis of ordinary readings of the Bible; an important learning of the project is that the dynamics of academic life rarely dispose its practitioners toward the perspectives of ordinary readers. A counter-culture is needed here! The interaction between spontaneous reading and exegesis introduces the question of the ethics of the interpretation, a subject that also merits much more thought.

But perhaps by far the most important task ahead is that of teaching ordinary readers to capitalize on their own potential and make it fertile, and the reverse: training theologians in dealing with the foreground of the Bible text, with how the text is read and could be reread here and now.

Conclusion

What a historic effect this anonymous woman of Sychar has brought about![2] The meeting with the Samaritan woman has been a source of inspiration for many artists. She has been proudly immortalized in marble, shaped in miniature in terracotta. She is pictured on copper, wood, paper, canvas, and cotton; she has been embroidered on velvet. She can be found in the catacombs. I see her walking the rice fields in India; black and proud she stands on an African plain. I see her in the Colombian cities, carried by the people in procession on one of the Sundays during Lent. She can be found in the France of the eighteenth century; in Italy in the twelfth, fourteenth, and sixteenth centuries; in the Netherlands of the golden age, in the work of Rembrandt and others. She has stood with the urn on her shoulders for more than a hundred years on the Plaza de Justicia in the center of blistering Zaragoza, Spain. Under Neapolitan trees she meekly talks to Jesus; against a background of blue mountains she stands in a Chinese landscape; high Indonesian palm trees look down upon her.

In the Orthodox tradition, the Samaritan woman is known by the name Photini, the holy carrier of light. In Greek sermons between the fourth and the fourteenth centuries, she is called the Apostle or the Evangelist. According to these traditions, after her baptism on Pentecost and after many missionary journeys, she left for Rome. Her attempt to convert Nero failed. His daughter did convert. Martyred, thrown in a deep pit, and starved, she finally entered the light of her Lord. Her five sisters and two sons had already preceded her.

We, too, owe this first evangelist a debt of gratitude. Hundreds of readers have tried to look at her through the eyes of another during the past few years. All of them drew from her well. The result is a wonderful collection of poems, prayers, songs, and artistic expressions. Yes, the Samaritan woman has given us many things: inspiration, encounter, broadening, faith, healing, new trust, liberation. We have kept asking her questions: Who are you? What was your name? How did it all turn out for you? Did you grow old? What did you look like? Who were all those men of yours?! I would like to give something back to you now. Something you yourself would never dare to dream of. A letter from one of the project participants, a woman, directed to you:

Dear Woman at the Well,

The story about what happened at Jacob's well long ago has been on my mind recently. Together with others I was allowed to discover what happened with you and to you. Your openness and vulnerable attitude stir my admiration. Your faith and trust in the man you wound up talking to make me jealous. You let the people in your town take part in your experience. You must have been contagiously enthusiastic with them. But what a pity that I don't know your name. Maybe I must, or rather *may*, call you "Woman at the Well." After all, you have become a well of joy to the people of your tribe and to those who are reading your story now. Thank you!

Of course, you wish to know who I really am. I slept on it, so I could come up with an answer to that question. Think of me as one of the people who live in your city, whom you invite to come along to see if that man isn't the promised Messiah. Or think of me as a disciple who still has a lot to learn. Or—especially—see me as a thirsty deer searching for living water.

Ineke

Notes

[1] W. Cantwell Smith, *What is Scripture?* (London: SCM Press, 1993).
[2] Janeth Norfleete Day, *The Woman at the Well: Interpretation of John 4:1–42 in Retrospect and Prospect* (Leiden, the Netherlands: E. J. Brill, 2002).

Appendix

List of participant groups

Country & group	Coordinator	Denomination	Participants[1]	Linked to
Africa				
Ghana				
Abetifi Pentecostal women	Jacolien Lambregtse	Pentecostal	10F	Philippines, ISACC staff
Abetifi church leaders at Ramseyer Training Centre	Jacolien Lambregtse	mixed	6M, 10F	Brazil, Feitoria Evangelical Lutherans
Abetifi youth group	Jacolien Lambregtse	Presbyterian	10M, 10F	the Netherlands, Hoek
Ashiyie Presbyterian Church group	Eric Anum	Presbyterian	14M, 13F	the Netherlands, Amsterdam
Bepong group	Jacolien Lambregtse	Methodist/ Presbyterian	40F	the Netherlands, Rheden
Elmina Presbyterian Church men	Eric Anum	Presbyterian	8M	Cuba, Matanzas group
Elmina Presbyterian Church women	Eric Anum	Presbyterian	20F	the Netherlands, Dordrecht
Komenda Presbyterian Bible study group	Eric Anum	Presbyterian	4M, 3F	the Netherlands, Halle
Komenda mixed Bible study group	Eric Anum	mixed	3M, 3F	Hungary, Budapest Reformed Church
Victory Presbyterian Church Twi group, Frafraha, suburb of Accra	Eric Anum	Presbyterian	4M, 4F	Scotland, Craigend group
Victory Presbyterian Church English group, Frafraha, suburb of Accra	Eric Anum	Presbyterian	5M, 6F	the Netherlands, Kampen
Kenya				
New Seventh Day Adventists, Kisii	Mary Getui	Seventh Day Adventist	6M, 2F	the Netherlands, Andijk
Nigeria				
Port Harcourt University students	Protus O. Kemdirim	mixed/ecumenical	12M	Peru, Lectura Pastoral de la Biblia group
South Africa				
Durban group, KwaZulu Natal	Mark Rathbone	Dutch Reformed	10M	
Ivory Park young people, near Midrand (Gauteng)	Gerald West	Methodist	6M, 10F	Colombia, Unidad Cristiana Univ. women

513

Country & group	Coordinator	Denomination	Participants	Linked to
South Africa				
Siyaphila Bible study, support group for people with HIV/AIDS, near Pietermaritzburg	Gerald West	mixed	1M, 10F	
Sokhanya Bible School, near Cape Town	Danie van Zyl	mixed	8M, 3F	the Netherlands, Zaandam
Stellenbosch men	Louis Jonker	Dutch Reformed	9M	USA, People's Seminary, lay pastor prog.
Stellenbosch women	Louis Jonker	Dutch Reformed	10F	El Salvador, Shékina Baptist Church
Young Christian Workers group, near Pietermaritzburg	Gerald West	mixed	4M, 11F	
Asia				
India				
Dalit wives of prisoners	Daniel Premkumar	mixed	10F	the Netherlands, Vlissingen
Perambur transsexual group, Chennai (Madras)	Daniel Premkumar	non-Christians	13M/F	the Netherlands, Zaandam OWZ
Shoolagiri Dalit group	Manohar Chandra Prasad	Dalit Christians	8M, 8F	Colombia, San Pablo BEC
Syrian Christian group, Chennai (Madras)	Sam P. Mathew	Syrian church	6M, 7F	the Netherlands, Zutphen
Indonesia				
Bandung group, Java	Jilles de Klerk	Roman Catholic	7F, 1M	Scotland, St. Aloysius CBS
Theological Seminary of Eastern Indonesia Macassar students, group 1	Jilles de Klerk	Protestant churches	4M, 6F	Cuba, Seminario Evangélico, Matanzas
Theological Seminary of Eastern Indonesia Macassar students, group 2	Jilles de Klerk	ecumenical, Reformed	5M, 3F	the Netherlands, Arnhem
Korea				
Hanil University and Theological Seminary students, Cheonju	Unha Chai	Presbyterian	2M, 6F	Colombia, Comunidad Cristiana de Crecimiento Integral
Philippines				
Christian Writers Fellowship, Mandaluyong	Evelyn Miranda-Feliciano	mixed/ecumenical	12F, 5M	Colombia, Grupo Estudio Bíblico, BEC
Institute for Studies in Asian Church and Culture (ISACC) staff, Quezon City		mixed	8M, 6F	Ghana, Abetifi Pentecostal women

Philippines

Group	Facilitator	Type		
Midlife fellowship group, Sambayanang Kristiyano sa Biga (Community Christian Church, SK)	Evelyn Miranda-Feliciano	Christian/mixed	7F	Bolivia, El Mesías
Samaritana staff workers	Evelyn Miranda-Feliciano	Evangelical	6F, 1M	Brazil, Second Presbyterian, Porto Alegre
Samaritana women, ex-prostitutes, Quezon City		mixed	9F	the Netherlands, Wichmond

Central America/Caribbean

Nicaragua

Centro Intereclesial de Estudios Teológicos y Sociales (CIEETS) students, Managua	Azucena López Namoyure	mixed	6M, 7F	the Netherlands, NijBeets
Filadelfia Baptist Church, Masaya	Azucena López Namoyure	Baptist	5M, 5F	Argentina, Santa Cruz BEC
Novia del Cordero, Managua		Pentecostal	5M, 5F	the Netherlands, Dagmaat Lisse

El Salvador

Bartolomé de las Casas men	Larry Madrigal	Unionists	24M	the Netherlands, Amstelveen
Bartolomé de las Casas women	Larry Madrigal	mixed	12F	the Netherlands, Geldrop
Colonia Los Dolores, San Salvador	Larry Madrigal	Roman Catholic	6F	the Netherlands, Voorschoten
San Rafael Cedros BEC	Larry Madrigal	Base Community	3M, 3F	Bolivia, Los Amigos
Shekiná Baptist Church, Santa Ana	Larry Madrigal	Baptist	1M, 20F	South Africa, Stellenbosch women

Cuba

Alamar group, outskirts of Havana	Pedro Triana	Baptist	7M, 9F	the Netherlands, Beverwijk
Instituto Bíblico Teológico Superior, Havana	Pedro Triana	Presby./Lutheran/ Baptist	3M, 5F	the Netherlands, Joure
Matanzas group	Pedro Triana	mixed	10M, 8F	Ghana, Elmina Presbyterian men's group
Sancti Spíritus group	Pedro Triana	mixed/ecumenical	5M, 5F	United States, Belmont Mennonite group
Santo Suárez group, Havana	Pedro Triana	Baptist	2M, 6F	the Netherlands, Langezwaag
Seminario Evangélico de Teología (SET), Matanzas	Pedro Triana	mixed	4M, 6F	Indonesia, Theol. Sem. Macassar students

North America

United States

The People's Seminary lay pastor training program, Burlington, Washington	Bob Ekblad	Lutheran/Presby./ Roman Catholic	5M, 4F	South Africa, Stellenbosch men
The People's Seminary Mexican women, Burlington, Washington	Bob Ekblad	mixed	5F	Colombia, ACODE

Country & group	Coordinator	Denomination	Participants	Linked to
United States				
Serendipity group, Belmont Mennonite Church, Elkhart, Indiana	Daniel Schipani	Mennonite	3M, 5F	Cuba, Sancti Spiritus
South America				
Argentina				
Santa Cruz BEC, Buenos Aires	Néstor Míguez	Roman Catholic	7F	Nicaragua, Filadelfia Baptist Church
Bolivia				
Los Amigos, La Paz	Abraham Colque/María Chávez	Quaker	6M, 4F	El Salvador, San Rafael Cedros
Aymara/Quechua group Jerusalem, La Paz		Methodist	7M, 7F	the Netherlands, Zwijndrecht
Comunidad Bet-El, El Alto, La Paz	Abraham Colque/María Chávez	Pentecostal/Lutheran	6M, 2F	the Netherlands, Ermelo
El Mesías, La Paz		Methodist	21F	Philippines, Midlife fellowship group, SK
Brazil				
Bairro das Rosas, Estância Velha	Nelson Kilpp	Protestant	7M, 8F	Colombia, Universidad Javeriana staff
Centro de Estudos Bíblicos (CEBI), Mato Grosso do Sul	Paulo Ueti	Ecumenical	7M, 1F	the Netherlands, Oudewater
Feitoria Evangelical Lutheran Congregation, São Leopoldo	Nelson Kilpp	Lutheran	2M, 8F	Ghana, Abetifi church leaders at Ramseyer
Second Presbyterian Church of Porto Alegre, Rio Grande do Sul	Nelson Kilpp	Presbyterian	6M, 3F	Philippines, Samaritana staff workers
Colombia				
ACODE Community and Development Association, Bogotá	Jairo Roa	Roman Catholic	11F	USA, People's Seminary, Mexican women
Comunidad Cristiana de Crecimiento Integral, Soacha township	Jairo Roa	mixed/ecum.	8F, 3M	Korea, Hanil University students
Grupo Estudio Bíblico BEC, Bogotá	Edgar López	Roman Catholic	5F, 3M	Philippines, Christian Writers Fellowship
Proyecto de Vida, Bogotá	Edgar López	Roman Catholic	6M, 8F	the Netherlands, Huizen
San Pablo BEC, Las Lomas, Bogotá	Edgar López	Roman Catholic	8F	India, Shoolagiri Dalit group
San Lucas BEC, Las Lomas, Bogotá	Edgar López	Roman Catholic	10M, 9F	the Netherlands, Apeldoorn

Group	Facilitator	Denomination	Gender	Linked group
Santa María de la Esperanza BEC, Puerto Rico, Bogotá	Edgar López	Roman Catholic	8F	the Netherlands, Waarde
Santiago BEC, Puerto Rico, Bogotá	Edgar López	Roman Catholic	14M/F	the Netherlands, Appingedam
San Ignacio BEC, Las Lomas, Bogotá	Edgar López	Roman Catholic	10F, 1M	Germany, Marburg student group 3
Unidad Cristiana Universitaria women's group	Jairo Roa	Evangelical	7F	South Africa, Durban group, KwaZulu Natal
Universidad Javeriana staff, Bogotá	Edgar López	Roman Catholic	5M	Brazil, Bairro das Rosas
Visión Mundial Colombia, Bogotá	Jairo Roa	Protestant/mixed	6M, 5F	the Netherlands, Santpoort
Ecuador				
Quito Pastoral Theology students	Helmud Rénard, Marcia Moya	Roman Catholic	2M, 8F	the Netherlands, Hilversum
Peru				
Italo Germán Delgado group	Italo Germán Delgado	Roman Catholic	7F, 1M	the Netherlands, Makkinga
Lectura Pastoral de la Biblia group, Lima	José Mizotti	Roman Catholic	5M, 5F	Nigeria, Port Harcourt University students
Europe				
Germany				
Marburg student group 1	Rainer Kessler	Protestant	4M, 4F	South Africa, Ivory Park young group
Marburg student group 2	Rainer Kessler	Protestant	2M, 4F	India, Chennai group 2, never started
Marburg student group 3	Rainer Kessler	Protestant	3F, 2M	Colombia, San Ignacio BEC
Schwenger group, Moringen, patients in a hospital for the criminally mentally ill		mixed	15M	not linked
Hungary				
Balatonszárszó group	Miklos Koscev	Reformed	3M, 5F	the Netherlands, Westmaas
Budapest Reformed Church	Miklos Koscev	Reformed	4M	Ghana, Komenda mixed study group
the Netherlands				
Amstelveen	Arie Moolenaar	mixed		El Salvador, Bartolomé de las Casas men
Amsterdam Johannes Groep	Arie Moolenaar	Dutch Reformed/ United Protestant	3M, 4F	Ghana, Ashiyie Presbyterian Church
Andijk	Arie Moolenaar			Kenya, New Seventh Day Adventists
Apeldoorn	Arie Moolenaar	United Protestant	7M, 5F	Colombia, San Lucas BEC

Country & group	Coordinator	Denomination	Participants	Linked to
the Netherlands				
Appingedam	Arie Moolenaar	United Protestant	2M, 6F	Colombia, Santiago BEC
Arnhem	Arie Moolenaar	mixed	11F	Indonesia, Macassar students group 2
Beverwijk	Arie Moolenaar	United Protestant	6F, 3M	Cuba, Alamar group
Dagmaat Lisse, Groningen	Arie Moolenaar	United Protestant/ Roman Catholic	2M, 11F	Nicaragua, Novia del Cordero
Dordrecht	Arie Moolenaar	United Protestant	8F	Ghana, Elmina Presbyterian women
Ermelo	Arie Moolenaar	United Protestant	7M, 6F	Bolivia, Comunidad Bet-El
Geldrop	Arie Moolenaar	United Protestant	5M, 6F	El Salvador, Bartolomé de las Casas women
Gorredijk	Arie Moolenaar	United Protestant	3M, 6F	Scotland, Kilmacolm CBS
Halle	Arie Moolenaar	United Protestant		Ghana, Komenda Presbyterian group
Hilversum	Arie Moolenaar	United Protestant	7M, 7F	Ecuador, Quito Pastoral Theology students
Hoek	Arie Moolenaar			Ghana, Abetifi youth group
Huizen	Arie Moolenaar	United Protestant	6M, 4F	Colombia, Proyecto de Vida
Joure	Arie Moolenaar	mixed	7M, 5F	Cuba, Instituto Bíblico Teológico Superior, Havana
Kampen	Arie Moolenaar	United Protestant	1M, 7F	Ghana, Victory Presby. English group
Langezwaag	Arie Moolenaar	United Protestant	4M, 5F	Cuba, Santo Suárez
Makkinga	Arie Moolenaar	United Protestant	3M, 6F	Peru, Italo Germán Delgado group
Middelburg	Arie Moolenaar	United Protestant	3M, 4F	Indonesia, Macassar students group 1
NijBeets	Arie Moolenaar	United Protestant	5M, 5F	Nicaragua, CIEETS students
Oudewater	Arie Moolenaar	United Protestant	8F	Brazil, CEBI Mato Grosso do Sul
Rheden	Arie Moolenaar	United Protestant	6M, 7F	Ghana, Bepong group
Santpoort	Arie Moolenaar	United Protestant	7M, 5F	Colombia, Visión Mundial Colombia
Vlissingen	Arie Moolenaar	United Protestant	13F	India, Dalit wives of prisoners
Voorschoten	Arie Moolenaar	United Protestant	5F	El Salvador, Colonia Los Dolores
Waarde	Arie Moolenaar	United Protestant	2M, 4F	Colombia, Santa María de la Esperanza BEC
Westmaas	Arie Moolenaar	United Protestant	4M, 5F	Hungary, Balatonszárszó group
Wichmond	Arie Moolenaar	United Protestant	2M, 4F	Philippines, Samaritana ex-prostitutes

Zaandam	Arie Moolenaar	United Protestant	7M, 6F	South Africa, Sokhanya Bible School
Zaandam OWZ (Oekumenische Werkplaats Zaandam)	Arie Moolenaar	Ecumenical	4M, 6F	India, Perambur transsexual group
Zutphen	Arie Moolenaar	United Protestant	3M, 5F	India, Syrian Christian group, Chennai
Zwijndrecht	Arie Moolenaar	United Protestant	7M, 7F	Bolivia, Aymara/Quechua group Jerusalem

Scotland

Craigend group, Glasgow	John Riches	Roman Catholic	8M, 14F	Ghana, Victory Presbyterian Twi group
Kilmacolm Scottish Contextual Bible Study group	John Riches	mixed	8F	the Netherlands, Gorredijk
St. Aloysius Scottish Contextual Bible Study group, Glasgow	John Riches	mixed	11F. 5M	Indonesia, Bandung group

Note

[1] Because in the course of the project the composition of various groups changed, the reader may notice some inconsistencies in data about number of participants.

Index of names

Cana · 136
Canaan · 39, 316, 389
Canaanites · 278, 483
Cape Coast, Ghana · 176
Cape Peninsula, South Africa · 58, 209, 279
Cape Town, South Africa · 196
Caravias, José Luis · 16, 51
Caribbean · 10, 13, 178, 515
Carroll R., M. Daniel · 53
Castro, Fidel · 34
Catholic Institute for International Relations · 285
Catholic parish of Resurrección · 144
Catholics. *See* Roman Catholics
Céligny, Switzerland · 493
Central America · xi, 28, 81, 123, 132, 454, 515
Central Sulawesi, Indonesia · 168
Centro Bartolomé de las Casas, San Salvador, El Salvador · 81, 82. *See also* Bartolomé de las Casas groups
Centro de Estudos Bíblicos (CEBI), Mato Grosso do Sul, Brazil · 224, 393, 516, 518
Centro Intereclesial de Estudios Teológicos y Sociales (CIEETS), Managua, Nicaragua · 249, 332, 394, 515, 518
Chai, Unha · 72, 514
Chandra, Manohar · 514
Chávez, María · 516
Chennai group 2, India · 517
Chennai Syrian church. *See* Syrian church in Chennai, Tamilnadu, India
Chennai, Tamilnadu, India · 22, 23, 242
Chicano · 138
China · 510
Christian Writers Fellowship, Mandaluyong, Philippines · 149, 155, 156, 158, 261, 264, 265, 266, 270, 351, 352, 353, 354, 355, 358, 514, 516
Cinderella · 335
Clines, David J. A. · 328
Cochrane, James R. · 476
Coenen, Harry · 303
Colombia · 34, 35, 36, 37, 57, 89, 117, 153, 154, 155, 156, 276, 293, 295, 307, 308, 310, 432, 351, 352, 353, 354, 355, 358, 368, 369, 376, 419, 457, 458, 466, 467, 468, 469, 471, 473, 510, 513, 514, 515, 516, 517, 518
Colombian Bible study group · 155
Colonia Los Dolores, San Salvador, El Salvador · 56, 82, 393, 515, 518
Colque, Abraham · 516
Comaroff, Jean · 476

Comaroff, John L. · 476
Commission of the Truth · 186
Community of Bible Institutes. *See* Comunidad de Institutos Bíblicos (CIB)
Comunidad Bet-El, La Paz, Bolivia · 392, 516, 518
Comunidad Cristiana de Crecimiento Integral, Soacha township, Colombia · 376, 466, 514, 516
Comunidad de Institutos Bíblicos (CIB) · 250
Cone, James H. · 287
Confucianism · 162
Conrad, Joseph · 282
Conrad, Sue · xi
Conradie, Ernst M. · 209, 409, 433
Contextual Bible Study (CBS) · 15, 165, 173, 175, 292, 464, 475, 519
Coote, Robert T. · 272
Costello, Tim · 358
Craigend group, Glasgow, Scotland · 394, 464, 465, 475, 513, 519
Croatto, J. Severino · 16, 50, 313
Cuba · x, 7, 21, 22, 34, 35, 38, 58, 69, 90, 106, 117, 167, 169, 170, 172, 173, 175, 178, 190, 191, 269, 351, 354, 358, 367, 372, 374, 376, 419, 420, 450, 504, 513, 514, 515, 516, 518
Cupach, William R. · 364, 365, 375
Curtis, Melissa C. · 328

D

Dagmaat group, the Netherlands. *See* Dagmaat Lisse, Groningen, the Netherlands
Dagmaat Lisse, Groningen, the Netherlands · 120, 122, 123, 124, 125, 126, 127, 128, 129, 130, 249, 251, 253, 255, 256, 257, 258, 259, 260, 308, 313, 314, 351, 352, 354, 355, 407, 515, 518
Dalit group. *See* Shoolagari Dalit group, Dalit wives of prisoners group
Dalit wives of prisoners group, India · 338, 367, 370, 376, 393, 422, 514, 518
Dalits · 10, 11, 17, 23, 148, 243, 285, 421, 495, 514
Davenport, T. R. H. · 286
Davies, Margaret · 53
Day, Janeth Norfleete · 511
Dayak · 169
de Groot, A. · 33, 52
De Groot Nieuws Bijbel (Good News Bible) · 95, 117
de Klerk, Jilles · 161, 514
de Wit, J. H(ans) · x, xi, 3, 50, 51, 53,

Mormons · 38
Morris, Leon · 317, 328, 329
Mosala, Itumeleng J. · 51
Moses · 363
Mt. Ebal · 316, 329
Mt. Gerizim · 96, 281, 329, 330, 427
Mt. Jeeri, Korea · 56
Mudge, Lewis S. · 475
Mugambi, J. N. K. · 195
Mugambi, J. N. Kanyua · 286
Mulder, Lambert · 53
Müller, B. A. · 42, 53
Mulrain, G. · 49
Munguía, Rodolfo · 358
Murrell, Nathaniel Samuel · 49
Muslims · 39, 58, 71, 99, 107, 109, 110, 148, 162, 168, 169, 172, 243, 244, 268, 299, 353, 354, 357, 358, 360, 364, 372, 493

N

Nablus · 316, 328
Nadar, Sarojini · 236
National Service Center of the Uniting Protestant Churches, Utrecht · 90, 91, 116, 117
Nazi Germany · 457
Nederlands Bijbel Instituut, Hogeschool voor Theologie, Utrecht, the Netherlands · 304
Nejapa, El Salvador · 83
Nero · 39, 511
the Netherlands · x, 7, 16, 18, 25, 28, 34, 35, 37, 43, 44, 54, 55, 56, 57, 59, 61, 63, 69, 70, 72, 75, 76, 80, 89, 90, 106, 107, 110, 111, 112, 114, 115, 122, 123, 124, 125, 126, 127, 145, 152, 154, 156, 165, 167, 170, 171, 172, 173, 174, 175, 196, 197, 205, 207, 243, 245, 249, 251, 256, 259, 262, 266, 270, 279, 285, 289, 297, 298, 305, 308, 309, 310, 311, 312, 313, 314, 337, 340, 348, 349, 351, 352, 353, 357, 358, 361, 363, 364, 367, 369, 370, 371, 374, 376, 378, 379, 404, 405, 406, 407, 408, 418, 419, 421, 422, 462, 498, 505, 506, 510, 513, 514, 515, 516, 517, 518
Netherlands Reformed Church (NRC) · 116, 119, 130
Neubert, Miriam · 52, 209, 333, 501
New Seventh Day Adventists, Kisii, Kenya · 393, 513, 517
New Translation. *See* Dutch Bible Society's New Translation
New York · 360
Newman, John Henry · 475
Ngada, N. H. · 287

Nicaragua · 35, 37, 38, 56, 62, 89, 117, 118, 122, 123, 124, 125, 126, 127, 128, 249, 256, 259, 260, 307, 312, 332, 351, 355, 357, 358, 368, 405, 406, 407, 408, 454, 515, 516, 518
Nicaraguan Baptist group. *See* Filadelfia Baptist Church, Masaya, Nicaragua
Nicaraguan Pentecostal group. *See* Novia del Cordero, Managua, Nicaragua
Nicaraguan theology students. *See* Centro Intereclesial de Estudios Teológicos y Sociales (CIEETS)
Nicodemus · 136
Nida, Eugene Albert · 270, 272
Nigeria · 7, 26, 54, 60, 63, 89, 178, 179, 181, 182, 187, 194, 323, 324, 326, 513, 517
Nigerian group. *See* Port Harcourt University group
NijBeets, the Netherlands · 515, 518
Nirmal, Arvind P. · 49
Norteños · 135
North America · xi, 31, 312, 378, 442, 454, 458, 482, 515
Northern Ireland · 464
Noth, Martin · 485
Novia del Cordero, Managua, Nicaragua · 35, 37, 118, 122, 123, 124, 125, 126, 127, 128, 249, 250, 251, 253, 255, 256, 257, 258, 259, 260, 307, 351, 394, 405, 504, 515, 518
Nthamburi, Z. J. · 286
Nyamiti, C. · 195

O

Ofo · 7, 61, 64, 323
Omkeer · 90, 116
Ong, Walter J. · 28, 52, 165, 166, 175, 414, 433
Oostwold, the Netherlands · 74
Open Doors · 358
Orange Order · 464
Orbe, Mark P. · 433
Orthodox · 39, 67, 486, 510
Osmer, Richard R. · 450
Ossewaarde–van Nie, Saskia · 118
Osu · 180, 181, 186, 323, 324
Otten, Willem Jan · 98, 117
Oudewater, the Netherlands · 516, 518

P

Paas, Marianne · 76
Packer, James · 264, 267, 272
Paddan-aram · 316
Padilla, Rene C. · 265, 272
Palestine · 17, 65, 149, 151, 157, 177, 241, 379
Palestinian Targum · 317

Rheden, the Netherlands · 76, 77, 81, 513, 518
Richard, Pablo · 17, 49, 51
Riches, John · x, 50, 51, 52, 53, 460, 491, 492, 519
Ricoeur, Paul · 8, 9, 14, 20, 22, 49, 51, 159, 304, 312, 417, 462, 463, 465, 472, 474, 475, 500, 501
Ridderbos, Herman N. · 317, 320, 328, 329, 330
Rincón, Alfonso · 160
Roa, Jairo · 516, 517
Robles, Rocío · 214, 219, 220, 226, 227, 228, 229, 230, 231, 235
Rogerson, J. W. · 53
Roman Catholic Church · 16, 37, 91, 124, 126, 331, 506
Roman Catholics · 63, 83, 84, 107, 110, 125, 144, 145, 148, 152, 153, 154, 158, 185, 233, 249, 312, 313, 349, 353, 371, 425, 428, 429, 464, 465, 504, 514, 515, 516, 517, 518, 519
Romans · 321
Rosenzweig, Franz · 497, 501
Rowland, Christopher · 285
Ruth · 256

S
Said, Edward W. · 273, 275, 276, 277, 285, 286, 287
St. Aloysius Scottish Contextual Bible Study group, Glasgow, Scotland · 164, 165, 170, 173, 514, 519
Salvador, Bahía, Brazil · 42
Samaritan Pentateuch · 218, 220
Samaritana group, Quezon City, Philippines · 34, 261, 264, 266, 270, 307, 351, 353, 354, 355, 376, 515, 518
Samaritana staff group, Philippines · 261, 515, 516
Sambayanang Kristiyano sa Biga (Community Christian Church, SK). See Midlife fellowship group
Samen op Weg church communities, the Netherlands · 44, 45, 76, 89, 90, 91, 116, 118, 121, 130, 143, 197, 206, 304, 313, 314, 358
Samen op Weg Gemeente of Warmond. See Warmond, the Netherlands
Samson · 483
San Ignacio BEC, Las Lomas, Bogotá, Colombia · 144, 148, 155, 158, 517
San Lucas BEC, Las Lomas, Bogotá, Colombia · 144, 151, 157, 376, 516, 517
San Pablo BEC, Las Lomas, Bogotá, Colombia · 144, 148, 155, 514, 516
San Rafael Cedros BEC, Cuscatlán, El

Salvador · 82, 393, 515, 516
Sancti Spiritus group, Cuba · 332, 376, 393, 515, 516
Santa Ana. See Shekiná Baptist Church, Santa Ana, El Salvador
Santa Cruz BEC, Buenos Aires, Argentina · 351, 352, 353, 354, 355, 392, 515, 516
Santa María de la Esperanza BEC, Puerto Rico, Bogotá, Colombia · 144, 152, 157, 158, 504, 516, 518
Santiago BEC, Puerto Rico, Bogotá, Colombia · 144, 152, 157, 517, 518
Santo Suárez group, Havana, Cuba · 195, 393, 515, 518
Santpoort, the Netherlands · 517, 518
Sarup, Madan · 285
Saunders, Christopher C. · 286
Schelling, Piet · x
Schertz, Mary H. · xi, 437, 441, 450
Schipani, Daniel S. · x, xi, 437, 442, 450, 451, 516
Schleiermacher, Friedrich · 449
Schnackenburg, Rudolf · 306, 313
Schreiter, Robert J. · 38, 51, 52, 463, 475, 486, 491
Schulz, Siegfried · 328, 459
Schwantes, Milton · 51
Schweitzer, Friedrich L. · 450
Schwenger group, Moringen, Germany · 266, 517
Scotland · x, 90, 106, 117, 175, 419, 464, 513, 514, 518, 519
Scott, James C. · 18, 212, 227, 229, 235, 237, 420, 433, 476
Scottish Conversations Group. See St. Aloysius Scottish Contextual Bible Study group, Glasgow, Scotland
Seattle, Washington · 57
Second Presbyterian Church of Porto Alegre, Rio Grande do Sul, Brazil · 393, 515, 516
Segovia, Fernando F. · 12, 50, 277, 285
Sekolah Tinggi Teologia di Indonesia Bagian Timur, Macassar, South Sulawesi, Indonesia, student group · 34, 69, 161, 162, 163, 164, 165, 166, 167, 168, 169, 170, 171, 172, 358
Seminario Evangélico de Teología (SET) students, Matanzas, Cuba · 164, 167, 169, 170, 171, 172, 173, 195, 351, 354, 358, 376, 393, 514, 515
Seminario Teológico Bautista, Managua, Nicaragua · 249
Serendipity group, Belmont Mennonite Church, Elkhart, Indiana, USA · 376, 515, 516
Seventh Day Adventists · 513

communities, the Netherlands
Universidad Javeriana. *See* Pontificia
Universidad Javeriana
University of Amsterdam, the Netherlands ·
493
University of Cape Coast, Cape Coast,
Ghana · 176
University of Glasgow, Scotland · 460
University of KwaZulu-Natal, Pietermaritz-
burg, South Africa · 211
University of Marburg, Germany · 452
University of Stellenbosch, South Africa ·
273, 315, 409
University of the Assemblies of God
(Universidad de las Asambleas de Dios)
· 251
University of the Western Cape, South
Africa · 409
Uthiramerur group, near Chennai
(Madras), Tamilnadu, India · 393
Utrecht, the Netherlands · 45, 89, 91,
116, 304, 348, 450

V

van de Beek, Abraham · 500
van der Ven, J. A. · 43, 53, 272, 417, 433
van Dijk Hemmes, Fokkelien · 455, 458
van Keulen, Dirk · 500
van Zyl, Danie · 196, 514
Vatican · 37
Verstraelen, F. J. · 52
Victory Presbyterian Church English
group, Frafraha, suburb of Accra, Ghana
· 393, 513, 518
Victory Presbyterian Church Twi group,
Frafraha, suburb of Accra, Ghana · 393,
513, 519
Virgin of Guadalupe · 139
Visión Mundial Colombia, Bogotá,
Colombia · 56, 517, 518
Vlissingen, the Netherlands · 367, 376,
514, 518
von Deutz, Rupert · 306, 314
Voorschoten, the Netherlands · 38, 371,
515, 518
Vroom, Hendrik M. · 51
Vrouw en Geloofbeweging (Women and
Faith Movement) · 78

W

Waarde, the Netherlands · 152, 157, 158,
517, 518
Warmond, the Netherlands · 164, 170,
171, 172
Warrior, R. A. · 49, 286
Washington · 360
Watzlawick, Paul · 290, 303
Weimar Republic · 497

Weinsheimer, Joel · 175
Wessel, Friedhelm · 316, 329, 330
West, Gerald O. · 14, 18, 50, 51, 52, 53,
182, 195, 211, 233, 235, 236, 237,
286, 292, 293, 295, 297, 474, 476,
514
Wester, Fred · 53, 303
Western Europe · 13, 202, 304, 305, 306,
307, 310, 311, 338
Westmaas, the Netherlands · 74, 351, 352,
354, 355, 517, 518
Wichmond, the Netherlands · 21, 261,
270, 351, 353, 354, 355, 370, 376,
515, 518
Wildervank, the Netherlands · 130
Williams, Rowan · 476
Willibrord translation · 95, 117
Wink, Walter · 444, 450
Wiseman, Richard L. · 375, 434
Witherington, Ben · 306, 308, 314
Witvliet, Theo · 493
Women and Gender Programme · 215
World Council of Churches · 117

X

Xhosa · 58, 196, 197, 202, 203, 209

Y

Yoder, Perry B. · 450
Young Christian Workers group, near
Pietermaritzburg, South Africa · 284,
394, 514
Youngnam area, Korea · 466

Z

Zaandam ecumenical base community
(Oekumenische Werkplaats Zandam,
OWZ), the Netherlands · 102, 394,
514, 519
Zaandam, the Netherlands · 196, 197,
198, 199, 201, 202, 203, 204, 205,
206, 207, 208, 275, 279, 280, 282,
284, 309, 313, 331, 394, 498, 514,
519
Zacchaeus · 109
Zending Werelddiakonaat
Ontwikkelingskerk (ZWO) · 77, 90,
91, 94, 113, 116
Zionists · 197, 504
Zondi-Mabizela, Phumzile · 215, 236
Zureck, Jorge · 160
Zutphen, the Netherlands · 21, 242, 243,
244, 245, 363, 368, 394, 514, 519
Zwijndrecht, the Netherlands · 394, 516,
519